Case 229.

In a provincial town a man was caught having intercourse with a hen. He was thirty years old and of high social position. The chickens had been dying one after another, and the man causing it had been "wanted" for a long time. When asked by the judge as to the reason for such an act, the accused said that his genitals were so small that coitus with women was impossible. Medical examination showed that his genitals were, in fact, extremely small. The man was *mentally quite sound*.

psychopathia sexualis

psychopathia sexualis

with especial reference to
contrary sexual instinct

a clinical-forensic study

by richard von krafft-ebing, m.d.

professor of psychiatry and neurology,
university of vienna

edited with an introduction by brian king

translated from the twelfth and final edition
complete and unabridged

bloat, a publishing company

a bloat book

The twelfth German edition of *Psychopathia Sexualis* [*Psychopathia sexualis, mit besonderer Berücksichtigung der konträren Sexualempfindung*] was first published in 1903 by Ferdinand Enke, Stuttgart.

The twelfth English edition of *Psychopathia Sexualis* was first published in 1906 by Medical Art Agency, New York, and translated by F. J. Rebman.

Book and cover design: Bloat

Associate editor: Susan King

Latin translator: Peter O'Neill

German translator of "The Significance of Menstruation in the Manifestation of Psychopathic States" ["Die Bedeutung der Menstruation für das Zustandekommen geistig unfreier Zustände," *Jahrbücher für Psychiatrie*, vol. 10, nos. 2 and 3, 1892]: Imogen von Tannenberg

ISBN 0-9650324-1-8

Wholesale distribution — USA & Canada:
LPC Group / INBOOK
1436 West Randolph Street, Chicago, Illinois 60607
phone 800 243 0138, fax 800 334 3892

Bloat
P. O. Box 254
Burbank, California 91503
email bloatbooks@hotmail.com
phone 818 759 6460

Printed in Hong Kong by Colorcraft Ltd.

table of contents

preface to the
first german edition (1886)
by richard von krafft-ebing, m.d.

FEW PEOPLE ever fully appreciate the powerful influence that sexuality exercises over feeling, thought, and conduct, both in the individual and in society. Schiller, in his poem, "Die Weltweisen," recognizes it with the words:

"Meanwhile, until Philosophy shall at last unite and maintain the world, Hunger and Love impel it onward."[1]

It is remarkable that the sexual life has received so little consideration from philosophers.

Schopenhauer (*Die Welt als Wille und Vorstellung,* 3d ed., vol. 2, p. 586ff.) thought it was strange that love had thus far been a subject for the poet alone, and that, with the exception of superficial treatment by Plato, Rousseau, and Kant, it had been foreign to philosophers.

What Schopenhauer and, after him, the philosopher of the unconscious, E. von Hartmann, discussed concerning the sexual relations is so imperfect, and in its consequences so distasteful, that the empirical psychology and metaphysics of the sexual side of human existence rest upon a foundation that is scientifically almost puerile. The treatment of the subject in the works of Michelet (*L'amour*) and Mantegazza (*Physiologie der Liebe*) should be considered more as brilliant discussions than as scientific treatises.

Although the poets may be better psychologists than the philosophers, they are men of feeling rather than understanding, and only one-sided in their consideration of the subject. They cannot see the deep shadow behind the light and sunny warmth of that from which they draw their inspiration. The poetry of all times and nations could furnish inexhaustible material for a monograph on the "psychology of love"; the great problem, however, can only be solved with the help of science, and especially with the aid of medicine, which studies the psychological subject at its anatomical and physiological source, and views it from all sides.

Perhaps it will be possible for medical science to gain a standpoint of philosophical knowledge midway between the despairing views of philosophers like Schopenhauer and Hartmann[2] and the gay, naïve views of the poets.

It is not the intention of the author to lay the foundation for a psychology of the sexual life, though undoubtedly psychopathology could contribute to psychology many important sources of knowledge.

Instead, the purpose of this treatise is to describe the pathological manifestations of the sexual life and to reduce them to conditions that can be approached from a legal standpoint. The task is a difficult one, and, in spite of years of experience as an alienist and medical jurist, the author is well aware that what he can offer must be incomplete.

The importance of the subject demands, however, that it should be examined scientifically, due to its forensic bearing and its effect upon the public welfare. The medico-legal expert, painfully aware of the incompleteness of our knowledge concerning the pathology of the sexual life, is nevertheless compelled to pass judgment upon his fellow men, where life, freedom, and honor are at stake. Only he can fully understand the significance of an attempt to gain definite views concerning it.

Even at the present time, the most erroneous opinions are expressed and the most unjust sentences are pronounced in the domain of sexual criminality, and these, in turn, influence laws and public opinion.

He who makes the psychopathology of sexual life the object of scientific study sees himself placed on a dark side of human life and misery, in the shadows of which the "images of God" wear hideous masks, and morals and aesthetics seem out of place.

It is the sad province of medicine, and especially of psychiatry, to continually regard the reverse side of life – human weakness and misery.

In this difficult profession, if we are able to ascribe to illness much of what frequently offends ethical and aesthetic feeling, perhaps some consolation can be gained and extended to the moral philosopher and aesthetician. Medicine undertakes to save the honor of mankind before the court of morality, and the honor of the individual before judges and his fellow men. In these studies, the duties and rights of medical science emanate from the high aim of the search for truth.

The author finds powerful the words of Tardieu (*Des attentats aux moeurs*): "Any physical or moral misery, any affliction, no matter how depraved it may be, should not frighten those who are dedicated to the knowledge of man and the sacred ministry of medicine, in that when one is obliged to see all things, one is allowed to speak of all things."[3]

The following pages are addressed to earnest investigators in the domain of natural science and jurisprudence. In order that unqualified persons should not become readers, the author found it necessary to choose a title understood only by the learned, and also, where possible, to express himself in technical terms. It also seemed necessary to write certain particularly revolting portions in Latin rather than in German.

It is hoped that this attempt to present to physicians and jurists facts from an important sphere of life will receive kindly acceptance and fill an actual gap in literature; for, with the exception of certain single descriptions and cases, current literature only presents the writings of Moreau and Tarnowsky, which cover but a portion of the field.

Dr Freiherr v. Krafft-Ebing

preface to the twelfth german edition (1902)
by richard von krafft-ebing, m.d.

THIS EDITION is entirely rewritten and considerably enlarged. The (exceptionally) favorable criticisms that former editions have been accorded in professional circles are a guarantee that the book exercises a beneficent influence upon legislation and jurisprudence, and will assist in removing erroneous ideas and superannuated laws.

Its commercial success is the best proof that large numbers of unfortunate people find in its pages instruction and relief in the frequently enigmatic manifestations of sexual life. The hosts of letters that have reached the author from all parts of the world substantiate this assumption. Compassion and sympathy are strongly elicited by the perusal of these letters, which are written primarily by men of refined thought and high social and scientific standing. They reveal sufferings of the soul, in comparison to which all the other afflictions dealt out by fate appear as trifles.

May it continue to convey solace and social elevation to its readers.

The number of technical terms has been increased, and the Latin language is more frequently utilized than in former editions.

May this edition be accorded the same kind of reception enjoyed by its predecessors. That it may be utilized in the service of science, justice and humanity is the wish of the author.

preface to the
twelfth english edition (1906)
by medical art agency, new york

THE PUBLISHERS sincerely trust that this revised translation from the twelfth German edition of *Psychopathia Sexualis* by Dr. R. von Krafft-Ebing will be received with favor by those for whom the book is written, and that its readers will derive that benefit which the author had in view.

Preparing and sifting the material for the twelfth edition of this work was the final task of the late author. When he was attacked by the fatal illness which carried him off, the manuscript was all ready for the printer.

Dr. Gugl and Dr. Stichl, pupils and for many years collaborators of the author, were entrusted by the family of the deceased with the revision of the proofs.

The sale of this book is strictly limited to members of the medical and legal professions, to teachers of and post-graduate students in the subject, educational institutions, libraries, book jobbers and bookstores, and not to the general public.

introduction to the
twelfth english edition (1939)
by victor robinson, m.d.,
professor of history of medicine,
temple university school of medicine.

SIR EDWARD Shepherd Creasy won his spurs in historiography by writing *Fifteen Decisive Battles of the World* (1852). A book on *Fifteen Decisive Books of the World* would necessarily include *Psychopathia Sexualis*.

Richard von Krafft-Ebing, professor at Strasbourg, Graz and Vienna, a prolific contributor to the literature of medical jurisprudence and nervous diseases, which he enriched with standard texts on forensic and clinical psychiatry, is now remembered as the author of *Psychopathia Sexualis* (Stuttgart, 1886), the first classic in sexual science which has had an enduring influence. After the rapid issue of several editions, the author saw that his book not only brought the solace of comradeship to bewildered victims of sexual deviations, but it brought rationalism to legislation and jurisprudence by helping to erase superannuated laws and superstitious ideas. *Psychopathia Sexualis* still molds sexual education.

Krafft-Ebing was a physician who wrote for physicians. He did not want the public to read his book, so he gave it a scientific title, employed technical terms, and inscribed the most exciting parts in Latin. Despite these handicaps, the author proved to be a magnificent reporter: the public swooped down on his book, and for a half-century have held it to their collective bosom. They regretted the technical terms not defined in any dictionary, and for the first time lamented their neglect of Latin in school. It was annoying not to understand the cryptic phrase in the lady's letter: "While you whine like a dog under the lashes of my servants, you shall witness another *favoritus sudorem pedum mihi lambit.*" What is meant by *paedicatio mulierum?* Is *uxorum* an obscene word? They read and stumbled and read on, for after all, the bulk of the book was in the vernacular, and to thousands of readers, fascinated and horrified, there was revealed the entire realm of sex turned upside down. *Psychopathia Sexualis* became the Adolescent's Handbook, but countless elders also tasted the forbidden apple in secret. In households today, behind innocent rows of Shakespeare and Dickens and Longfellow and Emerson, there is often hidden a Krafft-Ebing. Upon the whole, this enlightening book has accomplished an immense amount of good. It is an education in an inescapable subject which has not yet reached the college curriculum.

Krafft-Ebing did not possess the lyric fire of Mantegazza, or the literary grace of Havelock Ellis, but his style, masculine and muscular, suited his purpose. A diagnostician at the bedside of society, his statements were forthright and authoritative. A clinician who reported what he found, he stripped aside the twin veils of sham and shame which covered the pathology of sex. Krafft-Ebing could put much in a sentence, as witness, "The gratification of the sexual instinct seems to be the primary motive in man as well as in beast." He originated the combination, "syphilization and civilization." His comment on fashion was the terse remark, "The corset is the most disastrous error of woman's dress." His dictum, "It is questionable if the morality of mankind has improved in our times," is equally applicable to our times.

So graphic were the case histories of Krafft-Ebing, that at one time, whenever a homosexual wrote an intense autobiographical sketch, he was accused of imitating Krafft-Ebing, though in some cases it was shown that the writer had never heard of Krafft-Ebing. Krafft-Ebing's expression, "stepchildren of nature," which he applied to inverts, has frequently been quoted by the inverts themselves.

Krafft-Ebing devised the terms paranoia, sadism, masochism, psychic hermaphrodite, sexual bondage, and several others, described early cases of kleptolagnia, published the first complete case of transvestism, realized the rarity of erotic fetishism in the female but its frequency in the male, knew the tendency of female inverts to adopt the male method in urination, pointed out that the clitoris is the dominant erotogenic zone in the virgin, and that the vagina becomes eroticized only by coitus. When leading neurologists, such as Maudsley in England and

Spitzka in America, were emphasizing "masturbatory insanity," Krafft-Ebing scratched his pen through such nonsense. When the sexual impulse in the unmarried was unrecognized, he explained that prolonged ungratified desire is responsible for psychopathic and nervous conditions in man and woman. At a time when prudery was confused with purity, he declared that genius, art and poetry rest upon a sexual foundation. At a time when theology was sacrosanct, he was the first to show the relationship between religious ecstasy and sexual emotion, and did not hesitate to trace the identity of spiritual and sexual scatologic symbolism: the medieval ascetic, sucking the festering sores of the sick and the poor, and licking up human excrement, finding his counterpart in the urolagnic and coprolagnic rapture of the masochist.

In describing the numerous individuals whose sexual impulse was uncontrollable, but for whom normal coitus was impossible, Krafft-Ebing founded modern sexual pathology. Although he had no patience with metaphysical speculations, and preferred to report what he actually saw before him, he paid attention to the dreams of his patients and attempted to elicit any childhood experiences that might account for their psychopathic condition. With few of the faults and all the merits of the pioneer, his interpretive case histories are of permanent value. Through his hands, in consulting-room, clinic and law-court, passed a succession of the undersexed and the hypersexed, rapists, stranglers, rippers, stabbers, bloodsucking vampires and necrophiliacs, sadists who hurt their partners, masochists who thrilled at the sight of the whip, males in female clothes and females in male clothes, stuff-fetishists dominated by a shoe or handkerchief, lovers of fur and velvet, slaves of scatology, defilers of statues, despoilers of children and animals, frotteurs and voyeurs, renifleurs and stercoraires, pageists and exhibitionists, pedophiliacs and gerontophiliacs, satyriasists and nymphomaniacs, and again and again male-craving males and female-craving females, and the endless army of men who lusted after Woman in perverse ways, but had no desire for her vagina. The ability to enjoy and perform the sexual act, in the normal manner, appeared to be the most difficult of the arts.

"Sexual bondage should certainly constitute a cause for leniency in crimes committed through its agency," was the central theme of Krafft-Ebing's teaching. Letters carrying the most astounding confessions reached his desk, a correspondence to which he refers in one of the prefaces to his book: ". . . large numbers of unfortunate people find in its pages instruction and relief in the frequently enigmatic manifestations of sexual life. The hosts of letters that have reached the author from all parts of the world substantiate this assumption. Compassion and sympathy are strongly elicited by the perusal of these letters, which are written primarily by men of refined thought and high social and scientific standing. They reveal sufferings of the soul, in comparison to which all the other afflictions dealt out by fate appears as trifles." As edition after edition of *Psychopathia Sexualis* appeared, in the original and in translation, Krafft-Ebing found himself the father-confessor of the inverts and perverts of the world.

With few historical exceptions, it is the sad fate of the pioneer of one generation to become the reactionary of the next. Having advanced beyond his contemporaries, usually by overcoming tremendous obstacles, the old pioneer grows weary in his search for Truth, and rests in the shade of his achievements, looking with bitter eyes at the younger men who march beyond him with new viewpoints. Krafft-Ebing earned a reputation by his writings on homosexuality which he regarded as disease or degeneration. Since this was the prevailing belief, sanctioned by leading theologians, jurists and physicians, Krafft-Ebing was not called upon to change his convictions. But Krafft-Ebing's clinical experience and insight grew with the years, and after the age of sixty he possessed the mental resilience and the moral integrity to admit his error and to risk his reputation by declaring inversion a biological anomaly. In the first year of the new century, in his "New Studies in the Domain of Homosexuality," in the *Annual for Sexual Intermediate Stages* (Leipzig, 1901), edited by Magnus Hirschfeld, the old master published his new views:

"In view of the experience that contrary sexuality is a congenital anomaly, that it represents a disturbance in the evolution of sexual life, and of physical and mental development, in normal relation to the kind of reproductive glands which the individual possesses, it has become impossible to maintain in this connection the idea of disease. Not infrequently in the case of those with contrary sexuality do we find neuropathic and psychopathic predispositions, which may lead to the most severe aberrations of the sexual impulse. And yet we can always prove that, relatively speaking, heterosexuals are apt to be much more depraved than homosexuals. That contrary sexual sensation cannot thus be necessarily regarded as psychic degeneration, or even as a manifestation of disease, is shown by various considerations, of which one of the principal is that these variations of the sexual life may actually be associated with mental superiority. The proof of this is the existence of men of all nations whose contrary sexuality is an established fact, and who, nonetheless, are the pride of their nation as authors, poets, artists, leaders of armies, and statesmen. A further proof of the fact that contrary sexual sensation is not necessarily disease, nor necessarily a vicious self-surrender to the immoral, is to be found in the fact that all the noble activities of the heart which can be associated with heterosexual love can be equally associated with homosexual love, and also the passions and all the defects of love." Krafft-Ebing was a pioneer who remained a pioneer.

The foremost figures in the Sexual Science of the Twentieth Century are Iwan Bloch (1872-1922), Magnus Hirschfeld (1868-1935), Havelock Ellis (1859-1939), and Sigmund Freud (1856-   ), each of whom has placed a laurel leaf on the bier of the pathfinder. The critical Bloch testified: "Krafft-Ebing is, and remains, the true founder of modern sexual pathology." Hirschfeld inscribed his monumental work: "I dedicate this book to the spirit of Krafft-Ebing. If my *Sexual Pathology* does for our time what *Psychopathia Sexualis* did for his, then the goal at which I aimed has been reached." Ellis refers to Krafft-Ebing as "the first great clinician of sexual inversion." The first name cited in Freud's treatise, *Three Contributions to the Theory of Sex,* is Krafft-Ebing.

These lines are being composed on the eve of the centenary of the birth of Krafft-Ebing (1840-1902), on the occasion of a new printing of *Psychopathia Sexualis.* The writer of this Introduction was born in the year in which the first edition of *Psychopathia Sexualis* was published; he has been familiar with the work since his adolescence; he considers it an honor to write his name in the famous pages which have enlarged the boundaries of human understanding. Léon-Henri Thoinot, of Paris, distinguished for his contributions to the medico-legal aspects of moral offenses, used to say to his students: "There is a name that should be put above all others, that of Krafft-Ebing, of Vienna." There is no longer Vienna, but among the monuments bequeathed to science by the Viennese teachers, the *Psychopathia Sexualis* of Krafft-Ebing will not be forgotten.

the creation of a new science
by brian king

A BASIC yet salient fact: *sexual perversions* – sadism, masochism, fetishism, homosexuality, and countless other "aberrations" – did not exist before Krafft-Ebing's *Psychopathia Sexualis*. Of course, sexual perversions *did* exist in various forms and guises – since the beginning of civilization, no doubt – but they were not comprehensively defined and classified as such until the 1886 publication of *Psychopathia Sexualis* in Stuttgart, Germany. It marked the birth of *Sexualwissenschaft*, or "sexology" – the applied science and study of sexual behavior – and set the social and political standard of what we still consider to this day to be sexually "normal."

There were, to be sure, a handful of other books before Krafft-Ebing's that were devoted to the subject of *psychopathia sexualis* (literal translation: "sexual psychopathy"), especially in Germany. In 1823, a book by H. J. Löwenstein was published in Bonn that discussed, entirely in Latin, "abnormal sexual conditions"; in 1826, Joseph Häussler wrote a treatise published in Würzburg on "the relations of the sexual system to the psyche"; and, in 1844, Heinrich Kaan contributed a slim volume (124 pages), published in Leipzig and also written entirely in Latin, entitled *Psychopathia Sexualis*. These efforts, however, were only read by a select number of physicians and scientists, and therefore did not make a considerable impact.

In the latter half of the nineteenth century, however, European medicine and science, intoxicated with their relatively new systems of classification and examination, notably shifted toward a medicalization of sexuality in which every sexual whim, no matter how minor, was catalogued, given a name, and gazed upon from every angle. Sexual vice, previously a subject dealt with by the Church, rapidly became a matter of law dealt with by the State, which was advised in turn by the school of Medicine.

An archetypal case that illustrates this shift is related by Michel Foucault in *The History of Sexuality*. In 1867, Jouy, a farmhand, was arrested in the village of Lapcourt, France for playing a game called "curdled milk" with a local girl. He was examined by doctors, who studied his physiognomy in detail and asked him countless questions. Eventually acquitted, he was nonetheless hospitalized for an indeterminate amount of time, and a year later a medical journal published his case history. As pointed out by Foucault,

> What is the significant thing about this story? The pettiness of it all; the fact that this everyday occurrence in the life of village sexuality, these inconsequential bucolic pleasures, could become, from a certain time, the object not only of a collective intolerance but of a judicial action, a medical intervention, a careful clinical examination, and an entire theoretical elaboration (Foucault 1978).

The inexact theological notion of "vice" became the stringent medical fact of "perversion." Sexual acts of "sin" were now examined with biological, neurological, medical and pedagogical tools. As a result, "to a large extent the physician took over from the clergy as the keeper of normalcy" (Mosse 1985).

The keepers of sexual normalcy produced their own bible; a guidebook that exhibited, in clear clinical detail, a multitude of sexual perversions, individually identified and succinctly explained. *Psychopathia Sexualis* satiated the scientists with its plethora of detail, and Krafft-Ebing was the principal architect in the forensic and psychiatric demarcation between "normal" and "abnormal" sexuality.

[1] richard von krafft-ebing, m.d.

Regardless of its ultimate effect, *Psychopathia Sexualis* was significantly inspired by Krafft-Ebing's Catholic liberal upbringing. Born on August 14, 1840 in Mannheim, Germany, he was sent by his parents at an early age to attend the *Gymnasium* in

Heidelberg, where he lived with his mother's parents. His maternal grandfather was Karl Josef Mittermaier (1787-1867), a progressive criminal lawyer well-known as "the last hope of the damned." It was later noted in a Munich medical journal that "the German legal discipline owes to [Mittermaier] significant prison reforms, the introduction of humane punishments, and much other progress" (Fuchs 1903). Krafft-Ebing's parents later moved to Heidelberg (where his father was a high official in the local government). Krafft-Ebing stayed to study at the University of Heidelberg, and graduated with a doctoral degree in medicine in 1863.

Shortly before his graduation, however, Krafft-Ebing spent a summer semester recovering from an attack of typhoid fever in Zurich, where he attended a series of lectures given by psychiatrist Wilhelm Griesinger (1817-69). Krafft-Ebing later acknowledged Griesinger's lectures as a profound influence that directed him toward his career in psychiatry; Griesinger was also a notable influence on famed psychiatrist Theodor Meynert (1833-92) and one of his more gifted students, Sigmund Freud (1856-1939).

A year after obtaining his doctorate, Krafft-Ebing began his career as a neurologist and psychiatrist when he was appointed assistant physician at the Illenau insane asylum, where he worked under the supervision of founder and director Christian Roller (1802-78). He stayed at Illenau for four years; after his resignation in 1868, he moved to Baden-Baden to open a private practice as a neurologist. He served in the army during the Franco-Prussian War of 1870-71, stationed at a typhoid ward in Rastatt, and in 1872 was appointed professor of psychiatry at the University of Strasbourg (a city in German territory after the war), where he also opened a private clinic. Only one year later he was appointed director of the Feldhof Asylum near Graz, Austria, and he also became an Austrian citizen. In 1874 he was appointed professor of psychiatry at the University of Graz, where he stayed for the next fifteen years. Overwhelmed by his duties, however, he resigned his directorship at Feldhof in 1885, only to become the head of the university's psychiatric and neurological clinic and the founder of his own clinic in the nearby village of Mariagrün the following year.

Shortly after his arrival in Graz, Krafft-Ebing wrote his first major book, published in 1875: *Lehrbuch der gerichtlichen Psychopathologie, mit Berücksichtigung der Gesetzgebung von Österreich, Deutschland und Frankreich* (Textbook of Forensic Psychopathology, with Reference to the Legislation of Austria, Germany and France). An influential figure during this period of his life was colleague and friend Hans Gross (1847-1915), who later taught criminology at the University of Graz and wrote a seminal two-volume textbook on criminal investigation, *Handbuch für Untersuchungsrichter* (Handbook for the Examining Magistrate, 1893). Although he is now known as "the creator of modern crime detection" (Johnston 1972), Gross was also a notoriously conservative Catholic who once argued for the deportation of "degenerates" – tramps, anarchists, thieves, and especially gypsies – to colonies in Africa or the Pacific Islands (Le Rider 1993); he also supported the racist myth, prevalent at the turn of the century, of "Jewish ritual murder" (Nussbaum 1947). The substance of the myth: Christians, usually young children, were "not only bled white, but crucified, sometimes circumcised and crowned with thorns, tortured, beaten, stabbed, and sometimes finished off by wounding in the side in imitation of the murder of Christ. The blood taken from the child was mixed either in the powder state or otherwise into the Passover bread" (Leese 1938). Gross was also the father of Otto Gross, an erratic Nietzschean psychiatrist, anarchist and opium addict who propagated a theory of "sexual immoralism"; born in 1877, he died from pneumonia and drug abuse on February 13, 1920, after being found on the streets of Berlin.

Also during this period of time Krafft-Ebing married Luise Kissling (1846-1903), and had two sons and a daughter. In 1880 he contributed another important book to the field of psychiatry, the three-volume *Lehrbuch der Psychiatrie auf klinischer Grundlage für praktische Ärzte und Studirende* (published in English as the *Text-book of Insanity, Based on Clinical Observations* in 1905). Krafft-Ebing's *Lehrbuch*, required reading for many students of psychiatry, later motivated Carl Jung (1875-1961) to become a psychiatrist and marked the first usage of the term "paranoia" in its psychiatric application to persecutory delusions.

Krafft-Ebing was also renowned at this point in his life for his medical research, in which he established

the connection between general paralysis of the insane and syphilis. Although the original statistical association had been made by Esmark and Jensen in 1854, it had not gained wide recognition. Krafft-Ebing was, however, so convinced of this link that to prove it he inoculated nine paretics with syphilitic scrapings. None developed primary or secondary syphilis, and from this he felt justified in concluding that the paretic must have already been rendered immune by a previous syphilitic infection (Johnson 1973).

Since the beginning of his career, Krafft-Ebing had served as a psychiatric consultant for the courts of Austria and Germany. In this capacity as one of the first expert witnesses or "alienists," he kept an ever-expanding collection of case histories, individual stories detailing the sexual lives and peccadillos of a diverse grouping of patients, accused criminals, and others, gathered from a variety of sources — newspapers and journals, fellow physicians' letters, articles and books, and first-hand accounts that resulted from Krafft-Ebing's examinations.

His collection of case histories also contributed to his popularity as a teacher in Graz; his colleague Julius Wagner von Jauregg (1857-1940) later recalled:

> One had to be there to see how he was able to sustain the interest of a young audience in Graz during three-hour lectures; how it was obvious that he was fully involved in each case he presented as though it was as new to him as it was to his listeners; one had to see his almost holy dedication to his subject in order to recognize that the teaching profession was not a burden to him, but rather the expression and satisfaction of a noble drive. His natural inclinations and talents assisted him in this activity: a strong and pleasant voice, a perfect and fluent diction, and, most of all, a gift for clear and intelligible presentation, so that even laymen were in the habit of frequenting his lectures (Jauregg 1908).

In 1886, Krafft-Ebing sent his publisher in Stuttgart, Ferdinand Enke, the manuscript of his latest book. The first edition was only 110 pages long with 45 case histories. Its name: *Psychopathia Sexualis, mit besonderer Berücksichtigung der konträren Sexualempfindung. Eine klinisch-forensische Studie* (Psychopathia Sexualis, with Especial Reference to Contrary Sexual Instinct. A Clinical-Forensic Study).

[2] "psychopathia sexualis."

It is not known what motivated Richard von Krafft-Ebing to write *Psychopathia*

Sexualis. Perhaps he truly believed his book was going to be received by the public solely as a work of science, intended to illustrate in a scholarly manner his theories regarding the "anomalies of the sexual functions." And perhaps he was too close to the material, or too ensconced in the world of academia, to realize how explosive his prurient masterpiece was. What *is* known is this: even though the more obscene passages of the book were written in Latin, every child and adult in Europe with a *Gymnasium* or religious education was capable of reading these passages. Also, Krafft-Ebing never instructed his publisher to sell the book exclusively to a limited professional readership; it was available to the public without any restrictions. Whatever his motivations, the book's impact was spectacular and manifold. It was a huge commercial success, selling thousands upon thousands of copies, and was issued a dozen times in ever-revised and ever-enlarged editions, each one selling better than the previous edition.

Laymen saw for the first time a world some had hardly dreamed existed. This fat volume in German and Latin, impeccably medical, contained cases of lust-murder, sexual cannibalism and necrophilia; of a man who visited a Paris brothel to have prostitutes laid out in white shrouds; of coprophiliacs and fetishists; of a man whose great sexual delight was gathering pubic hair from brothel beds with his teeth. . . . Many such people were gentlemen and ladies with respectable family and public lives. Behind their social façade lay a cesspool of secret perversions and madness (Karlen 1971).

The social elite of Europe, especially in Vienna, also developed a fascination with *Psychopathia Sexualis* and its author. Krafft-Ebing became a bit of a celebrity; he was even rumored to count Crown Prince Rudolf of Austria as one of his patients. (If so, he was not much of a success in this unfortunate case; under mysterious circumstances, Rudolf shot his half-Greek mistress, Baroness Mary Vetsera, and himself on January 30, 1889, at his hunting lodge in Mayerling.) Austrian socialite Berta Szeps, daughter of Moriz Szeps (editor of the *Neues Wiener Tagblatt* newspaper) and wife of Emil Zuckerkandl (professor of anatomy at the universities of Graz and Vienna), recorded the following meeting with Krafft-Ebing in her diary:

Graz, June 15, 1886

Yesterday Professor Krafft-Ebing came to lunch. He gave me an inscribed copy of his *Psychopathia Sexualis,* the book that has made him world-famous. I like him very much.

In the course of our conversation I mentioned my father's friendship with the Crown Prince Rudolf, and in connection with it, we began to speak of King Ludwig of Bavaria. Krafft-Ebing is very well-informed about him, because the doctor in charge of Ludwig is an intimate friend of his.

"King Ludwig is quite insane," said Krafft-Ebing, "and I have warned my friend never to trust him so far as to go out for a walk with him unaccompanied by a male nurse. I received a letter from him today." And he began to read from it: " 'Dear friend, the King likes me very much, he is extremely friendly with me, and absolutely and entirely under my control. You really need not worry about my safety. . . .' "

Graz, June 17, 1886

. . . Yesterday, during a walk in the Royal Park at Munich, King Ludwig attacked his doctor and threw him into the lake. After a struggle in the water they were both drowned. . . . (Szeps 1939)

In the cafés of Paris, Berlin and Vienna, Krafft-Ebing's book was also a topic of discussion among the *literati.* Marcel Proust (1871-1922) read *Psychopathia Sexualis* and afterward disapprovingly commented to his friend Paul Morand, "It seems that even vice has now become one of the exact sciences" (Painter 1989). (It seems probable, however, that his reading of the book partly influenced his characterization of Charlus in *A la recherche du temps perdu.*) The famed Viennese writer Hugo von Hofmannsthal (1874-1929) bought the book when he was only fifteen to satisfy his curiosity about "nervous relaxation . . . dangerous game, risk of intellectual over-excitement" (Le Rider 1993). Frank Wedekind (1864-1918), author of the "Lulu" plays *Erdgeist* (Earth Spirit) and *Die Büchse der Pandora* (Pandora's Box), wrote the following entry in his diary on August 8, 1889:

Last night in bed I thought of the anecdote from Krafft-Ebing; the Parisian prostitute with the bulldog. I visualize it all in detail, thinking how the girl enters, walking on her hands, and collects money by holding her legs slightly apart. Then she gets monkeys to undress her, the whole point being her total passivity. Then at least three or four bulldogs are driven in and beaten. The girl lives and sleeps with a bitch for the sake of her spiritual aroma. I spend the entire afternoon trying to draw the girl (Wedekind 1990).

However popular Krafft-Ebing was among his readers, he became fairly controversial in certain circles of the medical and psychiatric establishment. In a review of the first English translation of *Psychopathia Sexualis* (seventh edition, 1893), an anonymous writer for the *British Medical Journal* could barely contain his revulsion for the book:

> We have taken some time to consider whether we should notice this book or not, and have, in the end, decided that the importance of the subject and the position of the author render it necessary to refer to it. It is, we believe, unique in the fulness with which the subject has been treated, but we question whether it need have been translated. Anyone wishing to study the subject might just as well have gone to the original, and some may be disposed to go even further and regret that the whole had not been written in Latin, and thus veiled in the decent obscurity of a dead language. There are many morally disgusting subjects which have to be studied by the doctor and the jurist, but the less such subjects are brought before the public the better (British Medical Journal 1893).

According to Viennese psychiatrist Moritz Benedikt (1835-1920), he had to talk the British Medico-Psychological Association out of canceling Krafft-Ebing's honorary membership because, due to the popularity of *Psychopathia Sexualis,* "the students of higher schools for girls were more knowledgeable on the theme of sexual perversions than we were as young physicians" (Ellenberger 1970).

As each edition of *Psychopathia Sexualis* came out, Krafft-Ebing included case histories that were autobiographies written by readers affected by previous editions of his book. He occasionally obliquely acknowledged this fascinating self-referential influence of his book on his own case histories (for instance, see case 148, p. 318, and case 137 in the appendix, pp. 603-4), and even used a later edition of his book as a vehicle to deflect an attack on the veracity of a case history by Dr. Hans Kurella regarding the book's effect on itself (see case 115, p. 224).

The accuracy of the case histories is still open to question; it seems that Krafft-Ebing primarily relied on his own professional instincts instead of any scientific form of analysis in the production and compilation of his cases. His colleague Julius Wagner von Jauregg said, "Clinical observations were his main strength: he carefully observed syndromes of disease and reflected his observations in a plain and rational manner" (Jauregg 1908). Certainly most of his contributors were highly regarded, reputable men of medicine and science. French psychologist Alfred Binet (1857-1911), for instance, whose theory on fetishism was an influence on *Psychopathia Sexualis,* later devised with Théodor Simon the "Binet-Simon scale," the first IQ test. Viennese sexologist Albert Moll's (1862-1939) writings on homosexuality and sexual development – a major influence on the "antipathic sexuality" section of Krafft-Ebing's book – were read and admired by Freud and British sexologist Havelock Ellis (1859-1939), among others. But not all of Krafft-Ebing's contributors can be vouched for – witness the bizarre story of French writer Léo Taxil.

Taxil's book *La prostitution contemporaine* (Paris, 1884) is occasionally cited in *Psychopathia Sexualis* without any question regarding its authenticity. Taxil, however, whose real name was Gabriel Jogand-Pagès, was an inflammatory journalist who reveled in public controversy. When he was a practicing Freemason he wrote a number of scandalous books and articles critical of the Catholic Church – one of his books, for instance, was entitled *Les amours secrètes de Pie IX* (The Secret Loves of Pius IX) – but in 1886 Taxil became a devout Catholic and wrote a series of exposés on the evils of Freemasonry. He then proceeded to carry out a bizarre hoax, proclaiming that he had met the high priestess of a Satanic-Masonic sect called the Palladium – her name, he said, was Diana Vaughan. Neither Diana Vaughan nor the Palladium existed, of course, but Taxil managed to keep the hoax alive for over ten years. He wrote of the Palladium's grotesque rituals, asserted he had successfully converted Diana to Catholicism, published her "autobiography" (which was read by the Pope himself), and accepted a papal benediction in her honor. (Diana never appeared in public, Taxil stated, due to death threats from depraved Palladium disciples.) Under pressure from Diana's followers, Taxil eventually announced that she would appear in public and answer questions from the Paris press on Easter Monday, 1897. On the appointed day, however, Taxil appeared instead and declared that he had created the persona of Diana Vaughan "to see how far he could go in duping the Church of Rome" (Webb 1974).

Krafft-Ebing also left himself open to criticism when he named a "perversion of the sexual instinct," *masochism,* after a living author – Leopold von Sacher-Masoch (1836-1895). (*Sadism,* named after the writer Donatien Alphonse François Sade [1740-1814] – the Marquis de Sade – was a psychiatric concept that had been in use as early as 1834.) He wanted to create a literary antonym to "sadism"; the nearest psychiatric definition at the time was the uninspired "passive algolagnia." Krafft-Ebing had heard the local gossip about the "perverse" sexual habits of Sacher-Masoch, the writer of the notorious *Venus im Pelz* (Venus in Furs, 1870) and an aristocratic dandy who also resided in Graz (he was, in fact, the son of Graz's police commissioner) – his slave-master liaisons with Anna von Kottowitz and Fanny von Pistor in the 1860s were still a hotly whispered topic among the high society of Graz in the 1880s. Sacher-Masoch was also, however, a respected author of "three substantial works of historical scholarship" that "contained original research and original views of Central European politics" (Cleugh 1967), and had been a professor of history at the University of Graz. He was recognized for his talent as an author in 1886 when "he made a triumphant journey to Paris where he was decorated and entertained by the *Figaro* and the *Revue des Deux Mondes*" (Deleuze 1971).

Put on the defensive by colleagues and friends of the late Sacher-Masoch, Krafft-Ebing exhibited his ungainly presumptuousness as a doctor *and* a critic by declaring in the twelfth edition of *Psychopathia Sexualis:*

> As a man Sacher-Masoch cannot lose anything in the estimation of his cultured fellow beings simply because he was afflicted with an anomaly of his sexual feelings. As an author he suffered severe injury as far as the influence and intrinsic merit of his work is concerned, because when he eliminated his perversion from his literary efforts he was a gifted writer, and as such would have achieved real greatness had he been driven by normal sexual feelings (p. 120).

Of course, one could go through the entire text of *Psychopathia Sexualis* and focus on Krafft-Ebing's unfortunate treatment of many subjects, and not just his disparagement of Sacher-Masoch – his antiquated *fin-de-siècle* attitude, for example, toward women, prostitution, masturbation and oral sex. For every negative, though, there is likely to be found a positive; e.g., his argument to repeal Paragraph 175, the law that jailed homosexuals for their sexual behavior. To get at the root of Krafft-Ebing's philosophy, however, one must look at the foundation of Krafft-Ebing's writings: his total and unquestioning belief in the theory of degeneration.

[3] "the psychic soil of degeneration."

The term "degeneration" had been used as an aesthetic criticism as early as the seventeenth century, but it was only after the publication in 1857 of Benedict Augustin Morel's *Traité des dégénérescences physiques, intellectuelles et morales de l'espèce humaine* (Treatise on the Physical, Intellectual and Moral Degeneration of Mankind) that it was used in a psychiatric, pathological and racial sense:

> Morel gave the term "degeneration" a medical meaning, but it derived from his interpretation of the Book of Genesis. Adam before the fall was the ideal human, the measure of man. However, as a result of the fall from Paradise, human beings can no longer escape external influences such as climate or nourishment, or the poisons, diseases, and environmental factors that carry some men furtherest away from the ideal type. They have degenerated from the standard once set (Mosse 1985).

And who was the classic "degenerate"? The most obvious were, in the mental category, the "idiots," "imbeciles," "feeble-minded," and "cretins"; in the physical category, persons with cleft palates, distorted ears, high-domed palates, and facial asymmetry; and, in the racial category, those who were insane as a result of "inbreeding" or "hereditary taint."

Krafft-Ebing was clearly a disciple of Morel, and offered in his 1880 textbook his own disturbing theory on insanity and its relation to "inbreeding":

> Statistics have been collected with great care to show the percentage of insanity in the various religious sects, and it has been shown that among the Jews and certain sects the percentage is decidedly higher. This fact stands in relation with religion only in so far as it constitutes a hindrance to marriage among those professing it; the more when its adherents are small in number, and there is consequent insufficient crossing of the race and increased inbreeding.

This is a phenomenon similar to that observed in certain highly aristocratic and wealthy families, whose members, either from motives of
honor or money, constantly intermarry, and thus have many insane relatives. In such cases the cause is not moral, but anthropologic (Krafft-
Ebing 1905).

Morel's theory of *dégénérescence* virulently spread across all of Europe. In France,
psychiatrists Valentin Magnan (1835-1916) and Jean-Martin Charcot (1825-1893)
took up the cause. The latter's espousal of degeneration in particular lent weight
to Morel's theory. Known as the *Napoléon des névroses,* Charcot taught at the famous
Salpêtrière in Paris, an asylum for insane and impoverished women. An important
influence on Freud and many other psychiatric figures, he was renowned for his
theatrical lectures that involved hypnotized female "hysterics" who twitched and
moaned for his packed audiences of students, actors and writers. In Italy, the
primary adherent of degeneration was Italian criminologist Cesare Lombroso
(1836-1909), who stated in his *L'uomo delinquente* (Criminal Man, 1876): "The aeti-
ology of crime . . . mingles with that of all kinds of degeneration: rickets, deafness,
monstrosity, hairiness, and cretinism, of which crime is only a variation"
(Lombroso 1911). In England, the writings of Morel were an influence on the
theories of Sir Francis Galton (1822-1911), the founder of eugenics.

In the United States, a slight variation of degeneration was devised in 1881 by
George M. Beard in his book *American Nervousness: Its Causes and Consequences.* He
named the condition "neurasthenia," and stated as its cause "modern civilization,
which is distinguished from ancient by these five characteristics: steam-power, the
periodical press, the telegraph, the sciences, and the mental activity of women"
(Beard 1881). Beard's book was immediately translated into German and embraced
by the German-Austrian medical and psychiatric community. As noted by historian
Sander L. Gilman, "a disease with no rigid symptomatology, [neurasthenia] was
defined negatively as not being hysteria, madness, melancholia, epilepsy, or any of
the numerous other endogenous or degenerate illnesses catalogued in the late
nineteenth century" (Gilman 1985).

Krafft-Ebing took Morel's theory of degeneration and Beard's theory of neurasthenia and severely applied them to his own theory of *psychopathia sexualis.* All forms
of sexual aberration – from excessive masturbation to necrophilia and cannibal-

ism – were essentially caused, according to Krafft-Ebing, primarily by the evils of bad heredity (which unnaturally predisposed one's sexual lust) and secondarily by the evils of modernity (which unnaturally excited one's sexual lust). Strewn throughout the text of *Psychopathia Sexualis* is an astonishing litany of imbecilic and inebriated relatives of the sexually pathological who reside in large cities – "hotbeds in which neuroses and low morality are bred" (p. 9).

The theory of degeneration seeped further into the public consciousness when Max Nordau's *Entartung* (Degeneration) was published in Germany in 1892. Nordau (1849-1923), a Hungarian journalist and physician who studied at one time under Charcot in Paris (his thesis was on "The Castration of Women"), took the degeneration theories of Morel, Lombroso and Krafft-Ebing and dogmatically applied them to the world of art and literature. *Entartung* opens with an epistolary dedication to Lombroso, in which Nordau elucidates his enormous critical task:

> Degenerates are not always criminals, prostitutes, anarchists, and pronounced lunatics; they are often authors and artists. These, however, manifest the same mental characteristics, and for the most part the same somatic features, as the members of the above-mentioned anthropological family, who satisfy their unhealthy impulses with the knife of the assassin or the bomb of the dynamiter, instead of with pen and pencil. . . . Now I have undertaken the work of investigating (as much as possible after your method) the tendencies of the fashions in art and literature; of proving that they have their source in the degeneracy of their authors, and that the enthusiasm of their admirers is for manifestations of more or less pronounced moral insanity, imbecility, and dementia (Nordau 1895).

And who were these aesthetic degenerates? Nietzsche, Ibsen, Zola, Wagner, Verlaine, Tolstoy, Baudelaire and Wilde, to mention just a few. Name for name, Nordau's list of degenerate writers and artists would later be cited as classic figures of modernism. *Entartung* was an international bestseller, and Nordau later cofounded Zionism with Theodor Herzl in 1897 before fading into obscurity.

Nordau's text was later a major source of inspiration for Adolf Hitler and the Nazis for their 1937 exhibition "Entartete Kunst." As compellingly argued by

George L. Mosse in his book *Toward the Final Solution,* the ties between the nine-teenth-century purveyors of degeneration – Morel, Lombroso, Krafft-Ebing, Nordau – and the twentieth-century racial biology theorists of National Socialism were deeply intertwined. Although Lombroso and Nordau were Jewish liberals, "their ideas became a staple of racist thought. . . . Nazi euthanasia was based upon the proposition that degeneration as exemplified by habitual criminality or insanity was structural and final" (Mosse 1978).

It is also worth noting that one of the coauthors of the first book to concretely propose governmental euthanasia was a contemporary of Krafft-Ebing's. Alfred Hoche was a professor of psychiatry at the University of Freiberg, and he co-authored (with Karl Binding, a retired jurist from the University of Leipzig) *Die Freigabe der Vernichtung lebensunwerten Lebens* (The Permission to Destroy Life Unworthy of Life, 1920). (In *Psychopathia Sexualis,* Krafft-Ebing references an early article by Hoche in a footnote concerning the laws on exhibitionism [p. 673].) According to Robert Jay Lifton in his book *The Nazi Doctors,* Hoche and Binding determined that the following were *Ballastexistenzen* ("human ballast") and there-fore unworthy of life: "not only the incurably ill but large segments of the mentally ill, the feebleminded, and retarded and deformed children" (Lifton 1986).

It is important to remember in this context, however, that Krafft-Ebing himself was a pacifist and a liberal; he undoubtedly would have been horrified by the evolu-tion of the nineteenth-century scientific theory of degeneration into National Socialism's murderous racist programs. In 1893, a time when anti-Semitism was entrenched throughout Europe, Krafft-Ebing contributed the following statement (reproduced in its entirety) to a publication which denounced racial and religious intolerance:

> There has arisen a rather disconcerting and regrettable development in the cultural life of Europe's well-civilized nations at the end of this century; it is the class and race hatred which serves only to disgrace our spirit.
> This spiritual epidemic is not new to anyone who is familiar with our cultural history. From a psychiatric standpoint, we must ask the question

whether we are dealing here with a childhood or mental disease which has its origin in the life of the peoples haunted by it.

I believe that we must assume the former, since the scope of development possible for the human spirit has not reached its limit so far. Quite the opposite is true; our present cultural stage is still relatively low. A large majority of people today, who pride themselves in having reached a state of humanistic morality, are still far removed from the gospel of the all-encompassing compassion preached to them by the holy founder of Christianity almost 1900 years ago, from his height of moral conviction, which can without question be said to serve as a moral code of truly international dimensions (Van Groningen 1893).

[4] therapeutic nihilism in fin-de-siècle vienna.

Krafft-Ebing was appointed in 1889 as a professor at the most celebrated Western school of medicine and science, the University of Vienna, and in 1892 succeeded Theodor Meynert (after Meynert's death) as the chair of the psychiatric department. Because of the accomplishments of the university's renowned medical faculty, Vienna was known as "the Mecca of Medicine" (Johnston 1972); for example, profound milestones in the fields of dermatology, ophthalmology, urology, anesthesia and surgery had been achieved. These triumphs in medicine, however, had their price – they were primarily realized due to the practice of "therapeutic nihilism," in which the patient was clinically observed by the medical faculty and students instead of cured. This was usually quite disastrous for the patients at the university's hospital, as is indicated by a journalist's account from 1899:

> It happens not infrequently that patients are submitted to examination when in their death agony. A doctor who visited the hospital told me he saw a party of students sounding a woman who was dying of pleurisy or pneumonia, in order that they might each hear the crepitation in her lungs as her last moments approached. She expired before they left the ward. He said something about treatment in another case to the professor who was lecturing these young men. The reply was, "Treatment, treatment, that is nothing; it is the diagnosis that we want" (O'Conor-Eccles 1899).

The mood in Vienna at the time of Krafft-Ebing's arrival could not have been more surreal – Crown Prince Rudolf had just killed his mistress and himself in Mayerling, and the Vienna press was reporting that Krafft-Ebing was attending to Rudolf's distraught mother Elisabeth, empress of the Hapsburg monarchy. Also, the scandal of the prince's death occurred during Vienna's annual carnival, the *Fasching,* a grotesque, extravagant celebration of masquerades and balls that lasted nearly two months. Krafft-Ebing participated in the festivities by attending the gala that traditionally ended the *Fasching,* which was held on the grounds of the university's insane asylum. Remarkably, some of the patients of the asylum were also in attendance:

> Milder cases were allowed to participate, usually in costumes they had made themselves. This year the Mayerling miasma seemed to have produced a horde of gory apparitions: executioners, cannibals, Blue-beards, Jack the Rippers, all hopping about frenzied to an all-inmate band "playing" waltzes on papier-mâché instruments (Morton 1979).

Legal and illegal commercial sex was another point of interest in *fin-de-siècle* Vienna; in a city of two million, there was an estimated population of between thirty to fifty thousand prostitutes, many of them underage. Accompanying the sexual commerce were the ostensible side effects of that time – syphilis, blackmail, and suicide. According to the writer Stefan Zweig, "one could read on the door of every sixth or seventh house, *Specialist for Skin and Venereal Diseases,* and to the fear of infection was added the horror of the disgusting and degrading forms of the erstwhile cures. . . ." (Zweig 1964).

Vienna was also beginning to experience a period rife with modernist achieve-ment that was later known as *die Wiener Moderne.* Synonymous with this era was a profusion of such notable minds as physicist and philosopher Ernst Mach (1838-1916), architect and designer Otto Wagner (1841-1918), composer and conductor Gustav Mahler (1860-1911), author and physician Arthur Schnitzler (1862-1931), Secession founder and painter Gustav Klimt (1862-1918), essayist and architect Adolf Loos (1870-1933), poet and playwright Hugo von Hofmannsthal (1874-1929), and *Die Fackel* founder and satirist Karl Kraus (1874-1936). The cafés of Vienna – especially the Griensteidl and the Central – greatly contributed to this impressive confluence of intelligentsia. It was a significant time, as noted by the historian Carl E. Schorske:

> Vienna in the *fin de siècle*, with its acutely felt tremors of social and political disintegration, proved one of the most fertile breeding grounds of our century's a-historical culture. Its great intellectual innovators – in music and philosophy, in economics and architecture, and, of course, in psychoanalysis – all broke, more or less deliberately, their ties to the historical outlook central to the nineteenth-century liberal culture in which they had been reared (Schorske 1981).

In this era of innovation, however, feuds and rivalries were somewhat commonplace, especially at the University of Vienna. For example, two famous and well-respected colleagues of Krafft-Ebing's, Josef Hyrtl (1810-1894) and Ernst Brücke (1819-1892), lived in the Anatomy Institute building (Hyrtl on the second floor, Brücke on the first). Upset over an largely imagined academic slight, Hyrtl

> took to using noisy tools when he knew that Brücke had company in the apartment below. Brücke retaliated by placing the dogs, on whom he conducted hunger experiments, under Hyrtl's windows, expecting to disturb him with their howling. To his amazement, however, Brücke found that the animals failed to lose weight as expected, until one day he discovered that Hyrtl secretly fed the poor beasts with meat that he threw down to them from his windows (Ellenberger 1970).

Krafft-Ebing was no exception, although he seemed to have avoided most of the political and personal battles normally engaged in within the halls of the university. Besides his controversial yet popular status as the bestselling author of *Psychopathia Sexualis*, Krafft-Ebing was also occasionally derided for his work in hypnosis; Moritz Benedikt, for instance, was so upset by Krafft-Ebing's hypnotic experiments that he wanted to force him to undergo "psychological analysis." Krafft-Ebing certainly did not help ease his colleagues' minds when he held a hypnotic "séance" at the home of his friend Berta Szeps. In attendance were sixty guests, including many members of the university's medical faculty. The most celebrated and respected surgeon in Vienna, Theodor Billroth (1829-94) – an old friend of

Krafft-Ebing's from his student days in Zurich – was also there. After Krafft-Ebing put a guest, a young female medium, into a trance, she unobtrusively removed a watch from another guest's pocket while under his spell. When, to the audience's surprise, she displayed the purloined watch to Krafft-Ebing, Billroth became furious and shouted, "Enough of these nasty tricks, this is a farce, an absolute scandal!" He then turned to Krafft-Ebing and exclaimed, "You are a swindler!" (Szeps 1939).

Perhaps Krafft-Ebing's most contentious relationship was with Sigmund Freud, which began when he criticized (with Meynert, Freud's mentor) Freud's cocaine experiments on neurotics. Freud was further angered after he delivered a lecture on April 21, 1896, before the Society for Psychiatry and Neurology, of which Krafft-Ebing was the chair. It was entitled "The Etiology of Hysteria," and was Freud's paper on his controversial "seduction theory," in which he believingly chronicled his patients' numerous stories of childhood sexual abuse supposedly committed by their servants, teachers, siblings, and parents. Freud later wrote to his friend Wilhelm Fliess what transpired afterward:

> A lecture on the etiology of hysteria at the psychiatric society was given an icy reception by the asses and a strange evaluation by Krafft-Ebing: "It sounds like a scientific fairy tale." And this, after one has demonstrated to them the solution of a more-than-thousand-year-old problem, *a caput Nili* [source of the Nile]! They can go to hell, euphemistically expressed (Freud 1985).

Incensed and feeling ostracized, Freud chose to not deliver another lecture in public for nearly ten years, even though he later rejected most of his paper's findings. (Krafft-Ebing's remark is especially interesting since he himself wrote of documented cases of infantile sexual abuse; Freud highlighted one such case in the margins of his own copy of *Psychopathia Sexualis* [see p. 624].)

Krafft-Ebing's relationship with Freud, however, was not altogether hostile. Freud had four inscribed copies of *Psychopathia Sexualis* in his library – the fifth, seventh, ninth and eleventh editions. The ninth edition of 1894 was inscribed: "To Herr Colleague Dr. Freud with friendly regards from the author." Krafft-Ebing's book was also a critical influence on Freud's position on bisexuality. Most important of all, Krafft-Ebing was, along with Professor Hermann Nothnagel (1841-1905), Freud's principal sponsor of his application for a paid position as a professor *extraordinarius* at the University of Vienna, which Freud ultimately was awarded in 1902. In a report dated May 10, 1897, Krafft-Ebing wrote that Freud possessed "unusual talent and [the] ability to direct scientific investigations into new pathways" (Sulloway 1979).

In 1901, Krafft-Ebing published a paper in Magnus Hirschfeld's *Jahrbücher für sexuelle Zwischenstufen* (Annual for Sexually Intermediate Stages) entitled "New Studies in the Domain of Homosexuality," in which he boldly reversed his previous position on homosexuality as a degenerative condition. Homosexuality was not a disease, he now argued, but a deviation – a normal, nonpathological variation of the sex drive:

> That contrary sexual sensation cannot thus be necessarily regarded as psychic degeneration, or even as a manifestation of disease, is shown by various considerations, one of the principal of which is that these variations of the sexual life may actually be associated with mental superiority. . . . The proof of this is the existence of men of all nations whose contrary sexuality is an established fact, and who, nonetheless, are the pride of their nation as authors, poets, artists, leaders of armies, and statesmen (Bloch 1908).

A psychiatrist of Krafft-Ebing's reputation declaring that homosexuality was similar to being colorblind or left-handed was a windfall for homosexual rights activists throughout Europe. Hirschfeld (1868-1935), founder of the Institute for Sexual Science in Berlin and an open homosexual, would later gratefully dedicate his book *Geschlechtsübergänge* (Sexual Pathology, 1917) in Krafft-Ebing's memory.

On March 11, 1902, Krafft-Ebing resigned from the University of Vienna due to ill health; according to the *British Medical Journal,* "he had long been suffering from a chronic affection of the kidneys" (British Medical Journal 1903). He retired to his home near Graz, where he revised the galleys of the twelfth and final edition of *Psychopathia Sexualis* and supervised the publication of his last book, *Psychosis menstrualis.*

Richard von Krafft-Ebing died on December 22, 1902, at the age of sixty-two. In his lifetime he had authored nearly four hundred articles and books, and collected over twenty thousand case histories. His successor at the University of Vienna, Julius Wagner von Jauregg (who would later win the Nobel Prize for Physiology and Medicine in 1927), paid homage in 1908 to Krafft-Ebing at a ceremony unveiling his statue at the university:

> In keeping with his deeply compassionate nature, it was a true satisfaction for him to wrench human weakness and flaws away from the judgment and outrage of the general public and to contribute to an understanding nurtured by pity and forgiveness. . . . By and by he sacrificed all distractions and enjoyments to his work; music, society, the enjoyment of nature; all had to recede more and more in the face of his all-encompassing drive to devote himself to his work. One can rightfully say that he worked himself to death (Jauregg 1908).

a note on the present edition.

This expanded edition of *Psychopathia Sexualis* utilized the following source material: the 1892 article "Die Bedeutung der Menstruation für das Zustandekommen geistig unfreier Zustände," published by the German psychiatric journal *Jahrbücher für Psychiatrie;* the 1893 seventh German edition and the 1903 twelfth German edition, published by Ferdinand Enke (Stuttgart); the 1893 seventh English edition, published by F. A. Davis Co. (Philadelphia) and translated by Charles Gilbert Chaddock; the 1906 twelfth English edition, published by Medical Art Agency (New York) and translated by F. J. Rebman in 1906; and the 1939 reissue of the 1906 Rebman edition, published by Pioneer Publications, with an introduction by Victor Robinson, M.D.

The two primary sources of text for this edition – the Chaddock and Rebman translations – were extensively edited, revised, corrected and checked against the German editions by myself and my associate editor, Susan King. Imogen von Tannenberg translated the *Jahrbücher für Psychiatrie* article and the German articles quoted in my introduction, and Peter O'Neill translated the passages written in Latin. The text that was originally in Latin has been set in a bold typeface to illustrate Krafft-Ebing's editorial choices of what he found to be "particularly revolting."

acknowledgments.

First and foremost, I would like to express my sincere gratitude to my sister and collaborator, Susan King, for all the time and energy she devoted to this project – as she well knows, it simply would not have been fully realized without her. Also, a note of thanks to her husband, Rob, for his patience.

During my stay in Vienna, the staff of the Institut für Geschichte der Medizin der Universität Wien were extremely helpful, especially director Karl Holubar and librarian Michael Oberhummer. I would also like to thank Dr. Felicitas Heimann-Jelinek, curator at the Jüdisches Museum der Stadt Wien, for her inspirational exhibition of *Ballastexistenzen* death masks, "Masken: Versuch über die Schoa."

My thanks also to Imogen von Tannenberg and Peter O'Neill for their translation work, Stefan Kloo at the Goethe Institute for his help, and my friends Eli Bonerz and Rebecca Cely for reading and proofing various revised drafts. Lastly, my loving thanks to Alexandra Patsavas for her support.

references.

Beard, George M. *American Nervousness: Its Causes and Consequences.* New York: G. P. Putnam, 1881.

Bloch, Iwan. *The Sexual Life of Our Time.* Translated by M. Eden Paul. New York: Allied Book Company, 1908.

British Medical Journal. Review of *Psychopathia Sexualis,* by Dr. R. von Krafft-Ebing. *British Medical Journal* (June 21, 1893): 1325-6.

———. "Freiherr von Krafft-Ebing, M.D." *British Medical Journal* (January 3, 1903): 53.

Cleugh, James. *The First Masochist: A Biography of Leopold von Sacher-Masoch.* New York: Stein and Day, 1967.

Deleuze, Gilles. *Masochism: An Interpretation of Coldness and Cruelty.* Translated by Jean McNeil. New York: George Braziller, 1971.

Ellenberger, Henri F. *The Discovery of the Unconscious: The History and Evolution of Dynamic Psychiatry.* New York: Basic Books, 1970.

Foucault, Michel. *The History of Sexuality.* Translated by Robert Hurley. New York: Vintage Books, 1978.

Freud, Sigmund. *The Complete Letters of Sigmund Freud to Wilhelm Fliess, 1887-1904.* Translated and edited by Jeffrey Moussaieff Masson. Cambridge, Massachusetts: The Belknap Press of Harvard University Press, 1985.

Fuchs, Alfred. "Hofrat Richard Freiherr v. Krafft-Ebing." *Muenchener Medizinische Wochenschrift* 4 (January 27, 1903): 167.

Gilman, Sander L. *Difference and Pathology: Stereotypes of Sexuality, Race, and Madness.* Ithaca, New York: Cornell University Press, 1985.

Jauregg, Julius Wagner von. "Richard v. Krafft-Ebing." *Wiener Medizinische Wochenschrift* 42 (October 17, 1908): 2305-11.

Johnson, John. "Psychopathia Sexualis." *The British Journal of Psychiatry* 122 (1973): 211-8.

Johnston, William M. *The Austrian Mind: An Intellectual and Social History 1848-1938.* Berkeley: University of California Press, 1972.

Karlen, Arno. *Sexuality and Homosexuality: A New View.* New York: W. W. Norton, 1971.

Krafft-Ebing, Richard von. *Text-book of Insanity, Based on Clinical Observations.* Translated by Charles Gilbert Chaddock. Philadelphia: F. A. Davis Company, 1905.

Le Rider, Jacques. *Modernity and Crises of Identity: Culture and Society in Fin-de-Siècle Vienna.* Translated by Rosemary Morris. Cambridge, England: Polity Press, 1993.

Leese, Arnold S. *My Irrelevant Defence, Being Meditations Inside Gaol and Out on Jewish Ritual Murder.* London: The I.F.L. Printing & Publishing Co., 1938.

Lifton, Robert Jay. *The Nazi Doctors: Medical Killing and the Psychology of Genocide.* New York: Basic Books, 1986.

Lombroso, Cesare. *Criminal Man.* New York: G. P. Putnam, 1911.

Morton, Frederic. *A Nervous Splendor: Vienna 1888/1889.* London: Weidenfeld and Nicolson, 1979.

Mosse, George L. *Toward the Final Solution: A History of European Racism.* New York: Howard Fertig, 1978.

————. *Nationalism and Sexuality: Respectability and Abnormal Sexuality in Modern Europe.* New York: Howard Fertig, 1985.

Nordau, Max. *Degeneration.* New York: D. Appleton and Company, 1895.

Nussbaum, Arthur. "The 'Ritual-Murder' Trial of Polna." *Historia Judaica* 9, no. 1 (1947): 57-74.

O'Conor-Eccles, C. "The Hospital Where the Plague Broke Out." *The Nineteenth Century* 46 (October 1899): 591-602.

Painter, George D. *Marcel Proust: A Biography.* London: Chatto and Windus, 1989.

Schorske, Carl E. *Fin-de-siècle Vienna.* New York: Vintage Books, 1981.

Sulloway, Frank J. *Freud, Biologist of the Mind: Beyond the Psychoanalytic Legend.* New York: Basic Books, 1979.

Szeps, Berta. *My Life and History.* Translated by John Sommerfield. New York: Alfred A. Knopf, 1939.

Van Groningen, J. *Freiheit, Liebe, Menschlichkeit! Ein Manifest des Geistes von hervorragenden Zeitgenossen* (Freedom, love, humanity! A manifesto of spirit by eminent contemporaries). Berlin: J. Van Groningen, 1893.

Webb, James. *The Occult Underground*. La Salle, Illinois: Open Court, 1974.

Wedekind, Frank. *Diary of an Erotic Life*. Translated by W. E. Yuill, and edited by Gerhard Hay. London: Basil Blackwell, 1990.

Zweig, Stefan. *The World of Yesterday*. Lincoln, Nebraska: University of Nebraska Press, 1964.

psychopathia sexualis

fragments of a system of psychology of sexual life

THE PROPAGATION of the human race is not left to mere accident or the caprices of the individual, but is guaranteed by the hidden laws of nature, which are enforced by a mighty, irresistible impulse. Sensual enjoyment and physical fitness are not the only conditions for the enforcement of these laws, but higher motives and aims, such as the desire to continue the species or the individuality of mental and physical qualities beyond time and space, exert a considerable influence. Man puts himself at once on a level with the beast if he seeks to gratify lust alone, but he elevates his superior position when, by curbing his animal desire, he combines with the sexual functions ideas of morality, the sublime, and the beautiful.

Placed upon this lofty pedestal he stands far above nature and draws from inexhaustible sources material for nobler enjoyments, for serious work, and for the realization of ideal aims. Maudsley (*Deutsche Klinik*, 1873, 2, 3) justly claims that sexual feeling is the basis upon which social advancement is developed: "If man were deprived of sexual distinction and the nobler enjoyments arising therefrom, all poetry and probably all moral tendency would be eliminated from his life."

Sexual life is no doubt the one mighty factor in the individual and social relations of man that discloses his powers of activity, of acquiring property, of establishing a home, and of awakening altruistic sentiments toward a person of the opposite sex, toward his own issue, as well as toward the whole human race.

Sexual feeling is really the root of all ethics, and no doubt of aestheticism and religion.

The most sublime virtues, even the sacrifice of self, may spring from sexual life, which, however, because of its sensual power, may easily degenerate into the lowest passion and basest vice.

Love unbridled is a volcano that burns down and lays waste all around it; it is an abyss that devours all – honor, substance and health.

It is of great psychological interest to follow up the gradual development of civilization and the influence exerted by sexual life upon habits and morality.[1] The gratification of the sexual instinct seems to be the primary motive in man as well as in beast. Sexual intercourse is done openly, and man and woman are not ashamed of their nakedness. The savage races, e.g., Australasians, Polynesians, and Malays of the Philippines, are still in this stage (see Ploss). Woman is the common property of man, the spoil of the strongest and mightiest who chooses the most winsome for his own; a sort of instinctive sexual selection of the fittest.

Woman is a "chattel," an article of commerce, exchange or gift, a vessel for sensual gratification, an implement for toil. The presence of shame in the manifestations and exercise of the sexual functions, and of modesty in the mutual relations between the sexes, are the foundations of morality. Thence arises the desire to cover the nakedness ("and they saw that they were naked") and to perform the act in private.

The development of this grade of civilization is furthered by the conditions of frigid climes which necessitate the protection of the whole body against the cold. It is an anthropological fact that modesty can be traced to much earlier periods among northern races.[2]

Another element that tends to promote the refined development of sexual life is the fact that woman ceases to be a "chattel." She becomes an individual being, and, although socially still far below man, she gradually acquires rights, independence of action, and the privilege to bestow her favors where she is inclined. She is wooed by man. Traces of ethical sentiments pervade the rude sensual appetite, idealization begins and the community of woman ceases. The sexes are drawn to each other by mental and physical merits and exchange favors out of preference. In this stage woman is conscious of the fact that her charms belong only to the man of her choice. She seeks to hide them from others. This forms the foundation of modesty, chastity and sexual fidelity, so long as love endures.

This development is hastened wherever nomadic habits yield to the spirit of colonization, where man establishes a household. He feels the necessity for a companion in life, a housewife in a settled home.

The Egyptians, the Israelites, the Greeks and the Teutonic races reached this level at early periods. Its principal characteristic is high appreciation of virginity, chastity, modesty and sexual fidelity, in strong contrast to the habits of other peoples where the host places the personal charms of the wife at the disposal of the guest.

The history of Japan furnishes a striking proof that this high grade of civilization is often the last stage of moral development, for in that country, as recently as twenty years ago, prostitution was not considered to impair in any way the social status of the future wife.

Christianity raised the union of the sexes to a sublime position by making woman the social equal of man and by elevating the bond of love to a moral and religious institution.[3] Thus the love of man, if considered from the standpoint of advanced civilization, can only be of a monogamous nature and must rest upon a stable basis. While nature can only lay claim to the law of propagation, a community (family or state) cannot subsist without the guarantee that the offspring thrive physically, morally and intellectually. From the moment woman was recognized as the peer of man, when monogamy became a law and was consolidated by legal, religious and moral conditions, the Christian nations obtained a mental and material superiority over the polygamous races, and especially over Islam.

Although Mohammed strove to raise woman from the position of the slave and mere handmaid of enjoyment to a higher social and matrimonial grade, she nevertheless remained far below man, who alone could obtain divorce on the easiest terms.

Above all things, Islamism excludes woman from public life and enterprise, and stifles her intellectual and moral advancement. The Mohammedan woman is simply a means for sensual gratification and the propagation of the species, while in the sunny balm of Christian doctrine her divine virtues and her qualities as housewife, companion and mother blossom forth. What a contrast!

Compare the two religions and their standard of future happiness. The Christian expects a heaven of spiritual bliss absolutely free from carnal pleasure; the Mohammedan expects an eternal harem, a paradise among lovely houris. Yet, in spite of the aid offered to him by religion, law, education and the moral code, the Christian (to subdue his sensual inclination) often drags pure and chaste love from its sublime pedestal and wallows in the quagmire of sensual enjoyment and lust.

Life is a never-ceasing duel between animal instinct and morality. Only willpower and a strong character can emancipate man from the meanness of his corrupt nature, and teach him how to enjoy the pure pleasures of love and pluck the noble fruits of earthly existence.

It is an open question whether the moral status of mankind has undergone an improvement in our times. No doubt society at large shows a greater veneer of modesty and virtue, and vice is not as flagrantly practiced as of yore.

The reader of Scherr (*Deutsche Kulturgeschichte*) will gain the impression that our moral code is not so gross as that of the Middle Ages, only because more refined manners have taken the place of former coarseness.

In comparing the various stages of civilization, it becomes evident that, despite periodic relapses, public morality has made steady progress, and that Christianity is the chief factor in this advance.

We are certainly far beyond the sodomitic idolatry, public life, legislation and religious exercises of ancient Greece, not to mention the worship of Phallus and Priapus in vogue among the Athenians and Babylonians, or the Bacchanalian feasts of the Romans and the privileged position held by the courtesans of those days.

In this slow progress there are stagnant and fluctuating periods, but they are only like the ebb- and flood-tide of sexual life in the individual.

The episodes of moral decay always coincide with the progression of effeminacy, lewdness and luxuriance of nations. These phenomena can only be ascribed to the higher and more stringent demands that circumstances place upon the nervous system. Exaggerated tension of the nervous system stimulates sensuality, leads the individual as well as the masses to excesses, and undermines the very foundations of society, as well as the morality and purity of family life. The material and moral ruin of the community is readily brought about by debauchery, adultery and luxury. Greece, the Roman Empire, and France under Louis XIV and XV, are striking examples of this assertion. In such periods of civic and moral decline the most monstrous excesses of sexual life may be observed; these, however, can always be traced to the psychopathological or neuropathological conditions of the nation involved.[4]

Large cities are hotbeds in which neuroses and low morality are bred; see the history of Babylon, Nineveh and Rome, and the mysteries of modern metropolitan life. It is a remarkable fact that among savages and half-civilized races, sexual intemperance is not observed (except among the Aleutians, as well as the Oriental and Nama-Hottentot women who practice masturbation).[5]

The study of sexual life in the individual naturally deals with its various phases, from the stage of puberty to the extinction of sexual feeling.

Mantegazza (*Physiologie der Liebe*) beautifully depicts the bodings and yearnings of awakening love; the mysterious sensations, foretastes and impulses that fill the heart long before the period of puberty has arrived. Psychologically speaking, this is, perhaps, the most momentous epoch of life, for the wealth of ideas and sentiments engendered through it forms the standard by which psychic activity may be measured.

The advance of puberty develops the impulses of youth, hitherto vague and undefined, into a conscious realization of sexual power. The psychological reactions of animal passion manifest themselves in the irresistible desires of intimacy, and in the longing to bestow the strange affections of nature upon others.

Religion and poetry frequently become the temporary haven of rest, even after the period of storm and stress has passed. Religious enthusiasm is more commonly seen in the young than in the old. The lives of the saints[6] are replete with remarkable records of temptations. The religious feasts of the ancients often degenerated into orgies, or into mystic cults of a voluptuous character. Even the meetings of certain modern sects simply dissolve themselves into obscene practices.

On the contrary, we find that the sexual instinct, when disappointed and unappeased, frequently seeks and finds a substitute in religion.

Even where psychopathological conditions are diagnosed beyond dispute, this relation between religious and sexual feelings can easily be established. The cause of religious insanity is often to be found in sexual aberration. In psychosis a motley mixture of religious and sexual delusions is observable; namely, in female lunatics who imagine that they are or will be the mother of God, and especially in persons who are slaves to masturbation. The cruel, sensual acts of chastisement, violation, emasculation, and even crucifixion, perpetrated upon oneself by religious maniacs, bear out this assertion.[7]

Anyone who attempts to explain the psychological relationship between religion and love encounters many difficulties, for numerous analogous instances present themselves.

Sexual inclinations and religious leanings (when considered as psychological factors) are composed of two elements.

Schleiermacher recognized the primary feeling of dependence as the paramount element in religion, long before modern anthropological and ethnographic research in the domain of primitive causes arrived at the same conclusions.

The secondary and truly ethical element, i.e., the love of God, enters the religious sentiment only when a higher stage of culture is attained. Initially, the double-faced, benevolent, yet angry, chimeras of complicated mythologies take the place of the evil spirits, until they in turn are dislodged by the benign form of the deity, the giver of perpetual happiness, whether it be in the shape of Jehovah as the author of all earthly blessings, or Allah who bestows physical delight in Paradise, or Christ who has gone before to prepare mansions of eternal light and bliss, or Nirvana who reigns in the heaven of the Buddhist.

The primary element of *sexual preference* is love, i.e., the expectation of unsurpassed pleasure. The secondary element is the feeling of dependence, although it is in reality the root from which all things grow, as the former may be entirely absent. It certainly exists in a stronger measure in woman, because of her social position and the passive part that she plays in the act of procreation; but at times it is also found in men who are of a feminine type.

Religion, as well as sexual love, is mystical and transcendental. In sexual love the real object of the instinct, i.e., propagation of the species, is not always present in the mind during the act, and the impulse is much stronger than could be justified by the gratification that can possibly be derived from it. Religious love strives for the possession of an object that is absolutely ideal, and cannot be defined by empirical knowledge. Both are metaphysical processes that give unlimited scope to the imagination.

They converge, however, in a similar *indefinite* focus; for the gratification of the sensual appetite promises a boon which far surpasses all other conceivable pleasures, and faith has in store a bliss that endures forever.

In either condition the mind is conscious of the enormous importance of the object to be obtained; thus impulses often become irresistible and overcome all opposing motives. Because at times neither of them can grasp the real object of their existence, however, they easily degenerate into fanaticism, in which intensity of emotion overbalances clearness and stability of reason. Expectation of unfathomed bliss is then coupled with reckless resignation and unconditional submission.

Due to this conformity, under high tension one dislodges the other, or both make their appearance together, for every violent upheaval in the soul must necessarily sweep along its surroundings. Nature, always the same, draws equally upon these two spheres of conception, initially forcing one, then the other, into stronger activity, even degenerating into acts of cruelty, either actively exercised or passively endured.

In religious life this may assume the shape of self-sacrifice or self-destruction, prompted by the idea that a victim is necessary for the material sustenance of the deity. The sacrifice is brought as a sign of reverence or submission, as a tribute, as an atonement for sins committed, or as a price wherewith to purchase happiness.

If, however, the offering consists in self-punishment – and that occurs in all religions! – it serves not only as a symbol of submission, or an equivalent in the exchange of present pain for future bliss, but everything that is thought to come from the deity, and all that is done in obedience to divine mandates or for the honor of the Godhead, is experienced directly as pleasure. Thus religious exuberance leads to ecstasy, a condition in which consciousness is so preoccupied with feelings of mental pleasure that distress is stripped of its painful quality.

Exaggerated religious enthusiasm also finds pleasure in the sacrifice of another person, when rapture combines with sympathy.

Similar manifestations may be observed in sexual life, as will be shown later on under the headings of "Sadism" and "Masochism."

Thus the relations existing between religion, lust, and cruelty[8] may be condensed into a formula: Religious and sexual hyperesthesia at the acme of development show the same volume of intensity and the same quality of excitement, and may therefore under given circumstances interchange. In certain pathological states, both will degenerate into cruelty.

Sexual influence is just as potent in awakening aesthetic sentiments. What other foundation is there for the plastic arts or poetry? From (sensual) love arises the warmth of fantasy that alone can inspire the creative mind, and the fire of sensual feeling kindles and preserves the glow and fervor of art.

This explains the sensual natures of great poets and artists.

The world of fantasy keeps pace with the development of sexual power. Whoever cannot be animated during this period by the ideals of all that is great, noble and beautiful remains a "Philistine" all his life. Even the dolt tries his hand at poetry when in love.

On the borders of physiological reaction, mysterious processes of maturing puberty can be observed that give origin to obscure yearnings and moods of despondency and *Weltschmerz,* rendering life tedious, coupled with the impulse to inflict pain and sorrow upon others (weak analogies of a psychological connection between lust and cruelty).

First love always gazes in a romantic, idealizing direction. It wraps the beloved object in a halo of perfection. In its incipient stages it is of a platonic character, and often turns to forms of poetry and history. With the approach of puberty it runs the risk of transferring the idealizing powers upon persons of the opposite sex, even when mentally, physically and socially such persons belong to an inferior class. To this may be easily traced many cases of misalliance, abduction, elopement and errors of early youth, and those sad tragedies of passionate love that are in conflict with the principles of morality or social standing, and often terminate in murder, self-destruction, or double suicide.

Purely sensual love is never true and lasting, and for this reason first love is usually but a passing infatuation, a fleeting passion.

True love is rooted in the recognition of the moral and mental qualities of the beloved person, is equally ready to share pleasures and sorrows, and is even ready to make sacrifices. True love shrinks from no dangers or obstacles in the struggle for the undisputed possession of the beloved.

Deeds of daring and heroism lie in its wake. Unless the moral foundation is solid, however, it will lead to crime, and jealousy often mars its beauty.

The love of the feeble-minded is based upon sentimentality, and, when unrequited, results in suicide.

Sentimental love is likely to degenerate into folly, especially when the sensual element lacks force (e.g., the Knight of Toggenburg, Don Quixote, and many of the minstrels and troubadours of the Middle Ages).

This kind of love is nauseating and has a repulsive or ludicrous effect on others, while true love and its manifestations command sympathy, respect, and even fear.

Love, when weak, is frequently turned away from its real object into different channels, such as voluptuous poetry, bizarre aesthetics, or religion. In the latter case it readily falls prey to mysticism, fanaticism, sectarianism, or religious mania. A smattering of all this can always be found in the immature love of early puberty. The poetical effusions of that period of life are then only worthy of perusal when they emanate from the pen of a truly endowed genius.

Ethical surroundings are necessary in order to elevate love to its true and pure form; sensuality, however, will ever remain its principal basis.

Platonic love is a platitude, a misnomer for "kindred spirits."

Because love implies the presence of sexual desire, it can only exist between persons of different sex capable of sexual intercourse. When these conditions are absent or destroyed, it is replaced by friendship.

The sexual functions of man exercise a marked influence upon the development and preservation of character. Manliness and self-reliance are not the qualities that adorn the impotent masturbator.

Gyurkovechky (*Männl. Impotenz,* Vienna, 1889) is correct in his observation that virility establishes the ratio of difference between old and young men, and that impotence impairs health, mental freshness, activity, self-confidence and imagination. The damage stands in proportion to the age of the subject and the extent of his debauchery.

The sudden loss of the virile powers often produces melancholia, or is the cause of suicide when life without love is a mere blank.

In cases where the reaction is less pronounced, the victim is morose, peevish, egotistical, jealous, narrow-minded, cowardly, as well as devoid of energy, self-respect and honor.

For instance, after castration the Skopzes rapidly degenerate.

This matter will be further elucidated under the heading of "Effemination."

In the sedate matron this condition is of minor psychological importance, although it is noticeable. The biological change barely affects her if her sexual career has been successful, and loving children gladden the maternal heart. The situation is different, however, when sterility has denied that happiness, or when enforced celibacy has prevented the performance of the natural functions.

These facts strongly characterize the differences that prevail in the psychology of sexual life in man and woman, and the dissimilarity of sexual feeling and desire in both.

Man has, without question, the stronger sexual appetite of the two. From the period of pubescence he is instinctively drawn toward woman. His love is sensual, and his choice is strongly prejudiced in favor of physical attractions. A powerful natural impulse makes him aggressive and impetuous in his courtship. The law of nature, however, does not completely fill his psychic being. Having won the prize, his love is temporarily eclipsed by other vital and social interests.

Woman, however, if physically and mentally normal, and properly educated, has but little sensual desire. If it were otherwise, marriage and family life would be empty words. For now, the man who avoids women, and the woman who seeks men, are sheer anomalies.

Woman is wooed for her favor. She remains passive. Her sexual organization demands it, and the dictates of good breeding come to her aid.

Nevertheless, sexual consciousness is stronger in woman than in man. Her need of love is greater – it is continual, not periodic – but her love is more spiritual than sensual. Man primarily loves woman as his wife, and then as the mother of his children; the first place in woman's heart belongs to the father of her child, the second to him as husband. Woman is influenced in her choice more by mental than physical qualities. As mother she divides her love between offspring and husband. Sensuality is merged in the mother's love. Thereafter the wife accepts marital intercourse not so much for sensual gratification as for proof of her husband's affection.

Woman loves with her whole soul. To woman love is life, to man it is the joy of life.

Misfortune in love bruises the heart of man, but it ruins the life of woman and wrecks her happiness. Whether woman can truly love twice in her life is a psychological question worthy of consideration. A woman's mind is certainly more inclined to monogamy than that of a man.

In the sexual demands of man's nature will be found the motives of his weakness toward woman. He is enslaved by her, and becomes more and more dependent upon her as he grows weaker, and the more he yields to sensuality. This accounts for the fact that in the periods of decline and luxury, sensuousness was the predominant factor. Thus arises the social danger when courtesans and their dependents rule the State and finally encompass its ruin.

History shows that great statesmen have often been the slaves of women in consequence of the neuropathic conditions of their constitution.

It shows a masterly psychological knowledge of human nature that the Roman Catholic Church enjoins celibacy upon its priests in order to emancipate them from sensuality, and to concentrate their entire activity on the pursuit of their calling. Nevertheless, it is a pity that the celibate state deprives the priest of the ennobling influence exercised by love and marital life upon the character.

Given that man by nature plays the aggressive role in sexual life, he is thus exposed to the danger of overstepping the limits set by law and morality.

The unfaithfulness of the wife, as compared with that of the husband, is morally of much wider bearing, and should always meet with severer punishment at the hands of the law. The unfaithful wife not only dishonors herself, but also her husband and her family, not to speak of the possible uncertainty of paternity.

Natural instincts and social position are frequent causes of disloyalty in the husband, while the wife is surrounded by many protecting influences.

Sexual intercourse is of different import to the spinster and the bachelor. Society expects of the bachelor modesty, but exacts of the spinster chastity as well. Modern civilization concedes only to the wife that exalted position in which woman sexually furthers the moral interests of society.

The ultimate aim, the ideal of woman, even when she is dragged in the mire of vice, ever is and will be marriage. Woman, as Mantegazza properly observes, seeks not only gratification of sensual desires, but also protection and support for herself and her offspring. No matter how sensual man may be, unless also thoroughly depraved, he seeks for a consort only that woman whose chastity he cannot doubt.

The emblem and ornament of woman aspiring to this state, truly worthy of herself, is modesty, so beautifully defined by Mantegazza as "one of the forms of physical self-esteem."

To discuss here the evolution of this, the most graceful of virtues in woman, is out of place, but most likely it is an outgrowth of the gradual rise of civilization.

A remarkable contrast may be found in the occasional exposure of physical charms, conventionally sanctioned by the world of fashion, in which even the most discreet maiden will indulge when robed for the ballroom, theatre, or similar social function. Although the reasons for such a display are obvious, the modest woman is fortunately no more conscious of them than of the motives that underlie periodic fashions, bringing certain forms of the body into undue prominence, to say nothing of corsets, etc.

In all times, and among all races, women are fond of fashion and finery. In the animal kingdom, nature has distinguished the male with the greater beauty. Men designate women as the beautiful sex, a gallantry which clearly arises from their sensual requirements. So long as woman seeks only self-gratification in personal adornment, and so long as she remains unconscious of the psychological reasons for thus making herself attractive, no objection can be raised against it; when done with the fixed purpose of pleasing men, however, it degenerates into coquetry.

Under analogous circumstances man would make himself ridiculous.

Woman far surpasses man in the natural psychology of love, partly because evolution and training have made love her proper element, and partly because she is animated by more refined feelings (Mantegazza).

Even the best of breeding concedes to man that he looks upon woman mainly as a means by which to satisfy the cravings of his natural instinct, though it confines him only to the woman of his choice. Thus civilization establishes a binding social contract which is called marriage, and grants by legal statutes protection and support to the wife and her issue.

It is important, and because of certain pathological manifestations (to be referred to later on) indispensable, to examine those psychological events that draw man and woman into that close union where the fullness of affection is concentrated only upon the beloved one to the exclusion of all other persons of the same sex.

If one could demonstrate design in the processes of nature (adaptation cannot be discounted), then the fact of fascination by one person of the opposite sex with indifference toward all others, as it occurs between true and happy lovers, would appear as a wonderful provision to ensure monogamy for the promotion of its object.

The scientific observer finds in this loving bond of hearts not only a mystery of souls, but also, almost always, a connection to certain physical or mental peculiarities in which the attracting power is qualified.

Hence the words *fetish* and *fetishism*. The word *fetish* signifies an object, or parts or attributes of objects, that by virtue of association to sentiment, personality, or absorbing ideas, exert a charm (the Portuguese *feitiço*) or at least produce a peculiar individual impression that is in no way connected with the external appearance of the sign, symbol or fetish.[9]

The individual valuation of the fetish, extending even to unreasoning enthusiasm, is called *fetishism*. This interesting psychological phenomenon may be explained by an empirical law of association, i.e., the relation existing between the notion itself and the parts thereof that are essentially active in the production of pleasurable emotions. It is most commonly found in religious and erotic spheres. Religious fetishism finds its original motive in the delusion that its object, i.e., the idol, is not a mere symbol, but possesses divine attributes, and ascribes to it peculiar wonder-working (relics) or protective (amulets) virtues.

Erotic fetishism makes an idol of physical or mental qualities of a person or even mere objects used by that person, etc., because they awaken powerful associations with the beloved person, thus initiating strong emotions of sexual pleasure. Analogies with religious fetishism are always discernible; for, in the latter, the most insignificant objects (hair, nails, bone, etc.) become at times fetishes which produce feelings of delight and even ecstasy.

The germ of sexual love is probably to be found in the individual charm (fetish) with which persons of opposite sex sway each other.

The case is simple enough when the sight of a person of the opposite sex occurs simultaneously with sexual excitement, whereby sexual excitement is intensified.

Emotional and optical impressions combine and are so deeply embedded in the mind that a recurring sensation awakens the visual memory and causes renewed sexual excitement, even orgasm and pollution (often only in dreams), in which case the physical appearance acts as a fetish.

Binet, among others, contends that mere peculiarities, whether physical or mental, may have the effect of the fetish, if their perception coincides with sexual emotion.

Experience shows that, in a large measure, chance controls this mental association; that the nature of the fetish varies with the personality of the individual, thus arousing the oddest sympathies or antipathies.

These physiological facts of fetishism often account for the affections that suddenly arise between man and woman; the preference of a certain person over all others of the same sex. Because the fetish assumes the form of a distinctive mark, it is clear that its effect can only be of an individual character. Because it is accentuated by the strongest feelings of pleasure, it follows that existing faults in the beloved are overlooked ("love is blind"), and an infatuation is produced that appears incomprehensible or silly to others. Thus it happens that the devoted lover who worships and invests his love with qualities that in reality do not exist is looked upon by others as simply mad. Thus love first exhibits itself as a mere passion, then as a pronounced psychic anomaly that attains what seemed impossible; it renders the ugly beautiful, the profane sublime, and obliterates all consciousness of existing duties toward others.

Tarde (*Archives de l'anthropologie criminelle,* vol. 5, no. 30) argues that although the form of this fetishism varies with persons as well as with nations, the ideal of beauty remains the same among civilized peoples of the same era.

Binet has more thoroughly analyzed and studied this fetishism of love.

From it springs the particular choice for slender or plump forms, for blondes or brunettes, for a particular shape or color of the eyes, tone of the voice, odor of the hair or body (even artificial perfume), contour of the hand, foot or ear, etc., which constitute the individual charm, the first link in a complicated chain of mental processes, all converging in that one focus, love; i.e., the physical and mental possession of the beloved.

This fact establishes the existence of *physiological* fetishism.

Without appearing as a pathological condition, the fetish may exercise its power so long as its leading qualities represent the integral parts, and so long as the love engendered by it encompasses the entire mental and physical personality.

Max Dessoir (pseudonym Ludwig Brunn)[10] in his article, "Der Fetischismus in der Liebe," cleverly says:

"Normal love appears to us as a symphony of tones of all kinds. It is roused by the most varied agencies. It is, so to speak, polytheistic. Fetishism recognizes only the tone-color of a single instrument; it issues forth from a single motive; it is monotheistic."

Even moderate thought will carry the conviction that the term "real love" (so often misused) can apply only where the entire person of the beloved becomes the physical and mental object of veneration.

Of course, there is always a sensual element in love, i.e., the desire to enjoy the full possession of the beloved object, and, in union with it, to fulfill the laws of nature.

Where the body of the beloved person is made the sole object of love, however, or if sexual pleasure alone is sought without regard to the communion of soul and mind, true love does not exist. Neither is it found among the disciples of Plato, who love the soul only and despise sexual enjoyment. In the one case the body is the fetish, in the other the soul, and love is fetishism.

Instances such as these simply represent transitions to pathological fetishism.

This assumption is enhanced by another criterion of true love, namely, the mental satisfaction derived from the sexual act.[11]

A striking phenomenon in fetishism is that among the many things that may serve as fetishes, there are some that gain significance more commonly than others; for instance, the hair, the hand, the foot of woman, or the expression of the eye. This is important in the pathology of fetishism.

Woman certainly seems more or less conscious of these facts. She devotes great attention to her hair and often spends an unreasonable amount of time and money upon its cultivation. How carefully the mother looks after her little daughter's hair! What an important part the hairdresser plays! The loss of hair causes despair to many young ladies. The author remembers the case of a vain woman who fell into melancholia because of this trouble, and finally committed suicide. A favorite subject of conversation among ladies is *coiffures*. Women are envious of each other's luxuriant tresses.

Beautiful hair is a powerful fetish with many men. In the legend of the Lorelei, who lured men to destruction, the "golden hair" she combs with a golden comb appears as a fetish. Frequently the hand or the foot possesses an attractiveness no less powerful; in these instances, however, masochistic and sadistic feelings often – though not always – assist in determining the peculiar kind of fetish.

By a transference through association of ideas, gloves or shoes obtain the significance of a fetish.

Max Dessoir (op. cit.) points out that, among the customs of the Middle Ages, drinking from the shoe of a beautiful woman (still to be found in Poland) played a remarkable part in gallantry and homage. The shoe also plays an important role in the legend of Aschenbrödel.

The expression of the eye is particularly important as a means of kindling the spark of love. A neuropathic eye frequently affects persons of either sex as a fetish. "Madame, your beautiful eyes cause me to die of love." (Molière).[12]

There are many examples showing that odors of the body become fetishes.

This fact is used to advantage by woman, either consciously or unconsciously, in the *ars amandi* ("art of love"). Ruth sought to attract Boaz by perfuming herself. The *demimonde* of ancient and modern times is noted for her lavish use of strong scents. Jäger, in his *Entdeckung der Seele,* calls attention to many olfactory sympathies.

Cases are known where men have married ugly women solely because their personal odors were exceedingly pleasing.

Binet makes it probable that the voice may also act as a fetish.

Belot, in his novel *Les baigneuses de Trouville,* makes the same assertion. Binet thinks that many marriages to singers are due to the fetish of their voices. He also observes that among the singing birds the voice has the same sexual significance that odors have among the quadrupeds. The birds allure with their song, and the male that sings most beautifully is joined at night by the charmed mate.

The pathological facts of masochism and sadism show that mental peculiarities may also act as fetishes, but in a wider sense.

Thus the fact of idiosyncrasies is explained, and the old proverb, "There is no disputing taste,"[13] retains its force.

With regard to fetishism in woman, science must, for the present time at least, be content with mere conjectures. It seems certain that as a physiological factor its effects are analogous to those in men, i.e., producing sexual sympathies toward persons of the same sex.

Details will come to our knowledge only when medical women enter into the study of this subject.

We may take it for granted that the physical as well as the mental qualities of man assume the form of the female fetish. In most cases, no doubt, the physical attributes of the male exercise this power without regard to the existence of conscious sensuality. On the other hand, it will be found that the mental superiority of man constitutes an attractive power when physical beauty is lacking. In the upper "strata" of society this is more apparent, even if we disregard the enormous influence exercised by "blue blood" and high breeding. The possibility that superior intellectual development favors advancement in social position and opens the way to a brilliant career does not seem to weigh heavily in the balance of judgment.

The fetishism of body and mind is of importance in procreation; it favors the selection of the fittest and the transmission of physical and mental virtues.

Generally speaking, the following masculine qualities impress woman; namely, physical strength, courage, nobility of mind, chivalry, self-confidence, self-assertion, insolence, bravado, and a conscious show of mastery over the weaker sex.

A "Don Juan" impresses many women and elicits admiration because he establishes the proof of his virile powers, although the inexperienced maiden can in no way suspect the many risks of syphilis and chronic urethritis she runs from a marital union with this otherwise interesting rake.

The successful actor, musician, vocal *artiste,* circus rider, athlete, and even the criminal, often fascinate the bread-and-butter miss as well as the maturer woman. At any rate, women rave over them, and inundate them with love letters.

It is a well-known fact that the female heart has a predominant weakness for military uniforms, preferring that of the cavalryman.

The hair of man – especially the beard, which is the emblem of virility and the secondary symbol of generative power – is a prevalent fetish with woman. To the degree that women bestow special care upon the cultivation of their hair, men who seek to attract and please women cultivate the elegant growth of the beard, especially the mustache.

The eye as well as the voice exert the same charm. Singers of renown easily touch woman's heart. They are overwhelmed with love letters and offers of marriage. Tenors have a decided advantage.

Binet (op. cit.) refers to this trait in an observation made by Dumas in his novel *La maison du vent,* in which a woman who falls in love with a tenor voice loses her virtue.

The author has not thus far succeeded in obtaining facts with regard to pathological fetishism in woman.

two

physiological facts

DURING THE time of the physiological processes in the reproductive glands, desires arise in the consciousness of the individual that have for their purpose the perpetuation of the species (sexual instinct).

Sexual desire during the years of sexual maturity is a physiological law. The duration of the physiological processes in the sexual organs, as well as the strength of the sexual desire manifested, vary, both in individuals and in races. Race, climate, heredity and social circumstances have a very decided influence upon it. The greater sensuality of southern races as compared with the sexual needs of those of the north is well-known. Sexual development in the inhabitants of tropical climes takes place much earlier than in those of more northern regions. In women of northern countries, ovulation, recognizable in the development of the body and in the occurrence of a periodic flow of blood from the genitals (menstruation), usually begins about the thirteenth to the fifteenth year; in men puberty, recognizable in the deepening of the voice, the appearance of hair on the face and mons pubis, and the occasional occurrence of pollutions, etc., takes place about the fifteenth year. In the inhabitants of tropical countries, however, sexual development starts several years earlier in women – sometimes as early as the eighth year.

It is worthy of remark that girls who live in cities develop about a year earlier than girls living in the country, and that the larger the town the earlier the development takes place, all else remaining the same.

Heredity, however, has a profound influence on desire and sexual power. Thus there are families with great physical strength and longevity where strong desire and virility are preserved until a great age, while in other families the sex life develops late and is extinguished early.

In woman the period of activity of the reproductive glands is shorter than in man, in whom sexual power may last until old age; ovulation ceases about thirty years after puberty. The period of waning activity of the ovaries is called the change of life (*climacteric, menopause*). This biological phase does not represent merely a cessation of functional potency and a final atrophy of the reproductive organs, but a transformation of the whole organism.

In Middle Europe the sexual maturity of man begins about the eighteenth year, and virility reaches its acme at forty. After that age it slowly declines. The power of procreation usually ceases at the age of sixty-two, but the power of coitus may be present much longer.

Although the existence of the sexual instinct is continuous during the time of sexual life, it varies in intensity. Under physiological conditions it is never periodic in the human male, as it is in animals; it manifests an organic variation of intensity in consonance with the collection and expenditure of semen. In women the degree of sexual desire coincides with the process of ovulation in such a way that sexual desire is intensified after the menstrual period.

Sexual instinct – as emotion, idea and impulse – is a function of the cerebral cortex. Thus far no definite region of the cortex has proven to be the exclusive seat of sexual sensations and impulses. This psychosexual center is nothing more than a junction and crossing of principal paths that lead, on the one hand, to the sensitive motor apparatus of the sexual organs, and, on the other hand, to those nerve centers of the visual and olfactory organs that are the carriers of the consciousness that distinguishes between the "male" and the "female."

Because of the close relations that exist between the sexual instinct and the olfactory sense,[1] it is to be presumed that the sexual and olfactory centers lie close together in the cerebral cortex. The development of sexual life has its beginning in the organic sensations that arise from the maturing reproductive glands. These excite the attention of the individual. Reading and the experiences of everyday life (which, unfortunately, are nowadays too early and too frequently suggestive), convert these notions into clear ideas, which are accentuated by organic sensations of a pleasurable character. With this accentuation of erotic ideas through lustful feelings, an impulse to induce them is developed (sexual desire).

Thus there is established a mutual dependence between the cerebral cortex (as the place of origin of sensations and ideas), and the reproductive organs. These organs, by reason of physiological processes (hyperemia, secretion of semen, ovulation), give rise to sexual ideas, images, and impulses.

The cerebral cortex, by means of preconceived or reproduced sensual ideas, reacts on the reproductive organs, causing hyperemia, production of semen, erection, and ejaculation. This is effected by the centers for vasomotor innervation and ejaculation, which are situated in the lumbar regions of the cord and lie close together. Both are reflex centers.

The center of erection (Goltz, Eckhard) is an intermediate station placed between the brain and the genital apparatus. The nervous paths that connect it with the brain probably run through the cerebral peduncle and the pons. This center may be excited by central (psychic and organic) stimuli, by direct irritation of the nerve tract in the cerebral peduncle, pons, or cervical portion of the cord, as well as by peripheral irritation of the sensory nerves (penis, clitoris and annexa). It is not directly subordinated to the will.

The excitation of this center is conveyed to the corpus cavernosum by means of nerves (nervi erigentes – Eckhard) running into the first three sacral nerves.

The action of the nervi erigentes, which renders erection possible, is inhibitory insofar as it inhibits the ganglionic nervous mechanism in the corpus cavernosum, upon which the action of the smooth muscle fibers of the corpus cavernosum are dependent (Kölliker and Kohlrausch). Under the influence of the action of the nervi erigentes, these fibers of the corpus cavernosum become relaxed, and their spaces fill with blood. Simultaneously, as a result of the dilation of the capillary network of the corpus cavernosum, pressure is exerted upon the veins of the penis and the return of blood is impeded. This effect is aided by the contraction of the bulbo cavernosus and erector penis muscles, which extend by means of an aponeurosis over the dorsal surface of the penis.

The erection center is under the influence of both exciting and inhibitory innervation arising from the cerebrum. Ideas and sense-perceptions of sexual content have an exciting effect. According to observations made on men that have been hanged, it is evident that the erection center may also be aroused by excitation of the tract of the spinal cord. Observations of the insane and those suffering from cerebral disease show that this is also possible as a result of organic irritation in the cerebral cortex (psychosexual center?). Spinal diseases (tabes, especially myelitis) affecting the lumbar portion[2] of the cord, in their earlier stages, may directly excite the erection center.

Reflex excitation of the center is possible and frequent in the following ways: by irritation of the (peripheral) sensory nerves of the genitals and surrounding parts by friction; by irritation of the urethra (gonorrhea), the rectum (hemorrhoids, pinworm), or the bladder (distention with urine, especially in the morning; irritation of calculi); by distention of the seminal vesicles with semen; by hyperemia of the genitals, occasioned by lying on the back and thus inducing pressure from the intestines upon the blood vessels of the pelvis.

The erection center may also be excited by irritation of the nervous ganglia, which are very abundant in the prostatic tissue (prostatitis, introduction of catheter, etc.).

The experiment of Goltz – according to whom, when (in dogs) the lumbar portion of the cord is severed, erection is more easily induced – shows that the erection center is also subject to inhibitory influences from the brain.

The fact that, in men, willpower and emotions (fear of unsuccessful coitus, surprise during the sexual act, etc.) can inhibit the occurrence of erection, and cause it, when present, to disappear, also indicates this.

The duration of erection is dependent upon the duration of its exciting causes (sensory stimuli), the absence of inhibitory influences, the nervous energy of the center, and the early or late occurrence of ejaculation (see below).

The central point of the sexual mechanism is the cerebral cortex. It is justifiable to presume that there is a definite region of the cortex (cerebral center) that gives rise to sexual feelings, ideas and impulses, and is the place of origin of the psychosomatic processes that we designate as *sexual life, sexual instinct,* and *sexual desire.* This center is susceptible to both central and peripheral stimuli.

Central stimuli, in the form of organic excitation, may be due to diseases of the cerebral cortex. Physiologically they are dominated by psychic impressions (memory and sensory perceptions, lascivious stories, touch, pressure of the hand, kiss, etc.). Auditory and olfactory perceptions certainly play but a very subordinate role. Under pathological conditions (see below), olfactory perceptions have a very decided influence in inducing sexual excitement.[3]

In beasts, the influence of olfactory perception on the sexual sense is unmistakable. Althaus ("Beiträge zur Physiol. u. Pathol. des Olfaktorius," *Arch. für Psych.,* vol. 12, no. 1) declares that the sense of smell is important with reference to the reproduction of the species. He shows that animals of opposite sexes are drawn to each other by means of olfactory perception, and that almost all animals, at the time of rutting, emit a distinct odor from their genitals. An experiment by Schiff confirms this. He extirpated the olfactory nerves in puppies, and found that, as the animals grew up, the male was unable to distinguish the female. Again, an experiment by Mantegazza (*Hygiene der Liebe*), who removed the eyes of rabbits and found that the defect constituted no obstacle to procreation, shows how important the olfactory sense is for the sex life in animals.

It is also remarkable that many animals (musk ox, civet cat, beaver) possess, on their sexual organs, glands that secrete substances with a very strong odor.

Althaus also shows that in man there are certain relations existing between the olfactory and sexual senses. He mentions Cloquet (*Osphrésiologie,* Paris, 1826), who calls attention to the sensual pleasure excited by the odor of flowers, and tells how Richelieu lived in an atmosphere laden with the heaviest perfumes in order to excite his sexual functions.

Zippe (*Wien. med. Wochenschrift,* 1879, no. 24), in connection with a case of kleptomania in a masturbator, likewise establishes such relations, and cites Hildebrand as an authority, who in his popular physiology says: "It cannot be doubted that the olfactory sense stands in remote connection to the sexual apparatus. Odors of flowers often occasion pleasurable sensual feelings, and when one remembers the passage in the 'Song of Solomon' – 'And my hands dropped with myrrh, and my fingers with sweet-smelling myrrh, upon the handles of the lock' – one finds that it did not escape Solomon's observation. In the Orient the pleasant perfumes are esteemed for their relation to the sexual organs, and the apartments of the Sultan's women are redolent with the fragrance of flowers."

Most, professor in Rostock (cf. Zippe), relates: "I learned from a sensual young peasant that he had excited many a chaste girl sexually, and easily landed his prey, by carrying his handkerchief in his armpit for a time while dancing, and then wiping his partner's perspiring face with it."

The case of Henry III shows that contact with a person's perspiration may be the exciting cause of passionate love. At the betrothal feast of the King of Navarre and Margaret of Valois, he accidentally dried his face with a garment of Maria of Cleves, which was moist with her perspiration. Although she was the bride of the Prince of Condé, Henry immediately conceived such a passionate love for her that he could not resist it, and made her, as history shows, very unhappy. An analogous instance is related about Henry IV, whose passion for the beautiful Gabriel is said to have originated at the instant when, at a ball, he wiped his brow with her handkerchief.

Professor Jäger, the "discoverer of the soul," refers to the same thing in his well-known book (*Entdeckung der Seel*, 2d. ed., 1880, chap. 15, p. 173); for he regards the sweat as important in the production of sexual effects, and as being especially seductive.[4]

One learns from reading the work of Ploss (*Das Weib*) that, in popular psychology, attempts to attract a person of the opposite sex by means of perspiration may still be discerned in many forms.

With reference to this, Jäger reports a custom still practiced by the natives of the Philippine Islands when they become engaged. When it becomes necessary for an engaged pair to separate, they exchange articles of wearing apparel, by means of which each becomes assured of faithfulness. These objects are carefully preserved, covered with kisses, and smelled.

The love of certain libertines and sensual women for perfumes[5] indicates a relation between the olfactory and the sexual senses.

A case mentioned by Heschl (*Wiener Zeitschr. f. prakt. Heilkunde,* March 22, 1861) is remarkable, where the absence of both olfactory lobes was accompanied by imperfectly developed genitals. It was the case of a man aged forty-five, in all respects well-developed, with the exception of his testicles, which were no larger than beans and contained no seminal canals, and his larynx, which seemed to be of feminine dimensions. Every trace of olfactory nerves was absent, as were the trigona olfactoria and the furrow on the undersurface of the anterior lobes. The perforations of the ethmoid plate were barely present, and occupied by nerveless processes of the dura instead of nerves. There was also an absence of nerves in the mucous membrane of the nose.

Finally, in mental diseases, the clearly defined relation of the olfactory and sexual senses is worthy of notice, for in the psychoses of both sexes superinduced by masturbation, as well as in insanity due to disease of the female organs (or during menopause), olfactory hallucinations are especially frequent, while in cases where a sexual cause is nonexistent, they are very infrequent.

I am inclined to doubt[6] that, under normal conditions, olfactory impressions in man, when contrasted with animals, play an important role in the excitation of the sexual center. Because of the importance of this consensus for the understanding of pathological cases, it is necessary here to thoroughly consider the relations existing between the olfactory and sexual senses.

With reference to these physiological relations, it may be mentioned as an interesting fact that there exists a certain histological conformity between the nose and the genitals, for both (as well as the nipple) have erectile tissue.

Interesting physiological and clinical observations by J. N. Mackenzie may be found in the *Journal of Medical Science,* April 1884. He finds: [1] that in certain women with normal olfactory organs a swelling of the erectile tissue of the nose regularly occurs with menstruation, and then disappears with the flow; [2] that menstruation is at times replaced by nosebleed, which disappears when the uterine flow begins, but in some cases always recurs with the menstrual functions; [3] that irritations of the nasal organs, such as violent sneezing, etc., occur at the time of sexual excitement; [4] stimulation of the genital tracts is occasioned by ailments of the nasal organs.

He also observes that nasal ailments in women grow worse during the time of menstruation; that venereal excesses produce inflammation of the Schneiderian membrane, or intensify it when it already exists.

He also points out that masturbators very frequently suffer from nasal disease, are troubled with abnormal sensations of olfaction, and are subject to nosebleed. According to his experience, there are ailments of the nose that stubbornly resist all treatment until the concomitant (and causal) genital disease is removed.

Other interesting observations and elucidations about the harmony between the nose and the genitals may be found in a book recently published by Fliess: *Die Beziehungen zwischen Nase und weiblichen Geschlechtsorganen,* Vienna (Deuticke), 1897; Cerviset, *Contribut. à l'étude du tissu érectile des fosses nasales,* Thèse de Lyon, 1887; Joal, *Revue mensuelle de laryngologie,* February 1888; Peyer, *Münch. med. Wochenschr.,* vol. 4, 1889; Endriss, dissertation, Würzburg, 1892.

The sexual sphere of the cerebral cortex may be excited, in the sense of an excitation of sexual concepts and impulses, by processes in the generative organs. This is possible as a result of all conditions that excite the erection center by means of centripetal influence (stimulus resulting from distention of the seminal vesicles; enlarged Graafian follicles; any sensory stimulus, however produced, about the genitals; hyperemia and turgescence of the genitals, especially of the erectile tissue of the corpus cavernosum of the penis and clitoris, as a result of a luxurious, sedentary life; abdominal plethora, high external temperature, warm beds, clothing; taking of cantharides [Spanish fly], pepper and other spices).

Sexual desire may also be induced by stimulation of the gluteal region (castigation, whipping).[7]

This fact is important for the proper understanding of certain pathological manifestations. It sometimes happens that in boys the first excitation of the sexual instinct is caused by a spanking, and they are thus incited to masturbate. This should be remembered by those who have the responsibility of children.

Because of the dangers caused by this form of punishment, it would be better if parents, teachers and nurses were to avoid it entirely.

Passive flagellation can excite sensuality, as is shown by the sects of flagellants[8] that were so widespread in the thirteenth and fifteenth centuries. They were accustomed to whip themselves, partly as an atonement and partly to mortify the flesh (in accordance with the principle of chastity promulgated by the Church – i.e., the emancipation of the soul from sensuality).

These sects were initially favored by the Church; but, because sensuality was only all the more excited by flagellation, and this fact became apparent in unpleasant occurrences, the Church was finally compelled to oppose it. The following facts from the lives of the two heroines of flagellation, Maria Magdalena of Pazzi and Elizabeth of Genton, clearly show the significance of flagellation as a sexual excitant. The former, the daughter of distinguished parents, was a Carmelite nun in Florence (about 1580), and, by her flagellations, and still more through the results obtained by them, she became quite celebrated, and is mentioned in the *Annals*. It was her greatest delight to have her hands bound behind her back by the prioress, and her naked loins whipped in the presence of the assembled sisters.

But the whippings, continued from her earliest youth, quite destroyed her nervous system, and perhaps no other heroine of flagellation had so many hallucinations ("raptures"). While being whipped her thoughts were of love. The inner fire threatened to consume her, and she frequently cried, "Enough! Fan no longer the flame that consumes me. This is not the death I long for; it comes with all too much pleasure and delight." Thus it continued. But the spirit of impurity wove the most sensual lascivious fantasies, and she was several times near losing her chastity.

It was the same with Elizabeth of Genton. As a result of whipping, she actually passed into a state of bacchanalian madness. As a rule she raved when, excited by unusual flagellation, she believed herself united with her "ideal." This condition was so exquisitely pleasant to her that she would frequently cry out, "O love, O eternal love, O love, O you creatures! cry out with me: 'Love, Love!' "

It is known, on the authority of Taxil (op. cit., p. 175), that rakes sometimes, just before the sexual act, have themselves flagellated or pricked until blood flows, in order to stimulate their diminished sexual power.

These facts find an interesting confirmation in the following experiences, taken from Paullini's *Flagellum Salutis* (1st ed., 1698; reprint, Stuttgart, 1847):

"There are some nations, namely, the Persians and Russians, where the women regard blows as a peculiar sign of love and favor. Strangely enough, the Russian women are never more pleased and delighted than when they receive hard blows from their husbands, as John Barclarus relates in a remarkable narrative. A German, named Jordan, went to Russia, and, pleased with the country, settled there and took a Russian wife, whom he loved dearly, and to whom he was always kind. But she always wore an expression of dissatisfaction, and went about with sighs and downcast eyes. The husband asked the reason, for he could not understand what was wrong. 'Aye,' she said, 'though you love me, you do not show me any sign of it.' He embraced her, and begged to be told what he had carelessly and unconsciously done to hurt her feelings, and asked to be forgiven, for he would never do it again. 'I want nothing,' was the answer, 'but what is customary in our country – the whip, the real sign of love.' When Jordan adopted the custom, his wife began to love him dearly.

"Similar stories are told by Peter Petreus of Erlesund, who adds that husbands, immediately after the wedding, provide themselves with, among other indispensable household articles, a whip."

On page 73 of this remarkable book, the author says further: "The celebrated Count of Mirandula, John Picus, relates of one of his intimate acquaintances that he was an insatiable fellow, but so lazy and incapable of love that he was practically impotent until he had been roughly handled. The more he tried to satisfy his desire, the heavier the blows he needed, and he could not attain his desire unless he had been whipped until the blood flowed. For this purpose he had a suitable whip made, which was placed in vinegar the day before using it. He would give this to his companion, and on bent knees beg her not to spare him, but to strike blows with it, the heavier the better. The good count thought this singular man found the pleasure of love in this punishment. Not being a bad man in other respects, he understood and hated his weakness."

Coelius Rhodigin relates a similar story, as does also the celebrated jurist, Andreas Tiraquell. In the time of the skillful physician, Otten Brunfelsen, there lived in Munich, then the capital of the Bavarian electorate, a debauchee who could never perform his sexual duties without a severe preparatory beating. Thomas Berthelin knew a Venetian who had to be beaten and driven before he could have intercourse, just as reluctant Cupid was driven by his followers with sprays of hyacinths. In Lübeck a few years ago there was a cheesemonger living on Mill Street who, on the basis of a complaint of unfaithfulness made to the authorities, was ordered to leave the city. The prostitute with whom he had been unfaithful went to the judges and begged on his behalf, telling how difficult intercourse had become for him. He could do nothing until he had been mercilessly beaten. At first the fellow, from shame and to avoid disgrace, would not confess, but after earnest questioning he could not deny it. There is said to have been a man in the Netherlands who was similarly incapable, and could do nothing without blows. By decree of the authorities, however, he was not only removed from his position, but also severely punished. A reliable friend, a physician in an important city of the kingdom, related to me how a woman of bad character had told a companion, who had been in the hospital a short time before, that she, with another woman of similar character, had been sent to the woods by a man who followed them there, cut rods for them, then exposed his naked buttocks and commanded them to belabor him well. They obeyed, and it is easy to conjecture what he then did with them. Not only have men been thus excited and inflamed to lasciviousness, but also women, so that they too might experience greater intensity of pleasure. For this reason the Roman woman had herself whipped and beaten by the *lupercis*. Thus Juvenal writes:

> "They die barren, and in vain
>   they sample Lyde's foreign nostrums guaranteed to induce conception,
>   or hold out eager hands to be struck by the Lupercus' goatskins."

It is a common proceeding for blasé and impotent men to have themselves whipped. A few years ago much noise was made about one such amateur who died while being whipped by several women in a house of prostitution in Moscow (Ibankow, *Archives d'Anthropol. criminelle,* vol. 14, p. 697).

In men, as well as in women, erection and orgasm, or even ejaculation, may be induced by irritation of various other regions of the skin and mucous membrane. These "hyperesthetic" zones in woman are, while she is a virgin, the clitoris, and, after defloration, the vagina and cervix uteri.

In woman, the nipple seems to particularly possess this quality. *Titallatio hujus regionis* plays an important part in the *ars erotica.* In his *Topograph. Anatomie,* 1865, vol. 1, p. 552, Hyrtl cites Val. Hildenbrandt, who observed a peculiar anomaly of the sexual instinct in a girl, which he called *suctusstupratio.* She had her breasts sucked by her lover, and after a while, by constantly pulling her nipples, she was able to suck them herself, an act that gave her the most intense pleasure. Hyrtl also calls attention to the fact that cows sometimes suck the milk from their own udders. L. Brunn (*Zeitg. f. Literatur,* etc., correspondent in Hamburg, 1889, no. 21), in an interesting article "Aus Liebe zum Schwachen, Unentwickelten, Hilflosen," points out how zealously the nursing mother gives herself to the nursing of the babe, "for love of the weak, undeveloped, helpless being."

Beside the ethical motives, it is easy to assume that a part is played by the fact that the sucking may be attended by feelings of physical pleasure. There is evidence that speaks in favor of this assumption. Brunn remarks that, according to Houzeau's experience, among the majority of animals, relations between mother and offspring are only close during the time of nursing, and indifferent thereafter; an observation that is correct in itself, though one-sided.

Bastian found the same thing (blunting of the feeling for the offspring after weaning) among savages.

Under pathological conditions, as shown by Chambard, other portions of the body (in hysterical persons) near the breasts and genitals may attain the significance of "hyperesthetic" zones.

In man, physiologically, the only "hyperesthetic" zone is the glans penis and perhaps the skin of the external genitals.

Under pathological conditions the anus may become a "hyperesthetic" area. Thus anal masturbation, which seems to be only too frequent, and passive pederasty would be explained. (Cf. Garnier, *Anomalies sexuelles,* Paris, p. 514; A. Moll, *Konträre Sexualempfindung,* 3d ed., p. 369; Frigerio, *Archivio di Psichiatria,* 1893; Cristiani, *Archivio delle Psicopatie sessuali,* p. 182, "Autopederastia in un alienato, affetto da follia periodica.")

The psycho-physiological process, comprehended in the idea of sexual instinct, is composed of

    [1] concepts awakened centrally or peripherally;
    [2] the pleasurable feelings associated with them.

The longing for sexual satisfaction (sexual desire) arises from them. This desire grows constantly stronger in dimension as the excitation of the cerebral sphere accentuates the feeling of pleasure with appropriate conceptions and activity of the imagination, and the pleasurable sensations are increased to lustful feelings by excitation of the erection center and the consequent hyperemia of the genitals (entrance of liquor prostaticus into the urethra, etc.).

If circumstances favor the satisfactory performance of the sexual act, the ever-increasing desire is gratified; if, however, conditions are unfavorable, inhibition occurs, checks the central erectile power, and prevents the sexual act.

To civilized man, the ready presence of ideas that inhibit sexual desire is distinctly important. The moral freedom of the individual, and the decision whether, under certain circumstances, excess, and even crime, be committed or not, depend, on the one hand, upon the strength of the instinctive impulses and the accompanying organic sensations; on the other, upon the power of the inhibitory ideas. Constitution, and especially organic influences, have a marked effect upon the instinctive impulses; education and cultivation of self-control counteract these influences.

The exciting and inhibitory powers are variable quantities. For instance, over-indulgence in alcohol is fatal in this respect because it awakens and increases sexual desire as it weakens moral resistance.

the act of cohabitation.[9]

The essential condition for the man is sufficient erection. Aujel (*Archiv für Psychiatrie,* vol. 8, no. 2) calls attention to the fact that in sexual excitement, not only is the erection center influenced, but the nervous excitement is distributed over the entire vasomotor system of nerves as well. The proof of this is the turgescence of the organs in the sexual act, injection of the conjunctiva, prominence of the eyeballs, dilation of the pupils, cardiac palpitation (resulting from paralysis of the vasomotor nerves of the heart, which arises from the cervical sympathetic nervous system, the resulting dilation of the cardiac arteries, and the increased stimulation of the cardiac ganglia induced by the consequent hyperemia of the cardiac walls). The sexual act is accompanied by a pleasurable feeling, evoked in the male by the passage of semen through the ejaculatory duct to the urethra, in consequence of the sensory stimulation of the genitals. This pleasurable sensation occurs earlier in the male than in the female, grows rapidly in intensity up to the moment of commencing ejaculation, reaches its acme at the instant of free emission, and disappears quickly after ejaculation.

In the female the pleasurable feeling occurs later and comes on more slowly, and generally outlasts the act of ejaculation.

The distinctive event in coitus is ejaculation. This function is dependent on a center (genital-spinal), which Budge has shown to be situated at the level of the fourth lumbar vertebra. It is a reflex center. The stimulus that excites it is the ejection of semen from the seminal vesicles into the pars membrana urethra, a reflex effect of stimulation of the glans penis. As soon as the collection of semen, with an ever-increasing pleasurable sensation, has reached a sufficient amount to be effectual as a stimulus of the ejaculation center, this center acts. The reflex motor path lies in the fourth and fifth lumbar nerves. The action consists of a convulsive excitation of the bulbocavernosus muscle (innervated by the third and fourth sacral nerves), which forces the semen out.

In the female as well, at the height of sexual and pleasurable excitement, a reflex movement occurs. It is induced by stimulation of the sensory genital nerves and consists of a peristaltic movement in the tubes and uterus as far down as the portio vaginalis, which presses out the mucous secretions of the tubes and uterus. Inhibition of the ejaculation center is possible as a result of cortical influence (absence of desire in coitus, emotions in general, influence of the will).

Under normal conditions, with the completion of the sexual act, sexual desire and erection disappear, and the psychic and sexual excitement is replaced by a comfortable feeling of lassitude.

three

anthropological facts[1]

EVERY INDIVIDUAL whose sexual development has been in accordance with the normal process represents physical and metaphysical attributes that are, as experience shows, typical of the sex to which the individual belongs. These sexual characteristics are either primary (sexual glands and organs of propagation) or secondary. The secondary sexual characteristics are bodily and psychic and are developed only during the period of puberty. Now and then cases of precocious, as well as retarded, sexual development are reported. As a rule they may be found to be due to abnormal evolutionary conditions in them, chiefly in individuals with a heavy neurotic taint.

The secondary sexual characteristics differentiate the two sexes; they designate the specific male and female types. The higher the anthropological development of the race, the stronger these contrasts between man and woman, and vice versa.

Important somatic secondary sexual characteristics are the skull, skeleton, pelvis (particularly), facial type, hair, larynx (voice), breasts, thighs, etc.

Important psychic characteristics are sexual consciousness (i.e., the knowledge of a special sexual individuality as man or woman) and a congruous sexual instinct, from both of which a long series of special features and individual peculiarities are evolved, such as psychic dispositions, inclinations, etc.

This differentiation of the sexes and the development of sexual types is evidently the result of an infinite succession of intermediary stages of evolution. The primary stage undoubtedly was bisexuality, such as still exists in the lowest classes of animal life as well as during the first months of fetal existence in man. The present stage of evolution is monosexuality, that is to say, a congruous development of the secondary bodily and psychic sexual characteristics belonging to the respective sexual glands.

Observation teaches that the pure type of the man or the woman is often enough missed by nature, that is to say that certain secondary male characteristics are found in woman and vice versa; to wit, men with an inclination for female occupations (embroidery, fashion, etc.), and women with a decided predilection for manly sports (without the influencing elements of early education). In both instances, particular cleverness in the inverted occupation and pronounced awkwardness in the originally proper occupation will be noticed. In this class belong castrates and women with a bass voice (abnormal development of the larynx), a narrow pelvis, a beard, undeveloped breasts, etc.

Of special scientific interest are the cases of gynecomastia, i.e., the development of breasts in the male individual, with concomitant inhibited development of the testicles during the period of puberty. Galen described and named this anomaly. Laurent's monograph[2] on this subject is worthy of mention.

As a rule the gynecomast is slender in build, has a smooth face and stunted testicles, is devoid of the secondary sexual characteristics of the man, has but little sexual desire for the opposite sex – is, in short, a sort of man-woman of moral and metaphysical inferiority.

It is a remarkable fact that gynecomastia only occurs in neurotically degenerated families and must be looked upon as the manifestation of an anatomical and functional degeneration.

Castration never produces gynecomastia, in which the glandular tissue but rarely develops, while the nipple becomes erogenous and capable of erection as in woman. Lactation has but seldom been observed. With involution even the breasts disappear. The true gynecomast betrays the signs of effemination – the voice is soft and has a high pitch, the hair on the mons pubis is that of a woman, the skin is soft, the pelvis wide; potency, though weak, is nevertheless heterosexual, and desire is absent. It cannot be denied that in these cases, through the interruption of evolutionary processes, the sexual characteristics of the man have been replaced by those of the woman, and, because of this substitution, the development of other physical and psychic sexual characteristics has been influenced in the sense of inversion. The possible combinations, of course, vary greatly.

An interesting and important question now arises, namely: "In the development of an individual having a definite sexual type, what is it that determines who will possess all the characteristics of a man or of a woman?"

One is tempted to look upon the development of the genital glands as the determining factor; these may be recognized even in the apparently bisexual fetus. For the primary sexual characteristics are present in the form of the sexual organs and may, with puberty, be developed into the secondary sexual characteristics.

That the sexual glands are important insofar as the sex itself is concerned is hardly open to controversy, but they are not necessarily the determining factor. As we shall see later on, the secondary characteristics (sexual sensations, attraction by the physical and psychic properties of the opposite sex, and the instinct to have sexual intercourse with persons of the opposite sex) may be inverted even at the very beginning of sexual development.

Again, the experience of gynecologists permits the following deductions. Hegar (Nothnagel's *Pathologie*, vol. 20, pt. 1, p. 371) points out:

[1] that despite congenital defects and rudimentary development of the ovaries, the feminine type may be thoroughly preserved;

[2] that the female sexual characteristics are relatively independent of the ovaries, as is proved by transverse hermaphroditism. The old axiom, *"Propter solum ovarium mulier est quod est"* ("It is only her ovaries that makes woman what she is"), therefore falls.

The sex-determining momentum is unknown. The form of the sexual glands is therefore not the qualifying element of sex-determination; instead we must look to sexual sensations and the sexual instinct.

All this directs our attention to the central domains of the nervous plexus that dominates the sexual functions and renders intermediary sexual gradations between the pure type of man and woman possible, quite in accordance with the original bisexual predisposition of the fetus. These grades may be due to some interference in the evolution of our present monosexuality (corresponding physical and psychic sexual characteristics) based upon degenerative, especially hereditarily degenerative, conditions.

The science of today can boast of but little positive knowledge regarding the evolutionary influence various departments of the sexual apparatus exercise upon each other. It is natural that we should study the influence exercised by the removal or total loss of the sexual glands upon the development or course of the sex life. That such an influence exists cannot be doubted; but the extent of the controlling power of peripheral factors might largely depend on whether the elimination of the sexual glands took place before or after the development of puberty; and again due regard must be given to the fact that the rise of psychic sexual characteristics may have considerably preceded physical development. Facts seem to prove that with the loss of the genital glands *previous* to puberty, the development of somatic and psychic sexual characteristics is stunted even to the point of *asexuality*. This is true for the human male and female as well as domestic animals.

Matters are different if the injury occurs *after* this biological phase. Here we are bound to find already existing physical as well as psychic characteristics, but their further development becomes stunted. The manner in which these organs succumb (through illness or surgical interference) is of no import; neither is the sex itself. The only condition needed is that the development of the secondary sexual characteristics had already begun, as this is plainly dependent upon central spheres. How far sexual development will then go depends chiefly upon the condition and the developing powers of these central factors, while its direction is governed by the biological energy of these bisexually predisposed centers.

If the development hitherto ran in heterosexual channels but was lacking in force, the sex simply experiences a check. If, however, the original bisexual predisposition had not yet received a definite sexual direction and possessed strength, sexual characteristics of the opposite sex and, under certain circumstances, even of an inverted nature may unfold. In most cases the characteristics of the opposite sex are only partially developed.

There are analogous cases in which the sexual glands were lost long after matured puberty. For instance, bearded women are frequently found in the postmortem without ovaries (*Dict. de méd. et de chirurg. prat. art. "ovario"*). In a similar manner pheasant hens with degenerated ovaries have the plumage and voice of the male.[3] (*Discuss. de la societé zoologique de Londres.*)

It is a well-known fact that many women grow a beard after menopause and that the voice drops to a lower register. If menopause is reached early and vitality remains strong, the opposite sex may even develop. See page 248 and cases 128 and 129.

A distinct difference may also be found in eunuchs, according to whether castration took place before or after psychic puberty. In the latter case the sex life is by no means a blank page, for although sexual feeling and instinct for the opposite sex are present, physical and psychic sexual characteristics of the male are stunted and feminism may take its place.

In rare cases – apparently in strongly developed bisexuality – signs of inverted sexuality may appear (Bedor's case in Cádiz of a eunuch with developed breasts).

These facts are not in favor of an exclusive effect of the sexual glands being exerted upon the development of the sex life, especially upon the psychic sexual characteristics. Undoubtedly these psychic sexual characteristics belong to those central spheres that normally come into functional force with the arrival of puberty, and thus determine the essential criterion of the sex (sexual instinct).

four

general pathology[1]
(neurological and psychological)

ANOMALIES OF the sexual functions are especially seen among civilized races. This fact is explained in part by the frequent abuse of the sexual organs, and in part by the circumstance that such functional anomalies are the primary signs of an inherited diseased condition of the central nervous system ("functional signs of degeneration").

Because the generative organs stand in important functional relation to the entire nervous system, and especially to its psychic and somatic functions, the frequency of general neuroses and psychoses arising from sexual (functional or organic) disturbances is easy to understand.

schedule of the sexual neuroses.

peripheral

[1] Sensory.
[a] *anesthesia* [b] *hyperesthesia* [c] *neuralgia.*

[2] Secretory.
[a] *aspermia* [b] *polyspermia.*

[3] Motor.
[a] *pollutions* (*spasm*) [b] *spermatorrhea* (*paralysis*).

s p i n a l   n e u r o s e s

[1] Affections of the erection center.

[a] *Irritation* (priapism) arises from reflex action of peripheral sensory irritants (e.g., gonorrhea); from direct organic irritation of the nerve tracts leading from the brain to the erection center (spinal disease in the lower cervical and upper dorsal regions), or from irritation of the center itself (certain poisons); or from psychic irritation.

With psychic irritation satyriasis exists, i.e., abnormal duration of erection with sexual desire. In reflex or direct organic irritation, sexual desire may be absent, and the priapism may give rise to disgust.

[b] *Paralysis* arises from the destruction of the center or the nerve tracts (nervi erigentes) in diseases of the spinal cord (paralytic impotence).

A milder form is that of lessened excitability of the center, resulting from over-stimulation (sexual excess, especially masturbation), or from alcoholic intoxication, abuse of bromides, etc. It may also originate from cerebral anesthesia, or anesthesia of the external genitals. In such cases cerebral hyperesthesia is more frequent (increased sexual desire, lust).

A peculiar form of diminished excitability is shown in cases where the center responds only to certain stimuli. Thus there are men for whom sexual contact with their virtuous wives does not supply the necessary stimulus for an erection, but in whom it occurs when the act is attempted with a prostitute, or in the form of some unnatural sexual act. Psychic stimuli may be inadequate (see below, paresthesia and perversion of sexual instinct).

[c] *Inhibition.* The erection center may become incapable of function through cerebral influence. This inhibitory influence is an emotional process (disgust, fear of contagion, or fear[2] of impotence). There are men who have an unconquerable

antipathy to woman, who fear infection, or who suffer from a perverse sexual instinct. In the latter category are those neuropathic individuals (neurasthenics, hypochondriacs), frequently weakened sexually (masturbators), who have reason, or who think they have reason, to mistrust their sexual power. This acts as an inhibitory impulse, making the act with the person of the opposite sex temporarily or absolutely impossible.

[d] *Irritable weakness.* In this condition there is abnormal impressionability of the center accompanied by rapid diminution of its energy. There may be functional disturbance of the center itself, weakness of the innervation through the nervi erigentes; or weakness of the erector penis muscle. Cases in which erection is abortive because of abnormally early ejaculation form a transition to the following anomalies:

[2] Affections of the ejaculation center.

[a] *Abnormally easy ejaculation* arises from absence of cerebral inhibition, the result of excessive psychic excitement or irritable weakness of the center. Here, under certain circumstances, the simple conception of a lascivious situation is sufficient to set the center in action (high degree of spinal neurasthenia, usually resulting from sexual abuse). It may also result from hyperesthesia of the urethra, whereby the escaping semen induces an immediate and excessive reflex action of the ejaculation center. In such cases, simple proximity to the female genitals (before insertion) may be sufficient to induce ejaculation.

In cases where hyperesthesia of the urethra is a cause, ejaculation may be accompanied by painful sensations instead of pleasurable ones. In cases where there is hyperesthesia of the urethra, there is usually also irritable weakness of the center. Both these functional disturbances are important to the production of excessive and daytime pollutions.

The accompanying pleasurable feeling may be pathologically absent. This occurs in defective men and women (anesthesia, aspermia?); as a result of disease (neurasthenia, hysteria); or from over-stimulation and the blunting thus induced (in prostitutes). The intensity of the pleasurable feeling accompanying the sexual act depends on the degree of psychic and motor excitement. Under pathological conditions this may become so pronounced that the movements of coitus assume the character of involuntary convulsive actions, and even pass into general convulsions.

[b] *Abnormally difficult ejaculation.* This is occasioned by inexcitability of the center (absence of desire, paralysis of the center: organic, from disease of the brain or spinal cord; functional, from sexual abuses, marasmus, diabetes, morphinism), usually in connection with anesthesia of the genitals and paralysis of the erection center. It may also be the result of a lesion of the reflex arc, peripheral anesthesia (urethra), or aspermia. In the course of the sexual act, ejaculation either does not occur at all, occurs tardily, or only occurs afterward in the form of a pollution.

[3] Cerebral neuroses.

[3.1] *Paradoxia* is sexual excitement that occurs independently of the period of the physiological processes in the generative organs.

[3.2] *Anesthesia* (absence of sexual instinct). Here all impulses, including organic impulses arising from the sexual organs, as well as visual, auditory and olfactory sense impressions, fail to sexually excite the individual. This is a physiological condition in childhood and old age.

[3.3] *Hyperesthesia* (increased desire, satyriasis). In this state there is an abnormally increased impressionability of the sex life in response to organic, psychic and sensory stimuli (abnormally intense desire, lustfulness, lasciviousness). The stimulus may be central (nymphomania, satyriasis), peripheral, functional or organic.

[3.4] *Paresthesia* (perversion of the sexual instinct). Excitability of the sexual functions to inadequate stimuli.

Subdivisions of *paresthesia* are:

[a] *Sadism.* Here the association of lust and cruelty, which is indicated in the physiological consciousness, becomes strongly marked on a psychically degenerated basis. The lustful impulse, when coupled with images of cruelty, rises to the height of powerful affects. This generates a force that strives to materialize these images

of fantasy. When hyperesthesia supervenes as a complication, or inhibitory moral counterimages fail to act, this is achieved.

The quality of the sadistic acts is defined by the relative potency of the tainted individual. If the sadist is potent, the impulse is directed to coitus coupled with preparatory, concomitant or consecutive maltreatment, even murder, of the consort ("lust murder"); the latter occurring chiefly because sensual lust has not been satisfied with consummated coitus.

If the sadist is psychically or spinally impotent, an equivalent of coitus will be seen in strangling, stabbing, flagellating (of women); ridiculously silly and seemingly senseless assaults upon the other person (symbolic sadism); or acts of violence upon any living and feeling object (whipping of school children, recruits, apprentices, cruel acts on animals, etc.).

[b] *Masochism* is the counterpart of sadism insofar as it derives the acme of pleasure from reckless acts of violence at the hands of the consort. It springs from the impulse to create a situation that by means of external physical force is in accordance with the individual psychic and spinal stage of potency, either as a preparatory and concomitant means to experience the voluptuous sensation of coitus, to increase it, or to make it a substitute for cohabitation. In direct ratio to the intensity of the perverse instinct and the remaining power of moral and aesthetic countermotives, it forms a gradation of behavior from the most abhorrent and monstrous to the most ludicrous and absurd (the request for personal castigation, humiliations of all sorts, passive flagellation, etc.).

[c] *Fetishism* invests imaginary presentations of separate parts of the body, articles of women's clothing, or even simply pieces of fabric, with voluptuous sensations. The pathological aspect of this manifestation may be deduced from the fact that fetishism of body parts never stands in direct relation to *sex*, but concentrates the whole sexual interest on one part abstracted from the entire body.

When the individual fetish is absent, coitus usually becomes impossible or can only be managed under the influence of the respective imaginary presentation, and even then grants no gratification. Its pathological condition is strongly accentuated by the circumstance that the fetishist does not find gratification in coitus itself, but rather in the manipulation of that portion of the body or that object which forms the interesting and effective fetish.

The fetish varies individually and is, no doubt, occasioned by some incident that determines the relation between a single impression and the voluptuous feeling.

[d] *Antipathic sexuality* is the total absence of sexual feeling toward the opposite sex. It concentrates all sexuality on its own sex. Only the physical and psychic properties of persons of the same sex exercise an aphrodisiac effect and awaken a desire for sexual union. It is purely a psychic anomaly, for the sexual instinct in no way corresponds with the primary and secondary physical sexual characteristics. In spite of the fully differentiated sexual type, in spite of the normally developed and active sexual glands, man is drawn sexually to man, because consciously or otherwise he has the instinct of the female.

From a clinical and anthropological standpoint this abnormal manifestation offers various grades of development.

[a] In predominant homosexual instinct, traces of heterosexual (psychic) hermaphroditism are to be found.

[b] If there is only inclination to one's own sex (homosexuality), the secondary physical sexual characteristics are normal, but the psychic elements may point to incipient inversion.

[c] The psychic sexual characteristics are inverted, i.e., they conform to the existing abnormal sexuality (*effemination-viraginity*).

[d] The secondary physical sexual characteristics approach that sex to which the individual, according to his instinct, belongs (*androgyny-gynandry*).

These cerebral anomalies fall within the domain of psychopathology. Although the spinal and peripheral anomalies may occur in combination with the cerebral anomalies, they usually affect persons free from mental disease. They may occur in various combinations, and become the cause of sexual crimes, for which reason they demand consideration. The cerebral anomalies, however, are of principal interest, because they frequently lead to the commission of perverse and even criminal acts.

[a] paradoxia.
sexual instinct manifesting itself
independently of physiological processes.

[1] sexual instinct manifested in childhood.

Every physician conversant with nervous affections and diseases incidental to childhood is aware of the fact that manifestations of sexual instinct may occur in very young children. The observations of Ultzmann concerning masturbation in childhood[3] are worthy of attention. It is necessary here to differentiate between [1] the numerous cases in which, as a result of phimosis, balanitis, or oxyuris in the rectum or vagina, young children have itching of the genitals, experience a kind of pleasurable sensation from manipulations occasioned thereby, and thus come to practice masturbation; and [2] those cases in which sexual ideas and impulses occur in the child as a result of cerebral processes without peripheral causes. Only the cases in this latter category pertain to premature manifestations of sexual instinct, which may always be regarded as an accompanying symptom of a neuro-psychopathic constitutional condition.

A case of Marc's (*Die Geisteskrankheiten,* etc., German translation by Ideler, vol. 1, p. 66) illustrates these conditions. The subject was a girl eight years of age, from a respectable family, who, devoid of all childlike and moral feelings, had masturbated from her fourth year; at the same time she consorted with boys aged ten or twelve. She had thought of killing her parents so that she might become her own mistress and give herself up to pleasure with men.

In these cases of premature manifestations of desire, the children begin to masturbate early; and, since they are greatly predisposed constitutionally, they often sink into dementia or become subjects of severe degenerative neuroses or psychoses.

Lombroso (*Archiv. di Psichiatria,* vol. 4, p. 22) has collected a number of cases of such children affected with decided hereditary taint. In one, a girl masturbated shamelessly and almost constantly at the age of three. Another girl began at the age of eight, and continued to practice masturbation when married – she even masturbated during pregnancy. She was pregnant twelve times. Five of the children died early, four were hydrocephalic, and two boys began to masturbate early – one at the age of seven, the other at the age of four.

Zambaco (*l'Encéphale,* nos. 1 and 2, 1882) tells the disgusting story of two sisters affected with premature and perverse sexual desire. The elder, R., masturbated at the age of seven, practiced lewdness with boys, stole whatever she could, seduced her four-year-old sister into masturbation, and at the age of ten had yielded to the practice of the most revolting vices. Even **a white-hot iron applied to her clitoris** had no effect in overcoming the practice, and she masturbated with the cassock of a priest while he exhorted her to reformation.

Cf. Magnan, *Psychiatr. Vorlesungen* (German translation by Möbius, nos. 2 and 3, p. 27), who relates a case of a premature and perverse sex life in a girl of twelve with hereditary taint. Other cases, ibid., pp. 120-121.

[2] reawakening of sexual instinct in old age.[4]

Cases in which the sexual instinct prevails until a great age are rare. "Indeed, vigor in old age brings greater esteem than years" (Zittmann). Oesterlen (Maschka, *Handb.,* vol. 3, p. 18) mentions the case of a man, aged eighty-three, who was sentenced to three years' imprisonment by a court in Würtemberg because of sexual misdemeanors. Unfortunately, nothing is said of the nature of the crime nor of the mental condition of the criminal.

The manifestation of sexual instinct in old age is not in itself pathological.

Presumption of pathological conditions must necessarily be entertained when the individual is decrepit and his sexual life has already long become extinct, and when the impulse – in a man whose sexual needs were not exceptional in his early life – manifests itself with greater strength, and strives for even perverse satisfaction in a shameless and impulsive manner.

In such cases a presumption of pathological conditions suggests itself at once. Medical science recognizes the fact that such an impulse depends upon morbid alterations of the brain that lead to senile dementia. This abnormal manifestation of sexual life may be the precursor of senile dementia, making its appearance long before there are any well-defined manifestations of intellectual weakness. The attentive and experienced observer will always be able to detect in this prodromal stage an alteration of character for the worse, and a deterioration of the moral sense accompanying the peculiar sexual manifestation.

The sexual desire of those passing into senile dementia is at first expressed in lascivious speech and gesture. The first objects of these senile subjects of brain atrophy and psychic degeneration are children. This sad and dangerous fact is explained by the better opportunity for success with children, but more, by the feeling of imperfect sexual power. Defective sexual power, and greatly diminished moral sense, explain the perversity of the sexual acts of such aged men. They are the equivalents of the impossible physiological act.

The annals of legal medicine distinguish perverse sexual acts as exhibition of the genitals,[5] lustful handling of the genitals of children,[6] inducement to perform masturbation on the seducer, and performance of masturbation[7] or flagellation on the victim.

Although in this stage the intellect may still be sufficiently intact to avoid publicity and discovery, the moral sense is too far gone to consider the moral significance of the act and to resist the impulse. With the progress of dementia, these acts are more and more shamelessly committed. Then care with respect to defective sexual power disappears, and adults also become the objects of the senile passion; but the defective sexual power necessitates equivalents for coitus. Sodomy often results, and, as Tarnowsky (op. cit., p. 77) points out, when the sexual act is performed with geese, chicken, etc., the sight of the dying animal and its death-struggles at the time of coitus afford complete gratification. Likewise, the perverse sexual acts with adults are equally horrible, and may be explained psychologically in the same way.

Case 49, in the author's *Lehrbuch der gerichtlichen Psychopathologie*, 3d ed., p. 161, demonstrates the enormous intensification of sexual lust during the course of senile dementia. **A lustful old man murdered his own daughter in a fit of jealousy, and experienced delightful pleasure at the sight of the dying girl's torn breast.**

Erotic delirium and states of satyriasis, with or without maniacal episodes, may occur in the course of the malady, as the following case shows:

Case 1.

J. René, always given to indulgence in sensuality and sexual pleasures, but always with a regard for decorum, had shown, since his seventy-sixth year, a progressive loss of intelligence and an increasing perversion of his moral sense. Previously bright and outwardly moral, he now wasted his property in concourse with prostitutes, frequented only brothels, asked every woman on the street to marry him or allow coitus, and thus became publicly so obnoxious that it was necessary to place him in an asylum. There the sexual excitement increased to a veritable satyriasis, which lasted until he died. He continuously masturbated, even before others; took delight only in obscene ideas; thought the men about him were women, and followed them with indecent proposals (Legrand du Saulle, *La folie,* p. 533).

Moreover, previously moral women, when affected with senile dementia, may manifest similar conditions of great sexual excitement (nymphomania, *furor uterinus*).

It can be seen from a reading of Schopenhauer[8] that, as a result of senile dementia, the abnormally excited and perverse instinct may be directed exclusively to persons of the same sex (see below). Gratification is obtained by passive pederasty, or, as I ascertained in the following case, by mutual masturbation:

Case 2.

Mr. X., aged eighty, of high social standing, from a family with hereditary taint. He was always very sensual, cynical, of uncontrollable temper, and, according to his own confession, reported that as a young man he preferred masturbation to coitus. However, he never showed signs of sexual perversion, and kept mistresses, raising a child by one. At the age of forty-eight he married, out of inclination, begot six children, and never gave his wife cause for complaint. I was unable to obtain a complete history of his family. What was ascertained, however, was that his brother was suspected of love for men, and that a nephew became insane as a result of excessive masturbation.

The patient's temper, always peculiar and quick, had for years been growing more violent. He had become exceedingly suspicious of others, and even slight opposition to his wishes induced attacks of anger that at times turned into actual raving, whereby he would then raise his hand, even against his wife. For a year there had been unmistakable signs of incipient senile dementia. The patient had become forgetful, had incorrectly localized past events, and had false ideas of time. For fourteen months it was noticed that he manifested affection for certain male servants, especially for a gardener's boy. Otherwise rude and overbearing to servants, he surfeited his favorite with favors and presents, and commanded his family and his house officials to treat the boy with the greatest respect. The aged patient awaited the hour of rendezvous in a state of true sexual excitement. He sent his family away so that he might be with his favorite undisturbed, and remained shut up with him for hours. When the doors were opened again, he was found lying on the bed exhausted. In addition to this object of his passion, the patient had intercourse episodically with other servants. He enticed them, asked them for kisses, exhibited himself, allowed manipulation of his genitals, and practiced mutual masturbation. As a result of these practices, absolute demoralization was brought about in the household. The family was powerless, for any opposition caused violent outbreaks of anger and even threats against them. The patient was completely without appreciation of his perverse sexual acts, and therefore the only course left to the afflicted family was to remove all authority from his hands and place him in an asylum. No erotic inclination toward the opposite sex was observed, though the patient occupied a bedroom with his wife. With reference to the perverse sexuality and the defective moral sense of this unfortunate man, it is worth noting that he questioned the servants of his daughter-in-law as to whether she had lovers.

[b] sexual anesthesia (absence of sexual feeling).

[1] as a congenital anomaly.

Only the cases in this category can be regarded as unquestionable examples of absence of sexual instinct dependent on cerebral causes, where, in spite of normally developed generative organs and the normal performance of their functions (secretion of semen, menstruation), the corresponding emotions of sexual life are absolutely nonexistent. These functionally sexless individuals are rare cases; indeed, they are always persons who have degenerative defects, and in whom other functional cerebral disturbances, states of psychic degeneration, and even anatomical signs of degeneration can be observed.

Case 3.

K., aged twenty-nine, civil servant, consulted with me because of his abnormal sexual condition. Because he was without relatives, he wanted to marry, but only on rational grounds. He claimed to have never experienced a sensual emotion. Sexual life was known to him only from what he had heard other men say about it or from what he had read in erotic novels, which, however, had never made any impression upon him. He had no dislike for the opposite sex, or special inclination toward his own sex, and had never masturbated. From his seventeenth year he had, at intervals, nocturnal pollutions, but without concomitant lascivious dreams. Erections occurred in the morning upon awakening, but disappeared at once after emptying his bladder. Except for the absence of sexual instinct, K. considered himself quite normal. No psychic defects could be detected. He was fond of solitude, of a frigid nature, without interest in the arts or the beautiful, but was a highly efficient and esteemed official.

Case 4.

W., aged twenty-five, merchant, claimed to be untainted; never had a severe illness; had never masturbated; rarely had pollutions after his nineteenth year, mostly without sensual dreams. Since his twenty-first year **coitus rarely, with the sexual act akin to masturbating inside a woman's body without any pleasurable feeling.** W. declared that he made these attempts solely through curiosity, and soon gave them up altogether as desire, gratification, and ultimately even erection were absent. He never had any leaning toward his own sex. His deficiency did not seem to cause him any worry. There were no abnormal manifestations in the ethical and aesthetic field.

Case 5.

P., aged thirty-six, common laborer, was received at my clinic in the beginning of November because of spastic spinal paralysis. He declared he came from a healthy family. A stutterer from his youth. Cranium microcephalic (circumference fifty-three centimeters). Somewhat imbecilic. He was never sociable, never had a sexual emotion. The sight of a woman was never enticing. He never had a desire to masturbate. Erections frequent, but only on awakening in the morning with a full bladder, and without a trace of sexual feeling. Pollutions infrequent – about once a year, in sleep – and usually while dreaming that he was involved with a female. These dreams, however, as well as his dreams in general, were not markedly erotic. He said the act of pollution was not accompanied by any pleasurable sensation. Patient did not feel the absence of sexual sensation. He was certain that his brother, aged thirty-four, was in exactly the same sexual condition as himself, and thought it likely that a sister, aged twenty-one, was in a similar state. A younger brother, he said, was sexually normal. The examination of his genitals revealed nothing abnormal beyond phimosis.

Further cases, see Krafft-Ebing, *Arbeiten aus dem Gesammtgebiet der Psychiatrie und Neuropathologie,* vol. 4, pp. 178, 179.

Hammond (*Sexuelle Impotenz,* German translation by Salinger, Berlin, 1889), even with his wide experience, reports only the following three cases of sexual anesthesia:

Case 6.

Mr. W., aged thirty-three; strong, healthy, with normal genitals. He had never experienced sexual desire, and had vainly sought to awaken his defective sexual instinct by means of obscene stories and intercourse with prostitutes. With such attempts he experienced only disgust, even nausea, and became nervously and mentally exhausted. Only once, when he forced the situation, did he have a transitory erection. W. had never masturbated, and had had pollutions about once every two months from his seventeenth year. Important interests demanded that he should marry. He had no *horror feminae,* and longed for a home and a wife, but felt that he was incapable of the sexual act. He died unmarried in the American Civil War.

Case 7.

X., aged twenty-seven, genitals normal; never felt sexual desire. Mechanical or thermic stimuli easily induced erection, but sexual desire was regularly replaced by a desire for alcoholic indulgence. Such excesses also induced erections, and he then sometimes masturbated. He had a disinclination for women and a loathing of coitus. If, with an erection, he made an attempt at coitus, it disappeared at once. Death in coma during an attack of cerebral hyperemia.

Case 8.

Mrs. O., normally developed, healthy, menstruated regularly; aged thirty-five; married fifteen years. She never experienced sexual desire, and never had any erotic excitement in sexual intercourse with her husband. She was not averse to coitus, and sometimes seemed to experience pleasure in it, but she never had a wish for repetition of cohabitation.

In connection with such genuine cases of anesthesia,[9] there should be considered other cases in which the mental side of the sex life is a blank page in the life of the individual, but where elementary sexual sensations manifest themselves at least in masturbation (cf. the transitional case 7). According to Magnan's ingenious classification – which, however, is not strictly correct and somewhat too dogmatic – in such cases the sexual life is so limited as to be designated spinal. Possibly in some such cases there exists virtually a mental side of the sex life, but it is very weak, and undermined by masturbation before it attains development. These represent the transitional cases from the congenital to the acquired (psychic) sexual anesthesia. This danger threatens many masturbators of vitiated constitution. It is psychologically interesting that when the sexual element is vitiated early, an ethical defect is then manifested.

The following two cases, previously published by me in the *Archiv für Psychiatrie*, vol. 7, are given here as illustrations worthy of consideration:

Case 9.

F.J., aged nineteen, student; mother was nervous, sister epileptic. At the age of four, acute brain affection, lasting two weeks. As a child he was not affectionate, and was cold toward his parents; as a student he was peculiar, retiring, preoccupied with self, and given to much reading. Well-endowed mentally. Masturbation from his fifteenth year. Eccentric after puberty, with continual vacillation between religious enthusiasm and materialism – first studying theology, then natural sciences. At the university his fellow students took him for a fool. He read Jean Paul almost exclusively, and wasted his time. Absolute absence of sexual feeling toward the opposite sex. Once he indulged in intercourse, experienced no sexual feeling in the act, found it absurd, and did not repeat it. Without any emotional cause whatsoever, he often had thoughts of suicide. He made it the subject of a philosophical dissertation, in which he contended that it was, like masturbation, a justifiable act. After repeated experiments, which he made on himself with various poisons, he attempted suicide with fifty-seven grains of opium, but he was saved and sent to an asylum.

Patient was destitute of moral and social feelings. His writings disclosed incredible frivolity and vulgarity. His knowledge had a wide range, but his logic was peculiarly distorted. There was no trace of emotionality. He treated everything (even the sublime) with incomparable cynicism and irony. He pleaded for the justification of suicide with false philosophical premises and conclusions, and, as one would speak of the most indifferent affair, he declared that he intended to accomplish it. He regretted that his penknife had been taken from him. If he had it, he would open his veins as Seneca did — in the bath. At one time a friend had given him, instead of a poison as he supposed, a cathartic. Instead of sending him to the other world, it sent him to the bathroom. Only the Great Operator could eradicate his foolish and fatal idea with the scythe of death, etc.

The patient had a large, rhombic, distorted skull, with the left half of the forehead flatter than the right. The occiput was very straight. Ears far back, widely projecting, and the external meatus forming a narrow slit. Genitals very lax; testicles unusually soft and small.

The patient occasionally suffered from onomatomania. He was compelled to think of the most useless problems, give himself over to interminable, distressing and worrying thoughts, and become so fatigued that he was no longer capable of any rational thinking. After some months the patient was sent home unimproved. There he spent his time in reading and frivolities, and busied himself with the thought of founding a new system of Christianity, because Christ had been subject to grand delusions and had deceived the world with miracles (!). After remaining at home some years, the sudden occurrence of a maniacal outbreak brought him back to the asylum. He presented a mixture of primordial deliria of persecution (Devil, Antichrist, persecution, poisoning, persecuting voices) and delusions of grandeur (Christ, redemption of the world), with impulsive, incoherent actions. After five months there was a remission of this intercurrent acute mental disease, and the patient then returned to the level of his original intellectual peculiarity and moral defect.

Case 10.

E., aged thirty, journeyman painter, was arrested while trying to cut off the scrotum of a boy he had caught in the woods. He reported that he wished to cut it off so that the world would not multiply. Often in his youth, for the same reason, he had cut into his own genitals.

It was impossible to learn anything of his ancestry. After his childhood he was mentally abnormal, violent, never lively, irritable, irascible, selfish and weak-minded. He hated women, loved solitude, and read much. He sometimes laughed to himself and did silly things. Lately his hatred for women had increased, especially for women who were pregnant, because they were responsible for the misery of the world. He also hated children, and cursed his father. He entertained communist ideas, berated the rich, the ministry and God, who had allowed him to come into the world so poor. He declared that it would be better to castrate all children than to allow others to come into the world, and whose only fate would be to endure poverty and misery. He had always had the intention, from his fifteenth year, of castrating himself, so that he might have no part in increasing unhappiness and adding to the number of men. He hated women because they were a means of procreation. Only twice in his life had he allowed women to masturbate him, and, with the exception of this, he had never had anything to do with them. Occasionally he had sexual desire, but never wanted a natural gratification of it. When nature did not help him, he occasionally helped himself by means of masturbation.

He was a powerful, muscular man. The formation of the genitals presented no abnormality. On the scrotum and penis were numerous scars, the results of his attempts at self-emasculation. These attempts, he asserted, were not carried out because of pain. Knock-kneed right leg. No evidence of masturbation could be discovered. He was moody, defiant, irritable. Social feelings were absolutely foreign to him. With the exception of imperfect sleep and frequent headaches, there were no functional disturbances.

A distinction must be made between cases of this kind, which are dependent upon cerebral causes, and others in which the absence of function arises from malformation of the generative organs, as in certain hermaphrodites, idiots and cretins.

Ultzmann's[10] observations show that sexual anesthesia is not caused simply by aspermia. He shows that even in cases of congenital aspermia, sex life and sexual power may be entirely satisfying; an additional proof that the origin of defective sexual desire lies in cerebral conditions.

The "frigid natures" of Zacchias are examples of a milder form of anesthesia. They are seen more frequently in women than in men. The characteristic signs of this anomaly are slight inclination to sexual intercourse, or pronounced disinclination to coitus without sexual substitute, with a failure of corresponding psychic, pleasurable excitation during coitus, which is indulged in only from a sense of duty. I have often had occasion to hear complaints from husbands about this. In such cases the wives were always proved to have been neuropathic from birth. Some were at the same time hysterical.

[2] acquired anesthesia.

Acquired diminution of sexual instinct, extending through all degrees to extinction, may depend on various causes. These may be organic and functional, psychic and somatic, central and peripheral. The diminution of sexual desire, as age advances, and its temporary disappearance after the sexual act, are physiological. Variations with respect to the duration of the sexual instinct are dependent upon individual factors. Education and manner of life have a great influence upon the intensity of the sex life. Intense mental activity (hard study), physical exertion, emotional depression, and sexual continence decidedly diminish sexual inclination. At first continence induces increase, but sooner or later, according to constitutional conditions, the activity of the generative organs decreases, and with it sexual desire. At all times, in a person sexually mature, a close connection exists between the activity of the generative glands and the degree of sexual desire. That this relation is not fixed is shown by the cases of sensual women, who, after the climacteric, continue to have sexual intercourse, and may manifest states of sexual excitement (cerebral). Also, eunuchs display sexual desire that may long outlast the production of semen.

On the other hand, however, experience teaches that sexual desire is essentially conditioned by the functions of the generative glands, and that the facts mentioned are exceptional manifestations. Peripheral causes of diminution or extinction of sexual desire may be castration, degeneration of the sexual glands, marasmus, sexual excesses in the form of coitus and masturbation, as well as alcoholism and abuse of cocaine. In the same way, the disappearance of sexual desire may be explained by general disturbances of nutrition (diabetes, morphinism, etc.). Finally, atrophy of the testicles, sometimes observed to follow focal lesions of the brain (cerebellum), should be noted.

A diminution of the sex life resulting from degeneration of the tracts of the cord and genito-spinal center occurs in diseases of the spinal cord and brain. A central interference with the sexual instinct may be organically induced by cortical disease (paralytic dementia in its advanced stages), or functionally induced by hysteria (central anesthesia?) and emotional insanity (melancholia, hypochondria).

[c] hyperesthesia
(abnormally increased sexual desire).

One of the most important anomalies of sexual life is an abnormal presence of sexual sensations and presentations that lead to frequent and violent impulses for sexual gratification. No doubt the outcome of the education and breeding of many centuries is that the sexual instinct – indispensable for the preservation of the race and therefore congenital in every normal individual – is not the predominant key in the chord of human sentiments, but rather forms episodes in the physical and psychic life of cultured man with periods of ebb and flow. As such, it is the generating element of higher and nobler social and moral sentiments, and leaves room for other spheres of activity, the object of which is the furtherance of interests affecting the individual as well as society at large.

Furthermore, the moral code and the common law require that civilized man satisfy his sexual instinct only within the barriers (established in the interests of the community) of modesty and morality, and that he, under all circumstances, control this instinct as soon as it comes in conflict with the altruistic demands of society.

If the normally constituted civilized individual were unable to comply with this rule, family and state would cease to exist as the foundations of a moral, lawful community.

Practically speaking, a normal, sane individual's sexual instinct is seen as not properly developed if it permeates all his thoughts and feelings, allows for no other aims in life, demands gratification tumultuously and in rut-like fashion without granting the possibility of moral and righteous counterpresentations, and ultimately resolves itself in an impulsive, insatiable succession of sexual enjoyments.

This would at once betray a pathological condition, episodically producing such a high degree of sexual feeling that self-consciousness becomes clouded, sanity impaired, and a true psychic calamity established that would lead to an irresistible impulse to commit sexual acts of violence.

Such psychosexual extravagances have received scant scientific study, though they are of great importance for the criminal forum because the individual so affected can scarcely be held mentally responsible. Fortunately for society and the criminal doctor, who is called upon to make the diagnosis, these cases, in which irresistible hypersensuality leads to the gravest of pathological sexual aberrations, are only encountered in that category of human beings classified as degenerates infected with hereditary taint.

Alas, their number is by no means small in modern society, which shows many marks of physical and psychic degeneration, especially in the centers of culture and refinement.

Coupled with perversions of sexual life and sexual imbecility, sprung from the same degenerated soil, and often helped along by alcohol, the most monstrous and horrible sexual excesses (cf. *sadism*) are perpetrated, which would disgrace humanity at large were they to be committed by the normal man.

The commission of these atrocious acts by degenerated and partially defective individuals is the outcome of an irresistible impulse or delirium. The mechanism behind these actions is indeed the property of psychic degeneration.

A particular act follows the direction given by the hereditary or acquired impulse, and is frequently determined by the relative potency or impotence of the agent. This pathological sexuality is a dreadful scourge for its victim, inasmuch as he is in constant danger of violating the laws of the state and morality, and of losing his honor, his freedom, and even his life. Alcohol and prolonged sexual abstinence are apt to produce powerful sexual feelings at any time in such degenerated persons.

In addition to these graver manifestations of pathological sexuality, we also find milder and more numerous gradations of hypersexuality; the lowest of these gradations, perhaps, belongs to those individuals who, impecunious though they may be while sexually potent, move in the better classes of society and have no other aim in life than to gratify their sexual desires. These individuals are not afflicted with a pathological sexual condition; they know how to measuredly control themselves, they observe the acknowledged rules of decency, they do not compromise themselves, and yet they allow no opportunity to pass by without utilizing their urges to the utmost. Another grade are the apron-hunters, the Don Juans, whose whole existence is an endless chain of sensual enjoyment and whose blunted moral sense does not keep them from seduction, adultery, and even incest.

Case 11.

P., caretaker, aged fifty-three; married; no evidence of hereditary taint; no epileptic antecedents; moderate drinker; no sign of premature senility; appeared, according to the statement of his wife, hypersexual, extremely libidinous, always potent, and, in fact, insatiable in his marital relations during the whole time of their married life of twenty-eight years. During coitus he became quite bestial and wild, trembled all over with excitement, and panted heavily. This nauseated the wife, who was by nature rather frigid and regarded the discharge of her conjugal duty as a heavy burden. Although he worried her with his jealous behavior, soon after the marriage he seduced his wife's sister, an innocent girl, and had a child by her. In 1873 he took mother and child to his home. He now had two women, but gave preference to the sister-in-law, which the wife tolerated as a lesser evil. As years went by his sexual desire increased, though his potency decreased. He often resorted to masturbation, even immediately after coitus, and without in the least minding the presence of the women. In 1892 he committed immoral acts with a girl of sixteen years, who was his ward, i.e., **he was in the habit of making the girl masturbate him.** He even tried to force her at gunpoint to have coitus with him. He made the same attempts on his own illegitimate child, so that often both had to be protected from him. At the clinic he was quiet and well-behaved. His excuse was hypersexuality. He acknowledged the wrongfulness of his actions, but said he could not help himself. The frigidity of his wife had forced him to commit adultery. There was no disturbance of his mental faculties, but the ethical elements were utterly nonexistent. He had had several epileptic fits, but no signs of degeneration.

We must concede that the degree of sexual desire is subject to a rise and fall in the untainted individual according to age, constitutional conditions, mode of life, and the various influences of health and illness on the body, etc. Sexual desire rapidly increases after puberty, until it reaches a marked degree; it is strongest from the twentieth to the fortieth year, and then slowly decreases. Married life seems to preserve and control the instinct. Sexual intercourse with many persons increases the desire.

Because woman has less sexual need than man, a predominating sexual desire in her arouses the suspicion of its pathological significance. Those living in large cities, who are constantly reminded of sexual things and incited to sexual enjoyment, certainly have more sexual desire than those living in the country. A dissipated, luxurious, sedentary manner of life, preponderance of meat for food, and the consumption of spirits, spices, etc., have a stimulating influence on the sexual life. In woman, sexual inclination increases after menstruation. At this point, excitement in neuropathic women may reach a pathological degree.

The great sexual desire of consumptives is remarkable, even during the very last stages of the disease. Sexual hyperesthesia is, in my opinion, a functional manifestation of degeneration. To what extent it may occur as an acquired, accidental, episodical condition in the untainted is worthy of scientific research. Excessive sexual desire may be peripherally or centrally induced, although the former manner of origin is less common. Pruritus and eczema of the genitals may cause it, as well as certain substances, such as cantharides, which powerfully stimulate sexual desire.

In women, sexual excitement often occurs at the climacteric period, occasioned by pruritus, as well as in cases where there is neuropathic taint. Magnan (*Annales médico-psychol.*, 1885, p. 157) reports the case of a lady who was afflicted in the mornings with attacks of frightful genital erethism, and the case of a man aged fifty-five who was tormented at night by unbearable priapism. In each case there was a neurosis.

The central origin of sexual excitement can often be traced[11] in persons having neurotic taint or hysteria, and in conditions of psychic exaltation. When the cortex and the psychosexual center are in a condition of hyperesthesia (abnormal excitability of the imagination, increased ease of association), not only visual and tactile impressions but also auditory and olfactory sensations may be sufficient to call up lascivious conceptions.

Magnan (op. cit.) reports the case of a young woman who had an increasing sexual desire from puberty, and satisfied it by masturbation. Gradually she grew to become sexually excited at the sight of any man she found pleasing to her; since she was unable to control herself, she would sometimes shut herself up in a room until the storm had passed. At last she gave herself up to men of her choice so that she might get rest from her tormenting desire, but neither coitus nor masturbation brought relief, and she went to an asylum.

In another case, a mother of five children, in despair about her inordinate sexual impulse, attempted suicide, and then sought an asylum. Although her condition there improved, she never trusted herself to leave.

Several illustrative cases involving men and women can be found in the author's article, "Ueber gewisse Anomalien des Geschlechtstriebs," cases 6 and 7 (*Archiv für Psychiatrie,* vol. 7, no. 2).

The following two cases show how powerful, dangerous and painful sexual hyperesthesia may become in those afflicted with this anomaly:

Case 12.
Sexual hyperesthesia. **Masturbated in front of his students in school.**

Z., thirty-six years of age, father of seven children, president of a school, confessed that he committed masturbation while sitting at his desk in his classroom. The act was not seen by the pupils, however, as the desk was encased all around. He had drunk more than usual on the preceding evening, had been provoked to anger before going to school, and had been excited by the sight of some very pretty girls attending his lecture. This produced a violent erection and led to masturbation. After the act he became conscious at once of his compromising position, but the thought that the pupils had not noticed his excitement helped him regain self-possession.

Because his previous conduct was without a blemish, the authorities suspected a pathological condition and insisted upon a medical examination by the author.

The facts elicited were the following: Z. came from healthy parents. Two close relations were epileptics. At the age of thirteen, Z. suffered a severe concussion of the brain, which produced an acute dementia lasting three weeks. Since that time, frequent spells of irritability and intolerance of alcohol.

At the age of sixteen, his sex life awakened with abnormal vigor and pronounced sexual emotions. Lascivious literature and pictures of women produced satisfying ejaculation. From the age of eighteen onward he indulged now and then in coitus. Usually, however, the touch of a woman's arm sufficed to produce orgasm and ejaculation. He married at the age of twenty-four and indulged in coitus three or four times daily; he also practiced masturbation, coupled with ideal coitus. (See footnote 11 on page 657.)

The birth of his fourth child (three years ago) forced Z., for economic reasons, to restrain himself from sexual intercourse because he despised contraceptive means. The female touch, which produced daily pollutions, proved unsatisfactory, as did masturbation. He suffered greatly from incessant sexual excitement, which at the end of periods of six weeks became so strong it visibly affected his mind and willpower. Only masturbation kept him from committing sexual violence on women. He became very irritable and flew easily into a fury, yelling and raging about the house, and even beating his wife and children.

Now it often happened that at the height of such a spell he would fall over and become unconscious, rattling from the throat in a peculiar manner. After a few minutes he would recover again with complete amnesia of what had happened. An attack of this kind had, however, not preceded the act with which he now stood charged, but had occurred three days afterward.

Z. was an intelligent, decent man, most penitent and filled with shame.

He understood quite well that he could no longer teach at a girl's school and bewailed his unnatural, unbridled sensuality.

Although he made no attempt to excuse his action in any way, he pointed out that his nervous system had been thoroughly shaken lately by insatiable sexual desire and over-work (lessons up to twelve hours daily).

Vegetative functions normal; parietal protuberance of cranium; genitals large, lax, but normal. Patellar reflexes much exaggerated.

In my report I pointed out that Z. suffered from a pathologically exaggerated sex life and most probably from epilepsy, and had committed the act while subject to a sexual affection that depressed the power of self-control to a minimum. Further legal proceedings were withdrawn. Z. was pensioned off.

Case 13.

On July 11, 1884, R., aged thirty-three, servant; was admitted suffering from persecutorial paranoia and sexual neurasthenia. Mother was neuropathic; father died of spinal disease. From childhood he had an intense sexual desire, of which he became conscious as early as his sixth year. From this age, masturbation; from fifteenth year, for lack of something better, pederasty; occasionally, sodomitic indulgences. Later, **abusive coitus with his wife during marriage.** An occasional perverse impulse to commit cunnilingus and to administer cantharides to his wife, because her sexual desire did not equal his own. His wife died after a short period of married life. Patient's circumstances became straitened, and he had no means to indulge himself sexually. Then masturbation again; employment of **a dog's tongue** to induce ejaculation. At times, priapism and conditions approaching satyriasis. He was then driven to masturbate in order to avoid committing rape. With gradually predominating sexual neurasthenia and hypochondria came beneficial diminution of excessive sexual desire.

A particular species of sexual hyperesthesia may be found in females for whom a most impulsive desire for sexual intercourse with certain men demands gratification. No doubt "unrequited love" for another man may often affect the married woman who does not psychically or physically (impotence of husband) experience connubial satisfaction; but the normal, untainted wife, guided by ethical reasoning, knows how to conquer herself.

Of course, pathological conditions change the situation.

Fetishism must be considered here. Sexual impulse is overpowering, at times periodically recurrent. Any attempt to overcome it produces the most painful attacks of worry and anxiety. This pathological want becomes so powerful that all considerations of shame, conventionality and womanly honor simply disappear, and it reveals itself in the most shameless manner even to the husband; the normal woman, however, endowed with full moral consciousness, knows how to conceal the terrible secret.

Magnan (*Psychiatr. Vorlesungen*, German translation by Möbius, nos. 2 and 3) quotes two striking instances from his own experience. One is especially instructive. A young woman, mother of three children, with a blameless past, but daughter of a lunatic, openly told her husband one day that she was in love with a certain young man and that she would kill herself if her intimate relations with him were impeded. She begged permission to live with him for six months to quench the fire of her passion, after which she would return to her family. Husband and children had no place in her heart with her present love. The husband took her to a foreign country and placed her under medical treatment.

This pathological love of married women for other men, a phenomenon in the domain of *psychopathia sexualis*, is sadly in need of scientific explanation. The author has had the opportunity of observing five cases belonging to this category. The pathological conditions were paroxysmal, in one case repeatedly recurrent, but always sharply distinct from the unaffected, healthy period, during which deep sorrow and contrition over the occurrence were manifested. (It was, however, sorrow over an unavoidable fatality caused by psychically abnormal conditions.)

While the pathological conditions continue, absolute indifference, even hatred, prevail toward husband and children, combined with an inability to grasp the meaning and consequences of the scandalous behavior that jeopardizes the honor and dignity of wife and family. It is remarkable that in all these cases the husband and relatives had come to the conclusion that the condition was caused by *psychopathia,* even before they had obtained expert opinion.

Compared to the "non-psychopathological" but otherwise abnormally libidinous nymphomaniacs, it is well worth noting that this sexual aberration is only an episode in the life of the otherwise honorable woman, and that the illicit intercourse is of a strictly monogamous character. This, when added to the circumstance that the unfortunate woman is not **the lover of many men,** but only the mistress of one man, establishes a distinct difference from nymphomania. In three of the cases mentioned above the grossly sensual momentum was missing; the real motive for marital infidelity was to be found in a fetish-like charm, in mentally superior qualities – in one case, in the voice of the charmer.

In two cases, unmistakable proof of sexual hyperesthesia and absolute impotence toward the husband were found; the merest touch of the other man produced orgasm, and the sexual act was the acme of pleasure. Of course, in these cases absolute sexual abandonment followed.

[d] paresthesia of sexual feeling (perversion of the sexual instinct).

In this condition there is perverse emotional coloring of the sexual ideas. Ideas physiologically and psychologically accompanied by feelings of disgust give rise to pleasurable sexual feelings, and the abnormal association finds expression in passionate, uncontrollable emotion. The results are perverse acts (perversion of the sexual instinct). This is more readily the case if the pleasurable feelings, when increased to passionate intensity, inhibit, with corresponding feelings of disgust, any opposing ideas; or when the influence of such opposing conceptions may be rendered impossible because of the absence or loss of all ideas of morality, aesthetics and law. This loss, however, is only too frequently found where the well-spring of ethical ideas and feelings (a normal sexual instinct) has been poisoned from the beginning.

Given the opportunity for natural satisfaction of the sexual instinct, every expression of it that does not correspond with the purpose of nature – i.e., propagation – must be regarded as perverse. The perverse sexual acts resulting from paresthesia are of the greatest importance clinically, socially and forensically; they must, therefore, receive careful consideration here; all aesthetic and moral disgust must be overcome.

Perversion of the sexual instinct, as will be seen farther on, is not to be confused with *perversity* in the sexual act, since perversity may be induced by conditions that are not psychopathological. The concrete perverse act, monstrous as it may be, is not decisive clinically. In order to differentiate between disease (*perversion*) and vice (*perversity*), one must investigate the whole personality of the individual and the original motive leading to the perverse act. Therein will be found the key to the diagnosis (see below).

Paresthesia may occur in combination with hyperesthesia. This association seems to be clinically frequent. Sexual acts are then confidently to be expected. The perverse direction of sexual activity may be toward the opposite sex or the same sex. Thus two great groups of perversions of sexual life may be distinguished.

sexual inclination toward persons of the opposite sex, with perverse activity of the instinct.

[1] sadism.[12]
association of active cruelty and violence with lust.

SADISM, ESPECIALLY in its rudimentary manifestations, seems to be common in the domain of sexual perversion. Sadism is the experience of sexually pleasurable sensations (including orgasm) that is produced by acts of cruelty and bodily punishment, either self-inflicted or witnessed in others, whether animals or human beings. It may also consist of an innate desire to humiliate, hurt, wound, or even destroy others in order to create sexual pleasure in oneself.

Thus it will happen that a lover in the grip of sexual heat will strike, bite,[13] or pinch the other, and kissing will degenerate into biting. Lovers and young married couples are fond of teasing each other; they wrestle together "just for fun," and indulge in all sorts of horseplay. The transition from these atavistic manifestations, that no doubt belong to the sphere of physiological sexuality, to the most monstrous acts of destruction of the consort's life, can be readily traced.

Where a husband forces his wife, with threats and other violent means, into the conjugal act, it can no longer be described as a normal physiological manifestation, but must be ascribed to sadistic impulses. It seems probable that this sadistic force is developed when the natural shyness and modesty of woman is juxtaposed against the aggressive manners of the male, especially during the earlier periods of married life, and particularly when the husband is hypersexual. Woman no doubt derives pleasure from her innate coyness, and the final victory of man affords her intense and refined gratification. Hence the frequent recurrence of these little love comedies.

A further strain of these sadistic traces may be found in men who demand the sexual act in unusual places, for this seems to offer to such a man an opportunity to show his superiority over woman, to provoke her defense, and to delight in her subsequent confusion and abashment.

Case 14.

One of my patients, hereditarily tainted, a crank, and married to an extremely handsome woman of vivacious temperament, became impotent when he saw her beautiful, pure white skin and her elegant clothes, but was quite potent with any ordinary wench, no matter how dirty (*fetishism*). It would happen, however, that during a lonely walk with her in the country, he would suddenly force her to have coitus in a meadow, or behind a shrub. The stronger her refusal the more excited he became, with perfect potency. The same would happen in places where there was a risk of being discovered in the act; for instance, in a railway train or the lavatory of a restaurant. At home in his own bed, however, he was quite devoid of carnal desire.

Modern civilized man, insofar as he is untainted, may exhibit a weak and rudimentary association between lust and cruelty. In persons known to have an abnormal (degenerative) predisposition, however, the occurrence of such associations may kindle monstrous manifestations of lust-driven cruelty. This susceptibility undoubtedly has its source in the sexual (feeling) and motor (instinctive) spheres.

In other words, a link between lust and cruelty is due to an awakening of latent psychic dispositions, occasioned by external circumstances that in no way affect the normal individual. They are not accidental deviations of sentiment or instinct in the sense of the modern doctrine of association. Sadistic sensations may often be traced back to early childhood and exist during a period of life when their revival can not be attributed to external impressions, much less to sexual temper.

Sadism must, therefore, like masochism and the antipathic sexual instinct, be counted among the original anomalies of the sex life. Sadism is a disturbance (a deviation) in the evolution of psychosexual processes sprouting from the soil of psychic degeneration.

That lust and cruelty often occur together is a fact that has long been recognized and is frequently observed. Writers of all kinds have called attention to this phenomenon.[14]

Blumröder (*Ueber Irresein,* Leipzig, 1836, p. 51) saw a man who had several bite wounds in his pectoral muscle that had been rendered by a sexually excited woman at the acme of lustful feeling during coitus. The same author ("Ueber Lust und Schmerz," Friedreich's *Magazin für Seelenkunde,* 1830, vol. 2, no. 5) calls especial attention to the psychological connection between lust and murder. He especially refers to the Indian myths of Shiva and Durga (Death and Lust); to human sacrifice with voluptuous mysteries; and to sexual instinct at puberty, with a lustful impulse to commit suicide, and with whipping, pinching, and pricking of the genitals, in a blind impulse to satisfy sexual desire. Lombroso (*Verzeni e Agnoletti,* Rome, 1874) also cites numerous examples of a desire to murder that occurs with greatly increased lust.

Ball quotes in his *Clinique St. Anne* the case of a powerful epileptic who, during coitus, bit off pieces of his consort's nose and swallowed them.

Ferriani (*Archiv. delle psicopatie sessuali,* vol. 1, 1896, p. 106) speaks of a young man who used to wrestle with his lover before coitus, and bit and pinched her during the act "because otherwise he felt no gratification." One day, however, he hurt the girl too much and she brought action against him.

On the other hand, when homicidal mania has been excited, lust often follows. Lombroso (op. cit.) alludes to the fact mentioned by Mantegazza, that generally added to the terrors of spoliation and plunder by bandits are those of brutal lust and rape.[15] These examples form transitions to the pronounced pathological cases.

The examples of the degenerate Caesars (Nero, Tiberius) are also instructive, inasmuch as they took delight in having youths and maidens slaughtered before their eyes. Not less so is the history of that monster, Marshall Gilles de Rais (Jacob, *Curiosités de l'histoire de France,* Paris, 1858), who was executed in 1440, on account of mutilation and murder practiced for eight years on more than eight hundred children. According to the monster's confessions, it was from reading Suetonius and the descriptions of the orgies of Tiberius, Caracalla, etc., that he acquired the idea of locking children in his castles, torturing them, and killing them. This inhuman wretch confessed that in the commission of these acts he enjoyed inexpressible pleasure. He had two assistants. The bodies of the unfortunate children were burned, and only a number of heads of particularly beautiful children were preserved – as memorials.

Cf. Eulenburg, op. cit., p. 58, where he gives satisfactory proof of Rais' insanity; also, in *Die Zukunft*, vol. 7, no. 26; Bossard and Maulle, *Gilles de Rays, dit Barbe-Bleu*, Paris, 1886 (Champion); Michelet, *Histoire de France*, vol. 6, p. 316-326; *Bibliothèque de Criminologie*, vol. 19, Paris, 1899, p. 245.

In an attempt to explain the association of lust and cruelty, it is necessary to return to a consideration of the quasi-physiological cases, in which, at the moment of most intense lust, very excitable individuals who are otherwise normal commit acts such as biting and scratching, usually out of anger. It must further be remembered that love and anger are not only the most intense emotions, but also the only two forms of robust (sthenic) emotion. Both seek their object, try to possess it, and naturally exhaust themselves in a physical effect on it; both throw the psychomotor sphere into the most intense excitement, and thus, by means of this excitation, reach their normal expression.

From this standpoint, it is clear how lust impels acts that are otherwise expressive of anger.[16] The one, like the other, is a state of exaltation, an intense excitation of the entire psychomotor sphere. Thus there arises an impulse to react on the object that induces the stimulus, in every possible way, and with the greatest intensity. Just as maniacal exaltation easily passes to raging destructiveness, so exaltation of the sexual emotion often induces an impulse to spend itself in senseless and apparently harmful acts. To a certain extent these are psychic accompaniments; but it is not simply an unconscious excitation of innervation of muscles (which also sometimes occurs as blind violence); it is true excess, a desire to exert the utmost possible effect upon the individual giving rise to the stimulus. The most intense means, however, is the infliction of pain.

Through such cases of infliction of pain during the most intense emotion of lust, we approach the cases in which a real injury, wound, or death is inflicted on the victim.[17] In these cases the impulse to cruelty that may accompany the emotion of lust becomes unbounded in a psychopathic individual; and, at the same time, due to a defect in moral feeling, all normal inhibitory ideas are absent or weakened.

In men, however, for whom such monstrous, sadistic acts are much more frequent than for women, there is another source in physiological conditions. In the intercourse of the sexes, the active or aggressive role belongs to man; woman remains passive, defensive.[18] It affords man great pleasure to win a woman, to conquer her; and in the *ars amandi,* the modesty of woman, who keeps herself on the defensive until the moment of surrender, is an element of great psychological significance and importance. Under normal conditions man meets obstacles in which it is his part to overcome, and for which nature has given him an aggressive character. This aggressive character, however, under pathological conditions may likewise be excessively developed, and express itself in an impulse to absolutely subdue the object of desire, even to destroy or kill it.[19]

If both these constituent elements occur together – the abnormally intensified impulse to a violent reaction toward the object of the stimulus, and the abnormally intensified desire to conquer the woman – then the most violent outbreaks of sadism occur.

Sadism is thus nothing other than an excessive and monstrous pathological intensification of phenomena – possible, too, in normal conditions in rudimental forms – that accompany the psychic sex life, particularly in males. It is of course not at all necessary, and not even the rule, that the sadistic individual should be conscious of his instinct. What he typically feels is only the impulse of cruel and violent treatment toward the opposite sex, and the coloring of the idea of such acts with lustful feelings. Thus arises a powerful impulse to commit the imagined deeds. Insofar as the actual motives of this instinct are not comprehended by the individual, the sadistic acts have the character of impulsive deeds.

When the association of lust and cruelty is present, not only does the lustful emotion awaken the impulse of cruelty, but also the reverse is true: cruel ideas and acts of cruelty cause sexual excitement, and in this way are used by perverse individuals.[20]

A differentiation of original and acquired cases of sadism is scarcely possible. Many individuals, tainted from birth, for a long time do everything to conquer the perverse instinct. If they are potent, they are able for some time to lead a normal sex life, often with the assistance of fantasies of a perverse nature. Later, when the opposing motives of an ethical and aesthetic kind have been gradually overcome, and when oft-repeated experience proves that the natural act provides incomplete satisfaction, the abnormal instinct suddenly bursts forth. Due to this late manifestation of an originally perverse disposition, the appearance is that of an acquired perversion. As a rule, however, it may be safely assumed that this psychopathic state exists from birth.

Sadistic acts vary in monstrousness according to the power exercised by the perverse instinct over the individual thus afflicted, and in accordance with the strength of opposing ideas that may be present, which nearly always are more or less weakened by original ethical defects, hereditary degeneracy, or moral insanity. Thus there arises a long series of forms, beginning with capital crime and ending with petty acts, that afford merely symbolic satisfaction to the perverse desires of the sadistic individual.

Sadistic acts may be further differentiated according to their nature; either taking place after consummated coitus, leaving the excessive sexual desire unsatisfied; or, with diminished virility, undertaken to merely stimulate the diminished power; or, finally, where virility is absolutely nonexistent, occurring as an equivalent of impossible coitus, and to induce ejaculation. In the last two cases, impotence notwithstanding, there is still intense desire; or there was, at least, intense desire in the individual at the time when the sadistic acts became habitual. Sexual hyperesthesia must always be regarded as the basis of sadistic inclinations. The impotence that occurs so frequently in the psychopathic and neuropathic individuals considered here, resulting from excesses practiced in early youth, is usually dependent upon spinal weakness. Often, too, there is a kind of psychic impotence, superinduced by concentration of thought on the perverse act with simultaneous fading of the idea of normal satisfaction. No matter what the external form of the act may be, the mentally perverse predisposition and instinct of the individual are essential to an understanding of it.

[a] lust murder[21]
(lust potentiated as cruelty, murderous
lust extending to anthropophagy).

The most horrible example, and one that most pointedly shows the connection between lust and the desire to kill, is the case of Andreas Bichel, which Feuerbach published in his *Aktenmässigen Darstellung merkwürdiger Verbrechen*.

Bichel killed and dissected the girls he raped. Referring to one of his victims, he expressed himself at his examination as follows: "I opened her breast and, with a knife, cut through the fleshy parts of the body. Then I arranged the body as a butcher does beef and, with an axe, hacked it into small pieces to fit into the hole which I had dug up in the mountain to bury it. I can say that while opening the body I was so greedy that I trembled, and could have cut out a piece and eaten it."

Lombroso, too ("Geschlechtstrieb und Verbrechen in ihren gegenseitigen Beziehungen," Goltdammer's *Archiv*, vol. 30), mentions cases that fall into the same category. A certain Phillipe indulged in strangling prostitutes after sex, and said: "I am fond of women, but it is sport for me to strangle them after having enjoyed them."

A certain Grassi (Lombroso, op. cit., p. 12) was seized one night with sexual desire for a relative. Irritated by her remonstrance, he stabbed her with a knife several times in the abdomen, and also murdered her father and uncle, who attempted to hold him back. Immediately thereafter, he hastened to visit a prostitute in order to cool his sexual passion in her embrace. This was not sufficient, however, for he then murdered his own father and slaughtered several oxen in the stable.

The foregoing makes it clear that a great number of so-called lust murders depend upon combined sexual hyperesthesia and paresthesia. As a result of this perverse coloring of the feelings, further acts of bestiality with the corpse may result – e.g., cutting it up and wallowing in the intestines. The case of Bichel points to this possibility.

A modern example is that of Menesclou (*Annales d'hygiène publique*), who was examined by Lasègue, Brouardel and Motet, declared to be mentally sound, and executed.

Case 15.

A four-year-old girl was missing from her parents' home on April 15, 1880. On April 16, Menesclou, one of the occupants of the house, was arrested. The forearm of the child was found in his pocket; the head and entrails, in a half-charred condition, were taken from the stove. Other parts of the body were found in the bathroom. The genitals could not be found. M., when asked of their whereabouts, became embarrassed. The circumstances, as well as an obscene poem found on his person, left no doubt that he had violated the child and then murdered her. M. expressed no remorse, asserting that his deed was an unhappy accident. His intelligence was limited. He presented no anatomical signs of degeneration; somewhat deaf and scrofulous.

Aged twenty; convulsions at the age of nine months. Later he suffered from disturbed sleep (bed-wetting), was nervous, and developed tardily and imperfectly. With puberty he became irritable, showed evil inclinations, was lazy and intractable, and in all trades proved to be of no use. He grew no better even in the house of correction. He was made a marine, but there, too, he proved useless. When he returned home he stole from his parents, and spent his time in bad company. He did not run after women, but gave himself up passionately to masturbation, and occasionally indulged in sodomy with bitches. His mother suffered from periodic menstrual mania. An uncle was insane; another was a drunkard. An examination of M.'s brain showed morbid changes to the frontal lobes, to the first and second temporal convolutions, and to a part of the occipital convolutions.

Case 16.

Alton, a clerk in England, went for a walk out of town. He lured a child into a thicket. Afterward, at his office, he made this entry in his notebook: "Killed today a young girl, it was fine and hot." The child was missed, searched for, and found cut into pieces. Many parts, among them the genitals, could not be found. A. did not show the slightest trace of emotion, and gave no explanation regarding the motive or circumstances of his horrible deed. He was a psychopathic individual, and occasionally subject to fits of depression with *taedium vitae*. His father had once had an attack of acute mania. A near relative suffered from mania with homicidal impulses. A. was executed.

Case 17.

Jack the Ripper. On December 1, 1887; July 7, August 8, September 30, one day in the month of October and November 9, 1888; and June 1, July 17, and September 10, 1889, the bodies of women were found in various lonely quarters of London ripped open and mutilated in a peculiar fashion. The murderer has never been found. It is probable that he first cut the throats of his victims, then ripped open the abdomen and groped among the intestines. In some instances he cut off the genitals and carried them away; in others he only tore them to pieces and left them behind. He does not seem to have had sexual intercourse with his victims, but most likely the murderous act and subsequent mutilation of the corpse were equivalents of the sexual act (McDonald, *Le criminal-type,* 2d ed., Lyon, 1884; Spitzka, *The Journal of Nervous and Mental Diseases,* December 1888; Kiernan, *The Medical Standard,* November-December 1888).

Case 18.

Vacher the Ripper. On August 31, 1895, Portalier, seventeen years old, a shepherd, was found naked in a field. The belly was ripped open and the body bore other wounds besides. Examination showed that the victim had been strangled first. On August 4, 1897, a tramp named Vacher was arrested on suspicion of having committed this crime. He confessed to it, as well as to numerous other acts of a similar nature that had been perpetrated in various parts of France since 1894. He claimed that at the time he committed the crimes he suffered from temporary insanity and irresistible impulse; he was, in fact, a madman. Medical examination, however, proved that Vacher was sane when he committed these atrocious deeds, fled after their commission, and had a clear memory of the facts.

V. was born in 1869 of honorable parents and belonged to a mentally sound family. He never had a severe illness, and was from his earliest infancy vicious, lazy, and shy of work. At twenty he immorally assaulted a small child. During his military service he acquired a very bad reputation and was discharged from his regiment in 1893 because of "psychic disturbances" (confused talk, persecution mania, threatening language, extreme irritability). In 1893 he wounded a girl because she refused to marry him, then made an attempt at suicide (he shot himself through the right ear, which left him deaf on that side and produced facial paralysis). He was sent to an insane asylum and treated there for persecution mania. On April 1, 1894, he was dismissed as cured. He began to tramp about the country and committed the following horrible crimes: On March 20,

1894, he strangled Delhomme, twenty-one years old, cut her throat, trampled upon her abdomen, tore out a portion of her right breast, and then had coitus with the corpse. He committed the same atrocity, but without ravaging the bodies, on November 20, 1894, on a girl named Marcel, thirteen years of age, and on May 12, 1895, on a girl named Mortureux, seventeen years of age. On August 24, 1895, he strangled and then ravaged a lady named Morand, fifty-eight years old, and on September 22 he cut the throat of Alaise, a sixteen-year-old girl, and attempted to rip her abdomen open. On September 29 he committed the same crime that he later committed on Portalier on a fifteen-year-old boy named Pelet; here, however, he also cut off the genitals of the boy and sexually assaulted the corpse.

On March 1, 1896, he attempted to rape Derouet, a girl eleven years old, but was scared off by the field police. On September 10 he committed his usual atrocity on a Mrs. Mounier, just married, nineteen years old, and on October 1 on Rodier, a shepherdess, fourteen years old. He cut out her genitals and carried them away. Toward the end of May 1897, he killed a tramp, a fourteen-year-old boy named Beaupied, by cutting his throat. He threw the corpse down into a well. On June 18 he murdered a shepherd boy, thirteen years old, named Laurent, and committed pederasty on the corpse. Soon afterward he made an attempt on a Mrs. Plantier, but she was rescued. Unfortunately the rescuers allowed him to go unpunished.

Lacassagne, professor of forensic medicine in Lyon, Pierrel, professor of psychiatry, and Rebatel, specialist in insanity, were the experts at this atrocious murder trial. They found no hereditary taints, no cerebral disease, and no traces of epilepsy. V. was not particularly bright, irascible from his earliest years, vicious, and fond of maltreating animals. No one retained him long in service. He entered a monastery, but was soon dismissed when he began to masturbate his comrades. He could not find employment because of his immorality and ill temper. He was not a drinker. In the army he was feared and shunned. One day, disappointed at not being made a corporal, he flew into a rage, attacked his superior and became delirious. He was taken to the infirmary and from there he was sent to the insane asylum. His comrades did not consider him normal. During his spells of rage he was uncontrollable and considered dangerous. He always threatened others with cutting their throats, and was thought capable of doing such an act. He slept badly, constantly dreamed of murder, and was often so delirious during the night, no one wanted to sleep near him.

At the asylum he was found to suffer from persecution mania and was considered a dangerous character. Nevertheless he was dismissed as cured.

Subsequently he was found to be guilty of eleven murders, which were acts of sadism; lust murders. The victims were strangled, their throats were cut, their abdomens were ripped open, and their corpses, especially the genitals, were mutilated and sexually ravaged.

It was definitively proven that V. acted in cold blood, that he was quite conscious of his actions, and that he suffered from no psychic abnormality.

He committed the crimes in various sections of France, traversing the country in every direction.

There were no marks of anatomical degeneration. His genitals were normally developed. In confinement he was lazy, irascible and quite intractable. On one occasion, out of sheer stubbornness and because he thought he had been slighted, he refused all food for a period of seven days. On another occasion he flew into a frightful rage when he was refused permission to go to church. He spoke cynically of his crimes, showed no remorse, insisted that they were the outcome of madness and insanity, and played insane, thus hoping to be sent to an insane asylum (where escape could be easier). The experts could establish no symptoms of mental disturbance.

Résumé of the experts: "V. is neither an epileptic nor subject to an impulsive disease. He is an immoral, passionate man, who once temporarily suffered from a depressing persecution mania coupled with an impulse to suicide. Of this he was cured, and thereafter became responsible for his actions. His crimes are those of an antisocial, sadistic, bloodthirsty being, who considers himself privileged to commit these atrocities because he was once treated in an asylum for insanity, and thereby escaped well-merited punishment. He is a common criminal and there are no ameliorating circumstances to be found in his favor." V. was sentenced to death (*Archives d'anthropologie criminelle,* vol. 13, no. 78).

In such cases it may even happen that appetite for the flesh of the murdered victim arises, and in consequence of this perverse coloring of the idea, parts of the body may be eaten.

Case 19.

Leger, vine dresser, aged twenty-four. From youth he was moody, silent, and shy of people. He started out in search of work. After wandering in the forest for about eight days, he caught a girl twelve years old. He violated her, mutilated her genitals, tore out her heart, ate part of it, drank her blood, and buried her remains. Arrested, he lied at first, but finally confessed his crime with cynical cold-bloodedness. He listened to his sentence of death with indifference, and was executed. At the postmortem examination, Esquirol found morbid adhesions between the cerebral membranes and the brain (Georget, *Darstellung der Prozesse Leger, Feldtmann,* etc., Darmstadt, 1827).

Case 20.

Tirsch, hospital beneficiary from Prague, aged fifty-five; silent, peculiar, coarse, irritable, grumbling, and revengeful. He was sentenced to twenty years' imprisonment for violating a girl ten years old. He had attracted attention because of his outbursts of anger over insignificant events, and because of *taedium vitae.* In 1864 the refusal of an offer of marriage he had made to a widow led him to develop a hatred toward women, and on July 8 he went about with the intention of killing one of the hated sex. **He attacked a poor old woman he came upon in the woods and demanded coitus; when she resisted, he knocked her down and, "crazy with rage," strangled her to death. He then cut a branch off of a birch tree because he wanted to flog the corpse, but he was unable to do so because of his conscience; he therefore cut off the breasts and genitalia with a knife, cooked them at home, and, for the next few days, ate them.** On September 12, when he was arrested, the remains of this meal were found. He gave as the motive for his act "inner impulse." He wished to be executed because he had always been an outcast. In confinement he refused food, showed great emotional irritability as well as occasional outbursts of fury, and this made isolation, lasting several days, necessary. It was authoritatively established that most of his earlier excesses were coincident with outbreaks of excitement and fury (Maschka, *Prager Vierteljahrsschrift,* 1866, vol. 1, p. 79; Gauster in Maschka, *Handb. der ger. Medizin,* vol. 4, p. 489).

In other cases of lust murder, violation is omitted for physical and mental reasons (see above), and the sadistic crime alone becomes the equivalent of coitus. The prototype of such cases is the following one of Verzeni. The life of his victim hung on the rapid or retarded occurrence of ejaculation. Because this remarkable case presents all the peculiarities known by modern science concerning the relation of lust to lust murder with anthropophagy, and especially because it was carefully studied, it receives a detailed description here:

Case 21.

Vincenz Verzeni, born in 1849; in prison since January 11, 1872. He was accused [1] of an attempt to strangle his nurse, Marianne, four years ago while she lay sick in bed; [2] of a similar attempt on a married woman, Arsuffi, aged twenty-seven; [3] of an attempt to strangle a married woman, Gala, by grasping her throat while kneeling on her abdomen; [4] on suspicion of the following murders:

In December, a fourteen-year-old girl, Johanna Motta, set out for a neighboring village between seven and eight o'clock in the morning. When she did not return, her master set out to find her, and discovered her body lying by a path in the fields near the village. The corpse was frightfully mutilated with numerous wounds. The intestines and genitals had been torn from the open body and were found nearby. The nakedness of the body and the abrasions on the thighs made it seem probable that there had been an attempt at rape; the mouth, filled with earth, pointed to suffocation. In the vicinity of the body, under a pile of straw, a portion of flesh torn from the right calf and pieces of clothing were found. The perpetrator of the deed was not discovered.

On August 28, 1871, a married woman, Frigeni, aged twenty-eight, set out into the fields early in the morning. When she did not return by eight o'clock, her husband went to fetch her. He found her dead, lying naked in a field, with the mark of a thong, with which she had been strangled, around her neck, and with numerous wounds. The abdomen had been ripped open, and the intestines were hanging out.

On August 29, at noon, as Maria Previtali, aged nineteen, went through a field, she was followed by her cousin, Verzeni. He dragged her into a field of grain, threw her to the ground and began to choke her. When he let go of her for a moment to ascertain whether anyone was near, the girl got up and, pleading for her life, induced Verzeni to let her go, after he had squeezed her hands together for some time.

Verzeni was brought before a court. He was then twenty-two years old. Cranium of more than average size, but asymmetrical. The right frontal bone narrower and lower than the left, the right frontal prominence less developed, and the right ear smaller than the left (by one centimeter in length and three centimeters in breadth); both ears defective in the inferior half of the helix; the right temporal artery somewhat atheromatous. Bullnecked; enormous development of the zygoma and inferior maxilla; penis greatly developed, frenum absent; slight divergent alternating strabismus (insufficiency of the internal rectus muscle, and myopia). Lombroso concluded from these signs of degeneration that there was a congenitally arrested development of the right frontal bone. As predicted, Verzeni had a bad ancestry – two uncles were cretins; a third, microcephalic, beardless, one testicle absent, the other atrophic. The father showed traces of pellagrous degeneration, and had an attack of pellagrous hypochondria. A cousin suffered from cerebral hyperemia; another was a confirmed thief.

Verzeni's family was bigoted and low-minded. Verzeni had ordinary intelligence, knew well how to defend himself, and sought to prove an alibi and cast suspicion on others. Although there was nothing in his past that pointed to mental disease, his character was peculiar. He was silent and inclined to be solitary. In prison he was cynical. He masturbated and made every effort to observe women.

Verzeni finally confessed his deeds as well as their motive. The commission of them gave him an indescribably pleasant (lustful) feeling, which was accompanied by erection and ejaculation. As soon as he had grasped his victim by the neck he experienced sexual sensations. It was entirely the same to him whether the women were old, young, ugly, or beautiful. Simply choking them had usually satisfied him, and he had then allowed his victims to live; in the two cases mentioned, however, the sexual satisfaction was delayed, and he had continued to choke them until they died. The gratification experienced in this garroting was greater than in masturbation. The dermal abrasions on Motta's thighs were produced by his teeth while sucking her blood in the most intense lustful pleasure. He had torn a piece of flesh from her calf and taken it with him to roast at home, but on the way he hid it under a haystack because he feared that his mother might suspect him. He also carried, for some distance, pieces of the clothing and intestines, because it gave him great pleasure to smell and touch them. The strength he possessed in these moments of intense lustful pleasure was enormous. He had never been a fool; while committing his deeds he saw nothing around him (apparently as a result of intense sexual excitement, annihilation of perception – instinctive action). After such acts he was always very happy, enjoying a feeling of great satisfaction. He had never had pangs of conscience. It had never occurred to him to touch the genitals of the martyred women, or to violate his victims. It had satisfied him to throttle them and suck their blood. The statements of this modern vampire seemed to rest on truth. Normal sexual impulses had apparently remained foreign to him. He had two sweethearts that he was satisfied to look at; it was very strange to him that he had no inclination to strangle them or squeeze their hands, but he had not had the same pleasure with them as he had with his victims. There was no trace of moral sense or remorse.

Verzeni himself said that it would be a good thing if he was kept in prison, because with freedom he could not resist his impulses. Verzeni was sentenced to imprisonment for life (Lombroso, *Verzeni e Agnoletti,* Rome, 1873). The confessions Verzeni made after he was sentenced are interesting:

"I had an unspeakable delight in strangling women, experiencing during the act erections and real sexual pleasure. It was even a pleasure just to smell female clothing. The feeling of pleasure I had while strangling them was much greater than what I experienced while masturbating. I took great delight in drinking Motta's blood. It also gave me the greatest pleasure to pull the hairpins out of the hair of my victims.

"I took the clothing and intestines because of the pleasure it gave me to smell and touch them. My mother finally came to suspect me, because she noticed spots of semen on my shirt after each murder or attempted murder. I am not crazy, but at the moment of strangling my victims I saw nothing else. After the commission of the deeds, I was satisfied and felt well. It never occurred to me to touch or look at the genitals or such things. It satisfied me to seize the women by the neck and suck their blood. To this very day I am ignorant of how a woman is formed. During and after the strangling, I pressed myself on the entire body without thinking of one part more than another."

Verzeni arrived at his perverse acts quite independently after he noticed, at twelve years old, that he experienced a peculiar feeling of pleasure while wringing the necks of chickens. He then often killed great numbers of them, saying later that a weasel had been in the hencoop (Lombroso, Goltdammer's *Archiv,* vol. 30, p. 13).

Lombroso mentions an analogous case (Goltdammer's *Archiv*) that occurred in Vitoria, Spain:

Case 22.

A certain Gruyo, aged forty-one, with a blameless past life and married three times, strangled six women in the course of ten years. Almost all were street prostitutes and quite old.

After strangling them he tore out their intestines and kidneys through the vagina. Some of his victims he violated before killing; others, because of impotence, he did not. He set about his horrible deeds with such care that he remained undetected for ten years.

[b] mutilation of corpses.

From the preceding group of horrible perversions come, naturally, the necrophiles. The perversion in these cases, as with lustful murderers, involves an idea that in itself awakens a feeling of horror, and before which a sane person would shudder. In these individuals, however, the perversion is accompanied by lustful feelings, and thus leads to the impulse to indulge in acts of necrophilia.

Although the cases of mutilation mentioned in the literature seem to be of a pathological character, with the exception of Sergeant Bertrand (see below), they are far from being described and observed with accuracy. In certain cases there may be nothing more than the possibility that unbridled desire sees in death no obstacle to its satisfaction. The seventh case mentioned by Moreau, perhaps, belongs here.

A man, aged twenty-three, attempted to rape a woman, aged fifty-three. In the struggle he killed her, violated her, threw her in the water, and fished her out again for renewed violation. The murderer was executed. The meninges of the anterior lobes were thickened and adherent to the cortex.

French writers have recorded numerous examples of necrophilia.[22] Two cases concerned monks performing the watch for the dead. In a third case the subject was an idiot, who also suffered from periodic mania, and after committing a rape he was sent to an insane asylum, where he mutilated female bodies in the mortuary.

In other cases, however, there is undoubtedly preference for a corpse over a living woman. When no other act of cruelty – cutting into pieces, etc. – is practiced on the cadaver, it is probable that the lifeless condition itself forms the stimulus for the perverse individual. It is possible that the corpse – a human form absolutely without will – satisfies an abnormal desire, in that the object of desire is seen as perfectly subjugated and without resistance.

Brierre de Boismont (*Gazette médicale,* July 21, 1859) relates the history of a corpse violator who, having bribed the watchman, then gained entrance to a room where there was the corpse of a sixteen-year-old girl from a family of high social position. At night a noise was heard in the death chamber, as if a piece of furniture had fallen over. The mother of the dead girl entered the room and saw a man dressed in his nightshirt spring from the bed where the body lay. It was first thought that the man was a thief; the real explanation, however, was soon discovered. It later became clear that the culprit, a man of good family, had often violated the corpses of young women. He was sentenced to imprisonment for life.

The story of a prelate, reported by Taxil[23] (*La prostitution contemporaine,* p. 171), is of great interest as an example of necrophilia. From time to time the prelate would visit a certain brothel in Paris and order a prostitute to be dressed in white like a corpse and laid out on a bier. At the appointed hour he would appear in the room, which, in the meantime, had been elaborately prepared as a room of mourning; he would then act as if he were reading a mass for the soul. Finally, he would throw himself upon the girl, who, during the entire time, was compelled to play the role of a corpse.[24]

The cases in which the perpetrator injures and cuts up the corpse are clearer. Such cases come next to those of lust murder, insofar as cruelty, or at least an impulse to attack the female body, is connected with lust. It is possible that a remnant of moral sense inhibits performing the cruel act on a living woman, and possibly the fancy passes beyond lust murder to rest on its results, the corpse. Here it is also possible that the idea of the defenselessness of the body plays a role.

C a s e   2 3 .

Sergeant Bertrand, a man of delicate physical constitution and peculiar character; from childhood silent and inclined to solitude.

The details of the health of his family were not satisfactorily known, but the occurrence of mental diseases in his ancestors was ascertained. It was said that while he was a child he was affected with destructive impulses that he himself could not explain. He would break whatever was at hand. In early childhood he taught himself to masturbate. At nine he began to feel inclinations toward persons of the opposite sex. At thirteen the impulse to have sexual intercourse was powerfully awakened in him. He began to masturbate excessively. At such times he imagined a room filled with women. He would imagine that he carried out the sexual act with them and then killed them. Immediately thereafter he would think of them as corpses, and of how he had defiled them. Occasionally in such situations the thought of carrying out a similar act with male corpses would come up, but it was always attended by a feeling of disgust.

In time he felt the impulse to carry out such acts with actual corpses. Lacking human bodies, he obtained those of animals. He would cut open the abdomen, tear out the entrails, and masturbate during the act. He declared that in this way he experienced inexpressible pleasure. In 1846 these bodies no longer satisfied him. He now killed dogs, and proceeded with them as before. Toward the end of 1846 he first felt the desire to make use of human bodies.

At first he was horrified by the idea. In 1847, by accident in a graveyard, he ran across the grave of a newly buried corpse. Then this impulse, with headaches and palpitation of the heart, became so powerful that, although there were people nearby and he was in danger of being discovered, he dug up the body. In the absence of a convenient instrument for cutting up the body, he satisfied himself by hacking at it with a shovel.

He reported that over a period of two weeks in 1847 and 1848 he was driven to commit brutalities on some fifteen corpses under the most difficult and dangerous of circumstances. He dug up the bodies with his hands, not at all aware in his excitement of the injuries he thus inflicted on himself. When he had obtained the body, he cut it up with a sword or pocketknife, tore out the entrails, and then masturbated. The sex of the bodies is said to have been a matter of indifference to him, though it was ascertained that this modern vampire had dug up more female than male corpses.

During these acts he declared himself to have been in an indescribable state of sexual excitement. After having cut up the bodies, he then reinterred them.

In July 1848 he accidentally came across the body of a girl of sixteen. Then, for the first time, he experienced a desire to carry out coitus with a cadaver.

"I covered it with kisses and pressed it wildly to my heart. All that one could enjoy with a living woman is nothing compared to the pleasure I experienced. After I had enjoyed it for about a quarter of an hour, I cut the body up, as usual, and tore out the entrails.

Then I buried the cadaver again." Only after this, B. declared, had he felt the impulse to use the bodies sexually before cutting them up, and had done it thereafter in three instances. The actual motive for exhuming the bodies, however, was then, as before, to cut them up; and the enjoyment in so doing was greater than in using the bodies sexually. The latter act had always been nothing more than an episode of the principal one, and had never quieted his desires; thus he had later always mutilated the body.

The medico-legal examiners gave an opinion of "monomania." Court-martial sentence of one year's imprisonment (Michéa, *Union méd.*, 1849; Lunier, *Annal. méd.-psychol.*, 1849, p. 153; Tardieu, *Attentats aux moeurs*, 1878, p. 114; Legrand, *La folie devant les tribun.*, p. 524).

Case 24.

Ardisson, born in 1872, belonged to a family of criminals and insane. At school he learned readily; he was not addicted to drink, had no epileptic antecedents, had never had an illness, but was rather weak-minded. The man who adopted him and with whom he lived was a moral outcast. When A. reached puberty, he practiced masturbation **and would drink his own semen** because "it would be a pity to lose it." He ran after the girls, but could not understand why they shunned him. **In places where women had urinated, he would drink the urine.** He did not think that there was anything wrong about this. He was looked upon in the village as a venal felon. With his adopter he shared the favors of the beggar women who stayed overnight at their house. He was fond of fornication, was a breast fetishist, and loved **to suck breasts.** Later on he fell into necrophilia. He exhumed cadavers of females ranging from three to sixty years of age, sucked their breasts, practiced cunnilingus on them, but rarely coitus or mutilation. Once he carried away the head of a woman, at another time the whole corpse of a little girl three and a half years old. After his ghoulish deeds he would properly rearrange the grave. He lived isolated by himself, was at times very morose, and never showed signs of warmth or sensitivity. As a rule, however, he was not of an evil disposition, even when in prison. Several times he worked as a stonemason. Remorse and shame over his misdeeds were unknown to him. In 1892 he worked temporarily as a gravedigger. He deserted from the army and then took to begging from house to house. He loved to eat rats and cats. When arrested and returned to the regiment he deserted again. He was not punished because he was not held responsible. Dismissed from the army, he again became a gravedigger. When a girl of seventeen who had very prominent breasts was buried, his old passion awoke again. He unearthed the cadaver and profaned it in his usual manner. This became a common occurrence. One time, he took home the head of a woman, covered it with kisses and called it his bride. He was caught after he had taken home the body of a child three and a half years old, which he had secreted in the straw. With this he gratified his sexual desires, even when the putrid body was falling to pieces. The stench that filled the house betrayed him. Laughingly he admitted everything. A. was of small stature, prognathous and feeble; skull symmetrical; general tremor; genitals normal, without sexual emotion; intelligence very limited; devoid of all moral sense. A. was pleased with prison life (Epaulard, *Vampyrisme*).

[c] injury to women (stabbing, flagellation, etc.).

Following lust murder and violation of corpses come cases closely allied to lust murder, where injury to the object of lust and sight of the victim's blood are a delight and a pleasure. The notorious Marquis de Sade,[25] after whom this combination of lust and cruelty has been named, was such a monster. Coitus excited him only when he could prick the object of his desire until the blood flowed. His greatest pleasure was to injure naked prostitutes and then dress their wounds.

The case of a captain belongs here, mentioned by Brierre de Boismont, who always forced the object of his affection to place leeches **on her genitals** before coitus, which was frequent. The woman finally became very anemic and, as a result of this, insane.

The following case, from my own practice, clearly shows the connection between lust and cruelty, with desire to shed and to see blood:

Case 25.
Mr. X., aged twenty-five; father syphilitic, died of paretic dementia; mother hysterical and neurasthenic. He was a weak individual, constitutionally neuropathic, and presented several anatomical signs of degeneration.

Hypochondria and imperative conceptions as a child; later, constant alternation between exaltation and depression. While still a child of ten, the patient felt a peculiar lustful desire to see blood flow from his fingers. Thereafter he often cut or pricked himself on the fingers, and took great delight in it. Erections were promptly added to this, and also occurred if he saw the blood of others; for example, once, when he saw the servant girl cut her finger, it gave him an intense lustful feeling. From this time his sex life became more and more powerful. Without any teaching he began to masturbate, and during the act there were always memory-pictures of bleeding women. It now no longer sufficed for him to see his own blood flow; he longed to see the blood of young females, especially those who were attractive to him. He could scarcely overcome the impulse to violate two cousins and a certain servant.

Any young woman, even an unattractive one, induced this impulse when she excited him by some peculiarity of dress or adornment, especially coral jewelry. At first he succeeded in overcoming these desires, but in his imagination thoughts of blood were always present, inducing lustful excitement. An inner relation existed between thoughts and feelings. Often there were other cruel fantasies. He imagined himself in the role of a tyrant who had the people in crowds attacked with grapeshot. He would imagine a scene of enemies taking a city to mutilate, torture, kill and rape the young women.

This patient, who in his normal state had a mild disposition and was not morally defective, was ashamed of and horrified by such cruel, lustful fantasies, which became at once latent when his sexual excitement was satisfied by masturbation.

After a few years the patient became neurasthenic. Then simple imaginary representations of blood and scenes of blood sufficed to induce ejaculation. In order to free himself from his vice and his cruel imagination, he began to indulge in sexual intercourse with females. Coitus was possible, but only when the patient called up the idea that the girl's fingers were bleeding. Without the assistance of this idea no erection was possible. The cruel thought of cutting was limited to the woman's hand. At the time of greatest sexual excitement, the mere sight of the hand of an attractive woman was sufficient to induce the most violent erections. Frightened by popular stories of masturbation's injurious results, he abstained and fell into a condition of severe general neurasthenia, with hypochondriacal dysthymia and *taedium vitae*. Careful and watchful medical treatment cured the patient after a few months. He remained mentally well for three years; though he again became very sensual, he was rarely troubled by his earlier ideas of flowing blood. He gave up masturbation altogether, found satisfaction in natural sexual indulgence, remained virile, and no longer found it necessary to call up ideas of blood.

The following case, reported by Tarnowsky (op. cit., p. 61), shows that such lustful, cruel impulses may be simply episodical, and occur in certain exceptional states of mind in neurotic individuals:

Case 26.

Z., physician; neuropathic constitution, reacting badly to alcohol. Under ordinary circumstances capable of normal coitus, but as soon as he had indulged in wine he found that his increased sexual desire was no longer satisfied by simple coitus. In this condition he was compelled to prick **a girl's buttocks,** or to make stabs with a lancet, to see blood, and to feel the entrance of the blade into a living body, in order to have ejaculation and experience complete satiety of his lust.

The majority of those afflicted with this form of perversion seem insensible to the normal stimulus of woman. In the first case (25), the assistance of the idea of blood was necessary to obtain erection. The following is that of a man who, by masturbation, etc., in early youth, had diminished his power of erection so that the sadistic act took the place of coitus:

Case 27.

The girl-stabber of Bozen (reported by Demme, *Buch der Verbrechen,* vol. 2, p. 341). In 1829, H., aged thirty, soldier, became the subject of a legal investigation. At different times and in different places he had wounded girls with pocketknives or penknives by stabbing them in the abdomen, preferably in the genitals. He cited heightened sexual impulse, increasing to the intensity of fury, as a motive for these acts, and this was only satisfied with the thought and act of stabbing persons of the female sex. The impulse would pursue him for days at a time. He would then pass into a confused mental state, which would clear away only when the impulse had been satisfied by the deed. In the act of stabbing he experienced the same satisfaction as that produced by completed coitus. This was increased by the sight of blood dripping from the knife. In his tenth year the sexual instinct became powerfully manifest. At first he yielded to masturbation, and felt physically and mentally weakened by it. Before he became a girl-stabber, he had satisfied his sexual lust by making immature girls practice masturbation on him, and by sodomy. Gradually the thought of how pleasurable it would be to stab a young and pretty girl in the genitals and take delight in the sight of the blood running from the knife came to him.

Among his effects were found copies of the objects of a phallic cult, as well as obscene pictures he painted of Mary's conception and the "thought of God injected" into the lap of the Virgin, were found. He was considered a peculiar, very irritable man, shy of people, fond of women, moody and glum. No traces of shame and regret for his deeds were ever found. He was apparently a person[26] who had become impotent through early sexual excesses and, by the continuance of intense sexual desire and heredity, was thus predisposed to perversion of sexual life.

Case 28.

In the 1860s the inhabitants of Leipzig were frightened by a man who had a habit of attacking young girls on the street by stabbing them in the upper arm with a dagger. Finally arrested, he was recognized as a sadist, who at the instant of stabbing had an ejaculation, and for whom the wounding of the girls was an equivalent of coitus. (Wharton, "A Treatise on Mental Unsoundness," § 623. Philadelphia, 1873).[27]

Impotence likewise exists in the next three cases. It may be psychic, however, because the principal tone of the sex life lies in sadistic inclination with distortion of the normal elements:

Case 29.

The girl-cutter of Augsburg (reported by Demme, *Buch der Verbrechen,* vol. 7, p. 281). Bartle, wine merchant. He was subject to lively sexual excitement at the age of fourteen, though decidedly opposed to its satisfaction with coitus; his aversion went so far as disgust for the female sex. At that time he already had the idea to cut girls, and thus satisfy his sexual desire. He refrained from it, however, because of lack of opportunity and courage. He disdained masturbation, but now and then had pollutions with erotic dreams of girls who had been cut. At the age of nineteen he cut a girl for the first time. During the act he had a seminal emission and experienced intense pleasure. From that time the impulse grew constantly more powerful. He chose only young and pretty girls, and typically asked them before the deed whether they were still single. The ejaculation or sexual satisfaction only occurred when he was sure that he had actually wounded the girls. After such an act he always felt tired and bad, and was also troubled with qualms of conscience. Up to his thirty-second year he pursued this process of cutting, but was always careful not to wound the girls dangerously. From that time until his thirty-sixth year he was able to control his impulse. He then sought to satisfy himself by simply pressing the girls on the arm or neck, but this only gave rise to erections and not to ejaculation. He then sought to attain satisfaction by pricking the girls with the knife left in its sheath, but this did not suffice. Finally, he stabbed with the open knife and had complete success, for he thought that, when stabbed, a girl bled more and suffered more pain than when merely cut. In his thirty-seventh year he was detected and arrested. In his lodgings a collection of daggers, sword canes, and knives were found. He said that just seeing these weapons gave him an intense feeling of sexual pleasure, with violent excitement, but grasping the weapons increased this pleasure. According to his own confession, he had injured fifty girls in all. His external appearance was rather pleasing. He lived in very good circumstances, but was peculiar and shy.

Case 30.

During the month of June 1896, on the street and in broad daylight, quite a number of young girls had been stabbed in the genitals. On July 2 the perpetrator was caught in the act. V., twenty years of age, was hereditarily heavily tainted; at fifteen he had been sexually excited to a high degree by the sight of a woman's buttocks. From that time on, this part of the female body attracted him in a sensuous manner and became the object of his erotic fantasies and dreams, accompanied by pollutions. Soon this was coupled with the lascivious desire to slap, pinch or cut the genitals of women. At the moment he performed this act in his dreams, pollution took place. Soon he was tempted to transfer his dreams into action. For a while he succeeded in mastering his morbid craving, but this produced feelings of anxiety and copious perspiration that would break out from his entire body. When orgasm and erection became vehement, he would be overcome with fear and confusion to such an extent that the impulse to cut became irresistible. At that psychic moment ejaculation would take place, and he felt relieved in body and mind (Magnan in Thoinot's *Attentats aux moeurs,* p. 451. For a more detailed account see Garnier in *Annales d'hygiène publique,* February 1900, p. 112).

Case 31.

J.H., aged twenty-six, came for consultation in 1883 concerning severe neurasthenia and hypochondria. Patient confessed that although he had practiced masturbation infrequently from his fourteenth to his eighteenth year, since that time he had been unable to resist the impulse. Until then he had had no opportunity to approach females, because as an invalid he had been anxiously cared for and never left alone. Although he had possessed no real desire for this unknown pleasure, he accidentally learned what it was when one of his mother's maids cut her hand severely on a pane of glass, which she had broken while washing windows. While helping to stop the bleeding, he could not keep from sucking up the blood that flowed from the wound, and during which he experienced extreme erotic excitement, with complete orgasm and ejaculation.

From that time on he sought in every possible way to see and, where practicable, to taste the fresh blood of females. He preferred the blood of young girls. He spared no pains or expense to obtain this pleasure. At first he availed himself of a young servant, who allowed her finger to be pricked with a needle or lancet at his request. When his mother discovered this, she discharged the girl. He was then driven to prostitutes as a substitute, and was often successful, though he had some difficulty. In the intervals he practiced masturbation alone and with a woman, which never afforded him complete satisfaction, but instead caused listlessness and self-reproach. Because of his nervous difficulties he visited many sanatoria, and twice was a voluntary patient in institutions. He used hydrotherapy, electricity, and strengthening cures, without particular success. For a time it was possible, by means of cold sitz baths, monobromate of camphor, and bromides, to diminish his sexual excitability and masturbatory impulse. However, when the patient again felt free, he would immediately fall into his old passion, and spare no pains or money to satisfy his sexual desire in the abnormal manner described.

Of special interest for the scientific proof of sadism is a case related by Moll (see case 29, ninth edition of this work [case 30 in the appendix, p. 520], and recently published by Moll himself in his book on *Libido sexualis*, p. 500).

This case clearly discloses one of the hidden roots of sadism – the impulse to achieve full subjugation of the woman, which here became consciously entertained. This is more remarkable because it occurred in a decidedly timid individual who was in other respects modest and even apprehensive. The case also clearly shows that powerful sexual desire impelling the individual to overcome all obstacles may be present at the same time that coitus is not desired, because the principal intensity of feeling is, from birth, connected to the cruel part of the sadistic (lustful and cruel) circle of ideas. This case also contains weak elements of masochism (see below).

Cases where men with perverse inclinations induce prostitutes, by paying them large sums, to allow themselves to be whipped and even wounded are common. Works on prostitution contain reports of these cases (see Coffignon, *La corruption à Paris*, etc.).

[d] defilement of women.

The perverse sadistic impulse to injure and humiliate women, and to treat them with contempt, is also expressed in the desire to defile them with disgusting or, at least, foul things.

The following case, published by Arndt (*Vierteljahrsschr. f. ger. Medizin,* vol. 17, no. 1), belongs here:

Case 32.

A., medical student at Greifswald, **was accused of frequently exposing his genitals in public to girls from respectable families; he would allow his private parts to protrude, completely exposed, out of his trousers, having previously kept them covered under his overcoat. Sometimes he chased the girls as they ran away, and, after catching them, he would smear them with his urine. All of this was performed in broad daylight; he never uttered a word as he performed these actions.**

A. was twenty-three years old, well-built, neatly dressed, and polite. Indication of an underdeveloped cranium; chronic pneumonia of the apex of the right lung, emphysema. Pulse, sixty; when excited, not more than seventy to eighty. Genitals normal. Occasional disturbances of digestion and hardness of the abdomen, vertigo, and excessive excitement of sexual desires, which led to early masturbation. Sexual desire was never directed toward a natural method of satisfaction. He had occasional attacks of depression, self-deprecating thoughts, and perverse impulses, for which he could find no motive, such as laughing at serious things, throwing his money in the water, and running about in the pouring rain. His father was of a nervous temperament, his mother subject to nervous headaches. A brother was subject to epileptic convulsions.

From his youth the culprit presented a nervous temperament, was inclined to convulsions and attacks of syncope, and when severely scolded would fall into a state of momentary stiffness. In 1869 he studied medicine in Berlin. In 1870 he went to war as a hospital assistant. His letters from this time betray a peculiar torpidity and softness. On returning home in 1871, his emotional irritability was noticed at once by those about him. Thereafter, frequent complaints of bodily ailments; unpleasantness resulting from a love affair. In November 1871 he pursued his studies diligently in Greifswald. He was considered very gentlemanly. In confinement he was quiet, calm, and sometimes self-absorbed. He attributed his acts to painful sexual excitement that lately had become excessive. He declared that he had been fully conscious of his perverse acts, and after committing them had always been ashamed of them. He had not experienced actual sexual satisfaction in their commission. He obtained no correct insight into his position. He considered himself a kind of martyr – a victim of an evil power. Presumption of irresponsibility as a result of absence of free will.

The impulse to defile occurs also, paradoxically, in the aged, when a reappearance of sexual instinct is so often expressed in perverse acts. Thus Tarnowsky reports (op. cit., p. 76) the following case:

Case 33.

I knew a patient who had a woman, dressed in a *décolleté* ball gown, lie down on a low sofa in a brightly lighted room. **Alone in the doorway of another bedroom, hidden in the dark, he observed the woman for a little while; roused to excitement, he jumped on top of her and defecated on her breasts. He confessed that, while he was doing this, he ejaculated.**

An officer of Vienna informed me that prostitutes were induced, with large sums of money, to suffer **men spitting, defecating and urinating into their mouths.**[28]

The following case by Dr. Pascal (*Igiene dell' amore*) also seems to belong here:

Case 34.

A man had a lover who would allow him to blacken her hands with coal or soot. She then had to sit before a mirror in such a way that he could see her hands in the reflection. While conversing with her, which was often for a long time, he constantly looked at her mirrored hands, and finally, after a while, he would take his leave, fully satisfied.

The following case, communicated by a physician, may be of interest with respect to this subject:

An officer was known in a brothel in K. only by the name of "Oil." "Oil" was only able to induce erection and ejaculation by having **a nude prostitute** step into a tub filled with oil while he rubbed the oil all over her body.

These acts lead to the presumption that certain cases of injury to women's clothing (e.g., sprinkling them with sulfuric acid, ink, etc.) depend upon a perverse sexual impulse; at any rate the motive seems to be to inflict an injury or pain of some sort. Those injured are always females, and the perpetrators males. In crimes of this kind, pains should always be taken to examine the sex life of the culprits.

The case of Bachmann, given below, throws a clear light on the sexual nature of such crimes; for, in this case, the sexual motive in the deed is proven.

Case 35.

B., aged twenty-nine, merchant; married; heavily tainted; since his sixteenth year, masturbation by means of a pocket electric battery; neurasthenic; impotent at the age of eighteen; for a while an absinthe drinker because of unrequited love. One day, on meeting a nursemaid wearing the type of white apron that his love used to wear, he could not resist the temptation to steal it. He took it home and, after masturbating into it, burned it with renewed masturbation. Returning to the street he met a woman wearing a white dress. The sight of it produced an impulse to stain her dress with ink. Having done it, he went home, reveled in the sensual situation thus provoked, and masturbated again. Another time, while strolling around on the street, he amused himself by cutting the dresses of women with a penknife. He was arrested as a pickpocket. On other occasions, a stain on a lady's dress made him experience orgasm and ejaculation. He obtained the same results from burning holes (with a cigar) in the clothing of women whom he passed (Magnan, reported by Thoinot, *Attentats aux moeurs,* p. 434, and by Garnier, *Annales d'hygiène publ.,* March 1900, p. 237).

Garnier (*Annales d'hygiène publ.,* February-March 1900) has given these cases of sadism special attention, reducing them to fetishism (see below). This is particularly apparent in case 35, where the fetish consisted of a blue dress covered with a white apron. The personality of the wearer was a matter of indifference; it was the fetish that fascinated, and the impulse was irresistible. Garnier calls these cases *sado-fetishism,* and points out their social and forensic importance, suggesting that such unfortunate individuals be confined in an insane asylum. Destructive actions like these upon the fetish as an object of desire and possession, which may also be thought of as sadism on lifeless objects, may be explained by the fact that, in sadistic natures, the fetish awakens sensual sensations that are coupled with the pleasure derived from acts of cruelty and destruction.

In well-developed fetishism, the fetish itself – abstracted from the personality of the wearer – dominates per se the whole sex life, bringing it into action and, under certain circumstances, awakening kindred regions of a sadistic nature that find gratification in the field of the (impersonal) fetish. The sadistic act is in itself often an equivalent for coitus rendered impossible by physical and psychic impotence. It may be practiced on boys, animals, or persons of the same sex, without relation to pedophilia, zoophilia, or homosexuality.

It is remarkable, and seems to prove the connection with lustful cruelty, that at the moment of the destructive act against the fetish (cutting off girls' tresses, stabbing women, defiling ladies' clothes, etc.), orgasm and ejaculation take place in the "sado-fetishist."

A. Moll (*Zeitschr. f. Medizinalbeamte*) has recently published a case which may be considered classical:

An academically cultured man, aged thirty-one, heavily tainted by heredity, offspring of a marriage between blood relations, always shy and retired; at the time of puberty (seventeen), would romp about with the playmates of his sister, girls of about eleven, and from the sight of their white underwear became a "laundry fetishist." He began to masturbate while thinking of girls clad in white garments. During this act, he also manipulated light-colored pieces of clothing that belonged to his female relatives.

At the age of twenty-three he began coitus with girls dressed in white. When twenty-five he saw a girl's white dress being bespattered with mud. This produced a very strong sexual emotion in him, and from that time on he felt an irresistible impulse to defile the apparel of women, to crush and tear it. This impulse was particularly provoked at the sight of women clad in white. He used a solution of ferrous sesquichlorate or ink, and thus produced orgasm and ejaculation. At times he had dreams of white female underwear that were accompanied by pollutions at the moment of touching or crushing the apparel. Insanity could not be established. He was fined the sum of fifty marks for unlawfully causing damage to personal property.

[e] other kinds of assault on females – symbolic sadism.

The foregoing groups do not exhaust the forms in which the sadistic impulse toward women is expressed. If the impulse is not overwhelming, or if there is yet sufficient moral resistance, it may happen that the perverse inclination is satisfied by an apparently quite senseless and silly act, which nevertheless has a symbolic meaning for the perpetrator. This seems to be the meaning of the two following cases:

Case 36.

(Dr. Pascal, *Igiene dell' amore.*) On a certain day once a month, a man made a habit of going to a lover to cut her "bangs." This gave him the greatest pleasure. He made no other demands on the girl.

Case 37.

A man in Vienna regularly visited several prostitutes only to lather their faces and then remove the lather with a razor, as if he were shaving them. He never hurt the girls, but became sexually excited and ejaculated during the procedure.[29]

[f] ideal sadism.

Sadism may eventually manifest itself solely in the imagination, i.e., in dream pictures that accompany the act of masturbation or accompany the process of pollution in sadistic fantasies.

That it remains an ideal act may only be due to lack of opportunity or courage to put it into practical action; or it may be due to latent ethics that forbid violence. Another alternative may be that when debility of the center of ejaculation is pronounced, a vivid sadistic impression suffices to provoke ejaculatory gratification. In this case sadism is merely an equivalent of coitus.

Case 38.

D., agent, aged twenty-nine years, family heavily tainted; masturbation at the age of fourteen, coitus at twenty, but without pronounced sexual desire or satisfaction; thereafter masturbation preferred. At first these acts were accompanied by the thought of a girl whom he could maltreat and subject to humiliating and infamous actions.

Reading about acts of violence on women excited him sexually, but he did not like to see blood on himself or on others. He hated the sight of a naked woman.

Because he disliked unnatural sexual intercourse, he never felt inclined to put his sadistic ideas into actual practice.

He could not account for his sadistic ideas. He made these statements at a consultation for neurasthenia.

Case 39.

Ideal sadism with "buttocks fetishism." P., aged twenty-two, of independent means, heavily tainted by heredity, accidentally saw the governess chastising his sister (fourteen years of age) **on the buttocks while holding the girl between her knees.** This made a deep impression on him, and he henceforth had a constant desire to see and touch his sister's buttocks. By some clever stratagem he succeeded. When seven years old he became the playmate of two small girls, one of whom was tiny and lean, the other rather plump. He played the role of a father chastising his children. The lean girl he simply spanked over her clothes. The other, however, allowed him to smack her bare bottom (she was then ten years old). This gave him great sexual pleasure and caused erection.

One day, after being chastised in this manner, the girl asked him to look at her pudenda. He refused the invitation, however, as this view did not interest him in the least.

At the age of nine he became acquainted with a boy a little older than himself. One day they came across a picture that represented a scene of flagellation in a monk's monastery. P. soon persuaded his companion to enact the scene. His companion consented to playing the passive role and found delight in it. This was often repeated. On one occasion, P. assumed the passive role, but it gave him no pleasure. The relation between the two continued until they grew into manhood, and P. always ejaculated during the flagellation. He dominated his friend, who looked upon him as a superior being. Only twice while this friendship lasted did P. attempt this procedure on other persons; once on a nursemaid whose bare bottom he smacked, and once on a girl, eleven years old, on the street. Her cries, however, drove him to hasty flight.

He never felt any inclination to masturbation, coitus with girls, nor antipathic sexual sensations. He confined himself to touching the buttocks of women when in a crowd, touching the buttocks of girls when mixing with them on the playground, looking under the dresses of women climbing the stairs of a bus, and watching little girls undressing themselves.

He practiced "sado-fetishism." He reveled in fantasy situations in which he flagellated his younger brother, a nursemaid or a nun; he invented stories which always ended in a scene of flagellation; answered advertisements such as: "Stern lady desires pupil," and derived the utmost delight from the correspondence that followed; made drawings of flagellation scenes and bare female buttocks, ransacked the libraries for books containing sadistic writings, made abstracts of the whole literature, collected pictures referring to this favorite subject, and designed such pictures himself in keeping with the progress he made in developing his perversion.

His flights of fantasy escalated from exhibition of the naked buttocks to smacking, flagellating and teasing them, and even to murder of the owner. Murder, however, frightened him. The ever-recurring ejaculations finally brought on severe neurasthenia. He could never make up his mind to seek medical advice. At last he found a woman with whom he could have coitus because she permitted him to flagellate her during the act (Regis, *Archives d'anthropologie criminelle,* no. 82, July 1899).

Case 40.

Merchant, forty years of age, abnormally early hetero- and hypersexuality. From his twentieth year occasional coitus and, for lack of something better, masturbation. As a consequence of being frightened (surprise during coitus), psychic impotence. Treatment unsuccessful. This affected his mind and he came near to despair. He then tried immature girls, with whom impotence could not cause him shame. His moral willpower, still unimpaired, eventually enabled him to resist this impulse, however, and he found satisfaction in being with girls legally of age and no longer innocent, but they had to be younger in appearance than their years. In such cases his impotence disappeared. One day he saw a lady slapping the face of her daughter, fourteen years old. This at once gave him a violent erection and orgasm. The thought of it had the same result. From that time he found it extraordinarily stimulating seeing girls, no matter how young, beaten; even reading or hearing about maltreatment of females had the same result.

That the retarded sadism in this case was not acquired but only latent is evident from the fact that it previously existed in an ideal form. It was part of his predominant sensual idea to introduce **"his arm, all the way up to the shoulder blade, into the vagina of a woman,"** and grope about within (other cases of ideal sadism, see Moll, *Libido sexualis,* pp. 324 and 500; Krafft-Ebing, *Arbeiten,* vol. 4, p. 163).

[g] sadism with any other object – whipping of boys.

The sadistic acts with females described above are also practiced on other living, sensitive objects – children and animals. There may be a full consciousness that the impulse is really directed toward women, and that, for lack of something better, only the nearest attainable objects (pupils) are abused. The condition of the perpetrator may be such, however, that the impulse to cruel acts enters consciousness accompanied only by lustful excitement, while its real object (which alone can explain the lustful coloring of such acts) remains latent.

The first alternative sufficiently explains the cases described by Dr. Albert (Friedreich's *Blätter f. ger. Med.,* p. 77, 1859) in which lustful teachers, without cause, whipped their pupils on the naked buttocks. We must think of the second alternative, the sadistic impulse without consciousness of its object, when the sight of punishment causes spontaneous sexual excitement in the witness and thus becomes the determining factor in his future sex life, as in the following cases:

Case 41.

K., aged twenty-five, merchant, applied to me in the fall of 1889 for advice concerning an anomaly of his sex life, which made him fear invalidism as well as the impossibility of future happiness in marriage.

Patient came from a nervous family. As a child he was delicate, weak and nervous. Healthy except for measles; later on he became more robust. At the age of eight, while at school, he saw the teacher punish the boys by taking their heads between his thighs and spanking them with a ferule. This sight caused the patient lustful excitement. "Without any idea of the danger and enormity of masturbation," he satisfied himself with it, and from that time often masturbated, always calling up the remembered image of a boy being punished.

This continued until his twentieth year. He then learned the significance of masturbation, and was terribly frightened; although he tried to overcome his impulse to masturbate he fell into the practice of psychic masturbation, which he regarded as innocuous and morally defensible, and during which he made use of the previously mentioned images of boys being whipped.

Patient now became neurasthenic, suffered from pollutions, and tried to cure himself by visiting brothels; but he could not induce erection. Then he sought to obtain normal sexual feelings by means of social intercourse with ladies, but recognized that he was entirely insensible to the charms of the fair sex.

The patient was an intelligent man, normally developed, and of aesthetic taste. There was no inclination toward persons of his own sex. My advice consisted of means by which to combat the neurasthenia and pollutions, including interdiction of psychic and manual masturbation, avoidance of all sexual excitants, and, possibly, hypnotic treatment to ultimately induce a return of the sex life to its normal condition.

Case 42.

Abortive sadism. N., student, came under observation in December 1890. He had practiced masturbation from early youth. According to his statements, he became sexually excited when he saw his father whip the children, and, later, when he saw his companions whipped by the teacher. As a spectator of such scenes, he always experienced lustful feelings. He could not say exactly when this first occurred, but it may have been at about the age of six. He could not tell exactly when he began to masturbate, but he stated with certainty that his sexual instinct was first awakened by the punishment of others, and thus he unconsciously came to practice masturbation. The patient remembered clearly that from the age of four to the age of eight he was frequently spanked, and that this caused him pain, never lustful pleasure.

Because he did not always have opportunity to see others whipped, he began to *imagine* how others were punished. This excited his lust, and he would then masturbate. Whenever he could, he managed to see others punished at school. Now and then he also felt the desire to whip others. At the age of twelve he induced a comrade to allow him to whip him. He found great sexual pleasure in this. When, however, his companion beat him in return, he experienced nothing but pain.

The impulse to beat others was never very strong. The patient experienced more satisfaction from filling his imagination with scenes of whipping. He never indulged in any other sadistic acts, and never had any desire to see blood, etc. Up to his fifteenth year his sexual indulgence consisted of masturbation, coupled with such fantasies. After dancing lessons and association with girls, the early fantasies disappeared almost entirely and were accompanied by only weak lustful feelings, so the patient gave them up entirely. In their place came thoughts of coitus in a natural way, without anything sadistic.

The patient indulged in coitus for the first time "because of his health." He was potent, and the act gratified him. He then tried to abstain from masturbation, but was not successful, though he often indulged in coitus with more pleasure than he had in masturbation. He wished to be freed from masturbation as if from something vicious. He had coitus once a month, but masturbated once or twice every night. He was sexually normal, excepting the masturbation. There was no neurasthenia; genitals normal.

Case 43.

P., aged fifteen, of high social position, came from a hysterical mother whose brother and father died in an asylum. Two children in the family died in early childhood of convulsions. Although the patient was talented, virtuous, and quiet, at times he was very disobedient, stubborn, and of violent temper. He had epilepsy, and practiced masturbation. One day it was learned that P., with money, induced a comrade of fourteen, B., to allow himself to be pinched on the arms, genitals, and thighs. When B. cried, P. became excited and struck at B. with his right hand, while with his left he made manipulations in the left pocket of his trousers. P. confessed that to maltreat his friend, of whom he was very fond, gave him peculiar delight, and that ejaculation while hurting his friend gave him much more pleasure than when he masturbated alone (Gyurkovechky, *Pathologie und Therapie der männlichen Impotenz.*, p. 80, 1889).

Case 44.

K., fifty years of age, without occupation, heavily tainted, satisfied his perverse sexual feelings exclusively on boys of ten to fifteen years of age, whom he seduced to mutual masturbation. At the acme of the situation he would pierce the lobe of the boy's ear. When this, later on, proved insufficient, he cut off the lobe of the boy's ear. He was arrested and sentenced to five years' imprisonment (Thoinot, op. cit., p. 452).

In all these cases of sadistic abuse of boys, there can be no thought of a combination of sadism and antipathetic sexual instinct, as often occurs (see below) in individuals of inverted sexuality. Aside from the absence of all positive signs, this is shown by a study of the next group, where, in association with the object of injury – animals – the instinct for women is seen to appear repeatedly.

[h] sadistic acts with animals.

In numerous cases, sadistically perverse men who are afraid of criminal acts with human beings or who only care to see the suffering of a sensitive being, will torture animals or observe dying animals[30] to stimulate or excite their lust.

The case of a man in Vienna, reported by Hofmann in his *Lehrbuch der gerichtlichen Medizin,* is noteworthy in relation to this. According to the evidence of several prostitutes, he was accustomed to excite himself before the sexual act by torturing and killing chickens, pigeons and other birds, and was therefore called *"Hendlherr"* ("Mr. Chicken").

For the elucidation of such cases, the observation of Lombroso is of value, according to whom two men would ejaculate when they killed or wrung the necks of chickens or pigeons.

The same author, in his *Uomo delinquente,* p. 201, speaks of a poet of some reputation who became powerfully excited sexually whenever he saw calves slaughtered or saw bloody meat.

Mantegazza (op. cit., p. 114) relates the prevailing practice among degenerate Chinese of sodomizing geese and, at the moment of ejaculation, cutting off their heads.

Mantegazza (*Fisiologia del piacere,* 5th ed., pp. 394-395) mentions the case of a man who once saw chickens killed, and from then on had a desire to wallow in their warm, steaming entrails, because he experienced a feeling of lust while doing it.

Thus, in these and similar cases, the sex life is so constituted from birth that the sight of blood, death, etc., excites lustful feeling. It is so in the following case:

Case 45.

C.L., aged forty-two, engineer, married, father of two children; from a neuropathic family; father irascible, a drinker; mother hysterical, subject to attacks of eclampsia. The patient remembered that in childhood he took particular pleasure in witnessing the slaughtering of domestic animals, especially swine. He thus experienced lustful pleasure and ejaculation. Later he visited slaughterhouses in order to delight in the sight of flowing blood and the death throes of the animals. When he could find an opportunity, he killed the animals himself, which always afforded him a vicarious feeling of sexual pleasure.

He first attained knowledge of his abnormality at the time of full maturity. Although the patient was not exactly uninclined to women, close contact with them seemed repugnant to him. On the advice of a physician, at twenty-five he married a woman who pleased him, in the hope of freeing himself of his abnormal condition. Although he was very partial to his wife, it was only seldom, and after great trouble and exertion of his imagination, that he was able perform coitus with her; nevertheless, he fathered two children. In 1866 he was in the war in Bohemia. The letters he wrote at that time to his wife were composed in an exalted, enthusiastic tone. He was missing after the battle of Königgrätz.

If, in this case, the capability of normal coitus was much impaired by the predominance of perverse ideas, in the following case it seems to have been entirely repressed:

Case 46.

A gentleman visited prostitutes, had them purchase a living fowl or rabbit, and made them torture the animal. He particularly reveled in the sight of the heads being cut off and the eyes and entrails being torn out. If he found a girl who would consent and be particularly cruel, he was delighted, paid her, and went his way without asking anything more of her (Pascal, *Igiene dell' amore*).

Also interesting is the awakening of sadistic feelings toward animals, as related in the following case of Féré:

Case 47.

B., thirty-seven years of age, tanner; tainted; began masturbation at the age of nine. One day, as he was about to masturbate with another boy on the corner of a street where the gradient was very steep, a heavily laden dray pulled by four horses came along. The driver yelled at the horses and whipped them. The horses slipped about a good deal and made sparks fly from the cobblestones. This excited B. very much and he ejaculated as one of the horses fell. Ever afterward a similar occurrence would have the same effect on him and he went in search of it. If the difficulty was overcome without extra exertion on the part of the horses or without the use of the whip, B. only became excited and had to resort to masturbation or coitus to find final satisfaction. Even after he was married and had children, sadism continued. When one of his children fell ill with chorea, B. had hysterical attacks (Féré, *L'instinct sexuel*, p. 255).

The last two sections, [g] and [h], show that the suffering of any living being may become a source of perverse sexual enjoyment to sadistically constituted persons, and that there may be sadism with almost any (living) object. However, it would be erroneous and an exaggeration to try to explain with sadistic perversion all the remarkable and surprising acts of cruelty that occur, and to assume sadism as the motive underlying all the horrors recorded in history or found in certain psychological manifestations among the peoples of the present time.

Cruelty arises from various sources and is natural to primitive man. Compassion, in contrast, is a secondary manifestation and acquired late. The instinct to fight and destroy, so important an endowment in prehistoric conditions, is long afterward operative; and, in the ideas engendered by civilization, like that of "the criminal," it finds new objects, so long as its original object – "the enemy" – still exists. That not simply the death, but also the torture of the conquered is demanded, is explained in part by the sense of power which satisfies itself in this way, and in part by the degree to which the impulse of vengeance is insatiable. Thus all horrors and historical enormities may be explained without recourse to sadism (which often enough may have been the motive, but should not be assumed as such, since it is a relatively rare perversion).

At the same time, there is another powerful psychic element to be taken into consideration, one that explains the attraction still exerted by executions, etc.; namely, the pleasure produced by intense, unusual impressions and rare sights, in contrast to which, in coarse and blunted beings, pity is silent.

Undoubtedly there are individuals for whom, however, in spite of or even by reason of their lively compassion, all that is connected with death and suffering has a mysterious attraction; who, with inward opposition, and yet following a dark impulse, occupy themselves with such things, or at least with pictures and notices of such things. Still, this is not sadism, so long as no sexual element enters into consciousness; and yet it is possible that, in unconscious life, slender threads connect such manifestations with the hidden depths of sadism.

[i] sadism in woman.

That sadism – a perversion often seen in men – is less frequent in women, may be easily explained. In the first place, sadism, in which the need for subjugation of the opposite sex forms a constituent element, thus represents, in accordance with its nature, a pathological intensification of the masculine sexual character; in the second place, the obstacles that oppose the expression of this monstrous impulse are, of course, much greater for woman than for man. Yet sadism occurs in women, and it can only be explained by the primary constituent element – the general hyperexcitation of the motor sphere. Only two cases have thus far been scientifically studied.

Case 48.

A married man presented himself with numerous scars from cuts on his arms. He explained their origin as follows: When he wished to approach his wife, who was young and somewhat "nervous," he first had to make a cut on his arm. She would then suck the wound and during the act become violently excited sexually.

This case recalls the widespread legend of the vampire, the origin of which may perhaps be attributed to such sadistic facts.[31]

In the second case of feminine sadism, for which I am indebted to Dr. Moll of Berlin, there is anesthesia in the normal activities of sexual life, as so frequently happens, accompanying the perverse impulse; there are also traces of masochism (see below).

Case 49.

Mrs. H., aged twenty-six, came from a family in which nervous or mental diseases were said to have not been observed; the patient herself, however, presented signs of hysteria and neurasthenia. Although married eight years and the mother of a child, Mrs. H. had never desired coitus. Very strictly educated as a young girl, until her marriage she remained almost innocent of any knowledge of sexual matters. She had menstruated regularly since her fifteenth year. Essential abnormality of the genitals was not apparent. To the patient coitus was not only not a pleasure, but was even an unpleasant act, and repugnance toward the act had constantly increased. The patient could not understand how anyone could call such an act the greatest delight of love, which to her was something far more sublime and unconnected with sensual impulse. At the same time it should be mentioned that the patient really loved her husband. In kissing him, too, she experienced a decided pleasure, which she could not exactly describe. But she could not conceive how the genitals could have anything to do with love. In other respects Mrs. H. was a decidedly intelligent woman of feminine character.

If she kissed her husband, she felt intense pleasure in biting him. It was extremely pleasurable to her to bite her husband so hard that he bled. She was happy if, instead of coitus, she was bitten by her husband and was allowed to bite him. She was sorry, however, if the biting was too painful for him (Dr. Moll).[32]

In history there are examples of famous women who, to some extent, had sadistic instincts. These "messalinas" are particularly characterized by their thirst for power, lust, and cruelty. Among them are Valeria Messalina herself, and Catherine de Médicis, the instigator of the Massacre of St. Bartholomew, whose greatest pleasure was to have the ladies of her court whipped before her eyes, etc.[33] (compare above).

[2] masochism.[34]
the association of passively endured cruelty and violence with lust.

MASOCHISM IS the opposite of sadism. While the latter is the desire to cause pain and use force, the former is the wish to suffer pain and be subjected to force.

By masochism I mean a peculiar perversion of the psychic sex life where the affected individual, in sexual feeling and thought, is controlled by the idea of being completely and unconditionally subject to the will of a person of the opposite sex; of being treated by this person as by a master, humiliated and abused. This idea is colored by lustful feeling; the masochist lives in fantasies, where he creates situations of this kind and often attempts to realize them. With this perversion his sexual instinct is often made more or less insensible to the normal charms of the opposite sex; incapable of a normal sex life, he is psychically impotent. This psychic impotence does not in any way depend upon a dread of the opposite sex, but rather upon the fact that the perverse instinct finds an adequate satisfaction by way of a deviation from the normal – in woman, to be sure, but not in coitus.

Cases also occur, however, where with the perverse impulse there is still some sensibility to normal stimuli, and intercourse under normal conditions takes place. In other cases the impotence is not purely psychic, but physical, i.e., spinal; for this perversion, like almost all other perversions of the sexual instinct, is developed only on the basis of a psychopathic and, for the most part, hereditarily tainted individuality; and, as a rule, such individuals are given to excesses, particularly masturbation, to which the difficulty of attaining what their fantasy creates drives them again and again.

I feel justified in calling this sexual anomaly "masochism," because the author Sacher-Masoch frequently made this perversion, up to his time quite unknown to the scientific world as such, the substratum of his writings. I thereby followed the scientific formation of the term "Daltonism," from Dalton, the discoverer of color blindness.

During recent years facts have been advanced proving that not only was Sacher-Masoch the poet of masochism, but also that he himself was afflicted with this anomaly.[35] Although these proofs were communicated to me without restriction, I refrain from giving them to the public. I refute the accusation that I have coupled the name of a revered author with a perversion of the sexual instinct, which has been made against me by some admirers of the author and by some critics of my book. As a man Sacher-Masoch cannot lose anything in the estimation of his cultured fellow beings simply because he was afflicted with an anomaly of his sexual feelings. As an author he suffered severe injury as far as the influence and intrinsic merit of his work is concerned, because when he eliminated his perversion from his literary efforts he was a gifted writer, and as such would have achieved real greatness had he been driven by normal sexual feelings. In this respect he is a remarkable example of the powerful influence exercised by the sex life – whether in the good or evil sense – over the formation and direction of man's mind.

The number of valid cases of masochism observed thus far is very large. Whether masochism occurs associated with normal sexual instincts or exclusively controls the individual; whether or not, and to what extent, the masochist strives to realize his peculiar fantasies; and whether or not masochism results in diminished virility will depend upon [1] the degree of intensity of the perversion in the single case, [2] the strength of opposing ethical and aesthetic motives, and [3] the relative power of the physical and mental organization of the affected individual. From the psychopathic point of view, the essential and common element in all these cases is *the fact that the sexual instinct is directed to ideas of subjugation and abuse by the opposite sex.*

Whatever has been said with reference to sadism about the impulsive character (indistinctness of motive) of the resulting acts and about the original (congenital) nature of the perversion, is also true for masochism.

In masochism there is a gradation of the acts from the most repulsive and monstrous to the silliest, regulated by the degree of intensity of the perverse instinct and the power of the remnants of moral and aesthetic countermotives. The extreme consequences of masochism, however, are checked by the instinct of self-preservation, and therefore murder and serious injury, which may be committed in sadistic excitement, have here no known passive equivalent. But the perverse desires of masochistic individuals may, in imagination, attain these extreme consequences (see below, case 50).

Moreover, the acts to which masochists refer are in some cases performed in connection with coitus, i.e., as preparatory measures; in others, as substitutes for coitus when coitus is impossible. This, too, depends exclusively upon the condition of sexual power, which has usually been diminished, physically and mentally, by the activity of the sexual ideas in the perverse direction, and not upon the nature of the act itself.

[a] the desire for abuse and humiliation as a means of sexual satisfaction.

Case 50.

Mr. Z., aged twenty-nine, technologist, came for consultation because of fear of tabes. Father nervous, died tabetic. Father's sister insane. Several relatives very nervous and peculiar. On closer examination the patient was found to have sexual, spinal and cerebral asthenia. He presented no symptoms of tabes dorsalis. Questions concerning abuse of the sexual organs brought out a confession of masturbation practiced since youth. In the course of the examination the following interesting psychosexual anomalies were discovered: At the age of five, sex life began with the impulse to whip himself, as well as the desire to see others whipped. In this he never thought of individuals as being of one sex or the other. For lack of something better, he practiced flagellation on himself, and, in time, this induced ejaculation. Long before this he had begun to satisfy himself with masturbation, and always during the act reveled in imaginary scenes of whipping. He twice visited brothels to have himself flogged by prostitutes. For this purpose he chose the prettiest girl he could find; he was disappointed, however, and did not even have an erection, to say nothing of ejaculation. He recognized that the flagellation was subsidiary, and that the idea of subjugation to the woman's will was the important thing. He realized this the second time. When he had the "thought of subjugation," he was perfectly successful. In time, by straining his imagination with masochistic ideas, he performed coitus without flagellation; finding little satisfaction in it, however, he performed sexual intercourse in a masochistic way. He found pleasure in masochistic scenes, in the sense of his original desire for flagellation, only when he was flagellated on his behind, or, at least, only when he called up such a situation in his imagination. At times of great excitability, it was even sufficient if he told stories of such scenes to a pretty girl. He would thus have an orgasm, and usually ejaculation.

A very effectual fetishistic idea was, toward the beginning, associated with this. He noticed that he was attracted and satisfied only by women wearing high heels and short jackets ("Hungarian fashion"). He did not know how he arrived at this fetishistic idea. Boys' legs with high heels also pleased him, but this charm was purely aesthetic, without any sensual coloring; he said he had never noticed anything homosexual in himself. The patient attributed his fetishism to his partiality for calves (legs). He was charmed by ladies' calves only when elegant shoes were on their feet. Nude legs – feminine nudity in general – did not affect him sexually. A subordinate fetishistic idea for the patient was the human ear. It was a lustful pleasure for him to caress the handsome ears of people. Although with men this pleasure was slight, with women it gave him great enjoyment.

He also had a weakness for cats. He thought them simply beautiful, and their movements were very attractive to him. The sight of a cat could raise him from the deepest depression. Cats seemed to him sacred; he saw something divine in them! He did not know the reason for this idiosyncrasy.

Of late he also frequently had sadistic ideas about punishing boys. In these imaginary flagellations both men and women played a part, but particularly women, at which time his enjoyment was much more intense.

The patient found that, in addition to what he recognized and felt as masochism, there was something else which he preferred to designate "pageism."

While his masochistic fantasies and acts were entirely of a coarse, sensual nature, his "pageism" consisted of the idea of being a page to a beautiful girl. His conception was perfectly chaste, but piquant; his relation to her that of a slave, but absolutely pure – a mere platonic submission. This reveling in the idea of serving as a page to such a "beautiful creature" was colored by a pleasurable feeling, but this was in no way sexual. In it, he experienced an exquisite feeling of moral satisfaction, in contrast with sensually colored masochism, and therefore he could regard it as something of a different nature.

At first sight there was nothing remarkable in the patient's appearance; his pelvis, however, was abnormally broad, and his ilia was flat; the pelvis, as a whole, was tilted and decidedly feminine. Eyes, neuropathic. He also mentioned that he often had itching and lustful irritation at the anus, and that there ("erogenous" area) he could satisfy himself with his finger.

The patient was troubled about his future. Help would be possible for him if he could only excite in himself an interest in women, but his will and imagination were too weak for that.

What the patient designated as "pageism" does not differ in any way from masochism, as may be seen [1] when it is compared with the following cases of symbolic masochism and others; [2] upon the consideration that in this perversion coitus is avoided as an inadequate act, and [3] from the fact that in such cases there is often a fantastic exaltation of the perverse ideal:

Case 51.

Ideal masochism. Mr. X., technologist, twenty-six years old. Mother of nervous disposition; suffered from neuralgia. In the father's family a case of spinal disease and one of psychosis. A brother suffered from nervousness. Mr. X. had only slight infantile affections; he learned easily at school, and developed normally. He was of manly appearance, but rather weakly and under medium size. The descent of the right testicle was imperfect, but could be noticed in the inguinal canal. Penis normally formed, but rather small.

At the age of five he felt sexual excitement while swinging on the crossbar with legs crossed and stretched out at full length. He repeated the exercise several times, but forgot about the sensation until he grew older. He then tried, without success, to induce this pleasurable feeling by repeating the exercise.

At the age of seven he took part in a big fight that occurred among the pupils of his school, after which the victors rode on the backs of the vanquished. This impressed X. considerably.

He thought the position of the prostrate boys was a pleasant one, and wanted to put himself in their place, imagining how, by repeated efforts, he could move the boy on his back near his face so that he might inhale the odor of his genitals. These thoughts, coupled with pleasurable feelings, afterward often recurred, although they never occasioned real sensations of lust; in fact, he considered these thoughts sinful and bad, and sought to fight them. He claimed to have had no knowledge at that time of sexual matters. It is remarkable that up to his twentieth year the patient was periodically troubled with bed-wetting.

Up to the time of puberty this masochistic fantasy of lying under the thighs of others, boys as well as girls, recurred periodically. Initially the objects were chiefly girls, but only exclusively when puberty was completed. Little by little these situations gained a different meaning, for soon the culminating point was the consciousness of being absolutely subject to the will and whims of a fully developed girl, coupled with corresponding humiliating acts and attitudes.

For instance, X. said:

"I am lying on my back on the floor. The mistress stands over my head with one foot on my breast, or she holds my head between her feet so that her genitals are directly in line with my vision. Or she sits astraddle my chest or on my face, using my body as a table. If I do not obey her commands promptly, she locks me up in a dark bathroom and leaves the house to find pleasure elsewhere. She introduces me to her friends as her slave and turns me over to them as a loan.

"She makes me perform the lowest menial work, wait upon her when she arises, in the bath **and when she urinates.** At times she uses my face for the latter purpose and makes me drink the voidance."

X. claimed that he never put these ideas into practical effect for fear of not realizing the anticipated pleasure.

One time he sneaked into the room of a pretty housemaid **in order to drink the girl's urine,** but he was much too disgusted to carry it out.

He stated that he fought in vain against these masochistic impulses, considering them to be of a painful and disgusting nature. They were still prevalent. He particularly pointed out that the *humiliation* connected with these imaginary acts was the principal attraction, and that the pleasure derived from causing pain to others was never associated with them.

He preferred as his "mistress" a slender maiden who would be about twenty years of age, have a pretty face, and wear a short light dress.

Ordinary intercourse with young women, dancing, or mixed society, never impressed him.

With puberty these masochistic ideas were accompanied by pollutions at times, but there were only weak emotions of lust.

At one time the patient resorted to friction of the glans penis, but he could not induce erection, much less ejaculation, and instead of pleasure he produced disagreeable paralytic feelings. This saved him from masturbation. After the age of twenty, however, he often experienced lustful emotions, with ejaculation, when performing gymnastic exercises on the horizontal bar, or when climbing poles or ropes. He never had a desire for sexual intercourse with women or for inverted sexual actions. At the age of twenty-six a friend urged him to engage in coitus, but on the way to the house "anxiety, restlessness, and decided disgust" crept over him. He became so nervous, with trembling and profuse perspiration, that he could not command an erection. Repeated attempts proved to be complete failures, but he was able to control his mental and physical excitement a little better than the first time.

Sexual desire was never present. Masochistic fantasies gave no assistance, because his mental faculties at such times were "as if paralyzed," and he could not call up the intense imaginary representations that he found necessary for an erection. Thus he gave up all attempts at coitus, partly because sexual desire was absent, and partly on account of his utter lack of confidence in success. Now and then he satisfied his weak sexual desires with the aid of gymnastic exercises. Occasionally, however, spontaneous or superinduced masochistic fantasies (when awake) would cause erection, but never ejaculation. Pollutions occurred at periods of six weeks.

The patient was highly intellectual, of refined manners, and a little neurasthenic. He complained that when he was in society, the feeling that he was being observed obtruded itself constantly. This caused him worry and embarrassment, though he was fully aware that all this was nothing but his imagination. He loved solitude, because he feared that others might discover his sexual abnormality.

This impotence did not cause him pain, for he scarcely had any desire. Nevertheless he would consider the cure of his sex life a great boon, because so much depended on it in social life, and he would be more self-possessed and manlier when among others.

His present existence he considered a misery, and his life a burden.

Case 52.

X., man of letters, aged twenty-eight, tainted. Sexually hyperesthetic from childhood. At the age of six he had dreams of being whipped on the buttocks by a woman. Upon awakening, intense lustful excitement; thus he came to practice masturbation. When eight years old, he once asked the cook to whip him. From his tenth year, neurasthenia. Until his twenty-fifth year he had dreams of flagellation or similar fantasies when awake, and indulged in masturbation. Three years ago he had an impulse to have himself whipped by a prostitute. The patient was disappointed, for neither erection nor ejaculation occurred. At twenty-seven, another effort, with the thought of forcing erection and ejaculation. This was finally made possible by the following artifice: While coitus was attempted the prostitute had to tell him how she mercilessly flogged other impotent men, and threaten him with the same. In addition to this, it was necessary for him to fantasize that he was bound, entirely in the woman's power, helpless, and most painfully beaten by her. Occasionally, in order to become potent, it was necessary to have himself actually bound. Thus coitus was possible. Pollutions were accompanied by lustful feeling only when he (infrequently) dreamed that he was abused, or that he looked on while one prostitute whipped another. He never had real lustful pleasure in coitus. The only things in women that interested him were the hands. Powerful women with big fists were his preference. At the same time, his desire for flagellation was only ideal because, with his great cutaneous sensitivity, a few strokes at the most were sufficient. Blows from men were repugnant to him. He wished to marry. From the impossibility of asking a decent woman to perform flagellation, and the doubt about being potent without flagellation, sprang his embarrassment and desire to recover.

passive flagellation and masochism.

Case 53.

D., aged thirty-two, sculptor; hereditarily tainted, marks of degeneration, constitutionally neuropathic, neurasthenic, weakly in his earlier years. First emotions of sexuality at the age of seventeen; it developed slowly and exclusively in a heterosexual, but masochistic, direction. He craved for floggings at the hands of a pretty woman (but there was no hand fetishism). He preferred women of haughty and imperious appearance. He never sought to put his masochistic desires into real practice. He could not explain them.

On four occasions he tried coitus, but without success. He practiced masturbation, which caused severe neurasthenia accompanied by phobia, whereupon he sought medical advice.

In three of the foregoing cases, passive flagellation, for the most part, serves the masochist as an expression of the desired situation of subjugation to the woman. The same means is needed by a large number of masochists. Passive flagellation, however, is a process which, as is known, has a tendency to induce erection reflexively by irritating the nerves of the buttocks.[36] The effect of flagellation is used by weakened debauchees to help their diminished power; this perversity – not perversion – is very common. It is, therefore, necessary to ascertain where passive flagellation of masochists stands in relation to those dissipated individuals who are not psychically perverse, but physically weakened.

It is not difficult to show that masochism is something essentially different from flagellation, and more comprehensive. For the masochist, the principal thing is subjugation to the woman; the punishment is only the expression of this relation – the most intense effect of it he can bring upon himself. For him the act only has a symbolic value, and is a means to the end of mentally satisfying his peculiar desires. On the other hand, the individual who is weakened and not subject to masochism, and who has himself flagellated, desires only a mechanical irritation of his spinal center.

Whether a given case is simple (reflex) flagellation or masochism is made clear by the individual's statements, and often by the secondary circumstances. The determination depends upon the following facts:

In the *first* place, the impulse to passive flagellation exists in the masochist from birth. The desire is felt before there has been any experience of the reflex effect, often first in dreams, as, for example, in case 55 (see below). *Second,* with the masochist, as a rule, flagellation is only one of many and various punishments that come into his mind as fantasies and are often realized. In these other punishments, and in the frequent acts accompanying flagellations that express purely symbolic humiliations, there can, of course, be no thought of a reflex physical irritative effect. *Third,* it is significant that, in the masochist, when the desired flagellation is carried out, it need have no aphrodisiac effect at all. Very often, indeed, there is a more or less defined disappointment; in fact, disappointment is always the result if the masochist is not successful in his desire to create, by means of the prearranged program, the illusion of the desired situation (to be in the woman's power), so that the woman ordered to carry out the act seems to be nothing more than the executive agent of his own will. In reference to this important point, compare the three foregoing cases with case 58.

Between masochism and simple (reflex) flagellation, there is a relation somewhat analogous to that existing between inverted sexual instinct and acquired pederasty. It does not lessen the value of this opinion that, in the masochist, the flagellation may also have the known reflex effect; or that a whipping received in childhood may have aroused lust for the first time, and thus simultaneously excited the latent masochistically constituted sex life. In this event, the case must be characterized by the conditions mentioned above, under the headings of *"second"* and *"third,"* in order to be masochistic. If the details of the origin of the case are not known, other circumstances, such as those mentioned above under *"second,"* would make it clearly masochistic. This is illustrated in the following two cases:

Case 54.

A patient of Tarnowsky's had a person in his confidence rent a house during his attacks, and instruct its personnel (three prostitutes) as to what was to be done with him. Whenever he went there he was undressed, masturbated and flagellated as ordered. He pretended to offer resistance, and begged for mercy; then, as ordered, he was allowed to eat and sleep. In spite of his protests, however, he was kept there, and beaten if he did not submit. Thus the affair would go on for some days. When the attack was over he was dismissed, and he returned to his wife and children, who had no suspicion of his disease. The attacks occurred once or twice a year (Tarnowsky, op. cit.).

Case 55.

X., aged thirty-four, greatly predisposed, suffered from antipathic sexual instinct. For various reasons he had no opportunity to satisfy himself with men, in spite of great sexual desire. Occasionally he dreamed that a woman whipped him, and then he would have a pollution.

Because of this recurring dream, he came to have prostitutes beat him as a substitute for love with men. Occasionally he would obtain a prostitute, undress himself completely (while she was not to take off her chemise), and have her tread upon him, whip and beat him. **This act produced a powerful lust; only by licking the woman's foot could he further increase his sexual desire and attain ejaculation.** Then disgust at the morally debasing situation occurred, and he retired as quickly as possible.

Case 56.

A gentleman of high standing, aged twenty-eight years, would go to a house of prostitution once a month. He always announced his coming with a note reading thus: "Dear Peggy, I shall be with you tomorrow evening between eight and nine o'clock. Whip and knout! Kindest regards. . . ."

He always arrived at the appointed time carrying a whip, a knout and leather straps. After undressing, he had himself bound hand and foot, and then flogged by the girl on the soles of his feet, calves and buttocks until ejaculation ensued. Other desires or wishes he never expressed. The fact that he disdained coitus seems to point to the fact that he resorted to this method simply as a means to gratify his masochistic inclination and not as a ruse to restore potency.

Cases occur, however, in which passive flagellation alone constitutes the entire content of the masochistic fantasies, without other ideas of humiliation, etc., and without well-defined consciousness of the real nature of this expression of submission. Such cases are difficult to differentiate from those of simple reflex flagellation. A knowledge of the primary origin of the desire, before any experience of reflex stimuli (see above, under *"first"*), is the only thing that renders the differential diagnosis certain, if weighed with the circumstance that genuine masochists are perverse from early youth, and that the realization of their desires is scarcely ever accomplished or proves to be a disappointment (see above, under *"third"*); for the whole thing chiefly belongs to the realm of the imagination.

The following is a case of typical masochism in which the whole circle of ideas peculiar to this perversion appears completely developed. This case, in which there is a detailed personal description of the whole psychic state, is different from case 49 in the eleventh edition only in that here there is no thought of a realization of the perverse fantasies, and that, notwithstanding the perversion of the sex life, normal stimuli are so effectual that sexual intercourse is possible under normal conditions.

Case 57.

"I am thirty-five years old, mentally and physically normal. Among all my relatives, in the direct as well as in the lateral line, I know of no case of mental disorder. My father, who at my birth was thirty years old, as far as I know had a preference for voluptuous, large women.

"Even in my early childhood I loved to revel in ideas about the absolute mastery of one man over others. The thought of slavery had something exciting in it for me, whether from the standpoint of master or servant. That one man could possess, sell or whip another, caused me intense excitement; and in reading *Uncle Tom's Cabin* (which I read at around the beginning of puberty) I had erections. Particularly exciting for me was the thought of a man being hitched to a wagon in which another man sat with a whip, driving and whipping him. Until my twentieth year these ideas were purely objective and sexless – i.e., the one in my fantasy in subjugation was another (not myself), and the master was not necessarily a woman. These ideas were, therefore, without effect on my sexual desires – i.e., on the way in which they took practical shape. Although these ideas caused erections, I have as yet never masturbated in my life, and from my nineteenth year I had coitus without the help of these ideas and without any relation to them. I always had a great preference for elderly, voluptuous, large women, though I did not scorn younger ones.

"After my twenty-first year my ideas became objective, and it became an essential thing that the 'mistress' should be a woman over forty years old, tall and powerful. *From this time I was always in my fantasies the subject;* the 'mistress' was a rough woman, who made use of me in every way, also sexually; who harnessed me to a carriage and made me take her for a drive, whom I had to follow like a dog, at whose feet I had to lie naked and be punished – i.e., whipped – by her. This was the constant element in my ideas, around which all others were grouped. In these fantasies I always found endless pleasurable comfort that caused erection, but never ejaculation. As a result of the induced sexual excitement, I would immediately seek a woman, preferably one corresponding exteriorly with my ideal, and have coitus with her without any actual aid of my fantasies, and sometimes also without any thought of them during the act. I also had, however, an inclination toward women of a different kind, and had coitus with them without being impelled by my fancy.

"Notwithstanding all this, my life was not exceedingly abnormal sexually; yet these ideas were certain to occur periodically, and they have remained essentially unchanged. With growing sexual desire, the intervals constantly grew shorter. At the present time the attacks come every two or three weeks. If I previously were to have coitus, the occurrence of the fantasies would, perhaps, be postponed. I have never attempted to realize my very definite and characteristic ideas – i.e., to connect them with the world outside of me – but I have contented myself with reveling in the thoughts, because I was convinced that my ideal would not allow even an approach to realization. The thought of a comedy with paid prostitutes always seemed so silly and purposeless, for a person hired by me could never take the place of my imagined 'cruel mistress.' I doubt whether there are sadistically constituted women like Sacher-Masoch's heroines. But, if there were such women, and I had the fortune (!) to find one; still, in a world of reality, intercourse with her would always seem only a farce to me. Indeed, I can say that were I to become the slave of a nymphomaniac, I believe that due to the other necessary renunciations, my desired manner of life would soon pall on me, and in my lucid intervals I would make every effort to obtain my freedom at all costs.

"Yet I have found a way in which to induce, in a certain sense, a realization. After my sexual desire has been intensely excited by reveling in my fantasy, I go to a prostitute and there call up before my mind's eye, with great intensity, some scene of the kind mentioned, in which I play the principal role. After thinking of such a situation for about half an hour, with erection always the result, I perform coitus with increased lustful pleasure and strong ejaculation. After ejaculation, the vision fades away. Ashamed, I depart as quickly as possible, and try not to think of the affair. Then for about two weeks I have no more such ideas! Indeed, after a particularly satisfactory act of coitus, it may happen that until the next attack I have no sympathy whatsoever with masochistic ideas. But the next attack is sure to come sooner or later. I must, however, state that I also have coitus without being prepared by such ideas, especially, too, with women who are acquainted with me and my position, and in whose presence I abhor such fantasies. *With these women, however, I am not always potent, while, with masochistic ideas, my virility is perfect.* It does not seem superfluous to add that otherwise in my thought and feeling I am very aesthetic, and despise anything like maltreatment of a human being. Finally, I must also mention the fact that the form of address is of importance. In my fantasies it is essential that the 'mistress' address me in the second person (*Du*), while I must address her in the third (*Sie*). This circumstance of being thus familiarly addressed by a person so inclined, as the expression of absolute mastery, has given me lustful pleasure from my youth, and continues to do so today.

"I was fortunate in finding a wife who is, in every way, especially sexually, attractive to me; though, as I scarcely need say, she in no way resembles my masochistic ideals. She is gentle, but voluptuous, for without voluptuousness I cannot conceive of such a thing as sexual charm. The first few months of married life were normal sexually; the masochistic attacks did not occur, and I had almost lost all thought of masochism. Then came the first confinement and the necessary abstinence. Punctually, then, with the occurrence of sexual desire, the masochistic fantasies returned, which, in spite of my great love for my wife, necessitated coitus with another, accompanied by masochistic ideas. It is worth noting here that marital coitus, which was later resumed, did not prove sufficient to banish the masochistic ideas, as masochistic coitus always does. As for the essential element in masochism, I am of the opinion that the ideas – i.e., the mental element – are the end and aim.

"If the realization of the masochistic ideas (i.e., passive flagellation, etc.) is the desired end, then it is in opposition to the fact that the majority of masochists never attempt realization; or when this is attempted great disappointment occurs, or at any rate the desired satisfaction is not obtained.

"Finally, I should mention that, according to my experience, the number of masochists, especially in big cities, seems to be quite large. The only sources of such information are – since men do not reveal these things – statements by prostitutes, and, because they agree on the essential points, certain facts may be assumed as proved.

"Thus there is the fact that every experienced prostitute keeps some suitable instrument (usually a whip) for flagellation; but it must be remembered that there are men who have themselves whipped simply to increase their sexual pleasure. These men, in contrast with masochists, regard flagellation as a means to an end.

"On the other hand, almost all prostitutes agree that there are many men who like to play 'slave' – i.e., like to be so called, and have themselves scolded and trod upon and beaten. As has been said, the number of masochists is larger than has yet been dreamed.

"As you can imagine, your chapter on this subject has made a deep impression on me. I should like to have faith in a cure, in a logical cure, so to speak, in accordance with the motto: 'To understand all is to cure all.'

"Of course the word *cure* is to be taken with some limitation, and there must be a distinction made between general feelings and concrete ideas. These general feelings can never be removed; they come like a streak of lightning, are there, and one does not know when or how they will strike.

"But the practice of masochism in the imagination by means of concrete associated ideas can be avoided, or at least restricted.

"Now things have changed. I say to myself: What! You busy your mind with things that offend not only the aesthetic sense of others, but also your own aesthetic sense? You regard as beautiful and desirable that which, in your own judgment, is at once ugly, coarse, silly, and impossible? You long for a situation which in reality you can never obtain? This opposing idea has an immediate inhibitory and undeceiving effect, and breaks the point of the fantasy. In fact, since reading your book (early this year), I have actually not reveled in my fantasy, though the masochistic tendencies have recurred at regular intervals.

"I must also confess that, in spite of its marked pathological character, masochism is not only incapable of destroying my pleasure in life, but it does not in the least affect my outward life. When not in a masochistic state, as far as feeling and action are concerned, I am a perfectly normal man. During the activity of the masochistic tendencies there is, of course, a great revolution in my feeling, but my outward manner of life suffers no change: I have a calling that makes it necessary for me to move much in public, and I pursue it in a masochistic condition as well as ever."

The author of the foregoing lines also sent me the following notes:

[1] "Masochism, according to my experience, is congenital under all circumstances, and never acquired by the individual. *I know positively that I was never spanked;* that my masochistic ideas were manifested from my earliest youth, and that, as long as I have been capable of thinking, I have had such thoughts. If the origin of them had been the result of a particular event, especially of a beating, I should certainly not have forgotten it. It is characteristic that *the ideas were present before there was any sexual desire.* At that time the ideas were absolutely sexless. I remember that when I was a boy it affected (not to say excited) me intensely when an older boy addressed me in the second person while I spoke to him in the third. I would keep up a conversation with him and have this exchange of address take place as often as possible. Later, when I had become more mature sexually, such things affected me only when they occurred with a woman, and one relatively older than myself."

[2] "Physically and mentally I am in all respects masculine. I have a superabundant growth of beard, and my whole body is very hairy. In my relations to the female sex that are not masochistic, the dominating position of the man is an indispensable condition, and any attempt to change it would meet with my energetic opposition. I am energetic, if not over-courageous; but lack of courage is not manifest when my pride is injured. I am not sensitive to events in nature (thunderstorms, storms at sea, etc.).[37]

"Again, my masochistic tendencies have nothing feminine or effeminate about them (?). Certainly, in these, the inclination to be sought and desired by the woman is dominant; but the general relation desired with her is not that in which a woman stands to a man; instead, it is that of the slave to the master, the domestic animal to its owner. If one regards the ultimate aim of masochism without prejudice, it must be acknowledged that its ideal is the position of a dog or horse. Both are owned by masters and punished by them, and the masters are responsible to no one. It is precisely this unlimited power of life and death, as exercised over slaves and domestic animals, that is the aim and end of all masochistic ideas."

[3] "The foundation of all masochistic ideas is sexual desire, and as this ebbs and flows, so do the masochistic fantasies. On the other hand, as soon as the ideas are present, they greatly intensify sexual desire. I am not by nature excessively sensual. However, when the masochistic ideas occur, I am impelled to engage in coitus at any cost (usually

I am driven to the lowest woman); and if these impulses are not promptly obeyed, sexual desire soon almost becomes satyriasis. One is almost justified in looking upon this as a depraved circle.

"Sexual desire occurs either in the course of time or as the result of special excitement (also of a kind that is not masochistic – e.g., kissing). In spite of its manner of origin, this sexual desire, by virtue of the masochistic ideas it engenders, is soon transformed into a masochistic and impure sexual desire.

"Moreover, there is no doubt that external accidental impressions, particularly those that loiter in the streets of a large city, greatly intensify the desire. The sight of beautiful and imposing female forms, *in nature* as well as in art, is exciting. For those subject to masochism – at least during the attacks – the whole external world becomes masochistic. The box on the ear administered by the teacher to the pupil and the crack of the driver's whip make deep impressions on the masochist, while they leave him indifferent or annoy him when he is not in the masochistic state."

[4] "In reading Sacher-Masoch, it struck me that in masochists there was also an occasional undercurrent of sadistic feeling. I have occasionally discovered in myself sporadic feelings of sadism. I must say, however, that the sadistic feelings are not so marked as the masochistic. Apart from the fact that they rarely appear, and then only as accessories, these sadistic fantasies never leave the sphere of abstract feeling, and, above all, never take the form of concrete, connected ideas. The effect of sexual desire, however, is the same for both."

If this case is remarkable because of the complete development of the psychic state that constitutes masochism, the following is noteworthy because of the great extravagance of the acts resulting from perversion. The case is also particularly suited to making clear the reason for the subjugation and humiliation at the hands of the woman, and the peculiar sexual coloring of the resulting situations:

Case 58.

Mr. Z., official, aged fifty; tall, muscular, healthy. Said to come from healthy parentage, but his father was thirty years older than his mother. A sister, two years older than Z., suffered from delusions of persecution. There was nothing remarkable in Z.'s external appearance. Skeleton entirely masculine; abundant beard, but no hair on his trunk. He characterized himself as a man of sanguine temperament, who could not refuse others anything; though irascible and hotheaded, he was quick to regret his outbursts.

Z. claimed that he had never masturbated. From his youth there had been nightly pollutions in which girls played a part, but were never included in the sexual act. For example, he dreamed that a pleasing woman lay heavily on him, or that as he lay sleeping on the grass she playfully walked up his back. Z. had always been averse to having coitus with women. This act seemed bestial to him. Nevertheless, he was drawn to women. It was only in the society of beautiful women and girls that he felt well and in his place. He was very gallant, without being forward.

When seated, a voluptuous woman with a beautiful figure, and particularly with a pretty foot, had the power to throw him into intense excitement. He was impelled to offer himself as a chair, in order "to support such grand beauty." A kick or a box on the ear from her would be heaven to him. He was horrified by the thought of having coitus with her. He felt the need to serve woman. He thought about how much ladies like to ride. He reveled in the thought of how fine it would be to be wearied by the burden of a beautiful woman in order to give her pleasure. He painted the situation in all colors; thought of the beautiful foot armed with spurs, the beautiful calves, the soft, full thighs. Every beautiful mature woman, every pretty female foot, always excited his imagination; but he never obeyed the peculiar feelings that seemed to him abnormal, and was able to control himself. He felt no need, however, to fight against them; on the contrary, it would have grieved him to be compelled to give up the feelings that had become so dear to him.

At the age of thirty-two, Z. happened to make the acquaintance of an attractive woman, aged twenty-seven, who had separated from her husband, and whom he found in need. He worked for her for months without any selfish motive. One evening she impatiently demanded sexual satisfaction from him, and almost used violence. Coitus was successful. Z. took the woman in, lived with her, and indulged in coitus moderately, but coitus was more of a burden than a pleasure: erections became weak, and he could no longer satisfy the woman. She finally declared that she would not have intercourse with him, because he was only excited without satisfying her. Though he loved the woman very much, he could not disclose his peculiar fantasies. After this he lived with her only in friendly relations, and deeply regretted that he could not serve her in the way she desired.

Fear of how she would receive his propositions and a feeling of shame kept him from confessing. He found a substitute in his dreams. Thus, for example, he dreamed that he was a proud, fiery steed, ridden by a beautiful lady. He felt her weight, the bit he had to obey, the pressure of the thighs on his flanks; he heard her beautiful, joyous voice. The exertion threw him into a sweat, the touch of the spurs did the rest, and always induced pollution with great lustful pleasure. Seven years ago, under the influence of such dreams, Z. overcame his reluctance in order to experience such things in reality. He was successful in creating a suitable opportunity. He speaks of it as follows: "I knew how to arrange it so that she would, on her own, seat herself on my back. Then I endeavored to make this situation as pleasant as possible, and easily arranged it so that on the next occasion she said spontaneously, 'Come, give me a little ride!' Being of tall stature, both hands braced on a chair, I made my back horizontal, and she mounted astride, in the manner of a man. I then did the best I could to imitate the movements of a horse, and loved to have her treat me like a horse, without consideration. She could beat, prick, scold, or caress me, just as she felt inclined. I could carry on my back persons weighing from sixty to eighty kilos for half or three-quarters of an hour, without interruption. At the end of this time I usually asked for a rest. During this, the conversation between my mistress and I was perfectly harmless, and without any relation to what had preceded. After about a quarter of an hour I was rested and placed myself again at the disposal of my mistress. When time and circumstances allowed it, I did this three or four times in succession. It sometimes happened that I practiced it both in the morning and in the afternoon. Afterward, I never felt weary or had uncomfortable feelings, but on such days I had very little appetite. I liked best to bare my trunk, when possible, so I could feel the riding whip more sharply. My mistress had to be decent. I liked her best in pretty shoes and stockings, with short closed drawers reaching to the knee; with the upper portion of her person completely dressed, and with hat and gloves."

Mr. Z. further said he had not performed coitus in seven years, but thought he was potent. The riding was a perfect substitute for that "bestial act," even when ejaculation was not induced.

For eight months Z. was determined to give up his masochistic play, and had persevered. He thought, however, that if a woman only moderately pretty were to address him directly and say, "Come, I want to ride you," he would not be strong enough to withstand the temptation. Z. wished to know if his abnormality was curable, if he was unworthy as a vicious man, or if he was an invalid deserving pity.

Even in the foregoing series of cases, the act of being walked upon has played a role, with other things, in expressing the masochistic situations of humiliation and pain. The exclusive and most extensive use of this means for perverse excitation and satisfaction, which has caused me to arrange a special group because it forms the transition to another kind of perversion (see below, [b]), is shown in the following classical case of masochism, reported by Hammond (op. cit., p. 28), from an observation by Dr. Cox[38] of Colorado:

Case 59.

X., a model husband, very moral, the father of several children, had times – i.e., attacks – in which he visited brothels, chose two or three of the largest girls, and shut himself up with them. He bared the upper portion of his body, lay down on the floor, crossed his hands on his abdomen, closed his eyes, and then had the girls walk all over his naked chest, neck and face, urging them at every step to press hard on his flesh with the heels of their shoes. Sometimes he wanted a heavier girl, or some other act even more cruel than this procedure. After two or three hours he had had enough. He paid the girls with wine and money, rubbed his blue bruises, dressed himself, paid his bill, and went back to his business, only to give himself the same strange pleasure again after a few weeks.

Occasionally it happened that he had one of the girls stand on his chest, then had the others turn her around until his skin was torn and bleeding from the turning of the heels of her shoes. Frequently one of the girls had to stand on him in such a way that one shoe was over his eyes, with its heel pressing on one eye, while the other shoe rested across his neck. In this position he endured the pressure of a person weighing about one hundred and fifty pounds for four or five minutes. The author speaks of dozens of similar cases that are known to him. Hammond presumes, with reason, that this man had become impotent with women; that in this strange procedure he found a substitute for coitus; and that, when the heels drew blood, he had pleasant sexual feelings, accompanied by ejaculations.

Case 60.

X., gentleman of the upper class of society; aged sixty-six; father hypersexual; two brothers said to be masochists. X. claimed that his masochism dated back to early childhood. At the age of five he asked little girls to undress him and spank his naked bottom. Later, he arranged with other boys or girls, when playing teacher, to flog him. At the age of fifteen he began to imagine that girls ambushed and then beat him. At that time he still had no idea about the sexual meaning of such proceedings; in fact, he was still unaware of sex. His craving for being beaten by women steadily increased. At the age of eighteen he learned how to satisfy his craving and had his first pollution during the act. When nineteen, first act of coitus with complete satisfaction and potency, and without masochistic representations. Normal sexual intercourse until he was twenty-one, when a girl suggested a masochistic scene. He accepted, and from that time never had coitus without a masochistic adventure preceding it. He soon recognized the fact that the stimulus proceeded from the idea of being in the power of a woman rather than from the act of violence itself. He succeeded in making a happy marriage, free of masochistic ideas, but admitted that from time to time he had to seek relief in some masochistic act with a girl, even though he then had grandchildren. The masochistic scene was always the prelude to coitus. He showed no psychopathic symptoms and was free from other perversions. He pointed out the frequency of masochism and the clever methods often applied by so-called masseuses. According to his experience, masochism was common in England, and English women were easily persuaded to practice it.

Case 61.

L., artist, aged twenty-nine; nervous disease and tuberculosis frequently occurred in his family. His sex life was suddenly aroused at the age of seven while being caned on his behind; at ten, masturbation. During the act he always thought of someone flagellating him. In later years, nocturnal pollutions were always accompanied by dreams of flagellation. The wish to be flogged was continually in his mind from the age of ten. From eleven to eighteen he had inclinations toward persons of his own sex, though they never overstepped the bounds of boyish friendship. During this homosexual period he was forever agitated by the desire to be beaten by his companions.

Coitus at nineteen, but without sufficient erection or gratifying pleasure. His heterosexual inclinations were always toward women older than himself. He was indifferent toward young girls. His craving for flagellation increased with the years.

At twenty-five he fell violently in love with a woman much older than himself, but refused marriage. The woman made every effort in her power to win him over to natural sexual intercourse. Although he detested this state of affairs and professed undying love for the woman, he insisted that his sexual feelings for her were only of a masochistic character. Now and then he succeeded in persuading her to flagellate him.

Because his sexual needs were strong, he had women flagellate him. He claimed that flagellation was the only adequate sexual act during which he could experience really pleasurable ejaculation. Coitus was of minor importance, and only on rare occasions did he couple it with the act of flagellation, probably because of psychic impotence.

Nevertheless, the two acts affected him in different ways. Coitus seemed to improve him both mentally and physically, while flagellation left bodily exhaustion and moral depression in its wake. He was persuaded that his masochism was a pathological condition; on those grounds he came for advice.

His appearance was undeniably masculine, his conduct decent and beyond criticism. He complained of cerebral neurasthenia (weakness of mind and willpower, absent-mindedness, irritability, shyness, anxiety of mind, pressure in the head, etc.). Genitals normal. Erections only in the morning.

He leaned toward the belief that if he could find a woman whom he could love, he might strip off his masochistic inclination in wedlock.

Therapeutic advice: auto-combating of masochistic thoughts, impulses and acts, with the aid of hypnotic suggestion, if necessary; strengthening of the nervous system, and removal of manifestations of irritating weakness by antineurasthenic treatment.

The cases of masochism thus far described, and the numerous analogous cases mentioned by those who report them, form a counterpart to the previously described group [c] of sadism. Just as in sadism men excite and satisfy themselves by maltreating women, so in masochism the same effect is sought in the passive reception of similar abuse.[39] Group [a] of the sadists, however – those who commit lust murder – is not, as strange as it may seem, without its counterpart in masochism. Taken to its extreme, masochism must lead to the desire to be killed by a person of the opposite sex, in the same way that sadism has its acme in active lust murder. But the instinct of self-preservation opposes such a result, so that the extreme is not actually carried out. When the whole structure of masochistic ideas is purely psychic, however, even the extreme may be reached in the imaginations of such individuals, as the following case shows:

Case 62.

A middle-aged man, married, a father, who came from a very nervous family but had always led a normal sex life, made the following communication: In his early youth he was powerfully excited sexually at the sight of a woman slaughtering an animal with a knife. From that time, for many years, he had reveled in the lustfully colored idea of being stabbed and cut, and even killed, by women with knives. Later on, after the beginning of normal sexual intercourse, these ideas completely lost their perverse stimulus for him.

This case should be compared with statements made by men who find sexual pleasure in being lightly pricked with knives by women who also threaten them with death.

Such fantasies, perhaps, provide the key to an understanding of the following strange case, for which I am indebted to Dr. Körber of Rankau, Silesia, whose letter is excerpted below:

Case 63.

"A lady sent me the following communication: While still a young and innocent girl, she was married to a man about thirty years old. On their wedding night he forced a bowl containing soap into her hands, and without any expression of endearment asked her to lather his chin and neck (as if for shaving). The inexperienced young wife did it, and was not a little astonished, during the first weeks of married life, to learn the secrets of marriage in absolutely no other form. Her husband always told her that it gave him the greatest delight to have his face lathered by her. Later, after she had sought the advice of friends, she induced her husband to perform coitus, and had three children in the course of time (by him, she stated with every assurance). The husband was industrious and reliable, but a moody man with a short temper; by occupation a merchant."

It may be inferred that this man conceived the act of being shaved (i.e., the lathering as a preparatory measure) as a rudimentary, symbolic realization of ideas of injury or death, and by means of this symbolism he had been sexually excited and satisfied. The perfect sadistic counterpart to this case is offered by case 37, which is a case of symbolic sadism.

symbolic masochism.

At any rate, there is a whole group of masochists who satisfy themselves with the symbolic representations of situations corresponding with their perversion; a group that corresponds with group [a] and [e] of sadism. Thus, just as the perverse longings of the masochist may, on the one hand, advance to "passive lust murder" (to be sure, only in the imagination), so, on the other hand, they may be satisfied with simple symbolic representations of the desired situations, which are otherwise expressed in acts of cruelty. This, of course, taken objectively, goes much farther than the idea of being murdered, but in fact not so far, due to the determining subjective conditions. Cases similar to 63 may be included here, in which the acts desired and planned by the masochists have a *purely symbolic* character, and to a certain extent serve to define the desired situation.

Case 64.

(Pascal, *Igiene dell' amore.*) Every three months a man of about forty-five years visited a certain prostitute and paid her ten francs for the following act. The prostitute had to undress him, tie his hands and feet, bandage his eyes, and draw the curtains of the windows. She then made her guest sit down on a sofa, and left him there alone in a helpless position. After half an hour she had to come back and unbind him. The man then paid her and left perfectly satisfied, to repeat his visit in about three months.

In the dark, with the aid of his imagination, this man seems to have extended the situation of being helpless at the hands of a woman. The following case, in which a complicated comedy, in the sense of masochistic desires, is again played, is even more peculiar:

Case 65.

(Pascal, op. cit.) A gentleman in Paris was accustomed to visit on certain evenings a house where a woman, the owner, acceded to his peculiar desire. He entered the salon in full dress, and she, likewise in evening dress, had to receive him with a very haughty manner. He addressed her as "Marquise," and she had to call him "dear Count." Then he spoke of his good fortune in finding her alone and his love for her, and would then attempt a bit of "hanky-panky." At this the lady had to feel insulted. The pseudo-count grew bolder and bolder, and asked the pseudo-marquise for a kiss on her shoulder. "There is an angry scene; the bell is rung; a servant, prepared for the occasion, appears and throws the count out of the house. He departs well-satisfied, and pays the actors in the farce handsomely."

Case 66.

X., aged thirty-eight, engineer; married, father of three children; married life unmarred. Periodically visited a prostitute who had to enact, previous to coitus, the following comedy. As soon as he entered her compartment, she took him by the ears and pulled him all over the room, shouting: "What do you want here? Do you know that you ought to be at school? Why don't you go to school?" She would then slap his face and flog him soundly, until he knelt before her begging forgiveness. She then handed him a little basket containing bread and fruit, such as children carry with them to school. He remained resistant until the girl's harshness gave him an orgasm; then he would call out: "I am going! I am going!," and then he would perform coitus.

It is probable that this masochistic comedy may have arisen from some scenes enacted during his school days and that in this way sexual desire became associated with them. Further details of X.'s sex life were not known (Carrara, *Archivio di Psichiatria,* vol. 19, no. 4).

ideal masochism.

A distinction must be made between "symbolic" and "ideal" masochism. In the latter, the psychic perversion remains entirely within the spheres of imagination and fantasy, and no attempt at realization is made. (Cf. cases 57 and 62.) Two other cases of ideal masochism are quoted here. The first is that of an individual mentally and physically tainted, bearing degenerative signs, in whom mental and physical impotence occurred early:

Case 67.

Mr. Z., aged twenty-two, single, was brought to me by his father for medical advice, because he was very nervous and plainly sexually abnormal. Mother and maternal grandmother were insane. His father begot him at a time when he was suffering severely from nervousness.

Patient was said to have been a very lively and talented child. At the age of seven he was noticed practicing masturbation. After his ninth year he became inattentive, forgetful, did not progress in his studies, and constantly required help and protection. With difficulty he got through the *Gymnasium,* and during his time of freedom had attracted attention because of his indolence, absent-mindedness, and various foolish acts.

Consultation was occasioned due to an occurrence on the street, in which Z. had forced himself on a young girl in an extremely impetuous manner and, in great excitement, had tried to have a conversation with her.

The patient said his reason was that, by conversing with a respectable girl, he wished to excite himself so that he could be potent in coitus with a prostitute!

His father characterized him as a man of perfectly good disposition, moral but lazy, dissatisfied with himself, often in despair about his lack of success in life, indolent, and interested in nothing but music, for which he possessed great talent.

The patient's exterior – his plagiocephalic head, his large, prominent ears, the deficient innervation of the right facialis around his mouth, the neuropathic expression of his eyes – indicated a degenerate, neuropathic individual.

Z. was tall, of powerful frame, and in all respects of masculine appearance. Pelvis masculine, testicles well-developed, penis remarkably large, mons pubis with abundant hair. The right testicle much lower than the left, the cremasteric reflex weak on both sides. The patient was intellectually below average. He was aware of his deficiency, complained of his indolence, and asked to have his will strengthened. His awkward, embarrassed manner, timid glances, and relaxed attitude pointed to masturbation. The patient confessed that from his seventh year until a year and a half ago he practiced it, years at a time, from eight to ten times a day. Until a few years ago, when he became neurasthenic (cephalic pressure, loss of mental power, spinal irritation, etc.), he said he always found great sensuous pleasure in it. Since then this had been lost, and the desire to masturbate had disappeared. He had grown increasingly more bashful and indolent, less energetic, and more cowardly and apprehensive. He had lost interest in everything, and attended to his business only from a sense of duty, feeling very low-spirited. He had never thought of coitus, and, from his standpoint as a masturbator, he could not understand how others could find pleasure in it.

Investigation in the direction of inverted sexual instinct yielded a negative result. He said he was never drawn toward persons of his own sex; instead, he occasionally thought that he had a weak inclination for females. He asserted that he came to masturbate independently. In this thirteenth year he first noticed ejaculations as a result of masturbatory manipulations.

It was only after long persuasion that Z. consented to entirely unveil his sex life. As his following statements show, he may be classified as a case of ideal masochism, with rudimentary sadism. The patient distinctly remembered that at the age of six, without any cause, he had "ideas of violence." He was compelled to imagine that a servant girl spread his legs apart and showed his genitals to another; that she tried to throw him into cold or hot water in order to cause him pain. These "ideas of violence" were attended by lustful feelings, and became the cause of masturbatory manipulations. Later the patient called them up voluntarily, in order to rouse himself to masturbation. They also played a part in his dreams; they never induced pollutions, however, apparently because the patient masturbated excessively during the day.

In time, other ideas of a sadistic nature were added to these masochistic "ideas of violence." At first they were scenes in which boys forcibly practiced masturbation on one another, or cut off the genitals. He often imagined himself as such a boy, first in an active, then in a passive role. Later he busied himself with mental pictures of girls and women exhibiting themselves to one another. He reveled in the thought, for example, of a servant girl spreading another girl's legs apart and pulling the genital hair; or in the thought of boys treating girls cruelly, and pricking and pinching their genitals.

Although such ideas always induced sexual excitement, he never experienced any impulse to carry them out actively, or to have them performed on himself passively. It satisfied him to use them for masturbation. Later on, with diminishing sexual imagination and desire, these ideas and impulses had become infrequent, but their content remained unchanged. The masochistic "ideas of violence" predominated over the sadistic. Whenever he saw a lady, he thought she had sexual ideas like his own. In this way, he partly explained his embarrassment in social intercourse. Having heard that he would get rid of his burdensome sexual ideas if he were to accustom himself to natural sexual indulgence, he had twice attempted coitus, although he only experienced repugnance and was not confident of success. On both occasions the attempt was a fiasco. The second time he made the attempt, he felt such aversion that he pushed the girl away and fled.

The second case, below, is an observation placed at my disposal by a colleague. Even though it is aphoristic, it seems particularly suited to illuminating the distinctive element of masochism – the consciousness of subjection in its peculiar psychosexual effect:

Case 68.

Z., aged twenty-seven, artist; powerfully built, of pleasing appearance, said to be free from hereditary taint. Healthy in youth, since his twenty-third year he had been nervous and inclined to hypochrondria. Although he bragged of sexual indulgence, he was not very virile. In spite of associations with females, his relations with them were limited to innocent attentions. At the same time, his covetousness for women who were cold toward him was remarkable. Since his twenty-fifth year he had noticed that females, no matter how ugly, always excited him sexually whenever he discovered anything domineering in their character. An angry word from the lips of such a woman was sufficient to give him the most violent erections. Thus, one day he sat in a café and heard the (ugly) female cashier scold the waiters in a loud voice. This threw him into the most intense sexual excitement, which soon induced ejaculation. Z. required the women with whom he was to have sexual intercourse to repulse and annoy him in various ways. He thought that only a woman like the heroines of Sacher-Masoch's romances could charm him.

These cases of ideal masochism plainly demonstrate that the persons afflicted with this anomaly do not aim at actually suffering pain. The term "algolagnia," therefore, as applied by Schrenck-Notzing and Eulenburg to this anomaly, does not signify the essence, i.e., the psychic nucleus of the element of masochistic sentiment and imagination. This essence consists rather of the lustfully colored consciousness of being subject to the power of another person. The ideal, or even actual, enactment of violence on the part of the controlling person is only the means to the end, i.e., the realization of the sentiment.

Cases like this, in which the entire perversion of the sex life is confined to the sphere of the imagination – to the inner world of thought and instinct – and only accidentally comes to the knowledge of others, do not seem to be infrequent. Their *practical* significance, like that of masochism in general (which does not have the great forensic importance of sadism), is confined to the psychic impotence to which such individuals, as a rule, become subject; and to the intense impulse to solitary indulgence, with adequate imaginary ideas, and all its consequences.

That masochism is a perversion of uncommonly frequent occurrence is sufficiently shown by the relatively large number of cases that have thus far been
studied scientifically, as well as by the agreement of the various statements
reported.

The works concerning prostitution in large cities also contain numerous statements concerning this matter.[40]

It is interesting and worthy of mention that one of the most celebrated of men was
subject to this perversion and describes it in his autobiography (though somewhat
erroneously). From Jean Jacques Rousseau's *Confessions* it is evident that he was
affected with masochism.

Rousseau, with reference to whose life and malady Möbius (*J. J. Rousseau's Krank-
heitsgeschichte,* Leipzig, 1890) and Chatelain (*La folie de J. J. Rousseau,* Neuchâtel,
1891) may be consulted, tells in his *Confessions* (pt. 1, bk. 1) how Mademoiselle
Lambercier, aged thirty, greatly impressed him when he was eight years old and
lived with her brother as his pupil. Her solicitude when he could not immediately
answer a question, and her threats to punish him if he did not learn well, made the
deepest impression on him. One day, when he had suffered blows at her hands, he
felt pain and shame, but also experienced sensuous pleasure, and this incited a
great desire to be whipped by her again. It was only for fear of disturbing the lady
that Rousseau failed to create other opportunities to experience this lustful, sensual
feeling. One day, however, he unintentionally triggered a whipping at Mademoiselle
Lambercier's hands. This whipping was the last, for Mademoiselle Lambercier must
have noticed something of the peculiar effect of the punishment; she did not allow
the eight-year-old boy to sleep in her room anymore. From then on, Rousseau felt a
desire to have himself punished by ladies pleasing to him, à la Lambercier, but he
asserts that until he became a youth he knew nothing of the relation of the sexes to
each other. As is known, Rousseau was first introduced to the real mysteries of love
in his thirteenth year, and lost his innocence with Madame de Warens. Until then
he had only had feelings and impulses attracting him to women in the nature of
passive flagellation and other masochistic ideas.

Rousseau extensively describes how he suffered from his great sexual desires
because of his peculiar sensuousness, which had undoubtedly been awakened by

his whippings, for he reveled in desire, and could not disclose his longings. It would be erroneous, however, to suppose that Rousseau was concerned merely with flagellation. Flagellation only awakened ideas of a masochistic nature. In these ideas, at least, the psychological nucleus of an interesting self-study can be found. The essential element for Rousseau was the feeling of subjection to the woman. This is clearly shown by the *Confessions,* in which he expressly emphasizes that, "To kneel before a domineering mistress, to obey her orders; this was for me a very sweet enjoyment."

This passage proves that the consciousness of subjection to and humiliation by the woman was the most important element.

Of course, Rousseau was mistaken in thinking that this impulse to be humiliated by a woman had arisen due to association of ideas with the idea of flagellation:

"Never daring to declare my tastes, I entertained myself at least with relations that maintained the idea."

It is only in connection with the numerous cases of masochism – the existence of which has now been established, and among which there are so many that are in no way connected with flagellation, illustrating the primary and purely psychic character of this instinct of subjection – that a complete insight into Rousseau's case is obtained and the error he made in analyzing his own condition is discovered.

Binet (*Revue Anthropologique,* vol. 24, p. 256), who analyzes Rousseau's case in detail, justly calls attention to its masochistic significance when he says: "What Rousseau likes in women is not only the furrowed brow, the raised hand, the stern look, the imperious attitude, but also the emotional state, of which these acts are the external signs; he loves the haughty, disdainful woman, crushing him under her feet with the weight of her regal wrath."

Binet finds the solution to this enigmatic psychological fact in his assumption that it is an instance of fetishism, while the difference is that the object of the fetishism – i.e., the object of individual attraction (fetish) – is not a portion of the body, like a hand or a foot, but a mental peculiarity. This enthusiasm he calls *"amour spiritualiste,"* in contrast with *"amour plastique,"* as manifested in ordinary fetishism.

Although this deduction is acute, it is only a term by which to designate a fact, not a solution of it. Whether an explanation is possible will occupy our attention later.

There were also elements of masochism (and sadism) in the French writer C. P. Baudelaire, who died insane.

Baudelaire came from an insane and eccentric family. From his youth he was psychically abnormal. His sex life was decidedly abnormal. He had love affairs with ugly, repulsive women – negresses, dwarfs, giantesses. About a very beautiful woman, he expressed the wish to see her hung up by her hands and thereby kiss her feet. This enthusiasm for the naked foot also appears in one of his fiercely feverish poems as the equivalent of sexual indulgence. He said women were animals who had to be shut up, beaten and fed well. The man displaying these masochistic and sadistic inclinations died of paretic dementia (Lombroso, *Der genial Mensch*, German translation by Fränkel).

In scientific literature, the conditions constituting masochism have not received attention until recently. Tarnowsky, however (*Die krankhaften Erscheinungen des Geschlechtssinns,* Berlin, 1886), relates that he has known happily married, intellectual men, who from time to time felt an irresistible impulse to subject themselves to the coarsest, most cynical treatment – to scoldings or blows from passive or active pederasts or prostitutes. It is worthy of remark that, as Tarnowsky observes, in certain cases, blows, even when they draw blood, do not bring the desired result (virility, or at least ejaculation during flagellation) to those persons given to passive flagellation. "The individual must then be undressed by force, his hands tied, fastened to a bench, etc., during which he shams opposition, scolds, and pretends to resist. Only under such circumstances do the blows induce excitement leading to ejaculation."

O. Zimmermann's work, *Die Wonne des Leids,* Leipzig, 1885, also contributes much to this subject,[41] taken from history and literature.

More recently this matter has attracted fuller attention.

A. Moll, in his work *Die Konträre Sexualempfindung,* pp. 133 and 155ff., Berlin, 1891, quotes a number of cases of complete masochism in individuals of inverted sexuality; among them is the case of a man suffering from sexual perversion, who sent twenty paragraphs of written instructions to a man engaged for this purpose, and who was to treat and abuse him like a slave.

In June 1891, Mr. Dimitri von Stefanowsky, Deputy Government Attorney in Jaroslaw, Russia, informed me that, about three years before, he had given his attention to the perversion of the sex life designated "masochism" by me, and called "passivism" by him; that a year and a half previously he had prepared a paper on the subject for Professor von Kowalewsky and the Russian Archives of Psychiatry; and that in November 1888 he had read a paper on this subject, considered in its legal and psychological aspects, before the Law Society of Moscow (printed in the *Juridischen Boten*, the organ of the society, in nos. 6 to 8).[42]

Schrenck-Notzing devotes several paragraphs in his work (*Die Suggestionstherapie bei krankhaften Erscheinungen des Geschlechtssinnes,* etc., Stuttgart, 1892) to masochism and sadism and quotes several observations of his own.

Professor E. Deak of Budapest points out that the favorite thought of the masochist, namely, to be used by a female person as a beast of burden, may be found in the ancient literature of India, e.g., *Pantschatandra* (Benfey, vol. 2, bk. 4), in the form of a narrative, "Woman's Wiles," the gist of which is: The wife of King Nenda (in consequence of some love quarrel) was very angry with her husband, but despite his most earnest entreaties would reconcile with him. He says to her: "Love, without thee I cannot exist. I throw myself at thy feet and implore thee to be kind to me." She replies: "If thou wilt let me put a bit in thy mouth, mount thee and goad thee on to run and neigh like a horse, I will forgive thee." He did it. (Cf. case 58 of this book.) Benfey found a similar story in a Buddhist narrative which was published in *Mémoires sur les contrées occidentales par Hionen Thsang, traduit du Chinois par St. Julien,* vol. 1, p. 124.

Sacher-Masoch's writings have been mentioned repeatedly in this book. Many perverts refer to this author as having given typical descriptions of their psychic conditions.

Zola has a masochistic scene in his *Nana,* and also in *Eugène Rougon.* The "decadent" literature of recent times in France and Germany often has sadism and masochism as its theme. According to Stefanowsky, the tendency of the Russian novel lies in the same direction. Johann George Forster (1754-94) mentions in his *Travels* that the same idea underlies Russian folklore. Stefanowsky finds the character of the "passivist" in an English tragedy by Otway, *Venice Preserved*, and also refers to Dr. Luiz's *Les fellatores, moeurs de la décadence*, Paris, 1888 (*Union des bibliophiles*).

Johannes Wedde (social democrat agitator, died 1890), of Hamburg, advocates in his lyrics the subjection of man to woman, who should be mistress instead of handmaid (cf. Max Hoffmann, *Magazin,* vol. 29, no. 2, p. 96).

A striking example of masochism can also be found in Northern European literature by J. P. Jacobsen, *Niels Lyne*.

[b] latent masochism – foot and shoe fetishists.

Following the group of masochists is the well-populated class of foot and shoe fetishists. This group forms the transition to the manifestations of another independent perversion, i.e., fetishism itself; it stands, however, in closer relationship to masochism than to fetishism, for which reason it is placed here.

By fetishists (see page 187), I mean individuals whose sexual interest is concentrated exclusively on certain parts of the female body, or on certain portions of female attire. One of the most frequent forms of this type of fetishism is that in which the female foot or shoe is the fetish and becomes the exclusive object of sexual feeling and desire. It is highly probable (and is shown by a correct classification of the observed cases) that the majority – perhaps all – of the cases of shoe fetishism rest upon a basis of a more or less conscious masochistic desire for self-humiliation.

In Hammond's case (case 59), a masochist found satisfaction in being trod upon. The subjects of cases 55 and 58 also had themselves trod upon. In case 59, *equus eroticus* (the erotic horse), the person loved a woman's foot, etc. In the majority of cases of masochism, the act of being trod upon is an easily accessible means of expressing the relation of subjection.[43]

Case 69.

Z., aged twenty-eight, hereditarily and constitutionally neuropathic, claimed to have had a pollution at the age of eleven when he was beaten by his mother on his buttocks. He often recalled the scene as a pleasurable experience. At the age of thirteen he developed a weakness for ladies' boots with high heels. He pressed them between his thighs and thus produced ejaculation. The very thought of it sufficiently effected the desired result. He soon added to this fantasy the idea that he lay at the feet of a pretty girl and allowed her to kick him with her pretty boots. This caused ejaculation. Until he was twenty-one he never had a desire for coitus or the female genitals. From twenty-one to twenty-five he suffered from tuberculosis, during which period the masochistic inclination almost disappeared. After recovery he tried coitus for the first time, but when he saw the nude form of the girl his desire vanished completely. He now confined himself to his masochistic fantasies, but hoped that some day he would meet with the ideal woman who, by means of sadistic acts, might lead him to normal sexual intercourse.

Such cases are numerous where, within a fully developed circle of masochistic ideas, the foot and the shoe or boot of a woman, conceived as a means of humiliation, have become the objects of special sexual interest. Through numerous degrees that are easily discriminated, they form the demonstrable transition to other cases in which the masochistic inclinations retreat more and more to the background, and little by little pass beyond the threshold of consciousness, while the interest in women's shoes alone, otherwise absolutely inexplicable, remains in consciousness. Frequent cases of shoe lovers, which, like all cases of fetishism, possess forensic interest (theft of shoes), occupy a position midway between masochism and fetishism. The majority or all may be looked upon as instances of latent masochism (the motive remaining unconscious) in which *the female foot or shoe, as the masochist's fetish,* has acquired an independent significance.

In cases 70 and 71, the female shoe possesses a subordinate interest, but unmistakable masochistic desires play an important part:

Case 70.

Mr. X., aged twenty-five, parents healthy, never previously ill, placed the following autobiography at my disposal: "I began to practice masturbation at the age of ten, without ever having any lustful thoughts during the act. Yet at that time – I am sure of this – the sight and touch of girls' elegant boots had a peculiar charm for me; my greatest desire was also to wear such shoes, a wish that was occasionally fulfilled at masquerades. But I was also troubled by a very different thought: *my ideal was to see myself in a position of humiliation; I would gladly have been a slave* and whipped; in short, I wished to receive the treatment that one finds described in many stories of slavery. I do not know whether the reading of such stories gave rise to my wish, or whether it arose spontaneously.

"Puberty began at the age of thirteen; with the occurrence of ejaculation lustful pleasure increased, and I masturbated more frequently, often two or three times a day. From my twelfth to my sixteenth year, during the act of masturbation, I always had the idea that I was forced to wear girls' boots. The sight of an elegant boot on the foot of a pretty girl intoxicated me; I avidly inhaled the odor of the leather. In order to smell leather during the act of masturbation, I bought a pair of leather cuffs, which I smelled while I masturbated. My enthusiasm for ladies' leather shoes remains the same today; since my seventeenth year, however, it has been coupled with the *wish to become a servant, to blacken shoes for distinguished ladies, to put on and take off their shoes for them, etc.*

"My dreams at night are made up of shoe scenes: either I stand before the show window of a shoe shop regarding the elegant ladies' shoes – particularly buttoned shoes – or I lie at a lady's feet and smell and lick her shoes. For about a year I have given up masturbation and go to prostitutes; coitus takes place by means of intense thought of ladies' buttoned shoes; or, if necessary, I take the shoe of the prostitute to bed with me. I have never again suffered from my previous habit of masturbation. I learn easily, have a good memory, and have never had a headache in my life. This much concerns myself.

"A few words about my brother: I am thoroughly convinced that he is also a shoe fetishist. Of the many facts that demonstrate this to me, it is only necessary to mention that it is a great pleasure for him to have a certain cousin (a very beautiful girl) tread upon him. As for the rest, I might try to determine whether or not a man who stands before a shoe shop and regards the shoes on display is a 'foot lover.' This anomaly is uncommonly frequent. When, in the circle of my acquaintances, I turn the conversation to the question of what woman's charm is, I frequently hear it said that it is much more in attire than in nudity; but everyone is careful not to reveal his especial fetish. I think an uncle of mine is also a shoe fetishist."

C a s e   7 1 .

Z., twenty-eight years, official, came from a neuropathic mother. Father died early; as to his family and health, no information was obtainable. Z. was from early childhood nervous and impressionable; began to masturbate early on his own accord; with puberty he became neurasthenic, avoided masturbation for a while, but was frequently troubled with pollutions; recovered somewhat at a hydropathic institute. Although he experienced strong sexual desire toward women, he never succeeded in coitus, partly because of diffidence in his sexual powers, partly from fear of infection. This upset him very much, especially as he relapsed, for lack of something better, into his secret habit.

Z., during a searching consultation on the subject of his sex life, proved to be a fetishist as well as a masochist, and revealed interesting relations between these two anomalies. He asserted that from his ninth year he had a weakness for women's shoes. This, he claimed, was caused by seeing, at that time, a lady mounting a horse while an attendant held the stirrup for her. This sight excited him very much, constantly recurred in his imagination, and steadily increased his lustful feelings. Later on his sensations during pollution were connected with women in high boots. Laced boots with high heels charmed him most when this idea was associated with the lustful thought that a woman trod upon him with her heel, and that he, while kneeling, kissed a woman's shoes. The only interesting thing about a woman was her shoe. Impressions of odor did not play any part in this. The shoe, as such, was insufficient; it had to be worn by a woman. Whenever he saw a woman with laced boots he became excited and masturbated. He believed that he could not command virile power with any woman unless her feet were clad with laced boots.

Lacking something better, he made a drawing of such a boot, and while masturbating reveled in gazing at it.

The following case is not only instructive because of the relations that are shown to exist between shoe fetishism and masochism, but is also of interest because of the cure of the sex life brought about by the patient himself.

C a s e   7 2 .

Mr. M., thirty-three years of age, from a good family, which had shown manifestations of psychic degeneration on the maternal side for generations, extending even to cases of moral insanity. The mother was neuropathic and her character was abnormal. He was strong, well-built, but neuropathic; he began as a small boy to practice masturbation spontaneously. At twelve years of age he had peculiar dreams of being tortured, whipped and kicked by men and women, especially by women. At about fourteen a weakness for women's boots came over him. They caused sexual excitement; he was forced to kiss and press them to him; this produced erection and orgasm, followed by masturbation. These acts were also accompanied by masochistic ideas of being kicked and tortured.

He recognized that his sex life was abnormal, and at the age of seventeen he sought a cure in coitus. He found himself quite impotent. At eighteen another attempt proved a failure; he continued masturbation assisted by shoe fetishism and masochistic fantasies.

At the age of nineteen he accidentally heard a man speak of flagellation by a girl as being a means to bring about virility. He now felt that he had found his remedy, and though he hastened to carry out the advice just received, he was completely disappointed. The whole situation disgusted him so thoroughly that no erection resulted.

He made no more similar attempts, and satisfied himself in the accustomed manner. When he was twenty-seven he met, by accident, a sympathetic and elegant girl, became intimate, and complained to her about his impotence. She laughed at him and said that at his age and with his constitution this was impossible.

He gained self-confidence, but only obtained potency after fourteen days of the greatest intimacy and with the aid of shoe fetishism and masochistic fantasies. This lasted several months. His condition improved, he could do without the secret aids, and his abnormal fantasies became latent. Then, for three years, because of psychic impotence with other women, he yielded again to masturbation and his former fetishism. In his thirtieth year he entered again into sympathetic relations with another girl; because he felt himself incapable of coitus without the aid of masochistic situations, however, he instructed her to treat him as her slave. She played her part well, made him kiss her feet, whipped him with a switch, and trod upon him. But it was all in vain. He only felt pain and utter confusion, and soon had these assaults discontinued. Ideal masochistic situations, however, aided him at times in accomplishing coitus.

He found little satisfaction, however, under these circumstances. He then came across my book *Psychopathia Sexualis* and found out the real condition of his anomaly. He wrote to his former acquaintance and again started intimate relations with her, but told her definitely that the former absurd scenes of "slavery" must not be enacted again, and that under no circumstances, even if he requested it himself, must she fulfill his masochistic ideas.

In order to free himself of shoe fetishism he adopted the following plan. He bought a lady's elegant boot and daily made these suggestions to himself while kissing the boot repeatedly: "Why should I have erections when kissing this boot, which is after all only a piece of ordinary leather?" This practice little by little stripped the object of its fetishistic charm. The erections disappeared, and finally the boot impressed him only as a boot. Intimate intercourse with the sympathetic person ran parallel to this suggestive self-treatment, and although at first he could not produce virility without the assistance of masochistic ideas, these gradually disappeared.

He was so pleased with his cure that he came to thank me for the valuable help he had found in the perusal of my book, which had shown him the right way to remedy his defect.

Since then he wrote that he was completely cured, that he met with no difficulties in his sexual intercourse, although from time to time masochistic representations faintly reappeared without, however, leaving any impression on his mind.

Case 73.

Reported by Mantegazza in his *Anthropologischen Studien*, 1886, p. 110. X., American, from good family, mentally and morally well-constituted; from the beginning of puberty capable of being excited sexually only by a woman's shoe. Her body and naked or stockinged foot made no impression on him; but the foot, when covered with a shoe, or a shoe alone, induced erection and even ejaculation. Sight alone was sufficient for him in the case of elegant shoes – i.e., shoes of black leather, with buttons up the side and with very high heels. His sexual desire was powerfully excited by touching, kissing, or putting such shoes on his feet. His enjoyment was increased by driving nails through the soles so that, when he walked, their points would penetrate his feet. This caused him terrible pain, but he enjoyed a real lustful feeling at the same time. His greatest enjoyment was to kneel down before the elegantly clad feet of ladies and have them step on him. If the wearer were an ugly woman, the shoes would not affect him, and his fantasy would cool. If the patient had only empty shoes at his disposal, his fantasy would be of a beautiful woman wearing them, and ejaculation would result. His nightly dreams were of the shoes of beautiful women. He considered the exposure of ladies' shoes in show windows immoral, while talk about the nature of women seemed harmless to him, though in bad taste. X. attempted coitus several times without success; ejaculation never occurred.

In the following case the masochistic as well as the sadistic element is in evidence (cf. "Torture of Animals," under "Sadism"):

Case 74.

A young, powerful man, aged twenty-six. Nothing in the opposite sex excited his sensual feeling except elegant shoes on the feet of a buxom woman, especially when they were made of black leather with high heels. The shoes without the wearer were sufficient. It gave him the greatest pleasure to see, touch, and kiss them. The feminine foot, when bare or covered with a stocking, had no effect on him. Since childhood he had had a weakness for ladies' fine shoes.

X. was potent; during the sexual act the female had to be elegantly dressed and, above all, have on pretty shoes. At the height of sexual excitement, cruel thoughts about the shoes arose. He was forced to think with delight of the death agonies of the animal from which the leather was taken. Sometimes he was impelled to take chickens and other animals with him to Phryne, in order to have her tread on them with her pretty shoes for his pleasure. He called this "sacrificing to the feet of Venus." At other times he had the woman walk on him with her shoes on, the harder the better.

Until the previous year it was sufficient – since he did not take the slightest sensual pleasure in women – to caress ladies' shoes that pleased him, thus attaining ejaculation and complete satisfaction (Lombroso, *Arch. di psichiatria,* vol. 9, fasc. 3).

The next case is reminiscent of case 73, because of the interest in the nails of the shoes (as capable of inflicting pain), and of case 74, because of the slight accompanying sadistic element:

Case 75.

X., aged thirty-four, married; of neuropathic parentage; suffered severely from convulsions as a child; remarkably precocious, but one-sided in development (could read at the age of three); nervous from childhood. At the age of seven he manifested an inclination to fondle shoes, especially the nails of women's shoes. The mere sight, but still more the touching and counting of the shoe nails, gave him indescribable pleasure.

At night he indulged in imagining how his cousins had their measurements taken for shoes; how he nailed horseshoes onto one of them or cut her feet off. In time the shoe scenes came upon him during the day, and involuntarily induced erection and ejaculation. Frequently he took shoes that belonged to female occupants of the house, and if he touched them with his penis he had an ejaculation. For a long time, as a student, it was possible for him to control his ideas and inclinations. There came a time, however, when he was compelled to listen to female footsteps on the pavement, which, like the sight of the nails being driven into ladies' shoes, or the sight of shoes in the windows of the boot shops, always swayed him with feelings of lustful pleasure. He married, and during the first months of his married life was free of these desires. Gradually he became hysteropathic and neurasthenic.

At this stage he began to have hysterical attacks when the shoemaker spoke to him of nails, or of driving nails, in ladies' shoes. The reaction was greater still if he chanced to see a pretty lady wearing shoes covered with nails. In order to induce ejaculation, it was necessary to cut soles out of pasteboard and cover them with nails; or, he would buy ladies' shoes, have them covered with nails in the shop, scrape them at home on the ground, and finally touch them with the end of his penis. Moreover, lustful shoe visions occurred spontaneously, during which he satisfied himself by masturbation.

X. was otherwise intelligent, skillful in his calling, but powerless in combating his perverse inclinations. He had phimosis; penis short, expanded at the root, and incapable of complete erection. One day the patient allowed himself to masturbate after he was excited by the sight of ladies' shoes covered with nails, in front of the window of a shoe shop, and thus he became a criminal (Blanche, *Archives de Neurologie*, 1882, no. 22).

Reference may be made here to a case of inverted sexuality, to be described later (case 137), in which the principal sexual interest was in the boots of male servants. The desire was to be trod upon by them, etc.

Case 76.

(Dr. Pascal, *Igiene dell' amore*.) X., merchant; from time to time (but particularly in bad weather) he had the following desire: He would accost some prostitute and ask her to go to a shoe shop with him, where he would buy her the handsomest pair of shoes made of patent leather on the condition that she put them on immediately. When this had taken place, she had to go about in the street, walking in manure and mud as much as possible, in order to soil the shoes. Then X. would lead her to a hotel, and, almost before they had reached a room, he would cast himself upon her feet, feeling extraordinary pleasure in licking them with his lips. When he had cleaned the shoes in this manner, he paid her and went on his way.

From these cases it may plainly be seen that the shoe is the fetish of the masochist, apparently because of the relation of the dressed female foot to the idea of being trod upon and other acts of humiliation. Therefore, when in other cases of shoe fetishism the female shoe appears alone as the excitant of sexual desire, one is justified in presuming that masochistic motives have remained latent. The idea of being trod upon, etc., remains in the depths of unconscious life, and the idea of the shoe alone, the means for such acts, rises into consciousness. Cases which would otherwise remain wholly inexplicable are sufficiently explained.[44] Although the above case demonstrates latent masochism, which may always be assumed to be the unconscious motive, the origin of the fetishism can often be proved to arise from an association of ideas with some particular event, as in cases 113 and 114.

Such cases of desire for ladies' shoes, without conscious motive and without demonstrable origin, are innumerable.[45] Three cases are given here as examples:

Case 77.
Minister, aged fifty. From time to time he went to houses of prostitution under the pretext of renting a room. He would enter the room with a girl. Then he would lustfully regard her shoes, take one off, and, **crazy with desire, kiss and bite her shoes. Finally he would press her shoes against his genitals, ejaculate, and rub his chest and nipples with the ejaculate;** then he would awake from his sexual ecstasy. He begged the woman to allow him to keep the shoe for a few days, and always, at the appointed time, would return it with thanks (Cantaranot, *La Psichiatria,* vol. 5, p. 205).

Case 78.
Z., student, aged twenty-three; from a tainted family. Sister was insane; brother suffered from male hysteria. The patient, peculiar from childhood, had frequent attacks of hypochondriacal depression, *taedium vitae,* and always felt that he was being slighted.

In a consultation due to mental trouble, I found him to be a very perverse, hereditarily predisposed man, with neurasthenic and hypochondriacal symptoms. A suspicion of masturbation was confirmed. Patient made interesting disclosures concerning his sex life. At the age of ten he was powerfully attracted to the foot of one of his comrades. At twelve he became an enthusiast for ladies' feet. It gave him a delightful sensation to revel in the sight of them. At fourteen he began to masturbate, thinking, at the same time, of the beautiful foot of a lady. At this time he reveled in the sight of the feet of his three-year-old sister. The feet of other females who attracted him induced sexual excitement. Only women's feet – no other part of them – interested him. The thought of sexual intercourse with women disgusted him. He had never attempted coitus. After his twelfth year he had no interest in the feet of male individuals. He was indifferent to the style of covering of the female foot; it was only necessary that the person seemed to be sympathetic. The thought of enjoying the feet of prostitutes was disgusting to him. For years he had been in love with his sister's feet. If he had the opportunity to obtain her shoes, the sight of them powerfully excited his sensuality. Kissing or embracing his sister did not have this effect. His greatest delight was to embrace and kiss the foot of a sympathetic woman, at which time ejaculation would result with a lively pleasurable sensation. Often he was impelled to touch his genitals with one of his sister's shoes; but he had been able, since that time, to master this impulse, especially because for two years (due to progressive irritable weakness of the genitals) the simple sight of the foot had induced ejaculation. From his relatives it was ascertained that the patient had a silly admiration for the feet of his sister, so that she avoided him and sought to hide her feet from him. The patient looked upon his perverse sexual impulse as pathological, and was painfully affected by the fact that the object of his vile fantasy was his sister's feet. He avoided opportunity as much as he could, and sought to help the matter by masturbation when, as in dreams accompanied by pollution, ladies' feet filled his imagination. However, when the impulse became too powerful, he could not avoid gaining a partial sight of his sister's feet. Immediately after ejaculation he would become angry with himself at having been weak again. His partiality for his sister's feet had cost him many a sleepless night. He often wondered if he could still love his sister. Although it seemed right to him that she should conceal her feet from him, he was often irritated because the concealment caused him to have pollutions. The patient gave assurances, confirmed by his relatives, of being moral in other respects.

Case 79.

S., New York, was accused of being a street thief. Numerous cases of insanity in his ancestry; father, brother and sister mentally abnormal. At seven, two violent cerebral concussions. At thirteen, struck by a beam. At fourteen, violent attacks of headache. Accompanying these attacks, or immediately after them, he had a peculiar impulse to take the shoes of female members of the family – usually only one shoe at a time – and hide them in some out-of-the way corner. Taken to task, he would lie, or declare that he had no recollection of the affair. This passion for shoes was unconquerable, and made its appearance every three or four months. On one occasion he attempted to take a shoe from the foot of one of the servants, and on another he stole his sister's shoe from her bedroom. In the spring two ladies had their shoes torn from their feet on the open street. In August, S. left his home early in the morning to go to his work as a printer. A moment afterward, on the open street, he tore the shoe from a girl's foot, fled to his place of work, and was arrested there as a street thief. He declared that he did not know much of his act; that the desire to possess the shoe, when he saw it, had come upon him like a stroke of lightning; he did not know why. He had acted while in an unconscious state. The shoe, as he correctly indicated, was found in his coat. In confinement he was so mentally excited that an outbreak of insanity was feared. Discharged, he then stole his wife's shoes while she was asleep. His moral character and habits of life were blameless. He was an intelligent workman, but the irregular employment that followed this incident made him confused and incapable of work. Pardoned (Nichols, *Am. Journal of Insanity*, 1859; Beck, *Medical Jurisprudence*, vol. 1, p. 732, 1860).

Pascal (op. cit.) has some similar cases, and many others have been mentioned to me by colleagues and patients.

[c] disgusting acts for the purpose of self-humiliation and sexual gratification – latent masochism – coprolagnia.

While in the manifestations thus far described the aesthetic treatment is at least, so far as appearances go, saved, and the lustful situation is kept within the confines of a symbolic or ideal character, there are many cases in which the desire for sexual gratification by way of self-humiliation before woman finds expression in acts that defile the moral and aesthetic feeling of the normal man.

Impressions obtained through the senses of smell and taste that produce in the normal man only feelings of nausea and disgust are made the basis of the most vivid emotions of lust, impulsively producing in the perverse subject intense orgasm and even ejaculation.

An analogy with the excesses of religious enthusiasm can even be traced. The religious enthusiast, Antoinette Bouvignon de la Porte, used to mix excreta with her foot in order to mortify herself (Zimmermann, op. cit., p. 124). The beatified Marie Alacoque licked up the excrement of sick people with her tongue to "mortify" herself, and sucked their festering toes! The analogy with sadism is also of interest in this connection, because here there are also manifestations in the sense of vampirism and anthropophagy arising from disgusting appetites of the organs of taste and olfaction, produce lustful feelings (cf. case 59, Bichel, Menesclou; and cases 18, 19, 20, 22). This impulse toward disgusting acts might well be named "coprolagnia." Its relation to masochism (as a subordinate form) has been indicated in case 51. The subsequent observation will render it clearer.

In some cases it seems that the masochistic element is unknown to the perverse subject, and that the instinct for nauseating acts alone is present (latent masochism). A striking instance of masochistic coprolagnia (combined with perverse sexuality) may be found in case 114 of the eighth edition of this work [case 114 in the appendix, p. 566]. The subject of this case not only revels in the thought of being the slave of male lover, referring for this purpose to Sacher-Masoch's *Venus im Pelz,* **but he even imagined asking his lover to let him smell his sweaty slippers and eat his excrement. Then he related how, lacking what he fantasized about and so strongly craved, he smelled his own sweaty slippers and ate his own excrement as a substitute; while doing this he had an erection, experienced intense pleasure, and ejaculated.**

Case 80.

Masochism – Coprolagnia. Z., fifty-two years of age; high position; father phthisical; family claimed to be untainted; always nervous, only child. He asserted that he had had peculiar emotions from the age of seven, when, by chance, he saw the servants take off their boots and stockings preparatory to scrubbing the floors of the house. Once he begged one of the maids to show him her toes and feet before she washed them. When he began going to school and reading books, he felt obsessively drawn to literature containing descriptions of refined cruelty and tortures, especially when they were executed at the demands of women. He devoured novels dealing with slavery and bondage and, while reading them, he became so excited he would masturbate. What excited him most was to imagine that he was the slave of a pretty young lady of his acquaintance who allowed him, after a long walk, **to lick her feet,**[46] **especially the soles and the spaces between the toes.** He thought of the young lady as particularly cruel and imagined her enjoyment of the tortures and whippings meted out to him. These fantasies were accompanied by masturbation. At the age of fifteen, while reveling in such fiction, he let a poodle lick his feet. One day he noticed how a pretty servant girl in his own home let a poodle lick her toes while she was reading. This caused in him erection and ejaculation. He persuaded the girl to let this happen frequently while he looked on. After a while he took the place of the poodle and ejaculated every time.

From his fifteenth to his eighteenth year he was at a boarding school and had no opportunity for practicing such evil habits. He was satisfied to excite himself every few weeks with the perusal of literature that discussed cruelties committed by women, imagining all the time that he was licking the feet of such women. This produced ejaculation accompanied by the highest lustful excitement. The female organs never had any attraction for him, and he never felt sexually drawn toward men. When he had attained puberty, he solicited girls and had coitus with them, but always sucked their feet before the act. He would also do this during the act, and asked the girls to tell him with what cruelties they would afflict him in case he did not lick their toes quite clean. Z. affirmed that he very often succeeded in this, and that the entire action was always pleasing to the girls.

He was especially attracted by well-bred women's feet deformed by narrow boots and unwashed for several days, but he could only stomach "slight, natural deposits, such as one might find upon the feet of clean well-bred ladies, and discolorations from the stockings, while sweating feet excited him only in his imagination, and disgusted him in reality." "Cruel tortures" also existed for him only in his imagination as a means of excitement; he abhorred them and never craved them in reality. Nevertheless, they played a preeminent part in his fantasy, and he never neglected to instruct the women with whom he kept in masochistic touch how they were to write him threatening letters. From the collection of such letters placed at my disposal by Z., one is given here because it clearly illustrates the line of thought and sentiment:

"Licker of women's sweaty feet! I take the utmost delight in conjuring up the moment when you will lick my toes, especially after a long walk. A facsimile of my foot I shall send you soon. It will intoxicate me like nectar when you will lick up my **sweaty feet.** And if you will not do it voluntarily, I shall force you; I shall treat you as my meanest slave.

You shall witness how another **lover licks the sweat from my feet,** while you shall whine like a dog under the lashes of my servants. I shall declare you outlawed. I shall find the most exquisite pleasure in seeing you in pain, breathing your last under the most cruel tortures, licking my toes in extreme agony. . . . You challenge my cruelty — very well, I shall crush you under my foot like a worm. . . . You ask me for a stocking? I shall wear it longer than usual. But I demand that you kiss it and lick it; that you soak the foot of it in water and then drink the water. If you do not carry out my pleasure absolutely, I shall chastise you with my riding whip. I demand unconditional obedience. If you do not obey, I shall have you whipped with my knout, I shall make you walk over a floor well-spiked with sharp nails, I shall have you bastinadoed and cast to the lions in the cage. It will give me the utmost delight to see how the wild beasts enjoy your flesh."

Z. looked upon such ridiculous tirades as a means to satisfy his perverse sexuality. These sexual monstrosities, which to him were only a congenital anomaly, he did not consider unnatural, although he acknowledged they would be disgusting to the normally constituted man. Otherwise he appeared to be a decent sort of a man with rather refined manners, but his otherwise meager aesthetic sentiments were overbalanced by a sensuality that gratified his perverse desires.

Z. gave me an insight into his correspondence with the literary champion of masochism, Sacher-Masoch.

One of these letters, dated 1888, showed as a heading the picture of a luxuriant woman of imperial bearing, only half-covered with furs, who held a riding whip as if ready to strike. Sacher-Masoch contended that "the passion to play the slave" was widespread, especially among the Germans and Russians. In this letter, the history was related of a noble Russian who loved to be tied and whipped by several beautiful women. One day he found his ideal in a pretty young French woman and took her to his home.

According to Sacher-Masoch, a Danish woman yielded her favor to no man until he acted the part of slave to her for a considerable time. **She would force her lovers to lick her feet and buttocks.** She had her adorers put in chains and whipped until they obeyed her **by licking her feet.** Once she had the "slave" fastened to her bedposts and thus made him witness her granting the highest favor to another. After the latter left her she had the fettered "slave" whipped by her servants until he yielded **by licking the buttocks of his mistress.**

If these assertions are true, which, of course, cannot be accepted from the poet without definite proof, they would constitute remarkable proofs of female sadism. At any rate they are psychologically interesting instances of thoughts and sentiments specific to masochism (my own observations, *Zentralblatt für Krankheiten der Harn- und Sexualorgane*, vol. 6, no. 7).

Case 81.

Z., aged twenty-four; Russian civil servant; mother neuropathic, father psychopathic. Z. was intelligent, of refined manners, physically normal, of pleasing appearance and aesthetic tastes; never had a severe illness. Claimed to have suffered from a nervous disposition since infancy; had, like his mother, neuropathic eyes, and lately suffered from cerebral asthenic troubles. His perverse sex life caused him much worry, bordering on despair, deprived him of self-esteem, and tempted him to suicide.

What oppressed him was the unnatural desire, recurring every four weeks, for **a woman to urinate into his mouth.** As cause he gave the following facts, interesting because of their genetic importance. At six years of age he accidentally put his hand **under the buttocks of a girl** who sat next to him in school. This caused him pleasure, and he did it repeatedly. The memory of these pleasant situations strongly aroused his imagination.

When he was a boy of ten, his nurse, in an impulse of sexual desire, clutched him against her own body and put her finger into her vagina. When he afterward happened to touch his nose with his finger, the smell was intensely pleasurable to him.

This immoral act developed into a lustful fantasy that made him believe **he was lying bound between a woman's thighs, and he was forced to sleep under her buttocks and drink her urine.**

In his thirteenth year these fictions disappeared. At fifteen his first act of coitus; at sixteen his second, quite normal and without fantasy representations.

Lacking money, he had to satisfy his intense, nagging sexual desire with masturbation.

At seventeen perverse ideas recurred. They became more powerful and he struggled against them in vain.

At eighteen he yielded to his impulse. **When a certain woman urinated into his mouth, he experienced the most intense pleasure.** He then had coitus with the vile woman. Since then he had felt the need to repeat the disgusting act every four weeks.

After indulging in this perverse action he was ashamed of himself and disgust overcame him. Although ejaculations rarely accompanied the act, he had erections and orgasms, and whenever ejaculation was absent, he gratified himself with coitus.

During the intervals between these excessive impulses, he was quite free from perverse thoughts and desires as well as from ideal masochism and fetishistic relations. Sexual desire during these intervals was slight and was easily gratified in a normal fashion without the assistance of perverse fiction. He often traveled miles from his country seat to the city to satisfy his cravings when these spells came over him.

Again and again the patient – refined as he was and disgusted with his own perversity – sought to resist the morbid impulse, but in vain; restlessness, anxiety, trembling and somnolence made life unbearable, until at last he found release from the psychic tension by gratifying his morbid cravings at any price. He attained this easily, but was at once overcome with self-reproach and self-contempt, bordering even on *taedium vitae.* These mental struggles enervated the patient and he complained of debility of memory, absent-mindedness, mental impotence, and cerebral pressure. His last hope was that medical science might succeed in freeing him from this monstrous affliction and reestablish his moral self.

Case 82.

Masochism – Fetishism – Coprolagnia. B., aged thirty-one, official; family neuropathically tainted, nervous from early childhood, weakly, nocturnal frights. First pollution at the age of sixteen. At seventeen fell in love with a French woman, twenty-eight years old and anything but pretty. Had a special weakness for her shoes. Whenever he could do so without being observed, he would cover them with kisses. This gave him sensual delight, but it never caused ejaculation. At that time, according to his statement, he had no knowledge of the difference in sexes. He could not understand his weakness for shoes. After he attained the age of twenty-two he had coitus about once a month, but did not derive psychic gratification from the act. One day he met a prostitute on the street whose haughty demeanor, fascinating eyes, and challenging mien made a peculiar impression on him. He felt an impulse to throw himself at her feet, kiss them, and follow her like a dog or slave. Her "majestic" feet clad in patent leather boots especially captivated him. He trembled with voluptuous excitement. During the night he could not sleep, for the thought of the woman haunted him. He imagined that he was kissing this woman's feet. This fantasy superinduced ejaculation. Shy by nature, he then resorted to psychic masturbation, and, having a dislike for prostitutes, he shunned henceforth the society of women altogether. He reveled in the thought of the pretty foot of an imperious woman, and associated this thought with the olfactory impression he would receive from its proximity. In erotic dreams he followed such women. Rain would begin to fall and the woman, raising her skirt, would show her pretty foot, ankle and calf, encased in a silken stocking. As soon as he grasped and fondled the warm form, so soft and yet so firm, he would ejaculate. On rainy days he used to patrol the streets to see such scenes in reality. If he saw what he came for he carried away the impression in his memory and it became the object of his nightly dreams and acts of psychic masturbation. To hasten the act, he sniffed, kissed, bit and chewed his own socks. His dreams and libidinous ecstasies were also mingled with fantasies of a purely masochistic character, e.g., a woman but slightly clad stood in front of him holding a whip in her hand, while he knelt at her feet like a slave. She would cut him with the whip, put her foot on his neck, face or mouth, until he consented **to thoroughly smell and suck the secretion between her naked toes.** During this mental act he smelled his own feet, the odor of which was repulsive to him when in his normal state. He varied these practices with acts of "buttocks fetishism" by using a girl's drawers **to press her dung up to his nostrils.** At other times the **vagina** was his fetish and he practiced ideal cunnilingus. For assistance he used pieces cut from the armpits of a woman's undervest, stockings, or shoes. After six years, during which neurasthenia had increased while his imaginative power had waned, he lost all power to accomplish these acts of psychic masturbation and came down to the level of a common masturbator. He later became acquainted with a girl of a similar masochistic tendency, and coitus became possible for both, but always by having recourse to some masochistic situation. The old fetishistic fascinations reappeared, however, and he found greater pleasures in appeasing this perverse appetite than in coitus, which he performed only out of respect. The end of this cynical sexual existence was a marriage – after his mistress had forsaken him – with a woman who had the same perverse inclinations as himself. They had children, but found sexual gratification chiefly in masochistic marital acts (*Zentralblatt für Krankheiten der Harn- und Sexualorgane*, vol. 6, no. 7).

Other cases of Cantarano's (*La Psichiatria*) belong here (**urination, even defecation by the girl onto the man's tongue before the act**), consumption of confects smelling like feces in order to become potent; and also the following case, likewise communicated to me by a physician:

"A Russian prince, who was very decrepit, was accustomed to having his mistress turn her back to him and defecate on his breast; this was the only way in which he could excite the remnant of sexual desire."

Another supported a mistress in an unusually brilliant style, with the condition that she eat marzipan exclusively. **To arouse sexual desire and his ability to ejaculate, he caught the woman's excrement in his mouth.** A Brazilian physician tells me of several cases of **a woman defecating into a man's mouth** that have come to his attention. Such cases occur everywhere, and are not at all infrequent. All kinds of secretions – saliva, nasal mucus, and even ear wax – are used in this way and swallowed with pleasure; **kissing the buttocks** and even **the anus** are indulged in. Dr. Moll (op. cit., p. 135) reports the same thing of a man affected with inverted sexuality. The perverse desire to practice cunnilingus, which is very widespread, probably often has its root in masochistic impulses.

Evidently the case quoted by Cantarano (*La Psichiatria*, vol. 5, p. 207) belongs here also, in which coitus is preceded by **biting and sucking** of the woman's toes, which have not been washed for some time. Also a case quoted by me in the eighth edition of this book, cf. ibid, case 68 [case 69 in the appendix, p. 538].

Stefanowsky (*Archives de l'anthropologie criminelle*, 1892, vol. 7) knows a Russian merchant **who was extremely delighted to drink what a girl in a brothel had, on his orders, spit into a dish.**

Neri, *Arch. delle psicopatie sessuali*, p. 108: Workman, aged twenty-seven, heavily tainted, facial tic, troubled with phobia (especially agoraphobia) and alcoholism. **He experienced the greatest pleasure if prostitutes defecated and urinated into his mouth. He poured wine over the bodies of harlots, and as it flowed down over their genitals he would lap it up with his mouth.** He was a fetishist of ladies' gloves and slippers; **he enjoyed kissing his sister's slippers, whose feet were usually moist with sweat. He achieved the greatest sexual satisfaction when he was insulted by girls or, even better, flogged until blood flowed. While being flogged, he would**

plead on his knees for the prostitute's forgiveness and mercy, and then begin to masturbate.

Pelanda (*Arch. di Psichiatria*, vol. 10, fascs. 3-4) relates the following case:

Case 83.

W., aged forty-five, predisposed, was given to masturbation at the age of eight. **From the age of sixteen he satisfied his sexual desire by drinking women's fresh urine. When he drank the urine, his pleasure was so intense that he could not taste or smell it.** After drinking he always experienced disgust and ill-feeling, and made firm resolutions to do it no more in the future. Once he had the same pleasure in drinking the urine of a nine-year-old boy with whom he once practiced fellatio. The patient suffered from epileptic insanity.

Still older cases belong here, which Tardieu (*Etude médico-légale sur les attentats aux moeurs*, p. 206) observed in senile individuals. He describes as "renifleurs" persons **"who, in secret places (no doubt convenient porticoes around the theatres where many women hurriedly urinate) seduce and pollute each other, having become excited by the stench of urine in their nostrils."** The "stercoraires" that Taxil (*La prostitution contemporaine*) mentions are, in relation to this subject, unique.

Eulenburg relates further monstrous facts belonging to this section. Cf. Zülzer's *Klin. Handbuch der Harn- und Sexualorgane*, vol. 4, p. 47.

[d] masochism in woman.

Woman's voluntary subjection to the opposite sex is a physiological phenomenon. Because of her passive role in procreation and long-existent social conditions, ideas of subjection are, in woman, normally connected with the idea of sexual relations. They form, so to speak, the harmonics which determine the tone-quality of feminine feeling.

Anyone conversant with the history of civilization knows in what a state of absolute subjection woman was always kept until a relatively high degree of civilization was reached;[47] and an attentive observer of life may still easily recognize how the custom of innumerable generations, in connection with the passive role with which woman has been endowed by nature, has given her an instinctive inclination to voluntary subordination to man; he will notice that exaggeration of customary gallantry is very distasteful to women, and that a deviation from it in the direction of masterful behavior, though loudly reprehended, is often accepted with secret satisfaction.[48] Under the veneer of polite society the instinct of feminine servitude is discernible everywhere.

Thus it is easy to regard masochism in general as a pathological growth of specific feminine mental elements – in other words, as an abnormal intensification of certain features of the psychosexual character of woman – and to seek its origin in that sex (see below, p. 172). It should, however, be noted that, in woman, an inclination to subordination to man (which may also be regarded as an acquired, purposeful arrangement, a phenomenon of adaptation to social requirements) is to a certain extent a normal manifestation.

Part of the reason that the masochist cannot achieve the "poetry" of the symbolic act of subjection is because man lacks the vanity of the weakling who gains satisfaction exclusively from the display of power (as the ladies of the Middle Ages did in their relations with the love-serving knights). Instead, man wants to achieve solid advantages. Thus, the barbarian has his wife plow for him, and the civilized lover speculates about her dowry; she willingly endures both.

Cases of the pathological increase of this instinct of subjection, in the sense of feminine masochism, are probably frequent enough, but custom represses their manifestation. Many young women like nothing better than to kneel before their husbands or lovers. Among the lower classes of Slavs it is said that the wives feel hurt if they are not beaten by their husbands. A Hungarian official informs me that the peasant women of the Somogyer Comitate do not think they are loved by their husbands until they have received the first box on the ear as a sign of love.

It would probably be difficult for the physician to find cases of feminine masochism.[49] Intrinsic and extraneous restraints – modesty and custom – naturally constitute in woman insurmountable obstacles to the expression of perverse sexual instinct. Thus it happens that, up to the present time, only three cases of masochism in woman have been scientifically established.

Case 84.

Miss X., twenty-one years of age; her mother was a morphine maniac and died some years ago from nervous disorders. Her uncle (mother's side) was also a morphine-eater. One brother of the girl was neurasthenic, another was a masochist (wished to be beaten with a cane by proud, noble ladies). Miss X. had never had a severe illness, but at times suffered from headaches. She considered herself to be physically sound, but periodically insane; namely, when she was haunted by the fantasies which she thus described:

Since her earliest youth she imagined herself being whipped. She simply reveled in these ideas, and had the most intense desire to be severely punished with a rattan cane.

This desire, she claimed, originated from the fact that at the age of five a friend of her father's took her across his knees for fun, pretending to whip her. Since then she had longed for the opportunity of being caned, but to her great regret her wish was never realized. During these periods she imagined herself as absolutely helpless and fettered. The mere mention of the words "rattan cane" and "to whip" caused her intense excitement. She had associated these ideas with the male sex only for the last two years. Previously she only thought of a severe schoolmistress or simply a hand.

She presently wished to be the slave of a man whom she loved; she would kiss his feet if he would only whip her.

She did not understand that these manifestations were of a sexual nature.

A few quotations from her letters demonstrate the masochistic character of this case:

"In former years I seriously contemplated going into a lunatic asylum whenever these ideas worried me. I fell upon this idea while reading how the director of an insane asylum pulled a lady by the hair from her bed and beat her with a cane and a riding whip. I longed to be treated in a similar manner at such an institute, and have therefore unconsciously associated my ideas with the male sex. I liked best, however, to think of brutal, uneducated female warders beating me mercilessly.

"Lying (in fantasy) before him, he puts one foot on my neck while I kiss the other. I revel in the idea of being whipped by him; but this often changes, and I fantasize quite different scenes in which he beats me. At times I take the blows as so many tokens of love — he is at first extremely kind and tender, and then, in the excess of his love, he beats me. I fantasize that to beat me for love's sake gives him the highest pleasure. Often I have dreamed that I was his slave — but, mind you, not his female slave! For instance, I have imagined that he was Robinson and I the savage who served him. I often look at the pictures in which Robinson puts his foot on the neck of the savage. I now find an explanation of these strange fantasies: I look upon woman in general as low, far below man, but I am otherwise extremely proud and quite indomitable; thus it arises that I think as a man (who is by nature proud and superior). This renders my humiliation before the man I love more intense. I have also fantasized myself to be his female slave; but this does not suffice, for after all every woman can be the slave of her husband."

Case 85.

Miss von X., aged thirty-five; from a greatly predisposed family. For some years she had been in the initial stages of persecutorial paranoia. This sprang from cerebro-spinal neurasthenia, the origin of which was found to be sexual hyperexcitation. At twenty-four she was given to masturbation. As a result of disappointment in an engagement, she began to practice masturbation and psychic masturbation. *Inclination toward persons of her own sex never occurred.* The patient said: "At the age of six or eight I conceived a desire to be whipped. Because I had never been whipped, and had never been present when others were thus punished, I cannot understand how I came to have this strange desire. I can only think that it is congenital. With these ideas of being whipped I had a feeling of actual delight, and pictured in my fantasy how fine it would be to be whipped by one of my female friends. I never had any thought of being whipped by a man. I reveled in the idea, and never attempted any actual realization of my fantasies, which disappeared after my tenth year. Only when I read Rousseau's *Confessions,* at the age of thirty-four, did I understand what my longing for whippings meant, and that my abnormal ideas were like those of Rousseau."

Because of its original character and the reference to Rousseau, this case may with certainty be called a case of masochism. The fact that it is a female friend who is conceived in her imagination as whipping her is explained by the circumstance that here the masochistic desire was present in the mind of a child before the psychic sex life had developed and the instinct for the male had been awakened. Antipathic sexual instinct is here expressly excluded.

Case 86.

A physician in the General Hospital of Vienna had his attention drawn to a girl who used to call on the medical assistants of the institution. When meeting one of them she would express great delight at meeting a medical man and ask him to at once undertake a gynecological examination of her. She said she would resist, but he must take no notice; instead, he was to ask her to be calm and to proceed with the examination. If Dr. X. consented, the scene would be enacted as she desired. She would resist, and thus work herself up into a high state of sexual excitement. If the medical man refused to proceed any further, she would beg him not to desist. It was quite evident that the examination was only requested for the purpose of inducing the highest possible degree of orgasm. When the medical man refused coitus, she felt deeply offended, but begged him to let her come again. She never accepted money.

It was apparent that orgasm was not induced by mere palpation of the genitals, but lay in the act of force, which was always demanded, and which became the equivalent of coitus. It was evidently a manifestation belonging in the province of masochism in woman.

an attempt to explain masochism.

The facts of masochism are certainly among the most interesting in the domain of psychopathology. An attempt at explanation must first seek to distinguish the essential from the unessential. The distinguishing characteristic in masochism is certainly the unlimited subjection to the will of a person of the opposite sex (in sadism, on the contrary, the unlimited mastery of this person), with the awakening and accompaniment of lustful sexual feelings to the degree of orgasm. From the foregoing it is clear that the particular manner in which this relation of subjection or domination is expressed (see above), whether merely in symbolic acts, or whether there is also a desire to suffer pain at the hands of a person of the opposite sex, is a subordinate matter.

While sadism may be looked upon as a pathological intensification of the masculine sexual character in its psychic peculiarities, masochism represents, rather, a pathological degeneration of the distinctive psychic peculiarities of woman. Masculine masochism is undoubtedly frequent, however, and it is this that comes most frequently under observation and almost exclusively makes up the series of observed cases. The reason for this has been previously stated.

Two sources of masochism can be distinguished in the sphere of normal phenomena. The first is that in the state of lustful excitement every impression made by the person giving rise to the sexual stimulus, no matter what method is employed, is pleasing to the individual excited.

It is entirely physiological that playful taps and light blows should be taken for caresses,[50]

> Like the lover's pinch, which hurts and is desired.
> – *Anthony and Cleopatra*, act 5, scene 2

From here the step is not far to a state where the wish to experience a very intense impression at the hands of the consort leads to a desire for blows, etc., in cases of pathological intensification of lust; for pain is always a ready means of producing intense bodily impressions. Just as in sadism the sexual emotion leads to a state of exaltation in which the excessive motor excitement implicates neighboring nervous tracts, so in masochism an ecstatic state arises in which the rising flood of a single emotion ravenously devours and covers with lust every impression coming from the beloved person.

The second and, indeed, most important source of masochism is to be sought in a widespread phenomenon, which, though it is extraordinary and abnormal, by no means lies within the domain of sexual perversion.

I refer here to the very prevalent occurrence in which one individual becomes dependent on another of the opposite sex in a very extraordinary and remarkable manner – even to the loss of all independent willpower; a dependence that forces the party in subjection to tolerate acts and suffering that greatly compromise personal interest, and often lead to offenses against both morality and law.

This dependence, however, differs from the manifestations of normal life only in the intensity of the sexual feeling that here comes into play, and in the slight degree of willpower necessary for the maintenance of its equilibrium. The difference is one of intensity, not of quality, as in masochistic manifestations.

This dependence of one person upon another of the opposite sex – abnormal but not perverse and of great interest when regarded from a forensic standpoint – I designate "sexual bondage,"[51] because the relations and circumstances attending it have in all respects the character of bondage. The will of the ruling[52] individual dominates that of the person in subjection, just as the master's does that of the servant.

This "sexual bondage," as has been said, is certainly an abnormal phenomenon. It begins with the first deviation from the normal. The degree of dependence of one person upon another, or of two upon each other resulting from an individual peculiarity in the intensity of otherwise normal motives, constitutes the usual standard established by law and custom. Sexual bondage is not a perverse manifestation, however; the instinctive activities at work here are the same as those that set in motion – although with less violence – the psychic sex life which moves entirely within normal limits.

Fear of losing the companion and the desire to keep the beloved always content, amiable, and inclined to sexual intercourse are the motives here of the individual in subjection. An extraordinary degree of love – which, particularly in woman, does not always indicate a high degree of sensuality – and a weak character are the simple elements of this extraordinary process.[53]

The motive of the dominant individual is egotism that finds unlimited room for action.

The manifestations of sexual bondage are various in form, and the cases are numerous.[54] At every step in life we find men who have fallen into sexual bondage. Among married men, henpecked husbands belong to this category, particularly elderly men who marry young wives and try to overcome the disparity of years and physical defects by unconditional submission to the wife's every whim. Unmarried men of ripe maturity, who seek to better their last chance of love by unlimited sacrifice, are also to be enumerated here. Also found in this category are men of any age, who, seized by hot passion for a woman, meet coldness and calculation, and have to capitulate on hard conditions; men of loving natures who allow themselves to be persuaded into marriage by notorious prostitutes; men who leave everything and jeopardize their future to run after adventuresses;

husbands and fathers who leave wife and child to lay the income of a family at the feet of a harlot.

Numerous as the examples of masculine "bondage" are, however, every observer of life who is at all unprejudiced must allow that they are far from equal in number and importance to the cases of feminine "bondage." This is easily explained. For a man, love is almost always only an episode, and he has many other and important interests; for a woman, on the other hand, love is the principal thing in life, and, until the birth of children, always her first interest. After this it is still often her first thought, but always takes at least second place. More important, man ruled by this impulse can easily satisfy it in embraces for which he finds unlimited opportunities. Woman in the upper classes of society, if she has a husband, is bound to him alone; and even in the lower classes there are still great obstacles to polyandry. Therefore, *a woman's husband means for her the whole sex,* and his importance to her becomes great. It must also be considered that the normal relation established by law and custom between husband and wife is far from being one of equality. In itself it expresses a sufficient predominance of woman's dependence. The concessions she makes to her lover to retain the love that would be almost impossible for her to replace only plunges her deeper into bondage; and this increases the insatiable demands of husbands resolved to use their advantage and traffic in woman's readiness to sacrifice herself.

Here may be placed the fortune hunter, who for money allows himself to be enveloped in the easily created illusions of a maiden; the seducer, and the man who compromises wives, calculating on blackmail; the gilded army officer and the musician with the lion's mane, who know so well how to stammer "Thee or death!" as a means to pay debts and provide a life of ease. Here, too, belong the kitchen soldier, whose love the cook returns with love *plus* the means to satisfy a different appetite; the drinker, who consumes the savings of the mistress he marries; and the man who, with blows, compels the prostitute, on whom he depends for a living, to earn a certain sum for him daily. These are only a few of the innumerable forms of bondage into which woman is forced by her greater need of love and the difficulties of her position.

It was necessary to give the subject of "sexual bondage" brief consideration here, for in it may be clearly discerned the soil from which the main root of masochism springs. The relationship of these two phenomena of psychic sexual life is immediately apparent. Bondage and masochism both consist of the unconditional subjection of the individual affected with this abnormality to a person of the opposite sex, and of domination of the former by the latter.[55] The two phenomena, however, must be strictly differentiated; they are not different in degree, but in quality.

Sexual bondage is not a perversion and is not pathological; the elements from which it arises – love and weakness of will – are not perverse; it is only their simultaneous activity that produces the abnormal result which is so opposed to self-interest, and often to custom and law. The motive, in obedience to which the subordinated individual acts and endures tyranny, is the normal instinct toward woman (or man), the satisfaction of which is the price of bondage. The acts of the person in subjection, by means of which the bondage is expressed, are performed at the command of the ruling individual to satisfy selfishness, etc. For the subordinated individual they have no independent purpose; they are only the means to an end – to obtain or retain possession of the ruling individual. Finally, bondage is a result of love for a particular person; it first appears when this love is awakened.

In masochism, which is decidedly abnormal and is a perversion, this is all very different. The motive underlying the acts and suffering of the person in subjection is through the charm afforded by the tyranny in itself. There may, at the same time, be a desire for coitus with the dominant person, but the impulse is directed to the acts which serve to express the tyranny as the immediate objects of gratification. The acts through which masochism is expressed are, for the individual in subjection, not the means to an end, as in bondage, but an end in themselves. Finally, in masochism the longing for subjection is present, *a priori,* before an inclination to any particular object of love.

The connection between bondage and masochism may be assumed by reason of the correspondence of the two phenomena in the objective condition of dependence, notwithstanding the difference in their motives; and the transformation of the abnormality into the perversion probably takes place in the following manner: Anyone living for a long time in sexual bondage becomes disposed to acquire a slight degree of masochism. Love that willingly bears the tyranny of the loved one then becomes an immediate love of tyranny. *When the idea of being tyrannized is for a long time closely associated with the lustful thought of the beloved person, the lustful emotion is finally transferred to the tyranny itself, and the transformation to perversion is completed.* This is the manner in which masochism may be acquired by cultivation.[56]

Thus a mild degree of masochism may arise from "bondage" – that is, become acquired; but genuine, complete, deep-rooted masochism, with its feverish longing for subjection from the time of earliest youth, is congenital.

The explanation of the origin of the perversion of fully developed masochism – infrequent though it may be – is most probably to be found in the assumption that it arises from the more frequent abnormality of "sexual bondage," through which, now and then, *this abnormality is hereditarily transferred to a psychopathic individual in such a manner that it becomes transformed into a perversion.* It has previously been shown how a slight displacement of the psychic elements under consideration may effect this transition. Whatever effects associating habits may have on possible cases of acquired masochism, the same effects are produced by the varying tricks of heredity upon original masochism. No new element is thereby added to "bondage," but, on the contrary, the very element is deleted which cements love and dependence, and thereby distinguishes "bondage" from masochism and abnormality from perversion. It is quite natural that only the instinctive element is transmitted.

This transition from abnormality into perversion, through hereditary transference, takes place very easily when the psychopathic constitution of the descendant presents the other factor of masochism – i.e., what has been previously called its main root – the tendency of sexually hyperesthetic natures to assimilate all impressions coming from the beloved person with the sexual impression.

From these two elements – from "sexual bondage" on the one hand and from the above-mentioned tendency to sexual ecstasy, which apperceives even maltreatment with lustful emotion, on the other – the roots of which may be traced back to the field of physiological facts, masochism arises from the basis of psychopathic predisposition, insofar as its sexual hyperesthesia initially intensifies all the physiological accessories of the sex life and, finally, its abnormal accompaniments, to the pathological degree of perversion.[57]

At any rate, masochism, as a congenital sexual perversion, constitutes a functional sign of degeneration in (almost exclusively) hereditary taint; and this clinical deduction is confirmed in my cases of masochism and sadism. It is easy to demonstrate that the peculiar, psychically anomalous direction of the sex life represented in masochism is an original abnormality, and not cultivated in the predisposed individual by passive flagellation or through association of ideas, as Rousseau and Binet contend. This is shown by the numerous cases of masochism – in fact, the majority – in which flagellation never appears, in which the perverse impulse is directed exclusively to purely symbolic acts expressing subjection without any actual infliction of pain, as in case 50, for example.

The same conclusion – namely, that passive flagellation is not the nucleus around which all the rest is gathered – is reached when closer study is given to the cases in which passive flagellation plays a role, as in cases 50 and 52. Case 58 is particularly instructive in relation to this, for in this instance there can be no thought of a sexually stimulating effect by punishment received in youth. Moreover, in this case, connection with an early experience is not possible, for the situation constituting the object of principal sexual interest absolutely cannot be carried out by a child.

Finally, the origin of masochism from purely psychic elements, when contrasted with sadism (see below), is convincingly demonstrated. That passive flagellation occurs so frequently in masochism is simply explained by the fact that it is the most extreme means of expressing the condition of subjection.

Again, the decisive points in the differentiation of simple passive flagellation from flagellation dependent upon masochistic desire are as follows: in the former, the act is a means to render coitus, or at least ejaculation, possible; in the latter, it is a means of gratifying masochistic desires.

As we have already seen, masochists subject themselves to all kinds of maltreatment and suffering in which there can be no question of reflex excitation of lust. Since such cases are numerous, we must seek to ascertain in these acts (as well as in flagellation in masochists, which has a similar significance) the relation in which pain and lust stand to each other. A masochist describes it is as follows:

The relation is not of such a nature that what causes physical pain is simply perceived here as physical pleasure; for the person in a state of masochistic ecstasy feels no pain, either because, by reason of his emotional state (like that of the soldier in battle), the physical effect on his cutaneous nerves is not apperceived, or because (as with religious martyrs and enthusiasts), in the preoccupation of consciousness with lustful emotion, the idea of maltreatment remains merely a symbol, without its quality of pain.

To a certain extent there is overcompensation of physical pain in the psychic pleasure, and the excess remains in consciousness as psychic lust. This also undergoes an increase, because, either through reflex spinal influence or through a peculiar coloring of sensory impressions in the sensorium, a kind of hallucination of bodily pleasure takes place, with a vague localization of the objectively projected sensation.

In the self-torture of religious enthusiasts (fakirs, howling dervishes, religious flagellants) there is an analogous state, with a difference in the quality of pleasurable feeling. Here the conception of martyrdom is also apperceived without its pain; for consciousness is filled with the pleasurably colored idea of serving God, atoning for sins, deserving heaven, etc., through martyrdom.

In order to give masochism its proper place in the sphere of sexual perversion, we must proceed from the fact that it is a manifestation of psychic characteristics of the feminine type that transcends into pathological conditions, insofar as its determining marks are suffering, subjection to the will of others, and subjection to force. Among people of a lower class of culture the subjection of woman is extended even to brutality. This flagrant proof of dependence can even be felt by woman as sensual pleasure and accepted as a token of love. It is probable that the woman of high civilization looks upon the role of being overshadowed by the male consort as an acceptable situation which forms a portion of the lustful feeling developed in the sexual act. The daring and self-confident demeanor of man undoubtedly exercises a sexual charm over woman. Thus, the masochist imagines himself in a passive, feminine role toward his mistress whereby his sexual gratification is governed by his experiencing a successful illusion of complete subjection to the will of the consort. The pleasurable feeling, call it lust, resulting from this act does not differ per se from the feeling which woman derives from the sexual act.

The masochistically inclined individual seeks and finds an equivalent for his purpose by endowing the consort, in his imagination, with certain masculine psychic sexual characteristics – i.e., he does so in a perverse manner, insofar as the sadistic female partner constitutes his ideal.

From this emanates the deduction that masochism is, properly speaking, only a rudimentary form of antipathic sexual instinct. It is a partial *effemination* which has only apperceived the secondary sexual characteristics of the psychic sex life.

This assumption is supported by the fact that heterosexual masochists consider themselves merely as individuals endowed with feminine feelings.[58] Observation shows that they really possess feminine traits of character.[59] This explains why the masochistic element is so frequently found in homosexual men.[60]

In the female masochist these relations to antipathic sexual instinct are also to be found. Cf. case 84. Moll quotes a typical case of homosexuality in a woman afflicted with passive flagellantism and coprolagnia:

Case 87.

Miss X., aged twenty-six. At the age of six, mutual cunnilingus; then up to seventeen, lacking opportunities, solitary masturbation. Since then cunnilingus with various female friends, at times playing the passive, at other times the active role, always producing ejaculation in herself. For years coprolagnia. **She experienced the greatest pleasure licking the anuses of her female lovers and licking her girlfriend's menstrual blood. The same pleasurable effect was gained by being flogged on the buttocks by a strong, nude mistress.** The thought of performing coprolagnia with a man was repulsive to her. She obtained satisfaction in cunnilingus performed by a man only when she imagined that the act was performed by a woman, not by a man. She disdained coitus with a man. Erotic dreams were always of a homosexual nature and were confined to active or passive cunnilingus. **During mutual kissing she experienced the greatest pleasure from biting her partner,** preferably on the lobe of the ear, causing pain and subsequent swelling.

X. had always leaned toward male occupations and loved to be among men as one of them. From her tenth to her fifteenth year she worked in a relative's brewery, clad, if possible, in trousers and a leather apron. She was bright, intelligent and good-natured, and felt quite happy in her perverse, homosexual existence. She smoked and drank beer. Female larynx (Dr. Flatau), small, badly developed breasts, large hands and feet (Dr. Moll, *Intern. Zentralbl. f. Physiol. und Pathol. der Harn- und Sexualorgane,* vol. 4, no. 3).

masochism and sadism.

The perfect counterpart of masochism is sadism. While in the former there is a desire to suffer and be subjected to violence, in the latter there is a wish to inflict pain and use violence.

The parallelism is perfect. All the acts and situations used by the sadist in the active role become the object of the desire of the masochist in the passive role. In both perversions these acts advance from purely symbolic acts to severe maltreatment. Even murder, in which sadism reaches its acme, finds, as is shown in case 62 – of course, only in fantasy – its passive counterpart. Under favorable conditions, both perversions may occur with a normal sex life; in both, the acts in which they express themselves are preparatory to coitus or substitutes for it.[61]

But the analogy does not exist only in external manifestations; it also extends to the intrinsic character of both perversions. Both are to be regarded as original psychopathologies in mentally abnormal individuals who are affected with psychic sexual hyperesthesia, and also, usually, with abnormalities. In addition, with each of these perversions two constituent elements may be demonstrated, which have their roots in psychic facts lying within physiological limits. In masochism, as shown above, these elements lie in the fact that [1] in the state of sexual emotion every impression produced by the consort, independent of the manner of its production, is, per se, attended with lustful pleasure, which, when accompanied by sexual hyperesthesia, may go so far as to overcompensate all painful sensation; and in the fact that [2] "sexual bondage," dependent on mental factors – in themselves not perverse – may, under pathological conditions, become a perverse, pleasurable desire for subjection to the opposite sex, which – even if its inheritance from the female side is not presupposed – represents a pathological degeneration of the instinct of subordination, a psychic and physiological fact of woman.

In harmony with this, there are, likewise, two constituent elements that explain sadism, the origin of which may also be traced back within physiological limits. These are: the fact that [1] in sexual emotion, to a certain extent as an accompanying psychic excitation, an impulse may arise to influence the object of desire in every possible way and with the greatest possible intensity, which, in individuals sexually hyperesthetic, may degenerate into a craving to inflict pain; and the fact that [2], under pathological conditions, man's active role of winning woman may become an unlimited desire for subjugation.

Thus masochism and sadism represent perfect counterparts. It is also in harmony with this that the individuals affected with these perversions regard the opposite perversion in the other sex as their ideal, as shown by case 57, and also by Rousseau's *Confessions*.

In addition, the contrast of masochism and sadism may be used to invalidate the assumption that the former has its origin in the reflex effect of passive flagellation, and that all the rest is the product of association of related ideas, as Binet, in his explanation of Rousseau's case, thinks, and as Rousseau himself believed. In the active maltreatment that forms the object of the sadist's sexual desire there is, in fact, no irritation of his own sensory nerves by the act of maltreatment, so that there can be no doubt of the purely psychic character of the origin of this perversion. Sadism and masochism, however, are so related to each other, and correspond so well on all points with each other, that the one allows, by analogy, a conclusion for the other; and this alone is sufficient to establish the purely psychic character of masochism.

According to the above detailed contrast of all the elements and phenomena of masochism and sadism, and as a résumé of all observed cases, lust in the infliction of pain and lust in inflicted pain appear to be simply two different sides of the same psychic process, where the primary and essential thing is the consciousness of active or passive subjection, and where the combination of cruelty and lustful pleasure has only a secondary psychological significance. Acts of cruelty serve to express this subjection; first, because they are the most extreme means for the expression of this relation; and second, because they represent the most intense effect that one person, with or without coitus, can exert on another.

Sadism and masochism are the results of associations, just the same as all complicated manifestations of psychic life are associations. After the production of the simplest elements of consciousness, the psychic life then simply consists of associations and disassociations between these elements.

The chief point gained by this analysis is that sadism and masochism are not merely the results of accidental associations, occasioned by chance or an opportune coincidence, but are the results of associations springing from causes that exist under normal circumstances and that are easily produced under certain conditions – e.g., sexual hyperesthesia. An abnormally intensified sexual instinct spreads in every direction. It reaches into adjacent spheres, and amalgamates with their contents, thus producing the pathological associations that are the real essence of both these perversions.[62]

Of course, this need not always be so, for there are cases of hyperesthesia without perversion. But these cases of pure sexual hyperesthesia – at least, those of striking intensity – seem to be of rarer occurrence than those of perversion.

The cases in which sadism and masochism occur simultaneously in one individual are interesting, but are somewhat difficult to explain. Such cases are, for instance, cases 50, 57 and 67 of the present edition, and especially case 29 of the ninth edition. From case 29 it is evident that it is particularly the idea of subjection that, both actively and passively, forms the nucleus of the perverse desires. Traces of the same thing are also to be observed, more or less clearly, in many other cases. At any rate, one of the two perversions is always markedly predominant.

Due to this marked predominance of one perversion and the later appearance of the other in such cases, it may well be assumed that the predominating perversion is *original,* and that the other has been *acquired* over the course of time. The ideas of subjection and maltreatment, colored with lustful pleasure, either in an active or passive sense, have become deeply imbedded in such an individual. Occasionally the imagination is tempted to try the same ideas in an inverted role. There may even be realization of this inversion. Such attempts in imagination and in reality, are, however, usually soon seen as inadequate and abandoned for the original inclination.

Masochism and sadism also occur in combination with antipathic sexual instinct, and, in fact, in association with all forms and degrees of this perversion. The individual of inverted sexuality may be a sadist as well as a masochist (cf. cases 55 of the present and 49 of the seventh edition [see appendix, p. 530] and numerous cases in the subsequent series of cases of sexual inversion).

Wherever a sexual perversion has developed on the basis of a neuropathic individuality, sexual hyperesthesia, which may always be assumed to be present, may induce the phenomena of masochism and sadism – first one, then both combined; one arising from the other. Thus masochism and sadism appear as the fundamental forms of psychosexual perversion, which may make their appearance at any point in the domain of sexual aberration.[63]

[3] fetishism –
the association of lust with the idea of
certain portions of the female person,
or with certain articles of female attire.

IN THE introduction to this work concerning the psychology of the normal sexual life, it was shown that, within physiological limits, the pronounced preference for a certain portion of the body of persons of the opposite sex, particularly for a certain form of this part, can attain great psychosexual importance. Indeed, for many men – in fact, the majority – the special power of attraction possessed by certain forms and peculiarities can be regarded as the real principle of individualism in love.

This preference for certain particular physical characteristics in persons of the opposite sex (beside which, likewise, a marked preference for certain psychic characteristics may be demonstrated), following Binet ("Du Fétischisme dans l'amour," *Revue Philosophique,* 1887) and Lombroso (introduction to the Italian edition of the second edition of this work), I have called "fetishism"; because this enthusiasm for certain portions of the body (or even articles of attire) and the worship of them, in obedience to sexual impulses, frequently call to mind the reverence for relics, holy objects, etc., in religious cults. This physiological fetishism has already been described in detail.

Together with this physiological fetishism, however, there is, in the psychosexual sphere, an undoubted *pathological, erotic fetishism,* about which there are already numerous cases presenting phenomena having great clinical and psychiatric interest, and, under certain circumstances, having forensic importance as well. This pathological fetishism does not confine itself to certain parts of the body alone, but is even extended to inanimate objects, which, however, are almost always articles of female clothing, and thus stand in close relation to the female person.

This pathological fetishism is connected, through gradual transitions, with physiological fetishism, so that (at least in body fetishism) it is almost impossible to sharply define the beginning of the perversion. Moreover, the whole field of body fetishism does not really extend beyond the limits of things that normally stimulate the sexual instinct. Here the abnormality consists only in the fact that the whole sexual interest is concentrated on the impression made by a part of the person of the opposite sex, so that all other impressions fade and become more or less indifferent. Therefore, the body fetishist is not to be regarded as a monster of excess, like the sadist or masochist, but rather as a monster of weakness. What is abnormal is not what stimulates him, but rather what does not affect him – the limitation of sexual interest that has taken place in him. Of course, this limited sexual interest, within its narrower limits, is usually expressed with a correspondingly high and abnormal intensity.

It would seem reasonable to assume, as the distinguishing mark of pathological fetishism, the necessity for the presence of the fetish as an essential condition for the performance of coitus. But when the facts are more carefully studied, it is seen that this limitation is really only indefinite. There are numerous cases in which, even in the absence of the fetish, coitus is possible, but incomplete and forced (often with the help of fantasies relating to the fetish), and particularly unsatisfying and exhausting. In addition, closer study of the distinctive subjective psychic conditions in these cases shows that there are transitional states that range from mere physiological preferences to psychic impotence in the absence of the fetish.

It is therefore better, perhaps, to seek the pathological criterion of body fetishism in purely subjective psychic states. The concentration of the sexual interest on a certain portion of the body that has no direct relation to sex (e.g., breasts and external genitals) – a peculiarity to be emphasized – often leads body fetishists to such a condition that they do not regard coitus as the real means of sexual gratification, but rather some form of manipulation of that portion of the body that is effectual as a fetish. This perverse instinct of body fetishists may be taken as the pathological criterion, whether actual coitus is still possible or not.

Fetishism of inanimate objects or articles of dress, however, in all cases, may well be regarded as a pathological phenomenon, since its object falls outside the circle of normal sexual stimuli. Even here there is a certain outward correspondence with processes of the normal psychic sex life, while the inner connection and meaning of pathological fetishism are entirely different. In the ecstatic love of a mentally normal man, a handkerchief or shoe, a glove or letter, the flower "she gave" or a lock of hair, etc., may become the object of worship, but only because they represent a mnemonic symbol of the beloved person – absent or dead – whose whole personality is reproduced by them. The pathological fetishist has no such relations. The fetish constitutes the entire content of his idea. When he becomes aware of its presence, sexual excitement occurs, and the fetish makes itself felt.[64]

According to all observations thus far made, pathological fetishism seems to arise only on the basis of a psychopathic constitution that is for the most part hereditary, or on the basis of existent mental disease.

Thus it happens that it often appears combined with other (original) sexual perversions that arise on the same basis. Not infrequently fetishism occurs in various forms in combination with inverted sexuality, sadism, and masochism. Indeed, certain forms of body fetishism (hand and foot fetishism) probably have a more or less distinct connection with sadism and masochism (see below).

If, however, fetishism also rests upon a general congenital psychopathic disposition, this perversion is still not, like those previously considered, essentially of an original nature; it is not congenitally perfect, as we can well assume sadism and masochism to be.

While in the sexual perversions described in the preceding chapters we have seen only cases of a congenital type, here we will see only *acquired* cases. Aside from the fact that often in fetishism the causative circumstance of its acquirement can be traced, the physiological conditions are nevertheless lacking, which in sadism and masochism, by means of sexual hyperesthesia, are intensified to perversions, and justify the assumption of congenital origin. In fetishism, every case requires an event which lays the groundwork for the perversion.

As has been said, it is, of course, physiological in sexual life to be partial to one or another of woman's charms, and to be enthusiastic about it; but concentration of the entire sexual interest on such a partial impression is the essential thing here, and for this concentration there must be a particular reason in every individual affected. Therefore, we can accept Binet's conclusion that *in the life of every fetishist there can be assumed to have been some event which determined the association of lustful feeling with the single impression.* This event must be sought in the time of early youth, and typically occurs in connection with the first awakening of the sex life. This first awakening is associated with some partial sexual impression (since it is always a thing standing in some relation to woman),[65] and stamps it for life as the principal object of sexual interest. The circumstances under which the association arises are usually forgotten; the result of the association alone is retained. The general predisposition to psychopathic states and the sexual hyperesthesia of such individuals are all that is original here.[66]

Like the other perversions thus far considered, erotic (pathological) fetishism may also express itself in strange, unnatural, and even criminal acts: gratification with the female person in an indecent place, theft and robbery of objects of fetishism, pollution of such objects, etc. Here, too, whether and to what extent such acts are performed depend upon the intensity of the perverse impulse and the relative power of opposing ethical motives.

The perverse acts of fetishists, like those of other sexually perverse individuals, may either alone constitute the entire external sex life, or occur parallel with the normal sexual act. This depends upon the condition of physical and psychic sexual power and the degree of excitability to normal stimuli that has been retained. Where excitability is diminished, the sight or touch of the fetish often serves as a necessary preparatory act.

The great practical importance which attaches to the facts of fetishism, in accordance with what has been said, lies in two factors. First, pathological fetishism is commonly a cause of *psychic impotence.*[67] Because the object upon which the fetishist's sexual interest is concentrated stands, in itself, in no *immediate* relation to the normal sexual act, it often happens that, due to his perversion, the fetishist diminishes his excitability to normal stimuli, or, at least, is capable of coitus only by concentrating his fantasy upon his fetish. In this perversion, and in the difficulty of its adequate gratification (just as in the other perversions of the sexual instinct), lie conditions favoring psychic and physical masturbation, which again deleteriously affects the constitution and sexual power. This is especially true for youthful individuals; particularly those who, because of opposing ethical and aesthetic motives, shrink from the realization of their perverse desires.

Second, fetishism is of great *forensic importance*. Just as sadism may extend to murder and the infliction of bodily injury, so may fetishism lead to theft and even to robbery for the possession of the desired articles.

Erotic fetishism has for its object either a certain portion of the body of a person of the opposite sex, or a certain article or material of wearing apparel of the opposite sex. (Only cases of pathological fetishism in men have thus far been observed, and therefore only portions of the female person and attire are spoken of here.) In accordance with this, fetishists fall into three groups.

[a] the fetish is a part of the female body.

Just as, in physiological fetishism, the eye, the hand, the foot and the hair of woman frequently become fetishes, likewise, in the pathological domain, the same portions of the body become the sole objects of sexual interest. What makes these cases pathological is the exclusive concentration of interest on these parts, beside which everything else feminine fades, and all other sexual value of woman may sink to nil, so that, instead of coitus, strange manipulations of the fetish become the object of desire.

Case 88.

X., aged thirty-four, teacher in the *Gymnasium*. In childhood he suffered from convulsions. At the age of ten he began to masturbate, with lustful feelings, which were connected with very strange ideas. He was particularly partial to women's eyes; but because he wished to imagine some form of coitus, and was absolutely innocent in sexual matters, he evolved the idea of making the nostrils the seat of the female sexual organs in order to avoid too great a separation from the eyes. His vivid sexual desires then revolved around this idea. He sketched drawings representing correct Greek profiles of female heads, but the nostrils were so large that **insertion of the penis** would have been possible.

One day, in an omnibus, he saw a girl in whom he thought he recognized his ideal. He followed her to her home and immediately proposed to her. Shown the door, he returned again and again, until arrested. X. had never had sexual intercourse (Binet, op. cit.).

Nose fetishism is seldom encountered. The following rare bit of poetry comes to me from England:

> O sweet and pretty little nose, so charming unto me;
> O were I but the sweetest rose, I'd give my scent to thee.
> O make it full with honey sweet, that I may suck it all;
> T'would be for me the greatest treat, a real festival.
> How sweet and how nutritious your darling nose does seem.
> It would be more delicious, than strawberries and cream.

Hand fetishists are numerous. The following case is not really pathological. It is given here as a transitional instance:

Case 89.

B., from a neuropathic family; very sensual, mentally intact. At the sight of the hand of a beautiful young lady he was always charmed and felt sexual excitement to the extent of erection. It was his delight to kiss and press such hands. As long as they were covered with gloves he felt unhappy. By pretexts he tried to get hold of such hands. He was indifferent to the foot. If the beautiful hands were ornamented with rings, his lust was increased. Only the living hand, not its image, caused him this lustful excitement. It was only when he was exhausted sexually by frequent coitus that the hand lost its sexual charm. At first the memory-picture of female hands disturbed him, even while at work (Binet, op. cit.).

Binet states that such cases of enthusiasm for the female hand are numerous. Here it may be recalled that, according to case 25, a man may be partial to the female hand as a result of sadistic impulses; and that, according to case 52, the same thing may be due to masochistic desires. Thus such cases have more than one meaning. It does not follow, however, that all, or even a majority, of the cases of hand fetishism allow or require a sadistic or masochistic explanation.

The following interesting case, which has been studied in detail, shows that, although at first a sadistic or masochistic element seems to have exercised an influence, at the time of the individual's maturity and the complete development of the perversion, the perversion contained neither of these elements. Of course, it is possible that, in the course of time, they disappeared; but here the assumption of the origin of the fetishism in an accidental association meets every requirement:

Case 90.

A case of *hand fetishism*, communicated by Albert Moll. P. L., aged twenty-eight, a merchant in Westphalia. Aside from the fact that the patient's father was remarkably moody and somewhat quick-tempered, nothing of an hereditary nature could be proved in the family. At school the patient was not very diligent; he was never able to concentrate his attention on any one subject for any length of time; on the other hand, from childhood he had a great inclination for music. His temperament was always nervous.

In August 1890 he came to me complaining of headaches and abdominal pain, which in every way gave the impression of being neurasthenic. The patient also said he had no energy. Only after specifically directed questions did the patient make the following statements concerning his sexual life. As far as he could remember, the beginning of sexual excitement occurred in his seventh year. Whenever he saw a boy of his own age urinate and caught sight of his genitals, he became lustfully excited. L. states with certainty that this excitement was associated with strongly accentuated erections. Led astray by another boy, L. learned to masturbate at the age of seven or eight. "Being of a very excitable nature," said L., "I practiced masturbation very frequently until my eighteenth year, without gaining any clear idea of the evil results or the meaning of the practice." He was particularly fond of practicing mutual masturbation with some of his school friends, but it was by no means a matter of indifference who the other boy was; on the contrary, only a few of his companions could satisfy him in this respect. When asked what particularly caused him to prefer this or that boy, L. replied that the *white, beautifully formed hand* of a school friend impelled him to practice mutual masturbation with him. L. further remembered that frequently, at the beginning of the gymnastic lesson, he would exercise by himself on an isolated bar. He did this for the purpose of exciting himself as much as possible, and he was so successful that, without using his hand and without ejaculation – L. was still too young – he had lustful pleasure. Another early event remembered by L. is interesting. One day his favorite companion, N., who practiced mutual masturbation with him, proposed that L. should try to get hold of his

(N.'s) penis, and he would do all he could to prevent it. L. acquiesced. In this way masturbation was directly combined with a struggle between the two, in which N. was always conquered. The struggle finally ended with N. being compelled to allow L. to practice masturbation on him. L. assured me that this kind of masturbation had given him, as well as N., special pleasure. In this way L. continued to practice masturbation very frequently until his eighteenth year. Warned by a friend, he then began to struggle with all his might against this evil habit. He became more and more successful, and finally, after the first performance of coitus, he stopped the practice of masturbation entirely. But this was only accomplished in his twenty-second year. It now seemed incomprehensible to the patient – who said he was filled with disgust at the thought – that he could have ever found pleasure in performing masturbation with other boys. Now, nothing could induce him to touch another man's genitals, the sight of which was even unpleasant to him. He had lost all inclination for men, and felt attracted to women exclusively.

It must be mentioned, however, that although L. had a decided inclination for the female sex, he presented an abnormal phenomenon.

The essential thing in woman that excited him was the sight of her beautiful hands. L. was far more impressed when he touched a beautiful female hand than he would have been had he seen the woman in a state of complete nudity. The extent of L.'s preference for beautiful female hands is shown by the following incident:

L. knew a beautiful young lady possessed of every charm, but her hands were quite large and not beautifully formed, and often they were not as clean as L. wished them to be. For this reason it was not only impossible for L. to conceive a deeper interest in the lady, but he was not able to even touch her. L. believed that there was nothing more disgusting to him than dirty fingernails; this alone would make it impossible for him to touch a woman who in all other respects was most beautiful. At one time L., as a substitute for coitus, would induce a prostitute to perform genital manipulation with her hand until ejaculation took place.

When asked what there was about a woman's hand that attracted him in particular; whether he saw in it a symbol of power, and whether it gave him pleasure to be directly humiliated by a woman, the patient answered that only the *beautiful form* of the hand charmed him; that it afforded him no gratification to be humiliated by a woman; and that he had never had any thought to regard the hand as the symbol or instrument of a woman's power. The preference for the hand was still so great that the patient had greater pleasure when his genitals were touched by it than when he performed coitus vaginally. Yet the patient preferred to perform coitus, because it seemed to him to be natural, while the former seemed abnormal. The touch of a beautiful female hand on his body immediately caused him to have an erection; he thought that kissing and other contacts did not exert nearly so strong an influence. Only in recent years had the patient performed coitus frequently, but it had always been very difficult for him to become determined to do it. Furthermore, in coitus he did not find the complete satisfaction he sought. When he found himself near a woman whom he would like to possess, however, sometimes the mere sight of her caused his sexual excitement to become so intense that ejaculation resulted. L. expressly said that during this process he did not intentionally touch or press his genitals; ejaculation under such circumstances afforded him much more pleasure than he experienced in actual coitus.[68]

The patient's dreams were never about coitus. When he had pollutions at night, they were almost always associated with thoughts other than those of the normal man. The patient's dreams were of events from his school days, when, besides the mutual masturbation described, he had ejaculations whenever he became anxiously excited. When, for example, the teacher dictated an extemporaneous exercise and L. was unable to follow in translation, ejaculation often occurred.[69] The pollutions that now occasionally occurred at night were accompanied only by dreams that had the same or a similar subject – i.e., the events at school just mentioned. Because of his unnatural feeling and sensibility, the patient thought he was incapable of loving a woman permanently.

Treatment of the patient's perversion was not possible.

This case of hand fetishism certainly does not depend on masochism or sadism, but is to be explained simply on the basis of early indulgence in mutual masturbation. Neither is there antipathic sexual instinct. Before the sexual appetite was clearly conscious of its object, the hands of schoolmates were used. As soon as the instinct for the opposite sex became evident, the interest for the hand was transferred to that of women.

In hand fetishists, who according to Binet are numerous, it is possible that other associations lead to the same result.

Next to the hand fetishists, naturally, come the *foot fetishists*. While glove fetishism, which belongs to the next group of object fetishism, seldom takes the place of hand fetishism, we find shoe and boot fetishism, of which innumerable cases are occurring everywhere, taking the place of enthusiasm for the naked female foot. It is easy to see the reason for this. The female hand is usually seen uncovered; the foot, covered. Thus the early associations which determine the direction of the sex life are naturally connected with a naked hand and a covered foot.

This assumption is certainly correct with regard to those who have grown up in large cities, and easily explains the scarcity of foot fetishism,[70] which will be elucidated by the following cases.

Case 91.

Foot fetishism. Acquired inverted sexuality. Mr. X., civil servant, twenty-nine years of age; mother neuropathic, father diabetic. He had good mental qualities, was of nervous disposition, but never suffered from nervous disease and showed no signs of degeneration. Patient distinctly recalled that even at the age of six he became sexually excited when he saw the naked feet of women, and was impelled to follow the women, or watch them when at work.

One night, at the age of fourteen, he slipped into the room where his sister slept and kissed her foot. At the age of eight he began to masturbate spontaneously, thinking all the while of the naked feet of women.

At sixteen he often took shoes and stockings of servant girls to bed with him and, while fingering them, excited himself into masturbation.

At the age of eighteen he began to have sexual intercourse with persons of the opposite sex. He had full power, and coitus satisfied him without the aid of a fetish. He did not have the slightest sexual inclination toward men or men's feet.

At the age of twenty-four a great change came over his sexual feelings and his physical condition. Patient became neurasthenic and began to experience sexual inclination toward males. No doubt excessive masturbation brought about neurosis and inverted sexuality, to which he was led by excessive sexual desire that had not been satisfied by coitus, and by the sight (accidental or otherwise) of female feet. As neurasthenia (sexual at first) increased, a rapid cessation of libido, power, and gratification set in with regard to women. At the same time, inclination toward his own sex developed and his fetishism was transferred to males.

By the age of twenty-five he had rarely enjoyed coitus with women, and without satisfaction. He had lost nearly all interest in the feet of women. The craving to have sexual intercourse with men grew stronger daily. When he was transferred to a large city he found the long-wished-for opportunity and actually reveled with intense passion in this unnatural love.

He ejaculated during these acts with the utmost voluptuousness. By and by the sight of a sympathetic man, especially if he were barefoot, sufficed.

The subject of his nocturnal pollutions was then intercourse with men in the fetishistic sense (feet). Shoes did not interest him. The naked foot was his charm. He often felt impelled to follow men in the street, hoping to find an occasion to take off their shoes. As a substitute he went barefoot himself. At times he was driven to walk along the street in his bare feet, thereby experiencing the most intense lustful feelings. If he resisted, agony, trembling, and palpitation of the heart set in. At night, for hours, he often yielded to this impulse, even in stormy, rainy weather, not minding the many risks and personal dangers to which, by so doing, he exposed himself.

He carried the shoes in his hand, became sexually excited, and found satisfaction only in spontaneous or induced ejaculation. He felt envious of navvies and the poor who could go barefoot without attracting attention.

His happiest moments were the times he spent in a hydropathic establishment, à la Kneipp, where he was allowed to go barefoot with the other men under treatment.

An awkward affair, the result of his perverse sexual practices, sobered him. He sought safety from his unnatural sexual existence by consulting a physician who sent him to me.

The patient did his utmost to abstain from masturbation and perverse connection with men. He underwent treatment for neurasthenia in a hydropathic institute and regained some interest in the gentle sex, with his foot fetishism serving as a bridge. He once had, with a degree of pleasure, coitus with a barefooted peasant girl who acceded to his wishes, and later on visited prostitutes a few times, but without gratification. He then turned again to persons of his own sex, backslid totally, and felt irresistibly drawn to tramps and farm laborers, whom he paid for the favor of kissing their feet. An attempt to rescue the unfortunate man with suggestive treatment was wrecked due to the impossibility of removing an enervation beyond therapeutic aid.

Case 92.

Foot fetishism with continued heterosexuality. Mr. Y., fifty years of age, bachelor, belonged to high society. Consulted a physician because of "nervous" troubles. Tainted, nervous from childhood, very sensitive to cold and heat, and troubled with delusions that assumed the character of transient persecutorial dementia. For instance, when he sat in a restaurant, he imagined that everybody stared at him, talked about him, and made fun of him. As soon as he rose from his chair this feeling left him and he no longer believed his fantasies.

He never felt settled for any length of time, and moved about from one place to another. Occasionally he engaged rooms at a hotel, but never went there because of his peculiar delusions.

He never had much libido. All his sentiments were heterosexual. Now and then he found gratification in coitus, which he claimed was normal.

Y. admitted that his sexual life was peculiar from early youth. Neither women nor men excited him sexually, but the sight of female feet, whether of children or of grown-up women, did excite him. No other parts of the female body attracted him.

If by chance he saw the naked feet of female gypsies or tramps, he would gaze at them for hours and was driven by a "terrible" impulse **to rub his genitals against their feet.** Thus far he had successfully resisted this impulse.

What annoyed him most was seeing these feet covered with dirt. He preferred to see them well-washed and clean. He could not say how this fetishism originated in him (from a communication by Professor Forel).

Moll, in his recent research on sexual desire, p. 288, relates a most interesting case of foot fetishism similar to case 91 above, insofar as the patient, due to the force of the fetish, became homosexual.

Shoe fetishism also finds its place in the category of dress fetishism, to be discussed later; however, because of its demonstrable masochistic character in the majority of cases, it has been, for the most part, already described above.

Besides the *eye, hand,* and *foot,* the *mouth* and *ear* often play the role of a fetish. Moll (op. cit.) mentions such cases, among others. (Cf. Belot's romance, *La bouche de Madame X,* which, Belot states, rests upon actual observation.)

The following remarkable case came under my personal observation:

C a s e   9 3 .

A gentleman of very bad heredity consulted me concerning impotence that was driving him almost to despair. While he was young, his fetish was women of plump form. He married such a lady, and was happy and potent with her. After a few months the lady fell very ill, and lost much weight. When, one day, he tried to resume his marital duty, he was absolutely impotent, and remained so. If, however, he attempted coitus with plump women, he was perfectly potent.

Even physical defects become fetishes.

C a s e   9 4 .

X., twenty-eight years of age; family heavily tainted; neurasthenic; lack of self-confidence and frequent depression, with fits of suicidal intentions, which he had great trouble warding off. The smallest worries threw him out of temper, and filled him with despair. He was an engineer in a factory in Russian Poland, a man of robust frame, without signs of degeneration. He complained of a peculiar mania, which caused him to doubt his sanity. In his seventeenth year he would become sexually excited at the sight of physical defects in women, especially lameness and disfigured feet. He was not conscious of the original associative connection between his libido and these defects in women.

From puberty he found himself under the bane of this fetishism, which was painful to him. Normal women had no attraction for him. If a woman, however, was afflicted with lameness or with contorted or disfigured feet, she exercised a powerful sensual influence over him, whether she was otherwise pretty or ugly.

In his dreams, accompanied by pollutions, the forms of limping women were always before him. At times he could not resist the temptation to imitate their gait, which caused vehement orgasm, with lustful ejaculation. He claimed to have strong libido, and suffered intensely when his sexual desire remained unsatisfied. Despite these facts, he had coitus for the first time when he was twenty-two years of age, and then only five times. He felt, however, not the slightest satisfaction, in spite of complete ability. He thought that the chance to mate with a limping woman would give him intense pleasure. At any rate, he never wished to marry anyone other than a lame woman.

From his twentieth year the patient manifested fetishism for garments. It often sufficed to put on female stockings, shoes and drawers. He bought such wearing apparel at times, and, putting it on secretly, became lustfully excited and ejaculated. Garments that had been worn by women had no attraction for him. He would gladly prefer to wear female garb, so as to keep up sensual emotions, but had not yet dared to do so for fear of being detected.

His sex life was reduced to these practices. He was definite in asserting that he was never addicted to masturbation. Quite recently he had been, in consequence of his neurasthenic afflictions, much troubled with pollutions.

Case 95.

Z., gentleman, family tainted. Even in early childhood he always felt great sympathy with the lame and the crippled. He used to limp about the room on two brooms in lieu of crutches or, when unobserved, go limping about the streets; at that time, however, no sexual significance was coupled with the idea. Gradually, the thought supervened that he would like "as a pretty lame child" to meet a pretty girl who would express sympathy for his affliction. Sympathy from men he disdained. Z. was brought up in a rich man's house by a private tutor, and claimed that up to his twentieth year he was unaware of the difference in sexes. His feelings were confined to the idea of being pitied by a pretty girl for being lame, or extending the same sympathy to a lame girl himself. Gradually, erotic emotions associated themselves with this fantasy and at the age of twenty he succumbed to temptation and masturbated for the first time. From then on he practiced this act often. Sexual neurasthenia supervened and an irritable weakness took hold of him, to such an extent that the very sight of a girl with a halting gait induced ejaculation. When masturbating, or in his erotic dreams, the idea of the limping girl was always the controlling element. The personality of the limping girl was a matter of indifference to Z., his interest being centered solely on the limping foot. He never had coitus with a girl thus afflicted. He never felt an inclination for it and did not think he could be potent under the circumstances. His perverse fantasies revolved only around masturbating against the foot of a lame female. At times he anchored his hope on the thought that he might succeed in winning and marrying a chaste lame girl; that, because of his love for her, she would take pity on him and free him of his crime by "transferring his love from the sole of her foot to the foot of her soul." He sought deliverance in this thought. His present existence was one of untold misery.

Case 96.

Mr. V., aged thirty, civil servant; parents neuropathic. From the age of seven he had, for many years, a lame girl of the same age as a playmate.

At the age of twelve, nervously disposed and hypersexually inclined, the boy began to masturbate spontaneously. At that time puberty set in, and undoubtedly the first sexual emotions toward the other sex coincided with the sight of the lame girl.

Subsequently, only limping women excited him sexually. His fetish was a pretty lady who, like the companion of his childhood, limped with the *left* foot.

Always heterosexual, but abnormally sensual, he promptly sought relations with the opposite sex, but was absolutely impotent with women who were not lame. Virility and gratification were most strongly elicited if the prostitute limped with the left foot, but he was also successful if the lameness was in the right foot. Due to his fetishism, the opportunities for coitus seldom occurred, so he resorted to masturbation, but found it a disgusting and miserable substitute. His sexual anomaly rendered him very unhappy, and he was often close to committing suicide, but regard for his parents prevented him.

This moral affliction culminated in the desire for marriage with a sympathetic lame lady. Unfortunately, because he could not love the soul of such a wife, but only her defect of lameness, he considered such a union a profanation of matrimony and an unbearable, ignoble existence. On this account he had often thought of resignation and castration.

When V. came to me for advice I obtained, in my examination of him, only negative results regarding signs of degeneration, nervous disease, etc.

I enlightened the patient on the subject, and told him that it was difficult, if not impossible, for medical science to obliterate a fetishism so deeply rooted in old associations, but expressed the hope that if he made a limping maid happy in wedlock he himself would find happiness also.

Descartes, who himself (*Traité des Passions,* vol. 136) expresses some opinions concerning the origin of peculiar affections in associations of ideas, was always partial to cross-eyed women, because the object of his first love had such a defect (Binet, op. cit.).

Lydston (*A Lecture on Sexual Perversion,* Chicago, 1890) reports the case of a man who had a love affair with a woman whose right lower extremity had been amputated. After separating from her he searched for other women with a similar defect. A negative fetish!

A peculiar variety of body fetishism may be found in the following case (strongly complicated with sadistic elements), in which *fine white virgin skin* is the fetish, and sadism leads to lustful acts of cruelty (as an equivalent to coitus), even to anthropophagy (cf. p. 90 et seq.), for which the deeply degenerated and probably epileptic patient seeks to find a substitute in self-mutilation and autophagy.

Case 97.

L., laborer, was arrested because he had cut a large piece of skin from his left forearm with a pair of scissors in a public park.

He confessed that for a long time he had been craving to eat a piece of the *fine white skin of a maiden,* and that for this purpose he had been lying in wait for such a victim with a pair of scissors; but, as he had been unsuccessful, he desisted from his intention and instead had cut his own skin.

His father was an epileptic, and his sister was an imbecile. Up to his seventeenth year he suffered from bed-wetting, was dreaded by everyone because of his rough and irascible nature, and was dismissed from school because of his insubordination and viciousness.

He began masturbation at an early age, and preferred to read pious books. His character showed traits of superstition, proneness toward the mystic, and showy acts of devotion.

When he was thirteen his lustful anomaly awoke at the sight of a beautiful young girl who had fine white skin. The impulse to bite off a piece of that skin and eat it became paramount. No other parts of the female body excited him. He never had any desire for sexual intercourse, and never attempted such.

Rather than use his teeth, he hoped to achieve his end more easily with the aid of scissors. Thus, for years he always carried a pair with him. On several occasions his efforts were nearly successful. Since the previous year he had found it most difficult to bear his failures any longer, so he decided upon a substitute – namely, each time he had unsuccessfully pursued a girl, he would cut a piece of skin from his own arm, thigh or abdomen and eat it. *Imagining that it was the skin of the girl whom he had pursued,* he would obtain orgasm and ejaculation while masticating his own skin.

Many large, deep wounds, as well as numerous scars, were found on his body.

During the act of self-mutilation, and for a long time afterward, he suffered severe pains, but they were overcompensated by the lustful feelings he experienced while eating the raw flesh, especially when the flesh dripped with blood and he succeeded in his illusion that it was **virgin skin.** The mere sight of a knife or scissors sufficed to provoke this perverse impulse, which threw him into a state of anxiety, accompanied by profuse perspiration, vertigo, palpitation of the heart, and a craving for **female skin.** He had to, with scissors in hand, follow the woman that attracted him, but he did not lose consciousness or self-control, for at the acme of the crisis he took from his own body what was denied him from the body of the girl. During the whole crisis he had erection and orgasm, and at the moment he began to chew the piece of his skin, ejaculation. After that he felt greatly relieved and comforted.

L. was quite conscious of the pathological aspect of his condition. Of course, this dangerous character was sent to an insane asylum, where he attempted suicide (Magnan, *Psychiatrische Vorlesungen,* German translation by Möbius, nos. 4-5, p. 49).

An interesting category is formed by the *hair fetishists.* The transition from "admirer of woman's hair" within physiological limits to pathological fetishism is easy. The beginning of the pathological series is formed by those cases in which the hair of a woman simply makes a sensual impression and incites the desire to cohabit. Next are those whose virility is only possible with a woman who possesses this particular fetish. Various senses (sight, smell, hearing, crepitant sounds, as well as touch, as with velvet and silk fetishists; see below) are possibly drawn into the activity of the hair fetishism as the fetishists receive lustful impulses.

The end of the series is formed by those for whom the hair of a woman suffices (even when it is severed from the body, and is no longer a part of the living body, per se, but is only matter, even a mercantile article) to excite libido and sensual gratification by way of physical or psychic masturbation, and eventually through contact of the genitals with the fetish.[71] An interesting instance of hair fetishism belonging to this last category is related by Dr. Gemy, under the title of "Historie des peruques aphrodisiaques," in *La médecine internationale,* September 1894.

Case 98.

A lady told Dr. Gemy that on her wedding night and the night that followed, her husband contented himself with kissing her, and running his fingers through her wealth of tresses. He then fell asleep. On the third night, Mr. X. produced an immense wig, with abundant long hair, and begged his wife to put it on. As soon as she had done so, he richly compensated her for his neglected marital duties. In the morning he again showed extreme tenderness while he caressed the wig. When Mrs. X. removed the wig, she at once lost all charm for her husband. Mrs. X. recognized this as a hobby, and readily yielded to the wishes of her husband, whom she loved dearly, and whose libido depended upon the wearing of the wig. It was remarkable, however, that a particular wig had the desired effect for only a fortnight or three weeks at a time. It had to be made of thick, long hair, but its color was unimportant.

The result of this marriage, after five years, was two children and a collection of seventy-two wigs.

The following case, observed by Magnan and reported by Thoinot (op. cit., p. 419), is that of a man with antipathic sexual instinct, to whom the actual existence of the fetish was an essential condition for potency.

Case 99.

X., aged twenty, inverted sexually. Only loved men with large bushy mustaches. One day he met a man who was his ideal. He invited him to his home, but was unspeakably disappointed when the man removed an artificial mustache. Only when the visitor returned the ornament to his upper lip did he exercise his charm over X. once more and restored X. to complete virility.

In those cases where the female hair as mere matter possesses the properties of a fetish, it frequently happens that the fetishist seeks to possess himself of woman's hair by unlawful acts. These cases belong to the group of hair despoilers, of no slight importance from the forensic aspect.[72]

Case 100.

A hair despoiler. P., aged forty, artistic, locksmith, single. His father was temporarily insane, and his mother was very nervous. Although well-developed and intelligent, he was affected early with tics and delusions. He had never masturbated. He loved platonically, and often busied himself with matrimonial plans. Although on rare occasions he had coitus with prostitutes, he felt disgusted rather than satisfied with such intercourse. Three years ago he was overtaken by misfortune (financial ruin), in addition to which he had a febrile disease, with delirium. These things had a very bad effect on his hereditarily predisposed nervous system. On August 28, 1889, P. was arrested at the Trocadéro in Paris, *in flagranti,* as he forcibly cut off a young girl's lock of hair. He was arrested with the hair in his hand and a pair of scissors in his pocket. He excused himself on the basis of momentary mental confusion and an unfortunate, irresistible passion; he confessed that on ten occasions he had cut off hair, which he took great delight in keeping at home. On searching his home, sixty-five switches and tresses of hair were found, sorted into packets. P. had already been arrested once, on December 15, 1886, under similar circumstances, but was released for lack of evidence.

P. stated that, for the last three years, when he was alone in his room at night, he felt ill, anxious, excited and dizzy, and was then troubled by the impulse to touch female hair. When it happened that he could actually take a young girl's lock of hair in his hand, he felt intensely excited sexually, and had erection and ejaculation without touching the girl in any other way. On reaching home, he would feel ashamed of what had taken place; the wish to possess hair, however, always accompanied by great sexual pleasure, became more

and more powerful in him. He wondered why previously, even in the most intimate intercourse with women, he had experienced no such feeling. One evening he could not resist
the impulse to cut off a girl's lock of hair. At home, with the hair in his hand, the sensuous process was repeated. He was forced to rub his body with the hair and envelop his
genitals in it. Finally, quite exhausted, he grew ashamed, and could not trust himself to go
out for several days. After months of rest, he was again impelled to possess female hair,
indifferent as to whose it might be. If he attained his goal, he felt himself possessed by a
supernatural power and unable to give up his booty. If he could not attain the object of his
desire, he became greatly depressed, hurried home, and there reveled in his collection of
hair. He combed and fondled it, and thus had intense orgasm, satisfying himself with
masturbation. Hair exposed in the showcases of hairdressers made no impression on him;
he required hair hanging down from a female head.

At the height of his act he was in such a state of excitement that he had only imperfect
apperception and subsequent recollection of what he had done. When he touched the
hair with the scissors he had erection, and, at the instant of cutting it off, ejaculation.
After his misfortune, about three years ago, he had weakness of memory, was easily
exhausted mentally, and troubled by sleeplessness as well as night terrors. P. deeply
regretted his crime.

Not only hair, but a number of hairpins, ribbons and other articles of the feminine *toilette,*
which had been given to him, were found in his possession. He had always had an actual
mania for collecting such things, as well as newspapers, pieces of wood and other worthless trash that he could never give up. He also had a strange, and, to him, inexplicable
fear of passing a certain street; to try it made him ill.

Medico-legal opinion showed him to be hereditarily predisposed, and proved the imperative, impulsive and decidedly involuntary character of the criminal acts, which had the
significance of an imperative act, induced by an imperative idea, and accompanied by
an overpowering abnormal sexual feeling. Pardon; asylum for the insane (Voisin, Socquet
and Motet, *Annales d'hygiène,* April 1890).

The following case is similar to the last, and also deserves attention, for it has
been well-studied, and can almost be called classical. It also places the fetish, as
well as the original associative awakening of the idea, in a clear light.

Case 101.

A hair despoiler. E., aged twenty-five. Maternal aunt, epileptic; brother had convulsions. He was fairly healthy as a child, and learned quite easily. At the age of fifteen he had an erotic feeling of pleasure, with erection, at the sight of one of the village beauties combing her hair. Until that time, persons of the opposite sex had made no impression on him. Two months later, in Paris, the sight of young girls with their hair flowing down over their shoulders excited him intensely. One day he could not resist an opportunity to twist a young girl's hair in his fingers. For this he was arrested and sentenced to imprisonment for three months. After that he served five years in the army. During this time hair was not dangerous for him, because it was not very accessible; sometimes, however, he dreamed of female heads with the hair braided or flowing. Occasional coitus with women, but without their hair being effective as a fetish. Once more in Paris, he again dreamed as before, and became greatly excited by female hair. He never dreamed about the whole form of a woman, only of heads with braids of hair. His sexual excitement due to this fetish had lately become so intense that he had resorted to masturbation. The idea of touching female hair, or better, possessing it, and masturbating while handling it, grew more and more powerful. Later, when he had female hair in his fingers, ejaculation was induced. One day he succeeded in cutting the hair of three little girls on the street (about twenty-five centimeters of hair), and it was in his possession when he was arrested during a fourth attempt. Deep regret and shame. He was not sentenced. After spending some time in the asylum, he improved so much that female hair no longer excited him. Once freed from the asylum, he thought of returning to his birthplace, where the women wore their hair done up (Magnan, *Archives de l'anthropologie criminelle,* vol. 5, no. 28).

A third case is the following, which is likewise suited to illustrate the psychopathic nature of such phenomena. The remarkable means which induced a cure are noteworthy:

Case 102.

Hair fetishism. Mr. X., between thirty and forty years old; from the higher class of society; single. Came from a healthy family, but from childhood had been nervous, vacillating and peculiar; since his eighth year he had been powerfully attracted to female hair, particularly the hair of young girls. When he was nine years old, a girl of thirteen seduced him. He did not understand it, and was not at all excited. A twelve-year-old sister of this girl also courted, kissed, and hugged him. He quietly allowed this, because the girl's hair pleased him so well. When about ten years old, he began to have erotic feelings at the sight of female hair that pleased him. Gradually these feelings occurred spontaneously, and memory-pictures of girls' hair were always immediately associated with them. At the age of eleven he was taught to masturbate by schoolmates. The associative connection of sexual feelings and a fetishistic idea were already established, and always appeared when the patient indulged in evil practices with his companions. With advancing years, the fetish grew more and more powerful. Even false hair began to excite him, but he always preferred natural hair. When he could touch or kiss it, he was perfectly happy. He wrote essays and poems on the beauty of female hair; he sketched heads of hair and masturbated. After his fourteenth year he became so powerfully excited by his fetish that he had violent erections. In contrast with his early taste as a boy, he was now charmed only by luxuriant, thick black hair. He experienced intense desire to kiss such hair, particularly to suck it. To touch such hair afforded him little satisfaction, however; he obtained much more pleasure from looking at it, and particularly from kissing and sucking it. If this were impossible, he would become unhappy, even to the extent of *taedium vitae.* He would then attempt to relieve himself, imagining fantastic "hair adventures" while masturbating. Often, on the street and in crowds, he could not keep from imprinting a kiss on ladies' heads. He would then hurry home to masturbate. Sometimes he could resist this impulse, but then it was necessary that he, filled with feelings of fear, run away as quickly as possible, in order to escape the domination of his fetish. Only once, while in a crowd, was he impelled to cut off a girl's lock of hair. In the act he was seized with fear, was not successful with his pocketknife, and, fleeing, he narrowly escaped detection.

When he became mature, he attempted to satisfy himself in coitus with prostitutes. He induced powerful erection by kissing their tresses, but could not induce ejaculation, and coitus did not satisfy him. At the same time, his favorite idea was the kissing of hair during coitus; but even this did not satisfy him, because it did not induce ejaculation. For lack of anything better, he once stole a lady's hair combings, put them in his mouth, and masturbated while projecting an image of the lady in his mind. In the dark, a woman could not interest him, because then he could not see her hair. Flowing hair also had no charm for him; nor did the hair around the genitals. His erotic dreams were all about hair. The patient later became so excited that he had a kind of satyriasis. He could not work, and felt so unhappy that he sought to drown his sorrow in alcohol. He drank large quantities, had alcoholic delirium, an attack of alcoholic epilepsy, and required hospital treatment. After the intoxication had passed, under appropriate treatment the sexual excitement soon disappeared; and when the patient was discharged, he was freed from his fetishistic idea, save for its occasional occurrence in dreams. The physical examination showed normal genitals and no degenerative signs whatsoever.

Such cases of hair fetishism, which lead to attacks on the hair of women, seem to occur everywhere from time to time. In November 1890, according to reports in American newspapers, several cities in the United States were troubled by such hair despoilers.

[b] the fetish is an article of female attire.

The great importance of adornment, ornament and dress in the normal sex life of man is generally recognized. Culture and fashion have, to a certain extent, endowed woman with artificial sexual characteristics, the removal of which, when woman is seen unattired, may exert an opposite influence in spite of the normal sexual effect of this sight.[73] It should not be overlooked that female dress often has a tendency to emphasize and exaggerate certain sexual peculiarities – secondary sexual characteristics (bosom, waist, hips). In most individuals, the sexual instinct awakens long before there is any possibility or opportunity of intimate intercourse, and the early desires of youth are concerned with the ordinary appearance of the attired female form. Thus it happens that often, at the beginning of the sex life, ideas of the persons exerting sexual charms and ideas of their attire become associated. This association may be lasting – the attired woman may always be preferred – if the individuals dominated by this perversion do not in other respects attain a normal sex life and find gratification in natural charms.

As a result of this, in psychopathic, sexually hyperesthetic individuals it actually happens that the dressed woman is always preferred to the nude female form. It may be recalled that in case 55 the woman was not to take off her chemise, and that in case 58, *equus eroticus* (the erotic horse), the woman was preferred dressed. Farther on a similar case will be cited.

Dr. Moll (op. cit., 2d ed.) mentions a patient who could not perform coitus with a nude prostitute; the woman had to at least wear a chemise. The same author (op. cit., p. 16) mentions a man affected with inverted sexuality, who is subject to the same dress fetishism.

The reason for this phenomenon is apparently to be found in the mental masturbation of such individuals. As a result of seeing innumerable clothed forms, their desires are in place before they see nudity.[74]

A more marked form of dress fetishism is that in which, instead of the dressed woman in general, a *certain kind of attire* in particular becomes a fetish. One can understand how, with an intense and early sexual impression that is combined with the idea of a particular garment on the woman, a very intense interest in this garment might be developed in hyperesthetic individuals.

Hammond (op. cit., p. 46) reports the following case, taken from Roubaud (*Traité de l'impuissance*, Paris, 1876):

Case 103.

X., son of a general. He was raised in the country. At the age of fourteen he was initiated into the pleasures of love by a young lady. This lady was a blonde and wore her hair in ringlets; and, in order to avoid being detected, during sexual intercourse with her young lover she always wore her usual clothing – gaiters, a corset, and a silk dress.

When his studies were completed, and he was sent to a garrison where he could enjoy freedom, he found that his sexual desire could only be excited under certain conditions. A brunette could not excite him in the least, and a woman in night clothes would stifle every bit of love in him. In order to awaken his desire, the woman had to be a blonde and wear gaiters, a corset and a silk dress – in short, she had to be dressed like the lady who had first awakened his sexual desire. He was always compelled to give up thoughts of matrimony, because he knew he would be unable to fulfill his marital duty with a woman in night clothes.

Hammond (p. 42) reports another case where marital coitus could only be performed with the help of a certain costume; and Dr. Moll mentions several similar cases in individuals of hetero- and homosexuality. The cause may often be shown to be an early association, and such may always be assumed. It is only in this way that one can explain why a certain costume is irresistible to such individuals, no matter who wears the fetish. Thus one can understand why, as Coffignon (op. cit.) relates, men at brothels demand that the women with whom they are concerned put on certain costumes, such as that of a ballet dancer, a nun, etc.;

and why these houses are furnished with a complete wardrobe for such purposes.

Binet (op. cit.) relates the case of a judge who was in love exclusively with Italian girls who came to Paris as artist's models and wore peculiar costumes. The cause here was an impression demonstrably made at the time of the awakening of the sexual instinct.

There is only one step from such cases to the complete absorption of the whole sex life by the fetish, the possession and manipulation of which may suffice to provoke orgasm and even ejaculation when irritable weakness of the ejaculation center prevails.

Case 104.

P., thirty-three years of age, businessman; mother suffered from melancholia and committed suicide. He was tainted with several signs of anatomical degeneration, was looked upon by his neighbors as a "type," and had the nickname *"l'amoureux des nourrices et des bonnes d'enfants"* ("the lover of wet nurses and nannies").

He became a nuisance to these girls with his obtrusive behavior, picked a quarrel with one of them who wore his fetish, and was arrested.

He claimed to have always been vehemently excited at the sight of wet nurses and nursemaids, not because they were of the female sex, but because they wore a certain costume. It was not certain portions, but the costume as a whole that attracted him. To be in the company of such persons was his greatest happiness. When he returned home from such encounters it was sufficient that he recall the impressions just received in order to have an orgasm.

An analogous case is related by Motet. It refers to a young man who only became sexually excited at the sight of a woman attired in a bridal costume. The individuality of the woman was a matter of indifference to him. To gratify his fetishistic cravings, he spent a great deal of his time at the door of a restaurant where many weddings were celebrated (Garnier, *Les Fétischistes,* p. 59).

A third form of dress fetishism, having a much higher degree of pathological significance, is by far the most frequent. In this form it is no longer the dressed woman herself, or even the woman dressed in a particular fashion, that constitutes the principal sexual stimulus; instead, the stimulus is constituted by some particular article of female attire upon which the sexual interest is so fixated that the lustful idea of this object is entirely separated from the idea of woman, and thus obtains an independent value. This is the real domain of dress fetishism, where an inanimate object – an isolated article of wearing apparel – is alone used for the excitation and satisfaction of the sexual instinct. This form of dress fetishism is also the most important forensically.

In a large number of these cases the fetishes are articles of female underwear, which, because of their private use, are suited to bringing about such associations.

Case 105.

K., aged forty-five, shoemaker, was reported to be without hereditary taint. He was peculiar, and had small mental endowment. He was of masculine appearance and without signs of degeneration. Previously blameless in conduct, he was discovered on the evening of July 5, 1876, removing stolen female undergarments from a place of concealment. Found with him were about three hundred articles of the female *toilette*; among them, chemises and drawers, nightcaps, garters, and a female doll. When arrested he was wearing a chemise. Since his thirteenth year he had been a slave to the impulse of stealing women's linen; after his first punishment for stealing, however, he became very careful, and stole with refinement and success. When this longing came over him, he grew anxious, and his head became full of ideas. He then could not resist the impulse, regardless of the consequences. He did not care from whom he took the articles. Before going to bed at night, he would put on the stolen clothing and create beautiful women in his imagination, thus inducing pleasurable feeling and ejaculation. This was apparently the motive for his thefts, inasmuch as he had never disposed of any of the articles, but had hidden them here and there.

He declared that, earlier in his life, he had indulged in normal sexual intercourse with women. He denied masturbation, pederasty, and other sexual acts. He said he was engaged at twenty-five, but, through no fault of his own, the engagement was broken. He was incapable of grasping the abnormality of his condition and the wrongfulness of his acts (Passow, *Vierteljahrsschr. f. ger. Mediz.*, vol. 28, p. 61; Krauss, *Psychologie des Verbrechens*, 1884, p. 190).

Case 106.

J., a young butcher. When arrested he was wearing, underneath his overcoat, a bodice, corset, vest, jacket, collar, jersey, and chemise, as well as fine stockings and garters.

When he was eleven he was troubled by the desire to wear his elder sister's chemise. He indulged in this pleasure whenever he could do so unnoticed and, since the age of puberty, the wearing of such a garment would bring on ejaculation. When he became independent he bought chemises and other articles of the female *toilette.* In his room a complete outfit of female attire was found. The great aim of his sexual instinct was to put on such garments. This fetishism ruined him financially. At the hospital he begged the attending physician to permit him to wear female attire. Inverted sexuality did not exist (Garnier, *Les Fétischistes,* p. 62).

Case 107.

Z., thirty-six years of age, scholar; had never heretofore felt interested in women, only in their attire, and had never enjoyed sexual intercourse. Besides being drawn to the elegance and smartness of the female *toilette* in general, certain underwear, chemises made of cambric and trimmed with lace, silk corsets, embroidered silk skirts and silk stockings formed his particular fetish. It gave him voluptuous pleasure to inspect and finger such female garments at the draper's. His ideal was the female form in a bathing costume, in silk stockings and a corset, or in a mourning dress with a long train.

He studied the costumes of the loose women of the street, but found them tasteless. He found more pleasure in gazing at the shop windows, but felt annoyed because the displays were not changed often enough. He found partial satisfaction in holding and studying fashion magazines, and in occasionally buying single garments of exceptional beauty. The height of pleasure for him would be to have access to the *toilette* arts of the boudoir or the fitting rooms of the dressmaker, or to be the chambermaid of some wealthy lady of the world and arrange her *toilette*. There were no traces of masochism or homosexual inclination to be found in this peculiar fetishist. He had a thoroughly manly presence (Garnier, *La folie à Paris,* 1890).

Hammond (op. cit.) reports a case of passionate interest in single articles of feminine apparel. Here, also, the patient's pleasure consisted in wearing a corset and other female garments (without any traces of antipathic sexual instinct). The pain of tight lacing, experienced by himself or induced by women, was a delight to him (sadistic-masochistic element).

A case probably belonging here is one reported by Diez (*Der Selbstmord,* 1893, p. 24), where a young man could not resist the impulse to tear female linen. While tearing linen, he always ejaculated.

A combination of fetishism with an impulse to destroy the fetish (in a certain sense, sadism with inanimate objects) seems to occur quite frequently (cf. case 120).

An article of dress that is not necessarily private in character, but that might be suggestive of undergarments and have sexual associations because of its material, color, and where it is worn, is the *apron* (cf. also the metonymic use of the word "apron" for "petticoat" in the saying, "To chase every apron," etc.). This explains the following case:

Case 108.

C., aged thirty-seven; from a badly tainted family; of small mental endowment; plagio-cephalic. At fifteen his attention was attracted by an apron hung out to dry. He put it on and masturbated behind a fence. From that time he could not see aprons without repeating the act. If he met anyone – whether man or woman – with an apron on, he was compelled to run after the person. In order to free himself from this constant stealing of aprons, he enlisted himself as a marine in his sixteenth year. In this calling he saw no aprons and had continual rest. At nineteen, he returned home, was again compelled to steal aprons, got into serious trouble as a result, and was locked up several times. He sought to free himself of his weakness by staying for several years with the Trappists. When he left them, he was just as bad as before. As a result of a new theft, he underwent a medico-legal examination, and was committed to an asylum. He never stole anything but aprons. It was a pleasure for him to revel in the memory of the first apron he ever stole. His dreams were filled with aprons. He occasionally used the memory of his thefts to make coitus possible, or for masturbation (Charcot and Magnan, *Arch. de Neurolog.,* 1882, no. 12).

In a case reported by Lombroso ("Amori anomali precoci nei pazzi," *Arch. di psich.,* 1883, p. 17), analogous to those of this series, a boy of very bad heredity had erections and great sexual excitement, at the age of four, at the sight of white garments, particularly underclothing. He was lustfully excited by handling and crumpling them. At the age of ten he began to masturbate at the sight of white, starched linen. He seemed to have been affected with moral insanity, and was later executed for murder.

The following case of *petticoat fetishism* is coupled with peculiar circumstances:

Case 109.

Z., aged thirty-five; civil servant; the only child of a nervous mother and a healthy father. From childhood he was "nervous," and at the consultation his neuropathic eyes, delicate, slender body, fine features, very thin voice, and sparse growth of beard attracted attention. The patient presented nothing abnormal except symptoms of slight neurasthenia. Genitals and sexual functions normal. Patient stated that he had only masturbated four or five times when he was very young. As early as the age of thirteen the patient was powerfully excited sexually by the sight of wet dresses, while the same dresses, when dry, had no effect upon him. His greatest delight was to look at women with wet garments in the rain. If he met a woman with a pleasing face under such circumstances he experienced an intense feeling of lustful pleasure, would have an erection, and felt impelled to perform coitus. He stated that he had never had any desire to steal wet dresses or to throw water on women. He could give no explanation of the origin of his peculiarity.

It is possible that, in this case, the sexual instinct was first awakened by the sight of a woman who exposed her charms by raising her skirts in wet weather. The obscure instinct, not yet conscious of its object, then became directed to the wet garments, as in other cases.

Lovers of women's handkerchiefs are frequent, and, therefore, forensically important. As to the frequency of handkerchief fetishism, it may be remarked that the handkerchief is the one article of feminine attire which, outside of intimate association, is most frequently displayed, and which, with its warmth from the person and specific odors, may by accident fall into the hands of others. The frequency of early association of lustful feelings with the idea of a handkerchief, which can always be presumed to have occurred in such cases of fetishism, is probably due to this.

Case 110.

A baker's assistant, aged thirty-two, single, previously of good repute, was discovered stealing a handkerchief from a lady. With sincere remorse, he confessed that he had stolen from eighty to ninety such handkerchiefs. He cared only for handkerchiefs, and, indeed, only for those belonging to young women attractive to him. In his outward appearance the culprit presented nothing peculiar. He dressed himself with taste. His conduct was peculiar, anxious, depressed and unmanly, and he often lapsed into whining and tears. Lack of self-reliance, weakness of comprehension, as well as slowness of perception and reflection were noticeable. One of his sisters was epileptic. He lived in good circumstances; never had a severe illness; was well-developed. In relating his history, he showed weakness of memory and lack of clearness; calculation was hard for him, though when young he learned and comprehended easily. His anxious, uncertain state of mind raised a suspicion of masturbation. The culprit confessed that he had indulged in this practice excessively since his nineteenth year. For some years, as a result of his vice, he had suffered from depression, lassitude, trembling of the limbs, pain in the back, and disinclination for work. Frequently a depressed, anxious state of mind came over him, during which he avoided people. He had exaggerated, fantastic notions about the results of sexual intercourse with women, and could not bring himself to indulge in it. Recently, however, he had thought of marriage. With great remorse and in a weak-minded way, he then confessed that six months ago, while in a crowd, he became violently excited sexually at the sight of a pretty young girl, and was compelled to crowd up against her. He felt an impulse to compensate himself for a less than satisfactory sexual passion by stealing her handkerchief. Thereafter, as soon as he was near attractive females, he would experience violent sexual excitement, palpitation of the heart, erection, and a desire for coitus, and the impulse would seize him to crowd up against them and steal their handkerchiefs. Although the consciousness of his criminal act never left him for a moment, he was unable to resist the impulse. During the act he was uneasy, which was partly due to his inordinate sexual impulse, and partly due to the fear of detection. The medico-legal opinion rightly gave weight to the congenital mental enfeeblement and the pernicious influence of masturbation, and referred the abnormal impulses to a perverse sexual impulse, calling attention to the presence of an interesting and well-known physiological connection between the olfactory and sexual senses. Inability to resist his pathological impulse was recognized. X. was not punished (Zippe, *Wiener med. Wochenschr.*, 1879, no. 23).

I am indebted to the kindness of Dr. Fritsch of Vienna for further facts concerning this handkerchief fetishist, who was again arrested, in August 1890, in the act of taking a handkerchief from a lady's pocket:

Authorities searching his house found four hundred and forty-six ladies' handkerchiefs. He stated that he had already burned two bundles of them. In the course of the examination it was further shown that X. had been punished with imprisonment for fourteen days in 1883 for stealing twenty-seven handkerchiefs, and was again imprisoned for three weeks in 1886 for a similar crime. Concerning his relatives, nothing more could be learned, except that his father was subject to congestions, and that a brother's daughter was an imbecile and constitutionally neuropathic. X. was married in 1879, and embarked on an independent business that became bankrupt in 1881. Soon after this his wife, who could not live with him, and with whom he did not perform his marital duty (denied by X.), demanded a divorce. Thereafter he lived as an assistant baker to his brother. He complained bitterly of an impulsive desire for ladies' handkerchiefs, and when the opportunity arose, unfortunately, he could not resist it. During the act he experienced a feeling of delight, and felt as if someone were forcing him. Sometimes he could restrain himself, but when the lady was pleasing to him he yielded to his initial impulse. He would be soaked with sweat, partly from fear of detection, and partly because of the impulse to perform the act. He said he had been sexually excited by the sight of women's handkerchiefs since puberty. He could not recall the exact circumstances of this fetishistic association. The sexual excitement occasioned by the sight of a lady with a handkerchief hanging out of her pocket had constantly increased. This had repeatedly caused erections, but never ejaculation. After his twenty-first year, he said, he had a desire for normal sexual indulgence, and had straightforward coitus without any ideas of handkerchiefs. As his fetishism increased, the appropriation of handkerchiefs afforded him much more satisfaction than coitus. Stealing the handkerchief of an attractive lady was the same to him as intercourse with her would have been. During the act he had true orgasm.

If he could not gain possession of the handkerchief he desired, he would become painfully excited, tremble, and sweat all over. He kept separate the handkerchiefs of ladies particularly pleasing to him, and reveled in the sight of them with intense pleasure. The odor of them also gave him great delight, though he stated that it was really the odor peculiar to the linen, and not the perfume, that excited him sensually. He rarely masturbated.

X. complained of no physical ailments except an occasional headache and vertigo. He greatly regretted the misfortune of his abnormal impulse – the evil spirit that impelled him to commit such criminal acts. He had but one wish: that someone might help him. Objectively there were mild neurasthenic symptoms, anomalies of the distribution of blood, and unequal pupils.

It was proved that X. had committed his crimes in obedience to an abnormal, irresistible impulse. Pardon.

Case 111.

Z. began to masturbate at the age of twelve. From that time he could not see a woman's handkerchief without having orgasm and ejaculation. He was irresistibly compelled to possess handkerchiefs. At that time he was a choirboy and used the handkerchiefs to masturbate in the bell tower close to the choir. He only chose handkerchiefs, however, that had black and white borders or violet stripes running through them. At fifteen he had coitus. Later on he married. As a rule, he was only potent when he wound such a handkerchief around his penis. Often he preferred coitus **between a woman's thighs** where he had placed a handkerchief. Whenever he spied a handkerchief he could not rest until he possessed it. He always had a number of them in his pockets and around his genitals (Rayneau, *Annales médico-psychol.,* 1895).

Such cases of handkerchief fetishism, where an abnormal individual is driven to theft, are numerous. They also occur in combination with inverted sexuality, as proved by the following case, which I borrow from page 162 of Dr. Moll's frequently cited work:[75]

Case 112.

Handkerchief fetishism in a case of antipathic sexual instinct. K., aged thirty-eight; mechanic; a powerfully built man. He made numerous complaints – weakness of the legs, pain in the back, headaches, lack of pleasure in work, etc. The complaints gave the decided impression of neurasthenia with a tendency to hypochondria. Only after the patient had been under Dr. Moll's treatment for several months did he state that he was also abnormal sexually.

K. had never had any inclination whatsoever for women; but handsome men, on the other hand, had a peculiar charm for him. Patient had masturbated frequently until he came to Dr. Moll. He had never practiced mutual masturbation or pederasty. He did not think that he would have found satisfaction in this, because, in spite of his preference for men, an article of *white linen* was his chief charm, though the beauty of its owner played a role. The *handkerchiefs* of handsome men particularly excited him sexually. His greatest delight was to masturbate in men's handkerchiefs. For this reason he often took his friends' handkerchiefs. In order to save himself from detection, he always left one of his own handkerchiefs with his friends in place of the stolen one. In this way he sought to escape suspicion of theft by creating the appearance of a mistake. Other articles of men's linen also excited K. sexually, but not to the extent that handkerchiefs did.

K. had often performed coitus with women, with erection and ejaculation, but without lustful pleasure. There was also nothing particularly about women that stimulated the patient to engage in coitus. Erection and ejaculation occurred only when, during the act, he thought of a man's handkerchief; and this was easier for the patient when he took a friend's handkerchief with him and had it in his hand during coitus. In accordance with his sexual perversion, his nightly pollutions with lustful ideas prominently featured men's linen.[76]

Far more frequent than the fetishism of linen garments, however, is that of *women's shoes.* These cases are, in fact, almost innumerable, and a great many of them have been studied scientifically. I have only a few thirdhand reports of similar glove fetishism, not including case 122 (see below), in which glove fetishism develops itself merely into "stuff fetishism." (Concerning the reason for the relative infrequency of glove fetishism, see [a] above.)

In shoe fetishism, the close relationship of the object to the feminine person, which explains linen fetishism, is absolutely lacking. For this reason, and because of the large number of well-observed cases in which the fetishistic enthusiasm for the female shoe consciously and undoubtedly arises from masochistic ideas, a masochistic origin, even when concealed, may always be assumed in shoe fetishism when no other manner of origin is concretely demonstrable. Therefore, the majority of the cases of shoe or foot fetishism have been given under "Masochism." There the constant masochistic character of this form of erotic fetishism has been sufficiently demonstrated by means of transitional conditions. The presumption of the masochistic character of shoe fetishism is weakened and removed only where another accidental cause for an association between sexual excitation and the idea of women's shoes – the occurrence of which is quite improbable *a priori* – can be proven. In the following two cases, however, there is such a demonstrable connection:

Case 113.

Shoe fetishism. Mr. v. P., from an old and honorable family, Pole, aged thirty-two, consulted with me in 1890 because of the "unnaturalness" of his sex life. He gave the assurance that he came from a perfectly healthy family. He had been nervous since childhood, and had suffered from chorea minor at the age of eleven. For ten years he had suffered from sleeplessness and various neurasthenic ailments. From his fifteenth year he had recognized the difference between the sexes and been capable of sexual excitation. At the age of seventeen he had been seduced by a French governess, but coitus was not permitted; intense mutual sexual excitement (mutual masturbation) was all that was possible. In this situation his attention was attracted by her elegant boots. They made a deep impression. His intercourse with this lewd person lasted four months. During this association her shoes became a fetish for the unfortunate boy. He began to have an interest in ladies' shoes in general, and actually went about trying to catch sight of ladies wearing pretty boots. The fetishism gained great power over his mind. He had the governess touch his penis with her shoes, and thus ejaculation with great lustful feeling was immediately induced. After separation from the governess he went to prostitutes, instructing them to perform the same manipulation. This was usually sufficient for satisfaction. Only seldom, as an auxiliary, did he resort to coitus, and his inclination for it diminished over time. His sex life consisted of dream pollutions, in which women's shoes played the exclusive role, and gratification with women's shoes **pressed against his penis,** but this had to be done by the prostitute. In the society of the opposite sex the only thing that interested him was the shoe, and only when it was elegant, of the French style, with heels, and brilliantly black, like the original.

In the course of time the following conditions became accessory: a prostitute's shoe that was elegant and chic; starched petticoats, and, if possible, black stockings. Nothing else in woman interested him. *He was absolutely indifferent to the naked foot.* Women did not have the slightest psychic charm for him. He had never had masochistic desires in the sense of being trod upon. In the course of years his fetishism had gained such power that when he saw a lady in the street of a certain appearance and with certain shoes, he was so intensely excited that he had to masturbate. Slight pressure on the penis sufficed to induce ejaculation when he was in this state of severe neurasthenia. Shoes displayed in shops, and recently even advertisements of shoes, sufficed to excite him intensely. In states of intense libido he made use of masturbation if shoes were not at his immediate command. The patient quite early recognized the pain and danger of his condition, and, even when he was free from neurasthenic ailments, he was morally very much depressed. He sought help from various physicians. Cold water cures and hypnotism were unsuccessful. The most celebrated physicians advised him to marry, and assured him that once he really loved a girl he would be free from his fetishism. The patient had no confidence in his future, but he followed the advice of the physicians. He was cruelly disappointed in the hope aroused in him by the authority of the physicians, though he led to the altar a lady distinguished by both mental and physical charms. The wedding night was terrible; he felt like a criminal, and did not approach his wife. The next day he saw a prostitute who possessed the required elegance. He was weak enough to have intercourse, in his way, with her. Then he bought a pair of elegant ladies' boots, hid them in bed, and, by touching them while in marital embrace, he was able, after a few days, to perform his marital duty. He ejaculated tardily, because he had to force himself to engage in coitus; after a few weeks this artifice failed because his imagination failed. He felt unspeakably miserable, and would have preferred to end his life. He could no longer satisfy his wife, who was sensual and much excited by their previous intercourse; he saw her suffering severely, both mentally and morally. He could not, and would not, disclose his secret. He experienced disgust in marital intercourse; he felt afraid of his wife; he feared the coming of night when he would be alone with her. He could no longer induce erection.

He again made attempts with prostitutes, and satisfied himself by touching their shoes. Then the prostitute had to touch his penis, and he would ejaculate; but, if this did not take place, he would attempt coitus with the lewd woman; without success, however, because ejaculation would occur immediately. In absolute despair, the patient came for consultation. He deeply regretted that, against his inner conviction, he had followed the unfortunate advice of the physicians and made a virtuous wife unhappy, deeply injuring her both mentally and morally. Could he answer to God for continuing such a marriage? Even if he were to expose his secret to his wife and she were to do everything for him, it would not help him because the familiar perfume of the *demimonde* was also necessary.

Aside from his mental pain, this unfortunate man presented no remarkable symptoms. Genitals perfectly normal. Prostate somewhat large. He complained that he was so much under the domination of his boot fetish that he would blush even when boots were discussed. His whole imagination was enthralled with such ideas. When he was on his estate, he often had to abruptly leave and travel a distance of ten miles to the city to satisfy his fetishism at shoe shops or with prostitutes.

This pitiable man could not bring himself to take treatment, for his faith in physicians had been greatly shaken. An attempt to ascertain whether the possibility existed of removing the fetishistic association through hypnosis proved abortive because of the mental excitement of the unfortunate man, who was exclusively controlled by the thought that he had made his wife unhappy.

Case 114.

X., aged twenty-four; from a badly tainted family (mother's brother and grandfather insane, one sister epileptic, another sister subject to migraine, parents of excitable temperament). During dentition he had convulsions. At the age of seven he was taught to masturbate by a servant girl. X. first experienced pleasure in these manipulations **when the girl happened by chance to touch his penis with her slippered foot.** Thus in the predisposed boy an association was established, as a result of which, from that time on, merely the sight of a woman's shoes, and, finally, merely the idea of them, sufficed to induce sexual excitement and erection. He now masturbated while looking at women's shoes, or while calling them up in imagination. The shoes of the schoolmistress excited him intensely, and in general he was affected by shoes that were partly concealed by women's garments. One day he could not keep from grasping the teacher's shoes – an act that caused him great sexual excitement. In spite of punishment he could not keep from performing this act repeatedly. Finally, it was recognized that there must be an abnormal motive in play, and he was sent to a male teacher. He then reveled in the memory of shoe scenes with his former schoolmistress; as a result, he had erections, orgasms, and, after his fourteenth year, ejaculation. At that time he also masturbated while thinking of a woman's shoe. One day the thought came to him to increase his pleasure by using such a shoe for masturbation. Thereafter he frequently took shoes secretly and used them for this purpose.

Nothing else in a woman could excite him; the thought of coitus filled him with horror. Men did not interest him in any way. At the age of eighteen he opened a shop, and, among other things, dealt in ladies' shoes. He was excited sexually by fitting shoes for his female patrons, or by manipulating shoes that came for mending. One day while doing this he had an epileptic attack, and, soon after, another attack while masturbating in his customary manner. He then recognized for the first time the injury to his health caused by his sexual practices. He tried to overcome his masturbation, sold no more shoes, and strove to free himself from the abnormal association between women's shoes and the sexual function. Then frequent pollutions, with erotic dreams about shoes, occurred, and the epileptic attacks continued. Though devoid of the slightest feeling for the female sex, he decided on marriage, which seemed to him the only remedy.

He married a pretty young lady. In spite of lively erections when he thought of his wife's shoes, he was absolutely impotent in attempts at cohabitation, because his distaste for coitus and for close intercourse in general was far more powerful than the influence of the shoe idea, which induced sexual excitement. Because of his impotence, the patient went to Dr. Hammond, who treated his epilepsy with bromides, and advised him to hang a shoe over his bed and look at it fixedly during coitus, while at the same time imagining his wife to be a shoe. The patient became free of epileptic attacks, and potent to the point that he could have coitus about once a week. His sexual excitation by women's shoes also diminished over time (Hammond, *Sexuelle Impotenz,* German translation by Salinger, 1889, p. 23).

These two cases of shoe fetishism,[77] which apparently depend upon subjective accidental associations, as is the case in fetishism generally, do not offer anything startling with reference to their objective cause, because, in the former case, it is only a matter of a partial impression of the general appearance of woman, and in the latter, a partial impression of the exciting manipulation.

But there are cases – up to now only two have been closely observed – in which the determining association has clearly not been brought about by any connection between the nature of the object and the otherwise normally exciting cause.

Case 115.

Shoe fetishism. Kurella, in his *Naturgeschichte des Verbrechers,* p. 213, tried to prove that the man described below was an imposter who invented an interesting nervous disease to conceal fraudulent activity. The author, however, arrived at a different conclusion.

O., born in 1865, student of theology, was tried before a magistrate as a fraud and mendicant. He came from a heavily tainted family, was afflicted with shoe fetishism, and had from his twenty-first year periodic episodes in which he was irresistibly forced to run away and abandon himself to drinking bouts, although by doing so he knowingly jeopardized his position and property. In the army he repeatedly deserted and became a veritable degenerate, as well as an enigma to his superiors, for at times his conduct was exemplary and beyond blemish.

Examined before a commission of army medical men, he was declared to have been suffering from "periodic insanity," unquestionably inherited. Consequently, this "congenital criminal" was dismissed from service. He sank deeper and deeper into the mire, became a tramp, lived by his wits, and was confined several times in an insane asylum.

The author found a pronounced asymmetry of the skull, as well as a right foot much larger than the left, etc.

O. was able to trace his shoe fetishism back to his eighth year. He had frequently dropped things at school so that he might have a reason to get close to the lady teacher's foot. Periodically the image of a woman's shoe impressed him so greatly that he could not resist the impulse to run away.

This same impulse had been the cause of his vagrancy. He held himself responsible for any punishable acts for which he was guilty. The author tested the existence of his shoe fetishism and found definite proof that it was not simulated. Kurella had assumed that the patient's shoe fetishism was a mere invention; that he had, in fact, derived the idea from reading the author's book, *Psychopathia Sexualis* (as other critics have done on similar occasions).

It became quite evident that O. had never seen or heard of the book. (Cf. the original report of Kurella, in which his reasons for labeling O. a criminal are extensively given.)

In this case the scientific observations made by the author were based upon the following points, namely: hereditary taint, asymmetry of the skull and other signs of degeneration, and sexual perversion with periodic psychic manifestations in which irresistible perverse impulses forced the patient to abnormal thoughts and acts.

Even during his lucid intervals, O. could not be held responsible for his actions, because nervous disturbances and other psychic anomalies, in the shape of moral defects, formed part of his degenerative psychopathic constitution.

O. suffered from an inherited degenerative mania, and was considered a danger to society (Alzheimer, *Archiv. f. Psychiatrie,* vol. 28, no. 2).

Case 116.

L., aged thirty-seven, clerk, from a tainted family. At five years old, he had his first erection when he saw his bedfellow – an aged relative – put on his nightcap. The same thing occurred later, when he saw an old servant put on her nightcap. Later, simply the idea of an old, ugly woman's head, covered with a nightcap, was sufficient to cause an erection. The sight of a cap or a naked woman or man alone made no impression, but the mere touch of a nightcap induced erection, and sometimes even ejaculation. L. was not a masturbator, and had never been sexually active until his thirty-second year, when he married a young girl with whom he had fallen in love. On his wedding night he remained cold until, from necessity, he brought to his aid the memory-picture of an ugly woman's head with a nightcap. Coitus was immediately successful. Thereafter it was always necessary for him to use this method. From childhood he had been subject to occasional attacks of depression, with suicidal tendencies, and occasional frightful hallucinations at night. When looking out a window, he became dizzy and anxious. He was a perverse, peculiar, and easily embarrassed man, of bad mental constitution (Charcot and Magnan, *Arch. de Neurol.,* 1882, no. 12).

In this very peculiar case, the simultaneous coincidence of the first sexual reference and an absolutely heterogeneous impression seems to have determined the association.

Hammond (op. cit.) also mentions a case of accidental associative fetishism that is quite peculiar. A married man, aged thirty, who, in other respects, was physically and mentally healthy, is said to have suddenly lost his sexual power after moving to another house, and to have regained it as soon as the furniture of the bedroom had been arranged as before.

[c] the fetish is some special material.

There is a third principal group of fetishists whose fetish is neither a portion of the female body nor a part of female attire, but some *particular material* which is so used, not because it is a material for female garments, but because it can in itself arouse or increase sexual feelings. Such materials are *furs, velvets* and *silks.*

These cases differ from previous instances of erotic dress fetishism in that these materials, unlike female linen, do not have any close relation to the female body; and, unlike shoes and gloves, they are not related to certain parts of the person having peculiar symbolic significance. Further, this fetishism cannot be due to an accidental association, as in the cases of the nightcaps and the arrangement of the bedroom; for these cases form an entire group having the same object. It must be presumed that in hyperesthetic individuals certain tactile sensations (a kind of tickling irritation distantly related to lustful sensations?) furnish the occasion for the origin of this fetishism.

The following is a personal observation of a man affected with this peculiar fetishism:

Case 117.

N., aged thirty-seven; from a neuropathic family; neuropathic constitution. He made the following statement: "From my earliest youth I have always had a deeply rooted partiality for furs and velvets, insofar as these materials cause me sexual excitement, and the sight and touch of them give me lustful pleasure. I cannot recall any event that caused this peculiarity (such as the simultaneous occurrence of the first sexual excitation by a woman dressed in these materials and an impression of the materials); in fact, I cannot remember when this enthusiasm began. I would not, however, exclude the possibility of such an event – of an accidental connection between a first impression and a conse-quent association; but I think it very improbable that such a thing took place, because I believe such an occurrence would have deeply impressed me. All I know is that even when I was a small child I had a lively desire to see and stroke furs, and thus had an obscure sexual pleasure. With the first occurrence of definite sexual ideas – i.e., the direction of sexual thoughts to women – the peculiar preference for women dressed in such materials was present. Since then, up to mature manhood, it has remained unchanged. A woman wearing furs or velvet, or, even better, both, excites me much more quickly and intensely than one devoid of these auxiliaries. Of course, these materials are not an essential condition of excitation; the desire also occurs without them in response to the usual stimuli; but, for me, the sight and, particularly, the touch of these fetish materials form a powerful aid to other normal stimuli and intensify erotic pleasure. Often merely the sight of only a passably pretty girl dressed in these materials causes me vivid excitement, and overcomes me completely. While the sight of my fetish materials gives me pleasure, the touch of them is even more pleasurable. (To the penetrating odor of furs I am indifferent – rather, I find it unpleasant – and I endure it only because of the association with pleasing visual and tactile impressions.) I have an intense longing to touch these materials while they are on a woman's person; to stroke, kiss, and bury my face in them. My greatest pleasure, during the act, is to see and feel my fetish on the woman's shoulder.

"Fur or velvet alone exerts on me the described effect; fur much more intensely than velvet. The combination of the two has the most intense effect. Again, female garments made of velvet and fur, seen and touched when off the wearer, cause me sexual excitement. In fact, the same effect is exerted by furs or robes having no relation to female attire, though to a lesser extent, as well as by the velvet and plush of furniture and drapery. Mere pictures of costumes of furs and velvet are objects of erotic interest to me; indeed, the very word 'fur' has a magic charm, and immediately calls up erotic ideas.

"Fur is such an object of sexual interest to me that a man wearing the type of fur that affects me [see below] makes a very unpleasant, repugnant, and disgusting impression on me, such as would be made on a normal person by a man in the costume and attitude of a ballet dancer. Similarly repugnant to me is the sight of an old or ugly woman clad in beautiful furs, because contradicting feelings are thus aroused.

"This erotic delight in furs and velvet is something entirely different from simple aesthetic pleasure. I have a lively appreciation for beautiful female attire, and a particular partiality for point lace; but this interest is purely aesthetic. A woman dressed in a point lace *toilette* (or in other elegant, elaborate attire) is more *beautiful* than another; but one dressed in my fetish material is more *charming*.

"Furs, however, exercise on me the effect described only when the fur has very thick, fine, smooth and rather long hair, which stands out like that of the so-called bearded furs. I have noticed that the effect depends upon this. I am entirely indifferent not only to the ordinary, coarse, bushy furs, but also to those that are commonly regarded as beautiful and precious, where the long hair has been removed (seal, beaver), or where the hair is naturally short (ermine); and likewise to those where the hair is overlong and lies flat (monkey, bear). The specific effect is exerted only by the standing long hair of the sable, marten, skunk, etc. Now, velvet is made of thick, fine, standing hairs (fibers); and its effect may be due to this. The effect seems to depend upon a very definite impression made by points of thick, fine hair upon the terminals of the sensory nerves.

"How this peculiar impression on the tactile nerves is related to sexual instinct is a perfect enigma to me. The fact is, this is the case for many men. I would also state expressly that beautiful female hair pleases me, but plays no more important a part than the other charms; and that while touching fur I have no thought of female hair (the tactile sensation, also, has not the least resemblance to that imparted by female hair). There is never an association with any other idea. Fur, per se, arouses sensuality in me – how, I cannot explain.

"The mere aesthetic effect, the beauty of costly furs, to which everyone is more or less susceptible, explains nothing here. Since Raphael's *Fornarina* and Reuben's *Helene Fourment,* the aesthetic effect of fur has been used as the foil and frame of female beauty by innumerable painters, and has played an important role in fashion – the art and science of female dress. Beautiful furs have the same aesthetic effect on me as they have on normal individuals, and affect me in the same way that flowers, ribbons, precious stones, and other ornaments affect everyone. Such things, when skillfully used, enhance female beauty, and thus, under certain circumstances, may have an indirect sensual effect. They have never had the direct, powerful, sensual effect on me that fetish materials have had.

"Although in me, and, in fact, in all 'fetishists,' the sensual and aesthetic effect must be strictly differentiated, this nevertheless does not prevent me from demanding in my fetish a whole series of aesthetic qualities in the way of form, style, color, etc. I could give a lengthy description of the qualities demanded by my tastes, but I omit it as not essential to the real subject at hand. I would only call attention to the fact that erotic fetishism is complicated by purely aesthetic tastes.

"The specific erotic effect of my fetish materials can be explained no better by their association with the idea of the female wearing them than by their aesthetic impression. In the first place, these materials affect me when entirely isolated from the body; and, in the second place, articles of clothing of a much more private nature that should call up associations exert a much weaker influence over me. Thus, for me, the fetish materials have an independent sensual value. Why is an enigma to me.

"Feathers in women's hats, fans, etc., have the same erotic fetishistic effect on me as furs and velvet (similar tactile sensation of airy, peculiar tickling). Finally, the fetishistic effect, with much less intensity, is exerted by other smooth materials (satin and silk). Rough goods, however, such as cloth and flannel, have a repelling effect.

"In conclusion, I will mention that somewhere I read an article by Karl Vogt on micro-cephalic man, according to which these creatures, at the sight of furs, rushed for them and stroked them with every manifestation of delight. I am far from any thought, on this basis, of seeing in widespread fur fetishism an atavistic retrogression to the taste of our hairy ancestors. Every cretin, with that simplicity belonging to its condition, touches anything that pleases him, and the act is not necessarily of a sexual nature; just as many normal men like to stroke a cat, or even velvet furs, and thus are not excited sexually."

In the literature on this subject, there are a few cases belonging here:

Case 118.

A boy, aged twelve, became powerfully excited sexually when, by chance, he covered himself with a foxskin. From that time on there was masturbation using furs, or by taking a furry dog to bed. Ejaculation would result, sometimes followed by a hysterical attack. His nocturnal pollutions were induced by dreaming that he lay entirely enveloped by a soft skin. He was absolutely insusceptible to stimuli coming from men or women. He was neurasthenic, suffered from delusions of being watched, and thought that everyone noticed his sexual anomaly. Because of this, he had *taedium vitae,* and finally became insane. He had marked taint; his genitals were imperfectly formed, and he presented other signs of degeneration (Tarnowsky, op. cit., p. 22).

Case 119.

C. was an especial lover of velvet. He was attracted in a normal way by beautiful women, but it particularly excited him to have the person with whom he was having sexual inter-course dressed in velvet. In this it was remarkable that it was not so much the sight as it was the touch of the velvet that caused the excitation. C. told me that stroking a woman's velvet jacket would excite him sexually to an extent scarcely possible in any other way (Dr. Moll, op. cit., p. 127).

A physician communicated to me the following case: In a brothel there was a man who was known by the name of "Velvet." He would dress a sympathetic prostitute in a garment made of black velvet, and would excite and satisfy his sexual desires simply by stroking his face with a corner of her velvety dress, without touching any other part of her at all.

Another authority assures me that this weakness for *furs, velvets, silks* and *feathers* is quite common among masochists (cf. case 50).[78]

The following is a very peculiar case of material fetishism. It is combined with the impulse to injure the fetish, which, in this case, represents an element of sadism toward the woman wearing the fetish, or impersonal sadism toward objects, which is common in fetishists (cf. p. 214). The impulse to cause injury made this a remarkable criminal case:

Case 120.

In July 1891, Alfred Bachmann, aged twenty-five, locksmith, was brought before Judge N. in the second term of the criminal court in Berlin. In April the police had received numerous complaints, according to which some evil hand had cut women's dresses with a very sharp instrument. On the evening of April 25 they were successful in arresting the perpetrator in the person of the accused. A policeman noticed how the accused, in a remarkable manner, pressed against a lady (who was in the company of a gentleman) while they were going through a passage. The officer asked the lady to examine her dress while he held the man under suspicion. It was ascertained that the dress had received quite a long slit. The accused was taken to the station, where he was examined. Found on him were a sharp knife, which he confessed he used for cutting dresses, and two silk sashes, such as ladies wear on their dresses. He confessed that he had taken the sashes from dresses in crowds. Finally, an examination of his person revealed a lady's silk neck scarf. The accused said he had found this. Since his statement in this case could not be refuted, the complaint was therefore based on the result of the search. In the two instances where a complaint was made by the injured parties, his acts were designated as injury to property, and in the other two instances as theft. The accused, a man who had often been punished before, gave before the judge, with a pale expressionless face, a strange explanation of his puzzling behavior. A major's cook had once thrown him downstairs because he was begging from her, and since that time he had entertained a great hatred for the whole female sex. There was a doubt about his responsibility, and he was therefore examined by a physician. The medical expert gave the opinion at the trial that there was no reason to regard the accused as insane, although he was of low intelligence. The culprit defended himself in a peculiar manner. An irresistible impulse forced him to approach women wearing silk dresses. *The touch of silk material gave him a feeling of delight,* and this went so far that, while in prison for examination, he would become excited if a silk thread happened to pass through his fingers as he unraveled rags. Judge Müller considered the accused to be simply a dangerous, vicious man, who should be made harmless for a long period of time. He advised imprisonment for one year. The court sentenced him to six months' imprisonment, with a loss of honor for one year.

A classical case of material fetishism (silk) is the following related by Dr. P. Garnier:

Case 121.

On September 22, 1881, V. was arrested in the streets of Paris while he interfered with the silk dress of a lady in a manner that aroused suspicion that he was a pickpocket. At first he was very confused, but finally, after many vain excuses, made a clean confession of his "mania." He was twenty-nine years of age, an assistant in a bookseller's shop; his father was a drunkard and a religious zealot, his mother of abnormal character. She wished to make a priest of him. Since his early youth he had felt an instinctive – and, he believes, congenital – impulse to touch silk. As a choirboy at the age of twelve he was allowed to wear a silk sash, which he could not finger often enough. He could not describe the peculiar sensation he experienced in doing this. Later, he became acquainted with a ten-year-old girl for whom he had a childish affection. On Sundays, when he met this girl, who was clad in a silk dress, he was impelled to lovingly put his arms around her and touch her dress. Later he derived intense pleasure from gazing at and touching the silk gowns displayed in a dressmaker's shop.

When they gave him remnants of silk material, he would promptly put them next to his body, and this immediately produced erection, orgasm and even ejaculation. These lustful desires made him so uneasy that he doubted his vocation to the priesthood and obtained his discharge from the seminary. As a consequence of habitual masturbation, he was, at that time, very neurasthenic. His silk fetishism swayed him as it always had. Only when a woman wore a silk gown could she charm him.

Even when he was a child, ladies with silk gowns played a prominent part in his dreams; later on the dreams were accompanied by pollutions. Because of his natural shyness, he did not resort to coitus until later in life, and then he could only succeed with a woman dressed in silk. He preferred instead to mix with crowds on the street and touch the silk gowns of ladies, which always produced ejaculation, accompanied by powerful orgasms and intense lustful feelings. What gratified him more than being with the prettiest woman was to put on a silk petticoat before going to bed.

The forensic medical opinion declared him to be a heavily tainted subject who gave way to abnormal desires under the strain of morbid impulses. Pardon (Dr. Garnier, *Annales d'hygiène publique,* 3d ser., vol. 29, no. 5).

The following case of *kid glove fetishism* is particularly adapted to show the origin of fetishistic associations, as well as the enormous influence permanently exercised by such an association, although it is itself based upon a psychic-physical, morbid predisposition.

Case 122.

Mr. Z., American, thirty-three years of age, manufacturer; for eight years had a happily married life, blessed with offspring; consulted with me for a peculiar and troublesome glove fetishism. He despised himself because of it, and said it brought him nearly to the verge of despair and even insanity.

He claimed to come from thoroughly sound parents, but had since infancy been neuropathic and excitable. By nature he was very sensual, while his wife was very frigid.

At the age of nine he was seduced by schoolmates to practice masturbation, which gratified him immensely, and he yielded to it with passion.

One day, when sexually excited, he found a small bag of chamois skin. He slipped it over his member and thereby experienced great sensual pleasure. After that he used it for masturbatory manipulations, put it around his scrotum, and carried it about with him day and night. This aroused in him an unusual interest for leather in general, but particularly for kid gloves.

With puberty, this interest centered entirely on ladies' kid gloves, which simply fascinated him. If he touched his penis with one such glove, it produced erection and even ejaculation.

Men's gloves did not excite him in the least, although he loved to wear them.

As a result, nothing about woman attracted him but her kid gloves. These were his fetish. They had to be long, with many buttons, and preferably worn-out, dirty and saturated, with perspiration at the fingertips. A woman wearing such gloves, even if she were ugly and old, had a particular charm for him. Ladies with silk or cotton gloves did not attract him. When meeting a lady he always looked at her gloves first. He took very little interest in the rest of the female sex.

When he would shake hands with a lady wearing kid gloves, the contact with the soft, warm leather would induce in him erection and orgasm.

Whenever he could get ahold of a kid glove, he would at once retire to a lavatory, wrap it around his genitals, and masturbate.

Later on, when visiting brothels, he would beg the prostitute to put on long gloves he provided for this purpose, which alone would excite him so much that ejaculation ensued forthwith.

Z. became a collector of ladies' kid gloves. He would hide away hundreds of pairs in various places. In his spare time he would count and gloat over them, "as a miser would over his gold," place them over his genitals, bury his face in a pile of them, put one on his hand, and masturbate. This gave him more intense pleasure than coitus.

He made covers or suspensories of them for his penis, wearing them for days. He preferred black, soft leather. He would fasten ladies' kid gloves around his waist in such a fashion that they would hang, apron-like, over his genitals.

After marriage, this fetishism grew worse. He was usually only virile when he put a pair of his wife's gloves near her head, so he could kiss them during coitus.

The acme of pleasure occurred when he would persuade his wife to put on kid gloves and thus touch his genitals prior to cohabitation.

Z. felt very unhappy because of this fetishism, and made repeated but vain attempts to free himself of the curse.

Whenever he came across the word "glove," or a picture of a glove in novels, fashion plates, advertisements, etc., he was simply fascinated. At the theatre, his eyes were riveted on the hands of the actresses. He could scarcely tear himself away from the show windows of glove dealers.

He would often stuff long gloves with wool or some such material to make them resemble arms and hands. Then he would **rub his member between the artificial limbs** until he had achieved his goal.

He routinely took ladies' kid gloves to bed with him and wrapped them around his penis until he could feel them like a large leathern priapus between his legs.

From the cleaners in larger towns he bought ladies' gloves that had not been reclaimed, but preferred those most soiled and worn. Although he admitted having yielded twice to the temptation of stealing such gloves, in every other respect his behavior was absolutely proper. When in a crowd he had to touch ladies' hands whenever possible. At his office he allowed no opportunity to pass without shaking hands with ladies, in order to feel for "at least a second the soft, warm leather." His wife had to wear, as often as possible, kid gloves or some such article made of chamois, with which he lavishly provided her.

At his office he always had ladies' gloves lying on his desk. Not an hour passed in which he did not touch and stroke them. When especially excited sexually, he put such a glove in his mouth and chewed it.

Other articles of the female *toilette,* as well as other parts of the female body, did not attract him. Z. felt very depressed because of this anomaly. He felt ashamed to look into the innocent eyes of his children, and prayed to God to protect them from the curse of their father.

The object of fetishism may also be found in a thing that only by *sheer accident stands in relation to the body of woman,* as may be gathered from the following instance related by Moll. Further, it proves how, by the mere accidental association of an apperception with a parallel sexual emotion – based, of course, upon a special psychic process – the object of such apperception may become a fetish, which may, in turn, some day again disappear.

The theory of association in connection with original perverse manifestations (based on organic-psychic motives) seems here quite acceptable. The same may be said of the data relating to masochism and sadism.

Case 123.

B., thirty years of age, apparently untainted, refined and sensitive; great lover of flowers; liked to kiss them, but without any sensual motive or sensual excitement; of a rather frigid nature; before twenty-one did not practice masturbation, and subsequently only for periods of time. At twenty-one he was introduced to a young lady who wore some large roses on her bosom. Since then large roses had dominated his sexual feelings. He incessantly bought roses; kissing them would produce erection. He took roses to bed with him, although he never touched his genitals with them. His pollutions, henceforth, were accompanied by dreams of roses. He dreamt of roses that had a fairy-like beauty; when he inhaled their fragrance, he ejaculated.

He became secretly engaged to his "lady of roses," but the platonic relations grew colder, and when the engagement was broken off the rose fetishism suddenly and permanently disappeared. It never returned, even when he became engaged again after a long spell of melancholia (A. Moll, *Zentralblatt f. d. Krankheiten der Harn- und Sexualorgane*, vol. 5, no. 3).

[d] beast fetishism.

In close relation to stuff fetishism, certain cases must be considered in which beasts exercise an aphrodisiacal influence over human beings. One feels tempted to call it *zoophilia erotica*.

This perversion seems to be rooted in a fetishism where the object is the skin of the beast.

The transmitting medium of this fetishism may, perhaps, be found in the peculiar idiosyncrasies of the tactile nerves, whereby the touching of furs or animal skins produces peculiar and lustful emotions (analogous to hair, braid, velvet, and silk fetishism). This may, perhaps, also explain the peculiar whim for cats and dogs sometimes seen in sexually perverted persons (see especially case 118). The following case, coming under my personal observation, seems to favor this assumption.

Case 124.

Zoophilia erotica, fetishism. Mr. N. N., twenty-one years of age, congenitally neuropathic, from a neuropathically tainted family. Even as a child he often felt impelled to behave with indifference for fear of encountering some untoward event. He learned easily, never had a severe illness, and early on had a great love for domestic animals, especially dogs and cats, because when petting them he experienced lustful emotions. For years he indulged in this play with animals, which sensually stimulated him, although, as it were, in an innocent fashion. When he arrived at the age of puberty he recognized the immorality of his acts and tried to free himself from the habit. He succeeded in this, but from then on he was troubled by such situations in his dreams, which produced pollutions. He then began masturbation. At first he practiced it by manipulation, accompanied by the idea that he was petting and stroking animals. After some time, he arrived at psychic masturbation, produced by vividly imagining such situations, and accompanied by orgasm and ejaculation. This made him neurasthenic.

He claimed that sodomitic ideas never entered his mind, that the sex of the animal never influenced his fantasies or actions, and that, in fact, he had given it no thought.

He never had homosexual instinct. Heterosexual desires were not foreign to him, however, although he never indulged in coitus because of absence of libido (due to masturbation and neurasthenia) and fear of infection. He was only drawn to women with a lithe figure and a proud gait.

The usual symptoms of cerebro-spinal neurasthenia were present. Patient was of slight build and anemic. He was greatly interested in knowing whether his lost virility could be restored, as this would raise his waning self-esteem.

Suggestions were made on how to avoid psychic masturbation, remove neurasthenia, strengthen the sexual centers, and satisfy the sex life in a normal way as soon as possible.

Epicritic. No bestiality, but fetishism. Very likely the petting of domestic animals, coupled with an abnormally premature sex life, coincided with a primary sexual emotion – probably originating from tactile sensations – and thus established an association between the two facts, which, by repetition, became permanent (*Zeitschrift für Psychiatrie,* vol. 50).

[4] antipathic sexuality.

AFTER THE attainment of complete sexual development, the most constant elements of self-consciousness in the individual include the knowledge of representing a definite sexual personality and the consciousness of desire, and, during the period of physiological activity of the reproductive organs (production of semen and ova), the ability to perform sexual acts corresponding with that sexual personality – acts which, consciously or unconsciously, have a procreative purpose.

Sexual instinct and desire, save for indistinct feelings and impulses, remain latent until the period of development of the sexual organs. The child is of neither gender; and though, during this latent period – when sexuality has not yet risen into clear consciousness, but is virtually present, and unconnected with powerful organic sensations – abnormally early excitation of the genitals may occur, either spontaneously or as a result of external influence, and find satisfaction in masturbation; notwithstanding this, however, the *psychic* relation to persons of the opposite sex is still absolutely lacking, and the sexual acts during this period exhibit more or less a reflex spinal character.

The existence of innocence or sexual neutrality is the more remarkable since very early in education, employment, dress, etc., the child undergoes a differentiation from children of the opposite sex. These impressions remain, however, devoid of psychic significance, because they are stripped of apparent sexual meaning; the central organ (cortex) of sexual emotions and ideas is therefore not yet capable of activity due to its undeveloped condition.

With the inception of anatomical and functional development of the generative organs, and the differentiation of form belonging to each sex (which go hand in hand, with boys as well as girls), rudimentary mental feelings corresponding with the sex are developed; and in regard to this, of course, education and external influences generally have a powerful effect upon the individual who is now beginning to observe.

If sexual development is normal and undisturbed, a definite character, corresponding with the sex, is developed. Certain well-defined inclinations and reactions in relation with persons of the opposite sex arise; and it is psychologically noteworthy with what relative rapidity each individual psychic type corresponding with the sex evolves.

For instance, while modesty during childhood is essentially an uncomprehended and incomprehensible exaction of education and imitation imperfectly expressed in the innocence and naïveté of the child, in the youth and maiden it becomes an imperative requirement of self-respect; and, if it is in any way offended, intense vasomotor reaction (blushing) and psychic emotions are induced.

If one's original constitution is favorable and normal, and factors injurious to the psychosexual development exercise no adverse influence, then a psychosexual personality is developed which is so unchangeable and corresponds so completely and harmoniously with the sex of the individual in question that subsequent loss of the generative organs (as by castration), menopause (the *climacteric*), or senility cannot essentially alter it.

This, however, must not be taken as a declaration that the castrated man or woman, the youth and the aged man, the maiden and the matron, the impotent and the potent man, do not essentially differ from each other in their psychic existence.

An interesting and important question for what follows is whether the peripheral influences of the generative glands (testes and ovaries) or central cerebral conditions are the determining factors in psychosexual development. The fact that congenital deficiency of the generative glands, or removal of them *before* puberty, have a profound influence on physical and psychosexual development, so much so that psychosexual development is stunted and assumes a type more closely resembling the opposite sex (eunuchs, certain viragoes, etc.), signifies in this respect their great importance.

That the physical processes taking place in the genital organs are cooperative and not exclusively the factors in the process of development of the psychosexual character is shown by the fact that, notwithstanding a normal anatomical and physiological state of these organs, sexual instinct can develop opposite of the sexual characteristic to which the individual belongs.

In this case the cause can only be found in a centrally conditioned anomaly – in an abnormal psychosexual constitution. This constitution, as far as its anatomical and functional foundation is concerned, is as yet unknown. Since, in nearly all such cases, the individual tainted with antipathic sexual instinct displays a neuropathic predisposition in several directions, and the neuropathic predisposition may be related to hereditary degenerate conditions, this anomaly of psychosexual feeling may be clinically called a functional sign of degeneration. This inverted sexuality appears spontaneously, without external cause, with the development of sexual life as an individual manifestation of an abnormal form of sexual life, and has the force of a *congenital* phenomenon; or it develops upon a sexuality which in the beginning was normal, as a result of definite injurious influences, and thus appears as an *acquired* anomaly. Upon what conditions this enigmatic phenomenon of acquired homosexual instinct depends still remains unexplained, and is a mere hypothetical matter. Careful examination of the so-called acquired cases make it probable that predisposition – also present here – consists of a latent homosexuality, or, at any rate, bisexuality, which, for it to become manifest, requires the influence of accidental stimulating causes to rouse it from its dormant state.

In so-called antipathic sexual instinct there are degrees of the phenomenon that correspond with the degrees of predisposition in the individuals. Thus, in the milder cases, there is simple hermaphroditism; in more pronounced cases, only homosexual feeling and instinct, limited, however, to the sex life; in still more complete cases, the whole psychic personality, and even bodily sensations, are transformed so they correspond with the sexual inversion; and, in the complete cases, the physical form is correspondingly altered.

The following division of the various phenomena of this psychosexual anomaly is therefore made in accordance with these clinical facts.

[a] homosexual feeling as an acquired manifestation in both sexes.

The determining factor here is the demonstration of perverse feeling for the same sex; not the proof of sexual acts with the same sex. These two phenomena must not be confounded with each other; *perversity* must not be taken for *perversion*.

Perverse sexual acts, without being dependent upon perversion, are often observed. This is especially true in reference to sexual acts between persons of the same sex, particularly in reference to pederasty. Here hyperesthesia, and not necessarily sexual paresthesia, is in effect, with natural sexual satisfaction physically or psychically impossible.

Thus we find homosexual intercourse in impotent masturbators or debauchees, or in sensual men and women who, lacking anything better, are in prisons, aboard ships, or in garrisons, bagnios, boarding schools, etc.

There is an immediate return to normal sexual intercourse as soon as the obstacles to it are removed. Frequently the cause of such a temporary aberration in youthful individuals is *masturbation* and its results.

Nothing is so prone to contaminate – under certain circumstances, even to exhaust – the source of all noble and ideal sentiments, which arise from a normally developed sexual instinct, as the practice of masturbation in one's early years. It despoils the unfolding bud of perfume and beauty, and leaves behind only the coarse, animal desire for sexual satisfaction. If an individual, thus depraved, reaches the age of maturity, there is lacking in him that aesthetic, ideal, pure and free impulse that draws the opposite sexes together. The glow of sensual sensibility wanes, and attraction toward the opposite sex is weakened. This defect influences the morals, character, fantasy, feeling and instinct of the youthful masturbator, male or female, in an unfavorable manner, even causing, under certain circumstances, desire for the opposite sex to become entirely absent; thus masturbation becomes preferable to the natural mode of sexual satisfaction.

Sometimes the development of nobler sexual feelings toward the opposite sex suffers because of hypochondriacal fear of infection in sexual intercourse; or because of an actual infection; or as a result of a faulty education that points out such dangers and exaggerates them. Again (especially in females), fear of the result of coitus (pregnancy), or abhorrence of men due to physical or moral defects, may direct into perverse channels an instinct that makes itself felt with abnormal intensity. Premature and perverse sexual satisfaction, on the other hand, injures not only the mind but also the body, inasmuch as it only induces neuroses of the sexual apparatus (irritable weakness of the centers governing erection and ejaculation, defective pleasurable feeling in coitus, etc.), while, at the same time, it maintains the imagination and libido in a state of continuous excitement.

Almost every masturbator eventually reaches a point where, frightened upon learning the results of the vice, or upon experiencing them (neurasthenia), or upon being led by example or seduction to the opposite sex, he wishes to free himself of the vice and reinstate his sex life.

The moral and mental conditions here are the most unfavorable possible. The pure glow of sexual feeling is destroyed, the fire of sexual instinct is absent, and self-confidence is lost, for every masturbator is more or less timid and cowardly. If the youthful sinner eventually attempts coitus, he is either disappointed because enjoyment is nonexistent due to defective sensual feeling, or he lacks the physical strength necessary to accomplish the act. This fiasco has a fatal effect and leads to absolute psychic impotence. A bad conscience and the memory of past failures prevent success in any further attempts. Constant sexual desire, however, demands satisfaction, and this moral and mental perversion distances itself farther and farther from woman.

For various reasons, however (neurasthenic complaints, hypochondriacal fear of results, etc.), the individual is also deprived of masturbation. Bestiality is resorted to, at times, under such circumstances. Intercourse with the same sex is then nearby as the result of seduction or feelings of friendship which, on the level of pathological sexuality, can be easily associated with sexual feelings.

Passive and mutual masturbation now become the equivalent of the avoided act. If there is a seducer – which, unfortunately, often happens – then the cultivated pederast is produced – i.e., a man who performs quasi acts of masturbation with persons of his own sex, and, at the same time, feels and prefers himself in an active role corresponding with his real sex, and who is mentally indifferent not only to persons of the opposite sex, but also to those of his own.

Sexual aberration reaches this degree in the *normally* constituted, *untainted,* mentally healthy individual. No case has yet been demonstrated in which perversity has been transformed into perversion – i.e., into an inversion of the sexual instinct.[79]

With *tainted* individuals, the matter is quite different. The latent perverse sexuality is developed under the influence of neurasthenia induced by masturbation, abstinence, etc.

Sexual excitation is thereby gradually induced in persons of the same sex. Related ideas are colored with lustful feelings and awaken corresponding desires. This decidedly degenerate reaction is the beginning of a process of physical and mental transformation, a description of which is attempted in what follows, and which is one of the most interesting psychological phenomena that have been observed. This metamorphosis presents different stages or degrees.

[1] degree: simple reversal of sexual feeling.

This degree is attained when a person exercises an aphrodisiac effect over another person of the same sex who reciprocates the sexual feeling. Character and instinct, however, still correspond with the sex of the individual presenting the reversal of sexual feeling. He feels himself in the active role; he recognizes his impulse toward his own sex as an aberration, and finally seeks aid.

With episodic improvement of the neurosis, initially even normal sexual feelings may reappear and assert themselves. The following case seems well suited to exemplify this stage of the psychosexual degeneration:

Case 125.

Acquired antipathic sexual instinct. "I am an official, and, as far as I know, come from an untainted family. My father died of an acute disease; my mother, still living, is *very nervous. My sister has been intensely religious for some years.*

"I myself am tall, and, in speech, gait and manner, give a perfectly masculine impression. Measles is the only disease I have had, but since my thirteenth year I have suffered from so-called nervous headaches.

"My sexual life began in my thirteenth year, when I became acquainted with a boy somewhat older than myself, **and with whom I amused myself by touching his genitals.** I had my first ejaculation in my fourteenth year. Seduced to masturbation by two older schoolmates, I practiced it partly with others and partly alone; alone, however, I always thought of persons of the female sex. My sexual desire was very intense, as it is today. I later tried to seduce a pretty, stout servant girl who had very large breasts; **I only succeeded in having her expose the upper part of her body in my presence and letting me kiss her mouth and breasts while she took my erect penis in her hand and rubbed it. Even though I vehemently sought coitus, she would only let me touch her genitals.**

"After going to the university, I visited a brothel and succeeded effortlessly.

"Then an event occurred which changed me. One evening I accompanied a friend home, and in a mild state of intoxication I grasped him **by his genitals.** He feigned slight opposition. I then went up to his room with him, and we practiced mutual masturbation. From then on we indulged in it quite frequently; in fact, we eventually engaged in fellatio, with resultant ejaculation. It is strange that I was not at all in love with this person, but passionately in love with another friend, for whom I never felt the slightest sexual excitement, and with whom I never connected sexual matters, even in thought. My visits to brothels, where I was gladly received, became more infrequent; in my friend I found a sexual substitute, and I did not desire sexual intercourse with women.

"We never practiced pederasty. That word was not even known between us. From the beginning of this relation with my friend, I again masturbated more frequently; naturally the thought of females receded more and more into the background, and I thought more and more about young, handsome, strong men with the largest possible genitals. I preferred young fellows, from sixteen to twenty-five years old, without beards, although they had to be handsome and clean. Young laborers dressed in trousers of Manchester cloth or English leather, particularly masons, especially excited me.

"Persons in my own position hardly had any effect on me; but, at the sight of one of those strapping fellows of the lower class, I experienced marked sexual excitement. It seems to me that the touch of such trousers, the opening of them and the grasping of the penis, as well as kissing the fellow, would be the greatest delight. My sensibility to female charms is somewhat dulled; yet in sexual intercourse with a woman, particularly when she has well-developed breasts, I am always potent without the help of my imagination. I have never attempted to make use of a young laborer, or the like, for the satisfaction of my evil desires, and never shall; but I often feel such a longing. I often impress on myself the mental image of such a man, and then masturbate at home.

"I am absolutely devoid of taste for female work. I rather like to move in female society, but dancing is repugnant to me. I have a lively interest in the fine arts. That my sexual sense is somewhat reversed is, I believe, in part due to greater convenience, which keeps me from entering into a relationship with a girl, as this is a matter of too much trouble. Constantly visiting houses of prostitution is, for aesthetic reasons, repugnant to me, and thus I always return to solitary masturbation, which is very difficult for me to avoid.

"Hundreds of times I have said to myself that, in order to have a normal sexual sense, it would be necessary for me, first of all, to overcome my irresistible passion for masturbation, a practice completely repugnant to my aesthetic feeling. Again and again I have resolved with all my might to fight this passion, but I am still unsuccessful. When I feel the sexual impulse gaining strength, I prefer to masturbate instead of seeking satisfaction in the natural manner because I feel I would enjoy myself more.

"And yet experience has taught me that I am always potent with girls, and also without trouble and the vision of masculine genitals. In one case, however, I did not attain ejaculation because the woman – it was in a brothel – was devoid of every charm. I cannot avoid the thought and severe self-accusation that, to a certain extent, my inverted sexuality is the result of excessive masturbation; and this especially depresses me, because I am compelled to acknowledge that I scarcely feel strong enough to overcome this vice by the force of my own will.

"As a result of my relations for years with the fellow student and pal mentioned in this communication – which, however, began while we were at the university, and after we had been friends for seven years – the impulse to unnaturally satisfy my libido has grown much stronger. I trust you will permit me to describe an incident which worried me for months:

"In the summer of 1882, I made the acquaintance of someone six years younger than myself, who, with several others, had been introduced to me and my friends. I soon became deeply interested in this handsome man, who was unusually well-proportioned, slim and healthy. After a few weeks our association ripened into friendship, and finally into passionate love, with feelings of the most intense jealousy. I soon noticed that, in this love, sexual excitation was also very marked; and, notwithstanding my determination, aside from everything else, to keep myself in check in relation to this man, whom I highly respected for his superior character, one night, after indulging freely in beer, as we were enjoying a bottle of champagne in my room, and drinking to good, true and lasting friendship, I yielded to the irresistible impulse to embrace him, etc.

"When I saw him the next day, I was so ashamed that I could not look him in the face. I felt the deepest regret because of my actions, and accused myself bitterly for having thus sullied our friendship, which had been and could have remained so pure and precious. In order to prove to him that I had lost control of myself only momentarily, at the end of the semester I urged him to make an excursion with me, and after some reluctance, the reason of which was only too clear to me, he consented. For several nights we slept in the same room without any attempt on my part to repeat my actions. I wished to talk with him about the event of that night, but I could not bring myself to do it; even when, during the next semester, we were separated, I could not induce myself to write to him on the subject; and when I visited him in March at X., it was the same. And yet I felt a great desire to clear up this dark point with an open statement. In October of the same year I was again in X., and this time found courage to speak without reserve; indeed, I asked him why he had not resisted me. He answered that it was partly because he wished to please me, and partly because he was somewhat apathetic due to his being a little intoxicated. I explained my condition to him, and also gave him *Psychopathia Sexualis* to read, expressing the hope that with the force of my own will I could fully and lastingly become master of my unnatural impulse. Since this confession, relations between us have been the most delightful and happy possible; there are the most friendly feelings on both sides, which are sincere and true, and hopefully they will endure.

"If I cannot improve my abnormal condition, I am determined to put myself under your treatment; the more so because, after a careful study of your work, I cannot count myself as belonging to the category of so-called homosexuals, and also because I have the firm conviction, or hope, at least, that a strong will, assisted and combined with skillful treatment, could transform me into a man of normal feeling."

Case 126.

Ilma S.,[80] aged twenty-nine; single, merchant's daughter; from a family with bad nervous taint. Father was a drinker and died by suicide, as did the patient's brother and sister. Another sister suffered from convulsive hysteria. Mother's father shot himself while insane. Mother was sickly, and became paralyzed after an attack of apoplexy. The patient never had a serious illness. She was bright, enthusiastic and dreamy. Menses at the age of eighteen without difficulty; but thereafter they were very irregular. At fourteen, chlorosis and catalepsy due to hysteria. Later, severe hysteria and an attack of hysterical insanity. At eighteen, relations with a young man that were not platonic. This man's love was passionately returned. From the patient's statements it seemed that she was very sensual, and after separating from her lover she practiced masturbation. She then led a romantic life. In order to earn a living, she put on male clothing and became a tutor; she gave up her job, however, because her mistress, not knowing her sex, fell in love with her and courted her. She then became a railway employee. In the company of her companions she was compelled, in order to conceal her sex, to visit brothels with them and hear the most vulgar stories. This became so distasteful to her that she gave up her job, resumed the dress of a female, and again sought to earn a living. She was arrested for theft and, due to severe hysterical epilepsy, was sent to the hospital. There inclination and impulses toward the same sex were discovered. The patient became troublesome due to a passionate love for female nurses and patients.

Her sexual inversion was considered congenital. Regarding this, the patient made some interesting statements:

"I am judged incorrectly if it is thought that I feel like a man toward the female sex. In my whole thought and feeling I am much more like a woman. Did I not love my cousin as only a woman can love a man?

"My feelings changed in Budapest when, dressed as a man, I had an opportunity to observe my cousin. I saw that I was completely deceived by him. This broke my heart. I knew that I could never love another man, and that I belonged to those who love but once. Of similar effect was the fact that, in the society of my companions at the railway, I was forced to hear the most offensive language and visit the most disreputable houses. As a result of this insight into men's motives gained in this way, I took an unconquerable dislike to men. Since I am, however, very passionate and need to have some loving person to depend on, to whom I can completely surrender myself, I felt myself more and more powerfully drawn toward intelligent women and girls who were sympathetic with me."

The antipathic sexual instinct of this patient, which was clearly acquired, expressed itself in a stormy and decidedly sensual way, and was further augmented by masturbation, since constant supervision in hospitals made sexual satisfaction with the same sex impossible. Character and occupation remained feminine. There were no manifestations of viraginity. According to information lately received by the author, this patient, after two years of treatment in an asylum, was entirely freed from her neurosis and sexual inversion, and was discharged as cured.

Case 127.
Mr. X., aged thirty-five, single, civil servant; mother insane, brother a hypochondriac.

Patient was healthy and strong, with a lively sensual temperament. He had manifested a powerful sexual instinct abnormally early, and even masturbated when he was a small boy. He had coitus for the first time at the age of fourteen, enjoyed himself and was completely potent. When he was fifteen years old, a man seduced and then masturbated him. X. became repulsed and freed himself from the disgusting situation. At the age of maturity he committed excesses in sexual desire with coitus; in 1880 he became neurasthenic and was afflicted with weakness of erection and premature ejaculation. He thus became less and less potent, and no longer experienced pleasure in the sexual act. During this period of sexual decadence he had what, for a long time, was previously foreign to him – and is still incomprehensible to him – an inclination to engage in sexual intercourse with immature girls of twelve or thirteen. His libido increased as his virility diminished.

Gradually he became attracted to boys of thirteen or fourteen. He sometimes felt the need to approach them.

Whenever he had the opportunity to touch boys who were attractive to him, he would have a violent erection, particularly when he was able to touch the boys' legs. Since then he did not desire women. Sometimes he forced women to have coitus, but his erection was weak and his ejaculation premature and devoid of pleasure.

Now only youths interested him. He dreamed about them and had pollutions. After 1882 he occasionally had an opportunity **to sleep with young men.** This sexually excited him, which he satisfied by masturbating. It was quite exceptional for him to touch his bedfellow and indulge in mutual masturbation. He shunned pederasty. For the most part he was compelled to satisfy his sexual needs by means of solitary masturbation. During the act he envisioned pleasing boys. After sexual intercourse with such boys, he always felt strengthened and refreshed, but morally depressed; he was conscious of having performed a perverse, indecent and punishable act. He found it painful that his disgusting impulse was more powerful than his will.

X. thought that his love for his own sex had resulted from excessive practice of natural sexual intercourse, and bemoaned his situation. When he consulted with me in December 1889, he asked me whether there were any means to bring him back to a normal sexual condition, since he was not horrified by women and would gladly like to marry.

This intelligent patient, free from degenerative signs, presented no abnormal symptoms except those relating, in a moderate degree, to sexual and spinal neurasthenia.

[2] degree: eviration and defemination.

If cases of antipathic sexual instinct develop and no restoration occurs, then deep and lasting transformations of the *psychic* personality may occur. The process completing itself in this way may be briefly designated *eviration* (*defemination* in woman). The patient undergoes a deep change of character, particularly in his feelings and inclinations, which ultimately become those of a female. After this, he also feels like a woman during the sexual act, desires only passive sex and, in certain circumstances, sinks to the level of a prostitute. In this condition of deep and more lasting psychosexual transformation, the individual is like a (congenital) high-grade homosexual. The possibility of restoring the previous mental and sexual personality seems, in such a case, precluded.

The following case is a classical example of this variety of lasting acquired antipathic sexual instinct:

Case 128.

Sch., aged thirty, physician, told me one day the story of his life and sickness, and asked for an explanation and advice concerning certain anomalies of his sex life. The following description gives, for the most part verbatim, the details of his autobiography; only in some portions has it been shortened:

"My parents are healthy. As a child I was sickly, but with good care I thrived and got on well at school. I was taught to masturbate by my playmates at the age of eleven, and indulged in it passionately. I learned easily until I was fifteen. Due to frequent pollutions I became less capable and did not get on well at school, and was uncertain and embarrassed when called on by my teacher. Frightened by my loss of capability, and recognizing that the loss of semen was responsible for it, I gave up masturbation; the pollutions, however, became even more frequent, often two or three a night. In despair, I consulted one physician after another. None were able to help me.

"Since I grew weaker and weaker, due to the loss of semen, and with my sexual appetite growing more and more powerful, I sought out houses of prostitution. At these houses, however, I was unable to find satisfaction; for, even though the sight of a naked female pleased me, neither orgasm or erection occurred, and even masturbation by a prostitute did not induce an erection. I would scarcely leave the house before the impulse would seize me again, and I would then have a violent erection. I grew ashamed before the girls and ceased to visit such houses. Thus a couple of years passed. My sexual life only consisted of pollutions. My inclination toward the opposite sex grew less and less. At nineteen I went to the university. The theatre had more attractions for me: I wished to become an actor. My parents were not willing. In the city I was occasionally compelled to visit girls with my comrades. I feared such a situation because I knew that coitus was impossible for me, and because my friends might discover my impotence. I therefore avoided, as much as possible, becoming the butt of their jokes and ridicule.

"One evening, in the opera house, an old gentleman sat near me. He courted me. I laughed heartily at the foolish old man, and became involved with his joke. **Unexpectedly he seized my genitals, which immediately caused my penis to become erect.** Frightened, I demanded to know what he intended. He said that he was in love with me. Having heard of hermaphrodites in the clinics, I thought I had one before me, and I was curious to see his genitals. The old man was very willing, and went with me into the bathroom. **As soon as I saw his large penis, fully erect, I became frightened and fled.**

"This man followed me, made strange proposals that I did not understand, and I fled. He did not give me any rest. I had learned the secrets of male love for males, and felt that my sexuality was excited by it. I resisted, however, the shameful passion (as I then regarded it), and, for the next three years, I remained free from it. During this time I repeatedly attempted coitus with girls in vain. My attempts to free myself of my impotence by means of medical treatment were also in vain. Once, when my sexual desire was troubling me again, I recalled what the old man had told me: that male-loving men were accustomed to meet on the E. Promenade.

"After a hard struggle with myself, and with a pounding heart, I went there, made the acquaintance of a blonde man, and allowed myself to be seduced. The first step was taken. This kind of sexual love was satisfactory to me. I always preferred to be in the arms of a strong man. Satisfaction consisted of mutual masturbation and occasionally **kissing the other man's penis.** I was then twenty-three years old. During the lectures in the clinic, just sitting with my comrades on the beds of patients excited me so intensely that I could scarcely listen to the lectures. In the same year I entered into a formal love-relation with a merchant of thirty-four. We lived as man and wife. X. played the man, and we fell more and more in love. I gave myself up to him, but occasionally I had to play the man. After a while I became tired of him; I became unfaithful and he grew jealous. There were terrible scenes, which led to a temporary separation and ultimately to an actual rupture. (X. afterward became insane and died by suicide.)

"I made many acquaintances, and loved the most ordinary people. I preferred those having a full beard, who were tall, middle-aged, and able to play the active role well. I developed an inflammation of the rectum (proctitis). My professor thought it was the result of sitting too much while preparing for examinations. I developed a fistula, and had to undergo an operation; but this did not cure me of my desire to let myself be used passively. I became a physician and went to a provincial town, where I had to live like a nun. I developed a desire to move in ladies' society, and was gladly welcomed there, because it was found that I was not so one-sided as most men, but was interested in *toilettes* and such feminine things. I felt, however, very unhappy and lonesome. Fortunately, in this town I made the acquaintance of a man, a 'sister,' who was like me. For some time I was taken care of by him. When he had to leave, I became depressed and full of despair, which was accompanied by thoughts of suicide.

"When it became impossible for me to endure the town any longer, I became a military surgeon in the capital. There I began to live again, and often made two or three acquaintances in one day. I had never loved boys or young people, only fully developed men. The thought of falling into the hands of the police was frightful. Thus far I have escaped the clutches of the blackmailer. At the same time, however, I could not keep myself from gratifying my impulse. After some months I fell in love with an official of forty. I remained true to him for a year, and we lived like a pair of lovers. I was the wife and was formally courted by him as the lover. One day I was transferred to a small town. We were in total despair. We spent the last night continually kissing and caressing one another.

"In the town of T., I was unspeakably unhappy, in spite of some 'sisters' whom I found. I could not forget my lover. In order to satisfy my sexual desire I slept with soldiers. My money obtained the men, but they remained cold, and I experienced no enjoyment with them. I was successful in being retransferred to the capital, where I found a new love-relation; but there was much jealousy, because my lover liked to venture into the society of 'sisters,' and was proud and coquettish. There was a rupture. I was very unhappy and glad to be transferred from the capital. I now stay in C., alone and in despair. Two infantry privates were brought into service, but with the same unsatisfactory results. When shall I ever find true love again?

"I am over medium height, well-developed, and look somewhat old; therefore, when I wish to make conquests, I use the arts of the *toilette.* My manner, movements and face are masculine. Physically I feel as youthful as a boy of twenty. I love the theatre, and especially art. My interest in the stage is in the actresses, whose every movement and gesture I notice and criticize.

"In the society of gentlemen I am silent and embarrassed, while in the society of those like myself I am free, witty, and as fawning as a cat if the man is sympathetic. When I am without love, I become deeply melancholic; the favors of the first handsome man, however, dispel my depression. In other ways I am frivolous and very ambitious. My profession means nothing to me. Masculine pursuits do not interest me. I prefer novels and going to the theatre. I am effeminate, sensitive, easily moved, easily injured and nervous. A sudden noise makes my whole body tremble, and I have to collect myself in order to keep from crying out."

Remarks: The above case was certainly one of acquired antipathic sexual instinct, since the sexual instinct and impulse were originally directed toward the female sex. Sch. became neurasthenic through masturbation.

As an accompanying manifestation of the neurasthenic neurosis, lessened impression-ability of the erection center and consequent relative impotence developed. As a result of this, sexual sensibility toward the opposite sex decreased, with simultaneous persis-tence of sexual desire. The acquired antipathic sexual instinct had to be abnormal, since the first touch by a person of the same sex was an adequate stimulus for the erection center. The perverse sexual feeling became complete – at first Sch. felt like a man in the sexual act; but more and more, as changes progressed, the feeling and desire for satis-faction changed into a form which, as a rule, characterizes the (congenital) homosexual.

This eviration induced a desire for the passive role, and, further, for (passive) pederasty. It made a deep impression on the character. The character became feminine; Sch. now preferred to move in the society of actual females, had an increasing desire for feminine occupations, and indeed made use of the art of the *toilette* in order to improve his fading charms and to make "conquests."

The above facts concerning acquired antipathic sexual instinct and effemination find an interesting confirmation in the following ethnological data:

Herodotus has described a peculiar disease that frequently affected the Scythians. The disease consisted of the following: men became effeminate in character, put on female garments, did the work of women, and even became effeminate in appearance. Explaining this insanity of the Scythians,[81] Herodotus relates the myth of how the goddess Venus, angered by the plundering of the temple at Ascalon by the Scythians, made women of these plunderers and their descendants.

Hippocrates, not believing in supernatural diseases, recognized that impotence was here a causative factor, and explained it, though incorrectly, as due to the custom of the Scythians to have themselves bled behind the ears in order to cure disease induced by constant horseback riding. He thought that these veins were of great importance in the preservation of the sexual powers, and that when they were severed, impotence was induced. Since the Scythians considered their impotence a result of divine punishment and incurable, they put on the clothing of females and lived as women among women.

It is noteworthy that, according to Klaproth (*Reise in den Kaukasus,* Berlin, 1812, vol. 5, p. 285) and Chotomski, even now impotence is extremely frequent, as a result of riding unsaddled horses, among the Tartars. The same is observed among the Apaches and Navajos of the western continent who ride excessively, scarcely walk, and are remarkable for their small genitals and mild libido and virility. Sprengel, Lallemand and Nysten recognize the fact that excessive riding may be injurious to the sexual organs.

Hammond reports analogous observations of great interest concerning the Pueblo Indians of New Mexico. These descendants of the Aztecs cultivate so-called *"mujerados,"* of which every Pueblo tribe requires one for the religious ceremonies (actual orgies in the spring), in which pederasty plays an important role. In order to cultivate a *mujerado,* a very powerful man is chosen, and he is made to masturbate excessively and ride constantly. Gradually such an irritable weakness of the genital organs is engendered that a great loss of semen is induced. This condition of irritability passes into paralytic impotence. Then atrophy of the testicles and penis sets in, the hair of the beard falls out, the voice loses its depth and compass, and physical strength and energy decrease. Inclination and disposition become feminine. The *mujerado* loses his position in society as a man. He takes on feminine manners and customs, and associates with women. Yet, for religious reasons, he is held in honor. It is probable that, at times other than during the festivals, he is used by the chiefs for pederasty. Hammond had the opportunity to examine two *mujerados.* One had become a *mujerado* seven years before, and was thirty-five years old at the time. Seven years earlier he was entirely masculine and potent. He had noticed gradual atrophy of his testicles and penis. At the same time he lost his libido and power of erection. He differed in no way, in dress and manner, from the women among whom Hammond found him. His genital hair was absent, his penis was shrunken, his scrotum lax and pendulous, and his testicles were extremely atrophied and no longer sensitive to pressure. The *mujerado* had large breasts like a pregnant woman, and asserted that he had nursed several children whose mothers had died. A second *mujerado,* aged thirty-six, who had been in his condition for ten years, presented the same peculiarities, though with less development of the breasts. Like the first *mujerado,* his voice was high and thin, and his body was plump.

[3] degree: stage of transition to a sexually paranoiac metamorphosis.

A further degree of development is represented by those cases in which *physical* sensation, in the sense of a change of sex, is also transformed. In this respect the following case is unique:

Case 129.

Autobiography. "I was born in Hungary in 1844, and for many years I was the only child of my parents; the other children died, for the most part, of general weakness. A brother who was born later is still living.

"I come from a family which has had numerous nervous and mental diseases. It has been said that I was very pretty as a little child, with blonde locks and transparent skin; I was very obedient, quiet and modest, so much so I was taken everywhere in the society of ladies without any offense on my part.

"With a very active imagination – my enemy through life – my talents developed rapidly. I could read and write at the age of four; my memory reaches back to my third year. I played with everything that fell into my hands – lead soldiers, stones, or ribbons from a toy shop; but a machine for working with wood that was given to me as a present I did not like. I liked best to be at home with my mother, who was everything to me. I had two or three friends with whom I got on in a good-natured way; I liked, however, to play with my aunts as well. They always treated me like a girl, which at first did not embarrass me. I must have already been on the path to become just like a girl; I can, at least, still remember well how it was always said: 'He is not supposed to be a boy.' In response to this I tried to play the boy – I imitated my companions in everything, and tried to surpass them in being wild. I succeeded in this. There was no tree or building too high for me to reach its top. I took great delight in playing soldier. I avoided girls more, because I did not wish to play with their toys; it always annoyed me that they treated me so much like one of them.

"In the society of mature people, however, I was always modest, and also always regarded with favor. Fantastic dreams about wild animals – which once drove me out of bed without waking me – troubled me frequently. I was always simply but elegantly dressed, and thus developed a taste for beautiful clothing. It seems peculiar to me that, from the time of my school days, I had a partiality for ladies' gloves, which I put on secretly as often as I could. Thus, when my mother was once about to give away a pair of gloves, I greatly opposed it, and told her, when she asked why I acted so, that I wanted them for myself. I was laughed at, and from that time I took great care not to display my preference for female things. Yet my enjoyment of them was very great. I took special pleasure in masquerade costumes – i.e., only in female attire. If I saw them, I envied their owners. What seemed to me to be the prettiest sight was two young men, beautifully dressed as white ladies, with masks on; and yet I would not have shown myself to others as a girl for anything, because I was so afraid of being ridiculed. At school I worked very hard, and was always among the first in my class. From childhood my parents taught me that duty came first, and they always set me an example. It was also a pleasure for me to attend school, for the teachers were kind, and the elder pupils did not plague the younger ones. We left my first home when my father was compelled, because of his business – which was dear to him – to separate from our family for a year. We moved to Germany. Here there was a stricter, rougher manner, partly with the teachers and partly with the pupils, and I was again ridiculed because of my girlishness. My schoolmates went so far as to give a girl, who had my exact features, my name, and they also gave me hers. Because of this I hated the girl, but I later became friendly with her after her marriage. My mother tried to dress me elegantly, but this was repugnant to me because it made me the object of taunting. So, I was finally delighted when I had the correct trousers and coats. These brought with them, however, a new annoyance. They irritated my genitals, particularly when the cloth was rough; and the touch of tailors while measuring me, because of their tickling, almost convulsed me and was unendurable, particularly around the genitals. Then I had to practice gymnastics; I simply could do nothing at all, or I could only indifferently do the things that even girls can do easily. While bathing I was troubled by feeling ashamed when undressed, but I liked to bathe. Until my twelfth year I had a weak back. I learned to swim late, but ultimately so well that I could take long swims. At thirteen, I had pubic hair and was about six feet tall, but my face was feminine until my eighteenth year, when my beard grew in abundance and ceased my resemblance to a woman. An inguinal hernia that I acquired in my twelfth year, and cured when I was twenty, gave me much trouble, particularly in gymnastics. From the age of twelve I also had problems with itching, burning and twitching that extended from my penis to my back; this would especially happen after sitting for a long period of time, and particularly while working at night. Sitting and standing was painful, and my condition became worse when I caught a cold. I did not suspect, however, that this could be connected with my genitals. Since none of my friends suffered in this way, it seemed strange to me. It required the greatest patience to endure the pain, especially since my abdomen also troubled me.

"Sexually I was still perfectly innocent; but now, as I was at the age of twelve or thirteen, I had a definite feeling of wanting to be a young lady. A young lady's form was more pleasing to me; her quiet manner, bearing, and particularly her attire, attracted me. I was careful to not allow this to be noticed, and yet I am sure that I would not have shrunk from the castration knife if it meant I could have attained my desire. If I had been asked to say why I preferred female attire, I would have said nothing more than it intensely attracted me; I perhaps also seemed to myself, because of my uncommonly white skin, more like a girl. The skin of my face and hands, in particular, was very sensitive. Girls enjoyed my company, and although I would have preferred their company constantly, I avoided them when I could; I had to exaggerate my circumstances in order to not appear feminine. In my heart I always envied them. I was particularly envious when one of my young girlfriends bought long dresses and wore gloves and veils. When I was on a journey at the age of fifteen, a young lady, with whom I was boarding, proposed that I disguise myself as a lady and go out with her; but since she was not alone, I did not acquiesce, much as I would have enjoyed it. While on this journey, I was pleased to see boys in one city wearing blouses with short sleeves that bared their arms. A lady elaborately dressed was like a goddess to me; even if her hand touched me coldly, I was happy and envious, and only too gladly would have put myself in her place – in beautiful garments, with a lovely form. Nevertheless, I studied assiduously, getting through the *Realschule* and the *Gymnasium* in nine years and passing my final examination with good marks. I remember, when I was fifteen, first expressing to a friend the wish to be a girl. When he asked me why, I could not give him a reason. At seventeen I entered fast society; I drank beer, smoked, and tried to joke with waitresses. The waitresses enjoyed my company, but they always treated me as if I wore petticoats. I could not take dancing lessons, they repelled me so; but if I could have gone in disguise, it would have been different. My friends loved me dearly; I hated only one, who seduced me into masturbation. Shame on those days, which injured me for life! I practiced it quite frequently, but during those days I saw myself as a 'double man.' I cannot describe the feeling; I think it was masculine, but mixed with feminine elements. I could not approach girls; I feared them, but they were not strange to me. They impressed me as being more like myself; I envied them. I would have denied myself all pleasures if, after my classes and at home, I could have been a girl and gone out as such. Crinoline and a smoothly fitting glove were my ideals. With every lady's gown I saw, I fantasized how I would feel in it – i.e., as a lady. I had no inclination toward men. I remember, however, that I was somewhat lovingly attached to a very handsome friend with a girl's face and dark hair; I think, though, I had no other wish than the desire that we both could be girls.

"At high school I finally had coitus once, **only I felt that I would have enjoyed intercourse with the girl if I had exchanged my penis with her vagina.** To her astonishment, the girl had to treat me as a girl, and she did this willingly; she treated me as if I were her (she was still quite inexperienced and therefore did not laugh at me).

"When I was a student I was wild at times, but I always felt that I assumed this wildness as a mask. I drank and duelled, but I could not take lessons in dancing because I was afraid of betraying myself. My friendships were close, but without other thoughts. It pleased me most to have a friend masked as a lady, or to study the ladies' costumes at the balls. I understood such things perfectly. I gradually began to feel like a girl.

"Due to my unhappy circumstances, I attempted suicide twice. Once, for no reason I did not sleep for fourteen days, had frequent hallucinations (visual and auditory at the same time), and was both living and dead. The latter habit of thought remains. I also had a friend (a lady) who knew about my hobby and put on my gloves for me, but she always looked upon me as a girl. I understood women better than other men did, and how they differed from men; they always treated me more like a woman – as if they had found in me a female friend. On the whole, I could not endure obscenity, and indulged in it myself only out of braggadocio when it was necessary. I soon overcame my aversion to foul odors and blood, and even liked them. Only some things nauseated me to look at. I was lacking in only one respect: I could not understand my own condition. I knew that I had feminine inclinations, but I also knew that I was a man. Yet I doubt whether – with the exception of the attempts at coitus, which never gave me pleasure (I ascribe this to masturbation) – I ever admired a woman without wishing I were her, or without asking myself whether I could not be like her, or wear her attire. I learned obstetrics with difficulty (I was ashamed for the exposed girls, and felt pity for them), and even now I have to overcome a feeling of fright with obstetrical cases; indeed, I sometimes think that I feel the forceps myself. After successfully filling several positions as a physician, I was in a military campaign as a volunteer surgeon. Riding was difficult for me; when I was a student, it was painful for me to ride because I wanted my genitals to have a more feminine feeling (I think it would have been easier to ride in the ladies' fashion).

"Still, I always thought I was a man with obscure masculine feelings, and whenever I associated with ladies I was still treated as an inexperienced woman. When I wore a uniform for the first time, I think I would have preferred slipping into a lady's costume with a veil; I was disturbed when the stately uniform attracted attention. In private practice I was successful in the three principal branches. I was then involved in another military campaign, and during this campaign I came to understand my nature; for I believe that, since the first jackass was born, no beast of burden has ever had to endure life with the patience I have shown. Military decorations were not absent, but I was indifferent to them.

"Thus I went through life, such as it was, never satisfied with myself, full of dissatisfaction with the world, and vacillating between sentimentality and a wildness that was affected for the most part.

"My experience as a candidate for matrimony was very peculiar. I would have preferred not to marry; family circumstances and my practice, however, forced me into it. I married an energetic, amiable lady from a family in which matriarchy was rampant. I was in love with her as much as one of us can be in love – i.e., what we love, we love with our whole hearts, and we live with this love, even though we do not show it as much as a genuine man does. We love our brides with all the love of a woman, almost as a woman might love her bridegroom. I cannot, however, say this for myself; I believed that I was just a depressed man who would come to his senses and discover himself with marriage. Even on my marriage night, however, I felt that I was just a woman in a man's body; it seemed to me that my place was beneath the woman. On the whole, we lived contented and happy, and for two years we were childless. After a difficult pregnancy (during which time I lay near death in enemy territory during the war), my wife gave birth to our first boy. This boy is still afflicted with a melancholy nature. Then came a second, who is very quiet; a third, full of peculiarities; a fourth, a fifth; and all are predisposed to neurasthenia. Since I always felt out of place, I went out often in gay society; I always worked, however, with as much human strength as I could endure. I studied and operated, and I experimented with many drugs and methods of cure, always on myself. I left the regulation of the house to my wife, as she understood housekeeping very well. My marital duties I performed as well as I could, but without personal satisfaction. Since the first time I had engaged in coitus, the masculine position had been repugnant and difficult for me. I would have very much preferred the other role. When I assisted with my wife's deliveries, it almost broke my heart, because I knew how to appreciate her pain. Thus we lived together for quite a while, until severe gout drove me to various baths and made me neurasthenic. I also became so anemic that every few months I had to take iron; otherwise I would become almost chlorotic, hysterical, or both. Constriction of my heart often troubled me; I would then have unilateral cramps of the chin, nose, neck and larynx, migraine, and cramps of the diaphragm and chest muscles. For about three years I had a feeling as if my prostate was swollen – a bearing-down feeling, as if giving birth to something. I also had pain in my hips, constant pain in my back, and similar ailments. Yet I fought against these ailments with the strength of despair – these illnesses impressed me as being female or effeminate – until three years ago, when a severe attack of arthritis completely broke me down.

"Before this terrible attack of gout occurred, however, in a state of despair I took hot baths (as close to my body temperature as possible) to lessen the pain of the gout. On one of these occasions I suddenly changed, and seemed to be near death. I sprang out of the bath with all my remaining strength; I felt exactly like a woman with a libido. This happened when Indian hemp extract became fashionable and was highly prized. Fearing a possible attack of gout (and feeling perfectly indifferent about life), I took three or four times the usual dose of the extract, and almost died of hashish poisoning. I laughed convulsively, experienced a feeling of unheard-of strength and swiftness, as well as a peculiar feeling in my brain and eyes, with millions of sparks streaming from my brain through my skin. But I could not force myself to speak. Suddenly I saw myself as a woman from my toes to my chest; I felt, as I had while in the bath, that my genitals had shrunken, my pelvis had broadened, and my breasts had become swollen. A feeling of unspeakable delight came over me. I closed my eyes, so at least I did not have to see my changed face. My physician looked like he had a gigantic potato for a head; my wife had the full moon on her thorax. I was strong enough, however, to briefly record my will in my notebook when they both left the room for a short time.

"But who could describe my fright when, the next morning, I awoke and found myself feeling as if I had completely changed into a woman; and when I stood up and started walking, I felt a vulva and breasts! When at last I raised myself out of bed, I felt that a complete transformation had taken place in me. During my illness a visitor said: 'He is too patient to be a man.' And the visitor gave me a plant in bloom, which seemed strange, but pleased me. From that time I was patient and would do nothing in a hurry; I became, however, as tenacious as a cat. At the same time, though, I was mild, forgiving, and no longer instilled with hatred – I had, in short, a woman's disposition. During my last sickness I had numerous visual and auditory hallucinations – I spoke with the dead, etc., saw and heard familiar spirits, and felt like a 'double person.' While lying ill, however, I did not notice that the man in me had been extinguished. The change in my disposition was a piece of good fortune, since I had a paralytic stroke that would have certainly killed me in my previous state. I then reconciled, but no longer recognized, myself. Since I still often confused neurasthenic symptoms with gout, I took many baths. My skin, however, became increasingly itchy (instead of diminishing), so much so that I gave up all external treatment (I also became more and more anemic from the baths), and toughened myself as best I could. But the imperative female feeling remained, and it became so strong that I wore only the mask of a man. In every other way I felt like a woman; gradually I lost memory of my former individuality. What was left of me after the gout, influenza ruined entirely.

"*Present condition:* I am tall, slightly bald, and my beard is growing gray. I am now beginning to stoop. Since having influenza I have lost about one-fourth of my strength. Due to a valvular lesion, my face looks somewhat red; full beard; chronic conjunctivitis; more muscular than fat. My left foot seems to be developing varicose veins, and it often goes to sleep; it appears to be thickened, though it is not.

"My mammary region, though small, swells out perceptibly. My abdomen is feminine in form; my feet are placed like a woman's, and my calves, etc., are feminine; and it is the same with my arms and hands. I can wear ladies' hose and gloves 7 $^1/_2$ to 7 $^3/_4$ in size. I also wear a corset without annoyance. My weight varies between 168 and 184 pounds. Urine, though without albumen or sugar, contains an excess of uric acid. When there is not too much uric acid in it, however, it is clear, and almost as clear as water after any excitement. Bowels usually regular, but if they are not regular, then all the symptoms of female constipation occur. Sleep is poor – for weeks at a time of only two or three hours' duration. Appetite quite good; but, on the whole, my stomach will not bear more than that of a strong woman, and reacts to irritating food with skin rashes and burning in the urethra. My skin is white, and, for the most part, feels quite smooth. There has been unbearable cutaneous itching for the last two years, which has diminished during the last few weeks, and is now only present in the popliteal spaces and on the scrotum.

"Tendency to perspire. Perspiration was previously as good as nonexistent, but now there are all the odious peculiarities of female perspiration, particularly around the lower part of my body; now I have to keep myself cleaner than a woman (I perfume my handkerchief, and use perfumed soap and *eau de cologne*).

"*General feeling:* I feel like a woman in a man's form, and even though I am often sensible of this form, it is always in a feminine sense. Thus, for example, I feel my penis as a clitoris; my urethra as a urethra and vaginal orifice, which always feels a little wet, even when it is actually dry; my scrotum as a labia majora; in short, I always feel a vulva. And only one who feels or has felt so knows what I mean. The skin all over my body feels feminine; it receives all impressions, whether a warm touch, or an unfriendly touch, as feminine, and I have the sensations of a woman. I cannot go out with bare hands, as both heat and cold trouble me. When the time is past when we men are permitted to carry sun umbrellas, I have to endure great sensitivity of the skin on my face, until sun umbrellas can be used again. On awakening in the morning, I am confused for a few moments, as if I were searching for myself; then the imperative feeling of being a woman awakens. I feel the sense of a vulva (that one is there), and always greet the day with a soft or loud sigh, for I fear again the farce that must be carried on throughout the day. I had to learn everything anew; the knife – apparatus, everything – felt different for the last three years; and with the change of muscular sense I had to learn everything over again. I have been successful, and only the use of the saw and bone chisel are difficult; it is almost as if my strength were not quite sufficient. I have, on the other hand, a keener sense of touch in working with the curette on the soft parts. It is unpleasant that, when examining ladies, I often feel their sensations; but this, indeed, does not repel them. The most unpleasant thing I experience is fetal movement. For a long time – several months – I was troubled by reading the thoughts of both sexes, and I still have to fight against this. I can endure it better with women; with men it is repugnant. Three years ago I had not yet consciously seen the world with a woman's eyes; this change in the relation of my eyes to my brain came almost suddenly, with a violent headache. I was with a lady whose sexual feeling was reversed, when suddenly I saw her changed in the sense I now feel about myself – namely, I saw her as a man – and I felt myself as a woman in contrast to her; I thus left her with ill-concealed displeasure. At that time she had not yet come to understand her own condition perfectly.

"Since then, all my sensory impressions are as if they were feminine in form and relation. My cerebral system almost immediately adjusted itself to the vegetative, so that all my ailments were manifested in a feminine way. The sensitivity of all my nerves, particularly the auditory, olfactory and trigeminal, increased to a condition of nervousness. If a window slammed, I was frightened inwardly, for a man does not dare to tremble at such things. If food is not absolutely fresh, I perceive a cadaverous odor. I could never depend on the trigeminal nerve, for the pain would jump whimsically from one branch to another – from a tooth to an eye. Since my transformation, however, I bear toothaches and migraines more easily, and have a less fearful feeling of constrictions in my chest. It seems to me a strange fact that I feel I am a fearful, weak being, and yet, when danger threatens, I am rather cool and collected. This is true in dangerous operations. My stomach rebels, resulting in belching or other symptoms, against the slightest indiscretion (in female diet) that is committed when I neglect to think of my female nature, and my stomach particularly rebels against abuse of alcohol. The indisposition that a man who feels like a woman experiences after intoxication is much worse than what any student could imagine. It almost seems to me as if feeling like a woman was entirely controlled by the vegetative system.

"Small as my nipples are, they demand room; as sometimes happens during puberty, they are swollen and painful. Because of this, white shirts, waistcoats and coats trouble me. I feel as though my pelvis is female, and I feel the same about my anus and buttocks. At first the sensation of a female abdomen was troublesome to me, because it cannot bear trousers and because it always possesses or induces a feminine feeling. I also have the imperative feeling of a female waist. It is as if I were robbed of my own skin and put in a woman's skin that fitted me perfectly, but which felt everything as if it covered a woman, and whose sensations passed through my male body and exterminated the masculine element. The testes, even though not atrophied or degenerated, are no longer testes, and often cause me pain. I feel like they should be in my abdomen, and should be nestled there; their mobility often bothers me.

"Every four weeks, at the time of the full moon, I physically and mentally have the menstrual discomfort of a woman for five days, only I do not bleed; I do, however, have the feeling of a loss of fluid, a feeling that my genitals and abdomen are swollen. A very pleasant period follows a day or two later when the physiological desire for procreation arrives, which with all its power permeates me as a woman. My whole body is then filled with this sensation, as an immersed piece of sugar is filled with water, or as full as a soaked sponge. It is like this: first I feel like a woman longing for love, and then I long for a man; and the desire, in fact, seems to me more a longing to be possessed than a wish for coitus. An intense natural instinct or feminine concupiscence overcomes my feeling of modesty, so that indirectly coitus is desired. I have never felt coitus in a masculine way more than three times in my life, and generally I was always indifferent about it. During the last three years, however, I have experienced it passively, like a woman, often with the feeling of feminine ejaculation, in fact, and I always feel that I have been impregnated. I am always fatigued as a woman is after coitus, and often feel ill, as a man never does. Sometimes it causes me such great pleasure that there is nothing to compare it to: it is the most blissful and powerful feeling in the world – at that moment the woman in me is simply a vulva that has devoured my whole person.

"For the last three years I have never lost for an instant the feeling of being a woman, and now, due to habit, this is no longer annoying to me, though during this period I have felt debased; for a man can endure feeling like a woman without desiring enjoyment, but when desire appears, happiness ceases! Then comes the burning, the heat, the feeling of turgor in my genitals (when my penis is not in a state of erection my genitals do not play any part). When in a state of intense desire, the feeling of sucking in my vagina and vulva is really terrible – a hellish pain of lust that can hardly be endured. If I have an opportunity then to perform coitus, it is better; due to a defective sense of being possessed by the other, however, it does not afford complete satisfaction; a feeling of sterility comes with its weight of shame and is added to a feeling of passive copulation and injured modesty. I almost feel like a prostitute. My reason does not help; the imperative feeling of femininity dominates and rules everything. The difficulty in carrying on one's occupation under such circumstances can easily be appreciated, but it is possible to force oneself to continue. It is, of course, almost impossible to sit, walk, or lie down – any one of these acts, at least, cannot be endured for long – and with the constant touch of my trousers, etc., it can be unendurable.

"Marriage then is like two women living together, one of whom regards herself as wearing the mask of a man (except during coitus when I, as a man, have to make myself feel like a woman). If the feeling of periodic menstruation fails to occur, then feelings of pregnancy or sexual satiety occur; a man never experiences these repugnant sensations of femininity, which can take possession of my whole being. I therefore gladly welcome the return of regular menstrual periods. When erotic dreams or ideas occur, I see myself in the form of a woman with an erect organ. Since my anus feels feminine, it would not be hard to become a passive pederast; only my religious convictions prevent it, as all other deterrents would be overcome. Since such conditions are repugnant, as they would be to anyone, I have a desire to be sexless, or to make myself sexless. If I had been single, I would have long ago removed my testes, scrotum and penis.

"What use is female pleasure when one does not conceive? What good comes from excitation of female love when one has only a wife for gratification (even though copulation is felt as though it were with a man)? What a terrible feeling of shame is caused by feminine perspiration! How the feeling for dress and ornament lowers a man! Even in his changed form, even when he can no longer recall masculine sexual feeling, a man would not want to be forced to feel like a woman. He still knows very well that heretofore he did not constantly feel sexual, that he was merely a human being uninfluenced by sex. Now he suddenly has to regard his former individuality as a mask, and now feels constantly like a woman. This feeling only changes every four weeks when he has his periodic sickness; in the intervals his insatiable female desire returns. If he could only awake without immediately being forced to feel like a woman! He longs for a moment when he at last might raise his mask; that moment, however, does not come. He can only make his misery more tolerable when he puts on some bit of female attire or finery, like an undergarment, since he would not dare go about as a woman. It is no trifle, to be compelled with fulfilling the duties obligated in being a woman costumed as a man, and with no end in sight. Religion alone saves him from a profound lapse, but it does not prevent the pain when temptation affects the man who feels as a woman; and so it must be felt and endured! When a respectable man who enjoys an unusual degree of public confidence and possesses authority must go about with a vulva – imaginary though it might be; when one, leaving his arduous daily task, is compelled to examine the *toilette* of the first lady he meets and criticize her with feminine eyes, reading the thoughts on her face; when a fashion journal possesses an interest equal to that of a scientific work (I felt this as a child); when one must conceal his condition from his wife, whose thoughts, the moment he feels like a woman, he can read in her face as it becomes perfectly clear to her that he has changed in body and soul – what must all this be? Misery caused by a feminine gentleness that must be overcome? Oftentimes, of course, when I am away and alone, it is possible for a time to live more like a woman. I wear female attire, for example, especially at night, keep my gloves on, or wear a veil or a mask in my room, so that my excessive libido is reduced. When feminine feeling has gained entry, however, it imperatively demands recognition. It is often satisfied with a moderate concession, such as the wearing of a bracelet above the cuff; it imperatively demands, however, some kind of concession. My only happiness is seeing myself dressed as a woman without a feeling of shame; indeed, when my face is veiled or masked, I prefer to see and think of myself that way. Like every one of fashion's fools, I have a taste for the prevailing mode, so greatly have I been transformed. To become accustomed to the idea of only feeling like a woman, to remember the previous contrasting manner of thought, and, at the same time, to express oneself as a man, requires a long period of time and an infinite amount of persistence.

"Nevertheless, in spite of everything, I occasionally betray myself with some expression of feminine feeling; either in sexual matters, when I say that I feel so and so, expressing what a man without the female feeling cannot know, or when I accidentally betray that my talent is female attire. In front of women this does not amount to anything, because a woman is greatly flattered when a man understands something of her affairs; this cannot, however, be displayed in front of my wife. How frightened I once was when my wife said to a friend that I had great taste in ladies' fashion! How astonished a haughty, stylish woman was when, as she was about to make a great error in the education of her little daughter, I described to her in writing and verbally all the feminine feelings! I definitely lied to her, saying that my knowledge had been gleaned from letters. Her confidence in me is as great as ever, and the child, who was on the road to insanity, is rational and happy. She had previously felt that all the feminine inclinations were sinful; now she knows what, as a girl, she must bear and control by will and religion, and she feels that she is human. Both ladies would laugh heartily if they knew that I had only drawn on my own sad experience. I also must add that I now have a finer sense of temperature, and I also have a sense of the elasticity of the skin and tension of the intestines, etc., in patients, that was unknown to me before; I also know that in operations and autopsies, poisonous fluids more readily penetrate my (uninjured) skin. Every autopsy causes me pain; examining a prostitute, or a woman with a discharge, cancerous odor, or something similar, is actually repugnant to me. In all respects I am now under the influence of antipathy and sympathy, from my sense of color to my judgment of people. Women usually see in each other symptoms of menstruation; therefore a lady wears a veil when she is not always accustomed to wearing one, and usually she perfumes herself (but only on her handkerchief or gloves) because her sense of smell in relation to her own sex is intense. Odors have an incredible effect on the female organism. For example, the odors of violets and roses quiet me, while other odors disgust me, and when I smell ylang-ylang I cannot contain my sexual excitement. Contact with a woman seems homogeneous to me; coitus with my wife only seems possible to me because she is somewhat masculine and has firm skin – and yet it is more like a form of lesbian love.

"Besides, I always feel passive. Often at night, when I cannot sleep due to excitement, coitus is accomplished **if I have my thighs apart, like a woman having intercourse with a man,** or if I lie on my side; an arm or bedclothes must not touch my breasts, however, or I cannot sleep, and there must be no pressure on my abdomen. I sleep best in a chemise and nightshirt, and with gloves on, because my hands can easily get cold. I am also comfortable in female drawers and petticoats, since they do not touch my genitals. I like women's dresses with crinoline lining best. Dresses do not annoy the feminine man, because he, like every woman, feels the dresses are part of him and not something foreign.

"My dearest associate is a lady suffering from neurasthenia, who, since her last confinement, feels like a man, but who, since I explained these feelings to her, abstains from coitus as much as possible. This is something I, as a husband, dare not do. She, by her example, helps me endure my condition. She has a perfect memory of feminine feelings, and has often given me good advice. If she were a man and I were a young girl I would attempt to win her; for her I would be glad to endure the fate of a woman. Her present appearance, however, is quite different from what it used to be. She is an elegantly dressed gentleman, notwithstanding bosom and hair; she also speaks quickly and concisely, and no longer takes pleasure in the things that please me. She has a kind of melancholy dissatisfaction with the world, but she bears her fate worthily and with resignation, finding her comfort only in religion and the fulfillment of her duty. During her menstrual cycle she almost dies. She no longer enjoys female society and conversation, and does not like delicacies.

"A young friend of mine felt like a girl from the very beginning, and had inclinations toward the male sex. His sister was the opposite; when her uterus demanded its right, and she saw herself as a loving woman in spite of her masculinity, she cut the matter short and committed suicide by drowning.

"Since complete effemination, the principal changes I have observed in myself are:

[1] The constant feeling of being a woman from head to toe.

[2] The constant feeling of having female genitals.

[3] The periodicity of the monthly menstrual cycle.

[4] The regular occurrence of female desire, though not directed to any particular man.

[5] The passive female feeling during coitus.

[6] After coitus, the feeling of impregnation.

[7] The female feeling when thinking of coitus.

[8] At the sight of women, the feeling of being similar to them, and having a feminine interest in them.

[9] At the sight of men, having a feminine interest in them.

[10] At the sight of children, the same feeling.

[11] A changed disposition and much greater patience.

[12] A final resignation to my fate, for which I have nothing to thank but religion; without it I would have committed suicide long ago.

"To be a man and feel that every woman is violently passionate or has sexual desire is hard to endure."

The foregoing autobiography, scientifically so important, was accompanied by the following no less interesting letter:

"Sir – I must beg your indulgence for troubling you with my communication. I lost all control, and thought of myself only as a monster before which I myself shuddered. Then your work gave me courage again, and I was determined to get to the bottom of the matter, examine my past life, and let the results be what they might be. It seemed a duty of gratitude to tell you the results of my recollection and observation, since I had not seen any description by you of an analogous case; and, finally, I also thought it might perhaps interest you to learn, from the pen of a physician, how such a worthless human, or masculine, being thinks and feels under the weight of the imperative idea of being a woman.

"It is not perfect; I no longer have the strength, however, to reflect upon it more, and have no desire to go into the matter more deeply. Much is repeated, but I beg you to remember that any mask may be allowed sometimes to fall off, particularly when it is not voluntarily worn.

"After reading your work I hope that, if I fulfill my duties as a physician, citizen, father and husband, I may still count myself among human beings who do not merely deserve to be despised.

"Finally, I wanted to lay the results of my recollection and reflection before you in order to show that one who thinks and feels like a woman can still be a physician. I consider it a great injustice to bar women from medicine. A woman using her instinct tracks many ailments which, in spite of all diagnostic skills, remain obscure to a man, especially with the diseases of women and children. If I could have my way, I would have every physician live the life of a woman for three months; he then would have a better understanding and more consideration in matters affecting the half of humanity from which he comes; he then would learn to value the greatness of woman, and appreciate the difficulty of her lot."

Remarks: The badly tainted patient was originally psychosexually abnormal, in that he felt like a woman in character and in the sexual act. This abnormal feeling remained purely a psychic anomaly until three years ago, when, due to severe neurasthenia, physical sensations essentially changed his sex; this now dominated his consciousness. To the patient's horror, he physically felt like a woman. Under the impulse of his unavoidable feminine sensations, he experienced a complete transformation of his former masculine feeling, thought and will; a transformation, in fact, of his entire sex life, in the true sense of eviration. At the same time, his ego was able to control these abnormal psychophysical manifestations and prevent a descent into paranoia – a remarkable example of neurotically tainted imperative feelings and ideas, which is of great value for an understanding of the manner in which a psychosexual transformation can happen. Three years later, in 1893, this unhappy colleague sent me an account of his present state. This corresponded essentially with his former state. His physical and psychic feelings were absolutely those of a woman; his intellectual powers were intact, however, and he was therefore saved from paranoia (see below).

A counterpart to this case, which is clinically and psychologically valuable, is that of a lady as given in:

Case 130.

Mrs. X., daughter of a high official. Her mother died from nervous disease. Her father was untainted and died from pneumonia at a good old age. Her brothers and sisters had inferior psychopathic dispositions; one brother was abnormal and extremely neuras-thenic.

As a girl Mrs. X. was decidedly inclined toward boys' sports. So long as she wore short dresses, she used to rove about the fields and woods in the freest manner, and climb the most dangerous rocks and cliffs. She had no taste for dresses and finery. Once, when she was given a dress made in a boys' fashion, she was extremely delighted; and when she was dressed up at school in boys' clothes on the occasion of some theatrical perfor-mance, she was filled with bliss.

Otherwise nothing betrayed her homosexual inclinations. Up to the time of her marriage (at the age of twenty-one), she could not recall a single instance in which she felt herself drawn to persons of her own sex. Men were also a matter of indifference. When she matured she had many admirers. This flattered her very much. She claimed, however, that the difference of the sexes never entered her mind; she was only influenced by the difference in clothes.

When attending her first and only ball, she was only interested in intellectual conversa-tion, and not in dancing or the dancers.

At the age of eighteen she started menstruating without difficulty. She always looked upon menstruation as an unnecessary and bothersome function. Her engagement with a man who, though good and rich, did not possess the slightest knowledge of a woman's nature, was a matter of utter indifference to her. She had neither sympathy for nor antipathy against matrimony. Her connubial duties were initially painful to her, and later on simply loathsome. She never experienced sexual pleasure, but became the mother of six children. When her husband began to observe *coitus interruptus,* because of the prolific consequences, her religious and moral sentiments were hurt. Mrs. X. grew more and more neurasthenic, peevish and unhappy.

She suffered from a prolapsed uterus and vaginal erosions, and became anemic. Gynecological treatment and visits to spas procured only slight improvements.

At the age of thirty-six she had an apoplectic stroke, which confined her to bed for two years with heavy neurasthenic ailments (insomnia, pressure in the head, palpitation of the heart, psychic depression, feelings of lost physical and mental power, which even bordered on insanity, etc.). During this long illness a peculiar change of her psychic and physical feelings took place.

The small talk of the ladies visiting her about love, *toilette,* finery, fashions, domestic and servants' affairs disgusted her. She was mortified at being a woman. She could not even make up her mind to look in the mirror. She loathed combing her hair and making her *toilette.* Much to the surprise of her own people, her hitherto soft and decidedly feminine features assumed a strongly masculine character, so much so that she gave the impression of being a man clad in female garb. She complained to her trusted physician that her periods had stopped — she did not want to involve herself at all, in fact, with such functions. When they recurred again she became ill-tempered, and found the odor of the menstrual flow most nauseating; she resolutely refused the use of perfumes, however, because they affected her in a similar unpleasant manner.

In other ways she felt that a peculiar change had come over her entire being. She had athletic spells and wanted to perform gymnastic exercises. At times she felt like she was twenty. She was startled — when her neurasthenic brain allowed thought at all — at the flight and novelty of her thoughts; at her quick and precise method of arriving at conclusions and forming opinions; at the curt and short way of expressing herself; and at her novel choice of words, which were not always becoming of a lady. An inclination to even use curse words and oaths was noticeable in this otherwise pious and correct woman.

She reproached herself bitterly, grieved because she had lost her femininity, and scandalized her friends with her thoughts, sentiments and actions.

She also perceived a change in her body. She was horrified to notice that her breasts were disappearing, her pelvis was becoming smaller and narrower, her bones were becoming more massive, and her skin was becoming rougher and harder.

She refused to wear a lady's nightgown or cap, and put away her bracelets, earrings and fans. Her maid and her dressmaker noticed a different odor coming from her body; her voice also grew deeper, rougher, and quite masculine.

When the patient was finally able to leave her bed, her bearing had changed; feminine gestures and movements were forced, and she could no longer bear to wear a veil over her face. Her previous period of life as a woman seemed strange to her, as if it did not belong in her history at all; she could no longer play the role of a woman. She assumed more and more the character of a man. She experienced strange feelings in her abdomen, and complained to her physician that she could no longer feel her internal organs of reproduction; she felt that her body was closed up, the region of her genitals enlarged, and she often had the sensation of possessing a penis and scrotum. She also showed unmistakable symptoms of male libido. All these observations affected her deeply, filled her with horror, and depressed her so much that she felt she was on the verge of insanity. With incessant efforts and kind advice, however, the family physician finally succeeded in calming the patient and piloting her safely over this dangerous point. She gained her equilibrium little by little in this novel, strange and morbid physical-psychical form. She took pains to perform her duties as a housewife and mother. It was interesting to observe that a truly masculine firmness of will had developed, and her softness of character had vanished. She assumed the role of the man in her house, a circumstance that led to many disagreements and misunderstandings. She became an enigma that her husband was unable to solve.

She complained to her physician that at times a "bestial masculine libido" threatened to overcome her; this made her despondent. Marital intercourse with the husband was extremely repulsive – impossible, in fact – to her. Periodically the patient experienced feminine emotions, but they became scarcer and weaker as time went by. During such periods she became conscious again of her female genitals and breasts, but these episodes painfully affected her; she felt that such a "second transmutation" would be unbearable and drive her to insanity.

She then became reconciled to the change of sex that was brought about by her severe illness, and, finding support in her religious convictions, bore her fate with resignation.

What affected her most keenly was the fact that, like an actress, she had to move in a strange sphere – i.e., in the role of a woman (*Status praesens,* September 1892).

[4] degree: sexually paranoiac metamorphosis.

A final possible stage in this disease process is the delusion of a transformation of sex. It arises on the basis of sexual neurasthenia, an absolute neurasthenia that results in a mental disease – paranoia.

The following cases show the development of this interesting neuropsychological process to its full potential:

Case 131.

K., aged thirty-six, single male, servant; received at the clinic on February 26, 1889. Typical case of persecutory paranoia, resulting from sexual neurasthenia, with olfactory hallucinations, sensations, etc.

He came from a predisposed family. Several brothers and sisters were psychopathic. Patient had a hydrocephalic skull, depressed in the region of the right fontanelle; eyes neuropathic. He had always been very sensual; began to masturbate at nineteen; had coitus at twenty-three; begot three illegitimate children. He gave up further sexual intercourse because he feared he would have more children; he was unable to provide for them. Abstinence was extremely painful for him. He also gave up masturbation, and was then troubled with pollutions. A year and a half ago he became sexually neurasthenic, had diurnal pollutions, and thereafter became ill and miserable. Generally neurasthenic, after a while he finally became paranoid.

A year ago he began to have paresthetic sensations – as if there were a great coil in the location of his genitals. Then he felt that his scrotum and penis were gone, and that his genitals had changed into those of a female.

He felt his breasts grow, thought that his hair was that of a woman, and that feminine garments were on his body. He thought he was a woman. The people in the street yelled at him: "Look at the woman! The old blowhard!" In a half-dreamy state, he felt as if he played the role of a woman during coitus with a man, which gave him the most intense feelings of pleasure. A remission of his paranoia occurred during his stay at the clinic, and, at the same time, his neurasthenia markedly improved. Feelings and ideas resulting from a developing sexual metamorphosis then disappeared.

The following is a more advanced case of eviration, on the path to a paranoiac change of sex:

Case 132.

Franz St., aged thirty-three; schoolteacher, single; probably from a tainted family; always neuropathic; emotional, timid, intolerant of alcohol; began to masturbate at eighteen.

At thirty there were manifestations of sexual neurasthenia (pollutions with consequent fatigue that soon began to occur during the day; pain in the region of the sacral plexus, etc.). Gradually spinal irritation, pressure in the head and cerebral neurasthenia also started to occur. Beginning in 1885 the patient gave up coitus because he no longer experienced pleasurable feeling. He masturbated frequently.

In 1888 he began to have delusions of paranoia. He noticed that he was avoided, and that he had unpleasant odors around him (olfactory hallucinations). He thought that this explained the altered attitude of people and their sneezing, coughing, etc.

He smelled corpses and foul urine. He recognized that these bad smells came from inward pollutions, as if fluids had flowed up from his symphysis toward his chest. The patient soon left the clinic.

In 1889 he was again received at the clinic in an advanced stage of persecutory and masturbatory paranoia (delusions of physical persecution).

In the beginning of May 1889 the patient attracted attention; he became cross when he was addressed as "mister." He protested because he said he was a woman. Voices told him this. He noticed that his breasts were growing. Some weeks before, others had touched him in a sensual manner. He heard it said that he was a whore. Lately, dreams of pregnancy. He dreamed that, as a woman, he indulged in coitus. During this hallucinatory act he felt the **insertion of a penis** and ejaculation.

Head straight; facial form long and narrow; parietal elevation prominent; genitals normally developed.

The following case, observed in the asylum at Illenau, is a pertinent example of lasting delusional alteration of sexual consciousness:

Case 133.

Metamorphosis of sexual paranoia. N., aged twenty-three, single, pianist, was received in the asylum at Illenau late in October of 1865. He came from a family in which there was said to be no hereditary taint; there was, however, phthisis (father and brother died of pulmonary tuberculosis). As a child the patient was weak and dull, although he was especially talented in music. He was always an abnormal character; silent, retiring, unsocial and sullen. He practiced masturbation after the age of fifteen. After a few years, neuras-thenic symptoms (palpitation of the heart, lassitude, occasional pressure in the head, etc.) and also hypochondriacal symptoms were manifested. During the last year he had worked with great difficulty. For about six months neurasthenia had increased. He complained of palpitation of the heart, pressure in the head, and sleeplessness; he was very irritable, and seemed to be sexually excited. He declared that he had to marry because of his health. He fell in love with an *artiste,* but at almost the same time (September 1865) he became ill from persecutory paranoia (ideas of enemies, derision in the street, poison in his food; obstacles were placed on the bridge to keep him from going to his *inamorata*). Due to increasing excitement and conflicts with those around him, whom he considered hostile, he was taken to the asylum. At first he presented the picture of typical persecutory paranoia with symptoms of sexual, and later general, neurasthenia; the delu-sions of persecution, however, did not rest upon this neurotic foundation. Occasionally the patient heard such sentences as: "Now the semen will be drawn from him. Now the bladder will be cut out."

In the course of the years 1866 to 1868, the delusions of persecution became less and less apparent, and for the most part were replaced by erotic ideas – a somatic and mental foundation for a lasting and powerful excitation of the sexual sphere. The patient fell in love with every woman he saw; he would hear voices that told him to approach, and beg for every woman's hand in matrimony, declaring that if he was not given a wife he would waste away. In 1869 he continued to masturbate, and signs of effemination became apparent. "He would, if he finds a wife, love her only platonically." The patient grew more and more peculiar, lived in a circle of erotic ideas, saw prostitution practiced in the asylum, and now and then heard voices that accused women of immoral conduct. For this reason he avoided the society of women, and only associated with them when two witnesses were with him, for the sake of music.

During 1872 his neurasthenic condition increased markedly. Persecutory paranoia again came into the foreground, and took on a clinical neurotic coloring. Olfactory hallucina-tions occurred. Magnetic influences were at work on him – "magnetic waves produced by striking an anvil" (false interpretation of sensations due to spinal asthenia). Due to continual and intense sexual excitement and excessive masturbation, the process of effemination constantly progressed. Only occasionally was he a man inclined toward women, complaining that the shameless prostitution of the men in the house made it impossible for a lady to approach him. He was dying of magnetically poisoned air and unsatisfied love. Without love he could not live. He was poisoned by a lewd toxin that affected his sexual desire. The lady whom he loved was surrounded by the lowest vice. The prostitutes in the house had fortune chains; that is, chains in which, without moving, a man could indulge in lustful pleasure. He was ready now to satisfy himself with prostitutes. He possessed a wonderful ray of thought that emanated from his eyes, which was worth twenty million francs. His compositions were worth five hundred thousand francs. Besides indications of delusions of grandeur, there were also indications of persecution – the food was poisoned with venereal excrement. He tasted and smelled poison, heard infamous accusations, and asked for appliances to close his ears.

The signs of effemination became more and more frequent, however, in August 1872. He became somewhat mannered, declaring that he could no longer live among men who drank and smoked. He thought and felt like a woman. He therefore decided he should be treated like a woman and transferred to a female ward. He asked for confections and delicate desserts. Due to tenesmus and cystospasm, he occasionally asked to be transferred to a ward hospital and treated as a very ill pregnant woman. The abnormal magnetism of masculine attendants had an unfavorable effect on him.

At times he still felt like a man, but in a way that indicated his abnormally altered sexual feeling. He pleaded for satisfaction only by means of masturbation, or marriage without coitus. Marriage for him was a sensual institution; the girl that he would take for a wife had to be a masturbator.

His personality became completely feminine at the end of December 1872. From that time onward he remained a woman. He had always been a woman, he said, but when he was a baby a French Quaker artist had put masculine genitals on him, and by rubbing and distorting his thorax had prevented the development of his breasts.

He thereafter demanded to be transferred to the female department, demanded protection from men who wanted to violate him, and asked for female clothing. Eventually he also desired employment in a toy shop where he could do crocheting and embroidery work, or a place in a dressmaking establishment with female work. From the time of his change of sex the patient began a new reckoning of time. He remembered his previous personality as being that of his cousin.

He always spoke of himself in the third person, and called himself the Countess V., the dearest friend of the Empress Eugenie, and asked for perfumes, corsets, etc. He took the other men of the ward for girls, tried to grow a head of hair, and demanded "Oriental hair remover" so that no one would doubt his gender. He took delight in praising masturbation, for "she had been a masturbator from the age of fifteen, and had never desired any other kind of sexual satisfaction." Occasionally neurasthenic symptoms, olfactory hallucinations and persecutory delusions were observed. All the events up to December 1872 belonged to the personality of the cousin.

The patient's delusion that he was the Countess V. could no longer be corrected. She proved her identity by the fact that the nurse had examined her, and found her to be a lady. The countess would not marry because she hated men. Since he was not provided with female clothing and shoes, he spent most of the day in bed, acted like an invalid lady of position, affected and modest, and asked for bonbons and such. His hair was done up in a knot as well as possible, and his beard was pulled out. Breasts were made of rolls of bread.

In 1874 caries began in the left knee joint, to which pulmonary tuberculosis was soon added. Death on December 2, 1874. Skull normal. Frontal lobes atrophic. Brain anemic. Microscopic (Dr. Schüle). In the superior layer of the frontal lobe, ganglion cells somewhat shrunken; in the adventitia of the vessels, numerous fat corpuscles; ganglia unchanged; isolated pigment particles and colloid bodies. The lower layers of the cortex normal. Genitals very large; testicles small, lax, and microscopically showed no change.

The delusion of sexual transformation, displayed in its conditions and phases of development in the foregoing case, is a manifestation remarkably infrequent in the pathology of the human mind. Besides the foregoing cases that I have personally observed, I have seen such a case, as an episodic phenomenon, of a lady who was sexually inverted (cf. case 159, p. 341), another case of a girl affected with original paranoia, and another case of a lady suffering from original paranoia.

Except for a case briefly reported by Arndt[82] in his textbook, one quite superficially described by Sérieux (*Recherches clinique,* p. 33), and the two cases known to Esquirol,[83] I cannot recall any cases of delusion of sexual transformation in literature.

I have already mentioned the interesting relations existing between the facts of delusional transformation of sex and the so-called insanity of the Scythians.

Marandon (*Annales médico-psychologiques,* 1877, p. 161), like others, has erroneously presumed that with the ancient Scythians there was an actual delusion, and that the condition was not merely that of eviration. According to the law of empirical actuality, such as delusion, so infrequent today, must have also been very infrequent in ancient times. Since it can only be conceived as arising from paranoia, there can be no question of its endemic occurrence; it can only be regarded as a superstitious manifestation of eviration (the result of the anger of the goddess), as is also evident from the statements of Hippocrates.

The facts of so-called Scythian insanity, as well as the facts recently learned about the Pueblo Indians, are also anthropologically noteworthy, insofar as general atrophy of the testes and genitals, and physical and mental similarity to the female type, were observed. This is all the more remarkable because, in men who have lost their reproductive organs, such a reversal of instinct is as unusual as it is in women, *mutatis mutandis,* after the natural or artificial phase of menopause.

[b] homosexual feeling as an abnormal congenital manifestation.[84]

The essential feature of this strange manifestation of the sexual life is the absence of sexual sensibility for the opposite sex (even to the extent of horror), while sexual inclination and impulse toward the same sex are present. Concurrently, the genitals are normally developed, the sexual glands perform their functions properly, and the sexual type is completely differentiated.

In cases of the complete development of the anomaly, feeling, thought, will and the whole character correspond with the peculiar sexual instinct, but not with the sex which the individual represents anatomically and physiologically. This abnormal mode of feeling may frequently be recognized in the manner, dress and career of the individuals, who may go so far as wearing the distinctive clothing that corresponds with what they feel to be their sexual role.

This abnormal manifestation anthropologically and clinically presents various degrees of development:

[1] Traces of heterosexual, with predominating homosexual, instinct (psychosexual hermaphroditism).

[2] There exists inclination toward the same sex only (homosexuality).

[3] The entire mental existence is altered to correspond with the abnormal sexual instinct (effemination and viraginity).

[4] The form of the body approaches that which corresponds to the abnormal sexual instinct. Actual transitions to hermaphroditism never occur, however, because such persons have completely differentiated genitals. Thus, just as it is in all pathological perversions of the sexual life, the cause must be sought in the brain (androgyny and gynandry).

The first definite communications[85] concerning this enigmatic phenomenon of Nature are made by Casper ("Ueber Notzucht und Päderastie," Casper's *Vierteljahrsschr.*, 1852, vol. 1), who, it is true, classes it with pederasty, but makes the pertinent remark that this anomaly is, in most cases, congenital, and also to be regarded as a form of mental hermaphroditism. Here there exists an actual disgust of sexual contact with women; the imagination is instead filled with beautiful young men, and statues and pictures of these men. It did not escape Casper that in such cases **insertion of the penis into the anus** (pederasty) is not the rule, but that, by means of other sexual acts (mutual masturbation), sexual satisfaction is sought and obtained.

In his *Klinischen Novellen* (1863, p. 33) Casper reproduces the interesting confession of a man showing this perversion of the sexual instinct, and does not hesitate to assert that (aside from vicious imagination and vice), as a result of overindulgence in normal sexual intercourse, there are numerous cases in which "pederasty" has its origin in a remarkable, obscure impulse that is congenital and inexplicable. Around the middle of the 1860s a certain assessor, Ulrichs, himself subject to this perverse instinct, declared in numerous articles, under the nom de plume "Numa Numantius,"[86] that the mental sex life was not connected with bodily sex; there were, he wrote, male individuals who felt like women toward men (a woman's mind in a man's body). He called these people "urnings," and demanded nothing less than the legal and social recognition of this sexual love of "urnings" as congenital and, therefore, within their rights; he also demanded the permission of marriage among them. Ulrichs failed, however, to prove that this congenital and paradoxical sexual feeling was absolutely physiological and not pathological.

Griesinger (*Archiv f. Psychiatrie,* vol. 1, p. 651) threw the first ray of light on these facts by pointing out anthropologically and clinically the marked hereditary taint of an individual who was under his observation.

We owe thanks to Westphal (*Archiv f. Psychiatrie,* vol. 2, p. 73) for the first systematic consideration of the manifestation in question, which he defined as "congenital reversal of the sexual feeling, with consciousness of the abnormality of the manifestation," and designated this manifestation with the name (now generally accepted) of *antipathic sexual instinct.* He also began to compile a series of cases that has now reached the number of approximately two hundred (those reported in this book not being included).

Westphal leaves undecided whether antipathic sexual feeling is a symptom of a neuropathic or psychopathic condition, or whether it may occur as an isolated manifestation. He holds fast to the opinion that the condition is congenital.

From the cases published up to 1877 I have designated this peculiar sexual feeling as a functional sign of degeneration and as a partial manifestation of a neuro- (psycho-) pathic state, in most cases hereditary – a supposition that has found renewed confirmation in consideration of additional cases. The following peculiarities may be presented as the signs of this neuro- (psycho-) pathic taint:

[1] The sexual life of individuals thus organized manifests itself, as a rule, abnormally early, and thereafter with abnormal potency. Other perverse manifestations are still frequently present, in addition to the abnormal method of sexual satisfaction, which is in itself conditioned by the peculiar sexual feeling.

[2] The psychic love manifest in these men is, for the most part, exaggerated and exalted in the same way as their sexual instinct is manifested, with a strange and even compelling force, in their consciousness.

[3] Besides the functional signs of degeneration evident in antipathic sexual

feeling, there are to be found other functional, and in many cases anatomical, evidences of degeneration.

[4] Neuroses (hysteria, neurasthenic, and epileptoid states, etc.) coexist. Almost invariably the existence of temporary or permanent neurasthenia can be proved. This is constitutional as a rule, having its root in congenital conditions. It is awakened and maintained by masturbation or enforced abstinence.

Due to these practices or congenital disposition, in male individuals there is ultimately sexual neurasthenia, which essentially manifests itself as irritable weakness of the ejaculation center. Thus it is explained that, in most cases, simply embracing and kissing, or even the sight of the loved person by itself, can induce ejaculation. Frequently this is accompanied by an abnormally powerful feeling of lustful pleasure, which may be so intense as to suggest a feeling of "magnetic" currents passing through the body.

[5] In the majority of cases, psychic anomalies (brilliant talent in art, especially music, poetry, etc., as well as poor intellectual powers or a unique form of eccentricity) are present, which may extend to pronounced conditions of mental degeneration (imbecility, moral insanity).

In many homosexuals, temporary or permanent insanity of a degenerative character (pathological emotional states, periodic insanity, paranoia, etc.) can appear.

[6] In almost all cases where an examination of the physical and mental peculiarities of the ancestors and blood relations has been possible, neurosis, psychoses, degenerative signs, etc., have been found in the families.[87]

The depth of congenital antipathic sexual feeling is shown by the fact that the lustful dream of a male-loving homosexual has for its content only male individuals, and that of a female-loving woman only female individuals, with corresponding situations.

The observation of Westphal – that the consciousness of a person who is congenitally defective in their sexual desire toward the opposite sex is painfully affected by the impulse toward the same sex – is true in only a number of cases. Indeed, in many instances the consciousness of the abnormal condition is absent. The majority of homosexuals are happy in their perverse sexual feeling and impulse, and only unhappy insofar as social and legal barriers stand in the way of the satisfaction of their instinct toward their own sex.

The study of antipathic sexual feeling points directly to anomalies of the cerebral organization of the affected individuals. The very fact that in these cases (with a few exceptions) the sexual glands are found anatomically and functionally quite normal seems to favor this assumption.

This enigmatic manifestation in the nature of man has led to many attempts at explanation.

Among lay persons, antipathic sexual feeling is called a *vice;* in the language of the law, it is called a *crime.* Those tainted with it, although recognizing it as an abnormality (since it is based upon a freak of nature), claim the same rights and privileges that are accorded to those who enjoy normal heterosexual love. In antipathic sexual circles, from Plato down to Ulrichs, this standpoint has been maintained. Plato's *Banquet,* chapters 8 and 9, can be quoted for this purpose, namely: "There is no Aphrodite without an Eros. There are, however, two goddesses. The older Aphrodite came into existence without a mother; because she is the daughter of Uranus, she is called Urania. The younger Aphrodite is the daughter of Zeus and Dione, and she is called Pandemos. Therefore, the Eros of the former must be Uranus, and the Eros of the latter must be Pandemos. With the love of Eros, Uranus did not choose a female but a male; this is the love for boys. Whoever is inspired with this love turns to the male sex." An impression can be gained from many of the classics that the love of Urania attains a higher position than the love of her sister Pandemos. More recent explanations of the homosexual instinct have come from philosophers, psychologists and natural scientists.

One of the most peculiar explanations is advanced by Schopenhauer (*Die Welt als Wille und Vorstellung*), who seriously contends that nature seeks to prevent old men (i.e., over fifty years of age) from begetting children, since experience teaches that the offspring never turn out decently. For this purpose, nature in her wisdom has turned sexual instinct in old men toward their own sex! The great philosopher and thinker evidently was not aware that sexual inversion, as a rule, exists from birth, and that pederasty occurring in senility is only sexually perverse, but by no means proves the presence of perversion.

Binet attempts to explain these peculiar manifestations from a *psychological* stand-point, thinking (with Condillac) to reduce them – together with other *bizarre* psychic phenomena – to the law of association of ideas (i.e., association of ideas with regard to the state of developing). This clever psychologist assumes that the instinct, not as yet sexually differentiated, is determined by the coincidence of a vivid sexual emotion with the simultaneous sight of or contact with a person of the opposite sex. In this manner a forceful association is created, which takes root by repeating itself, while the original associative process is forgotten or becomes latent. Even today, Schrenck-Notzing and others lean toward this opinion in their efforts to explain inverted sexual instinct (especially when acquired); it cannot, however, withstand serious criticism. Psychological forces insufficiently explain manifestations of so thoroughly degenerated a character (see below).

Chevalier (*Inversion sexuelle,* Paris, 1893) rightly disagrees with Binet by noting that these attempts at psychological explanation do not explain the precocity of homo-sexual impulses (that exist long before sexual feelings are associated with the imag-ination), aversion toward the opposite sex, or the early appearance of secondary psychic-sexual manifestations. Nevertheless, Binet's subtle remark that the lasting presence of such associations is only possible in predisposed (tainted) individuals is noteworthy.

The explanations attempted by physicians and naturalists also do not prove satis-factory. Gley (*Revue philosophique,* January 1884) maintains that those afflicted with inverted sexual instinct have a female brain (!) with masculine sexual glands, and that an existing morbid condition of the brain determines the sexual life, while normally the sexual glands influence the sexual cerebral functions. Magnan (*Annales méd. psychol.,* 1885, p. 458) also speaks of a female brain in the body of a man and vice versa. Ulrichs (*Memnon,* 1868) comes closer to the point when he speaks of a woman's mind in an innately male body, and thus seeks to explain congenital effemination. According to Mantegazza, (op. cit., 1886, p. 106), anatomical anomalies exist in such persons, in that the natural plexus of the genital nerves terminates in the rectum, thus misdirecting thither all lustful desires. But surely Nature is never guilty of such leaps or errors. Neither does she burden a masculine body with a female brain. The author of this hypothesis, otherwise so insightful, completely overlooks the fact that sexually inverted individuals, as a rule, abhor the use of the anus – namely, pederasty. Mantegazza goes back, as a support for his hypothesis, to the communications he received from a well-known prominent author, who assured him that he was not as yet satisfied in his own mind whether he derived greater pleasure from coitus or defecation. Even if we admit the veracity of this statement, it would only prove that its author was sexually abnormal and that he derived only a minimum amount of pleasure from coitus. One might also conclude that the mucous membrane of his rectum was erogenous in some abnormal manner.

Bernhardi (*Der Uranismus,* Berlin, 1882) casually found in five hermaphrodites ("*pathici*") the absence of spermatozoa (in four cases, not even sperm crystals), and thought to find the solution of this "enigma of many thousand years" in the assumption that the *pathicus* was a "monster of the feminine sex, having nothing else in common with the male other than the male genitals, which in some cases are only imperfectly developed." This author could not even base his contention upon an autopsy, which undoubtedly would have eventually established a case of hermaphroditism.

Those who practice active viraginity and gynandry he names "monsters of masculine gender, in opposition to which the passive lesbian is as perfect a woman as the active predator is a perfect man."

The author of this book made an attempt to utilize facts of heredity for an explanation of this anomaly. Proceeding from the experience that manifestations of sexual perversion are frequently found in the parents, he suspects that the various grades of congenital sexual inversion represent various grades of sexual anomaly inherited by birth, acquired by ascendency, or otherwise developed. In this connection the law of progressive heredity must also be considered.

All attempts at explanation made hitherto on the basis of natural philosophy or psychology, or those of a merely speculative character, are insufficient.

Recent research, however, proceeding on embryological (ontogenetic and phylogenetic) and anthropological lines, appears to promise good results.

The research of Frank Lydston (*Philadelphia Med. and Surg. Recorder,* September 1888) and Kiernan (*Medical Standard,* November 1888) suggests [1] that bisexual organization is still found in the lower animal kingdom, and [2] that monosexuality gradually develops from bisexuality. Kiernan assumes, in trying to subordinate sexual inversion to the category of hermaphroditism, that, in individuals thus affected, retrogression into the earlier hermaphroditic forms of the animal kingdom may, at least functionally, take place. These are his own words: "The original bisexuality of the ancestors of the race, shown in the rudimentary female organs of the male, could not fail to cause functional, if not organic, reversions when mental or physical manifestations were hindered by disease or congenital defect. It seems certain that a femininely functioning brain can occupy a male body and vice versa."

Chevalier's research (op. cit., p. 408) proceeds from the idea of original bisexual life in the animal kingdom and original bisexual predisposition in the human fetus.

According to Chevalier, the difference in gender, with marked physical and psychic sexual characteristics, is only the result of endless processes of evolution; psycho-psychic sexual difference runs parallel with the high level of the evolving process. In addition, an individual being must itself pass through these grades of evolution. Although it is originally bisexual, in the struggle between the male and female elements, one or the other is conquered, and a monosexual being evolves that corresponds with the type of individual in the present stage of evolution. Traces of the conquered sexuality, however, remain. Under certain circumstances, these latent sexual characteristics may arrive at Darwin's definition, i.e., they may provoke manifestations of inverted sexuality. Chevalier does not, however, look upon such processes as a retrogression (atavism), in the sense of Lombroso's opinion and that of others, but rather considers them, with Lacassagne, as disturbances in the present stage of evolution.

If the structure of this opinion is pursued, the following anthropological and historical facts may emerge:

[1] The sexual apparatus consists of [a] the sexual glands and organs of reproduction; [b] the spinal centers, which act either as a check or a stimulus upon [a]; [c] the cerebral regions, in which the psychic processes of the sex life are enacted.

Since the original predisposition of [a] is of a bisexual character, the same must be said for [b] and [c].

[2] The tendency of nature in the present stage of evolution is the reproduction of monosexual individuals, and the law of experience teaches that the normally developed cerebral center corresponds with the sexual glands (the "law of sexually homologous development").

[3] This destruction of antipathic sexuality is, at present, not yet complete. In the same manner that the vermiform appendix in the intestinal tube points to former stages of organization, so may be found in the sexual apparatus – in the male as well as in the female – residue that points to the original ontogenetic and phylogenetic bisexuality (not to speak of hermaphroditic malformations), which may be looked upon as merely partial excesses of development or disturbances in the formation of sexual organization (especially in regard to the *external* genitals).

The residue referred to are, in the male, the prostatic utricle (remnants of the Müllerian duct) and the nipple, and, in the female, the paroophoron (remnants of the original renal portions of the Wolffian body), and the epoophoron (remnants of the Wolffian body, and analogous with the epididymis in the male). Beigel, Klebs, Fürst, and others have found indications in the human female of the Wolffian body in the form of the so-called Gartnerian canals, which in the female ruminants are usually present in the lateral wall of the uterus.

[4] Furthermore, a long line of clinical and anthropological facts favor this assumption.

I will only call attention to the frequent cases of individuals with characteristics of mixed or (in the sense of sexual inversion) predominating physical and psychic sexuality ("female men and male women"); to the appearance of psychic and physical female characteristics in men after castration (eunuchs), and of male characteristics in women after the removal of the ovaries in early youth; and also to the manifestations of viraginity in the premature climacteric, even to the point of development of a second gender.

Professor Kaltenbach shows a remarkable instance of such a second (antipathic) sex life, which developed after the premature climacteric.

On February 17, 1892, he consulted with me about "a woman, thirty years of age, married for two years, who used to have irregular menstruation."

Beginning in June 1891 a sudden series of manifestations developed that corresponded with the process of masculine puberty: full beard, darkened hair on the head, and the eyebrows, mons pubis, chest and abdomen covered with hair like a man.

There was an increased activity of the sudoriferous and sebaceous glands. On her chest, back and face, heavy miliary and acne marks were prominent, although previously the tint had been classically white and smooth. Her voice, once a rich soprano, was now a "lieutenant's voice." Her entire facial expression had changed. She experienced a complete change of carriage: chest broad, waist gone, abdomen prominent with adipose tissue, short thickset neck, masculine all over. The lower part of her face became broad, and her breasts became flat and masculine. Psychic changes: formerly mild and tractable, she was now energetic, hard to control, and even aggressive. Inadequate sexual desire from the beginning of her marriage, with no trace of inversion.

In the sexual organs highly interesting changes were also found. "Thus this young woman has changed, for all intents and purposes, into a man."

My explanation of the case:

"Premature climacteric, loss of previous feminine sexuality. Physical and psychic development of male sexuality, hitherto latent. Interesting illustration of the bisexual predisposition, and of the possibility of continued existence of a second sexuality in a latent state, under conditions hitherto unknown."

Unfortunately, I could obtain no further information about the subsequent metamorphosis of this case or the presence of probable hereditary taint.

See also cases 129 and 130. In these two cases, severe neurasthenia was the causative element of the change of sex, which was also based upon heavy taint; the change, however, was only psychic, and did not affect the physical sexual character.

[5] These manifestations of inverted sexuality are evidently found only in persons with *organic taint*.[88] In normal constitutions the law of monosexual development, homologous with the sexual glands, remains intact. That the cerebral center is developed under other conditions, quite independent from the peripheral sexual organs (including the sexual glands), is evident from the cases of hermaphroditism (at least, so far as pseudohermaphroditism is concerned), in which the law referred to above remains intact in the sense of monosexual development, analogous to the sexual glands. In true hermaphroditism, however, a mutual influence of both centers is obtained, physically as well as psychically; thus, a neutralization of the love life occurs, even assumes a state of asexuality, and tends to physically and psychically combine and put into operation both of these sexual traits.

Hermaphroditism and sexual inversion, however, stand in no relation to each other. This is clear from the fact that the hermaphrodite (or, practically speaking, the pseudohermaphrodite) follows the law of evolution quoted above, and does not present signs of inverted sexuality; nor has hermaphroditism ever been anatomically observed in cases of antipathic sexual instinct. This conforms with the difference of conditions under which they originate, for in sexual inversion we must look for the cause in central (cerebral) defects, and in hermaphroditism in the anomalies affecting the peripheral sexual apparatus.

The facts quoted in the cases above seem to support an attempt to historically and anthropologically explain sexual inversion.

Sexual inversion is a disturbance of the law of the development of the cerebral center, homologous to the sexual glands (homosexuality), and also a disturbance of the law of the monosexual formation of the individual (psychic "hermaphroditism"). In case 129, it is the center of bisexual predisposition, antagonistic to the gender represented by the sexual gland, which in a paradoxical manner conquers what was originally intended to be superior; yet the law of monosexual development prevails.[89]

In case 130, victory lies with neither center; an indication of the tendency of monosexual development remains, however, insofar as one center is predominant, usually the center motivated toward the opposite sex. This is all the more remarkable in that it does not have the support of a corresponding sexual gland – not even a peripheral sexual apparatus, in fact, which is more proof that the cerebral center is autonomous and, in its development, independent of the sexual glands.

In case 129, it must be assumed that the center, which rightfully should have won, was too weak. This fact may be recognized in the subsequently weak libido in the sexual character, which was markedly feeble in physical and psychic conditions.

In case 130, both centers were too weak for one to obtain victory and superiority.

This defect of the natural laws must, from an anthropological and clinical stand-point, be considered a manifestation of degeneration. In fact, in all cases of sexual inversion a taint of a hereditary nature can be established. What causes produce this factor of taint and its activity is a question which cannot be adequately answered by science in its present stage.[90]

There are plenty of analogous cases to be found in tainted individuals, because the symptoms of influences that disturb physical and psychic evolution, and that are clearly found in the germ of procreation, exhibit themselves in many other manifestations of a defective or perverse character (signs of anatomical, func-tional, somatic and psychic degeneration).

The antipathic sexual instinct is the strongest mark left by a whole series of exhibi-tions of the partial development of psychic and physical inverted sexual character-istics (see above), and one can easily say that the more indistinct the psychic and physical sexual characteristics appear in the individual, the deeper it is below the present level of a perfect homologous monosexuality attained in the evolution of thousands of years.

The cerebral center mediates the psychic and also, indirectly, the physical sexual characteristics. The various grades of congenital antipathic sexuality correspond with the intensity of the various grades of taint.

The same is true in regard to "acquired" sexual inversion, which exhibits itself only later in life. An untainted man can never become sexually inverted from masturbation or seduction by a person of the same sex, because as soon as the extrinsic influences cease, he returns to normal sexual functions. The tainted individual, however, whose psychosexual center is originally weak, is in a different position. All possible psychic and physical deficiencies, especially those of a neurasthenic nature, can impair his weakened sexuality, homologous though it may have been, until this time, in relation to his sexual glands. These evil influences can render him most profoundly psychically bisexual, then invertedly monosexual, and can eventually cause effemination by producing physical and psychic characteristics of sexuality in the sense of predominating antipathic feelings or the destruction of primordial centers. On page 240 I have attempted to show how far neurasthenia can provide the impulse for the development of antipathic sexuality.

congenital antipathic sexual instinct in man.

The sexual acts in which male homosexuals seek and find satisfaction are multifarious. There are individuals of fine feeling and strength of will who occasionally satisfy themselves with platonic love; they run the risk, however, of becoming nervous (neurasthenic) and insane as a result of this enforced abstinence. In other instances, masturbation is practiced for the same reasons that may lead normal individuals to avoid coitus.

In homosexuals with nervous systems congenitally irritable or injured by masturbation (irritable weakness of the ejaculation center), simple embraces or caresses, with or without contact of the genitals, can sufficiently induce ejaculation and consequent satisfaction. The sexual act in less irritable individuals consists of masturbation by the beloved person, mutual masturbation, or imitative coitus between the thighs. In homosexuals morally perverse and sexually potent, sexual desire is satisfied by pederasty – an act, however, which is repugnant to perverted individuals who are not morally defective (much as it is the same way with normal men). The overall testimony of the homosexual is remarkable: an adequate sexual act with a person of the same sex gives him a feeling of great satisfaction and strength, while satisfying himself with solitary masturbation or coitus with a woman affects him unfavorably, making him miserable and increasing his neurasthenic symptoms.

Regarding the frequency[91] of the occurrence of the anomaly, it is difficult to reach an accurate conclusion, since those affected do not often break from their reserve, and in criminal cases the homosexual with a perversion of the sexual instinct is usually classified with the person inclined to pederasty for simply vicious reasons. According to the experiences of Casper and Tardieu, as well as my own, this anomaly is much more frequent than reported cases would lead us to presume.

Ulrichs (*Kritische Pfeile*, p. 2, 1880) declares that there is, on the average, one person affected with antipathic sexual instinct to every 200 mature men, or to every 800 of the population, and that the percentage among the Magyars and the southern Slavs is still greater – statements which may be regarded as untrustworthy. The subject of one of my cases personally knows fourteen homosexuals in his home-town of 13,000 inhabitants. He further declares that he is acquainted with at least eighty in a city of 60,000 inhabitants. Presumably this man, otherwise trustworthy, makes no distinction between the congenital and the acquired anomaly.

[1] psychic hermaphroditism. [92]

The characteristic mark of this degree of inversion of the sexual instinct is that – besides a pronounced sexual instinct and desire for the same sex – a desire toward the opposite sex is present. Homosexuality is primary and, in time and intensity, constitutes the most striking feature of the sex life, while a desire for the opposite sex is much weaker and is only manifested episodically.

Although the heterosexual instinct may be rudimentary, simply manifesting itself in the unconscious (dream) state, it may also be (episodically, at least) powerfully exhibited.

Sexual instinct toward the opposite sex can be strengthened by exercising will and self-control; by moral treatment and possibly hypnotic suggestion; by improvement of the constitution and the removal of neuroses (neurasthenia); and especially by abstinence from masturbation.

There is always the danger, however, that homosexual feelings, in that they are the most powerful, may become permanent and lead to an enduring and exclusive antipathic sexual instinct. This is especially to be feared because of the influences of masturbation (just as in acquired inversion of the sexual instinct), its resultant neurasthenia, and the consequent exacerbations. Furthermore, it is to be found as a consequence of unfavorable experiences in sexual intercourse with persons of the opposite sex (defective feeling of pleasure in coitus, failure in coitus because of weakness of erection and premature ejaculation, infection).

On the other hand, it is possible that aesthetic and ethical sympathy with persons of the opposite sex can favor the development of heterosexual desire. Thus it happens that an individual, according to the predominance of favorable or unfavorable influences, can alternately experience heterosexual and homosexual feelings.

It seems probable that such hermaphrodites with constitutional taint are rather numerous.[93] Because they socially attract very little attention, and because the secrets of married life are only brought to the knowledge of the physician, it is immediately apparent why this interesting and clearly important transitional group to absolute inverted sexuality has thus far escaped scientific investigation.

Many cases of frigidity involving married couples may possibly be a result of this anomaly. Sexual intercourse with the opposite sex is, in itself, possible. At any rate, in cases of this degree, no fear of the opposite sex exists. There is a fertile field here for the application of medical and moral therapeutics (see below).

The differential diagnosis from acquired antipathic sexual instinct may present difficulties because, in such cases, as long as remnants of a normal sexual instinct are not absolutely lost, the actual symptoms are the same (see below).

Sexual satisfaction of homosexual impulses in the first degree consists of passive and mutual masturbation and coitus between the thighs.

Case 134.

Antipathic sexual instinct with sexual satisfaction in heterosexual intercourse. Mr. Z., aged thirty-six, consulted with me because of an anomaly of his sexual feelings that had become a matter of anxiety to him in connection with an intended marriage. Patient's father was neuropathic, and suffered from nightmares and night terrors. His grandfather was also neuropathic, and his father's brother was an idiot. Patient's mother and her family were healthy and mentally normal. The patient had three sisters and one brother; the brother was subject to moral insanity. Two of the sisters were healthy and enjoying happy married lives.

As a child, the patient was weak, nervous, and subject to night terrors, like his father; he never had any severe illnesses, however, except coxitis, which resulted in a slight limp. Sexual impulses were manifested early. At the age of eight, without any instruction, he began to masturbate. First ejaculation at the age of fourteen. He was mentally well-endowed, and principally interested in art and literature. He was always physically weak, and had no inclination for boyish sports nor, later, for manly occupations. He had a certain interest in the female *toilette,* ornaments, and occupations. From the time of puberty the patient noticed in himself an inexplicable inclination toward males. Youths of the lowest classes were extremely attractive to him. Cavalrymen especially excited him. He experienced a lustful desire to press himself against such individuals from behind. In crowds it was occasionally possible for him to do this, and he would then experience an intense feeling of pleasure. On such occasions, after the age of twenty-two, he would, at times, ejaculate. Afterward ejaculation would occur when a sympathetic man laid his hand on the patient's thigh. He was now in a state of great anxiety, fearing that he might sometime sexually assault a man. Men of the lower classes wearing tight brown trousers were especially dangerous for him. His greatest pleasure would have been to embrace such a man and press himself against him; unfortunately, the morality of his country would not allow such a thing. Pederasty seemed disgusting to him.

It gave him great pleasure to see the genitals of men. He was always compelled to look at the genitals of every man he met. In circuses, theatres, etc., only male performers interested him. Patient had never noticed any inclination for women. He did not avoid them, and even occasionally danced with them, but he never felt the slightest sensual excitation under such circumstances.

The patient was neurasthenic at the age of twenty-eight as a result of his excessive masturbation.

Frequent pollutions while asleep then occurred, which weakened him very much. It was only on occasion that he dreamed of men, but never women, when he had pollutions. A lascivious dream-picture of pederasty only occurred once. He dreamt of death scenes and being attacked by dogs, etc. After these dreams he suffered, as before, from intense sexual desire. There often appeared before him such lascivious thoughts as gloating over the death of animals in a slaughterhouse, or allowing himself to be whipped by boys; he always overcame such desires, however, and he also overcame the impulse to dress in a military uniform.

In order to cure himself of masturbation, and to thoroughly satisfy his libido, he decided to frequent brothels. At the age of twenty-one, he first attempted sexual intercourse with a woman, after overindulging in wine. The beauty of the female form, and female nudity in general, made no impression on him. He was able to enjoy the act of coitus, however, and thereafter visited brothels regularly for "purposes of health."

From this time he took great pleasure in hearing men tell stories of their sexual relations with the opposite sex.

Ideas of flagellation would also come to him while in a brothel, but the retention of such fantasies was not essential for the performance of coitus. He considered sexual intercourse with prostitutes to be simply a remedy against the desire for masturbation and men – a kind of safety valve to prevent compromising himself with some man.

The patient wished to marry; he feared, however, that not only could he not love a decent woman, but that he also might be impotent when engaging in coitus with her. He therefore decided he needed medical advice.

The patient was very intelligent and in all respects was of masculine appearance. In dress and manner he presented nothing that would attract attention. Gait, voice and frame (especially the pelvis) were masculine in character. Genitals normally developed. Abundant growth of hair for a male. The patient's relatives and friends did not have the slightest suspicion of his sexual anomalies. In his inverted sexual fantasies he never felt like a woman toward men. For a few years he had been entirely free from neurasthenic troubles.

He could not answer whether he considered himself a subject of congenital sexual inversion. It seems probable that he had a congenitally weak inclination for the opposite sex and a greater inclination for the same sex that was a result of early masturbation in consequence of the homosexual instinct, which increasingly weakened his attraction to the opposite sex, but did not make it nonexistent. When he stopped masturbating, his feeling for women became significantly more natural, but only in a coarse, sensual way.

The patient explained that, for reasons of family and business, it was necessary for him to marry, so it was impossible to eliminate this delicate point.

Fortunately the patient confined himself to the question of his virility as a husband. It was necessary to reply that he was virile, and that he would probably be virile in conjugal intercourse with the wife of his choice if she were sympathetic; he was also told that he could always improve his potency by exercising his imagination in the right direction.

The main objective was to strengthen his sexual inclination for the opposite sex, which was defective, but not absolutely nonexistent. This could be done by avoiding and opposing all homosexual feelings and impulses, possibly with the help of the artificial inhibitory influences of hypnotic suggestion (removal of homosexual desires by suggestion); by exciting and exercising normal sexual desires and impulses; by completely abstaining from masturbation; and by eradicating remnants of the neurasthenic condition of the nervous system with hydrotherapy and, possibly, general faradization.

Case 135.

V., aged twenty-nine, official; father hypochondriacal, mother neuropathic; four other children normal; one sister homosexual.

V. was very talented, learned easily, and had an excellent religious education. Extremely nervous and emotional. At the age of nine he began to masturbate on his own accord. At the age of fourteen he recognized the danger of this practice and fought with some success against it; he began to rave about male statuary, however, and also about young men. When puberty set in, he took slight interest in women. At the age of twenty he had coitus for the first time with a woman; although he was potent, he derived no satisfaction from it. Afterward, only because he lacked something better, heterosexual intercourse (about six times).

He admitted that he frequently had intercourse with men (**mutual masturbation, coitus between the thighs, sometimes in the mouth**). He took either the active or passive role.

At the consultation he was in despair and wept bitterly. He abhorred his sexual anomaly, and said that he had desperately battled against it, but without success. With women he found only moderate animal satisfaction, and psychic gratification was totally absent. He craved, however, for the happiness of family life.

Except for an abnormally broad pelvis (100 centimeters), there was nothing in his character or personal appearance that lacked masculine qualities.

Case 136.

K., aged thirty; on his mother's side of the family there were several cases of insanity.

Both parents were neurasthenic, irritable and excitable, and lived unhappily together.

From his early childhood, K. had sympathy only for men, especially for male servants.

Pollutions at the age of fourteen, often with homosexual dreams. Descriptions of bull-fights and the torture of animals greatly excited him sexually.

At fifteen he began masturbating on his own accord. At the age of twenty-one, homosexual intercourse with men (mutual masturbation only), and sporadic psychic masturbation associated with thoughts of men.

His inclination to women was of a transient nature. When he was pressed to marry, he could not decide in its favor.

He never had coitus with a woman, partly because he had no confidence in his virility, and partly from fear of infection.

For years he was highly neurasthenic, which rendered him for whole periods of time psychically unfit for any kind of work. He was listless and devoid of energy, but structurally and personally appeared masculine. Genitals normal.

Advice: Treatment for neurasthenia, energetic combat against homosexual desires with the company of ladies, and eventually coitus with condoms. Wedlock, when suitable, inasmuch as his station in life demanded it.

K. returned after four months. He had conscientiously acted upon the medical advice, was successful in coitus, dreamed of women, disdained the idea of sexual relations with men, but during summer he still experienced homosexual impulses (due to exacerbation of neurasthenia, superinduced by the hot weather).

He hoped to marry at an early date, and anticipated much happiness from marriage.

Case 137.

Psychic hermaphroditism. Heterosexual feeling interfered with early by masturbation, but episodically very intense. Homosexual feeling from birth that was perverse (sexual excitation by men's boots).

Mr. X., high social position, aged twenty-eight. He came to me in September 1887, in a despairing mood, to consult with me due to a perversion of his sex life. This perversion made life seem almost unbearable to him and had repeatedly brought him close to suicide. The patient came from a family in which neuroses and psychoses had been of frequent occurrence. In his father's family there had been marriage between first cousins for three generations. His father was said to have been a healthy man and to have lived morally during his years of marriage. His father's preference for fine-looking servants, however, seemed remarkable to the son. His mother's family was described as eccentric. His mother's grandfather and great-grandfather died melancholic, her sister was insane, and a daughter of the grandfather's brother was hysterical and had nymphomania. Only three of his mother's twelve brothers and sisters were married. Of these siblings, one brother was a homosexual and was always nervous as a result of excessive masturbation. The patient's mother was said to have been a bigot of small mental endowment, nervous, irritable, and inclined to melancholia.

The patient had a sister and a brother. The brother was neuropathic, frequently melancholic, and, though mature, had never shown the slightest trace of sexual inclination. The sister was an acknowledged beauty and was greatly sought by gentlemen. This lady was married, but childless, reportedly due to her husband's impotence. She had always been indifferent to the attention men gave her; she was charmed by female beauty, however, and was actually in love with some of her female friends.

With respect to himself, the patient asserted that when he was four years old he dreamt of handsome jockeys wearing shining boots. He never dreamt of women when he grew older. His nightly pollutions were always induced by "boot dreams." From the age of four he had a peculiar partiality for men or, more correctly, for lackeys wearing shining boots. At first they only excited his interest, but with the development of his sexual functions the sight of them caused powerful erections and lustful pleasure. It was only servants' boots that affected him; the same kind of boots on persons of a similar social position did not affect him. In a homosexual sense, there was no sexual impulse connected with these situations; even the thought of such a possibility was disgusting to him. At times, however, he had sensually colored ideas, such as being his servant's servant and pulling off his boots; the idea of being stepped on by him or shining his boots was extremely pleasing. The pride of the aristocrat would rise up against such thoughts. In general, these notions about boots were disgusting and painful to him.

His sexual instinct was early and powerfully developed. It first found expression indulging in sensual thoughts about boots and, after puberty, in dreams accompanied by pollutions; otherwise, his mental and physical development was undisturbed. Patient was mentally well-endowed – he learned easily, finished his studies, and became an officer. Because of his distinguished, manly appearance and his high position, he was greatly sought by others in society.

He characterized himself as a clever, quiet, strong-willed, but superficial man. He asserted that he was a passionate hunter and rider, and that he never had any inclination for feminine pursuits. In the society of ladies he had always been reserved; dancing always tired him. He never had an interest in any lady of high social position. As for women, only buxom peasant girls, like the models of painters in Rome, had taken his fancy. He had, however, never felt any sexual interest, even in such representatives of the female sex. At the theatre and circus only male performers were attractive to him; at the same time, however, they gave him no sensual feeling. As for men, only their boots excited him and, indeed, only when the wearers belonged to the servant class and were handsome men. Men of his own position wearing ever-so-fine boots were absolutely unexciting to him.

In reference to his sexual inclinations, the patient was still uncertain whether he felt these inclinations more toward the opposite sex or his own. He originally thought that he was more attracted to women, but that this attraction was, in any case, very weak. He stated with certainty that the sight of a naked man made no impression on him, and that the sight of male genitals was even repugnant to him. As for women, this was not exactly the case; even the most beautiful feminine form did not excite him sexually. As a young officer, he was occasionally compelled to accompany his comrades to brothels. He was all the more easily persuaded to get involved because he wanted to get rid of his vile partiality for boots; he was impotent, however, unless he brought the image of boots to his aid. Under these circumstances the act of cohabitation was normally performed, but without any pleasurable feeling. The patient felt no impulse to engage in intercourse with women and always required some external cause or persuasive idea. Left to himself, his sex life consisted of reveling in ideas about boots and corresponding dreams with pollutions. The impulse to kiss his servant's boots, to pull them off, etc., became more and more connected with these dreams and ideas, and the patient was determined to use every means to rid himself of this disgusting desire, which deeply wounded his pride. At that time, twenty years old and living in Paris, he recalled a very beautiful peasant girl who lived in his distant hometown. He hoped to free himself of his sexual perversion with her assistance. He went home and tried to win the girl's favor. He asserted that at the time he was deeply in love with this person, and that the sight of her or the touch of her dress gave him sensual pleasure. One time, when she kissed him, he had a powerful erection. After about a year and a half, the patient succeeded in achieving his desire with this person.

He was potent, but ejaculated tardily (ten to twenty minutes), and never had a pleasurable feeling during the act.

After about a year and a half of sexual intercourse with this girl, his love for her grew cold because he did not find her so "fine and pure" as he wished. Then it was necessary for him to call upon images of boots (which had been latent) in order to be potent during sexual intercourse. As these ideas spontaneously arose, his potency proportionately failed. He thereafter had coitus with other women. The act occasionally took place without any assistance from his imagination, especially when the woman was sympathetic.

The patient once committed rape. It is remarkable that on this single occasion he had a pleasurable feeling during the (forced) act. Immediately after the deed he had a feeling of disgust. One hour after the forced indulgence, he had coitus with the same woman, with her consent, and experienced no feeling of pleasure.

With the decline of his virility – i.e., when it was maintained only with ideas about boots – his libido for the opposite sex decreased. The patient's slight libido and weak inclination for women were evinced by the fact that, while he still sustained sexual relations with the peasant girl, he began to masturbate. He learned about the vice from Rousseau's *Confessions;* the book accidentally fell into his hands. The boot fantasies immediately became linked with the corresponding impulses. He then experienced violent erections and would often masturbate. This gave him a lively feeling of pleasure, which was denied to him during coitus; he initially felt mentally brighter and fresher as a result of masturbation.

In time, however, symptoms of sexual neurasthenia and, later, general neurasthenia with spinal irritation, appeared. He then temporarily gave up masturbation, and sought his first love; she, however, was now more than ever indifferent to him. He finally became impotent (even when he summoned ideas of boots to his aid), gave up women entirely, and again practiced masturbation, which protected him from the impulse to kiss and blacken servants' boots. At the same time he felt his sexual position keenly. He again occasionally attempted coitus, and was successful as soon as he thought of blackened boots. After continued abstinence from masturbation, he was occasionally successful in coitus without any artificial aid.

The patient said that his sexual needs were intense. If ejaculation did not occur for a long time, he became congestive, psychically greatly excited, and tormented by repugnant images of boots. He was therefore forced to have coitus or, preferably, to masturbate.

During the past year his moral position became painfully complicated by the fact that – as the last of a wealthy line of high position, and because of the importunate desire of his parents – he had to marry. The bride possessed a rare beauty, and she was perfectly sympathetic with him mentally; as a woman, however, she was as unappealing to him as any other woman. She satisfied him aesthetically "as any work of art would"; in his eyes, she was simply ideal. To honor her in a platonic way would be happiness worth striving for; to possess her as a wife, however, was a painful thought. He was certain beforehand that he would be impotent with her, except with the help of ideas about boots. Such means, however, opposed his respectful, moral and aesthetic feelings for the lady. If he were to soil her with such thoughts, she would lose, in his eyes, all her aesthetic value; then he would become impotent with her, and she would become repugnant to him. The patient considered his position one of despair, and confessed that he had lately been repeatedly close to suicide.

He was a man of great intelligence, and of decidedly masculine appearance, with an abundant growth of beard, a deep voice, and normal genitals. His eyes had a neuropathic expression. No signs of degeneration. Symptoms of spinal neurasthenia. It was possible to reassure the patient and give him hope for his future.

Medical advice consisted of instructions to combat his neurasthenia; masturbation and indulgence in fantasies about boots were interdicted. It was hoped that, with the removal of the neurasthenia, cohabitation without ideas would become possible, and that, in time, the patient would become morally and physically capable of marriage.

In the latter part of October 1888, the patient wrote to me that he had resolutely resisted masturbation and his imagination. In the meantime he had only had one dream about boots, and scarcely any pollutions. He had been free from homosexual inclination; in spite of this, however, there was often considerable sexual excitement, but without any adequate sexual desire for women. In spite of this deplorable situation, circumstances nevertheless compelled him to marry in three months.

[2] homosexual individuals, or urnings.

In contradistinction from the preceding group of psychosexual hermaphrodites, there are here, from birth, predominant sexual desires and inclinations for persons of the same sex exclusively; in contrast with the following group, however, the anomaly is limited to the sex life, and does not more deeply and seriously affect character and mental personality.

The sex life of these homosexuals (or urnings), *mutatis mutandis,* is entirely like normal heterosexual love. Because it is the exact opposite of natural feeling, however, it becomes a caricature, and the more so as these individuals are also, as a rule, subject to sexual hyperesthesia. Due to this, their love for their own sex is emotional and passionate.

The homosexual loves and deifies the male object of his affection, just as the normal man idealizes the woman he loves. He is capable of the greatest sacrifice, and experiences the pangs of unhappy, often unrequited, love; he suffers from the disloyalty of his beloved object, and is subject to jealousy, etc.

The male-loving man is only attracted to male dancers, actors, athletes, statues, etc. The sight of female charms is unimportant to him, if not repulsive. A naked woman is disgusting to him, while the sight of male genitals, hips, etc., affords him infinite pleasure.

Bodily contact with a sympathetic man induces a thrill of delight and, since these individuals are in most cases sexually neurasthenic (congenitally, from masturbation, or from enforced abstinence from sexual intercourse), under such circumstances ejaculation is easily induced. During the most intimate forms of intercourse with women, ejaculation cannot be induced at all, or only by artificial means. The sexual act with a man provides pleasure in many instances and leaves behind a feeling of comfort. Should the homosexual be able to force himself to engage in coitus – in which, as a rule, disgust has an inhibitory effect and makes the act possible – then his feeling is something like that of a man compelled to take disgusting food or drink. However, experience shows that homosexuals belonging to this group frequently marry, due to either ethical or social considerations.

Such unfortunates are relatively potent to the extent that, in marital intercourse, they incite their imagination and, instead of thinking of their wives, call up the image of some beloved man. Coitus is a great sacrifice, however, and affords no pleasure. It makes them, for days afterward, nervous and miserable. If these homosexuals are not able to overcome their inhibitory feelings and ideas (by means of powerful stimulation of their fantasies, or under the influence of alcoholic drink, or by erections induced by an overfilled bladder, etc.), then they are completely impotent; the mere touch of a man, however, can induce an intense erection, and even ejaculation.

Dancing with a woman is unpleasant to a homosexual; dancing with a man, however, especially one with an attractive form, is the greatest of pleasures to him.

The male homosexual who is highly cultured is not opposed to non-sexual intercourse with women; with intelligence and refinement, they can make conversation charming. It is only woman in her sexual role that he abhors.

Character and occupation correspond with the individual's sex in this degree of sexual degeneration. Sexual perversion remains an isolated anomaly in the mentality of the individual, deeply affecting his social existence. Accordingly, these individuals feel during the sexual act the same way they would feel if they naturally engaged in heterosexual intercourse.

Transitions to group three can occur, however, inasmuch as the passive role that corresponds with homosexual feeling is sometimes thought of or desired, or at least forms the content of dreams. Moreover, leanings to occupations and tendencies of taste are manifested that do not correspond with the sex of the individual. In many cases, one gets the impression that such symptoms are artificial, the result of educational influences; in other cases, that they represent deeper acquired degenerations of the original anomaly, superinduced by perverse sexual activity (masturbation), and analogous to the signs of progressive degeneration observed in acquired sexual inversion.

Regarding the manner of sexual satisfaction, it must be stated that with many male homosexuals a mere embrace is sufficient to induce ejaculation, subject as they are to irritable weakness of the sexual apparatus. In cases of sexual hyperesthesia and moral paresthesia, homosexuals attain great pleasure by engaging in intercourse with persons of the lowest condition.

On the same basis, desire to commit pederasty (active, of course) and other similar aberrations can occur, though such acts are infrequent. Apparently active pederasty is indulged in only in cases of moral defect and excessive sexual desire in individuals who are especially passionate.

The sexual desire of mature homosexuals, *in contradistinction to old and decrepit debauchees who prefer boys (and indulge in pederasty by preference), never seems to be directed toward immature males.* Only in cases of violent passion, or for lack of anything better, does the homosexual become dangerous to boys.

Case 138.

Z., aged thirty-six, wholesale merchant. His parents were said to have been healthy; physical and mental development normal; typical childhood diseases. At the age of fourteen he masturbated on his own accord; at the age of fifteen he began to rave about boys his own age. He never took the slightest notice of the opposite sex.

At the age of twenty-four he went to a brothel for the first time, but fled when he saw a nude woman.

At the age of twenty-five he engaged in sexual intercourse with men of his own kind (fervent embraces with ejaculation, occasional mutual masturbation).

For business reasons, and thinking he could cure his abnormal passion, at the age of twenty-eight he married a lady endowed with many physical and mental charms. With the aid of his imagination (thinking of intercourse with a handsome young man), Z. succeeded in being potent with his wife, whom at heart he loved passionately. This strain, however, superinduced neurasthenia. When his child was born, he gradually withdrew from his wife (who was somewhat frigid anyway), primarily because he was haunted by the fear of procreating offspring afflicted with his own anomaly.

Homosexual feelings and thoughts began to sway him again, which he sought to eradicate by masturbating.

He fell in love with a handsome young man, but overcame his weakness at the cost of his own health; his severe struggle brought on a pronounced attack of cerebral neurasthenia. He came to me for advice, because his homosexual tendency had become too powerful to be resisted any longer. He was afraid that his secret affliction might be discovered, thus rendering his position impossible in society. Like many of his fellow sufferers, he had taken to drink. Although he found that alcohol relieved his nervous disorders (physical weakness, psychic inertness and depression), his libido had increased.

Z. was a man of refined thought, mentally well-endowed, and appeared masculine and normal. He deeply deplored his position and loathed his weakness to masturbation (also mutual at times).

Mutual kisses and embraces satisfied him. Morally, he said, he had sunk so low he could imagine abandoning himself to this perverse passion, were it not for his wife and child.

My advice was to strenuously combat these homosexual impulses, perform his marital duties whenever possible, eschew alcohol and masturbation (which increases homosexual feelings and kills the love for women), and undergo treatment for neurasthenia. If he could not find relief and the situation became unbearable, he must confine himself to kisses and embraces with the male.

Case 139.

V., aged thirty-six, merchant; mother psychopathic; sister healthy; brother neuropsychopathic.

V. was drawn early to persons of his own sex. At first he was attracted to schoolmates and playmates, and later (at puberty) to adults, but never to persons of the opposite sex, whose charms had no interest for him. At the age of six he felt annoyed at not being a girl. He always preferred dolls and girls' games.

At twelve a schoolmate seduced him to masturbate. His dreams (with pollutions when virile) were exclusively of a homosexual character. He practiced mutual masturbation with men, **coitus between the thighs** and, exceptionally, **sucking the other man's member.** During this he had felt a pronounced tendency toward either the active or the passive role. Although he was potent during the act when he thought of a man, he never experienced real pleasure. The sexual act with a woman seemed to him a miserable substitute for the homosexual act. During recent years, intimate relations with a young man.

V. acknowledged the abnormality of his sex life.

Genitals normal. The secondary physical and psychic sexual characteristics are thoroughly masculine. No pathological conditions. After being arrested for having committed mutual masturbation, he was tried, found guilty, and sent to prison. He felt his sentence keenly, but only because it brought dishonor to him and his family. He could not help feeling and acting in an abnormal manner.

Case 140.

H., aged thirty, member of high society; mother neuropathic.

As a boy he felt drawn to his schoolmates. At the age of fourteen an older playmate committed pederasty on him. Although he liked it, he nevertheless felt pangs of conscience and never allowed the act to be repeated. He then practiced mutual masturbation. As neurasthenia increased, embracing and pressing a companion to himself was sufficient to produce ejaculation. He confined himself to this method when seeking satisfaction. He never had a liking for persons of the other sex and was unconscious of his anomaly. At twenty, however, he made some attempts, with prostitutes, to cure his sex life. Up to that time he had looked upon his abnormal practices as merely a youthful aberration. Although he was potent in coitus, he derived no gratification from it, and thus he again turned to men. His weakness was for young men eighteen to twenty years of age. He had no sympathy for men older than that. He never played a well-defined role in his relations with other men, but his social situation affected him keenly. He was continually haunted by the fear of detection, and said he could never survive the shame of it. There was nothing in his habits or behavior that betrayed antipathic sexual instinct. Genitals normal. No signs of degeneration. He had no faith in ever changing his abnormal sexuality. He had no taste whatsoever for women.

Case 141.

Y., aged forty, manufacturer; father was neuropathic and died of cerebral apoplexy; mother's family was tainted with insanity; two other children in the family, though sexually normal, were constitutionally neuropathic. At eight, masturbation of his own accord. At fifteen he felt drawn to handsome boys his own age, several of whom he seduced to masturbation. With puberty he was attracted to youths seventeen to twenty years of age, but they had to be beardless and have pretty, soft and girl-like features. Girls had no charm for him.

Although he soon recognized the pathological character of his sex life, he considered his method of satisfying these abnormal needs to be in accordance with nature and felt no remorse. To touch a woman was loathsome to him. He had twice attempted coitus, but without success. He likewise viewed masturbation as a filthy act. Regarding his antipathic sexual instinct, he declared that he had honestly striven to strip off this dreadful impulse, inasmuch as it made him an outcast before the whole world. All his efforts were in vain, however, for he felt forced by nature to seek satisfaction in his own manner. He always played the active role and confined himself entirely to acts not prohibited by the law of the land. He nonetheless became involved in an affair, as a result of which he lost a position that was one of confidence and good renumeration. He then became a vagabond until he decided to cross the ocean and begin a new life. Being clever and honorable, he succeeded.

When I first met Y., he was in despair and firmly contemplated suicide, especially because a medical man had failed with hypnotic treatment; Y. had not reacted to suggestion.

He was inclined to neurasthenia. Penis small. No pathological symptoms. Masculine in every respect.

Case 142.

T., aged thirty-four; merchant; mother neuropathic and weakly; father healthy. At the age of nine a schoolmate taught him how to masturbate. He practiced mutual masturbation with a brother who slept with him in the same bed. Once **he put his brother's member into his mouth.** On one occasion, when still a boy, **he licked the place where a soldier had urinated earlier.** At fourteen, first love for a schoolmate of ten. At the age of seventeen he took a dislike to handsome young men and subsequently focused his affection on decrepit old men.

One night he heard his aged father "give a groan of sexual satisfaction." This excited him immensely as he imagined his father performing the marital act. Since that time the picture of old men performing the homosexual act enlivened his dreams (with pollution) and was present in his mind during masturbation. The more aged, decrepit, and feeble the man was, the stronger was T.'s sexual excitement, even to the point of ejaculation. Although at twenty-three he sought a cure with a prostitute, erection failed him, and he made no further attempts at that time. Young men and boys left him cold.

At twenty-nine he developed a violent love for an old man whom he had accompanied for years on the man's daily walks. Although intimate relations were precluded, T. often had ejaculations on these walks. To free himself of this humiliating situation, he once more went to a prostitute, but it proved to be a fiasco. He then fell upon the idea of hiring a decrepit old man and making him have coitus with a prostitute while he looked on. This idea caused erection in him, and he was thus able to have coitus himself. Although the act gave him no pleasure, he felt psychically relieved, especially when he was potent in the absence of the old man. This, however, did not last long. He became sexually and generally neurasthenic, depressed, shy, and impotent, eventually giving himself up to psychic masturbation coupled with thoughts of old men in homosexual situations.

T. was masculine in appearance and presented no special marks beyond his heavy sexual neurasthenia.

Case 143.

Z., aged twenty-eight, merchant; father very nervous and irritable; mother hysteropathic. Z. was constitutionally nervous, suffered from enuresis until his eighteenth year, and was a frail boy. Proper physical development did not really begin until he was twenty years of age. The first sexual emotions he experienced were when, as a boy of eight, he witnessed other boys being caned on the buttocks. Although he felt compassion for the boys, he nevertheless had a feeling of lustful pleasure that pervaded his whole body. Some time afterward, he was late for school. On the way the anticipation of a caning on his buttocks excited him so much that for a short time he had a violent erection and could not move.

At eleven he fell in love with a "beautiful, blonde boy who had wondrously lovely, intelligent, and lustrous eyes."

It gave him immense pleasure to see this boy home, and he often craved for kisses and caresses from him. He recognized the unbecoming nature of this desire, however, and did not allow the boy to have an inkling of it.

At that time he met a girl, two years his junior, who pleased him so much that he once covered her with kisses. This, however, remained a solitary episode.

At thirteen he was seduced to masturbation. He did not cultivate the habit, however, inasmuch as he found protection in his "more refined feelings for young men" and disdained "dragging his pure, divine love" in the gutter.

At seventeen he became desperately enamored with a companion who had "lovely brown eyes, noble features and a dark complexion." He suffered untold tortures because of this unhappy love for two and one-half years, after which he was separated from his companion. If ever he were to meet him again, the old fire would be certain to flare up anew. On two other occasions he fell in love with comrades, but not as violently as in the first instance. Although at twenty he had coitus, he derived no pleasure from the act. He continued his relations with women to avoid masturbation, to appear potent, and to mask his homosexual tendency.

Although he had no *horror feminae,* women did not excite him. "A woman is a work of art, a statue."

Endowed with a strong willpower, he was able to master his abnormal inclination. He regarded his sexual position as unsatisfactory, however, especially because he looked upon coitus as a coarsely sensual enjoyment, and because erection had become difficult.

In the consultation no abnormal signs could be detected. He appeared to be virile and mentally sound.

Case 144.

P., aged thirty-seven; his mother was very nervous and suffered from migraines. As a boy he was subject to attacks of severe hysteria. He was always drawn to handsome young men and became highly excited when he could see their genitals. With puberty he practiced mutual masturbation with men who had to be between twenty-five and thirty years old. He played the female role in the sexual act. He loved with the whole intensity of a woman and, like an actor on the stage, only posed as a man. Other boys sneered at him because of his girlish ways and habits. He married in the hope of correcting his sex life. He forced himself to engage in coitus with his wife and produced potency by imagining her to be a young man. They had one child. He became neurasthenic, however, his imagination waned, and he became impotent. For two years he avoided coitus, resumed his homosexual practices, and was apprehended by the police in the act of mutual masturbation with a young man.

He pleaded that because of prolonged sexual abstinence, he had become unduly excited by the sight of a man's genitals and had yielded, in his confusion, to the impulse.

There was no amnesia. Thoroughly virile. Decent appearance. Genitals normal. Short imprisonment.

Case 145.

N., aged forty-one, unmarried. Although his father and mother were closely related to each other, they were both psychically normal. An uncle on the father's side was insane. N.'s brothers were hyper- and heterosexual. At the age of nine he felt strong inclinations toward other boys. At fifteen, mutual masturbation and coitus between the thighs.

At sixteen, a love affair with a young man. He declared that his homosexual love developed just as the love affairs between men and women do in novels.

Only handsome young men between twenty and twenty-four attracted him. His erotic dreams were solely homosexual. He played the female role in actual intercourse with men.

He said his soul had a feminine character. He only cared for cooking and girls' work, and never for boys' games. He disdained manly sports, smoking, and drinking. He led a varied life and was greatly satisfied serving as a cook in a foreign country. He lost his position, however, because he entered into a love affair with the son of his employer.

At twenty-two he recognized the abnormality of his sexual position. He became alarmed and, although he began to frequent brothels to cure himself of his perverse habits, erection absolutely failed him.

When his family discovered the true state of affairs, he became confused with shame and made an attempt on his own life. He nevertheless recovered and, cast out by his family, he went abroad, disgusted with himself and his unhappy life. His only hope was that, with old age, relief would come. He came for medical advice to find "honor and rest." The secondary physical sexual characteristics were quite normal and of the masculine type. Genitals normal. He thought of castration or entering a monastery.

Advice: Suggestive treatment.

Case 146.

On a summer evening, at twilight, X. Y., a physician of a city in North Germany, was committing a misdemeanor with a countryman in a field when he was detected by a watchman. He practiced masturbation on him and then **put the other man's member into his mouth.** X. escaped legal prosecution by flight. Because there had been no publicity, and because **insertion of the member into the anus** had not taken place, the authorities dismissed the complaint. An extensive correspondence of a perverse sexual character was found among X.'s effects. It revealed that he had had perverse intercourse for years with all classes of people.

X. came from a neurotic family. His paternal grandfather committed suicide while insane. His father was a weak, peculiar man. One brother masturbated at the age of two. A cousin was sexually perverse and practiced perverse acts similar to X.'s when he was a youth. He became weak-minded and died of spinal disease. A paternal great-uncle was a hermaphrodite. His mother's sister was insane. His mother was said to have been healthy. X.'s brother was nervous and irascible.

X. was likewise nervous as a child. The mewing of a cat would create great fear in him, and if anyone were to merely imitate the voice of a cat, he would cry bitterly and run to others for protection. Slight physical disturbance caused violent fever. He was a quiet, dreamy child with an excitable imagination, but only slight mental capabilities. He did not indulge a great deal in boyish games, preferring instead feminine pursuits. It gave him especial pleasure to curl the hair of the housemaid or his brother.

At thirteen, X. went to an institute where he practiced mutual masturbation and seduced his comrades. His cynical conduct made him unmanageable to the point that he had to be taken home. His parents then found love letters with lascivious contents that indicated perverse sexuality. From the age of seventeen he studied under the strict surveillance of a professor in his *Gymnasium,* but made sad progress. His only talent was for music.

After finishing his studies, the patient entered the university at the age of nineteen. He attracted attention with his cynical character and by associating with young persons who were thought to be involved with masculine love. He began to be dandified, wearing striking cravats and low-cut shirts. He forced his feet into narrow shoes and curled his hair in a remarkable way. This peculiarity disappeared when he left school and returned home.

At the age of twenty-four he was neurasthenic for a lengthy period of time. From then until his twenty-ninth year, although he was earnest and skillful in his profession, he avoided the society of the opposite sex and constantly associated with men of doubtful character.

The patient would not allow a personal examination. In writing, he made the excuse that it would be of no use, inasmuch as his impulse to his own sex had existed from his earliest childhood and was congenital. He had always had *horror feminae* and had never been inclined to avail himself of the charms of women. He felt himself to be in the role of a man toward men. He recognized his impulse toward his own sex as abnormal, and excused his sexual indulgence as being the result of an abnormal natural condition.

Since his flight, X. has lived in southern Italy and told me in his letter that now, as before, he indulged in perverse love. X. was an earnest, stately man, with masculine features, a well-grown beard, and normally developed genitals. A short time ago, Dr. X. furnished me with his autobiography, and the following excerpts are worthy of mention:

"When, at the age of seven, I entered a private school, I felt very uncomfortable, and found very little sympathy from my companions. Toward only one of them, a very handsome child, did I feel attracted, and I loved him wildly. In childish games I always knew how to arrange it so that I could appear in feminine attire. My greatest pleasure was to form intricate coiffures for our servant girls. I often regretted that I was not a girl.

"My sexual instinct awakened when I was thirteen, and from the moment of its appearance it was directed toward youthful, strong men. At first I was not really certain that this was abnormal, but consciousness of its abnormality came when I saw and heard how my companions were characterized sexually. I began to masturbate at the age of thirteen. At seventeen I left home and went to the *Gymnasium* of a large capital. I was put to board in the home of a married professor from the *Gymnasium,* with whose son I later had sexual relations. It was with him that I first attained sexual satisfaction. Thereafter I made the acquaintance of a young artist, who soon noticed that I was abnormal, and confessed to me that he was in the same condition. I learned from him that this abnormality was very frequent, and this knowledge overcame the trouble that I had had in supposing that I was alone in my abnormality. This young man had an extensive acquaintance with persons in like condition, to whom he introduced me. I then became the object of general attention, for on all sides I was declared to be very attractive physically. I soon became insanely loved by an old gentleman; not finding him to my taste, however, I endured him for only a short time, and then gave my ear to a young and handsome officer who lay at my feet. He was really my first love.

"After passing my final examination at the age of nineteen and free from the discipline of school, I made the acquaintance of a great number of people like myself, among them Karl Ulrichs ('Numa Numantius').

"When I later took up the study of medicine and associated with many normal youths, I was often in a position where I was compelled to visit public prostitutes. After having consorted, to no purpose, with various prostitutes, some of whom were very beautiful, the opinion was spread among my acquaintances that I was impotent. I strengthened this idea by telling of previous sexual excesses. At that time I had numerous superficial relations with women who prized my physical qualities, which were considered very beautiful. The result of this was that I was exciting somebody all the time, and I received such a mass of love letters that I was often in a state of embarrassment. The acme of this situation was reached later, when, as a physician, I lived in the hospital. I was treated like a celebrated person there, and the scenes of jealousy that took place on my account almost led to the discovery of the whole thing. Shortly after this, I fell ill with an inflammation of my shoulder joint, from which I recovered after three months. During this illness I received injections of morphine several times daily, which were suddenly discontinued. I secretly kept up the morphine injections after my recovery. For the purpose of special study before entering into private practice, I spent some months in Vienna, where, by means of some recommendations, I gained entrance to various circles of people like myself. I learned that the abnormality in question, in its various forms, is spread through the lower classes as well as the higher, and that commonly those who can be approached for money are found among the higher classes.

"When I established myself in the country, I hoped to cure myself of the morphine habit by means of cocaine, and then I became a victim of cocaine. After only three relapses, however, I was able to rid myself of this habit (about two years ago). It was impossible for me, in my position, to find sexual satisfaction, and I noticed with pleasure that the use of cocaine had overcome my desire. When, at the urgent request of my aunt, I had first emancipated myself from cocaine, I traveled for a few weeks in order to improve my health. The perverse impulses were then reawakened to their former strength, and while I was out in the fields by the city amusing myself with a man one evening, I noticed that I had been detected by the authorities and advertised. The act of which I was accused was not punishable, however, in accordance with the opinion expressed by the highest court of the German kingdom. I therefore had to be careful; for the announcement of the crime had already been heralded everywhere. I saw after this that I had to leave Germany and find a new home where neither the law nor public opinion would be opposed to an impulse that, like all abnormal instincts, could not be overcome by the will. Because I was never deceived for a moment about recognizing my impulses as opposing my social behavior, I repeatedly attempted to become master of them; these efforts, however, only increased their power. This same observation has been noted by my acquaintances. Because I was drawn exclusively toward strong, youthful and masculine individuals who were seldom inclined to yield to my wishes, I was compelled to buy them. My desire was limited to persons of the lower classes, and so I was always able to find those who could be obtained with money. I hope that the following statements will not awaken your repugnance. At first I intended to omit them, but I am including them for the completeness of this communication, because they serve to enrich the clinical material. I am compelled to perform the sexual act in the following way:

"I put the young man's penis in my mouth and move it about with my mouth in such a way that my lover ejaculates semen; I then spit the sperm onto his perineum, tell him to press his thighs together, and rub my penis against and between his closed thighs. The young man, meanwhile, must embrace me as passionately as he can. What I have just described gives me the same pleasure as ejaculation. Inserting my penis into his anus or rubbing it manually produces ejaculation, but this gives me no pleasure whatever.

"I have found, however, that those who take my penis and do what I have described above completely satisfy my desires.

"Concerning my physical appearance and related matters, I should mention the following: I am 186 centimeters tall, have a masculine appearance, and I am healthy, with the exception of abnormal irritability of the skin. My hair and beard are black and thick. My genitals are of medium size and normally formed. I am able, without any trace of fatigue, to perform the sexual act from four to six times in twenty-four hours. My life is very regular. I use alcohol and tobacco very sparingly. I play the piano quite well, and some of my unpretentious compositions have been much applauded. I have recently finished a novel, which, as my first work, has been very favorably received by my friends. The subject matter of the story has several problems taken from the lives of homosexuals.

"Among the large number of fellow sufferers who are personally known to me, I have naturally been in a position to make observations concerning the condition and the degrees of abnormality. The following information may thus be of service to you:

"The most abnormal thing that I became acquainted with was the impulse of a gentleman who lived in Berlin. Above all others, he preferred young fellows with unwashed feet, and he would lick the feet passionately. A gentleman in Leipzig had a similar desire. When it was possible, he would **lick the genitals and anus,** preferring the parts to be unwashed. Several people have assured me that the sight of riding boots or parts of military uniforms induced in them such excitement that spontaneous ejaculation resulted. A man in Paris compelled a friend **to urinate into his mouth.**

"Regarding the degree to which many men feel like women, which is not the case for me, two persons in Vienna are examples. They both have feminine names. One is a barber who calls himself 'French Laura'; the other was formerly a butcher who calls himself 'Butcher Fanny.' They have never missed an opportunity, during the carnivals, to show themselves in very fantastic feminine masks. In Hamburg there is a person who many people believe to be a woman, because he always goes about the house in feminine attire, and though he only occasionally leaves the house, it is always in such clothing. He wished to stand as godmother at a christening, and this caused quite a scandal.

"Feminine timidity, frivolity, obstinacy and weakness of character are the rule of such individuals.

"Several cases of perverse sexuality are known to me where epilepsy and psychoses are present. Hernias are remarkably frequent. In my practice many persons come to me, on the recommendation of friends, to be treated for diseases of the anus. I saw two syphilitic and one local chancre, as well as several fissures. At present I am treating a gentleman for condyloma of the anus, which form a rounded tumor as large as a fist. In Vienna I saw one case of primary affection of the soft palate in a young man who used to frequent fancy-dress balls in girl's attire and entice young men. He would pretend to be menstruating and thus induce others to use him **by means of his mouth.** The assertion was made that he had deceived fourteen men in this way in one evening. Because I have found nothing concerning the intercourse of pederasts in any of the publications I have seen on antipathic sexuality, I will venture, in conclusion, to say something on this subject:

"As soon as individuals affected with inverted sexuality become acquainted, there is a detailed narration of their experiences, loves, and seductions, insofar as the social difference between them allows for such entertainment. Only rarely is this amusement not done with new acquaintances. They call themselves 'aunts' and, in Vienna, 'sisters.' Two very masculine public prostitutes in Vienna, who lived in a perverse sexual relation with each other and with whom I accidentally became acquainted, told me that for the corresponding condition in women the name 'uncle' was used. Since becoming conscious of my abnormal instinct, I have met thousands of such individuals.

"Almost every large city has some meeting place, as well as a so-called promenade. In smaller cities there are relatively few 'aunts,' although in a small town of 2300 inhabitants I found eight, and in one town of 7000 I found eighteen of whom I was absolutely sure – to say nothing of those whom I suspected. In my own town of 30,000 inhabitants, I personally know around 120 'aunts.' The majority of these 'aunts' (and I, especially) possess the capability of immediately judging whether another is like us or not. In the language of the 'aunts,' such a person is called 'reasonable' or 'unreasonable.' My acquaintances are often astounded by the certainty of my judgment. Individuals who seem absolutely masculine I recognize as 'aunts' at first sight. On the other hand, I am able to behave in such a masculine way that my genuineness is doubted in the circles to which I have been introduced by acquaintances. When I am in the mood, I can act exactly like a girl.

"The majority of 'aunts,' like myself, do not regret their abnormality, but would be sorry if their condition were changed. Furthermore, according to my own and all other experience, this congenital condition cannot be influenced. Therefore, all our hope rests upon the possibility of a change in the relevant laws, so that only rape or the commission of public offense, when such can be proved at the same time, shall be punishable."

[3] effemination.

There are various transitions from the foregoing cases to those of this category that are characterized by the degree to which the psychic personality, especially regarding the general manner of feeling and inclinations, is influenced by the abnormal sexual feeling. In this group are fully developed cases in which males are females in feeling, and in which females are males in feeling. This abnormality of feeling and character development is often apparent in childhood. The boy likes to spend his time with girls, play with dolls, and help his mother about the house; he likes to cook, sew, knit; he develops tastes in the female *toilette,* and even becomes the adviser of his sisters. As he grows older he eschews smoking, drinking and manly sports and, instead, finds pleasure in the adornment of persons, art, *belles lettres,* etc., even to the extent of involving himself entirely in the cultivation of the beautiful. Because woman possesses parallel inclinations, he prefers to move in the society of women.

If he can assume the role of a female at a masquerade, it is his greatest delight. He seeks to please his lover, so to speak, by studiously trying to represent what pleases the female-loving man of the opposite sex – modesty, sweetness, taste for aesthetics, poetry, etc. Efforts to approach the female appearance in gait, attitude and attire are frequently seen.

With reference to the sexual feeling and instinct of homosexuals whose entire mental being is so thoroughly permeated, the men, without exception, feel themselves to be females. Thus they are as antagonistic to men who are constituted like them as they are like them in form. On the other hand, they are drawn toward members of their own sex who are homosexual or sexually normal. The same jealousy that occurs in normal sexual life also occurs here, when rivalry is threatened. Indeed, because there is usually sexual hyperesthesia, this jealousy is often boundless.

In cases of completely developed inverted sexuality, heterosexual love is looked upon as absolutely incomprehensible; sexual intercourse with a person of the opposite sex is unthinkable, impossible. Such an attempt brings on the inhibitory concept of disgust or even horror, which makes erection impossible. Of my cases that were transitional to the third category, only two had the ability, when aided by imagining that the female in question assumed the role of man, to have coitus for the time being. The act, however, which yielded no gratification, was a great sacrifice and afforded no pleasure.

In the act of homosexual intercourse, effeminated man always feels as a woman and assumes the female role. Where there is irritable weakness of the ejaculation center, the methods of indulgence include simply lying underneath the partner or allowing coitus between the thighs. In other cases, the methods include passive masturbation, or having **the lover ejaculate into the mouth.** Some have a desire for passive pederasty; occasionally a desire for active pederasty occurs. In one attempt of this kind, the man desisted because of the disgust that seized him when the act reminded him of coitus.

There was no inclination for immature persons (boy love). Not infrequently there were only platonic desires.

Case 147.

E., aged thirty-one, son of an inveterate drunkard. No other taint in his family. Grew up in a village. At the age of six he began to feel happy when he was in the company of men who had beards. At the age of eleven he began to blush whenever he met a handsome man, and he dared not look at him. He was at ease in the company of women. He wore girl's garments up to his seventh year, and was very unhappy when he was deprived of them. He liked occupation in the kitchen and about the house best. His school time passed without incident. Although now and then he had an intimate liking for a certain schoolmate, this wore off.

Dreams of men who had beards and were clad in blue clothes became more frequent.

He joined an athletic society so that he might converse with men. He liked to go to balls, not because of the girls, who were a matter of indifference to him, but to see the fine men, thinking all the time that he was locked in an embrace with one of them. He felt lonely, however, and dissatisfied, and gradually became conscious of being quite unlike the other young fellows. All his thoughts and aims concerned finding a man who could love him.

At seventeen he was seduced by another man to mutual masturbation. He reacted with delight, shame and fear. He recognized the abnormality of his sexual feelings, became depressed, and seriously considered suicide. Although he finally became reconciled with his abnormal position and craved for men, he was shy by nature and thus found little opportunity. He felt uneasy when girls sought his company. At twenty-six he went to live in a large city and then found plenty of opportunities for homosexual intercourse. For some time he lived with a man of his own age as husband and wife. He felt happy in the role of a woman. Sexual gratification was obtained by mutual masturbation and coitus between the thighs.

He was a skillful workman, well-liked, and masculine in appearance and behavior. Genitals normal. No signs of degeneration.

His younger brother was also homosexual.

Two sisters, who both died young, avoided men, preferred work in the stable to work in the kitchen, and were skillful in all men's handicrafts.

Case 148.

C., aged twenty-eight, gentleman of leisure; father neuropathic; mother very nervous. One brother suffered from paranoia, another was psychically degenerated. Three younger members of the family were normal.

C. was neuropathically tainted; he had a slight convulsive tic. For as long as he can remember he felt drawn to male persons, though only to his schoolmates at first. When puberty set in, he fell in love with male teachers who used to come to his house to visit his parents. He felt himself to be in the female role. His dreams, with pollutions, were always about men. He was gifted in music and poetry, and loved the theatre. He had no talent for science, especially mathematics, and passed his final examinations with difficulty.

He declared that he was psychically a woman. He loved to play with dolls and preferred women's affairs, disdaining all the pursuits of men. He liked the society of young girls best, because they were sympathetic and had a soul-like affinity. In the company of men he was as shy and confused as a maiden. He never smoked and disliked alcoholic drinks. Most of all, he liked to spend his time cooking, knitting and embroidering. He had no libido. Although he had experienced a few episodes of sexual intercourse with men, his ideal on such occasions was to play the role of the woman. He abhorred coitus with a woman. After reading *Psychopathia Sexualis* he became alarmed, was afraid of coming in conflict with the police, and avoided sexual relations with men. Pollutions became very frequent, however, and neurasthenia supervened. He came for medical advice.

C. had an abundant beard and was a decidedly masculine type, with the exception of soft features and remarkably fine skin. Genitals normal, except for a deficient prolapse of one of the testicles. In his behavior, gait, and appearance there was nothing unusual, though he imagined that everyone noticed his abnormal sexual proclivity, and he therefore shunned society. Lascivious talk made him blush like a maiden. Once, when someone turned the topic of conversation to antipathic sexual instinct, he fainted. Music caused a heavy perspiration to occur all over his body. Closer acquaintance revealed his psychic femininity; he was as timid as a girl and without a vestige of independence. Nervous restlessness, convulsive tics, and numerous neurasthenic complications stamped him as a constitutionally tainted neuropathic individual.

Case 149.

B., waiter, forty-two years of age, unmarried, was sent to me by his own physician (with whom he had fallen in love) as a case of sexual inversion. In modest language, B. readily gave an account of his life, with an emphasis upon his sexual life. He seemed pleased to obtain at last an authentic explanation of the abnormal state that he had always considered a disease.

B. possessed no knowledge of his grandparents. His father had an irascible, excitable nature, strong sexual needs, and was a drinker. After begetting twenty-four children with the same woman, he obtained a divorce, and later had three children by his house-keeper. The mother was a healthy woman. Of the twenty-four children, only six are now living. Although several of them suffered from nervous affections, they were all sexually normal, with the exception of one sister who had always run after men.

B. asserted that he had always been delicate and sickly. His sex life awoke at the age of eight. He began to masturbate and derived much pleasure from **putting the erect penis of other boys into his mouth.** At the age of twelve he began to fall in love with men, prefer-ring those in the thirties who had mustaches. At that time his sexual needs were extraor-dinary, and erections and pollutions were frequent. He masturbated daily, thinking of a man he loved. His ambition was always **to put an erect penis into his mouth,** which was thought to cause ejaculation accompanied by the utmost lust. Thus far, however, he had only succeeded in doing this twelve times. He never felt nausea with the penis of a sympathetic man; on the contrary. Active as well as passive pederasty disgusted him thor-oughly, and he never accepted such offers. During the perverse act he played the role of a woman. His love for sympathetic men was boundless. He would do anything for the man he loved and, when he beheld him, he trembled with excitement and lustful feelings.

At nineteen, although he was lured by his companions to a brothel several times, coitus did not please him, and only at the moment of ejaculation did he experience a sort of gratification. He could only be virile with a woman when, during the act, he thought of her as the man he loved. He would have much rather preferred that the woman had allowed him **to put his penis into her mouth,** but she refused. For lack of something better, he indulged in coitus; twice he was even a father. The younger of the two chil-dren, now a girl of eight, had already begun masturbation and mutual masturbation, which troubled him very much. Was there no remedy for this?

The patient said that during sexual intercourse and otherwise he always felt as a woman toward men. He believed that this sexual perversion originated from the fact that when he was born his father had wished for a girl. The other children of the family always teased him because of his girlish ways and manners. To sweep the rooms and wash the dishes were always pleasant occupations for him. His housework was always much admired and praised because he was more clever than the girls.. Whenever he could, he would don girl's attire. He always wore a female mask at the Mardi Gras balls. His female nature made him a capital coquette.

Drinking, smoking, and manly sports and occupations never suited him, but he was passionately fond of sewing and was often upbraided as a boy because of his weakness for dolls. At the circus or the theatre his attention was drawn only by the male performers. He had an irresistible desire to loiter about bathrooms in order to get a look at the men's genitals.

Female charms never attracted him. Coitus was only possible when he was aided by the thought of a beloved man. Nocturnal pollutions were always produced by lascivious dreams about men.

Despite numerous sexual excesses, B. had never suffered from sexual neurasthenia, nor were there symptoms of neurasthenia of any kind.

Features delicate; sparse side whiskers and mustache, which did not begin to grow until he was twenty-eight. Except for a light, swinging gait, his external appearance did not indicate his female nature. He observed that he was often teased because of his womanish carriage. His manners were highly modest. Genitals large, well-developed, quite normal, with an abundance of hair; pelvis masculine. Cranium rachitic, slightly hydrocephalic; parietal bones rather bulging. Countenance exceptionally small. Patient said he was easily provoked to wrath.

Case 150.

Taylor had occasion to examine a certain Eliza Edwards, aged twenty-four. It was discovered that she was of masculine sex. E. had worn female clothing from her fourteenth year and had also been an actress. The hair was worn long, in the manner of females, and parted in the middle. Although the form of the face was feminine, the body was otherwise masculine. The beard was carefully pulled out. The masculine, well-developed genitals were artfully fixed in an upward position with a bandage. The condition of the anus indicated passive pederasty (Taylor, *Med. Jurisprudence*, 1873, vol. 2, pp. 278 and 473).

Case 151.

An official of middle age, who was married to a virtuous woman, and had been happy for some years in family life, presented a peculiar manifestation of antipathic sexual feeling.

One day, through the indiscretion of a prostitute, the following scandal became public: About once a week, X. would appear in a house of prostitution, where he would dress himself up as a woman; he always required, as a part of his costume, a coiffure. When his *toilette* was completed, he would lie down on the bed and have the prostitute perform masturbation. He very much preferred, however, to have a male person (a servant of the house) perform this act. This man's father was hereditarily tainted, had been insane several times, and was afflicted with hyperesthesia and sexual paresthesia.

[4] androgyny.

Forming direct transitions from the foregoing groups are individuals of antipathic sexuality in whom not only the character and the feelings agree with the abnormal sexual instinct, but also the frame, features, voice, etc. Thus, the individual approaches the opposite sex anthropologically, and in more than a psychic and psychosexual way. This anthropological form of the cerebral anomaly seems to represent an extremely high degree of degeneration. That this variation, however, has an entirely different basis than the teratological manifestation of hermaphroditism, in an anatomical sense, is clearly shown by the fact that thus far, in the domain of inverted sexuality, no transitions to hermaphroditic malformation of the genitals have been observed. The genitals of these persons always prove to be fully differentiated sexually, though there are often anatomical signs of degeneration (epispadias, etc.), in the sense of an arrest of development in otherwise well-marked organs.

Nevertheless, there is an insufficient record of cases that belong to this interesting group of women in masculine attire with masculine genitals. Every experienced observer of his fellow men remembers masculine persons who were remarkable for their womanish character and type (wide hips, a form rounded by abundant development of adipose tissue, absence or insufficient development of beard, feminine features, delicate complexion, falsetto voice, etc.).

In persons who belong to the fourth group, as well as in certain persons who belong to the third who form transitions to the fourth, there seems to be a feeling of (sexual) shame toward persons of the same sex, though none toward persons of the opposite sex.

Case 152.

Androgyny. Mr. v. H., aged thirty, single; neuropathic mother. It was reported that neither nervous nor mental diseases had occurred in the patient's family, and his only brother was said to be completely normal, both mentally and physically. Because the patient's physical development was delayed, he spent much of his time at the seashore and climatic resorts. From childhood he was of neuropathic constitution and, according to his relatives, unlike other boys. His disinclination for masculine pursuits and his preference for feminine amusements were noted early. Thus, while he avoided all boyish games and gymnastic exercises, he found doll play and feminine occupations to be particularly pleasing. Although subsequently he developed well physically and escaped severe illnesses, he remained mentally abnormal, incapable of an earnest aim in life, and decidedly feminine in thought and feeling.

In his seventeenth year pollutions occurred, became more frequent, and finally took place during the day; the patient grew weak and manifested various nervous disturbances. Symptoms of spinal neurasthenia made their appearance, and although they lasted for many years, they became milder, with a decrease in the number of pollutions. Masturbation was denied, but was highly probable. An indolent, effeminate, dreamy habit of thought became more and more noticeable at puberty. All efforts to induce the patient to take up an earnest pursuit in life were in vain. His intellectual functions, though formally quite undisturbed, were never equal to the motive of an independent character and the higher ideals of life. He remained dependent, an overgrown child, and nothing more clearly indicated his original abnormal condition than his actual inability to take care of money, added to his own confession that he had no ability to use money reasonably, and that he had wasted it on curios, toilet articles, and the like.

Incapable as he was of a reasonable use of money, the patient was no more capable of leading a social existence; indeed, he was incapable of gaining an insight into its significance and value.

He learned very poorly, spending his time with the *toilette* and artistic nothings, particularly painting, for which he evinced a certain capability; lacking perseverance, however, he accomplished nothing in this direction. He could not be moved to take up any earnest thought; he had a mind only for externals, was always distracted, and serious things quickly wearied him. Preposterous acts, senseless journeys, waste of money and debts repeatedly occurred throughout the course of his later life; and even with these positive faults in his life, he lacked understanding. Self-willed and intractable, he never did well when an attempt was made to put him on his feet and point out to him his own interests.

With these manifestations of a congenitally abnormal and defective mind, there were notable indications of perverse sexual feeling, which were also indicated in the somatic condition of the patient. Sexually, the patient felt like a woman toward men, and had inclinations toward people of his own sex, with indifference, if not actual disinclination, for females.

Although the patient asserted that in his twenty-second year he had sexual intercourse with women, and was able to perform the act of coitus normally, he soon ceased to indulge in such intercourse. This was partly because of an occasional increase of neurasthenic symptoms after coitus, and partly because of fear of infection – but it was really because of an absence of satisfaction. Concerning his abnormal sexual condition, he was not quite clear. Although he was conscious of an inclination toward the male sex, he confessed, in a shamefaced way, that he had certain pleasurable feelings of friendship for masculine individuals, which, however, were not accompanied by any sensual feelings. He did not exactly abhor the female sex; he could even bring himself to marry a woman who, through a similarity in artistic tastes, could have an attraction for him. It would be necessary, however, for him to be freed from conjugal duties, because they were unpleasant to him, and because performing them made him tired and weak. Although he denied having had sexual intercourse with men, his blushing and embarrassment, and, more important, an occurrence some time ago in N., where the patient provoked a scandal by attempting to have sexual intercourse with youths, showed that he was being dishonest.

Also, the patient's external appearance, condition, form, gestures, manners, and dress were remarkable, and decidedly recalled the feminine form and characteristics. *Although his thorax and pelvis were of decidedly feminine form,* he was above average in height. *His body was rich in fat; his skin was well-groomed, delicate and soft.* The impression of a woman in masculine dress was further increased by *a thin growth of hair on his face,* shaven except for a small mustache; his mincing gait; his shy, effeminate manner; his feminine features; the swimming, neuropathic expression of his eyes; the traces of powder and paint; the curtailed cut of his clothing, with a bosom-like prominence to the upper garments; the fringed feminine cravat; and his hair, smoothly brushed down from the brow to the temples. The physical examination left no doubt about the feminine form of his body. His external genitals were well-developed, though his left testicle had remained in the canal; *his mons pubis was unusually rich in fat and prominent, with a thin growth of hair. His voice was high and without masculine timbre.*

The occupation and manner of thought of v. H. were decidedly feminine. He had a boudoir and a well-supplied *toilette* table, where he spent many hours beautifying himself with all kinds of arts. He abhorred the chase, practice with arms, and such masculine pursuits. Calling himself an aesthete, he spoke with preference of his paintings and attempts at poetry. He was interested in and pursued feminine occupations (e.g., embroidery), which he called his greatest pleasure. He could spend his life in an artistic and aesthetic circle of ladies and gentlemen, in conversation, music and aesthetics. He preferred conversation about feminine things – fashions, needlework, cooking and household work.

The patient was well-nourished, but anemic. He had a neuropathic constitution, and presented symptoms of neurasthenia, which were maintained by a bad manner of life, lying abed, living indoors, and effeminateness.

He complained of occasional pain and pressure in the head, and had habitual constipation. He was easily frightened; he complained of occasional lassitude, fatigue, and drawing pains in the extremities, in the direction of the lumbar-abdominal nerves. After pollutions, and regularly after eating, he felt tired and relaxed; he was sensitive to pressure over the spinous processes of the dorsal vertebrae, as well as to pressure along accessible nerves. He felt peculiar sympathies and antipathies toward certain persons, and fell into a condition of peculiar fear and confusion when he met people for whom he felt repugnance. His pollutions, though they later rarely occurred, were pathological, in that they occurred by day and were unaccompanied by any sensual excitement.

Opinion:

[1] Mr. v. H., according to all observations and reports, was a mentally abnormal and defective person, and had been, in fact, from birth. His antipathic sexual instinct represented a part of his abnormal physical and mental condition.

[2] This condition, in that it was congenital, was incurable. There existed defective orga-

nization of the highest cerebral centers, which rendered him incapable of leading an independent life, and of obtaining a position in life. His perverse sexual instinct prevented him from exercising normal sexual functions, and this was attended by all the social consequences of such an anomaly, as well as the danger of satisfaction of perverse impulses that arose out of his abnormal organization, with consequent social and legal conflicts. Fear of such conflicts, however, was not great, because the (perverse) sexual impulse of the patient was weak.

[3] Mr. v. H. was not irresponsible in the legal sense of the word, and was neither fit for, nor in need of, treatment in a hospital for the insane.

Although he was only an overgrown child, and incapable of personal independence, it was possible for him to live in society if he was under the care and guidance of normal individuals. It was possible for him, to a certain extent, to respect the laws and restrictions of society, and to judge his own acts. With respect to possible sexual errors and conflicts with criminal laws, however, it must be emphasized that his sexual instinct was abnormal, had its origin in organic pathological conditions, and this circumstance had to eventually be used in his favor. Because of his notorious lack of independence, he had to be kept under parental care or guardianship; to do otherwise would have caused him to be ruined financially.

[4] Mr. v. H. was also physically ill. He presented signs of slight anemia and spinal neurasthenia.

A rational regulation of his manner of life, tonic regimen, and, if possible, hydrotherapeutic treatment, seemed necessary. The suspicion that this trouble had its origin in early masturbation had to be entertained. There was also the possibility of the existence of spermatorrhea, which was of importance etiologically and therapeutically (personal case, *Zeitschrift f. Psychiatrie*).

congenital sexual inversion in woman.[94]

Science in its present stage has little data to fall back on regarding the occurrence[95] of homosexual instinct in woman as compared to man.

It would not be fair to then conclude that sexual inversion in woman is rare, for if this anomaly is really a manifestation of functional degeneration, then degenerative influences will prevail in the female as well as in the male.

The causes of apparent infrequency in woman may be found in the following facts: [1] It is more difficult to gain the confidence of the sexually perverse woman; [2] this anomaly, insofar as it leads to sexual intercourse between women, does not fall under the criminal code (in Germany at any rate), and therefore remains hidden from public knowledge; [3] sexual inversion does not affect woman as it does man, inasmuch as it does not render woman impotent; [4] woman (whether sexually inverted or not) is not by nature as sensual nor certainly as aggressive in the pursuit of sexual needs as man, thus the inverted sexual intercourse among women is less noticeable, and is considered by outsiders mere friendship. Indeed, there are cases on record (psychic hermaphroditism, even homosexuality) in which the causes of the wife's frigidity remain unknown, even to the husband.

Certain passages in the Bible,[96] the history of Greece ("sapphic love"), and the moral history of ancient Rome and the Middle Ages[97] all offer evidence that sexual intercourse between women took place in every era, just as it is practiced nowadays in harems, female prisons, brothels and young ladies' seminaries (see below, "Lesbian Love").

It must nonetheless be admitted that many of these cases should be reduced to instances of perversity rather than perversion.[98]

The primary reason why inverted sexuality in woman remains covered with the veil of mystery is that, insofar as woman is concerned, the homosexual act does not fall under the law.

I cannot stress enough the fact that sexual acts between persons of the same sex do not necessarily constitute antipathic sexual instinct. This instinct exists only when the physical and psychic secondary sexual characteristics of the same sex exert an attracting influence over the individual that provokes the impulse toward sexual acts.

Through many years of experience I have gained the impression that inverted sexuality occurs in woman as frequently as it does in man. The chaste education of the girl, however, deprives the sexual instinct of its predominant character; the seduction to mutual masturbation is less frequent; the sexual instinct in the girl only begins to develop when she is introduced, at puberty, to the society of the other sex, and is thus led primarily into heterosexual channels. All these circumstances work in her favor; they often serve to correct abnormal inclinations and tastes and force her into the ways of normal sexual intercourse. We may safely assume, however, that many cases of frigidity or anaphrodisia in married women are rooted in undeveloped or suppressed antipathic sexual instinct.

The situation changes when the predisposed female is tainted by other anomalies of a hypersexual character and then led or seduced by other females to masturbation or homosexual acts.

In these cases we find situations that are analogous to what has been described as existing in men afflicted with "acquired" antipathic sexual instinct.

The possible sources from which homosexual love in woman may spring include the following:

[1] Constitutional hypersexuality that impels masturbation. This leads to neurasthenia and its evil consequences, as well as to anaphrodisia in normal sexual intercourse, as long as the libido remains active.

[2] Hypersexuality also leads, for lack of anything better, to homosexual intercourse (inmates of prisons, daughters of the higher classes of society who are carefully guarded in their relations with men, or who are afraid of impregnation – this latter group is commonly seen). The seducers are often female servants, female friends with perverse sexual inclinations, or female teachers in seminaries.

[3] Impotent husbands who can sexually excite but not satisfy their wives, thus producing in the wife unsatisfied sexual desire, recourse to masturbation, feminine pollutions, neurasthenia, nausea for coitus and, ultimately, disgust with the male sex in general.

[4] Prostitutes of gross sensuality who, disgusted with intercourse involving perverse and impotent men who use them to perform the most revolting sexual

acts, seek compensation in the sympathetic embrace of persons of their own sex. These cases are extremely common.

Careful observation of the ladies of large cities soon reveals that homosexuality is by no means a rarity. Homosexuality may nearly always be suspected in females who wear their hair short, who dress in the fashion of men, who pursue the sports and pastimes of their male acquaintances, or in opera singers and actresses who appear on the stage in male attire by preference.

Regarding the clinical aspect I can be brief, inasmuch as this anomaly shows the same characteristics for both man and woman, *mutatis mutandis,* and runs through the same grades. Many psychically hermaphroditic and homosexual women do not betray their anomaly either by external appearances or by mental (masculine) sexual characteristics. It is worth mentioning, however, that Dr. Flatau (Moll, op. cit., p. 334), in examining the larynx of twenty-three homosexual women, found a decidedly masculine formation in several of them.

In the transition to the subsequent grade, i.e., that of *viraginity* (analogous to effemination in the male), strong preference for male garments will be found. In dreams, as well as in the ideal or real homosexual function, the individual in question plays an indifferent sexual role.

The woman in whom viraginity is fully developed definitely assumes the masculine role.

In this grade modesty only finds expression toward the same but not the opposite sex.

In such cases the sexual anomaly often manifests itself by strongly marked characteristics of male sexuality.

The female homosexual may be found most often in the haunts of boys. She is the rival in their play, and prefers the rocking horse, soldier play, etc., to dolls and other girlish occupations. The *toilette* is neglected and rough boyish manners are affected. Love for art finds a substitute in scientific pursuits. At times, smoking and drinking are cultivated with passion.

Perfumes and sweetmeats are disdained. The consciousness of being a woman and being thus deprived of gay college life, or being barred from a military career, produces painful reflections.

The masculine soul that heaves in the female bosom finds pleasure in the pursuit of manly sports and manifestations of courage and bravado. There is a strong desire to imitate male fashion in dressing the hair and in general attire, and, under favorable circumstances, to even don male attire and impose in it. Arrests of women in men's clothing are by no means of rare occurrence. The case of a woman who successfully posed for years as a man (hunter, soldier, etc.) is related by Müller in Friedreich's *Blätter;* another is related by Wise (op. cit.); and other such cases exist.

The ideals of such *viragoes* are certain female characters from the past or the present who have excelled by virtue of genius and brave, noble deeds.

Gynandry represents the extreme grade of degenerative homosexuality. The woman of this type only possesses the feminine qualities of the genital organs; thought, sentiment, action, and even external appearance are those of a man.

Often enough in life one comes across such characters, whose frame, pelvis, gait, appearance, coarse masculine features, rough deep voice, etc., betray a man rather than a woman. Moll (op. cit., p. 331) has provided many interesting details about the mode of life of these men-women and the way in which they satisfy their sexual needs.

Mutatis mutandis, the situation is the same as with the man-loving man. These creatures seek, find, recognize, love one another, and often live together as "father" and "mother" in pseudo-marriage. Suspicion may always be turned toward homosexuality when one reads in the advertisement columns of the daily papers: "Wanted, by a lady, a lady friend and companion."

Numerous psychic hermaphrodites and even homosexuals of the female gender enter upon matrimony with men partly through ignorance of their own anomaly, and partly because they wish to be provided for. Some of these marriages linger on, in a way. The husband, perhaps, is psychically sympathetic, and thus renders the marital act possible for the unhappy wife. In most cases, however, after one or two children have been born, she seeks to avoid the connubial duty under all kinds of pretexts.

More frequently, however, incompatibility wrecks these unions. Homosexual intercourse continues after marriage, just as with the homosexual man.

When viraginity prevails, marriage is impossible, for the very thought of coitus with a man arouses disgust and horror.

The intersexual gratification among these women seems to be reduced to kissing and embracing. This seems to satisfy those who have a weak sexual instinct, and produces ejaculation in sexually neurasthenic females.

Masturbation, for lack of anything better, seems to occur in all grades of the anomaly the same as in men.

Strongly sensual individuals may resort to cunnilingus or mutual masturbation.

In grades three and four, the desire to adopt the active role toward the beloved person of the same sex seems to invite the use of a priapus.

Case 153.

Psychic hermaphroditism. Mrs. X., twenty-six years of age, suffered from neurasthenia. She was hereditarily tainted and suffered periodically from delusions. She had been married seven years and had two healthy children, a boy of six and a girl of four. There was success in gaining the confidence of the patient. She confessed that she was always more inclined toward persons of her own sex, and that, although she esteemed and liked her husband, sexual intercourse disgusted her. After the birth of the younger of the two children she had prevailed upon him to give it up altogether. When at the seminary she had interested herself in other young ladies in a manner that she could only describe as love. At times, however, she also found herself drawn to certain gentlemen, and especially her virtue had recently been sorely tried by an admirer to whose advances she was afraid she might succumb. For this reason, she avoided being alone with him. Such episodes, however, were only of a transient character when compared with her passionate liking for persons of her own sex. Her whole desire was to be kissed, embraced, and have the most intimate intercourse with them. She suffered a great deal from nervousness because she could not always realize these desires. The patient was not aware that this inclination to persons of the same sex had a sexual character; for beyond kissing, embracing, or fondling them, she would not know what to do with them. Patient thought herself to be of a sensual nature. It was likely that she was addicted to masturbation.

She considered her sexual perversion to be "unnatural, morbid."

There was nothing in the behavior, manners, or external appearance of this lady that betrayed in the least her anomaly.

Case 154.

Psychic hermaphroditism. Mrs. M., forty-four years of age. She claimed to be an example illustrating the fact that in *one* and *the same* human being, whether a man or a woman, the inverted as well as the normal direction of sexual life can be combined. The father of this lady was very musical, generally possessed a considerable talent for art, was a great admirer of the gentle sex, and was of exceptional beauty. He died, after repeated apoplectic attacks, with dementia in an asylum. His brother was neuropsychopathic. As a child he was afflicted with somnambulism, and later with sexual hyperesthesia. Although married and the father of several married sons, he fell desperately in love with Mrs. M., then eighteen years of age, and attempted to abduct her.

Her grandfather (on the paternal side) was a very eccentric and well-known artist, who had originally studied theology, but for love of the dramatic art became a mimic and a singer. He was given to excess in *Baccho et Venere* (drink and sex). He was extravagant and fond of splendor, and died at the age of forty-nine from a cerebral hemorrhage. Her mother's father, as well as her mother, died of pulmonary phthisis.

She had eleven brothers and sisters, but only six survived. Two brothers died of tuberculosis at the ages of sixteen and twenty. One brother was suffering from laryngeal phthisis. Like Mrs. M., four living sisters were physically like the father, as well as very nervous and shy. Two younger sisters were married, in good health, and both had healthy children. Another one, a maiden, was suffering from nervous affection.

Mrs. M. was the mother of four children, mostly delicate and neuropathic.

There was nothing of importance in the history of the patient's childhood. She learned easily, had a gift for poetry and aesthetics, was somewhat affected, and loved to read novels and sentimental literature. She had a neuropathic constitution and was very sensitive to changes of temperature; the slightest draft would make her flesh creep. It is noteworthy, however, that at ten years of age she imagined one day that her mother did not love her. She thereupon put many sulphur matches in her coffee and, in order to draw her mother's love, drank it to make herself ill.

Puberty began without difficulty at the age of eleven, with subsequent regular menses. Even before this, her sexual life had awakened and been potent ever since. The first sentiments and emotions lay in the homosexual direction. She conceived a passionate, though platonic, affection for a young lady, wrote love songs and sonnets to her, and was never happier than when she had once been able to admire the "charms of her beloved" in the bath, and then gaze upon the neck, shoulders and breasts of this lady while she dressed. She resisted with difficulty the desire to touch these physical charms. As a girl she was deeply in love with the *Madonna* of Raphael and Guido Reni. She was irresistibly impelled to follow pretty girls and ladies by the hour, no matter how inclement the weather might be, admiring their air of refinement and watching for a chance to show them favor, give them flowers, etc. The patient asserted that up to her nineteenth year she did not have the slightest knowledge of the difference between the sexes, since she had been brought up by a prudish old maiden aunt like a nun in a cloister. As a consequence of this crass ignorance she fell victim to a man who loved her passionately and insidiously betrayed her virtue. She became the wife of this man, gave birth to a child, and although she led an "eccentric" sexual life with him, she felt satisfied with the sexual intercourse. A few years later she became a widow. Subsequently her affections turned again to persons of her own sex. The patient declared that the principal reason for this was a fear of the results of sexual intercourse with men.

At the age of twenty-seven she entered upon a second marriage with a man who had an infirm constitution. It was not a love match. Although she thrice became a mother and fulfilled all the conditions of maternity, her health worsened, and during the latter years of her marriage her dislike for coitus steadily increased, primarily because of her husband's infirmity. Her desire for sexual gratification, however, remained strong.

Three years after her second husband's death, she discovered that her daughter by the first husband, now nine years of age, was given to masturbation and was going into decline. She read an article about this vice in the *Encyclopedia,* could not resist the temptation to try it herself, and thus became a masturbator. She hesitated giving a full account of this period of her life. She stated, however, that she became so excited sexually that she had to send her two daughters away from home in order to preserve them from something "terrible." The two boys were able to remain at home.

Patient became neurasthenic due to masturbation (spinal irritation, pressure in the head, languor, mental constipation, etc.), at times even dysthymic, with worrying *taedium vitae.*

Her sexual inclinations alternated between men and women. She controlled herself, however, and suffered much from her abstinence, especially since she used masturbation only as a last resort because of her neurasthenic afflictions. At the age of forty-four – still having regular periods – the patient suffered from a violent passion for a young man with whom she was bound to be in constant contact because of her avocation.

The patient did not offer anything extraordinary in her external appearance. Though she had a graceful build, her form was slight. Pelvis decidedly feminine, but arms and legs large, and of pronounced masculine type. Female boots did not really fit her, and she had quite crippled and malformed her feet by forcing them into narrow shoes. Genitals quite normal. Excepting a prolapsed uterus with hypertrophy of the vaginal portion, no changes were noticeable. She still claimed to be essentially homosexual, and declared that her inclination and desire for the opposite sex were only periodic and grossly sensual. Although she had strong sexual feelings toward the man aforementioned, she found her greatest and noblest pleasure in pressing a kiss upon the soft cheek of a sweet girl. This pleasure she enjoyed often, for she was the "favorite aunt" among these "dear creatures," to whom she unstintingly rendered the services of a "cavalier," always feeling herself in the role of the man.

Case 155.

Homosexuality. Miss L., fifty-five years of age. No information about her father's family. The parents of her mother were described as irascible, capricious and nervous. One brother of her mother was an epileptic, another was eccentric and mentally abnormal.

Mother was sexually hyperesthetic, and for a long time she was a nymphomaniac. She was considered to be psychopathic and died at the age of sixty-nine of cerebral disease.

Miss L. developed normally and had only slight illnesses in childhood. Although she was mentally well-endowed, she had a neuropathic constitution, was emotional, and was troubled with numerous trifling concerns.

At the age of thirteen, two years previous to her first menstruation, she fell in love with a girlfriend ("a dreamy feeling, quite free of sensuality").

Her second love was for a girl (a bride) who was older than herself; this was accompanied by tantalizing sensual desires, jealousy, and an "undefined consciousness of mystical impropriety." She was refused by this lady and subsequently fell in love with a married woman, who was a mother and twenty years her senior. Because she controlled her sensual emotions, this lady never divined the true reason for the enthusiastic friendship, which lasted twelve years. Patient described this period as a veritable martyrdom.

At the age of twenty-five she began to masturbate. Although the patient seriously thought she might save herself through marriage, her conscience objected when she considered that her children might inherit her weakness, or that she might make a sincere husband unhappy.

At the age of twenty-seven she was approached by a girl who made direct proposals, denounced abstinence as absurd, plainly described the homosexual instinct that ruled her, and was very impetuous in her demands. Although she suffered the caresses of the girl, she would not consent to sexual intercourse because sensuality without love disgusted her.

She was mentally and bodily dissatisfied as the years flew by and left the consciousness of a spoiled life. Now and then she became enthusiastic about ladies of her acquaintance, but controlled herself. She also rid herself of masturbation.

At thirty-eight years of age she became acquainted with a girl who was nineteen years her junior and of exceptional beauty. She came from a demoralized family and had been seduced at an early age to mutual masturbation by her cousins. It could not be ascertained whether this girl (A.) was a case of psychic hermaphroditism or of acquired sexual inversion. The former hypothesis seems the likelier of the two.

The following is taken from an autobiography of Miss L.:

"Miss A., my pupil, began to show me her idolatrous love. She was sympathetic to the highest degree. Since I knew that she was entangled in a hopeless love affair with a dissolute fellow, and that she maintained intimate intercourse with demoralized female cousins, I decided not to repulse her. Compassion and the conviction that she was surely drifting into moral decay determined that I suffer her advances.

"I did not consider her affection as dangerous, as I did not think it possible (considering her love affair) that in *one* soul *two* passions (one for a man and another for a woman) could exist simultaneously. Moreover, I was certain of my powers of resistance. I therefore kept Miss A. about me, renewed my moral resolutions, and considered it my duty to use her love for me for the purpose of ennobling her character. The folly of this I soon found out. One day, while I lay asleep, Miss A. took occasion to satisfy her lust on me. Although I woke up just in time, I did not have the moral strength to resist her. I was highly excited – intoxicated, as it were – and she prevailed.

"What I suffered immediately after this occurrence defies description: worry over the broken resolutions, which I had made such strenuous efforts to keep; fear of detection and subsequent contempt; exuberant joy to at last be rid of the tortured watchings and longings of the single state; unspeakable sensual pleasure; and wrath against the evil companion mingled with feelings of the deepest tenderness toward her. Miss A. calmly smiled at my excitement, and soothed my anger with caresses.

"I accepted the situation. Our intimacy lasted for years. We practiced mutual masturbation, but never to excess or in a cynical fashion.

"Little by little this sensual companionship ceased. Miss A.'s tenderness weakened; mine, however, remained as before, although I no longer felt the same sensual cravings. Miss A. was thinking of marriage, partly in order to find a home, but especially because her sensual desires had turned onto a normal path. She succeeded in finding a husband. I sincerely hope she will make him happy, but I doubt she will. Thus I have the prospect before me of lingering on in the same joyless, peaceless life of youthful days.

"It is with sadness that I remember the years of our loving union. It does not disturb my conscience to have had sexual intercourse with Miss A., inasmuch as I succumbed to her seduction after having honestly endeavored to save her from moral ruin and to bring her up as an educated and moral being. In this I honestly think I succeeded after all.

Besides, I rest in the thought that the moral code is only established for normal human beings, and is not binding for anomalies. Of course, the human being who is endowed by nature with sentiments of refinement, but whose constitution is abnormal and outside the conventionalities of society, can never be truly happy. But I experienced a sad tranquility and felt happy when I thought Miss A. was happy too.

"This is the history of an unhappy woman who, by the fatal caprice of nature, is deprived of all joy in life and made a victim of sorrow."

The author of this woeful story was a lady of great refinement. She had, however, coarse features and a powerful (but completely feminine) frame. She passed through menopause without trouble, and had since been entirely free from sensual worry. She had never played a defined sexual role toward the woman she loved. She never felt the slightest inclination for men.

Miss L.'s statements about the family relations and health of her paramour established Miss A.'s heavy taint beyond doubt. The father died in an insane asylum, the mother was deranged during the period of her menopause, neuroses frequently occurred in the family, and Miss A. herself suffered (heavily, at times) from hysteropathy with hallucinations and delirium.

Case 156.

Homosexuality. S. J., aged thirty-eight, governess. She came to me for medical advice because of nervous trouble. Father was periodically insane and died from cerebral disease. Patient was an only child. She suffered early from anxiety and alarming fantasies; e.g., that she would wake up in a coffin after it had been fastened down; that she would forget something when going to confession and thus receive holy communion unworthily. Although she was often troubled with headaches, very excitable, and easily startled, she nevertheless had a great desire to see exciting things such as funerals, etc.

From earliest youth she was subject to sexual excitement and spontaneously practiced masturbation. At the age of fourteen she began to menstruate. Her periods were often accompanied by colicky pains, intense sexual excitement, neuralgia, and mental depression. At the age of eighteen she successfully gave up masturbation.

The patient never experienced any inclination toward a person of the opposite sex. To her, marriage only meant finding a home. She was, however, powerfully drawn to girls. Although at first she considered this affection to be mere friendship, the intensity of her love for girlfriends and her deep longings for their constant company soon caused her to recognize that it meant more than simple friendship.

It was inconceivable to her that a girl could love a man, although she was able to comprehend the feeling of a man toward a woman. She always took the deepest interest in pretty girls and ladies, the sight of whom caused her intense excitement. Her desire was always to embrace and kiss these dear creatures. She always dreamed only of girls and never of men. To revel in looking at them was the acme of pleasure. Whenever she lost a "girlfriend" she was in despair.

Patient declared that she never felt herself to be in a defined role toward her girlfriends, even in her dreams. Her appearance was thoroughly feminine and modest. Feminine pelvis, large breasts, no indication of beard.

Case 157.

Homosexuality. Mrs. R., aged thirty-five, of high social position, was brought to me in 1886 by her husband for advice.

Father was a physician; very neuropathic. Paternal grandfather was healthy, normal, and reached the age of ninety-six. Facts concerning paternal grandmother were absent. All children from the father's family were said to have been nervous. The patient's mother was nervous and suffered from asthma. The mother's parents were healthy. One of the mother's sisters had melancholia.

From her tenth year, the patient had been subject to habitual headaches. With the exception of measles, she had no illness. She was gifted and enjoyed the best of training, having especial talent for music and languages. It became necessary that she prepare herself for work as a governess, and thus during her earlier years she was mentally overworked. At seventeen she passed through an attack of melancholia, of some months' duration, without delirium. The patient asserted that she had always had sympathy for her own sex only, and merely had an aesthetic interest in men. She never had any taste for female work. As a little girl, she preferred to play with boys.

She said she remained well until her twenty-seventh year. Then, without external cause, she became depressed and considered herself a bad, sinful person, had no pleasure in anything, and was sleepless. During this time of illness she was also troubled with delusions; she was compelled to think of her own death and that of her relatives. Recovery after about five months. She then became a governess and, though overworked, remained well, except for occasional neurasthenic symptoms and spinal irritation.

At twenty-eight she made the acquaintance of a lady five years her junior. She fell in love with her and her love was returned. The love was very sensual and was satisfied by mutual masturbation. "I loved her as if she were a god; hers is a noble soul," she said, when speaking of this love bond. It lasted four years and was ended by the (unfortunate) marriage of her friend.

In 1885, after much emotional strain, the patient became ill with symptoms of hystero-neurasthenia (dyspepsia, spinal irritation, and tonic spasmodic attacks; attacks of hemianopia with migraine and transitory aphasia; **itching of the genitals and anus**). In February 1886 these symptoms disappeared.

In March she became acquainted with her present husband, whom she married without taking much time for reflection, inasmuch as he was rich, deeply in love with her, and his character was in sympathy with her own.

On April 6 she read the sentence, "Death misses no one." Like a flash of lightning in a clear sky, the former delusions of death returned. She was forced to meditate on the most horrible manner of death for herself and those about her, and constantly imagined death scenes. She lost rest and sleep, and took no pleasure in anything. Her condition then improved. Late in May 1886 she married, though she was still troubled by painful thoughts that she would bring misfortune on her husband and those around her.

First act of coitus on June 6, 1886. She was morally deeply depressed by it. She had had no such conception of matrimony. The husband, who really loved his wife, did all he could to quiet her. He consulted physicians, who thought all would be well after pregnancy. The husband was unable to explain the peculiar behavior of his wife. She was friendly toward him and suffered his caresses. During coitus, which was actually carried out, she was entirely passive. After the act she was tired, exhausted all day long, nervous, and troubled with spinal irritation.

A bridal tour brought about a meeting with her old friend, who had lived in an unhappy marriage for three years. The two ladies trembled with joy and excitement as they sank into each other's arms. They then became inseparable. The husband saw that this friendly relation was a peculiar one and hastened their departure. He later had the opportunity of ascertaining, through the correspondence of his wife with this friend, that the letters they exchanged were like those of two lovers.

Mrs. R. became pregnant. During pregnancy the remains of depression and delusions disappeared. In September, during about the ninth week of pregnancy, miscarriage took place. After that, renewed symptoms of hysterical neurasthenia. In addition to this, forward flexion and right lateral position of the uterus, anemia, and an atonic ventricle.

At the consultation the patient gave the impression of a very neuropathic, tainted person. The neuropathic expression of her eyes cannot be described. Appearance entirely feminine. With the exception of a very narrow arched palate, there was no skeletal abnormality. The patient was brought without difficulty to her account of the details of her sexual abnormality. She complained that she had married without knowing what marriage between men and women meant. Although she loved her husband dearly for his mental qualities, marital intercourse was painful for her; she did it unwillingly and without ever finding any satisfaction in it. After the act, she was weary and exhausted all day long. Although she was better since the miscarriage and the interdiction of sexual intercourse by the physicians, she thought of the future with horror. She esteemed her husband and loved him mentally; if he would only avoid her sexually in the future, however, she would do anything for him. She hoped to have sexual feeling for him in time. When he played the violin, she seemed to feel the beginning of an inclination for him that was something more than friendship; it was only transitory, however, and she was not assured of the future from it. Her greatest happiness was in correspondence with her former lover. Although she felt that this was wrong, she could not give it up, because to do so made her miserable.

Case 158.

Homosexuality. Miss X., of the middle class of a large city. At the end of my observations she was twenty-two years of age.

She was considered a beauty; much admired by men; decidedly sensual; a born Aspasia; refused all proposals of marriage. She nevertheless reciprocated the advances of one admirer, a youthful scholar, and entertained relations with him. That is, she allowed him to kiss her, but not as a lover. On one occasion, when Mr. T. thought he had obtained the aim of his attentions, she tearfully begged him to stop, alleging that her refusal was not based upon moral principles, but was rooted in deeper psychic reasons. Subsequent correspondence between the two disclosed the existence of sexual inversion.

Her father was a drinker and her mother was hysteropathic. The patient had a neuro-pathic constitution, a large bust, and the appearance of an exceptionally handsome woman. She was, however, strikingly mannish in her manners, had masculine tastes, loved gymnastics and horseback exercise, smoked, and had a masculine carriage and gait. She wished to appear on the stage.

She had recently caused much talk because of her enthusiastic friendships with young ladies. One young lady lived with her. They slept in the same bed.

Miss X. declared she had been sexually indifferent up to the onset of puberty.

At the age of seventeen, while at a spa, she made the acquaintance of a young foreigner whose "royal" appearance fascinated her. On one occasion she was happy when she danced with him the whole evening. The next evening, at twilight, she happened to witness, directly opposite her window in the shrubbery of the gardens, the revolting scene of this charming young man **having intercourse like a wild beast with a woman who was menstruating.** Miss X. was horrified, almost annihilated, **at the sight of the flowing blood and the almost bestial sexual lust of the man,** and felt it was difficult to recover her mental balance. For a long time thereafter she could neither sleep nor eat, and from then on she saw in man the embodiment of coarse vulgarity.

Two years later, in a public park, she was approached by a young lady who smiled and looked upon her in such a peculiar fashion that she felt a thrill pass through her soul.

The day after, Miss X. was irresistibly impelled to go to the park again. The young lady was already there and seemed to be waiting for her. They greeted each other like old acquaintances, talked and joked together, and had daily rendezvous. After some time, as the weather turned inclement, they then met at the young lady's boudoir.

"One day," Miss X. relates in her confidential revelations, "she led me to her divan and, while she was seated, I knelt at her feet. She locked her timid eyes upon me, stroked my hair away from my forehead, and said, 'Ah! if only I could love you once really! May I?' I consented, and while we sat together thus, gazing into each other's eyes, we drifted into that current which allows of no retreat. . . . She was enchantingly beautiful. All I wanted was to possess the power of the artist to immortalize that form upon the canvas. To me it was a novel experience. I was intoxicated. We abandoned ourselves to each other without restriction, drunk with the ravages of sensual feminine pleasure. I do not believe that man can ever grasp the exuberance of such piquant tenderness; man is not sufficiently refined; he is much too coarse. . . . Our wild orgy lasted until I sank down exhausted, powerless, unnerved. I fell asleep on her bed. Suddenly I awoke with an unspeakable thrill, hitherto unknown to me, running through my whole being. She was upon me, **performing cunnilingus** – the highest pleasure for her. **I could only kiss her breasts,** which caused her to quiver convulsively.

"This relationship lasted for a whole year, when the removal of her father to another city separated us."

Miss X. admitted that in this homosexual relationship she always felt she was in the role of a man toward the woman, and that on one occasion, for lack of anything better, she granted cunnilingus to one of her male admirers.

Case 159.

Homosexuality. Mrs. C., aged thirty-two, wife of an official; a large, not uncomely woman, feminine in appearance; came from a neuropathic and emotional mother. A brother was psychopathic, and died of drink. Patient was always peculiar, obstinate, silent, quick-tempered, and eccentric. Her brothers and sisters were excitable. Pulmonary phthisis had been frequent in the family. As a girl of only thirteen, with signs of great sexual excitement, she attracted attention with her enthusiastic love for a female friend her own age. Her education was strict, though the patient secretly read many novels and wrote innumerable poems. She married at eighteen to free herself from unpleasant circumstances at home.

The patient said she had always been indifferent toward men. In fact, she avoided balls. Female statues pleased her. Her greatest happiness was to think of marriage with a beloved woman. She was not aware of her sexual peculiarity until marriage, and it had remained inexplicable to her. She did her marital duty and bore three children, two of whom were subject to convulsions. She lived pleasantly with her husband, but she only esteemed him for his moral qualities. She gladly avoided coitus. "I would have preferred intercourse with a woman."

Until 1878 she had been neurasthenic. When she made a sojourn to a spa, she made the acquaintance of a female homosexual (whose history I have reported as case 6 in the *Irrenfreund*, no. 1, 1884).

The patient came home a changed person. Her husband said: "She was no longer a woman, no longer had any love for me and the children, and would have no more of my marital approaches. She was inflamed with passionate love for her female friend and had taste for nothing else." After the husband forbade the entry of her lover into the house, there was an exchange of letters that contained such expressions as "My dove! I live only for you, my soul." There were meetings and frightful excitement when an expected letter did not come. The relation was not in any way platonic. From certain indications it was presumed that mutual masturbation had been the means of sexual satisfaction. This relation lasted until 1882 and made the patient decidedly neurasthenic.

Because she absolutely neglected the house, her husband hired a woman of sixty years as a housekeeper, and he also hired a governess for the children. The patient fell in love with both, who, at least, allowed caresses, and profited materially through the love of their mistress.

She developed pulmonary tuberculosis in late 1883 and, therefore, had to go south. There she became acquainted with a Russian lady, forty years old, and fell passionately in love with her. Her romantic love, however, was not returned. One day insanity became manifest. She thought the Russian lady was a nihilist, that she was magnetized by her, and she presented formal persecutory delusions. She fled, but was caught in an Italian city and placed in a hospital, where she soon became quiet. Presently, however, she worried the lady again with her love, felt very unhappy, and planned suicide.

Greatly depressed because she did not have the lady, she was harsh toward her family when she returned home. A delusional, erotic state of excitement flourished around the end of May 1884. She danced, shouted, and called herself a man; she demanded her former lover, and said she was of royal blood. She escaped from the house in male attire and was taken to the asylum in a state of erotomaniacal excitement. After a few days, the exaltation disappeared. The patient became quiet and made a desperate attempt at suicide, after which she was mentally in great anguish, with *taedium vitae.* The perverse sexual feeling became less and less noticeable as tuberculosis progressed. The patient died of phthisis in early 1885.

Examination of the brain presented nothing unusual insofar as architecture and arrangement of convolutions were concerned. Weight of brain 1150 grams. Skull slightly asymmetrical. No anatomical signs of degeneration. External and internal genitals without anomaly.

Case 160.

Homosexuality in transition to viraginity. Mrs. v. T., wife of a manufacturer; aged twenty-six; married only a few months; was brought by her husband for consultation because after a banquet she had fallen upon the neck of a lady guest, covered her profusely with kisses, and caressed her like a lover, thus causing a scandal.

Mrs. T. said that before their marriage she had explained to her husband her antipathic sexual feelings and had told him that she esteemed him solely for his mental qualities. She accepted her conjugal duties as a simple matter of unavoidable necessity. Her only condition was that she should be on top during coitus. In this position she obtained a sort of gratification, inasmuch as she imagined his body to be that of a beloved woman beneath her.

Her father was neuropathic, of the feminine type, suffered from hysteria, and was very weak in his sexual needs. One of his sisters, it was said, bought the conjugal rights from her husband for a sum of money, giving him full liberty to find sexual satisfaction elsewhere. The mother was hypersexual and was known as a nymphomaniac. She made her daughter sleep in the same bed with her until she reached the age of fourteen. At fifteen v. T. was sent to a girl's school. She was extraordinarily bright, learned quickly, and soon excelled over all the other girls in her class.

At the age of seven she had a psychic trauma when a friend of the family exhibited himself before her.

Menses, which began at twelve, were regular and without nervous concomitants. At that age she began to be powerfully drawn to the other girls. Although for several years she never associated these yearnings with sexual feelings, she looked upon them as an anomaly. She only felt bashful when undressing in the presence of persons of her own sex. At twenty her sexual instinct awoke. She turned at once to girls for gratification, avoiding men entirely. She had sensual love affairs with girls by the scores. When she returned home from school, she had no supervision and plenty of money, and thus found it easy to give her passion full sway. She always felt like a man with women. **Masturbation with a beloved woman** was the common occurrence in her orgies until a female cousin taught her the mysteries of lesbian love. She now coupled the act with cunnilingus. She always played the active role and never allowed others to satisfy themselves with her body. Homosexual women she disdained. She gave preference to unmarried women of high standing, endowed with mental gifts; with a voluptuous, Diana-like figure; and of a modest and retiring disposition. (She did not care for sensual women.) Whenever she met such a woman, she would become so erotically excited that she fell upon the woman's body like a hungry, wild beast. She said that at such moments everything seemed imbued with a reddish gleam, and consciousness was obliterated for the time being. Her nerves were easily unstrung, and she could not master her feelings.

At the age of twenty-three she became acquainted with a young woman who, to all appearances, was not homosexual, but very hypersexual. The woman could not find sexual satisfaction because of her husband's impotence. Relations with this woman stimulated T.'s homosexuality to an extremely high pitch and increased her sexual needs. She furnished an apartment away from home, where she had regular orgies **with her finger and tongue,** sometimes for hours, until she collapsed in a state of exhaustion. She had a love affair with a dressmaker's model, with whom she had herself photographed in men's attire and, thus costumed, visited places of amusement with her. She was finally arrested on one of these occasions. She escaped with a warning and gave up wearing male attire outdoors.

A year before her marriage she had a period of melancholia. At that time she considered suicide and wrote a farewell letter to an intimate lady friend, a sort of confession, from which a few passages are given:

"I was born a girl, but a misdirected education soon forced my fiery imagination into the wrong direction. I had a mania at twelve to pose as a boy and court the attention of ladies. I recognized this abnormal impulse as a mania, but it grew, like fate, with the years. The power to rid myself of it was lost. It was my hashish, my happiness, and it grew into an overpowering passion. I felt like a man, forced to play the active role. My exuberant disposition, fierce sensuousness and deep-rooted perverse instinct gradually forged me into the chains of lesbian love. Although I took a certain interest in men, a single touch by a woman made my whole nervous system tremble. I have suffered untold tortures from the bane of this passion.

"The reading of French novels and the company of lascivious companions taught me all the tricks of perverse erotics, and the latent impulse became a conscious perversity. Nature has made a mistake in the choice of my sexuality and I must do a lifelong penance for it, for the moral power to suffer the unavoidable with dignity is lost. Irresistibly I have been drawn into the maelstrom of passion and shall be swallowed up by it. . . .

"I languished for your sweet body. I was jealous of your Victor as one rival is of the other. In my jealousy I suffered the tortures of hell. I hated that man and wished for his death. I cursed the fate that made me a woman. I was satisfied playing a stupid comedy with you by putting on an artificial penis, which only increased the heat of my passion. I lacked the courage to tell you the truth, because it would have made me feel so miserable and ludicrous. Now you know all. You will not despise me, though; you will only feel what I have suffered. All my joys resemble more a momentary intoxication than the real gold of happiness. It was all but an illusion. I have fooled life and life has fooled me. We are quits. I say goodbye. Think sometimes in the hour of happiness of your poor, comical fool who loved you truly and so well . . ."

The sex life of this woman also contained traces of masochism and sadism. If the woman whom she worshiped had chided or even struck her, it would have been a delight — so she claimed — and at the time of sexual excitement she felt more like biting than kissing the object of her love.

She was highly cultured and intellectual, and although she felt her false position painfully, it was because of her family rather than herself. She looked upon it all as fate, over which she had no control. She bewailed it, declaring herself ready to do anything to rid herself of this perversion and become a true wife and a good mother, for she would take good care that her child was brought up in the right way. She would do anything to placate her husband and perform her marital duties, but she could not bear his mustache, and she must first rid herself of her unfortunate impulsive passion.

The physical and psychic secondary sexual characteristics were partly masculine, partly feminine. Her love for sport, smoking and drinking; her preference for clothes cut in the fashion of men; her lack of skill in and liking of female occupations; her love for the study of obtuse and philosophical subjects; and her gait and carriage, severe features, deep voice, robust skeleton, powerful muscles and absence of adipose layers bore the stamp of the masculine character. Her pelvis (small hips) also approached the masculine figure – distance of the spine twenty-one centimeters, cristae twenty-six centimeters, and trochanter thirty-one centimeters. Vagina, uterus, ovaries normal; clitoris rather large. Breasts well-developed, hair on female mons pubis.

I sent her to a hydropathic establishment where an experienced colleague succeeded in freeing this patient from her homosexual affliction by means of hydropathic and suggestive treatment. Sexually, at least, she became a decent, neutral person. The relatives with whom she lived for a considerable time afterward found her behavior absolutely correct.

Case 161.

Viraginity. Miss N., twenty-five years of age. Her parents were reportedly healthy. Her brothers and sisters were all neuropathic. Three of her sisters were married. She was very talented, especially in the fine arts. Even in her earliest childhood she preferred playing "soldiers" and other boys' games. She was bold and tomboyish, and even tried to surpass her little companions of the other sex. She never had a liking for dolls, needlework or domestic duties. Puberty at fifteen. She soon fell in love with young ladies, but only in a platonic fashion, for she was a "respectable girl." For several years after this her libido was very strong. She could hardly restrain herself. Her dreams had a lascivious character, were only about females, and she was in the role of a man. She was desperately in love with a woman of forty, whom she tormented with her jealous conduct.

Miss N. was indifferent to men. Although she could safely live in the same room with a man, toward persons of her own sex she was most bashful.

She was quite conscious of her pathological condition.

Masculine features, deep voice, manly gait, small breasts, but no beard; she cropped her hair short and made the impression of a man in woman's clothes.

Case 162.

Viraginity. C. R., maidservant, aged twenty-six; suffered from the time of her development with original paranoia and hysteria. As a result of her delusions, her life had been somewhat romantic and, in 1884, in Switzerland, where she had gone as a result of her delusions of persecution, she came under the observation of the authorities. It was ascertained at this time that R. was affected with sexual inversion.

Concerning her parents and relatives, there was no information at hand. With the exception of an inflammation of the lungs at the age of sixteen, R. asserted that she had never been severely ill.

First menstruation at fifteen, without any difficulties; it was thereafter often irregular and abnormally excessive. The patient declared that she had never had inclinations toward the opposite sex and had never allowed the approach of a man. She could never understand how her friends could describe the beauty and amiability of men. She was charmed and inspired, however, when imprinting a kiss on the lips of a beloved female friend. She had a love for girls that was incomprehensible to her. She had passionately loved and kissed some of her female friends and would have given up her life for them. Her greatest delight would have been to live continually with such a friend and possess her absolutely.

In this regard she felt toward the beloved girl as a man would feel. Even as a little child she had an inclination only for the play of boys; she loved to hear shooting and military music, was always much excited by them, and would have gladly gone as a soldier. The chase and war have been her ideals. In the theatre only feminine performers interested her. Although she knew very well that the whole of her inclination was unwomanly, she could not help it. It had always been a great pleasure for her to go about in male clothing; also, she had always preferred masculine work, and had shown unusual skill. The opposite was true, however, with reference to feminine occupations, especially handiwork. The patient also had a weakness for smoking and spirits. The patient had persecutory delusions and, in order to rid herself of them, she had often gone about in male attire and played the part of a man. She did this with such natural skill that she was able, as a rule, to deceive people concerning her sex.

It was authoritatively established that for a long time in 1884 the patient went about in male attire, first in the garments of a civilian, then in the uniform of a lieutenant. In

August of the same year, dressed as a male servant, she fled to Switzerland as a result of delusions of persecution. There she found service in a merchant's family and fell in love with the daughter of the house, "the beautiful Anna," who, not recognizing the sex of R., fell in love with the handsome young man.

Concerning this episode, the patient made the following characteristic statement: "I was madly in love with Anna. I don't know how it came about, and I cannot put myself right concerning this impulse. In this fatal love lies the reason why I played the role of a man for so long. I have never felt any love for a man, and I believe that my love is for the female and not the male sex. I can in no way understand my condition."

From Switzerland, R. wrote letters home to her friend Amelia, which were produced at the examination. The letters showed a passionate love that went beyond the bounds of friendship. She apostrophized her friend: "My flower, sun of my heart, longing of my soul." She was her greatest happiness on earth; her heart was hers. And in her letters to her friend's parents she wrote: "You, too, should watch my 'flower,' for if she should die, I would also be unable to endure life."

For the purpose of investigating her mental condition, R. remained for some time in an asylum. On one occasion, when Anna was allowed to pay R. a visit, there was no end of passionate embraces and kisses. The visitor freely acknowledged that they had previously secretly embraced and kissed in the same way.

R. was a tall, slim, stately person, of feminine form in all respects, but with masculine features. Cranium regular; no anatomical signs of degeneration. Genitals normal and indicative of virginity. R. made the impression of a morally pure and modest person. All the circumstances indicated that she had only indulged in platonic love. Eyes and appearance were indicative of a neurasthenic person. Severe hysteria, occasional cataleptic attacks, with visionary and delirious states. The patient was very easily brought into a state of somnambulism by hypnotic influence, and was susceptible in this condition to all possible suggestions (personal case, Friedreich's *Blätter*, 1881, no. 1).

Case 163.

Viraginity. Miss O., twenty-three years of age. Mother constitutionally and heavily hysteropathic. Mother's father insane. Father's family untainted.

Father died early of pneumonia. Patient was brought to me by her trustees because she had recently run away from home in male attire in order to roam the world and become an "*artiste*." Very gifted in music.

For several years she attracted a great deal of attention with her bold, mannish behavior, and by wearing her hair and attire in male fashion. From the age of thirteen she had been demonstrative in her love for girlfriends, whom she often wearied with her fervent embraces.

She did not seek to conceal her passionate fondness for persons of her own sex. She asserted that since her thirteenth year she had been fully conscious of the fact that she could love only women. She felt as a man toward women. Because she looked like a man, she would much rather wear men's clothes.

A short time ago she seriously asked a relative who was in the police department to obtain permission for her to go about in male attire.

Her erotic dreams exclusively involved intimate intercourse with female friends. She never took the slightest interest in men and never thought of marriage.

She felt quite happy in her abnormal sexual condition and did not recognize it as pathological. She could not comprehend that her sexual instinct differed from that of other women.

The circumference of her head was 51 centimeters. Frame quite feminine, but her feet were exceptionally large and more of a masculine type. Carriage, attitude and gait quite masculine. Female voice. Monthly periods regular since her thirteenth year.

Case 164.

Viraginity. On October 5, 1898, W., aged thirty-six, a charwoman, was brought to my clinic by police for examination pertaining to her sanity. She had engaged herself to a young girl on the pretext that she was a man and belonged to an aristocratic family. Examination proved this to be a classical case of original paranoia. When she was five, she imagined that the couple with whom she lived were only her foster parents; when she was eighteen, that she came from a distinguished family; and when she was twenty-nine, that her father was a king and her mother was a countess. Circumference of cranium 53 centimeters, parietal bones slightly bulging. Ears abnormally small, of uneven size, misformed; the right lobe joined groin-like to the cheek, the left properly developed. Palate very narrow and steep. Teeth decayed, many missing (rickets). Stature medium size, willowy. Chest strongly arched. Waist and region of hips smaller than normal. A prominent gynecologist examined the pelvic area and found a small pelvis, narrow at the inferior outlet, almost typically masculine in form. Ilium less inclined than normal.

The hard lines and severe features of her face gave it a rather masculine appearance. Her hair was cut short. Gait and bearing masculine. Skin very rough, adipose layers sparse, breasts stunted. Genitals normal, hymen intact. She was loath to speak of her sex life, but wanted an explanation as to why she had no desire for men and only for persons of her own sex. Her "genitals could not be right." Menses at the age of sixteen; the flow of blood, however, came only rarely, and then very sparsely. With the advent of puberty, she was attracted to persons of her own sex. She was never sensual. Her sexual ideas were always about the female sex in general and were never concentrated on an individual. Although she had lived with another girl of her own age, their relations had been one of sisters; sexual acts had never taken place between them. She felt toward women as a man feels. She loathed the idea of sexual intercourse with a man. As a child she preferred playing with boys. When playing "robbers," she would be the captain and choose a girl for her wife, but without any sexual moment. At sixteen she thought she possessed the qualities of a man. She was then in a convent and learned masturbation from a woman. The thought of this woman was always present when she masturbated and acted as a sexual stimulus. She later thought of other females during the act, but without decided individuality.

At thirty-three she became neurasthenic and successfully gave up the practice of masturbation. She bewailed the fact that she had not been born a man, inasmuch as she generally hated feminine things and dress. She would have much rather been a soldier. She disdained sweetmeats, preferring a cigar. She was a bright, intelligent person. Larynx and voice feminine. I succeeded in convincing her that she could not marry a woman and, with the promise that her perverse sexual inclinations could be conquered, she was dismissed.

Case 165.

Miss X., aged thirty-eight, consulted with me late in the fall of 1881 because of severe spinal irritation and obstinate sleeplessness. Her attempts to combat such had caused her to become addicted to morphine and chloral. Her mother and sister were nervous, but the rest of the family was healthy. Although the patient had been subject, as a girl, to muscular cramps and hysterical symptoms, she declared that her present trouble dated from a fall on her back in 1872, at which time she was terribly frightened. Following this shock, a neurasthenic and hysterical neurosis developed, with predominating spinal irritation and sleeplessness. Hysterical paraplegia, lasting as long as eight months, and hysterical hallucinatory delirium, with convulsive attacks, episodically occurred. In the course of this, symptoms of morphinism were added. A stay of some months in the hospital relieved the symptoms of her morphinism, and considerably improved her neurasthenic neurosis, in the treatment of which general faradization exerted a remarkably favorable influence.

Even at the first meeting, the patient produced a remarkable impression because of her attire, features and conduct. She wore a gentleman's hat, closely cut hair, eyeglasses, a gentleman's cravat, a coat-like outer garment of masculine cut that reached well down over her gown, and boots with high heels. Her coarse, somewhat masculine features and harsh, deep voice rather made the impression of a man in female attire than that of a lady, when one overlooked the bosom and the decidedly feminine form of the pelvis. Observation of her during the lengthy interview never revealed signs of erotism. When questioned concerning her attire, she would only respond that the style she chose suited her better. It was gradually ascertained that even as a small girl, she had had a preference for horses and masculine pursuits, and never any interest in feminine occupations. Later she developed a particular pleasure in reading, and prepared herself to be a teacher. Dancing had never pleased her; it had always seemed silly to her. The ballet had never interested her. The circus had always given her the greatest pleasure. Until her sickness in 1872 she had had no inclination for persons of the opposite sex or for those of her own sex. From that time she had a peculiar friendship with females, particularly for young ladies, which was remarkable to her. She also had a desire, which she satisfied, to wear hats and coats of a masculine style. Since 1869 she had worn her hair short and parted it on the side, as men do. She asserted that she was never sexually excited in the company of men, but that from the time mentioned, her friendship and self-sacrifice for sympathetic ladies was unbounded. At the same time, she experienced repugnance for gentlemen and their society.

Her relatives reported that, before 1872, the patient had a proposal of marriage, which she refused; and that in 1874, when she returned from a sojourn at a spa, she was sexually changed, and occasionally showed that she did not regard herself as a female.

From that time she would associate only with ladies, had a kind of love relation with one or another, and made remarks that indicated her view of herself as a man. This predilection for women was decidedly more than mere friendship, inasmuch as it expressed itself in tears, jealousy, etc.

In 1874, when she was stopping at a spa, a young lady who took her for a man in disguise fell in love with her. When this lady later married, the patient was depressed for a long time and spoke of unfaithfulness. Moreover, since her illness began, her relatives had been struck by her desire for masculine attire, her masculine conduct, and her disinclination for feminine pursuits; while previously, at least sexually, she had presented nothing unusual.

Further investigation showed that the patient had a love relation, which was not purely platonic, with the lady described in case 159, to whom she wrote affectionate letters like those of a lover to his beloved. In 1887 I saw the patient again, in a sanatorium, where she had been placed because of hystero-epileptic attacks, spinal irritation, and morphinism. The inverted sexual feeling existed unchanged, and only the most diligent supervision kept the patient from improper advances toward her fellow patients.

Until 1889 the patient's condition remained quite unchanged. Her health then began to fail, and she died of "exhaustion" in August 1889. The autopsy showed, in the vegetative organs, amyloid degeneration of the kidneys, fibroma of the uterus, and a cyst on the left ovary. The frontal bone was much thickened, uneven on the inner surface, with numerous exostoses; dura adherent to vault of cranium. Long diameter of skull, 175 millimeters; lateral diameter, 148 millimeters; weight of the edematous, but not atrophied, brain, 1175 grams. The meninges delicate, easily removed. Cortex pale. Convolutions broad, not numerous, regularly arranged. Nothing abnormal in the cerebellum and great ganglia.

Case 166.

Gynandry.[99] History: On November 4, 1889, the father-in-law of a certain Count Sandor complained that Sandor had swindled him out of 800 francs under the pretense of requiring a bond as secretary of a stock company. It was ascertained that Sandor had entered into matrimonial contracts and escaped from the nuptials in the spring of 1889; and it was further revealed that the ostensible Count Sandor was no man at all, but a woman in male attire – Sarolta (Charlotte), Countess V.

S. was arrested and, on the basis of deception and forgery of public documents, was brought to be examined. At the first hearing, S. confessed that she was born on September 6, 1866; she stated that she was a female, Catholic, single, and worked as an authoress under the name of Count Sandor V.

From the autobiography of this man-woman I have gleaned the following remarkable facts, which have been independently confirmed:

S. came from an ancient, noble and highly respected family of Hungary, in which there had been eccentricity and family peculiarities. A sister of the maternal grandmother was hysterical, a somnambulist, and had lain seventeen years in bed because of imagined paralysis. A second great-aunt spent seven years in bed because of an imagined fatal illness, and at the same time gave balls. A third had the whim that a certain table in her salon was bewitched. When anything was laid on this table, she would become greatly excited and cry, "Bewitched! bewitched!" and run with the object into a room she called the "Black Chamber," the key to which she never let out of her hands. After the death of this lady, a number of shawls, ornaments, bank notes, etc., were found in this chamber. A fourth great-aunt did not leave her room for two years, during which time she neither washed nor combed her hair. All these ladies were, nevertheless, intellectual, finely educated, and amiable.

S.'s mother was nervous and could not bear the light of the moon.

She inherited many of the peculiarities of her father's family. One line of the family was almost entirely devoted to spiritualism. Two blood relations on the father's side shot themselves. The majority of her male relatives were unusually talented; the females were decidedly narrow-minded and domesticated. S.'s father had a high position, which, however, he lost as a result of his eccentricity and extravagance (he wasted over a million and a half).

Among the many foolish things that her father encouraged in her, one was exemplified by the fact that he brought her up as a boy, called her Sandor, allowed her to ride, drive and hunt, and admired her muscular energy.

This foolish father likewise allowed his second son to go about in female attire and had him brought up as a girl. This farce ceased, however, when the son was sent to a higher school at the age of fifteen.

Sarolta-Sandor remained under her father's influence until her twelfth year. She then came under the care of her eccentric maternal grandmother in Dresden, by whom – when the masculine play became too obvious – she was placed in an institute and made to wear female attire.

At thirteen, representing herself as a boy, she had a love relation with an English girl and ran away with her.

Sarolta returned to her mother, who, unable to do anything, was compelled to allow her daughter to again become Sandor, wear male clothes, and fall in love with persons of her own sex, which the girl did at least once a year.

At the same time, S. received a careful education and made long journeys with her father; always, of course, as a young gentleman. She became independent early and visited cafés, even those of doubtful character. Indeed, she boasted one day that in a brothel she had had a girl sitting on each knee. She was often intoxicated, had a passion for masculine sports, and was a very skillful fencer.

She felt herself drawn particularly toward actresses or others of similar position and, if possible, toward those who were not very young. She asserted that she had never had any inclination for a young man and had felt an increasing dislike for young men over time.

"I preferred to go into the society of ladies with ugly, ill-favored men, so that none of them could put me in the shade. If I noticed that any of the men awakened the sympathies of the ladies, I felt jealous. I preferred ladies who were bright and pretty; I could not endure them if they were fat or much inclined toward men. It delighted me if the passion of a lady was disclosed under a poetic veil. All immodesty in a woman was disgusting to me. I had an indescribable aversion for female attire – indeed, for everything feminine – but only insofar as it concerned me; I was otherwise extremely enthusiastic for the beautiful sex."

During the last ten years S. had lived almost constantly away from her relatives in the guise of a man. She had enjoyed many liaisons with ladies, traveled much, spent a great deal, and incurred debts.

At the same time, she carried on literary work and was a valued collaborator on two noted journals of the capital.

Her passion for ladies was changeable; constancy in love was entirely lacking.

Only once, many years before, did such a liaison last for a significant period of time. At Castle G., S. made the acquaintance of Emma E., who was ten years older than herself. She fell in love with her, they made a marriage contract, and lived together as man and wife for three years at the capital.

A new love, which proved fatal to S., caused her to sever her matrimonial relations with E., who would not have it so. Only with the greatest sacrifice was S. able to purchase her freedom from E., who still looked upon herself as a divorced wife and regarded herself as the Countess V.! That S. also had the power to excite passion in other women was shown by the fact that when she had grown tired of a Miss D., having spent thousands of guilder on her, D. threatened to shoot S. if she was unfaithful. (This incident occurred before S.'s marriage to E.)

It was in the summer of 1887, while at a spa, that S. made the acquaintance of a distinguished official's family. She immediately fell in love with the daughter, Marie, and her love was returned.

S.'s mother and cousin tried in vain to break up the affair. During winter the lovers corresponded zealously. In April 1888, Count S. paid her a visit, and attained her wish in May 1889; namely, that Marie (who had recently given up a position as a teacher) became her bride. The ceremony was performed in an arbor by a pseudo-priest in Hungary, in the presence of her lover's friend. S. and her friend forged the marriage certificate. The pair lived happily and, without the interference of the father-in-law, this false marriage would have probably lasted much longer. It was remarkable that during the comparatively long existence of the relation S. was able to completely deceive the family of her bride about her true sex.

S. was a passionate smoker, and in all respects her tastes and passions were masculine.

Her letters and even her legal documents reached her under the name of "Count S." She often spoke of having to drill in military exercises. From the remarks of the father-in-law it appeared that S. knew how to imitate a scrotum by stuffing handkerchiefs or gloves in her trousers. The father-in-law once noticed something resembling an erect member on his future son-in-law (probably a priapus). S. had also occasionally remarked that she was obliged to wear a suspensory bandage while riding. S. had, in fact, worn a bandage around her body, possibly as a means of retaining a priapus.

Although S. frequently had herself shaved for the sake of appearance, the servants in the hotel where she lived were convinced that she was a woman, because the chambermaids found traces of menstrual blood on her linen (which S. explained, however, as hemorrhoidal). They also claimed to have convinced themselves of her real sex by looking through the keyhole when S. took a bath.

From the statements of Marie's family it seemed likely that for a long time she was deceived about the true sex of her false bridegroom. The following passage in a letter from Marie to S. on August 26, 1889, speaks in favor of the incredible simplicity and innocence of this unfortunate girl: "I don't like children anymore, but if I had a little Bezerl or Patscherl by my Sandi – ah, what happiness, Sandi mine!"

A large number of S.'s manuscripts allow conclusions to be drawn concerning her mental individuality. The handwriting possessed the character of firmness and certainty. Her fictional characters were genuinely masculine. The same peculiarities repeated themselves everywhere – wild, unbridled passion; hatred and resistance to all that opposes the heart that thirsts for love; poetical love unmarred by a single ignoble blot; enthusiasm for the beautiful and the noble; appreciation of science and the arts.

Her writings betrayed a wonderfully wide range of reading in the classics of all languages, as well as in citations from poets and prose writers of all lands. The statements of those qualified to judge literary work showed that S.'s poetical and literary ability was by no means small. The letters and writings concerning her relation with Marie were psychologically worthy of notice.

S. wrote of the happiness she had by M.'s side, expressing boundless longing to see her beloved, if only for a moment. After such happiness she wanted only one wish – to exchange her cell for the grave. The most bitter thing was the knowledge that now Marie also hated her. She had shed hot tears, enough to drown herself in, over her lost happiness. Whole quires of paper were devoted to the apotheosis of this love and to reminiscences of the time of their first love and acquaintance.

S. complained that her heart would not be directed by reason, and she expressed emotions that could only be felt, not simulated. On the other hand, there were outbreaks of the most silly passion, with the declaration that she could not live without Marie. "Thy dear, sweet voice; the voice whose tone, perchance, would raise me from the dead; that has been for me like the warm breath of Paradise! Thy presence alone was enough to alleviate my mental and moral anguish. It was a magnetic stream; it was a peculiar power that your being exercised over mine, which I cannot quite define; and, therefore, I cling to that ever-true definition: I love you because I love you. In the night of sorrow I had but one star – the star of Marie's love. That star has lost its light; now only its shimmer remains – the sweet, sad memory that lights with its soft ray even the deepening night of death – a ray of hope."

This writing ended with the apostrophe: "Gentlemen, learned in the profession of law, psychologists and pathologists, do me justice! Love led me to take the step I took; all my deeds were conditioned by it. God put it in my heart.

"If he created me so and not otherwise, am I then guilty; or is it the eternal, incomprehensible way of fate? I relied on God that one day my emancipation would come; for my thought was only love itself, which is the foundation, the guiding principle, of His teaching and His kingdom.

"O God, Thou All-pitying, Almighty One! Thou seest my distress; Thou knowest how I suffer. Incline Thyself to me; extend Thy helping hand to me, deserted by all the world. Only God is just. How beautifully does Victor Hugo describe this in his *La Légende des Siècles*! How sad do Mendelssohn's words sound to me: 'Nightly in dreams I see thee . . .'"

Though S. knew that none of her writings reached her lover, she did not grow tired of writing of her pain and delightful love in page after page of the deification of Marie. She wrote: "And to induce one more pure flood of tears, on one still, clear summer evening, when the lake was aglow with the setting sun like molten gold, and the bells of St. Anna and Maria-Wörth, blending in harmonious melancholy, gave tidings of rest and peace – for that poor soul, for this poor heart, that beats for thee till the last breath."

Personal examination: The first meeting the experts had with S. was a time of some embarrassment for both sides; for them, perhaps, because S.'s somewhat dazzling and forced masculine carriage impressed them; for her, because she thought she was to be marked with the stigma of moral insanity. She had a pleasant and intelligent face, which, in spite of a certain delicacy of features and diminutiveness of all its parts, gave a decidedly masculine impression, notwithstanding for the absence of a mustache. It was even difficult for the experts to realize that they were concerned with a woman, despite her female attire and the constant association. Interaction with the man Sandor, on the other hand, was much more free, natural, and apparently correct. The accused also felt this. As soon as she was treated like a man she immediately became more open, more communicative, and more free.

In spite of her inclination for the female sex, which had been present from her earliest years, she asserted that she first felt a trace of sexual feeling in her thirteenth year. This expressed itself in kisses, embraces, and caresses, accompanied by sexual pleasure, on the occasion of her elopement with the redheaded English girl from the Dresden institute. At that time only feminine forms appeared to her in dream-pictures. In sensual dreams ever since then, she had felt herself in the role of a man and had also occasionally experienced ejaculation.

She knew nothing of solitary or mutual masturbation. Such a thing seemed disgusting to her and not conducive to manliness. She had also never allowed her genitals to be touched by others, because it would have revealed her great secret. Although her menses began at seventeen, they were always scanty and without pain. It was plain to see that S. was horrified speaking of menstruation; it was repugnant to her masculine consciousness and feeling. She recognized the abnormality of her sexual inclinations, but had no desire to have them changed, inasmuch as in the perverse state she felt both well and happy. The idea of sexual intercourse with men not only disgusted her, she also thought it would be impossible.

Her modesty was so great, she preferred to sleep among men than among women. Thus, when it became necessary for her to answer the calls of nature or to change her linen, she had to ask her cell companion to turn her face to the window, so that she might not see her.

When occasionally S. came in contact with this companion – a woman from the lower walks of life – she experienced a sexual excitement that made her blush. Indeed, without being asked, S. related that, in her cell, she was overcome with actual fear when she was compelled to force herself into the unusual female attire, and her only comfort was that she was at least allowed to keep a shirt. What was remarkable and speaks for the significance of olfactory sensations in her sex life was her statement that (on the occasions of Marie's absence) she had sought and smelled the places where Marie's head had reposed in order to experience the delight of inhaling the odor of her hair. Women who were beautiful, voluptuous, or quite young did not particularly interest her. She made the physical charms of women subordinate. She felt magnetically drawn to those between twenty-four and thirty. She found sexual satisfaction exclusively in the female body (never in her own person) in the form of masturbation of the beloved woman or cunnilingus. Occasionally she availed herself of a stocking stuffed with oakum as a priapus. S. made these admissions unwillingly and with apparent shame, just as in her writings immodesty or cynicism were never found.

She was religious, had a lively interest in all that was noble and beautiful – men excepted – and was very sensitive to the opinion others entertained of her morality.

She deeply regretted that in her position she had made Marie unhappy. She regarded her sexual feelings as perverse, and saw as morally reprehensible such a love of one woman for another among normal individuals. She had great literary talent and an extraordinary memory. Her only weaknesses were her great frivolity and her inability to manage money and property reasonably. She was conscious of these flaws, however, and did not care to talk about them.

She was 153 centimeters tall, of delicate build, thin, but remarkably muscular chest and thighs. Her gait in female attire was awkward. Her movements were powerful and not unpleasing, though they were somewhat masculine and lacking in grace. She greeted one with a firm handshake. Her whole carriage was decided, firm and somewhat self-conscious. Her glance was intelligent; mien somewhat diffident. Feet and hands remarkably small, having remained in an infantile stage of development. Extensor surfaces of the extremities were remarkably well-covered with hair, while there was not the slightest trace of beard, in spite of all shaving experiments. The hips did not correspond in any way with those of a female. Waist lacking. Pelvis so slim and so lacking in prominence that a line drawn from the axilla to the corresponding knee was straight – not curved inward by the waist or outward by the pelvis. The skull slightly oxycephalic, and in all its measurements below the average of the female skull by at least one centimeter.

Circumference of the head 52 centimeters; occipital half-circumference, 24 centimeters; line from ear to ear, over the vertex, 23 centimeters; anterior half-circumference, 28.5 centimeters; line from glabella to occiput, 30 centimeters; ear-chin line, 26.5 centimeters; long diameter, 17 centimeters; greatest lateral diameter, 13 centimeters; diameter at auditory meatus, 12 centimeters; zygomatic diameter, 11.2 centimeters. Upper jaw strikingly projecting, its alveolar process obtruding beyond the under jaw about 0.5 centimeter. Position of the teeth not fully normal; right upper canine not developed. Mouth remarkably small; ears prominent; lobes not differentiated, passing over into the skin of the cheek. Hard palate, narrow and high; voice rough and deep; breasts fairly developed, soft and without secretion. Mons pubis covered with thick, dark hair. Genitals completely feminine, without trace of hermaphroditic appearance, but at the stage of development of a ten-year-old girl. The labia majora touched each other almost completely; labia minora had a cock's-comb-like form and projected under the labia majora. Clitoris small and very sensitive. Frenulum delicate; perineum very narrow; entrance to vagina narrow; mucous membrane normal. Hymen lacking (probably congenitally); likewise the hymenal caruncles. Vagina so narrow that the insertion of a virile member would be impossible, also very sensitive; certainly coitus had not taken place. Uterus felt, through the rectum, to be about the size of a walnut, immovable and retroflected.

Pelvis generally narrowed (dwarf pelvis), and of decidedly masculine type. Distance between anterior superior spines 22.5 centimeters (instead of 26.3 centimeters). Distance between the crests of the ilia, 26.5 centimeters (instead of 29.3 centimeters); between the trochanters, 27.7 centimeters (31); the external conjugate diameter, 17.2 centimeters (19 to 20); therefore, the internal conjugate presumably 7.7 centimeters (10.8). Because of narrowness of the pelvis, the direction of the thighs not convergent, as in a woman, but straight.

The opinion showed that in S. there was a congenitally abnormal inversion of the sexual instinct, which, indeed, expressed itself anthropologically in anomalies of development of the body that were the result of great hereditary taint; further, that the criminal acts of S. had their foundation in her abnormal and irresistible sexuality.

S.'s characteristic expressions – "God put love in my heart. If He created me so and not otherwise, am I then guilty; or is it the eternal, incomprehensible way of fate?" – were really justified.

The court granted pardon. The "countess in male attire," as she was called in the news-papers, returned to her home, and presented herself again as Count Sandor. Her only distress was her lost happiness with her beloved Marie.

A married woman in Brandon, Wisconsin, whose case is reported by Dr. Kiernan (*The Medical Standard,* November and December 1888), was more fortunate. In 1883 she ran away with a young girl, married her, and lived with her as her husband undisturbed.

An interesting "historical" example of androgyny is a case reported by Spitzka (*Chicago Medical Review,* August 20, 1881). The gentleman in question was the Governor of New York and lived in the reign of Queen Anne. He was apparently affected with moral insanity, was terribly licentious, and, in spite of his high posi-tion, could not keep himself from going about in the streets in female attire, coquetting with all the allurement of a prostitute.

In a picture of him that has been preserved, his narrow brow, asymmetrical face, feminine features, and sensual mouth immediately attract attention. It is certain that he never actually regarded himself as a woman.

complications of antipathic sexual instinct.

In individuals afflicted with sexual inversion, the perverse sexual feeling and incli-nation may be further complicated by other perverse manifestations. Thus, acts that are analogous to the antipathic sexual instinct may be performed by individu-als who have a natural inclination toward persons of the opposite sex.

Because abnormally increased sexuality is almost a regular accompaniment of antipathic sexual feeling, acts of lustful sadistic cruelty for the satisfaction of libido are easily possible. A remarkable example of this is the case of Zastrow (Casper and Liman, 7th ed., vol. 1, p. 160; vol. 2, p. 487), who bit one of his victims (a boy), tore his prepuce, slit his anus, and strangled him.

Z. came from a psychopathic grandfather and melancholic mother. His brother indulged in abnormal sexual pleasures and ultimately committed suicide.

Z. was a congenital homosexual who was masculine in build and occupation. There was phimosis. Mentally, he was a weak, perverse, and socially useless man. Women horrified him, and he felt as a woman toward a man in his dreams. He was painfully conscious of his perverse instinct and lack of normal sexual feeling, and sought satisfaction in mutual masturbation, with a frequent desire for pederasty.

Similar sadistic feelings of this kind in those afflicted with antipathic sexual instinct are found in some of the foregoing histories (cf. case 96 of the sixth edition; also, Moll, *Kontr. Sexualempfindung,* second edition, p. 189; Krafft-Ebing, *Jahrb. f. Psychiatrie,* vol. 12, pp. 357 and 389; Moll, *Untersuchungen über Libido sexualis,* cases 26 and 27).

As examples of perverse sexual satisfaction dependent upon antipathic sexual instinct, one reported by Athenaeus should be mentioned of the Greek who was in love with a statue of Cupid and defiled it in the temple of Delphi; and in addition to the monstrous cases reported by Tardieu (*Attentats,* p. 272), there is the terrible one reported by Lombroso (*L'uomo delinquente,* p. 200) of a certain Artusio who wounded a boy in the abdomen and abused him sexually *by using the incision.*

Cases 92, 110 and 115 (eighth edition) show that fetishism may also occur with antipathic sexual instinct; in addition, there is a case of shoe fetishism related by me in *Jahrbücher f. Psychiatrie,* vol. 12; Moll, op. cit., second edition, p. 179; Garnier, *Les Fétichistes,* p. 98.

The following case, taken from Garnier, is a classical example of boot fetishism. At times, masochism is a complication of sexual inversion. Cf. Moll, *Kontr. Sexualempfindung,* 2d ed., p. 172 (case 12) and p. 190; Hem, *Internat. Zentralbl. f. d. Physiol. und Pathol. der Harn- und Sexualorgane,* vol. 4, no. 5 (homosexuality in a woman with passive flagellantism and coprophagy); Krafft-Ebing, case 43 in sixth edition of this book, also case 137 of this edition and 114 of ninth edition; also *Jahrbücher für Psychiatrie,* vol. 12, p. 339 (homosexuality, abortive masochism), p. 351 (psychically hermaphroditic masochism).

Case 167.

Homosexuality. X., twenty-six years of age, from the upper class, was arrested for having practiced masturbation in a public park. Heavily tainted by heredity; skull abnormal; peculiar from earliest youth; psychically abnormal. At the age of ten he began to show a peculiar interest in patent leather shoes. He began to masturbate at thirteen; in order to achieve ejaculation, however, he had to fasten his eyes upon patent leather shoes. He never felt any inclination toward women, and when, at the age of twenty-one, he attempted coitus at a brothel, he derived no satisfaction from the act. At twenty-four his homosexual instinct increasingly asserted itself. He was only drawn, however, toward young men who wore elegant clothes and patent leather boots. He masturbated while thinking of such men. His ideal was to live with such a man and practice mutual masturbation. Unable to realize his wishes, he would introduce a ball into his anus and, while moving it in and out, he imagined having coitus with his ideal young man, who would be wearing patent leather boots. He masturbated simultaneously. During this imitation of passive pederasty he wore drawers made of red silk. For some time he was accustomed to stick notices on public buildings to this effect: "My buttocks are at the disposal of handsome gentlemen who wear patent leather boots." While writing such notices and looking at his own patent leather shoes, he would have an erection. At the age of sixteen, when young men began to interest him, he only had eyes for their patent leather boots. He loved to loiter about the show windows of boot shops as well as the drilling grounds of the military school, where he had an opportunity to admire the officers in their patent leather boots. One day he bought a pair for himself and became quite intoxicated from gazing at them. The very smell of them was sufficient to excite him to a high degree sexually. He finally put them on so that he might make conquests in them, but was not successful. He then used them for another purpose. He would masturbate and ejaculate into them. He derived the most intense lustful pleasure from putting one of the shoes to his anus or between his thighs and rubbing it around thus while masturbating. One day, when X. found a defect on the upper of one of these shoes, which he always saved most carefully, he was very dejected. He felt like a person who has just discovered the first wrinkle in the face of his beloved. One day in the park he thought that a young man made advances to him according to his own desire; he was highly elated and could not resist exposing himself. He was arrested, but not sentenced. He was sent to an insane asylum (Garnier, *Les Fétichistes,* p. 114).

In general, the *acquired* cases show the following characteristics:

[1] The homosexual instinct appears as a secondary factor, and may always be referred to influences (mental or masturbatory neurasthenia) that disturbed normal sexual satisfaction. It is, however, probable here that in spite of powerful sensual libido, the feeling and inclination for the opposite sex were weak from birth, especially in a spiritual and aesthetic sense.

[2] The homosexual instinct, as long as sexual inversion has not yet taken place, is looked upon by the affected individual as vicious and abnormal, and only practiced for lack of something better.

[3] The heterosexual instinct long remains predominant, and the impossibility of satisfying it produces pain. As the homosexual feeling gains in strength, the heterosexual instinct weakens proportionally.

On the other hand, in *congenital* cases:

[a] The homosexual instinct is the one that primarily occurs and becomes dominant in the sex life. It appears as the natural manner of satisfaction and also dominates the dream life of the individual.

[b] The heterosexual instinct fails completely, or, if it should make its appearance in the history of the individual (psychosexual hermaphroditism), it is nevertheless only an episodic phenomenon that has no root in the mental constitution, and is essentially simply a means to satisfaction of sexual desire.

After a consideration of the foregoing characteristics, the differentiation of the above groups of congenital inverted sexuality from one another, as well as from the cases in which the anomaly is acquired, will present no difficulties.

In any event, the prognosis of the cases of acquired antipathic sexual instinct is much more favorable than that of the congenital cases. In the acquired cases, the occurrence of effemination (the mental inversion of the individual, in the sense of perverse sexual feeling) is the limit beyond which there is no longer hope of benefit from therapy. In the congenital cases, the various categories established in this book form as many stages of psychosexual taint, and benefit is only *probable* within the category of the psychic hermaphrodites, and only *possible* (see Schrenk-Notzing's case) in that of the homosexuals.

The prophylaxis of these conditions thus becomes most important – for the congenital cases, prohibition of the reproduction of such unfortunates; for the acquired cases, protection from the injurious influences that experience dictates may lead to the fatal inversion of the sexual instinct.

Numerous *predisposed* individuals meet this sad fate because parents and teachers have no suspicion of the danger to children that masturbation leaves in its wake.

In many schools and academies, masturbation and vice are actually cultivated. At present, too little attention is given to the mental and moral peculiarities of the pupils.

Nothing more is asked of pupils than that their tasks be completed. That many of them are thus ruined in body and soul is never considered.

In obedience to affected prudery, the sex life is made a mystery to the developing youth, and not the slightest attention is given to the excitations of his sexual instinct. During the years of children's development, how few family physicians are ever called in to give advice to the patients who are often so greatly predisposed!

It is thought that all must be left to Nature. In the meantime, Nature rises in her power and leads the helpless, unprotected innocent onto dangerous bypaths.

diagnosis, prognosis and therapy of antipathic sexual instinct.

The diagnosis of antipathic sexual instinct is of great import clinically and especially forensically. At first glance it presents some difficulties, inasmuch as the symptoms are rather of a subjective nature and the perverse acts offer so many aspects that may mean perversion as well as perversity. Much depends on the veracity of the patient, and in many cases that leaves much to be desired. Autobiographies are to be taken with a grain of salt and should be discounted. The expert will soon be able, nonetheless, to weed out exaggeration and untruth. Antipathic sexual instinct is such a complicated psychic anomaly that only the experienced specialist can quickly distinguish between truth and fiction.

True knowledge is most easily ascertained from those who, though they despair of their existence and contemplate suicide (frequently found in those who have cultured minds and realize the anomaly of their position), come as a last resort to the medical man for advice; also from those who are confronted with legal proceedings, or who are forced by circumstances into marriage and doubt their virility. These patients have an urgent need for help and will tell the truth. In strong contrast to these truly unfortunate beings stand those individuals, generally of limited ethical and intellectual worth, who seek to enrich medical knowledge with fatuous gossip about their disease. Every case of genuine homosexuality has its etiology, its concomitant physical and psychic symptoms, its reactions upon the whole psychic being, and must be reduced to an abnormal sexual instinct that is diametrically opposed to the physical sex of the affected individual, as it can be explained upon that basis only. The diagnosis is to be found in the anamnesis, the etiology, the previous life, and the psychosexual development of the case. To form a clear opinion it is best to judge the case from the standpoint of the anthropological clinical history of its development, and to collect synthetically all the various details.

The opinion will then be as definitely established as in any other clinical case.

The first important point, based upon ripe experience, is the fact that antipathic sexual instinct as an anomaly of sexual life is only found in individuals who are tainted, as a rule, hereditarily. Initially, particular stress should be laid upon this point. In all cases in which anamnesis has been proved, this taint will be readily found. By itself this proof is of no value, for perversity also grows in this soil. But it assumes importance when the same frailty is found to exist in several members of the same family, or appears in the form of other perversions of the sexual life, either in the individual who is under consideration or in other members of his family. Often enough the patient presents other psychic or neurotic anomalies, even psychic diseases, defects or the like. They are so frequent and numerous that one is often led to doubt whether the manifestation under observation belongs in the neuropathic or psychopathic sphere.

These neurotic and psychopathic manifestations demand a most careful scrutiny as to their meaning. Not uncommonly they are signs of taint or degeneration of value equivalent to antipathic sexual instinct; or they may be reactions that emanate from external defects to which tainted individuals are more subject than normal man is, and that are often indirectly dependent upon antipathic sexual instinct on the basis of psychic conflicts in which these unfortunates are frequently implicated by virtue of their sexual perversions; or they may be found to spring from the imperfect or perverse gratification of their sexual needs (masturbation).

It is certain that these persons are usually also abnormal as far as character is concerned. Neither man nor woman, they are a mixture of both, with secondary psychic and physical characteristics of the one sex as well as the other, that grow out of the interfering influences of a bisexual predisposition and disturb the development of a well-defined and complete being. This peculiarity, however, is only found in fully developed cases. A psychic disease is not, per se, a necessary adjunct to antipathic sexual instinct. All nations and all eras have produced perverse men, whose renown and greatness adorn the history of their mother country or that of the world.

This abnormality must not be looked upon as a pathological condition or as a crime, but as the development of the sex life with its reacting effects upon the mind and the moral sense. It may also proceed with the same harmony and satisfying influence as in the normally disposed, a further argument in favor of the assumption that antipathic sexual instinct is an equivalent for heterosexuality. If ethical and intellectual defects are present, they may be looked upon merely as complicated anomalies resulting from the taint.

An important factor is precocity in sexual life, which, together with its antithesis, retarded puberty, is the distinguishing mark of a degenerated constitution. This is demonstrated when the sex life takes an inverted course at an early period, particularly at a time when evil influences or bad examples cannot be at work; for instance, when little boys prefer male adults to their female relations; or show a predilection for girls' games and occupations, or particular skill in sewing, knitting, embroidering, etc.; or show an inclination for the female *toilette,* and find pleasure in wearing girls' clothing, choose girls' characters in private theatricals or in masquerades and betray great cleverness in impersonating the female character, etc.

Homosexual acts (mutual masturbation, etc.) previous to puberty are not a proof of antipathic sexuality. They may spring from hypersexuality, precocity or some external influences. They do not necessarily lead to inverted sexuality unless the individual is predisposed. It is at the time of puberty that the sex life is developed and receives its direction for the rest of life. An unconscious desire for sexual union, often enough stimulated by individuals of the same sex, brings the play-mates together, and, although tickling and other tactile irritations – quite apart from the genuine sexual instinct – may lead to acts of masturbation, they are not coupled with psychic feelings in the sense of homosexual acts. Analogous manifes-tations may be observed in young animals.

Antipathic sexuality rarely develops, however, from this horseplay. Puberty teaches the youthful sinner to know his true sex soon enough. From the sexual instinct, based upon a series of physical and psychic attractions, emanates the sexual leaning to persons of the opposite gender, and the earlier homosexual encounters are remembered with shame and confusion. But the homosexual act committed *after* puberty has set in is *the decisive* step in the wrong direction. The stage of sexual differentiation sometimes covers a long period and often reaches far beyond that of physical sexual development.

Of great value in diagnosing a case is to ascertain the patient's dream life and other activities of sleep. The true status of the sexual instinct is often pitifully portrayed. Nocturnal pollutions are found to be colored [a] predominantly in cases of psychic hermaphroditism, and [b] in all the other grades of the anomaly in the exclusive sense of homosexuality. In cases of effemination (viraginity) they are accompanied by dream-pictures that delineate the passive role (in man) or the active role (in woman) during the sexual act.

The presence of physical or psychic abnormal characteristics may aid diagnosis if they are coupled with other more distinctive signs. By themselves they prove nothing, inasmuch as they are also found in individuals who are not tainted; for instance, in *gynecomasts,* bearded women, etc.

In the well-pronounced cases of antipathic sexual instinct (effemination and viraginity) the physical and psychic characteristics of inverted sexuality are so plentiful that a mistake cannot occur. They are simply men in women's garb, and women in men's attire, especially if they have full freedom of action. Psychically they consider themselves as belonging to the opposite sex. We have seen female homosexuals in the army and male homosexuals among the waitresses in restaurants. They act, walk, gesticulate and in every way behave exactly as if they were persons of the gender they simulate. I have known male homosexuals who surpassed woman in wiles, loquacity, coquetry, etc.

In pronounced cases, bashfulness and timidity will be observed in the homosexual individual when he is in the presence of persons of his own sex.

That homosexuals know each other instinctively is a fable. They recognize one another by their gait, natural shyness and other signs, just as normal persons of opposite sexes do if they go adventure hunting.

The higher grades of homosexuality reveal *horror feminae* to the extent of absolute impotence. Imagination sometimes assists in producing erection and rendering coitus possible. Diagnosis is definitely established when absolute proof is at hand that a homosexual person is permanently attracted to a person of the same sex (while no such attractions exist with persons of the opposite sex), is led to a sexual act that grants full satisfaction to the sexual instinct with that person, and disgust for persons of the opposite sex is insurmountable.

The distinction between congenital and acquired (or rather retarded) homosexuality is considered to be of theoretical as well as therapeutic value.

Some authors claim that congenital homosexuality does not exist, but that the anomaly is acquired from others. I cannot accept their arguments, however, for they do not explain the presence of the distinguishing symptoms that are so often found in the earliest years of the individuals afflicted; i.e., at a period in which external influences may be absolutely excluded.

Case 168.

Taken from Moll, *Libido sexualis,* case 69, p. 726. A young man, thirty-four years of age, was first drawn to young men at the age of seventeen, and had no liking for girls. He was an effeminate character, had a girl's nickname, and played with dolls. When he was drunk, he allowed men to masturbate him. When sober, however, he would not permit it, because he thought it was stupid.

The experiences detailed in this and numerous other scientific works on masturbation provide valuable suggestions for parents and teachers.

Educators are often too "naïve" in their views, and their power of observation is too limited to notice the sexual abuses that are rampant among the boys entrusted to their care and even practiced during lesson time. In a few exceptional cases, educators have become seducers of boys. Everything conducive to unduly furthering the development of the sex life – prolonged sitting at school, the use of alcoholic drinks, etc. – should be strictly avoided. A boy with inverted sexuality should be rigidly excluded from all public educational institutions for boys and sent to a hospital for nervous disorders. Boys should not be permitted to sleep together at home. Swimming lessons and bathing *en masse* should be under the careful and strict supervision of a competent person.

Neither should a child with antipathic sexual instinct be placed under the isolated instruction of a tutor or private master, because often the first object of homosexual love is the instructor at home. Care should be taken that tainted children are not caressed and fondled by persons of the same sex. **Flagellation on the buttocks** should never be permitted.

The best place for children who are perversely inclined (sexually) is the public school, where coeducation of the sexes prevails. An early preference for games, occupations and pastimes of the opposite sex should be strongly discountenanced and interdicted. There should be a careful watch for masturbation in both sexes. Early signs of antipathic sexual instinct should be noted at once and hypnotic and suggestive treatment applied, because there is more hope for eradicating the evil in its earlier stages than when the individual so tainted has already been lost in the quagmire of sexual perversion.

The lines of *treatment,* when antipathic instinct exists, are the following:

[1] Prevention of masturbation and removal of other influences that are injurious to the sex life.

[2] Cure of the neurosis (universal and sexual neurasthenia) that arises out of the unhygienic conditions of the sex life.

[3] Mental treatment to combat homosexual feelings and impulses, and to encourage heterosexual ones.

The momentum of the treatment lies in fulfilling the third indication, particularly with reference to masturbation.

In only a very few cases where acquired antipathic sexual instinct has not significantly progressed can the fulfillment of [1] and [2] be sufficient, as is proved in a case that was fully reported by the author in the *Irrenfreund,* 1885, no. 1. Cf. case 128, ninth edition of this book.

Physical treatment will not usually prove sufficient, even when reinforced morally by good advice regarding the avoidance of masturbation, the repression of homosexual feelings and impulses, and the encouragement of heterosexual desires. This is true even in cases of acquired sexual inversion.

All that can really benefit the patient is a method of mental treatment – hypnotic suggestion.

I know of only one case in which auto-suggestion proved successful, cf. case 129, ninth edition.

As a rule, only *suggestion that comes from a second person* by means of *hypnosis* promises success.

The object of post-hypnotic suggestion in such cases is to remove the impulse to masturbation and homosexual feelings, and to encourage heterosexual emotions with a sense of virility.

The possibility of inducing hypnosis of sufficient intensity is, of course, a prerequisite. Unfortunately, it is in these very cases of neurasthenia that this proves impossible, inasmuch as the subject is often excited, embarrassed, and in no condition to concentrate his thoughts.

Because of the great benefit that can be given to such unfortunates, and with Ladame's case in view (see below), in all such cases, everything should be done to force hypnosis – the only means of salvation. The result, in the three following cases, was satisfactory:

Case 169.

Antipathic sexual instinct acquired through masturbation. Mr. X., merchant, aged twenty-nine. Father's parents healthy. Nothing nervous in father's family.

Father was an irritable, peevish old man. One brother of the father was a man-about-town, and died unmarried.

Mother died in her third confinement when the patient was six years old. She had a deep, rough, masculine voice, and a coarse appearance. Of the children, one brother is irritable, "melancholic," and indifferent to women.

As a child the patient had scarlet fever with delirium. Up to his fourteenth year he was lighthearted and social; after that, however, he was quiet, solitary, and "melancholic." The first trace of sexual feeling appeared in his tenth or eleventh year, at which time he learned masturbation from other boys, and practiced mutual masturbation with them.

At the age of thirteen or fourteen, ejaculation for the first time. Patient had felt no evil results of masturbation until the last three months.

At school he learned easily, but was troubled with headaches. Pollutions after the age of twenty, in spite of a daily practice of masturbation. With pollutions occurred "procreative" dreams, as a man and wife might perform the act. In his seventeenth year he was seduced into mutual masturbation by a man who loved men. He found satisfaction in this, inasmuch as he was always very passionate sexually. It was a long time before the patient again sought new opportunities for intercourse with males, which he did simply to rid himself of semen.

He felt no friendship or love for the person with whom he had intercourse. He felt satisfaction only when he played the passive role; i.e., when masturbation was practiced on him. Once the act was completed, he had no respect for the individual. If he later came to respect the man, he ceased to indulge in the act with him. Later it became a matter of indifference to him whether he masturbated or had masturbation practiced on him. During solitary masturbation, he always thought of attractive men practicing masturbation on him. He preferred a hard, rough hand.

The patient thought that he would have arrived at a natural method of satisfying his sexual desires had he not been led astray. He never felt love for his own sex, though he had pleased himself with the thought of loving men. He had initially had sensual inclinations toward the opposite sex. He had found pleasure in dancing and, although pleased with women, had been more interested in the figure than in the face. He had had erections at the sight of women who pleased him. He had never attempted coitus because of a fear of infection. Thus, he did not know whether he was potent with women. He thought he could no longer be so, because his feeling for women had grown cold, especially in recent years.

Although his sensual dreams had previously involved both men and women, in recent years he had dreamed only of encounters with men, and could not remember if he had dreamed of sexual relations with a woman. At the theatre, as well as at the circus and ballet, the feminine figure had always interested him. In museums, masculine and feminine statues had affected him equally.

Patient was a heavy smoker, a beer drinker, loved male society, and was an athlete and skater. Anything dandified was repugnant to him, and he had never felt any desire to please men; he would have even preferred to please women.

He now felt his position to be painful, because masturbation had obtained the upper hand. Although it had previously been practiced without evil effects, it now began to disclose its bad results.

He had suffered from neuralgia of the testicles since July 1889. The pain occurred particularly at night, at which time there was also trembling (increased reflex excitability).

Sleep was not refreshing, and he would awaken with pain in his testicles. He was now inclined to indulge more frequently in masturbation. He was afraid of the consequences of the habit. He hoped that his sexual life might still be turned into normal channels. He thought now of the future; he had a relation with a girl who was attractive to him, and the thought of possessing her as a wife was pleasing.

Although he had abstained from masturbation for five days, he could scarcely believe that he would be strong enough to overcome the habit on his own. Lately he had been extremely depressed, had become tired of life, and had lost all desire for work.

Patient was tall, powerful, well-nourished, and had a thick growth of beard. Skull and skeleton normal. Knee jerks very prompt, with more rapid deep reflexes in the upper extremities. Pupils dilated, equal, with prompt reactions. Carotids of equal caliber; urethral hyperesthesia; cords and testicles not sensitive; genitals normal.

The patient was calmed and given hope for the future on the condition that he give up masturbation and attempt to transfer his sexual desires from persons of his own sex to females.

Prescription: hip baths, 20°-24° C; extr. secal. with water, 0.5; antipyrin, 1.0 per day; potassium bromide, 4.0 evenings.

December 13. The patient arrived in a disturbed condition of mind. He complained that he was unable, on his own, to resist the impulse to masturbate, and asked for help.

An attempt at hypnosis induced a condition of deep lethargy in the patient.

He was given the following suggestions:

[1] I can not, must not, and will not masturbate again.

[2] I abhor the love of my own sex and shall never again think men handsome.

[3] I shall and will become well again, fall in love with a virtuous woman, be happy, and make her happy.

December 14. While the patient was out walking he saw a handsome man, and felt powerfully drawn toward him.

Hypnotic sittings were subsequently held every second day with the above suggestions.

December 18 (fourth sitting). Somnambulism occurred; the impulse toward masturbation and interest in men disappeared.

At the eighth sitting, "complete virility" was added to the above suggestions. The patient felt morally elevated and physically strengthened. The neuralgia of the testicles had disappeared. He found he was without sexual feeling.

He believed himself to be free from masturbation and inverted sexual inclination.

After the eleventh sitting he thought further help was unnecessary. He wished to go home and marry. He felt well and potent. Early in January 1890, treatment ceased.

In March 1890, the patient wrote: "I have since had several occasions on which it has been necessary to use all my moral strength to overcome my habit, and, thank God, I have been successful in freeing myself from this vice. Several times I have had the opportunity for sexual intercourse, and I have found pleasure in it. I look calmly on my happy future."

Other cases successfully treated by suggestion may be found in Wetterstrand, *Der Hypnotismus und seine Anwendung in der praktischen Medizin*, 1891, p. 52ff.; Bernheim, *Hypnotisme*, Paris, 1891, etc., p. 38.

The foregoing details of the successful results of hypnotic suggestion in cases of acquired sexual inversion make it seem possible that unfortunates afflicted with congenital perversion may also be helped to some degree by the same means.

Of course, in cases of a congenital anomaly the proposition is different. To correct a morbid psychosexual existence is a most difficult problem.

The most favorable cases are those of *psychosexual hermaphroditism,* in which rudimentary heterosexual feelings, at least, may be strengthened by suggestion and brought into active practice.

Case 170.

Mr. von X., aged twenty-five, landed proprietor. He came from a neuropathic, irascible father, who was said to have been sexually normal. His mother was nervous, as were her two sisters. His maternal grandmother was nervous, and his maternal grandfather was a *roué* who was prone to much venery. The patient was like his mother and an only child. From birth he was weak, frequently suffered from migraines, and was nervous. He passed through several illnesses. At fifteen he began masturbation without having been taught.

Although until his seventeenth year he had never had any feeling for men, or, in fact, any sexual inclination, at this time desire for men arose. He fell in love with a comrade. His friend returned his love. They embraced and kissed and indulged in mutual masturbation. Occasionally the patient practiced coitus **between the man's thighs.** He abhorred pederasty. His lascivious dreams were concerned only with men. In the circus and the theatre males alone interested him. His inclination was for men of about twenty years. Handsome, tall forms were enticing to him. He was quite indifferent to all other characteristics of the men. In his sexual affairs with men, his role was always that of a man.

After his eighteenth year, the patient was always a source of anxiety to his highly respected parents, for at that time he began a love affair with a male waiter, who fleeced him and made him an object of remark and ridicule. He was taken home. He then consorted with servants and hostlers, causing a scandal. He was sent away to travel about. In London he got into a "blackmailing scrape," but succeeded in escaping to his home.

He did not profit in any way from this bitter experience and again showed disgraceful inclinations toward men. Patient was sent to me to be cured of his fatal peculiarity (December 1888). Tall, stately, robust, well-nourished, of masculine build; large, well-formed genitals. Gait, voice, and attitude masculine. Pronounced masculine passions. He smoked sparingly, and only cigarettes; drank little, and was fond of confectionery. He loved music, arts, aesthetics, flowers, and moved in ladies' society by preference. He wore a mustache, but his face was otherwise clean-shaven. His garments were not remarkable in any way. He was a soft, blasé fellow, and a do-nothing. He would lie in bed mornings, and could scarcely be made to rise before noon. He said he had never regarded his inclination toward his own sex as abnormal. He looked upon it as congenital; taught, however, by his evil experiences, he wished to be cured of his perversion. He had little faith in his own will. Although he had tried to reform, he had always lapsed into masturbation, which he found injurious, inasmuch as it caused (slight) neurasthenic symptoms. There was no moral defect. Intelligence was slightly below average. A careful education and aristocratic manners were apparent. Exquisite neuropathic eyes betrayed a nervous constitution. The patient was not a complete and hopeless homosexual. *Although he had heterosexual feelings, his sensual inclinations toward the opposite sex were nevertheless manifested weakly and infrequently.* At nineteen he was first taken to a brothel by friends. He experienced no *horror feminae.* He had efficient erections and some pleasure in coitus, but it was not the instinctive delight he experienced while embracing men.

The patient asserted that since then he had engaged in coitus six times, twice unaided. He gave the assurance that he was always capable of it, but, as with masturbation, he did it only as a substitute for intercourse with men when the sexual impulse troubled him. He had thought of the possibility of finding a sympathetic lady and marrying her. He would regard marital cohabitation and abstinence from intercourse with men as hard duties.

Since there were rudiments of heterosexual feelings present, and the case could not be looked upon as hopeless, it seemed that treatment was indicated. Although the indications were clear enough, there was no support for them in the will of the indolent patient, who was so unconscious of his own position. Thus it seemed necessary to seek support for the moral influence in hypnosis. The fulfillment of this seemed doubtful, however, because the famous Hansen had tried several times, in vain, to hypnotize him.

Nonetheless, because of the most important social interests of the patient, it was necessary to make another attempt. To my great surprise, Bernheim's procedure immediately induced a condition of deep lethargy, with the possibility of post-hypnotic suggestion.

At the second sitting, somnambulism was induced by merely looking at him. The patient yielded easily to suggestions of all kinds; indeed, contracture was induced by stroking him. He was awakened by counting three. Once awake, the patient had amnesia for all the events of the hypnotic state. Hypnosis was induced every second or third day and the hypnotic suggestions were given. At the same time, moral and hydrotherapeutic measures were employed.

The hypnotic suggestions were as follows:

[1] I abhor masturbation because it makes me weak and miserable.

[2] I no longer have inclination toward men, because love for men is against religion, nature and law.

[3] I feel an inclination toward woman, because woman is lovely, desirable, and created for man.

During the sittings the patient always repeated these suggestions verbatim. After the fourth sitting, he reported that when he went into society he paid court to the ladies. Shortly thereafter, when a famous prima donna sang, he was very enthusiastic for her. Some days later, the patient sought the address of a brothel.

Although he still preferred the society of young gentlemen, the most careful observation failed to reveal anything suspicious.

February 17. Patient asked to be allowed to indulge in coitus, and was very well-satisfied with his experience with one of the *demimonde*.

March 16. Up to this time, hypnosis twice a week. The patient always passed into deep somnambulism by simply being looked at, and repeated the suggestions as requested. He was susceptible to all kinds of post-hypnotic suggestion and was completely unaware in the waking state of the influences that had been exerted on him in the hypnotic state. In the hypnotic condition he always gave the assurance that he was free from masturbation and sexual feeling for men. Because he gave the same answers in hypnosis – e.g., that on such and such a date he practiced masturbation for the last time, and that he was too much under the will of the physician to be able to lie – his assertions deserved belief. This was further supported by the circumstance that he looked well, he was free from all neurasthenic symptoms, and, when he was in the society of men, not the slightest suspicion rested on him. An open, free, and manly bearing was developed.

Moreover, because on his own he now and then indulged in coitus with pleasure, and his occasional pollutions were induced by lascivious dreams that involved women, there could be no doubt about the favorable change in his sex life. Thus it was presumed that the hypnotic suggestions had developed into auto-suggestive inclinations that directed his feelings, thoughts and will. Although the patient will probably always remain frigid, he more often spoke of marriage and of his intention to win a wife as soon as he had become acquainted with a sympathetic lady. Treatment was stopped (author's own case, *Internat. Zentralblatt für die Physiol. und Pathol. der Harn- und Sexualorgane,* vol. 1).

In July 1889 I received a letter from his father telling me of his son's good health and conduct.

On May 24, 1890, I met my former patient by chance while on a journey. His bright, healthful appearance allowed the most favorable opinion of his condition. He told me that though he still had a sympathetic feeling for some men, it was never anything like love. He occasionally had pleasurable coitus with women and now thought of marriage.

As a test, I hypnotized him in the former manner and asked for the commands I had given him. In a deep condition of somnambulism and in the same tone of voice as before, the patient repeated the suggestions he had received in December 1888 – an excellent example of the possible duration and power of post-hypnotic suggestion.

Other cases may be found in the eighth edition, cases 137, 138, 140, 141; and ninth edition, case 133, of this book.

The cases quoted by the author, as well as those given by Ladame in which suggestion removed the homosexual instinct (or, at least, neutralized it as a protection from shame and law), seem to furnish proof that even the gravest cases of congenital sexual inversion may benefit from the application of hypnotism.

Wetterstrand (cf. Schrenck-Notzing, op. cit., case 49), Bernheim (cf. Schrenck-Notzing, case 51), Müller (cf. Schrenck-Notzing, case 53), Schrenck-Notzing (op. cit., cases 66, 67), go so far as to report complete success in displacing the homosexual instinct with the heterosexual instinct, coupled with virility. Schrenck-Notzing (op. cit., cases 62, 63) also succeeded in cases of effemination.

Decided and lasting results may be hoped for only when hypnotism produces deep somnambulism. But such results are, after all, nothing more than suggestive training, not a real cure. Although they are marvelous "artifacts" of hypnotic science practiced on abnormal human beings, they are by no means "transformations" (cf. Schrenck-Notzing) of a psychosexual existence.

Very instructive in this respect is a case related by Schrenck-Notzing. After the "cure" was effected, the individual in question says of himself: "I am always conscious of a certain insuperable coercion that does not rest upon moral principles, but I believe must be directly referable to treatment." At any rate, such "cures" afford no proof whatsoever against the assumption of an original condition of sexual inversion.

It is necessary here to warn the reader against illusions about the true value of hypnotic therapy.

Repeated attempts have been made to question the right of the medical adviser to treat cases of antipathic sexuality. The advice given to such unfortunates has been to become reconciled with their anomaly and to eschew homosexual intercourse. Success has been achieved in some cases where the libido was weak or the sense of morality was not entirely blunted. It was pointed out to these unfortunate beings the many other dreadful afflictions, such as trigeminal neuralgia or malignant tumors, that man must bear with resignation. Unfortunately, this view involves a defective knowledge of the meaning and bearing of antipathic sexual instinct, for if the advice is adopted, this affliction means nothing more or less than a hopeless existence, a life without love, an undignified comedy before human society, and moral and psychic marasmus. For the individual who rejects such advice, on the other hand, eventual loss of social position, civic honor and liberty are involved.

Castration is out of the question, because it is difficult to justify such an operation. Although sexual desire would be diminished, the antipathic sexual instinct and its attendant psychic tortures cannot be extirpated by this process.

To confine such people in an insane asylum is a monstrous idea. There can only be justification for it when the perverse individual also suffers from a psychosis that renders confinement imperative.

Another objection that has been made against treatment is that the welfare of society is jeopardized insofar as an opportunity is given to tainted individuals to propagate their perversions.

This objection appears comical in the face of the fact that no one has yet thought of prohibiting the marriage of the congenital libertine or the habitual drunkard. My experience teaches me that by no means do the sexual perverts in general constitute the worst type of degeneration. The progeny of individuals thus tainted, whom I have had occasion to observe, has offered no pronounced manifestations of neuropathic constitution or taint.

Psychopathia sexualis is seldom perceived as a family failing or a mark of heredity.

The number of cases that have actually been cured of this anomaly will always be limited, inasmuch as many of these unfortunates refrain from taking even the medical man into their confidence. Others despair beforehand of the efficacy of treatment, while some who practice homosexual intercourse and find satisfaction in it hesitate to exchange their method for something uncertain. Still others demur for fear of becoming potent and thus transmitting their own weakness to the offspring. Many present psychic impediments that seem insurmountable, or they do not react to hypnotic influence or suggestion, thus rendering treatment futile.

If an individual afflicted with antipathic sexual instinct demands treatment for ethical, social, or any other reasons, surely it cannot be denied him. It is the sacred duty of every medical man to give advice and aid to the best of his ability and knowledge whenever it is asked of him. The health and welfare of the patient must forever be paramount to that of society at large. Hygiene and prophylaxis will always enable him to recompense the community for any damage he may have done in an isolated case.

Furthermore, in the majority of cases, the patient is quite satisfied when he becomes sexually neutral, and under these circumstances medical skill has rendered a notable service to both the individual and society.

five

special pathology

the manifestations of abnormal sexual life in the
various forms and states of mental disturbance

arrest of mental development.

SEXUAL LIFE in idiots is, generally speaking, only slightly developed. It is lacking entirely in idiots of high grade. In such instances the genitals are frequently small and deformed, and menstruation is late or does not occur at all. There is either impotence or sterility. Even in idiots of low grade, sexuality is not prominent. In rare cases it is manifested with a certain periodicity, and then with greater intensity. At such times it may find expression in sudden impulses, and be violently satisfied. Perversions of the sexual instinct do not seem to occur at the lowest levels of mental development.

When, in these cases, the desire for sexual satisfaction is opposed, great passion is excited, and thus arises a danger of murderous assault on the persons attacked. It is to be expected that idiots do not exercise choice, and will even attempt to satisfy the sexual instinct on their nearest relatives.

Thus Marc and Ideler report the case of an idiot who attempted to rape his sister, and had almost strangled her when he was discovered.

Friedreich reports an analogous case (Friedreich's *Blätter*, 1858, p. 50).

I have repeatedly had occasion to give opinions in cases that involved attempts to rape little girls.

Giraud (*Annal. méd. psych.*, 1885, no. 1) also reports a case of this kind. Although consciousness of the significance of the act is always lacking, an instinctive knowledge that such obscene acts are not publicly permitted is often present, causing the act to be undertaken in a deserted place.

In imbeciles the sexual instinct is usually developed as it is in normal individuals. Because the moral inhibitory ideas are cloudy, however, the sexual impulse is more or less openly manifested. For this reason imbeciles are sources of disturbance in society. Abnormal intensity and perversion of the sexual instinct are infrequent.

The most frequent manner of satisfying the sexual desire is masturbation. The weak-minded seldom make sexual attacks on adults of the opposite sex.

Sexual satisfaction with animals is frequently attempted. The great majority of cases of sexual injury to animals must be attributed to imbeciles. In addition, children are quite often their victims.

Emminghaus (Maschka's *Handb.*, vol. 4, p. 234) draws attention to the frequency of unrestricted manifestation of sexual instinct among imbeciles, which comprises open masturbation, exhibition of the genitals, attacks on children and those of the same sex, and sodomy.

Giraud (*Annal. méd. psychol.*, 1855, no. 1) has reported a whole series of immoral attacks on children:[1]

[1] H., aged seventeen; imbecile; enticed a little girl into a barn by giving her nuts. There he exposed her genitals and showed his own, making movements of coitus on the child's abdomen. He had no idea of the moral significance of the act.

[2] L., aged twenty-one; imbecile; degenerate. He was watching cattle when his sister of eleven years and her playmate of eight years came and told him how some unknown man had attempted violence with them. L. led the children to a deserted house and attempted coitus with the younger child. He let her go, however, because emission was unsuccessful and because the child cried out. On the way home he promised to marry her if she would not say anything. At the trial it became clear that he thought he could right the wrong he had done by marriage.

[3] G., aged twenty-one; microcephalic, imbecile; had masturbated since his sixth year, and had practiced active and passive pederasty. He had repeatedly tried to perform pederasty with boys, and had attacked little girls. He was absolutely without an understanding of his acts. His sexual desires were manifested periodically and intensely, as in animals.[2]

[4] B. aged twenty-one; imbecile. While alone in a forest with his sister of nineteen, he demanded that she allow coitus. She refused. He threatened to strangle her and stabbed her with a knife. After the frightened girl wrenched his penis, however, he left her and quietly went on with his work. B. had a deformed, microcephalic skull and no sense of the significance of his act.

Emminghaus (op. cit., p. 234) reports the case of an exhibitionist:

Case 171.

A man, aged forty; married; had for sixteen years exhibited himself in parks, at dusk, to little girls and servants, having drawn their attention by whistling. Although the frequent punishment he received caused him to avoid these places, he carried on his practice elsewhere. Hydrocephalus. Mental weakness of slight degree. Mild sentence passed.

Case 172.

X., from a tainted family; imbecile; defective and perverted in intellect, feeling and will. For help and protection he was brought before an officer. The complaint was that he had repeatedly exposed his genitals to servant girls, and had shown himself at windows with the upper portion of his body naked. No other manifestations of inverted sexual instinct. No masturbation reported (Sander, *Archiv f. Psych.,* vol. 1, p. 655).

Case 173.

Pederasty with a child. On April 8, 1884, at ten o'clock in the morning, while X. was sitting in the street holding a boy of eighteen months on her lap, a certain Vallario approached and took the child from X., saying he was going to take him for a walk. He went the distance of half a kilometer, and when he returned, he said that the child had fallen from his arms and had thus injured his anus. The anus was torn, and blood was pouring from it. At the place where the deed had been done, traces of semen were found. V. confessed his horrible crime. He acted so strangely at his final trial that an examination of his mental condition was made. He had impressed the prison attendants as being an imbecile. V., aged forty-five, mason; defective morally and intellectually; dolichomicrocephalic; narrow, deformed facial bones; the halves of the face and the ears asymmetrical; brow low and retreating; genitals normal. V. showed general diminution of cutaneous sensibility, was imbecilic, and had no ideas. He lived in the present, had no ambition, and did nothing of his own will. He had no desires and no emotional feeling. He had never had coitus. Nothing more could be ascertained about his sex life. Proofs of intellectual and moral idiocy due to microcephaly; the crime was ascribed to a perverse, uncontrollable sexual impulse. Sent to an asylum (Virgilio, *Il Manicomio,* vol. 5, no. 3).

A case mentioned by L. Meyer (*Arch. f. Psych.,* vol. 1, p. 103) shows how female imbeciles may indulge in shameless prostitution and immorality.[3]

states of acquired mental weakness.

The numerous anomalies of the sex life seen in cases of senile dementia have been described in the section on "General Pathology." In other conditions of acquired mental weakness – those due to apoplexy, an injury to the head, the secondary stages of psychoses, or inflammatory processes in the cortex (syphilis, paretic dementia) – perversions of the sexual instinct seem to be infrequent; and here the immoral sexual acts seem to depend on abnormally increased or uninhibited sexual feeling, which is not in itself abnormal.

[1] dementia consecutive to psychoses.

Casper (*Klin. Novellen,* case 31) reports a case that belongs here. It is that of a physician, aged thirty-three, who attempted rape on a child. He was weakened mentally as a result of hypochondriacal melancholia. He excused his deed in a very silly way and had no appreciation of the moral and criminal meaning of the act, which was apparently the result of a sexual impulse that, because of his mental weakness, could not be controlled.

Case 21, in Liman's *Zweifelhafte Geisteszustände,* is an analogous case (dementia after melancholia; offense against morals with exhibitionism).

[2] dementia after stroke.

Case 174.

B., aged fifty-two. After having a cerebral attack, he was no longer able to carry on his business as a merchant.

One day, in the absence of his wife, he locked two girls in the house, gave them liquor to drink, and carried out sexual acts with them. He commanded them to say nothing and left the house. The medical expert established mental weakness, a result of repeated strokes. B., who had previously been well-behaved, said he committed the criminal act because of an uncontrollable and incomprehensible impulse; and that, when he came to himself, he was ashamed and sent the girls away. After his stroke, B. had been weak-minded, incapable of business, and hemiplegic. Soon after his arrest he made an unskillful attempt at suicide. He often cried childishly. His moral and intellectual energy in opposing his sexual impulses was certainly much weakened. No sentence (Giraud, *Annal. méd. psychol.,* March 1881).

[3] dementia after cerebral stroke.

Case 175.

K., at the age of fourteen, was injured on the head by a horse. His skull was fractured in several places, and several pieces of bone required removal.

From that time, K. had been mentally weak, irascible, and ill-tempered. Gradually he developed an inordinate and truly beastly sensuality, which drove him to the most immoral acts. One day he raped a girl of twelve, strangling her from a fear of discovery. Arrested, he confessed. The medical experts declared him responsible, and he was executed.

The autopsy revealed ossification of almost all the sutures, remarkable asymmetry of the halves of the skull, and evidence of healed fractures. The affected hemisphere had bands of scar tissue running through it and was one-third smaller than the other hemisphere (Friedreich's *Blätter,* 1885, no. 6).

[4] acquired mental weakness, probably resulting from syphilis.

Case 176.

X., officer, had repeatedly committed immoral acts with little girls. Among other things, he had induced them to perform masturbation on him, had exposed his genitals, and had handled theirs.

X., formerly healthy and with a blameless life, was infected with syphilis in 1867. In 1879 paralysis of the left abducens nerve occurred. Thereafter mental weakness was noticed, in addition to a change in his disposition and character. Headache, occasional incoherence of speech, failure of power of thought and logic, occasional inequality of pupils, and paresis of the right facial muscles were observed.

X., aged thirty-seven, showed no trace of syphilis when examined. The paralysis of the left abducens nerve was still present. The left eye was amblyopic. He was mentally weak. Concerning the trial before him, he said it was nothing but a harmless misunderstanding. Indications of aphasia. Weakness of memory, particularly for recent events. Superficial emotional reaction; rapid exhaustion of memory and ability to speak. Conclusion: the ethical defect and the perverse sexual impulse were the symptoms of an abnormal condition of the brain induced by syphilis.

Suspension of criminal proceedings (personal case, *Jahrbücher für Psychiatrie*).

[5] paretic dementia.

Here the sexual life is usually abnormally affected; in the incipient stages of the disease, as well as in episodic states of excitement, it is intensified and sometimes perverse. In the final stages, libido and sexual power usually become nonexistent.

Just as in the prodromal stage of the senile forms, one sees here, in connection with more or less evident losses in the moral and intellectual spheres, expressions of an apparently intensified sexual instinct (obscene talk, lasciviousness in intercourse with the opposite sex, thoughts of marriage, frequenting of brothels, etc.), which are characteristic of the clouding of consciousness.

Seduction, abduction and public scandal are the order of the day here. At first there is still some appreciation of the circumstances, though the cynicism of the acts is striking enough. As the mental weakness increases, such patients become criminal because of exhibitionism, masturbation in the streets, and attempts at immoral acts with children.

With the occurrence of conditions of mental excitement, attempts at rape, or, at least, grossly immoral acts are committed; e.g., the patient attacks women on the street, appears in public in a state of imperfect dress; or, half-clothed, tries to force his way into strange houses to cohabit with the wife of an acquaintance, or marry the acquaintance's daughter on the spot.

Numerous cases belonging to this category are cited by Tardieu (*Attentats aux moeurs*); Mendel (*Progr. Paralyse der Irren*, 1880, p. 123); and Westphal (*Archiv f. Psych.*, vol. 7, p. 622). A case by Petrucci (*Annal. méd. psychol.*, 1875) shows that bigamy may also occur here.

Characteristic of this disease is the brutal disregard of consequences with which patients in the advanced stages attempt to satisfy their sexual needs.

In a case reported by Legrand (*La folie*, p. 519), the father of a family was found masturbating in the open street. After the act he consumed his semen.

A patient seen by me, who was an officer from a prominent family, made attacks on little girls at a spa in broad daylight.

A similar case is reported by Dr. Régis (*De la dynamie ou exaltation fonctionelle au début de la paral. gén.*, 1878).

Cases reported by Tarnowsky (op. cit., p. 82) show that pederasty and bestiality can also occur in the prodromal stages and elsewhere in the course of this malady.

epilepsy.

Because epilepsy often leads to acquired states of mental weakness, it is thus allied to them, and therefore all the possibilities of reckless satisfaction of the sexual impulse that have been mentioned may occur. Moreover, in many epileptics the sexual instinct is very intense. It is usually satisfied by masturbation, occasional attacks on children, and pederasty. Perverse sexual acts seem to be infrequent.

Much more important are the numerous cases in literature in which epileptics who present no signs of active sexual impulse between epileptic attacks will manifest them in connection with such attacks, or during the time of equivalent or post-epileptic exceptional mental states. Although these cases have thus far scarcely been studied clinically, and not at all studied forensically, they deserve careful scrutiny. In this way certain cases of violence and rape would be understood, and murders prevented.

It will certainly be clear from the following facts that the cerebral changes accompanying the epileptic outbreak may induce an abnormal excitation of the sexual instinct.[4] Besides, in their exceptional mental states, epileptics are unable to resist their impulses because of the disturbance of consciousness.

A young epileptic of bad heredity, whom I have known for years, always attacks his mother and tries to violate her after his frequent epileptic seizures. After a time he comes to himself, and has no recollection of his acts. In the intervals he is morally strict, with only slight sexual inclination.

Some years ago I became acquainted with a young peasant who masturbated shamelessly during epileptic attacks, but during the intervals was above reproach.

Simon (*Crimes et délits,* p. 220) mentions an epileptic girl of twenty-three, well-educated and of the best morals who, during attacks of vertigo, would shout out obscene words, raise her dress, make lascivious movements, and try to tear open her undergarments.

Kiernan (*Alienist and Neurologist,* January 1884) reports the case of an epileptic who always had, as an aura, the vision of a beautiful woman in lascivious positions, which induced ejaculation. After some years of treatment with potassium bromide, the vision was changed to that of a devil attacking him with a pitchfork. The instant the vision reached him, he became unconscious.

The same author speaks of a respectable man who had epileptic attacks of furor and dysthymic disorder, with impulses to pederasty, two or three times a year for a period of one or two weeks; and of a lady with epilepsy who had a sexual desire for boys that occurred during menopause.

Case 177.

W., of good heredity, previously healthy; he was mentally sound, quiet, kind and temperate before and after his attacks. On April 13, 1877, he had no appetite. The next day, in the presence of his wife and children, he demanded coitus, first of his wife's friend, who was present, then of his wife. Taken away, he had an epileptoid attack, after which he became wildly maniacal and destructive, throwing hot water on those who tried to approach him, and throwing a child in the stove. Although he soon became quiet, for some days he remained confused, and finally came to himself with no recollection of the events of his attack (Kowalewsky, *Jahrbücher f. Psych.*, 1879).

Another case, examined by Caspar (*Klin. Novellen,* p. 267), may be attributed to epilepsy (latent). A respectable man attacked four women, one after another, on the open street (one before two witnesses). He violated one of them, "notwithstanding that his young, pretty and healthy wife" lived nearby.

In the following cases, the epileptic significance of the sexual acts is unequivocal:

Case 178.

L., an official, aged forty; a kind husband and father. Over the course of four years he had offended public morals twenty-five times, for which he had to endure long imprisonment.

In each of the first seven complaints he was accused of exposing his genitals to girls from eleven to thirteen years old while passing them on horseback, having caught their attention with obscene words. During his confinement he exposed his genitals at a window that opened onto a popular street.

L.'s father was insane; his brother was once seen on the street wearing only a shirt. During his military service L. had had two attacks of severe fainting. After 1859 he suffered peculiar attacks of vertigo, in which he was weak, tremulous, and deathly pale. At such times he experienced darkness before his eyes, saw bright stars, and was forced to get support in order to keep upright. After these violent attacks, great weakness, and profuse sweating.

After 1861 he had been very irritable. Respected though he was as an official, this caused him much trouble in his work. His wife noticed the change in him. He had days when he would run about the house as if insane, holding his head between his hands, striking the wall, and complaining of a headache. In 1864 he fell to the ground four times, where he would lay stiff with his eyes open. He had also demonstrated confused states of consciousness.

L. declared that he did not have the slightest memory of the crime of which he had been accused. Observation showed further and more violent attacks of epileptic vertigo. L. was not sentenced. In 1875 paretic dementia rapidly developed with fatal results (Westphal, *Arch. f. Psych.*, vol. 7, p. 113).

Case 179.

A rich man of twenty-six had lived for a year with a girl with whom he was very much in love. Although he cohabited only rarely, he was never perverse.

Twice during the year, after excessive indulgence in alcohol, he had had epileptic attacks. One evening after dinner, when he had taken much wine, he hurried to the house of his mistress and went into her bedroom, although the servant had told him she was not at home. From there he hastened into a room where a boy of fourteen was sleeping, and began to violate him. At the cry of the child, whose foreskin and hand he had injured, the servant rushed to the boy's aid. He left the boy and raped the maid; after that he went to bed and slept twelve hours. When he awoke, he had an indistinct memory of intoxication and coitus. Thereafter he had repeated epileptic attacks (Tarnowsky, op. cit., p. 52).

Case 180.

X., of high social position, for some time led a dissolute life and had epileptic attacks. He became engaged. On his wedding day, shortly before the ceremony, he appeared before the assembled guests on his brother's arm. When he appeared before his bride, he exposed his genitals and began to masturbate. He was at once taken to an expert in mental disease. On the way he constantly masturbated, and for some days was driven by this impulse, which gradually decreased in intensity. After this paroxysm, the patient had only a confused memory of the events, and could give no explanation for his acts (Tarnowsky, op. cit., p. 53).

Case 181.

Z., aged twenty-seven; very bad heredity; epileptic. He violated and killed a girl of eleven, then lied about the deed. Absence of memory, i.e., mental confusion at the time of the crime, was not proved (Pugliese, *Arch. di Psich.,* vol. 8, p. 622).

Case 182.

V., aged sixty, physician; violated children. Sentenced to imprisonment for two years. Dr. Marandon later proved the existence of epileptoid attacks of apprehensiveness, dementia, erotic and hypochondriacal delusions, and occasional attacks of fear (Lacassagne, *Lyon méd.,* 1887, no. 51).

Case 183.

On August 4, 1878, H., aged about fifteen, was picking gooseberries with several little girls and boys. She suddenly threw L., aged nine and a half, to the ground and exposed her, ordering A., aged seven and a half, and O., aged five, to bring about **contact of the genitals** with the girl, which they obeyed.

H. had a good character. For five years she had been subject to irritability, headaches, vertigo and epileptic attacks, which had arrested her mental and physical development. Although she had not menstruated, she manifested menstrual symptoms. Her mother was suspected of being epileptic. For three months, after seizures, H. had frequently done strange things, and had no memory of them afterward.

H. seemed to have been deflowered. Mental defect was not apparent. She said she had no memory of the act of which she had been accused. According to her mother's testimony, she had an epileptic attack on the morning of August 4, and therefore had been told by her mother not to leave the house (Pürkhauer, Friedreich's *Blätter f. ger. Med.,* 1879, no. 5).

Case 184.

Immoral acts of an epileptic in states of abnormal unconsciousness. T., revenue collector; aged fifty-two; married. He was accused of seventeen years of immorality with boys; namely by practicing masturbation on them and by inducing them to carry out the act on himself. A respected officer, the accused was overcome by the terrible crime attributed to him, and declared that he knew nothing of such deeds. His mental integrity was questionable. His family physician of twenty years emphasized his peculiar, retiring disposition and his mercurial moods. His wife asserted that on one occasion, T. tried to throw her in the water, and that he sometimes had outbreaks in which he tore off his clothing and attempted to throw himself out of a window. T. knew nothing of these attacks. Other witnesses testified to strange changes of mood and peculiarities of character. A physician reported observing in him occasional attacks of vertigo and convulsions.

T.'s grandfather was insane; his father was affected with chronic alcoholism and, in recent years, epileptoid attacks. His father's brother was insane and had killed a relative while in a delirious state. Another uncle of T. had killed himself. Of T.'s three children, one was weak-minded, another cross-eyed, and the third subject to convulsions. The accused asserted that he had occasional attacks in which consciousness was reduced to the point that he did not know who he was. These attacks were ushered in by an aura-like pain in the back of his neck. He was then impelled to go outside for air, after which he did not know where he went. His wife had perfectly satisfied him sexually. For eighteen years he had had chronic eczema (actual) of the scrotum, which had often caused him to have extraordinary sexual excitement. The opinions of the six experts were contradictory (ranging from diagnoses of sanity to attacks of latent epilepsy). The jury disagreed, however, and he was dismissed. Dr. Legrand du Saulle, who was called as an expert witness, found that until his twenty-second year T. had urinated in bed from ten to eighteen times a year. Although after that time the nocturnal enuresis had ceased, states of mental confusion, lasting from an hour to a day, had since then occurred occasionally. The patient, however, was left without any memory of them. Soon T. was arrested again for public immorality, and sentenced to imprisonment for fifteen months. In prison he grew sick, and apparently much weaker mentally. For this reason he was pardoned, but the mental weakness increased. T. was considered to have had repeated epileptoid convulsions (tonic convulsion with tremor and loss of consciousness). (Auzouy, *Annal. méd psychol.*, November 1874; Legrand du Saulle, *Etude méd. légale*, etc., p. 99.)

The following cases of immoral acts with children, observed by the author and reported in Friedreich's *Blätter*, will serve to conclude this group,[5] which is so important in its legal bearings. It is all the more important because a state of unconsciousness was established at the time of the act, and because the facts related in Latin [translated, in bold typeface] show how a complicated and refined act becomes possible in such a state of unconsciousness.

Case 185.

P., aged forty-nine; married; hospital beneficiary. He was accused of having committed the following terrible acts with two girls – D., aged ten, and G., aged nine – whom he had taken to his workshop on May 25, 1883.

D. testified: "I was in the meadow with G. and my sister J., aged three. P. called us into his shop and locked the door. **Then he kissed us, tried to put his tongue in my mouth, and licked my face; he held me on his lap, opened his trousers, lifted up my skirt, tickled my genitals with his finger, and rubbed my vulva with his member until I became moist.** When I cried, he gave me twelve kreutzers, and threatened to shoot me if I exposed him. Finally he tried to persuade me to come again the next day."

G. testified: **"P. kissed D.'s buttocks and genitals, and attempted to do the same with me. He then took his young son, three years old, in his arms, kissed him, undressed him, and held the boy against his exposed genitals. Afterward he asked us our names and said that he thought that D.'s genitals were much bigger than mine. He even forced us to look at his member, hold it in our hands, and see how erect it was."**

At his examination on May 29, P. said he had only an indistinct recollection of having fondled, caressed and given presents to a little girl a short time before. If he had done anything more, it must have been in an irresponsible condition. Besides, he had suffered for years with weakness in his head as a result of an injury. On June 22 he knew nothing of the events of May 25, and nothing of his examination on May 29. This amnesia was also shown on cross examination.

P. came from a family affected with cerebral disease; a brother was epileptic. P. had been a drinker. Years ago he actually received an injury to his head. After that he had had occasional attacks of mental disturbance introduced by moroseness, irritability, tendency to alcoholic excesses, apprehension, and delusions of persecution sufficient to induce threats and deeds of violence. At the same time he would have auditory hyperesthesia, vertigo, headache and cerebral congestion, as well as great mental confusion and amnesia for the whole period of the attack, which sometimes lasted for weeks.

During the intervals he was subject to headaches that started from the point of injury on the head (a small scar in the skin over the right temple), which was painful when pressed. With exacerbation of the headache, he would become very irritable and morose, to such an extent that he was suicidal, and mentally like someone drunk. In 1879, while in such a state, he made an impulsive attempt at suicide, about which he later had no memory. Soon after this, having been sent to the hospital, he gave the impression of being epileptic, and for a long time was treated with potassium bromide. At the end of 1879 he was taken to the infirmary; no actual epileptic attack had been observed.

During his lucid intervals he was a virtuous, industrious, good-natured man, and had never shown any sexual excitement. Furthermore, until this time he had never shown any sexual inclinations, even during his mental confusion. Until recently he had lived with his wife. At the time of the criminal act he had shown signs of an approaching attack, and had asked the physician to prescribe potassium bromide.

P. asserted that after the injury to his head he had been intolerant of heat and alcohol, which immediately brought on headaches and confusion. The medical examination proved the truth of his assertions regarding mental weakness, irritability and poor sleep.

If P. felt pressure at the location of the trauma, he became congested, irritable, confused, and trembled all over; he appeared excited, his consciousness was disturbed, and this condition remained like so for hours.

At times, when he was free of the sensations that originated from the scar, he seemed kind, free, willing and open, though he was mentally weak and cloudy. P. was not sentenced (see Friedreich's *Blätter* for full report).

periodic insanity.

Just as in cases of non-periodic mania (see below, "Mania"), an abnormal intensity or a noticeable prominence of the sexual sphere is often manifested in periodic attacks.

The following case, reported by Servaes (*Arch. f. Psych.*), shows that such a sexual manifestation may also be perverted:

Case 186.

Catherine W., aged sixteen. She had not yet menstruated and was previously healthy. Father very irascible.

Seven weeks before admission (on December 3, 1872), melancholic depression and irritability. November 27, maniacal outbreak, lasting two days; thereafter, melancholic. December 6, normal condition.

December 24 (twenty-eight days after the first maniacal attack), silent, shy, depressed. December 27, exaltation (jolly, laughing, etc.), with violent love for attendant (female). December 31, sudden melancholic catalepsy, which disappeared after two hours. January 20, 1873, a new attack resembling the previous one. A similar one on February 18, with traces of menses. The patient had no recollection whatsoever for what occurred during the paroxysms; she blushed scarlet with astonishment and shame when she was told about them.

Subsequently there were abortive attacks, which entirely disappeared in June and were replaced by a normal mental condition.

In a case of probable circular insanity reported by Gock (*Arch. f. Psych.*, vol. 5), a man of very bad heredity manifested a sexual feeling for men during a state of exaltation. Because the patient thought himself a girl, however, it is questionable whether the sexual inclination was induced by the delusion or by an antipathic sexual instinct.

In connection with such cases of abnormal manifestation of the sexual instinct are those that manifest, as a symptom of mania, an abnormal and often perverse sexual instinct in an impulsive way, analogous to dipsomania; although, in the intervals, the sexual instinct is neither intense nor perverse.

The following is a genuine case of such periodic *psychopathia sexualis* connected with the process of menstruation, reported by Anjél (*Arch. f. Psych.*, vol. 15, no. 2):

Case 187.

A quiet lady, near menopause. Very bad heredity. In her youth, attacks of petit mal. Always eccentric, quick-tempered; very moral; childless marriage.

Several years ago, after a violent emotional disturbance, she had a hystero-epileptic attack with post-epileptic insanity of several weeks' duration. Subsequently there was sleeplessness for several months. Following this was menstrual insomnia, as well as an impulse to embrace, kiss, and fondle the genitals of ten-year-old boys. During this excitement there was no desire for coitus; certainly not for intercourse with adults.

The patient often spoke openly of this impulse and asked to be watched, as she was not to be trusted. During the intervals she anxiously avoided all talk of it, was very modest, and not at all passionate sexually.

With reference to the still imperfectly known cases of periodic *psychopathia sexualis* of this kind, Tarnowsky (op. cit., p. 38) had made valuable contributions, though his cases were not all of a periodic nature.

Tarnowsky reports cases where married, cultured men, who were the fathers of families, were occasionally compelled to perform the most terrible sexual acts; although during the intervals they were sexually normal, abhorred their paroxysmal sexual acts, and shuddered before the expectation of their repetition.

If a new paroxysm came on, the normal sexual instinct disappeared; a state of mental excitement arose, and with it insomnia, thoughts and impulses to commit perverse sexual acts, anxious confusion, and an increasing impulse to the abhorred indulgence. In this state the act was a relief, because it ended the condition. The analogy with dipsomania is complete.

For other cases (of periodic pederasty), see Tarnowsky, op. cit., p. 41. The case reported there, on page 46, belongs in the category of epilepsy.

The following case, reported by Anjél (*Arch. f. Psych.*, vol. 15, no. 2), is one of the most typical of the convulsive-like occurrence of sexual excitement:

Case 188.

A gentleman of high social position, aged forty-five; generally respected and beloved; heredity good; very moral; married fifteen years. Previously normal sexually, the father of several healthy children, and in a happy marriage. Eight years ago he had a sudden fright. For some weeks thereafter he had an apprehension of cardiac attacks. Then came attacks, at intervals of several months to a year, of what the patient called his "moral catarrh." He became sleepless. Three days later, loss of appetite, increasing irritability, strange appearance; fixed stare, staring into space; paleness that alternated with redness; tremor of his fingers; red, shining eyes with a peculiar glassy expression; and violent, quick manner of speech. There was a desire for girls from five to ten years old; even for his own daughters. He would beg his wife to guard the children. He would shut himself in his room for days at a time while in this state. Previously he had been compelled to pass schoolgirls on the street, finding a peculiar pleasure in exposing his genitals before them by acting as if he was about to urinate.

Out of a fear of exposure, he shut himself in his room. He was morose, incapable of movement, and torn by feelings of fear. Consciousness seemed to be undisturbed. The attacks lasted from eight to fourteen days. The cause of their return was not clear. Improvement was sudden, at which time there was a great desire for sleep. After this was satisfied, he was well again. In the interval there was nothing abnormal. Anjél assumed an epileptic foundation, and considered the attacks to be the psychic equivalents of epileptic convulsions.

mania.

With the general excitation that exists here in the psychic organ, the sexual sphere is likewise often implicated. For maniacal females, this is the rule. In certain cases, it may be questionable whether the instinct, which is not in itself intensified, is simply recklessly manifested or present in actual abnormal intensity. The latter is usually the correct assumption – certainly so when sexual delusions and their religious equivalents are constantly expressed. In accordance with the degrees of the disease's intensity, the intensified instinct is expressed in different forms.

Observation of simple maniacal exaltation in men reveals courting, frivolity, lasciviousness in speech, and frequenting of brothels. Women show an inclination for the society of men, personal adornment, perfumes, talk of marriage and scandals, and suspicion of the virtue of other women. There is, on the other hand, the religious equivalent – pilgrimages, missionary work, desire to become a monk or the servant of a priest; and in this case there is much talk about innocence and virginity.

At the height of mania there may be seen invitations to engage in coitus, exhibitionism, obscenity, great excitation at the sight of women, a tendency to smear the body with saliva, urine, and even feces; religio-sexual delusions (of being under the protection of the Holy Ghost, having given birth to Christ, etc.); as well as open masturbation and pelvic movements of coitus.

In maniacal men care must be taken to prevent shameless masturbation and sexual attacks on women.

nymphomania and satyriasis.[6]

The description of these conditions is simply an addendum to the attempt made on page 70 to explain sexual hyperesthesia, insofar as we take into consideration temporary sexual affects emanating therefrom, whether they are occasioned by abstinence or are of a permanent character. They may become so predominant that they completely sway the field of imagination and desire, and imperatively demand the relief of the affect in the corresponding sexual act. Although in acute and severe cases ethics and willpower lose their controlling influence entirely, in chronic and milder cases restraint is still possible to a certain degree. At the acme of the paroxysm, hallucinations, delirium and benumbed consciousness make their appearance, and often continue during a prolonged period.

Such cases have led to the classification of nymphomania as a proper psychic disease. This is an error, however, for nymphomania is only a syndrome within the sphere of psychic degeneration. As such, it may manifest itself as an *acute paroxysmic* condition, analogous to dipsomania, that frequently coincides with menstrual phases, recurring either in stated periodic cycles or at irregular intervals. Or it may be a complication or combination of other conditions, and appear episodically in senile dementia, menopausal psychosis, mania in degenerates, and acute delirium ("acute deadly nymphomania").

Moreau (op. cit.) reports an interesting case. A young girl suddenly became a nymphomaniac after being forsaken by her betrothed; she reveled in cynical songs and expressions, as well as lascivious attitudes and gestures. She refused to put on her garments, had to be held down in bed by muscular men (!), and furiously demanded coitus. Insomnia, congestion of the facial nerves, a dry tongue, and rapid pulse. Within a few days lethal collapse.

Louyer-Villermay (op. cit.): Miss X., aged thirty; modest and decent, she was suddenly seized with an attack of nymphomania, with an unlimited desire for sexual gratification and obscene delirium. Death from exhaustion within a few days. Cf. three other cases with deadly results by Maresch, *Psychiatr. Zentralblatt,* 1871.

Although *chronic nymphomania* is more frequently seen, it seems to occur only in individuals who are psychically degenerated. It is the result of sexual hyperesthesia and exacerbations thereof, and extends even to the state of sexual affects that manifest themselves in impulsive acts or, in milder cases, are complicated with delusions. These, however, do not necessarily lead to involuntary acts, inasmuch as ethical considerations may counterbalance the milder forms of sexual excitement, and because recourse to solitary masturbation as a means of temporary relief is here always possible.

These milder cases of nymphomania claim our sympathy no less than those unfortunate women who, because of irresistible impulses, are forced to sacrifice feminine honor and dignity; for even such milder cases are fully conscious of their painful situation. They are a toy in the grip of a morbid imagination that revolves solely around sexual ideas and grasps even the most distant points as an aphrodisiac. Even in their sleep they are pursued by lascivious dreams. In the daytime the slightest stimulus will produce a crisis in which they are tormented by a veritable cerebro-sexual hyperirritability coupled with painful sensations (pressure, vibration, pulsation, etc.) in the genitals. Temporary relief comes eventually in the form of genital neurasthenia, which reacts promptly on the center of ejaculation and readily causes pollutions in lascivious dreams, or in the form of some erotic crisis when awake. They cannot find full gratification, however, any more than their unfortunate fellow sufferers who abandon themselves to men. This frigidity explains to a large extent the persistence of the sexual affect; i.e., a nymphomania that heaps crisis upon crisis.

Sexual neurasthenia, which inhibits orgasm and sensual gratification, no doubt fully explains the frigidity that restrains the beneficent assuagement of sexual emotions while it maintains an incessant craving (insatiable libido) that forces the woman, who is now morally devoid of all power of resistance, to auto-masturbation or psychic masturbation, and eventually (as a nymphomaniac) to prostitution, where satisfaction and relief is found with one man after another.

This neurasthenia is often caused by an abnormally early and powerful sexual instinct that prescribes masturbation; or it may be reduced to an enforced continence that coexists with a strong sexual appetite.

Case 189.

Mrs. V.; from earliest youth, mania for men. Of good ancestry, highly cultured, good-natured, very modest, blushed easily, but always terrified of her family. **When she was alone with a person of the opposite sex, unconcerned whether he was a child, in the prime of life, or an old man, handsome or repulsive, she would immediately undress and either violently demand sexual satisfaction or attack him.** She resorted to marriage as a cure. **She loved her husband very much, but was unable to restrain herself from demanding coitus from any male she happened to find alone, whether he was a friend, laborer or schoolboy.**

Nothing could cure her of this failing. Even when she was a grandmother, she still remained a nymphomaniac. **She once enticed a boy of twelve into her bedroom, determined to violate him.** He tore himself away and fled, and his brother gave her a severe punishment. But it was all in vain. Upon being sent to a convent, she was a model of good conduct, and committed not the slightest act of indiscretion. The moment she returned home, however, she resumed her perverse practices. The family sent her away, giving her a small allowance. She worked hard to earn the money she needed for "buying her lovers." One would never suspect, when looking at the trim, neat matron of sixty-five years of age, with her modest manners and most amiable disposition, how shamelessly needy she was, even then, in her sexual life.

At last she was sent to an insane asylum, where she lived until May 1858, when in her seventy-third year she succumbed to a stroke of cerebral apoplexy. Although her behavior at the asylum while under surveillance was beyond reproach, if left to herself she utilized every opportunity in the same old fashion, even to within a few days before her death. No other signs of mental anomaly could be detected (Trelat, *Folie lucide*).

Case 190.

Chronic nymphomania. Mrs. E., aged forty-seven. An uncle on father's side insane. Father suffered from self-conceit and was given to sexual excess. A brother died from acute cerebral inflammation. Always nervous, eccentric and erotic, she began coitus at the age of ten. Married at nineteen. Although her husband was virile, she maintained a number of male friends. Fully conscious of the abominable nature of her conduct, she was powerless in restraining her insatiable appetite. She kept up appearances, however. Later she claimed that she had suffered from a "monomania for men."

She had six confinements. One day she was thrown from a carriage and sustained a brain concussion. This caused melancholia and persecutory paranoia. With approaching menopause, her menses became frequent and profuse, but her libido gradually disappeared. Slight degree of descended uterus and prolapsed anus.

Chronic conditions of nymphomania are apt to weaken public morality and lead to offenses against decency. Woe unto the man who falls into the meshes of such an insatiable nymphomaniac, whose sexual appetite is never appeased. Heavy neurasthenia and impotence are the inevitable consequences. These unfortunate women disseminate a spirit of lewdness, demoralize their surroundings, become a danger to boys, and are also liable to corrupt girls, for there are homosexual nymphomaniacs as well.[7] They lure men by exposing their feminine charms, even with exhibitionism. Nymphomaniacs endowed with the world's riches purchase lovers. In many instances they resort to prostitution.

The conditions of *satyriasis* in men are analogous to nymphomania. It is a central disturbance, either of an acute or chronic character. In the acute stage it may lead to hallucinations of erotic content, or to furious mania and acute delirium, where compensation of the sexual affect is rendered impossible.

This pathological sexual affect, stigmatized by its abnormal intensity and duration, fills the entire psychic life. Occurrences of the most common and indifferent nature are taken as sensual hints or suggestions. The lustful coloring of thoughts, ideas, or natural sensual perceptions is strongly exaggerated. At the acme of the crisis the patient is in a "rut-like" condition, in which consciousness is clouded and a general physical excitement, similar to what is experienced during coitus (cf. p. 40), pervades the entire body. Ejaculation may be linked with a renewed phase of orgasm in which the genital organs retain a permanent turgescence (priapism). The individual afflicted with satyriasis is forever exposed to the peril of committing rape, and thus becomes a danger to all persons of the opposite sex. For lack of anything better he resorts to masturbation and sodomy. Luckily, satyriasis is a rare disease. It is not due to poisoning with cantharides, as some claim, which only produces priapism; that is, though cantharides initially cause erotic sensations and erection, after repeated doses they produce the opposite effect.

Analogous with nymphomania, mild chronic conditions of a mild satyriasis exist in men (chiefly after sexual abuse) who, although they suffer from sexual neurasthenia, masturbation and subsequent impotence, are still the slaves of an insatiable libido. The imagination (as in acute cases) is highly excited and consciousness is completely filled with obscene pictures and situations. For these men, the whole train of thought and the entire realm of desire is directed to sexual matters. Impotence and frigidity, assisted by perverse fantasies, lead them to the worst perversities possible in the sexual act and render them particularly dangerous to children. They give offense by practicing exhibitionism, masturbation, and sexual acts with persons of the other sex in public. They are lascivious in speech, revel in filthy language, etc.

Mild satyriasis is often observed in the incipient stages of paralytic dementia and senility.

Case 191.

Satyriasis. Acute delirium due to abstinence. On May 29, 1882, F., aged twenty-three, unmarried, cobbler, was received at the psychiatric clinic at Graz. Father irascible, mother neuropathic, uncle on mother's side insane.

Patient had never had a severe illness, was not addicted to drink, but was sexually very needy. Five days previously he had been attacked with an acute psychic disease. In broad daylight, and in the presence of two witnesses, he made two separate attempts at rape; he went into a fit of delirium, raved about obscene matters when arrested, constantly masturbated, and became a raving maniac with violent motoric irritability and fever. Treatment with ertogamine brought relief.

On January 5, 1888, he was arrested again in a fit of raving mania. The day before he had been morose, irritable, squeamish, and sleepless. He became furious when foiled in two assaults on women. On January 6 his condition became very much aggravated; heavy acute delirium (disturbance of consciousness, jactation, grinding of teeth, facial contortions and other motoric manifestations, temperature 40.7° C). Masturbation as if by instinct. Recovery under treatment with ertogamine until January 11.

When again restored to health, he gave some interesting details about his illness.

His sexual needs had always been great. Coitus at sixteen. Continence caused headaches, great psychic irritability, dislike for work, laziness, sleeplessness. When he had no opportunity for coitus, he resorted to masturbation once or twice daily.

For two months he did not have sexual intercourse. As sexual excitement increased, masturbation failed as a means of compensation, although the desire for coitus became more vehement than ever. At the acme of the attack his memory failed him. In his normal state he was a decent man who looked upon his state as a pathological condition that filled him with alarm for his future.

Case 192.

On the afternoon of July 7, 1874, C., engineer, while traveling on business from Trieste to Vienna, left the train at the town of Bruck, and, as he passed through the town to the neighboring village of St. Ruprecht, attempted to rape an old woman, aged seventy, whom he found alone in a house. He was seized by the neighbors and arrested by the local police. At his hearing he declared that he had tried to find the dog pound in order to satisfy his sexual desire with a bitch. He said that he often suffered from such sexual excitement. He did not deny his act, but excused it as the result of disease. The heat, the motion of the cars, and an anxiety about being away from his family had confused him and made him ill. Shame and remorse were not shown. His conduct was open, his mien gay; eyes red and bright, head hot, tongue coated; pulse full, soft, beating over one hundred; fingers somewhat tremulous. The statements of the accused were precise but hurried; his glance was uncertain, with an unmistakable expression of lasciviousness. He gave the medical expert summoned to examine him an impression of one suffering from disease – as if he were in the beginning of alcoholic insanity.

C. was forty-five years old, married, father of one child. He did not know what diseases had afflicted his parents or other members of his family. In childhood he was weak and neuropathic. At the age of five his head had been injured by a blow with a hoe. A scar one-half centimeter broad by one centimeter long, situated on the right parietal and frontal bones, dated from that injury. The bone here was somewhat depressed. The overlying skin was united to the bone. Pressure at this point caused pain, which radiated along the lower branch of the trigeminus. This spot was also at times spontaneously painful. In his youth he suffered "fainting spells"; before puberty, pneumonia, rheumatism and intestinal catarrh. At the age of seven he experienced a peculiar inclination for men – i.e., for a certain superior. Whenever he saw this man he had a peculiar feeling in his heart; he kissed the ground he walked on. At ten he fell in love with a certain deputy. Later he had an enthusiasm for men, though it was entirely platonic. He began to masturbate at the age of fourteen; first intercourse at seventeen. The earlier manifestations of inverted sexual feeling then disappeared entirely. At that time he passed through a peculiar acute psychopathic condition, which he described as a kind of clairvoyance. At fifteen, hemorrhoids, with symptoms of abdominal plethora. After profuse hemorrhoidal hemorrhage, which usually occurred every three or four weeks, he was better. At other times, he was constantly in a condition of painful sexual excitement, which he satisfied partly by masturbation and partly by coitus. Every woman he met excited him; even when, among female relatives, he was impelled to make indecent proposals. Sometimes it was possible for him to master his desire; sometimes he was driven to indecent acts. Subsequent ejection from the household seemed perfectly right to him, because he thought he needed such correction and support against his powerful and burdensome impulse. No periodicity in this sexual excitement was recognizable.

Until 1861 he committed excesses in sexual intercourse and was infected several times with gonorrhea and chancres. In 1861, marriage. Although he was sexually satisfied, he became a burden to his wife because of his great sensuality. In 1864 he had an attack of mania in the hospital at Fiume. During the same year he again fell ill, and was taken to the insane asylum at Ybbs, where he remained until 1867. There he suffered from recurrent mania accompanied by great sexual excitement. He said that intestinal catarrh and anxiety were the causes of his illness at that time.

Thereafter he was well, but suffered a great deal because of his excessive sexual desire. Even a short absence from his wife caused his impulse to become so powerful that man and animal were the same for the satisfaction of his lust. In summer these impulses were much stronger and were always accompanied by abdominal plethora. Something he remembered from medical reading made him think that in his case the ganglionic system was more powerful than the cerebral. In October 1873, on account of business, he had to leave his wife. From that time until Easter, with the exception of occasional masturbation, there was no sexual indulgence. After that he made use of women as well as bitches. From the middle of June until July 7, he had no opportunity for sexual indulgence. He felt nervously excited, relaxed, and as if he were going crazy. Lately he had slept badly. A longing for his wife, who lived in Vienna, drove him to leave his business. He obtained a leave of absence. The heat and the noise of the train confused him, and he could no longer hold out against his sexual excitement and the pressure of blood in his abdomen. Everything danced before his eyes. He left the train at Bruck, and was absolutely confused, not knowing where he went. For a moment the thought came to him to throw himself in the water; everything appeared as in a mist before his eyes. He then saw a woman, exposed his genitals, and tried to embrace her. She cried for help, and he was thus arrested.

After the attempt it suddenly became clear to him what he had done. He openly confessed his crime, which he remembered in all its details, but which seemed to him to be something abnormal. He said he could not help it. For some days after this, C. suffered from headaches and congestions, was occasionally excited and restless, and slept badly. Although his mental functions were undisturbed, he was, nevertheless, a congenitally peculiar man, with a character that was weak and devoid of energy. His facial expression had something lascivious and peculiar about it. He suffered from hemorrhoids. His genitals presented nothing abnormal. The cranium was narrow and retreating at the forehead. Body large and well-nourished. With the exception of diarrhea, there was no disturbance of the vegetative functions.

Case 193.

For three years D., farmer, much respected, married, aged thirty-five, had manifested states of sexual excitement with increasing frequency and severity that had become true paroxysms of satyriasis during the past year. It was impossible to discover hereditary or other organic causes. D. was occasionally compelled, when his sexual excitement was excessive, to perform the sexual act from ten to fifteen times in twenty-four hours, without deriving any feeling of satisfaction. Gradually he developed a condition of general nervous hyperirritability (general erethism) with increased emotional irritability, to the extent of pathological outbreaks of anger and an impulse to overindulge in alcohol, which induced symptoms of alcoholism. His attacks of satyriasis became so violent that they interfered with his consciousness; the patient raged about, blindly and impulsively engaging in sexual acts. He demanded that his wife give herself to other men or to animals in his presence; that she allow copulation with him **in the presence of his daughters,** because this would afford him greater enjoyment. Memory of the events of these attacks, in which the extreme irritability even led to outbreaks of maniacal rage, was entirely lacking. D. himself thought that he must have had moments in which he no longer had control of his senses, and where, without satisfaction from his wife, he would have been compelled to seize the next best female. After an attack of violent emotion, these attacks of sexual excitement suddenly disappeared (Lenz, *Bulletin de la société de méd. mentale de Belgique,* no. 21).

melancholia.

The thoughts and feelings of melancholiacs do not favor the excitation of sexual desires. At the same time, these patients sometimes masturbate. In my experience, such cases have always been hereditarily predisposed and previously given to masturbation. The act does not seem to be so much due to a lustful desire as it is when induced by habit, ennui, anxiety, and an impulse to temporarily change the painful mental condition.

hysteria.

In this neurosis the sexual life is frequently abnormal; indeed, in predisposed individuals it is always abnormal. All the possible anomalies of the sexual function may occur here, with sudden changes and peculiar activity. Furthermore, on a degenerate hereditary basis and in moral imbecility, these anomalies may appear in the most perverse forms. The abnormal change and inversion of the sexual feeling are never without effect upon the patient's disposition.

The following case, reported by Giraud, is one of this nature that is worthy of repeating:

Case 194.

Marianne L., of Bordeaux. At night, while the household was asleep under the influence of narcotics that she had administered, she gave the children of the house to her lover for sexual enjoyment, and also made them witness immoral acts. It was found that L.

was hysterical (hemianesthesia and convulsive attacks), although before her illness she had been a moral, trustworthy person. Since her illness she had become a shameless prostitute and had lost all moral sense.

In the hysterical the sexual sphere is often abnormally excited. This excitement may be intermittent (menstrual?). Shameless prostitution, even in married women, may result. In a milder form the sexual impulse expresses itself in masturbation, walking around in a room naked, smearing the body with urine and other filthy substances, wearing male attire, etc.

Schüle (*Klin. Psychiatrie*, 1886, p. 237) frequently finds an abnormally intense sexual impulse "that disposes girls and even happily married women to become nymphomaniacs."

The author cites known cases in which brides made attempts to flee with men they had accidentally met during the honeymoon; in addition, there are cases where respected wives entered into liaisons and sacrificed everything to their insatiable impulse.

In hysterical insanity, the abnormally intense sexual impulse may express itself in delusions of jealousy, unfounded accusations against men for immoral acts,[8] hallucinations of coitus,[9] etc.

Occasionally frigidity may occur, with an absence of lustful feeling. This is usually due to genital anesthesia.

paranoia.

In the various forms of paranoia, abnormal manifestations in the sexual sphere are not infrequent. Many of these cases develop because of sexual abuse (masturbatory paranoia) or sexual excitement. Furthermore, experience has shown that in psychically degenerated individuals who have other functional signs of degeneracy, the sexual sphere is usually deeply implicated.

In religious and erotic paranoia the abnormally intense and, under certain circumstances, perverse sexual instinct is most clearly manifested. In religious paranoia, however, the condition of sexual excitation is expressed not so much through a direct satisfaction of the sexual desires as (there are exceptions) through platonic love; i.e., an enthusiastic admiration of a person of the opposite sex who is aesthetically pleasing. Under certain circumstances, the enthusiasm is for an imaginary person, a portrait, or a statue.

A love for the opposite sex that is weak and purely mental also often has its basis in a weakness of the genitals resulting from long-continued masturbation. Furthermore, under the guise of virtuous admiration for a beloved person, great lasciviousness and sexual perversion are often concealed. Episodically, especially in women, violent sexual excitement can occur as nymphomania.

Religious paranoia typically rests upon sexuality that manifests itself in an abnormally early and intense sexual impulse. The libido finds satisfaction in masturbation or religious enthusiasm, the object of which may be, for example, a certain minister or saint.

The psychopathological relations between the sexual and religious domains have been described in detail on p. 10 et seq.

Apart from masturbation, sexual crimes are relatively frequent in religious paranoia.

Marc's work (*Uebers*, with Ideler, vol. 2, p. 160) contains a remarkable example of religious insanity. Giraud (*Annal. méd. psychol.*) has reported a case of immorality with a little girl by a religious paranoiac, aged forty-three, who was temporarily erotic. A case of incest also belongs here (Liman, *Vierteljahrsschrift f. ger. Med.*).

Case 195.

M. impregnated his daughter. His wife, mother of eighteen children, and herself pregnant by her husband, lodged the complaint. M. had had religious paranoia for two years. "It was revealed to me that I should beget the Eternal Son with my daughter. Then a man of flesh and blood would arise by my faith, who would be 1800 years old. He would be a bridge between the Old and the New Testament." This command, which he deemed divine, was the cause of his insane act.

Sexual acts that have a pathological motive occasionally occur in states of persecutory paranoia.

Case 196.

A woman of thirty enticed a boy of five who played near her with a promise of money and food. She handled his genitals and attempted coitus. She was a teacher who had been betrayed and then cast off. Although previously moral, for some time after this she had given herself to prostitution. The explanation given for her immoral change was that she had various delusions of persecution, and thought she was under the secret influence of her seducer, who impelled her to engage in sexual acts.

She also believed that the boy had been put in her way by her seducer. Coarse sensuality as a motive for her crime was given less consideration, as it would have been easier for her to satisfy her sexual desire in a natural way (Küssner, *Berl. klin. Wochenschrift*).

Case 197.

Immoral acts with children – paranoia. On May 26, X., aged forty-six, railway official, was arrested in the act of sucking the penis of an eight-year-old boy on the public highway. On the way to prison he committed the same offense on a fellow prisoner, who was riding in the same vehicle with him. Later he attacked another prisoner. He was sent to the psychiatric ward of the hospital, where he made similar attempts. He was then isolated.

The medical examination proved persecutory paranoia, developed from constitutional neurasthenia. X. was heavily tainted by heredity. His illusion was that the administration under which he had served had been persecuting him and had tried to force him to resume his former duties. He had noticed that persons who were friendly to him, especially his superiors, tried to show him a way in which he could rid himself of this fear of persecution. They did so by putting a finger in their mouth and sucking it. Still plainer were the suggestions of his buddies who, while pointing to a dog (meaning himself), spoke of "licking." This started the idea in him that if he could be apprehended in the act of licking somebody's genitals, his superiors would become disgusted with him and dismiss him from service, in which way he would regain his freedom.

Although for a long time he could not muster up the courage to commit such an act, the idea became so strong that at first he resorted to cunnilingus with prostitutes, who invited him with cunning looks to this delectable feast. Because these women, however, refused to denounce him to the authorities, he then attacked boys and girls – the sex was immaterial – who, he imagined, invited him to engage in the act with gestures. He could not understand why he should come in conflict with the police by committing an act that had been suggested to him by his superiors – and all this in spite of the continued persecution of the railway administration.

It is strange that X. should have had recourse to such an abominable and nauseating sexual act and not to theft or some other act of dishonesty, unless it is explained on the basis of an increasing neurasthenia, coupled with a perversion of the sexual instinct and subsequent impotence. He was always hypersexual with a heterosexual predisposition, suffered for years from sexual neurasthenia, and derived no satisfaction from coitus. As erection became difficult over time, he consulted several physicians who advised abstinence. His excessive libido rendered it difficult to follow this advice, and impotence prevented coitus. This suggested cunnilingus, which granted a certain amount of sexual gratification and at times even produced ejaculation. This also compensated him for the nausea he experienced during the act and paved the way to his folly with children.

Although he claimed that he found sexual satisfaction in this act, the chief object for it was always to rid himself of persecution by his superiors. This passion calmed down under treatment at the hospital, and he became a decent man when put under domestic supervision.

Cullerre ("Perversions sexuelles chez les persécutés," in *Annal. médico-psychol.,* March 1886) has reported similar cases. One involved a patient who, suffering from persecutory sexual paranoia, tried to violate his sister, giving as a reason that the impulse had been given to him by Bonapartists.

In another case, a captain suffering from delusions of persecution by electromagnetism was driven to pederasty – a thing he abhorred. In a similar case, the persecutor impelled the patient to engage in masturbation and pederasty.

pathological sexuality in its legal aspects[1]

THE LAWS of all civilized nations punish those who commit perverse sexual acts. Inasmuch as the preservation of chastity and morals is one of the most important reasons for the existence of the commonwealth, the state cannot be too careful as a protector of morality in the struggle against sensuality. This contest, however, is unequal. Only a certain number of the sexual crimes can be combated legally, and the infractions of the laws by so powerful a natural instinct can be influenced only slightly by punishment. It also lies in the nature of the sexual crimes that only a fraction of them ever reaches the knowledge of the authorities. Public sentiment, in that it looks upon them as disgraceful, lends much aid.

Criminal statistics prove the sad fact that sexual crimes are progressively increasing in our modern civilization.[2] This is particularly the case for immoral acts with children who are under the age of fourteen.

In the early 1860s, Casper (*Klinische Novellen*) drew attention to this deplorable fact. As a criminal physician (Berlin), he had 52 cases of crimes against morality under observation from 1842-51, but during the decade of 1852-61 the number had risen to 138.

According to the *Comptes rendus de la justice criminelle en France,* although during the period of 1826-40 *"attentats aux moeurs"* ("crimes against morality") formed only 20 percent of the criminal proceedings, from 1856-60 the average rose to 53 percent. Sexual atrocities on children were only one-thirteenth of all cases tried before the criminal forum from 1826-30, but were one-third of all cases during the period of 1856-60.

Oettingen (*Moralstatistik*) quotes 136 cases of rape on children committed in France in 1826, but 805 in 1867.

For the year 1872, Moreau (*Aberrations du sens génésique*) quotes 682 cases of immoral attacks on children in France; for the year 1876, the number had increased to 875.

In England, similar offenses on children numbered 167 for the period 1830-34, and 1395 for the period 1855-57.

In Prussia, according to Oettingen, sexual attempts were in the proportion of 325:925; sexual crimes in the proportion of 1477:2945. Ortloff also finds (*Die strafbaren Handlungen*) a considerable increase in immoral offenses on children under the age of fourteen. We are indebted to Thoinot for interesting statistics of moral offenses dealt with by the criminal courts of France (*Attentats aux moeurs et perversions du sens génital,* 1898, Paris). Sexual criminal cases seem to be on the wane in France. In 1860 there were 830 (2.3 to a population of 100,000) offenders sentenced; in 1892 only 679 (1.7 to a population of 100,000). The proportion of crimes committed on adults and children in 1860 was 180:650 (1:3.6), while in 1892 it fell to 78:601 (1:7.7). In 1885 it reached the lowest point, 1:9.5.

The moralist sees in these sad facts nothing but the decay of general morality, and in some instances can come to the conclusion that, in comparison with the severity of the laws punishing sexual crimes in past centuries, the laws' present mildness is partly responsible for this.

The medical investigator is driven to the conclusion that this manifestation of modern social life stands in relation to the predominating nervous condition of later generations, in that it begets defective individuals, excites the sexual instinct, leads to sexual abuse and, where the continuance of lasciviousness is associated with diminished sexual power, induces perverse sexual acts.

The following discussion will clearly demonstrate how such an opinion is justified, especially with respect to the increasing number of sexual crimes committed on children.

The relative increase of sexual offenses on children seems to point to an advance in the physical decadence (impotence) and psychic degeneration of the adult population.

This view seems to be supported by Tardieu, Brouardel and Bernard, who find that attacks on children are more frequent in large cities, while those on adults, especially rape, occur more often in the country.

The statistical facts compiled by Tardieu and Brouardel, according to which the proportion of sexual offenses on children is in ratio with the age of the offender – i.e., the older the criminal the younger the victim – as well as the factor that acts of immorality by very old men are only committed on children, seem to demonstrate that coital impotence and moral decay (senile dementia) are the fundamental causes of these horrible crimes.

From the foregoing it is immediately evident that neuropathic and even psychopathic states largely determine the commission of sexual crimes. Thus, nothing less than the responsibility of many of the men who commit such crimes is here called into question.

Psychiatry cannot be denied the credit of having recognized and proved the psychopathological significance of numerous monstrous, paradoxical sexual acts.

Law and Jurisprudence have thus far given only scant attention to the facts resulting from investigations in psychopathology. In this, Law is opposed to Medicine, and is constantly in danger of passing judgment on individuals who, in the light of science, are not responsible for their acts.

Due to this superficial treatment of acts that deeply concern the interests and welfare of society, it becomes very easy for justice to treat a delinquent (as dangerous to society as a murderer or a wild beast) as a criminal, and, after punishment, to release him to prey on society again. On the other hand, scientific investigation shows that a man who is mentally and sexually degenerate from birth, and therefore irresponsible, must be removed from society for life, but not as a form of punishment.

A judge who only considers the crime and not its perpetrator is always in danger of injuring not only important interests of society (general morality and safety), but also those of the individual (honor).

In no domain of criminal law is cooperation of judge and medical expert so much to be desired as it is in that of sexual delinquencies; and here only anthropological and clinical investigation can provide illumination and knowledge.

The *nature of the act* can never, in itself, determine whether it lies within the limits of mental pathology or within the bounds of mental physiology. *The perverse act does not, per se, indicate perversion of instinct.* At any rate, the most monstrous and most perverse sexual acts have been committed by persons of sound mind. *The perversion of feeling must be shown to be pathological.* This proof is obtained by learning the conditions attending its development, and by proving its role in an existing general neuropathic or psychopathic condition.

Although the form of the act is important, it, too, allows only presumptions, inasmuch as the same sexual act committed by an epileptic, a paralytic, or a man of sound mind, respectively, takes on other features and peculiarities in accordance with the manner in which it is done.

Periodic recurrence of the act under identical circumstances, as well as an impulsive manner in carrying it out, give rise to weighty presumptions that it is of pathological significance. The decision, however, must follow a referral of the act to its psychological motive (abnormalities of thought and feeling), as well as a demonstration that this elementary anomaly is but one symptom of a general neuropathic condition – either an arrest of mental development, a condition of psychic degeneration, or a psychosis.

The cases discussed in the portion of this work devoted to general and special pathology will certainly be useful to the medical expert in assisting his discovery of the motive of the act.

To obtain the facts that are necessary to decide whether immorality or abnormality occasioned the act, a medico-legal examination is required. Such an examination is made according to the rules of science, and takes account of both the past history of the individual and the present condition; i.e., the anthropological and clinical data.

Proof of the existence of an *original,* congenital anomaly of the sexual sphere is important, and points to the need for an examination in the direction of a condition of psychic degeneration. An *acquired* perversity, to be pathological, must be found to depend upon a neuropathic or psychopathic state.

Practically, paretic dementia and epilepsy must first come to mind. The decision concerning responsibility will depend on a demonstration of the existence of a psychopathic state in the individual charged with a sexual crime.

This is indispensable, in order to avoid the danger of covering simple immorality with the cloak of disease.

Psychopathic states may lead to crimes against morality while removing the conditions necessary to the existence of responsibility under the following circumstances:

[1] There may be no moral or legal notions to oppose the normal or intensified sexual desire, due to [a] the fact that they may have never been developed (states of congenital mental weakness); or to [b] the fact that they have been lost (states of acquired mental weakness).

[2] When the sexual desire is increased (states of psychic exaltation), consciousness may be simultaneously clouded and the mental mechanism too disturbed to allow the opposing ideas, virtually present, to exert their influence.

[3] When the sexual instinct is perverse (states of psychic degeneration). It may, at the same time, be so intensified as to be irresistible.

Cases of sexual delinquency that occur outside of states of mental defect, degeneration, or disease can never be excused on the basis of irresponsibility.

In many cases, instead of an abnormal psychic condition, a neurosis (local or general) is found. Inasmuch as the transitions from a neurosis to a psychosis are easy, and elementary psychic disturbances are frequent in neurosis and constant in profound perversion of the sexual life, the neurotic disturbance – e.g., impotence, irritable weakness, etc. – exerts an influence on the motive of the incriminating act. Thus a judge who is just, notwithstanding the lack of legal irresponsibility due to mental defect or disease, will recognize the circumstances that ameliorate the heinousness of the crime.

For various reasons the practical jurist will call medical experts to make a psychiatric examination in all cases of sexual crimes.

To be sure, his own conscience and judgment must be the guides when necessity makes them his only reliance. Under the following circumstances indicators are apparent that point to a pathological condition:

The accused is senile. The sexual crime is committed openly, with remarkable cynicism. The manner of obtaining sexual satisfaction is silly (exhibitionism), or cruel (mutilation or murder), or perverse (necrophilia, etc.).

Among the sexual acts that occur, experience dictates that rape, mutilation, pederasty, lesbian love and bestiality may have a psychopathological basis.

In cases of lust murder – insofar as its ulterior object goes beyond the murder itself – and likewise in cases of corpse mutilation, psychopathic conditions are probable.

Exhibitionism and mutual masturbation seem to indicate the probable existence of pathological conditions. Although masturbation of another as well as passive masturbation may occur in connection with senile dementia and inverted sexual feeling, they also occur with mere sensuality.

Cunnilingus and fellatio (**putting the penis into a woman's mouth**) have not thus far been shown to depend upon psychopathological conditions.

These horrible sexual acts seem to be committed only by sensual men who have become satiated or impotent from excessive indulgence in a normal way. **Putting a penis into a woman's mouth** does not seem to be psychopathic; instead it is a practice of married men of low morality who wish to prevent pregnancy, and of satiated cynics in non-marital sexual indulgence.

The practical importance of the subject makes it necessary that sexual acts threatened with punishment as sexual crimes be considered by jurists from the standpoint of the medico-legal expert. Thus there is an advantage gained, in that the psychopathological acts, according to their circumstances, are placed in the right light by comparison with analogous acts that fall within the domain of physiological psychology.

[1] offense against morality in the form of exhibitionism.[3]

[Austrian statutes, Paragraph 516; abridgment, Paragraph 195. German statutes, Paragraph 183.]

In man's present condition of civilization, modesty is a characteristic and motive so firmly fixed by centuries of education that presumption of a psychopathological element necessarily arises when *public* decency is coarsely offended.

The presumption is justifiable that an individual who has in this way offended public decency and his own self-respect was either incapable of the feelings of morality (idiots) or had lost them (states of acquired mental weakness); or that he acted while in a clouded state of consciousness (transitory insanity, states of partial consciousness).

A distinctive act belonging here is that of *exhibitionism* (exposure). The cases thus far recorded are exclusively those of men who ostentatiously expose their genitals to persons of the opposite sex, whom in some instances they even pursue; without, however, becoming aggressive.

The silly manner of this sexual activity (or really sexual demonstration) points to intellectual and moral weakness; or, at least, to temporary inhibition of the intellectual and moral functions, with excitation of libido dependent upon a decided disturbance of consciousness (abnormal unconsciousness, mental confusion), while also calling the virility of these individuals into question. Thus there are various categories of exhibitionists.

The first category includes *acquired states of mental weakness* in which consciousness is clouded because of the causative cerebral (or spinal) disease interfering with the ethical and intellectual functions. In this condition there can be no resistance to a sexual desire that has either always been intense or has been intensified by the disease process. At the same time impotence exists, which no longer permits expression of the sexual instinct in violent acts (rape), but only in acts that are silly.

The majority of reported cases[4] fall in this category. They consist of individuals who are afflicted with senile dementia, paretic dementia, or mental defects due to alcoholism, epilepsy, etc.

Case 198.

Z., high official, aged sixty; widower, father of a family. He gave offense in that, during fourteen days, he had repeatedly exposed his genitals at his window to an eight-year-old girl who lived opposite him. After a few months, under similar circumstances, this man repeated his indecent act. At his examination he acknowledged the depravity of his action and could give no excuse for it. Death, a year later, due to cerebral disease (Lasègue, op. cit.).

Case 199.

Z., aged seventy-eight; seaman. He had repeatedly exhibited his genitals on children's playgrounds and in the neighborhood of girls' schools. This was the only way in which he was sexually active. He was married and the father of ten children. Twelve years previously he had suffered a severe head injury, which left a deep scar, indenting the bone. Pressure on this scar caused pain; at the same time his face would become flush, his expression would become fixed, and he would grow somnolent, with convulsive movements in the right upper extremity (apparent epileptoid state in connection with cortical disease). Moreover, there was senile dementia and advanced old age. It is not reported whether the exhibitionism coincided with epileptoid attacks. Senile dementia proved; pardoned (Dr. Schuchardt, op. cit.).

Pelanda (op. cit.) has reported a number of cases of this kind:

[1] Paralytic, aged sixty. At the age of fifty-eight he began to exhibit himself to women and children. In the asylum at Verona he was lascivious for a long time thereafter, and also attempted fellatio.

[2] A drinker, aged sixty-six, suffering from recurrent madness. His exhibitionism was first noticed in church during divine service. His brother was likewise an exhibitionist.

[3] A drinker, predisposed, aged forty-nine. He was always very excitable sexually; in an asylum because of chronic alcoholism. He exhibited himself whenever he saw a woman.

[4] A man, aged sixty-four; married; father of fourteen children. Great predisposition. Rachitic, microcephalic head. For years he had been an exhibitionist, in spite of repeated punishment.

Case 200.

X., merchant, born in 1833; single. He had repeatedly exhibited himself to children, sometimes even urinating at the same time. Once, under these circumstances, he had kissed a little girl. Twenty years previously, X. had had a severe attack of mental disease, of two years duration, which was said to have been an apoplectic attack. Later, after loss of his fortune, he indulged in drink, and in recent years had often appeared absent-minded. His condition was that of alcoholism, premature senility and mental weakness. Penis small; phimosis; testicles atrophic. Proof of mental disease; pardoned (Dr. Schuchardt, op. cit.).

Although such cases recall the lasciviousness of youthful, sexually excited persons who are still more or less boyish, they also evoke that of many mature cynics of low morality; those who find pleasure in defiling the walls of public restrooms, etc., with drawings of male and female genitals – a kind of ideal exhibitionism that is still widely separated, however, from actual exhibitionism.

Another category of exhibitionists is made up of *epileptics*.[5] This category is *essentially* to be distinguished from the foregoing, because a conscious motive for the exhibitionism is lacking. Thus it appears much more like an *impulsive* act which, without any consideration of external circumstances, is performed as if it were an abnormal organic necessity.

At the time of the act there is always a state of imperfect consciousness; and thus it is explained that the unfortunate individual, without consciousness of the meaning of his act, or, at least, *without cynicism,* practices exhibitionism in obedience to a blind impulse. If there is no permanent mental weakness, he regrets and abhors the act after regaining consciousness.

As with other impulsive acts, the prime motive in this state of imperfect consciousness is a feeling of apprehensive oppression. If a sexual feeling becomes associated with it, the ideas are then given a certain direction in the sense of a corresponding (sexual) act.

The way in which temporary sexual ideas easily arise in epileptics may be understood from the discussion on p. 391.

Once such an association has been formed, and if, during an attack, a particular act has taken place, that act is all the more easily repeated in every subsequent attack; for, so to speak, a known track has been established in the path of motivity.

The feeling of anxiety that accompanies the state of imperfect consciousness causes the associated sexual impulse to appear as a command; thus, an inner force is acted upon in a purely impulsive manner and in a state of absolute irresponsibility.

Case 201.

K., a subordinate official, aged twenty-nine; from a neuropathic family; living in a happy marriage; father of one child. He had repeatedly, especially at dusk, exhibited himself to servant girls. K. was tall, slim, pale, nervous and hasty in manner. *There was imperfect memory of the crimes.* Since childhood there had been frequent severe congestive attacks, with intense flushing of the face, a rapid, tense pulse, and a fixed, absent stare. At the same time, occasional confusion and vertigo. In this (epileptic) exceptional state K. would answer only after repeated questioning, and then *it was as if he were waking from a dream.* K. stated that he had always felt excited and restless for some hours before his criminal acts, experiencing a feeling of fear, with oppression and congestion in his head. In this condition he had often been giddy, with an indistinct feeling of sexual excitement. At the height of such states he had left his house, without any purpose in mind, and exposed his genitals anywhere. After returning home, he had only a dreamy remembrance of what had occurred, and felt very weak and depressed. It was also remarkable that, while exhibiting his genitals, he used lighted matches to make them visible. Although the opinion was to the effect that the criminal acts depended upon epilepsy and were imperative impulses, he was, nevertheless, sentenced, with the assumption of extenuating circumstances (Dr. Schuchardt, op. cit.).

Case 202.

L., aged thirty-nine; single; tailor. His father was probably a drinker; he had two epileptic brothers, one of whom was insane. The patient himself had slight epileptic attacks, and occasional states of imperfect consciousness in which he ran about aimlessly, and afterward did not know where he had been. Although he had been considered a moral man, he was now accused of having exhibited and played with his genitals in a strange house five or six times. His memory of these acts was very imperfect.

Because of repeated desertion from the army (probably also while in epileptic states of imperfect consciousness), L. had been severely punished. In imprisonment he became insane with "epileptic insanity," was sent to the Charité, and from there discharged as "cured." As far as the criminal acts were concerned, cynicism and wantonness could be excluded. That they were committed in a state of imperfect consciousness was probable from the fact that, among other things, to the policeman who arrested him, the "imbecile" appeared to be in a remarkably cloudy state of mental consciousness (Liman, *Vierteljahrsschr. f. ger. Med.*, vol. 38, no. 2).

Case 203.

L., aged thirty-seven. From October 15 to November 2, he had given offense many times by exhibiting himself to girls on the open street in broad daylight, as well as in schools he had forcibly entered. It occasionally happened that he wanted the girls to perform masturbation or allow coitus and, when refused, he performed masturbation before them. In G., in a public house, he rapped on the window with his exposed penis so that the children and servant girls in the kitchen were forced to see it.

After his arrest it was ascertained that since 1876, although L. had frequently caused trouble by exhibitionism, he had always escaped punishment, due to the demonstration of mental disease by physicians. On the other hand, he had been punished for desertion and theft in the army and later, as a civilian, on one occasion for stealing cigars. L. had repeatedly been in asylums because of insanity (attacks of insanity?). In addition, he was often remarkable because of his changeable, quarrelsome character, occasional excitement, and inconstancy.

L.'s brother died of paralysis. He himself presented no degenerative signs; no epileptic antecedents. At the time of observation he was neither insane nor mentally weakened.

He behaved himself very well and expressed great regret for his sexual crimes, which he explained in this way: though not a drinker, he occasionally had an impulse to drink. Soon after he began to drink, congestion of the head, vertigo, restlessness, anxiety and oppression occurred. He then passed into a dreamy state. An irresistible impulse then forced him to expose himself, after which he experienced a feeling of relief and breathed more easily. Once he had exposed himself, he knew nothing more of what he did. A short time before such attacks, he often had flames before his eyes and vertigo. He had only an obscure, dreamy memory about the interval of his clouded state of consciousness.

Only later did sexual ideas and impulses become associated with these apprehensive, cloudy states of consciousness. Years ago, while in such states, without motive and with great danger, he had deserted. Once he had jumped from a third-story window; on another occasion he had left a good position to wander about aimlessly in a neighboring country, where he was immediately arrested for exhibitionism.

One time, when he was not experiencing an abnormal period, L. became intoxicated; there was no exhibitionism. In the lucid state his sexual feeling and interaction were perfectly normal (Dr. Hotzen, Friedreich's *Blätter*, 1890, no. 6).

A clinical group that very nearly approaches the epileptic exhibitionists is made up of certain *neurasthenic* individuals, in whom there may likewise occur attacks (epileptoid?) of imperfect consciousness[6] in connection with a feeling of apprehensive oppression. Sexual impulses may be associated with this, resulting in acts of exhibitionism that have an impulsive character.

Case 204.

Dr. S., academic teacher, had aroused public indignation by being repeatedly seen running around in the Tiergarten in Berlin, before ladies and children, with his genitals hanging out. Although S. admitted this, he denied all thought or consciousness of causing public offense, and excused himself by saying that his running around with exposed genitals afforded him relief from nervous excitement. Mother's father was insane, and died by suicide; his mother was constitutionally neuropathic, a somnambulist, and had been temporarily insane. He was neuropathic, had been a somnambulist, and had had a continuous aversion to engage in sexual intercourse with females. In his youth he practiced masturbation. He was a neurasthenic man, shy, torpid, easily embarrassed and confused. He was always much excited sexually. He frequently dreamed that he was running around with exposed genitals, or that he hung from a horizontal bar, with his head downward, dressed only in a shirt, so that the shirt fell down and exposed his erect penis. His dreams would induce pollutions, after which he would then have rest for a few days or an entire week.

Often, while awake, the impulse would come upon him to run around with exposed genitals, just as he would in his dreams. As he was about to expose himself, he became very hot and then ran around aimlessly. Although his member would become moist with secretion, pollution was never induced. When his penis had finally become flaccid, he put his genitals back in his pants and came to his senses, glad if no one had seen him. In such conditions of excitement *he seemed to be in a dream, as if intoxicated*. He had never intended to offend women. S. was not epileptic. His declarations had the mark of truth. He had never actually followed or spoken to women while in this condition. Frivolity and coarseness were excluded. No doubt S.'s acts were due to pathological sensations and ideas, and S. was in a state of pathological disturbance of mental action at the time of the commission of his acts (Liman, *Vierteljahrsschrift für gerichtl. Med.,* vol. 38, no. 2).

Case 205.

X., aged thirty-eight; married; father of one child. Always sullen and silent. Suffered frequently from headaches. *Very neurasthenic,* though not insane. He was much troubled at night by pollutions. He repeatedly followed saleswomen, for whom he had lain in wait, and then exposed and handled his genitals. In one case he even followed a girl into a shop (Trochon, *Arch. de l'anthropologie criminelle,* vol. 3, p. 256).

In the following case the exhibitionism seems subsidiary to the impulsive desire to satisfy sudden, intense libido by means of masturbation:

Case 206.

R., coachman, aged forty-nine; Vienna; married since 1866; childless. Father neuropathic and given to sexual excesses; died of cerebral disease. He presented no degenerative signs.

At the age of twenty-nine he suffered a severe concussion as a result of falling from a high place. Up to that time his sex life had been normal. Afterward, however, he had been seized every three or four months with a painful sexual excitement accompanied by an intense desire to masturbate. A feeling of weariness and discomfort, with a desire for alcoholic indulgence, preceded this. In the intervals he was sexually cold and only rarely desired his wife, who, moreover, had been sick and incapable of cohabitation for five years.

He gave the assurance that, as a young man, he had never masturbated. Also, in the intervals between his attacks, he had never thought of satisfying himself sexually in this way.

The impulse to masturbate during the attack was always excited by certain feminine charms – short cloak, pretty foot and ankle, elegant appearance. Age made no difference; even little girls excited him. The impulse was sudden and unconquerable. R. described the situation and act as characteristically impulsive. Although he had often tried to resist it, he would then grow hot and terribly frightened, his head would burn, and he would seem to be in a fog. He never, however, lost consciousness. At the same time he would have violent, darting pain in his testicles and spermatic cords. He regretted his actions, but had to confess that the impulse was stronger than his will. Such a situation forced him to masturbate, no matter where he might be. After ejaculation he would become calm and regain his self-control. He regarded this as a terrible affliction. Defense showed that R. had been punished six times for similar offenses – exhibitionism and masturbation in the open street. Although an examination by experts into his mental condition was demanded by his counsel, the court refused on the grounds that the proceedings had raised no doubt as to his responsibility.

On November 4, 1889, while in his worst condition, R. happened to be on the street as a crowd of schoolgirls went by. This awakened his unconquerable impulse. He had no time to run to a closet because he was too excited. There was immediate exhibitionism, masturbation in front of a house, great scandal and immediate arrest. R. was not weak-minded and had no ethical defect. He bemoaned his fate, deeply regretted his act, and feared new attacks. He regarded his condition as abnormal – as a fate against which he thought he was powerless.

He believed he was still virile. Penis abnormally large. Cremasteric reflex present; patellar reflex increased. Weakness of the sphincter of the bladder, which had existed for some years. Various neurasthenic difficulties.

Opinion showed that R. was subject to the influence of abnormal conditions and had acted impulsively. Patient was sent to an asylum, from which he was discharged after a few months.

In the foregoing case the clinically important point lies not in his existing neurosis, but rather in the impulsive character of the act (exhibitionism dependent on masturbation).

With the enumeration of the categories of imbeciles, mentally weakened individuals, and exhibitionists who are in a neurotic (epileptic or neurasthenic) state of benumbed consciousness, the clinical and forensic side of this phenomenon is still apparently unexhausted. In addition to these, there is another class, the representatives of which, *due to deep hereditary taint* (*hereditary degenerative neurosis?*), are impelled to periodic, impulsive exhibitionism.

With reference to these conditions of periodic *psychopathia sexualis* (cf. "Periodic Insanity"), in which the accidentally awakened impulse to exhibitionism is only a partial manifestation of a clinical whole (as is the craving for drink in periodic dipsomania), Magnan,[7] from whom I borrow the following instructive cases, justly lays the greatest stress upon the impulsive, periodic feature of these abnormal impulses; and no less upon the fact that they are often accompanied by terrible anxiety, which is replaced by a feeling of relief after the realization of the impulse.

These facts, and to an equal extent the clinical picture of degeneracy that is usually referable to injurious hereditary conditions, or to conditions that exercise an injurious effect on the development of the brain in early years (rickets, etc.), are of decisive medico-legal importance.

Case 207.

G., aged twenty-nine, waiter in a café. In 1888, while standing in the doorway of a church, he exhibited himself to several girls working on the other side of the street. He confessed to the act, as well as that he had been guilty many times of the same crime, which he had committed in the same place and at the same time of day, and for which he had been punished the year before with imprisonment for one month.

G. had very nervous parents. His father was mentally unstable and very irascible. His mother was insane at times and suffered from a severe neurotic disturbance.

G. had always had nervous twitching of the face, as well as a constant alternation of causeless depression (accompanied by *taedium vitae*) with periods of elation. At the ages of ten and fifteen, for little reason, he wished to commit suicide. When excited, he also had nervous twitching of the extremities. He presented constant general analgesia. When first in prison, he was beside himself with shame about the disgrace he had brought upon his family, and said he was the worst of men, deserving the severest punishment.

Until his nineteenth year G. had satisfied himself with solitary and mutual masturbation. On one occasion he had practiced masturbation with a girl. From that time the female customers in the café where he worked had excited him so intensely that ejaculation was often induced. He suffered from almost constant priapism, and his wife said that in spite of coitus, it often disturbed his rest at night. For seven years he had repeatedly exhibited himself at his window and exposed himself naked to female neighbors living opposite.

In 1883 he married for love. Marital intercourse did not satisfy his needs. At times his sexual excitement was so intense that he had headaches, seeming confused (as if drunk), strange, and incapable of work.

During a recent attack he had exhibited himself before ladies on two different streets in Paris (May 12, 1887). Since then he had been fighting a desperate battle against these morbid impulses that had now become almost permanent, and that at their height made him morose, confused, and caused him to weep all night. In spite of all his efforts he backslid again and again. *Opinion:* Proof of hereditary degeneration with delusions and irresistible impulses ("delirious perversion of the genital sense"). Pardon (Magnan, *Arch. de l'anthropologie criminelle,* vol. 5, no. 28).

Case 208.

B., aged twenty-seven; from a neuropathic mother and an alcoholic father. He had one brother (a drinker) and a hysterical sister. Four blood relations on the paternal side were drunkards, and one female cousin was hysterical.

After his eleventh year, masturbation, solitary and mutual. After his thirteenth year, impulses to exhibitionism. He attempted it at a street urinal, and although he felt pleasure in it, he also had immediate twinges of conscience. If he attempted to oppose his impulse thereafter, he became apprehensive and had a feeling of oppression in his chest. As a soldier he was often impelled to expose himself to his comrades under various pretexts.

After his seventeenth year he had sexual relations with women. It gave him great pleasure to show himself naked before them. He continued his exhibitionism on the street. Because he could only rarely count on female spectators at urinals, he went instead to churches. In order to exhibit himself at such places, he always had to strengthen his courage by drinking. Under the influence of alcohol, the impulse, at other times controllable with difficulty, became irresistible. He was not sentenced. He lost his position, and then drank more. Not long after, he was again arrested for exhibitionism and masturbation in a church (Magnan, idem).[8]

Case 209.

X., aged thirty-five; barber's assistant. Repeatedly punished for offenses against decency, he was again arrested for the following incident. Over the course of three weeks he had been hanging around girls' schools, trying to attract the attention of the pupils, and, when he had succeeded in this, had exhibited himself. Occasionally he had promised them money, with the words, **"I have a very beautiful penis, come with me and suck it."**

At his examination X. confessed to everything, but did not know how it had come about. Although he was the most reasonable of men in other respects, he had had the impulse to commit this crime and could not overcome it.

While in the army in 1879, he was once out on leave, and had run around exhibiting himself to children: imprisonment for a year. The same crime in 1881. He chased the crying children and "stared" at them: imprisonment for one year and three months. Two days after his discharge, he said to two little girls: **"If you want to see my penis, come with me into this inn."** He denied these words and claimed drunkenness: imprisonment for three months.

In 1883 renewed exhibitionism; during the act he said nothing. At his examination he stated that he had suffered from such excitations since a severe illness eight years previously: imprisonment for one month.

In 1884 exhibitionism before girls in a churchyard; again in 1885. He declared: "I understand my crime, but it is like a disease. When it comes over me, I cannot stop myself from engaging in such acts. It sometimes happens that, for quite a long time, I am free from these inclinations." Imprisonment for six months.

Discharged on August 12, 1885, he had a relapse on August 15. The same excuse was given. This time he underwent medical examination. The examination revealed no mental disturbance. Sentenced to three years. After discharge, a new series of exhibitionism. Examination on this occasion revealed the following:

His father suffered from chronic alcoholism and was said to have been guilty of the same crime. Mother and a sister nervously ill, and the whole family of excitable temperament.

From his seventh to his eighteenth year X. suffered from epileptic convulsions. First cohabitation at sixteen; later, gonorrhea, and, it was stated, syphilis. After that, normal sexual intercourse until his twenty-first year. At that time he often had to pass a playground where he would occasionally urinate, and it happened that the children watched him out of curiosity.

He occasionally noticed that being watched in this manner caused him sexual excitement, inducing erection and even ejaculation. He then found more pleasure in this kind of sexual gratification, became indifferent about coitus, and satisfied himself only in this manner. He felt that his every thought was ruled by this. He dreamed, with pollutions, only of exhibitionism. His attempts to control his impulse became more and more ineffectual. It came over him with such force that he noticed nothing around him, saw and heard nothing, and was like one "devoid of reason" – like "a bull trying to butt his head through a wall."

X. had an abnormally broad head; small penis; left testicle deformed. Patellar reflex absent. Symptoms of neurasthenia, especially cerebral. Frequent pollutions. For the most part his dreams were about normal coitus and only infrequently about exhibitionism before little girls.

With reference to his sexual acts, he stated that the impulse to seek and approach little girls was primary; only when he had succeeded **in directing their attention to his exposed genitals did he become erect and ejaculate.** He did not lose consciousness during the act. Afterward he was troubled about his deed and, if undiscovered, said to himself, "Once more I have escaped the authorities."

In prison he did not have the impulse; instead, he was troubled by dreams and pollutions exclusively. With freedom he had daily sought an opportunity to satisfy himself through exhibitionism. He would give ten years of his life to be free from the impulse; "this life of constant anxiety, this alternation between freedom and imprisonment, is unendurable."

The opinion assumed a congenital (?) perversity of the sexual instinct with unmistakable hereditary taint, neuropathic constitution, asymmetry of the cranium, and defective development of the genitals.

It is also worthy of remark *that the exhibitionism began when the epilepsy ceased, so that one might think of it as a vicarious phenomenon.*

The sexual perversity developed, with predisposition, through accidental association of ideas of sexual content (children looking at him urinating) with an act that was, in itself, purposeless.

The patient was not sentenced, but sent to an asylum (Dr. Freyer, *Zeitschr. f. Medizinalbeamte,* vol. 3, no. 8).

Case 210.

At nine o'clock at night in the spring of 1891, a lady, very much in great trepidation, went to a policeman in the city park of X. and stated that a man, his front absolutely naked, had approached her from the shrubbery, after which she had run away frightened. The officer went at once to the place indicated and found a man who exposed **his naked belly and genitals.** Although the man attempted to escape, he was overtaken and arrested. He stated that he had been sexually excited by alcohol and had been at the point of going to a prostitute. On his way through the park, however, he recalled that exhibitionism gave him much more pleasure than coitus, in which he seldom, and only for lack of anything better, indulged. After pulling up his shirt, he posted himself in the shrubbery, and when two women came up the path, he approached them with exposed genitals. During such exhibitionism he had a pleasurable feeling of warmth, and the blood rushed to his head.

The accused worked in a factory, and his employer stated that he was faithful, thrifty, sober and intelligent.

In 1886 B. had been punished because he had twice exhibited himself publicly – once in broad daylight and once at night, under a street lamp.

B., aged thirty-seven, single, made a peculiar impression because of his dandified dress and affected manner. His eyes had a neuropathic, languishing expression; around his mouth played a smile of self-satisfaction. He was said to have come from healthy parents. A sister of his father and a sister of his mother were insane. Other relatives were thought of as religiously eccentric.

B. had never had any severe illness. From childhood he was eccentric and imaginative. He loved romances about knights and others, was entirely absorbed by them, and even went so far as to identify himself, in fantasy, with the heroes. He always thought of himself as slightly better than others, and thought a great deal of elegant dress and ornaments. When he strutted about on Sundays he imagined himself as a high official.

B. had never shown epileptic symptoms. In youth moderate indulgence in masturbation; later, moderate indulgence in coitus. At that time he never had any perverse sexual feelings or impulses. Retired manner of life; reading during leisure hours (popular novels, heroic tales, Dumas and others). B. was not a drinker. On rare occasions he made himself a kind of punch, which always excited him sexually.

Some years later, and with a marked decrease of libido, he had developed after such alcoholic indulgence the "accursedly silly thought," as well as the desire **to publicly expose his genitals to women.**

If he got into this state, he felt warm, his heart beat violently, blood rushed to his head, and he could then no longer resist the impulse. He heard and saw nothing more, and became absolutely absorbed in his lust. Afterward he had often pounded his crazy head with his fists and firmly resolved never to do such a thing again; the crazy ideas, however, had always returned.

When he exhibited himself, his penis became only half-erect and ejaculation never occurred; even in coitus it was always tardy. In exhibitionism he was satisfied with **looking at his genitals** and would have the lustful thought that this sight must be very pleasant to women, since he himself liked so much to see **the genitals of women.** He was capable of coitus only when the prostitute showed that she was partial to him; without this, he preferred to pay and leave without doing anything. In his dreams he exhibited himself to young, voluptuous women.

The medico-legal opinion recognized the hereditary psychopathic character of the culprit, and the perverse, impulsive desire to perform the incriminating acts. It further pointed out the remarkable fact that for B., who was otherwise sober and reserved, the impulses to indulge in alcohol depended on abnormal conditions that recurred periodically and forced him to indulge. That B. had been, during his attacks, in an exceptional psychic state, in a kind of mental confusion, and was absolutely absorbed in his perverse sexual fantasy, was clearly shown by the form of the act. Thus was explained the fact that he became aware of the approach of the police only when it was too late to try to escape. It is interesting to note in this hereditary and degenerate impulsive exhibitionism how the perverse sexual impulse was awakened from its latency by the influence of alcohol.

The foregoing cases seem to justify the assumption of a psychopathological meaning of "exhibitionism" in the sense of sexual demonstration.

A forensically important variety of exhibitionism is made up of the so-called *frotteurs* (men who sexually rub themselves against women). Clinically speaking, this class certainly rests upon a similar neurotic and degenerate foundation, and expresses itself in a peculiar act which is conditioned by violent libido (sexual hyperesthesia) and is associated with diminished virility.

The three following cases, borrowed from Magnan (op. cit.), are typical:

Case 211.

D., aged forty-four; hereditarily predisposed; drinker; suffering from lead poisoning. Until the previous year he had masturbated frequently, and had often drawn pornographic pictures which he showed to his acquaintances. He had repeatedly dressed himself, in secret, as a woman.

For a period of two years after he became impotent, he had felt the desire, while in crowds at dusk, **to expose his penis and rub it hard against a woman's buttocks.** Once, after being discovered in the act, he was sentenced to imprisonment for four months.

His wife owned a milk shop. **He could not help repeatedly immersing his genitals into a pail full of milk.** During the act he felt lustful pleasure, "as if touched with velvet." He was cynical enough to use this milk for himself and the customers. During imprisonment he developed alcoholic persecutory insanity.

Case 212.

M., aged thirty-one; married six years; father of four children; badly predisposed; subject to occasional melancholia. Three years before, he had been discovered by his wife while he was wearing a silk dress and masturbating. One day he was discovered, in a shop, engaging in the act of *frottage* on a lady. He was very repentant and asked to be severely punished for his irresistible impulse.

Case 213.

G., aged thirty-three; badly predisposed hereditarily. At a bus station he was discovered engaging in the act of *frottage* with his penis on a lady. Deep repentance; he stated, however, that at the sight of the noticeable posterior of a lady, he was irresistibly impelled to practice *frottage,* and that he then became confused and did not know what he did. Sent to an asylum.

Case 214.

A *frotteur.* Z., born in 1850; previously of blameless life; of good family; private official. He was well-to-do financially; untainted. After a short married life he became a widower in 1873. For some time he had attracted attention in churches because he crowded up behind women, whether old or young, and toyed with their "bustles." He was watched and one day arrested in the act. Z. was terribly frightened and in despair about his situation. In making a full confession he begged for pardon, saying that nothing but suicide remained for him.

For two years he had been subject to the unhappy impulse to go into crowds of people – in churches, at box offices of theatres, etc. – and press up behind females, manipulate the prominent portion of their dresses, and thus have orgasm and ejaculation.

Z. stated that he had never indulged in masturbation, and had never been perverse sexually. Since the early death of his wife, he had gratified his great sexual desire in temporary love affairs, having always had an aversion for prostitutes and brothels. The impulse to engage in *frottage* had suddenly seized him, two years ago, while he happened to be in church. Though he was conscious that it was wrong, he could not help yielding to it immediately. Since then he had been excitable about the posteriors of females, and had actually been impelled to seek opportunity for *frottage.* The only thing on women that excited him was the "bustle"; every other part of the body and attire was a matter of indifference to him; nor did he mind whether the woman was old or young, beautiful or ugly. Since this began, he no longer desired natural gratification. Later, *frottage* scenes appeared in his dreams.

During *frottage* he was fully conscious of his situation and the act, and tried to perform it so as to attract as little attention as possible. Afterward he was always ashamed of what he had done.

Although the medical examination revealed no sign of mental disease or mental weakness, it did reveal symptoms of sexual neurasthenia (from libidinous abstinence ?) which was also proved by the detail that even the mere touch of the fetish by the unexposed genitals sufficed to induce ejaculation. Apparently Z., who was libidinous, though weakened sexually and distrustful of his virility, had come to practice *frottage* by having the sight of the female posterior coincide accidentally with sexual excitement. This associative combination of a perception with a feeling permitted the former to attain the significance of a fetish.

Because of the limited number of cases thus far observed, it can hardly be decided whether these *frotteurs* (if considered as men who, in consequence of disturbed

virility, have become either temporarily or permanently hypersexually degenerated) should come under the category of exhibitionists, or should be classified with
the fetishists, as Garnier does (*Les fétichistes,* p. 73).

Whether or not exposure of the genitals takes place cannot affect this decision,
for such exposure may derive from the intensity of the *frotteur's* orgasm (which
may even lead to lustful ecstasy), or from external circumstances that are favorable to this loathsome impulse. The very fact that in pathological fetishism, up
until now, the fetish has never included the genital (or surrounding) areas, seems
to upset Garnier's theory regarding fetishism of the female buttocks (cf. p. 187).

The simplest explanation seems to be that "*frottage*" is the masturbatory act of a
hypersexual individual who is uncertain about his virility with a woman's body.
This would also explain the motive of the assault being made from behind (cf.
case 211). That fetishism may be involved seems to follow from case 212, which
clearly proves silk fetishism. Very likely the lady in question wore a silk gown, and
the indecent attack was directed upon the dress, not the buttocks. In case 214 the
act is evidently qualified by the "bustle" and not by the particular part of the body.

As acts that offend public morals and are, therefore, punishable, the *violation of
statutes* – a whole series of cases Moreau (op. cit.) has collected from ancient and
modern times – may be enumerated here. They are, unfortunately, presented too
much like anecdotes to allow satisfactory judgment of them. They always give the
impression of being pathological – like the story of a young man (related by
Lucianus and St. Clemens of Alexandria) who made use of a Venus of Praxiteles
for the gratification of his lust; and the case of Clisyphus, who violated the statue of
a goddess in the Temple of Samos after having placed a piece of meat on a certain
part. In modern times, the *Journal L'événement* of March 4, 1877, relates the story of
a gardener who fell in love with a statue of the Venus de Milo and was discovered
attempting coitus with it. At any rate, these cases stand in etiological relation with
abnormally intense libido and defective virility or courage, as well as lack of opportunity for normal sexual gratification.

The same thing must be assumed in the case of the so-called "voyeurs"[9] – i.e., men so
cynical they seek to view coitus to assist their virility, or seek the sight of an excited
woman to have orgasm and ejaculation. Concerning this moral aberration which, for

various reasons, cannot be further described here, it will suffice to refer to Coffig-non's book *La corruption à Paris*. This book contains horrible revelations in the domain of sexual perversity (and also perversion, which this book distinguishes).

[2] rape and lust murder.

[Austrian statutes, Paragraphs 125, 127; Austrian abridgment, Paragraph 192; German statutes, Paragraph 177.]

By the term *rape,* the jurist means coitus with an adult that occurs outside of marital relations and is enforced by means of threats or violence; or with an adult who is in a condition of defenselessness or unconsciousness; or with a girl who is under the age of fourteen years. **Fellatio** or, at least, **contact of the genitals** (Schütze) is necessary to establish the fact. Today, rape of children is remarkably frequent. Hofmann (*Ger. Med.*, vol. 1, p. 155) and Tardieu (*Attentats*) report horrible cases.

The latter establishes the fact that, from 1851 to 1875 inclusive, 22,017 cases of rape came before the courts in France, and of these, 17,657 were committed on children.

The crime of rape presumes a temporary, powerful excitation of sexual desire, induced by excess in alcohol or by some other condition. It is highly improbable that a man who is morally intact would commit this most brutal crime. Lombroso (Goltdammer's *Arch.*) considers the majority of men who commit rape to be degenerate, particularly when the crime is perpetrated on children or old women. He asserts that he has found actual signs of degeneracy in many such men.

It is a fact that rape is often the act of degenerate male imbeciles,[10] who, under some circumstances, do not even respect the bond of blood.

Cases that are a result of mania, satyriasis and epilepsy have occurred, and are to be kept in mind.

The crime of rape may be followed by the murder of the victim.[11] There may be unintentional murder, murder to destroy the only witness of the crime, or murder out of lust (see above). Only for cases of the latter kind should the term *lust murder*[12] be used.

The motives of lust murder have been previously considered. The cases given in illustration are characteristic of the manner of the deed. The presumption of a murder out of lust always exists when injuries of the genitals are found, the character and extent of which cannot be explained by a brutal attempt at coitus alone; or, further, when the body has been opened, and parts (intestines, genitals) have been torn out and are absent.[13]

Lust murders dependent upon psychopathic conditions are never committed with accomplices.

Case 215.

Weak-mindedness; epilepsy; attempt at rape; murder. On the evening of May 27, 1888, Blasius, a boy eight years old, was playing with other children in the neighborhood of the village of S. An unknown man came along and enticed the boy into the woods.

The next day the boy's body was found in a ravine with his abdomen slit open, an incised wound in his cardiac region, and two stab wounds in his neck.

Because a man answering to the description of the boy's murderer had attempted to attack a six-year-old girl on May 21 in a similar manner, and had only accidentally been prevented, it was presumed to be a case of lust murder.

The body had been found in a heap, with only the shirt and jacket on. In addition to the other wounds, there was also a long incision in the scrotum.

Although suspicion fell upon a farmhand, E.; confrontation with the children determined that it was not possible to identify him as the stranger who had enticed the boy into the woods. Besides, he provided an alibi with the help of his sister.

The untiring efforts of the officers brought new evidence to light, and finally E. confessed. He had enticed the girl into the woods, thrown her down, exposed her genitals, and was about to abuse her; she had, however, a lesion on her head and was crying loudly, so his desire cooled and he fled.

After he had enticed the boy into the woods, under the pretext of showing him a bird's nest, he was taken with a desire to abuse him. Because the boy refused to take off his trousers, E. did it for him; and when the boy began to cry out he stabbed him twice in the neck. He then made an incision, just above the pubes, in imitation of female genitals, in order to use it to satisfy his lust. Because the body grew cold immediately, however, he lost his desire, and – after cleaning his knife and hands near the body – he fled. When he saw the boy was dead, he was filled with fear, and his member became flaccid.

During his examination E. toyed apathetically with a rosary. He had acted in a state of mental weakness. He could not understand how he came to do such a thing. He must have been beside himself, because he often became so weak in his head that he would almost fall down. Previous employers reported that he had periods when he was confused and stubborn, did no work all day, and avoided others.

His father stated that E. learned with difficulty, was unskillful at work, and was often so obstinate that one dared not punish him. At such times he would not eat, and occasionally ran away and remained away from home for days. During these periods he also seemed quite lost in thought, would screw his face up, and say senseless things.

As a youth he still sometimes wetted the bed, and often came home from school with wet or soiled clothing. He was so restless in sleep that no one could sleep beside him. He had never had playmates. He had never been cruel, bad, or immoral.

His mother gave similar testimony. She further said that E. had convulsions for the first time in his fifth year, and that he once lost the power of speech for seven days. Sometime about his seventh year he once had convulsions for forty days, and was also dropsical. Later, he also often suffered from seizures in his sleep, at which time he often talked in his sleep. After such nights his bed was found completely wet in the morning.

At times it was impossible to do anything with him. Because his mother did not know whether his behavior was due to viciousness or disease, she did not venture to punish him.

Since the convulsions in his seventh year, his mind had failed so much that he could not even learn the common prayers; he also became very irascible.

Neighbors, persons prominent in the community, and teachers state that E. was peculiar, weak-minded, and irascible; that he was very strange at times and apparently in an exceptional mental state.

The examinations of the medical experts gave the following results:

E. was tall, slim, and poorly nourished. His head measured 53 centimeters in circumference. The cranium was rhombic, and flattened in the occipital region.

His countenance was devoid of intelligence; his glance was fixed, expressionless; his attitude was careless, and his body was bent forward. Movements were slow and heavy. Genitals normally developed. E.'s whole appearance pointed to torpidity and mental weakness.

There were no signs of degenerative marks, no abnormality of the vegetative organs, and no disturbances of motility or sensibility. He came from a perfectly healthy family. Although he knew nothing of convulsions or of wetting his bed at night, he stated that he had recently had attacks of vertigo and loss of mind.

At first he denied the murder point-blank. Later, in great contrition before the examining judge, he confessed all, and gave a clear motive for his crime. He stated that he had never had such a thought before.

He had been prone to masturbation for years; he even practiced it twice daily. He stated that, lacking courage, he had never ventured to ask coitus of a woman, though his dreams involved only such scenes. Neither in dreams nor in the waking state had he ever had perverse instincts; in particular, no sadistic or antipathic sexual feelings. The sight of the slaughter of animals had never interested him. When he enticed the girl into the woods, his desire, of course, was to satisfy his lust with her; but he could not explain how it happened that he tried such a thing with a boy. He thought he must have been out of his mind at the time. The night after the murder he could not sleep because of fear; he had twice confessed already, to ease his conscience. He was only afraid of being hanged. This should not be done, as he had done the deed in a weak-minded condition.

He could not explain why he had cut open the boy's abdomen. It had not occurred to him to grope among the intestines, smell them, etc. He stated that he had experienced convulsions, one during the day, after the attempt on the girl, and another during the night, after the murder of the boy. At the time of his crime he was indeed conscious, but he had given no thought as to what he was doing.

He often suffered from headaches; could not endure heat, thirst, or alcohol; there were times when he was perfectly confused. The test of his intelligence showed a high grade of weak-mindedness.

The opinion (Dr. Kautzner of Graz) showed the imbecility and neurosis of the accused, and made it probable that his crime, for which he had only a general recollection, had been committed in an exceptional (pre-epileptic) mental state, qualified by the neurosis. Under all circumstances E. was considered dangerous, and probably required commitment to an asylum for life.

Case 216.[14]
Rape of a little girl by an idiot. Death of the victim.

On the evening of September 3, 1889, Anna, aged ten years, daughter of a laborer, went to the village church, about two miles distant, but did not return. The following day her body was found about fifty paces from the main road, in a copse. Her face was turned to the ground, her mouth was gagged with moss, and there were signs of criminal assault in the area of her anus.

Suspicion fell upon a young laborer, K., nineteen years of age, because on September 1 he had attempted to entice the child into the woods when she was returning from church.

K. was arrested. Although at first he denied the deed, afterward he made a complete confession. He had strangled the child and, when she stopped kicking and resisting, **he perpetrated an act of sodomy upon the child's anus.**

During the preliminary examination no one had raised the question as to the mental condition of this monster. Consequently, shortly before the trial, when his counsel asked for an examination of the mental condition of his client, the request was refused on the grounds "that the previous proceedings contained nothing that could warrant the plea of insanity."

By accident, counsel for the defense succeeded in establishing the fact that the great-grandfather as well as the paternal aunt of the accused had been insane, and that the father was an inveterate alcoholic since earliest youth and a cripple on one side of his body. These facts were verified during the trial.

Such facts, however, made no impression. The defense finally prevailed upon the medical adviser of the court to suggest that K. be sent for observation to an insane asylum for a period of six weeks.

The opinion of the physician at the institute established K.'s idiocy, thus rendering him not responsible for his deed.

He appeared insipid, stolid, apathetic; had forgotten nearly all he had ever learned at school; he betrayed neither by voice nor mien the slightest emotions of compassion, contrition, shame, hope, or fear of the future. His face was as immovable as a mask.

Head quite abnormal; bullet-shaped. There was proof that his brain was already diseased during the fetal period or during the earliest years of development.

Upon this report K. was permanently interned at the asylum.

Through the indefatigable efforts of a brave lawyer, the court was saved from committing a judiciary murder, and the honor of society was sustained.

Case 217.

Lust murder; moral imbecility. N., a man of middle age, born in Algeria; said to be of Arabic descent. He had served for several years in the colonial troops, and had then traveled as a sailor between Algeria and Brazil. Later, in the hope of finding lighter employment, he had gone to North America. He was known among his acquaintances as lazy, cowardly and brutal. Several times he had been sentenced for vagrancy; it was said that he was a thief of the lowest kind; that he knocked about with women of the lowest class, and participated in whatever were their activities. His perverse sexual relations and acts were also well-known. On several occasions he had bitten and beaten women with whom he had had sexual relations. Because of the description given of him, the authorities thought they had finally arrested a certain unknown party who had scared the women in the streets at night by embracing and kissing them, and who had the nickname "Jack the Kisser."

He was a tall man (over six feet), slightly bent forward. Low forehead, very prominent cheekbones, massive jawbones; small, narrow, inflamed eyes, piercing look; big feet, hands like birds' claws; shambling gait. His arms and hands were tattooed all over. One thing that was remarkable was the picture of a woman in colors around which the name "Fatima" was inscribed, because tattooing the female form upon the body is considered to be disgraceful among the Arabs of the Algerian army, and because prostitutes generally have a cross tattooed on their skin. His general appearance gave the impression of a low grade of intelligence.

N. was convicted of the murder of an elderly female with whom he had spent the night. The corpse bore various wounds, some remarkable for their length. The abdomen was ripped open, pieces of the intestines were cut out, in addition to one of the ovaries; other parts were strewn around the corpse. Several of the wounds were like crosses; one was in the shape of a crescent. The murderer had strangled his victim. He denied the deed, as well as any inclination to commit such an act (Dr. MacDonald, Clark University, Mass.).

[3] bodily injury, injury to property, torture of animals dependent on sadism.

[Austrian statutes, Paragraphs 152, 411; German statutes, Paragraph 223 (bodily injury). Austrian statutes, Paragraphs 85, 468; German statutes, Paragraph 303 (injury to property). Austrian police regulations; German statutes, Paragraph 360 (torture of animals).]

Aside from lust murder, which has previously been described, milder expressions of sadistic desires also occur; among them, impulses to stab, flagellate, or defile females, to flagellate boys, or to maltreat animals.

The deep degenerative significance of such cases is clearly demonstrated by the series of examples given under "General Pathology." Should such mentally degenerate individuals be unable to control their perverse impulses, they can only be cared for in asylums.

Case 218.
Sadism on boys and girls committed by a moral idiot.

K., fourteen years and five months old, killed a small boy in a cruel manner. The trial, in fact, revealed two cases of murder and seven cases in which K. had cruelly tortured little boys. These children ranged in age from seven to ten years. K. would lure them into a hidden place, strip them naked, bind them hand and foot, tie them against some object, and gag their mouths with a handkerchief. He would then beat them with a stick, a strap, or a piece of rope, slowly, pausing for minutes at a time – grinning throughout and not uttering a word. He forced one of the boys under a threat of death to repeat the Lord's Prayer twice, to promise secrecy under oath, and to repeat curse words and oaths after him. In another instance, he pricked the boy's cheeks with a needle, played with his genitals, and stabbed him in the pubic region. He then ordered him to lie on his stomach while he jumped on his back and danced all over his body. Finally, he stabbed him in the buttocks and dug his teeth into them. He bit another boy on the nose and stabbed him with a knife.

He enticed the eighth victim, a little girl, into his mother's shop, fell upon her from behind and, putting one hand over her mouth, cut her throat with the other. The body was found in a dark corner, completely covered with ashes and manure. The head was severed from the body, the flesh cut away from the bones, and the whole body covered with cuts and wounds. The largest cut was on the inner side of the left thigh, penetrating through the genitals into the abdomen. Another cut extended obliquely from the iliac fossa to the abdomen. The clothes and linen were torn and cut into shreds.

The corpse of the ninth victim was found with his throat slit, blood flowing from his eyes, and his heart pierced by innumerable stabs. A number of stab wounds were found in the abdomen. The scrotum was ripped open, the testicles were hanging out, and the glans penis was cut off.

K. first lured the boy to him as he had the little girl. He then cut his throat and stabbed him all over.

K., whose hereditary conditions were not known, had suffered from a severe illness during the entire first year of his life, and had thus become extremely emaciated. He then began to recover, and reported that he was not further afflicted with bad health (with the exception of frequent complaints about pain in his head and eyes and vertigo) until he was eleven, when he went through a "severe illness" that made him delirious. Headaches would suddenly seize him, so that he would run away from play, and only return after a considerable amount of time. When asked on such occasions about his conduct, he would answer slowly, "My head, my head."

He was intractable, disobedient and beyond control. He exhibited sudden and extreme moods, desires and opinions. At three years old he was seen one day, with a knife, torturing a chicken. He lied with every appearance of truth. At school he was a disturbing element, making faces, constantly talking to himself; he was obstinate and disrespectful. Punishment to him was an injustice; he was recalcitrant. In the house of correction he was secluded, preoccupied with himself, suspicious, disliked by his comrades – in fact without any friend. His intellectual powers were good; he possessed sagacity, reason and a good memory. He exhibited great defect in ethical direction. He betrayed not the slightest signs of sorrow or penitence for his deeds, or the least consciousness of his responsibility. Only for his mother did he seem to have a sort of tender feeling. He could assign no object for his actions. He calmly discussed his chances: they would not condemn him to death because he was only fourteen years of age; they had not been accustomed to hang boys of his age before, and they would surely not start with him. What motive he had for his deeds cannot be ascertained from him. Once he said that reading a description of the tortures performed by the Red Indians had tempted him to imitate them. He had once even thought of running away from home to join the Indians. Whenever he espied a victim, his imagination would be filled with images of cruel actions.

On the morning of such days he would wake up with vertigo and pressure in his head, and this condition would last all day.

As for physical anomalies, only an exceptionally large penis and very big testicles are mentioned. Mons pubis completely and thickly covered with hair; in fact, the genitals were as fully developed as those of an adult. No symptoms of epilepsy (Dr. MacDonald, Clark University, Mass.).

Case 219.

Sadism; bodily injury. B., seventeen years of age, tinsmith, bought a long knife on January 4, 1893; went to a prostitute, had repeated sexual intercourse with her, gave her money, and made her sit undressed on the edge of the bed. He then stabbed her with a knife, slightly, three times in the chest and abdomen while his member was erect. When the girl began to yell and people came to her assistance, B. fled, but immediately gave himself up to the police. Although at first he said he had stabbed the girl in a quarrel, he later stated he had had no motive for his deed. Several blood relations of his father had been insane. B. was not tainted, not a drunkard, had not gone through any severe illness, had never masturbated, but had practiced coitus for two years. Genitals normal.

He seemed, under observation, mentally normal; he was ashamed of his actions, to which the experts properly ascribed a sexual motive. In spite of definite proof of mental sanity, he was released (Coutagne, *Annal. méd. psych.*, July-August 1893).

Case 220.

Acts of violence emanating from sadism. M., sixty years of age, worth several million francs, happily married, father of two daughters, one eighteen, the other sixteen, was convicted of seduction of minors and acts of violence on females. He would go to the house of a procuress, where he was known as *"l'homme qui pique"* ("the man who pricks"), and there, lying upon a sofa in a pink silk dressing gown lavishly trimmed with lace, he would await his victims – three nude prostitutes. They had to approach him single file, silent and smiling. They gave him needles, cambric handkerchiefs, and a whip. While kneeling before one of the girls, he would stick about a hundred needles into her body and fasten with twenty needles the handkerchief upon her breast, which he would then suddenly tear away. He would then whip the girl, tear the hair from her mons pubis, squeeze her breasts, etc., while the other two girls would wipe the perspiration from his forehead and strike lascivious artificial poses. Excited to the highest pitch, he would then have coitus with his victim. Later, for the sake of economy, he was satisfied to perform his brutality with one girl alone. Consequently, this girl became severely ill, and in her distress asked him for help. He reported this "extortion" to the police, who then made inquiries and brought a charge against him. At first he denied the facts; when convicted, however, he expressed his surprise that such a fuss should be made over a mere trifle. M. was described as a man of repulsive appearance, with a receding forehead. He was sentenced to six months' imprisonment, a fine of 200 francs, and 1000 francs damages to his victim (*Journal Gil Blas,* August 14 and 16, 1891).

A less revolting case, that of a young man, is related by Ferrioni, *Archivio delle psicopatie sessuali,* vol. 1, p. 106, 1896. To induce virility, this young sadist would first wrestle with the girl, and then bite and pinch her, during the act, in order to produce satisfaction. One day, however, he bit the girl so hard that she brought charges against him.

Case 221.

Murder through sadism. Married man, thirty years of age at the time of this crime. He had lured a girl to the bell tower of the church where he was the sexton and killed her.

When circumstantial evidence forced him to admit the deed, he confessed to another similar murder. Both corpses showed numerous contusions around the fleshy parts of the head, as well as fractures of the skull and extravasations under the dura mater and in the brain. No other bodily injuries were found; the genital organs were intact.

Sperm stains were found on the underwear of the criminal, who was arrested soon after the deed was committed. L. had a pleasing appearance, dark complexion, beardless. There were no details about his hereditary relations, antecedents, sexual life before the act, etc.

By his own admission, his motive was "lust of the cruelest and most abominable kind" (Dr. MacDonald, Clark University, Mass.).

Guillebeau,[15] professor at the Veterinary College in Bern, has collected a number of cases in which horrible acts of sadistic violence were committed upon dumb animals.

[1] Injuries to the vaginas of six cows. Offender unknown.

[2] Mortal injuries on four calves and goats, committed with the sharp point of a stick by a nineteen-year-old youth. He had become an imbecile at the age of four because of meningitis. He confessed that the act was one of sexual lust. Considered irresponsible.

[3] Repeated and numerous injuries with a stick to cows and goats in the anus and vagina by a stable boy (aged twenty-four). He confessed that when milking or otherwise attending the animals he became sexually excited and had violent erections and sensations of fear. At first he used his hand, but later he used a stick, which he would introduce into the orifice. It was always an impulsive act and only occurred when he suffered from sleeplessness, nervousness, and sexual excitement. Although always tormented later by pangs of conscience, he could not help relapsing. Considered irresponsible.

[4] A similar offense (an imitation of the former) in the same stable by a feeble-minded cowherd, eighteen years old, on the rectum of an ox.

Case 222.

X., aged twenty-four. Parents healthy; two brothers died from tuberculosis, one sister suffered from periodic fits. At the age of eight, X. began to experience pleasurable feelings with erection when he pressed his abdomen against his school desk. He often did this. Later he practiced mutual masturbation with a schoolmate. First ejaculation at the age of thirteen. In his first attempt at coitus (at eighteen), he was impotent. He continued to masturbate. After reading a popular book describing the dreadful consequences of masturbation, he became very neurasthenic. Although hydrotherapy brought improvement, a second attempt at coitus was a fiasco. Return to masturbation. In time this also failed him. Instead he would pick up a living bird by the bill and swing it around in the air. The sight of the tortured animal provoked erection, and then, when the flapping wing touched his penis, ejaculation would ensue with enormous sexual lust (Dr. Wachholz, Friedreich's *Blätter f. ger. Med.* 1892, no. 6, p. 336).

See also *Rivista sperimentale*, 1897, vol. 23, p. 702, and 1898, vol. 24, fasc. 1; Kölle, *Ger. psych. Gutachten*, case 4, p. 48.

[4] masochism and sexual bondage.

Masochism[16] may under certain circumstances attain forensic importance, for modern criminal law no longer recognizes the principle *"volenti non fit injuria"* ("no injustice if willing"), and the present Austrian statute in Paragraph 4 says expressly: "Crimes may also be committed on persons who demand their commission on themselves."

Psychologically speaking, the facts of *sexual bondage* are of greater criminal importance (cf. p. 175).

If sensuality is predominant – that is, if a man is held in fetishistic servitude and his moral power of resistance is weak – he may be goaded into the very worst crimes by an avaricious or vindictive woman, into whose bondage his passion has led him. The following case is a striking instance:

Case 223.

Murder of a family through sexual bondage. N., soap manufacturer in Catania; thirty-four years of age; previously of good character; stabbed his wife to death in her sleep on December 21, 1886, and strangled his two daughters, one seven years and the other six weeks old. Although at first he denied the deed and tried to throw suspicion upon others, he finally confessed and begged to be hanged.

N. came from a sound family, was healthy himself, was a good businessman, highly respected, and had married well. For several years, however, he had been under the fascinating influence of a mistress who had captivated and completely controlled him.

He had kept this matter a secret from the world as well as from his wife.

By playing on his jealousy and declaring that only by marriage could he possess her in the future, this monster of a woman had brought the weak and infatuated N. to become the murderer of his wife and children. After the deed he induced his young nephew to chain him so it would appear as if he himself had been the victim of the villains, and commanded him to silence under the threat of death. He played for the neighbors the role of the unhappy, maltreated father.

After a full confession he showed the deepest contrition. During the two years of the subsequent trial, N. never showed signs of mental derangement.

He could only explain his mad love for his mistress as an infatuation. He had never had cause to find fault with his wife. There were no traces of abnormal or perverse sexual instinct in this exceptional criminal. His sorrow and contrition over the deed gave sufficient proof that no moral defect was present. His mental condition was declared to be sound. Exclusion of irresistible impulse (Mandalari, *Il Morgagni,* February 1890).

Case 224.

Sexual bondage in a lady. Mrs. X., thirty-six years of age; mother of four children. Came from a neuropathic and heavily tainted mother. Father psychopathic. She began to masturbate at the age of five, and had an attack of melancholia at the age of ten, during which she was troubled by the delusion that she could not go to heaven because of her sins. This made her nervous, excitable, emotional and neurasthenic. At seventeen she fell in love with a man who was denied her by her parents. She then showed symptoms of hysteria. At twenty-one she married a much older man who had little sexual appetite. Their conjugal relations never satisfied her; coitus produced severe genital erethism that she could not then satisfy with masturbation. She suffered tortures from this insatiable sexual desire, yielded more and more to masturbation, and became heavily hystero-neurasthenic, capricious and quarrelsome; marital relations grew increasingly colder.

After nine years of mental and physical anguish, Mrs. X. succumbed to the blandish-ments of another man, in whose arms she found the gratification for which she had so long desired.

Then, however, she was tormented by the consciousness of having broken her marriage vow and often feared she would become insane. Only the love of her children prevented her from committing suicide.

She scarcely dared to appear before her husband, whom she highly esteemed for his noble character, and felt dreadful qualms of conscience because she had to conceal the awful secret from him.

Although she found full gratification and immense sensual pleasure in the arms of the other man, she repeatedly made attempts to give up this liaison. Her efforts were in vain. She got deeper and deeper into the bondage of this man, who by recognizing and abusing his power had merely to feign that he would leave her in order to possess her without restraint. He abused the bondage of this miserable woman only to gratify his sexual appetite, gradually even in a perverse manner. She was unable to refuse him any demand.

When in her despair Mrs. X. came to me for professional advice, she declared that she could no longer continue such a life of misery and anguish. An insuperable libido, disgusting to herself, drew her to this man, whom she could not love but could neither do without; on the other hand, she was constantly tormented by the danger of discovery and by self-reproach because of her offense against the law of God and man.

The greatest mental pain was caused by the thought of losing her paramour, who often threatened to leave her if she did not yield to his wishes, and who controlled her so thor-oughly that she would do anything and everything at his bidding.

The soundness of mind in the horrible case 223 and in many other analogous cases cannot be called into question. As matters stand nowadays, when the public cannot comprehend the more refined analysis of the motives in a tragedy, and when the legal profession eschews psychology in favor of logical formalism, it can hardly be expected that judge and jury will give weight to *sexual bondage* – especially because in this condition the incentive to the crime is not the result of a diseased state, and the intensity of the incentive itself cannot be addressed.

Nevertheless, in such cases it is proper to consider whether the accused was possibly still susceptible to countermotives, or whether these were excluded from an effective presence. If the latter is the case, it would be equivalent to a disturbance of the psychic equilibrium.

In these cases a sort of acquired moral weakness is undoubtedly produced that impairs the soundness of mind. *Sexual bondage* should certainly constitute a cause for leniency in crimes committed through its agency.

[5] bodily injury, robbery and theft dependent on fetishism.

[Austrian statutes, Paragraph 190; German statutes, Paragraph 249 (robbery). Austrian statutes, Paragraphs 171, 460; German statutes, Paragraphs 242 (theft).]

It is seen from the section on fetishism, under "General Pathology," that pathological fetishism may become the cause of crimes. As such, there are now recognized hair despoiling; robbery or theft of women's linen, handkerchiefs, aprons; shoes; and silks. It cannot be doubted that such individuals are the subjects of deep mental taint. To prove the assumption of an absence of mental freedom and consequent irresponsibility, however, it must be shown that there was an irresistible impulse, which, either because of the strength of the impulse itself or because of the existence of mental weakness, rendered impossible any control over the criminal perverse impulse.

Such crimes and the peculiar manner in which they are carried out (and in this they very much differ from common robbery and theft) always demand a medico-legal examination. That the act per se does not necessarily arise from psychopathological conditions, however, is shown by the infrequent cases of hair despoiling[17] that occur simply for the purpose of gain.

Case 225.

P., laborer, aged twenty-nine. Family heavily tainted. Emotional, irritable; had masturbated since childhood. At ten years old he saw a boy masturbate into a woman's handkerchief. This gave the direction to P.'s sex life. He stole handkerchiefs from pretty girls and masturbated into them. His mother tried every means to break him of this habit. She admonished him, took the stolen handkerchiefs away and bought him new ones, all in vain. He was caught by the police and punished for theft. He then went to Africa and served in the army with an excellent record. On his return to France he resumed his old practices. He was only potent if the prostitute held a white handkerchief in her hand during the act. He married in 1894 and sustained his virility by grasping a handkerchief during coitus.

The fetishistic crisis always came suddenly, like a paroxysm, especially at moments of laziness. He would feel out of sorts, psychically moody, sexually excited, and impelled to masturbate. Soon the fantasy image of a handkerchief would appear and take full possession of his thoughts and feelings. If he then caught sight of a woman's handkerchief, he would choke with fear, palpitation of the heart would set in, he would tremble, and profuse perspiration would break out all over his body. Although conscious of the risk involved, he was irresistibly forced to steal the handkerchief. He was arrested on one such occasion, but the examining physician declared him irresponsible. During the time of detention he was free from the obsession. He hoped to master his weakness in the future. He estimated that he had stolen one hundred handkerchiefs. He used each handkerchief only once, then threw it away (Magnan with Thoinot, *Attentats aux moeurs,* p. 428).

Case 226.

Handkerchief fetishism; repeated thefts of handkerchiefs belonging to women.

D., forty-two years of age, manservant, single, was sent by the police on March 11, 1892, to the district asylum of Deggendorf (Niederbayern) for observation of his mental faculties.

He was 1.62 meters high, muscular and well-fed. Head submicrocephalic; expression of face blank. The eyes distinctly neuropathic. Genital organs normal. With the exception of a moderate degree of neurasthenia and increased patellar reflexes, there was nothing abnormal in D.'s nervous system.

In 1878, D. received his first sentence of one and a half years' imprisonment at Straubing for stealing handkerchiefs.

In 1880, he stole a handkerchief from a tradeswoman in the yard of an inn, and was sentenced to fourteen days.

In 1882, on a public road, he made an attempt to pull a handkerchief from the hand of a peasant girl. Charged with attempted robbery, he was found not guilty on the strength of medical opinion, which reported weakness of mind and a morbid disturbance of his mental faculties at the time of the crime.

In 1884, he was tried before a jury for having committed, under similar circumstances, robbery of a woman's handkerchief. He was found guilty and sentenced to four years' imprisonment.

In 1888, in a public marketplace, he took a handkerchief from the pocket of a woman. Sentence, four months.

In 1889, for a similar offense, nine months.

In 1891, ditto, ten months. Otherwise his record shows only a few fines or detentions at the police station for carrying a concealed weapon (a knife) and vagrancy.

All the thefts of handkerchiefs were from young females. They usually occurred in broad daylight, in the presence of other people, and so clumsily and impudently that each time he was arrested on the spot. During the proceedings, not the slightest hint could be found of the theft of other articles, no matter how insignificant.

On December 9, 1891, D. was again released from jail. On December 14 he was caught in a crowd at the annual fair stealing a handkerchief from a peasant girl. He was immediately arrested; when searched, the police found two more women's white handkerchiefs.

In addition, on previous occasions whole collections of women's handkerchiefs had been found on his person (1880, thirty-two pieces; 1882, fourteen, nine of which he wore next to his skin; on another occasion, twenty-five; in 1891, seven white handkerchiefs were found on him).

When questioned as to his motive for stealing handkerchiefs, he always said that he was drunk at the time, and had taken the handkerchiefs as a joke.

He maintained that the handkerchiefs found on him had been bought or swapped for something else, or had been given to him by women with whom he had had relations.

Under observation, D. showed weakness of mind, and appeared run down because of vagrancy, drink and masturbation. He was, however, good-natured, obedient, and by no means afraid of work.

He knew nothing of his parents and grew up without supervision. As a child he made a living by begging; at thirteen he was a stableboy, and at fourteen was used by others for pederasty. He declared that very early he felt a strong sexual instinct; at that time he began to have coitus and to practice masturbation. At fifteen, he was told by a coachman that great pleasure could be derived by applying the handkerchiefs of young women to his genitals. He tried it, found it to be the case, and then sought to obtain, in any way possible, such handkerchiefs. This craving became so strong that whenever he saw a pleasing young woman with a handkerchief in her hand or pocket, violent sexual excitement would seize him. He was then impelled to follow the woman and take her handkerchief.

When sober he generally contrived to resist this impulse for fear of punishment. When he had drink in him, however, he could not resist. While serving in the army, he had often induced young and pleasing girls to give him their used handkerchiefs. After he had used these handkerchiefs for a while, he exchanged them for others.

When he slept with a girl, he generally exchanged his own handkerchief for the girl's. He often bought handkerchiefs specifically to exchange with those used by women.

New and unused handkerchiefs had no effect on him. The girl had to carry it around and use it before it excited him sexually.

According to the trial proceedings, in order to bring unused handkerchiefs into contact with women, he would sometimes throw one in the road, in front of an approaching woman, so that she might step on it. Once he fell upon a girl, pressed a handkerchief against her neck, and ran away.

As soon as he possessed a handkerchief touched by a woman, he would have an erection and orgasm. He would then put the handkerchief **on his nude body,** or preferably on his genitals, and thus produce a pleasurable ejaculation.

He never asked such women to have coitus with him, partly because he feared a refusal, but primarily because he preferred the handkerchief to the girl.

D. made all these confessions piecemeal and with great reserve. He repeatedly broke into tears and refused to say more because he was "so ashamed" of himself. "I am not a thief, and have never stolen a penny's worth, even when I was in dire distress. I never could have brought myself to sell one of these handkerchiefs. I am not a bad man. It is just that when I do these stupid things I am beside myself."

The favorable opinion given by the authorities of the asylum attributed his misdeeds to an abnormal mental condition producing a morbid, irresistible impulse to commit these acts, coupled with a weakness of intellect to a moderate degree. Free pardon from theft.

Case 227.
Violation of ladies' toilettes *emanating from cloth fetishism.*

X., heavily tainted (great uncle insane, father a drunkard, sister an idiot), was arrested while pushing up against ladies in an office. He had been cutting pieces of fur, velvet or cloth from their apparel with a pair of scissors. A large collection of such cuttings was found in his pockets and in his room.

From his tenth year X. had shown a weakness for woolly and fluffy materials. Just the sight of them, but more the touch of them, would bring on orgasm and ejaculation. Fur particularly had this effect on him, and after that, satin. This explained why a number of cuttings of satin ribbons were found in his collection.

He induced lustful emotions by placing the stolen pieces of cloth next to his skin. If ejaculation was not spontaneous, he assisted with masturbation. Neither woman in her capacity as woman, nor sexual intercourse with her, had any charm for him (Garnier, *Les Fétichistes pervertes,* p. 49, Paris, 1896).

notes on the question of responsibility in sexual offenses caused by delusion.[18]

The question of delusion in the sexual affects that occur in fetishism, sadism and exhibitionism presents many difficulties. The all-important point is to find the motive for the act that results from either fetishism or sadism, inasmuch as it is a sexual offense (likely an equivalent for impossible coitus) that claims our attention, and not, for instance, a theft. The offender, out of shame from his act, is apt to mislead the examining judge. Particular stress should be laid upon the fact that the act emanated from an irresistible impulse, a delusion that voids responsibility. The patient, although not fully robbed of consciousness, is nevertheless unable to shake off the delusion and finds relief only in committing the imperative act, which is usually accompanied by strong paroxysms of fear and anxiety. The organic source of this fear may be found in powerful somatic, vasomotoric manifestations. Of psychic importance is the consciousness that the mind is inhibited in forming free thoughts; that the willpower is impaired and quite impotent in the presence of the delusion. This may be accompanied by hypersexuality, and the affect of fear may be overcompensated by an anticipated pleasurable feeling. Thus the patient, though conscious of the wrongfulness of the act and its consequences, determines to end the situation by yielding to the impulse, which is, after all, the only psychologically possible way out of the difficulty. The offender is merely an automaton, the slave of a driving idea.

The situation is an organic force, an impulse to rid oneself of an intolerable position that involves one's very existence. Beneficent freedom from the constraint and the predominating idea is indeed experienced after the commission of the deed. Delusions (in the narrower sense) that struggle against the prevailing impulse and fear, the cardinal symptom of which is the presence of consciousness, must not be confused with:

[1] *The sexual acts of psychically defective individuals* in whom the sensual appetite, by virtue of ethical and intellectual insufficiency, finds prompt satisfaction in some adequate sexual act, but without psychic affects or a conflict with moral principles.[19]

[2] *Impulsive sexual acts committed by heavily degenerated individuals* by virtue of

preeminent sexual feelings during sexual hyperesthesia. These feelings suddenly grow, even from birth, into a powerful sexual affect that occludes the spheres of willpower and consciousness, becoming either a sexual delusion colored with the character of a psychic reflex or a quasi-psychic convulsion.

Alcohol and prolonged sexual abstinence are the provocative causes of such affects in many degenerates. The corresponding acts of violence usually consist of rape.[20] They originate from epileptic[21] and hysterical neuroses or from overindulgence in alcohol, while acts emanating from delusions maintain clinical relations to neurasthenia.

[3] *The sexual acts (primarily exhibitionism) committed under exceptional episodic psychic conditions,* with or without delirium and hallucinations. These occur in individuals afflicted with general neuroses (epilepsy, hysteria) or alcoholism, when consciousness is clouded and memory is paralyzed. They generally present the character of an impulsive act.[22]

These perversions may be observed in heterosexual as well as homosexual individuals; likewise in those who are sexually or otherwise impotent.

The perversions that occur in the performance of the sexual act, or any other act serving as an equivalent for coitus consist of:

[a] (for heterosexual, potent individuals) imaginary representations of the female sexual organs (Raymond and Janet, *Névroses et idées fixes,* vol. 2, p. 162); gazing at the genitals of women (Petres and Régis, *Obsessions,* p. 40); **holding the genitals against women's feet** (case 76); **a woman urinating into a sick man's mouth** (case 68); bestiality (cases 199, 201, 203); periodic pederasty (Tarnowsky, *Die krankhaften Erscheinungen des Geschlechtssinnes,* p. 38).

[b] (for heterosexual, impotent individuals) sadistic acts.

For homosexual individuals, the same manifestations may be observed, only *mutatis mutandis.*

The question of responsibility in the individual case depends upon the psychic conditions by which the offender was driven. In many instances, the culprit is devoid of all moral worth as well as ethical and intellectual understanding; he is, in fact, in the transitory stage of becoming a psychically defective sexual criminal. In other instances, the powerful motives that lead to the criminal act are prolonged sexual abstinence or the complicating influences of alcohol, with its erogenous and demoralizing effects (primarily in cases of exhibitionism). *Forensic responsibility* in these cases is determined by whether or not the offender succumbed to an irresistible impulse. To what extent the offender is to be held accountable for having consciously and in a reckless manner impaired his moral willpower by intoxication is for the jurist to decide. If the act is the result of a delusion, it cannot be considered in the light of a punishable act.

An episode of psychic perversion – especially when manifested in the form of a delusion – cannot possibly be designated as a mental disease; instead it is a temporary confusion of consciousness, a morbid state of the mind, a transitory disturbance of the psychic life.

Nevertheless, the offender is a danger to the common welfare, and the interests of society are best served by his confinement to an insane asylum, where abstinence from alcohol is enforced and proper treatment (if necessary, hypnotic suggestion) offers the promise of a final cure.

[6] violation of individuals under the age of fourteen.

[Austrian statutes, Paragraphs 128, 132; Austrian abridgment, Paragraphs 189, 191; German statutes, Paragraphs 174, 176.]

By violation of sexually immature individuals, the jurist means all the possible immoral acts committed upon persons under fourteen years of age that are not included in the term "rape." The term "violation," in the legal sense of the word, includes the most horrible perversions and acts that are only possible for a man who is a slave to lust, morally weak, and usually lacking in sexual power.

A common feature of the crimes committed on persons who really still belong, more or less, to childhood, is that they are unmanly, knavish, and often silly. It is a fact that these acts, with the exception of pathological cases such as those of imbeciles, paretics, and the senile, are committed almost exclusively by young men who lack courage or have no faith in their virility; or by *roués* who have, to some extent, lost their power. It is psychologically incomprehensible that a mentally sound adult of full virility should indulge in sexual abuse of children.

non-psychopathological cases.

Non-psychopathological cases of immoral acts with children may be summarized in the following categories:

[1] Debauchées who have tasted all the pleasures of normal and abnormal sexual pleasures with women. The only motive that can be found for the infamous act is in a morbid psychic craving to create a novel sexual situation and to revel in the shame and confusion of the child victim. A subordinate motive may be sexual impotence that leads the adult to seek a new stimulus in extraordinary coitus with an immature female. Should virility also fail here, sexual contact with boys is very likely resorted to, especially in the form of pederasty. In large cities the markets for these filthy needs are well-stocked. (Cf. Tardieu's revelations of Paris, and Tarnowsky's revelations of St. Petersburg.) Casper tells us that lewd mothers often prepare their little daughters for the use of these libertines.

[2] Young men who are afraid of the adult female or are diffident about their own virility. These are mostly recruited from the groups of masturbators who suffer from either psychic impotence or some irritable weakness of the sexual organs that renders coitus with a woman impossible. They then seek a compensatory equivalent in the manipulation of the female organs in the child, which usually suffices to produce orgasm and ejaculation in themselves. If potency is still unimpaired, **insertion of the penis** will be attempted in almost every case.

Casper, in his *Klin. Novellen*,[23] cases 4 and 5, shows that even brothers have proved to be dangerous fiends toward their little sisters.

[3] Lewd servant girls, governesses and nursemaids, not to mention female relatives, represent a large percentage of cases. These women abuse, for sexual purposes,[24] the little boys entrusted to their care and often even infect them with gonorrheal poison.

The cases in which lascivious tutors, governesses, etc., cane or spank their pupils without provocation are open to investigation as to the pathological condition of the malefactor.[25]

The manner in which acts of immorality are committed on children differs widely, especially where libertines are concerned. Such methods consist primarily of libidinous manipulations of the pudenda, active masturbation (using the child's hand for masturbation), flagellation, etc. Less frequent are cunnilingus, fellatio with boys or girls, pederasty with boys, coitus between the thighs, and exhibitionism. The possibilities in this direction, however, are inexhaustible.

The finer feelings of man revolt at the thought of counting these monsters among the psychically normal members of human society. One can only presume that such individuals have suffered a shipwreck in the sphere of morality and potency. This, however, should not preclude the moral responsibility of the perpetrator, as sheer moral depravity may be at the bottom of the act. This is especially true for lascivious characters, drunkards, or those individuals who are oversated with natural sexual intercourse. Judgment of the act should be guided by its monstrosity and the degree to which it psychically and physically differs from the natural act.

psychopathological cases.

A great number of these cases, however, certainly depend upon pathological states.

A review of the psychopathological cases of immorality with children shows that the largest number may be reduced to conditions of *acquired* mental weakness. First of all we must mention senile dementia[26] (Kirn, *Allg. Zeitschr. f. Psychiatrie*, no. 39, p. 217), then chronic alcoholism,[27] paralysis,[28] mental debility due to epilepsy,[29] injuries to the head and apoplexy,[30] and syphilis of the brain.[31] These are followed by *original* mental defects[32] and states of degeneration.[33]

The cause of these offenses may also be found in states of morbid unconsciousness.

These outrages on morality are frequently due to overindulgence in alcoholic stimulants or epilepto-psychic conditions of an exceptional character, and are also occasionally due to an error in sex or personality. They may be explained on the grounds of sexual excitement concomitant with these conditions, especially in epileptic subjects.[34] Rape and pederasty frequently occur under these circumstances. In the states of psychic weakness, the extent to which there is command over virility may determine the quality of the sexual act.

In addition to the aforesaid categories of moral renegades and those afflicted with psychic-moral weakness (whether congenital or superinduced by cerebral disease or episodic mental aberration), there are cases in which the sexually needy subject is drawn to children not because of degenerated morality or psychic or physical impotence, but rather because of a morbid disposition, a *psychosexual perversion,* which may at present be named *erotic pedophilia.*[35]

In my own experience I have come across only four such cases, all of which involve men. The first case is of more value than the others, inasmuch as it appears in the form of platonic love. It manifests its sexual character, however, in the fact that this (paranoiac) lover of children is stimulated only by little girls. He is quite callous toward the grown-up woman and also appears to be a hair fetishist.

Observation number two represents a man tainted by heredity. From puberty (which came very late, at the age of twenty-four) he had sensual emotions toward little girls who were from five to ten years of age. Although the mere sight of such a girl brought on ejaculation, a touch from her caused absolute sexual paroxysm, with only a succinct recollection as to its duration. The marital act gave some slight gratification, and thus enabled him to control, for a time, his desire for little girls. A heavy neurasthenia supervened, however (primarily due to *coitus interruptus*), at which time he became a criminal, either because his moral powers of resistance slackened, or his sexual appetite increased.

The third case is a man tainted by heredity and constitutionally neurasthenic; cranium abnormal. Although he was never normally inclined to the adult woman, during coitus he was like an animal at rutting time. To immorally touch little girls gave him the highest possible pleasure. He became a pedophile when he was only twenty-five years old.

The fourth case is a man, tainted, who found sexual charm in immature girls. For mature women he felt little attraction. When impotence (due to syphilis?) and paralytic dementia set in, he could no longer resist his morbid impulse.

The cases quoted here under the heading of "erotic pedophilia" (in the sense of sexual perversion) have the following traits in common:

[1] The afflicted individual is tainted.

[2] The affection for immature persons of the opposite sex is of a primary nature (quite in opposition to the debauchée); the imaginary representations have an abnormal aspect and are marked very strongly, indeed, by lustful feelings.

[3] The libidinous acts – if you exclude the one case in which virility was present – consist only of immodest touches or masturbation of the victim. Nevertheless they adduce the gratification of the subject, even though ejaculation is not attained.

The following cases taken from Magnan (*Psychiatrische Vorlesungen,* German translation by Möbius, nos. 2 and 3, p. 41) clearly show that erotic pedophilia also occurs in women.

Magnan's first case is a lady, twenty-nine years of age, tainted by heredity; she suffered from delusions and phobias.

For eight years she had a strong desire for sexual union with one of her (five) nephews. Her desire was first directed toward the oldest when he was five years of age. She then transferred this desire to each of them, in turn, as they grew up. The sight of the child in question was sufficient to produce orgasm and even pollution. She was able to resist her inclination, which she cannot explain. She had no desire for mature men.

The second case is a woman, thirty-two years of age, mother of two children; heavily tainted by heredity; separated from her husband because of brutal treatment.

For several months she had neglected her children in order to visit a friend's house every day when the son of the house was returning from school. She hugged and kissed the child, occasionally saying that she was in love with him and wanted to marry him.

One day she told his mother that the boy was ill and unhappy. She wanted to cohabit with him in order to cure him.

Although she was forbidden to enter the house, she laid siege to it.

One day she tried to force her way in. She was afterward sent to an asylum, where she continued to rave about the boy.

That erotic pedophilia may occur periodically is demonstrated by Anjél's observation (see above, cases 187 and 188).

To the same degree, however, that antipathic sexual instinct can be compared to heterosexual instinct, so is the predilection for the immature here equally abnormal and exceptional. Thus, practically speaking, acts of immorality committed on boys by sexually inverted men are extremely rare.

I have already laid stress upon this fact in my pamphlet *Der Konträr-sexuale vor dem Strafrichter,* second edition, p. 9. In it I have pointed out that the real seducer of youth is the weak-minded man who is born sexually normal; the *roué* who is impotent or at least sexually perverted and morally depraved; and the senile man who, though morally enfeebled, remains sexually excited.

Under such accidental conditions, the sexually inverted individual may also eventually become a danger to boys (cf. case 127 of the present and 109 of the ninth edition of this book). This has nothing to do with pedophilia, however, because in these cases the boys were near puberty, while in cases of genuine pedophilia the subject is drawn only to the sexually quite immature. The first case of Magnan seems to be the most instructive in this regard, for in it the desire turned from the older boy to each of the younger ones as they, in turn, grew from the age of three to five years.

The following case, reported by Pacotte and Raynaud (*Archives d'Anthropologie criminelle,* vol. 10, p. 435), may be looked upon as proof that erotic pedophilia also may occur in cases of antipathic sexuality.

Case 228.

X., thirty-six years of age, journalist; heavily tainted by heredity; ethically and intellectually defective; from early youth afflicted with epileptoid spells; intolerant of alcohol; face asymmetrical; never cared for women; masturbated since he was eighteen; attempts at coitus found him cold and impotent.

Boys of ten to fifteen years of age, however, excited him very much. Although he was conscious of the criminality of the act, he could not resist the impulse to practice pederasty with them. Many times he was sated by their "enchanting looks and sweet smiles."

Neither adults nor little girls possessed any charm for him. Only at the age of twenty-two, when a twelve-year-old boy forced sexual intercourse upon him, did he become a pedophile. At that time he refused his seducer; soon, however, he could no longer resist the desire awakened in him by that incident, although he had repeatedly been sentenced and imprisoned for this offense. His life was blighted by this unfortunate weakness, and he made several attempts at suicide.

Expert opinion established congenital sexual inversion, and, within the limits of homosexuality, a special anomaly; namely, love that was exclusively for boys of a certain age and of delicate constitution.

It was asserted that degenerative mental disturbance affected the soundness of his mind and rendered him a danger to the community.

X. was inconsolable over the result of his trial, for he was sent to an insane asylum. He had anticipated a free pardon.

In my *Arbeiten* (no. 4, pp. 119-124) I have published three other cases of erotic pedophilia that came under my personal observation. Two other cases in my possession have never been published. It seems to me as if all these cases might be reduced to fetishism. This would at once account for the paradox apparent in the manifestations of erotic pedophilia. As it stands, this perversion can only be explained on the basis of heavy taint, for a strongly marked degenerative predisposition can always be found in these individuals. That these cases are not of everyday occurrence and require a fetishistic impulse may also account for their rarity.

Pseudopedophilia, which occurs in individuals who have lost their libido for the adult through masturbation and subsequently turn to children for the gratification of their sexual appetite, is much more frequently observed. (Cf. case 106 of the tenth edition of this book.)

Another classical case may be found in my *Arbeiten,* no. 4, p. 125.

Irresponsibility should not, as a rule, be claimed in these cases, for experience teaches that a pedophile's impulses can be mastered, unless a weakening or total loss of willpower has been superinduced by pathological conditions, such as severe neurasthenia or paralytic dementia. A plea for ameliorating circumstances, however, may be indicated. Nevertheless a criminal inquiry should always be made in flagrant cases of erotic pedophilia. The question of responsibility *in concreto facto* depends entirely on the synthetic comprehension of all the characteristics of the individual involved. Hypersexuality, overindulgence in alcoholic drinks, moral weakness, etc., should be carefully considered, inasmuch as they frequently counteract the freedom of action.

At any rate, these unfortunate beings should always be looked upon as a common danger to the welfare of the community, and put under strict surveillance and medical treatment. The proper place for such persons is a sanitarium[36] established for that purpose, not a prison.[37]

That a cure is possible is evidenced by two severe cases that came under my observation and treatment.

Unfortunately, the presumption that psychopathological conditions are present cannot always be proved. But the fact that pathological moments are not absent should be carefully weighed. At any rate, a thorough investigation of the mental status of the individual must be made. This is especially the case when old men seduce children. Moral and intellectual idiocy, heavy psychic degeneration, defects springing from acquired organic causes and mental aberrations are frequently at the bottom of these excesses. The beginning of senile or paralytic dementia is not always sufficiently pronounced to allow a proper diagnosis. Proper care must therefore be exercised.

[7] u n n a t u r a l   a b u s e   (s o d o m y).[38]

[Austrian statutes, Paragraph 129; abridgment, Paragraph 190; German statutes, Paragraph 175.]

[a] v i o l a t i o n   o f   a n i m a l s   (b e s t i a l i t y).[39]

Violation of animals, as monstrous and revolting as it may seem to mankind, is by no means always due to psychopathological conditions. Low morality and great sexual desire, along with a lack of opportunity for natural indulgence, are the principal motives for this unnatural means of sexual satisfaction, which is resorted to by women as well as by men.

To Polak we owe the knowledge that bestiality is frequently practiced in Persia because of the delusion that it cures gonorrhea; just as in Europe the idea is still prevalent that intercourse with children heals venereal disease.

Experience teaches that bestiality with cows and horses is somewhat common. Occasionally the acts may be undertaken with goats, bitches, and, as shown in a case of Tardieu's and one of Schauenstein's (*Lehrb.*, p. 125), with hens.

The action of Frederick the Great in the case of a cavalryman who had committed bestiality with a mare is well-known: "The fellow is a pig, and shall be reduced to the infantry."

The intercourse of females with beasts is limited to dogs. A monstrous example of the moral depravity in large cities is related by Maschka (*Handb.*, vol. 3); it is the case of a Parisian woman who, for ten francs a head, showed herself in the sexual act with a trained bulldog to a secret circle of *roués*.

C a s e   2 2 9 .

In a provincial town a man was caught having intercourse with a hen. He was thirty years old and of high social position. The chickens had been dying one after another, and the man causing it had been "wanted" for a long time. When asked by the judge as to the reason for such an act, the accused said that his genitals were so small that coitus with women was impossible. Medical examination showed that his genitals were, in fact, extremely small. The man was *mentally quite sound.*

There were no statements concerning any abnormalities at the time of puberty, etc. (Gyurkovechky, *Männl. Impotenz*, 1889, p. 82).

Case 230.

On the afternoon of September 23, 1889, W., aged sixteen, shoemaker's apprentice, caught a goose in a neighbor's garden, and committed bestiality on the fowl until the neighbor approached. On being accused by the neighbor, W. said, "Well! Is there anything wrong with the goose?" and then went away. Although at his examination he confessed to the act, he excused himself on the grounds of a temporary loss of his mind. After a severe illness in his twelfth year, he had attacks, with heat in his head, several times a month. During the attacks he was intensely excited sexually, could not help himself, and did not know what he was doing. He had consummated the act with the goose during such an attack. He answered for himself in the same way at the trial, and stated that he knew nothing about the form of the act except what he had learned from the statements of the neighbor. His father stated that W., who came from a healthy family, had always been sickly after an attack of scarlet fever in his fifth year, and that, at the age of twelve, he had a febrile cerebral disease. W. had a good reputation, learned well in school, and later helped his father in his work. He was not prone to masturbation.

The medical examination revealed no intellectual or moral defect. The physical examination revealed normal genitals; greater than average development of the penis; marked exaggeration of the patellar reflexes. In other respects, negative results.

The history of his condition at the time of the deed was not reliable. There was no proof of previous attacks of mental disturbance, and no attacks occurred during the six weeks of observation. There was no perversion of the sex life. The medical opinion allowed the possibility that some organic cause (cerebral congestion), dependent upon cerebral disease, may have exercised an influence at the time of the commission of the criminal act (from the opinion of Dr. Fritsch, Vienna).

There is another group of cases, however, that fall well within the category of bestiality, in which a decided pathological basis exists, indicated by heavy taint, constitutional neuroses, impotence for the normal act, and an impulsive manner of performing the unnatural act. Perhaps the purpose would be better served by placing such cases under the heading of a special appellation; using, for instance, the term "bestiality" for those cases that are not of a pathological character, and reserving the term "zooerasty" for those cases that are of a pathological nature.

Case 231.

Impulsive sodomy. A., aged sixteen; gardener's boy; born out of wedlock; father unknown; mother deeply tainted, hystero-epileptic. A. had a deformed, asymmetrical cranium, as well as deformity and asymmetry of the bones of the face. In addition, the whole skeleton was deformed, asymmetrical and small. He had been a masturbator since childhood; always morose, apathetic, and fond of solitude; irritable and pathological in his emotional reaction. He was an imbecile, probably much reduced physically by masturbation, and neurasthenic. Moreover, he presented hysteropathic symptoms (limitation of the visual field, dyschromatopsia [partial color blindness]; diminution of the senses of smell, taste and hearing on the right side; anesthesia of the right testicle, clavus, etc.).

A. was convicted of having committed masturbation and sodomy on dogs and rabbits. At the age of twelve he saw how boys masturbated a dog. He imitated it and could not stop thereafter from abusing dogs, cats and rabbits in this vile manner. Much more frequently, however, he committed sodomy on female rabbits – the only animals that had a charm for him. At dusk he often repaired to his master's rabbit pen in order to gratify his vile desire. Rabbits with torn rectums were repeatedly found. The act of bestiality was always done in the same manner. There were actual attacks that came on every eight weeks, always in the evening, and always in the same way. A. would become very uncomfortable and feel as if someone were pounding his head. He felt as if he were losing his reason. He struggled against the imperative idea of committing sodomy on the rabbits, and thus had an increasing feeling of fear and an intensification of headaches, until it became unbearable. At the height of the attack there were sounds of bells, cold perspiration, trembling of the knees, and, finally, loss of resistive power, with impulsive performance of the perverse act. As soon as this was done he lost all anxiety; the nervous cycle was completed, he was again his own master, deeply ashamed of the deed, and fearful of the return of an attack. A. stated that, when in such a condition, if he were called upon to choose between a woman and a female rabbit, he would choose the rabbit. Also, between attacks, he is partial only to rabbits. In his exceptional states, simple caressing or kissing, etc., of the rabbit typically sufficed to afford him sexual satisfaction; but sometimes, when doing this, he experienced such sexual passion that he was forced to wildly perform sodomy on the animal.

The acts of bestiality mentioned were the only acts that afforded him sexual satisfaction, and they constituted the only manner in which he was capable of sexual indulgence. A. declared that he never had a lustful feeling during the act, only satisfaction, inasmuch as he was thus freed from the painful condition into which he was brought by the imperative impulse.

The medical evidence easily proved that this human monster was a psychic degenerate, an irresponsible invalid, and not a criminal (Boeteau, *La France médicale,* vol. 38, no. 38).

Case 232.

X., peasant, aged forty; Greek-Catholic. Father and mother were hard drinkers. From his fifth year the patient had epileptic convulsions – i.e., he would fall down unconscious, lie still for two or three minutes, and then get up and run around aimlessly with staring eyes. Sexuality was first manifested at seventeen. The patient had inclinations neither for women nor for men, only for animals (fowl, horses, etc.). He had intercourse with hens and ducks, and later with horses and cows. He had never masturbated.

The patient painted pictures of saints; he was of very limited intelligence. He had religious paranoia with states of ecstasy for years. He felt an "inexplicable" love for the Virgin, for whom he would sacrifice his life. Taken to the hospital, he proved to be free from infirmity and signs of anatomical degeneration.

He had always had an aversion for women. During his only attempt at coitus with a woman he was impotent; with animals, however, he was always potent. He was bashful before women; he regarded coitus with women almost as a sin (Kowalewsky, *Jahrb. für Psychiatrie,* vol. 7, no. 3).

Case 233.

T., thirty-five years of age. Father an inebriate; mother psychopathic. Never had a severe illness; never showed special peculiarities. At the age of nine, immorality with a hen; later, with other domestic animals. His bestial desires disappeared when he began to have sexual relations with women. He married at twenty and found sexual satisfaction.

At twenty-seven he began to drink, and this awakened his former perverse inclinations. One day he took a female goat to a neighboring village to have her bred. Although he felt a strong desire to commit sodomy on her, he initially overcame the impulse. Then, however, palpitation of the heart, pain in the chest, and a violent orgasm made him succumb. T. declared that these bestial acts gave him greater lustful gratification than coitus with a woman.

His acts of bestiality remained unnoticed. He was finally sent to an insane asylum because of *delirium tremens.* When he was examined upon admission, he made the above revelations (Boissier and Lauchaux, *Annal. médico-psychol.,* July-August 1893, p. 381).

In the explanation of zooerasty, great difficulties are encountered. Any attempt to reduce it to fetishism, as is possible in *zoophilia erotica* (cf. p. 235), cannot possibly succeed.

Whether zoophilia can ever lead to sexual acts with beasts and eventually bestiality is questionable. If it is in reality a fetishistic manifestation, this possibility cannot be based upon the present knowledge of fetishism.

Even in the case of fetishistic *zoophilia erotica* (p. 235), acts of bestiality were never committed; in fact, the sex of the animals in question was never considered. The only thing that can be done at present is to consider zooerasty an original perversion of the sex life, and place it on the same level as antipathic sexuality.

Although only rudimentary and abortive, the following case seems to support this theory as well as establish complete unconsciousness of the motive for the impulse.

C a s e   2 3 4 .

Y., twenty years of age, intelligent, well-educated; claimed to be free from hereditary taint; physically sound except for evidence of neurasthenia and urethral hyperesthesia; said he never masturbated. Always fond of animals, especially dogs and horses. Although with puberty his love for animals increased, sexual ideas in connection with sport seem to have been absent.

One day, upon mounting a mare for the first time, he experienced a sensation of lust; two weeks later, on a similar occasion, he had the same sensation with erection.

During his first ride he ejaculated. A month later, the same thing happened. Patient felt disgusted by the occurrence and was angry with himself. He gave up the saddle. From then on, however, he had pollutions almost daily.

The sight of men on horseback, or dogs, caused erections. Almost every night he had pollutions accompanied by dreams in which he rode on horseback or was training dogs. Patient came for medical advice.

Treatment with sounds removed the urethral hyperesthesia and the diminished pollutions. The patient reluctantly followed the advice of the physician to have coitus. This reluctance was based partly on his dislike for women and partly on his diffidence about his virility.

Although he made abortive attempts at coitus, he could not even bring about an erection. The moment he saw a man on horseback, however, an erection occurred. This depressed him; he considered his condition abnormal and beyond remedy.

Continued medical treatment. A further attempt at coitus was successful with the assistance of fantasized images of riders and dogs, which stimulated erection.

Patient grew more virile; his love for animals waned; erections at the sight of riders and dogs disappeared, nocturnal pollutions with dreams of animals became less frequent; he then dreamed of girls. Erection (which did not at first support premature ejaculation) and pathological coitus grew normal under treatment with sounds. Patient found normal sexual gratification and was freed from his perverse sexual impulse (Dr. Hanc, *Wien med. Blätter,* 1887, no. 5).

The preceding case justifies the assumption of an original perversion, because instead of the idea of the normal object (woman), it is the idea of commonly seen animals (dogs and horses) that awakens sexual feelings and desires. There may have been a latent sadistic element in the case, because the riding of horses and the training of dogs played a prominent part, at least in the sex life of his dreams.

The following case, that of a **rapist of animals,** is of pathological interest.

Case 235.

Mr. X., forty-seven years of age, of high social position, came to me for advice because of a troublesome anomaly of his sex life. He was about to be married and, in his present condition, considered it morally impossible to enter into matrimony.

X. was evidently heavily tainted. His father, two of his sisters, and one brother were highly neurotic. His mother was presumed to have been a healthy woman.

The sexual instinct awoke early in X., and he began to spontaneously masturbate at the age of eleven.

He was decidedly hypersexual, practiced masturbation with passion, and at the age of fourteen he forgot himself and sodomized bitches, mares and other female animals. He ascribed these acts to excessive sexual desire and to a lack of opportunity to satisfy his cravings in the normal way (he had spent his childhood and boyhood in a lonely part of the country and later went to boarding school).

X. admitted that he was quite conscious of the abomination of his acts, and said that he fought with all his willpower against these bestial impulses. The greed, the lust, and the pleasure they always gave, however, overpowered him. When he grew into manhood, he had neither homosexual desires nor an inclination for women.

From this part of his confession the opinion seemed justified that his bestiality was only a perversity that was rooted in his habits, and was not a perversion.

It struck one as peculiar, however, that his erotic dreams were always about bestial inter-course, and that when he sought at twenty-five to improve his condition by having coitus with a woman, he derived not the slightest gratification from it, although he was quite potent, and the prostitute was pleasing and sympathetic.

He had the same experience in other repeated attempts during the subsequent twenty-two years. He described coitus as a mere mechanical act devoid of lustful excitement. He stated he might as well have coitus with a piece of wood. Although normal coitus simply disgusted him, he experienced the height of pleasure with an animal.

The mere sight of animals excited him wildly. The society of ladies bored him. When he engaged in coitus with a girl, she had to resort to all kinds of manipulations to prepare him for the act.

For a period of two months prior to his first visit to me, X. had exerted all his willpower to resist the impulses of masturbation and bestiality.

Physically he was a peculiar being, evidently a superior degenerate. There were no symptoms of anatomical degeneration, and no traces of neurasthenia.

I made strong suggestions that he be on his guard against masturbation and bestiality, and that he seek more often the society of ladies; prescribed anaphrodisiacs; advised frugality, slight hydrotherapy, plenty of open-air exercise, and steady occupation. At the end of ten months, I had the satisfaction of learning that the patient experienced a slight gratification in repeated sexual intercourse with a woman and was almost free from his former perverse desires.

An analogous case is reported by Moll in his work *Libido sexualis,* p. 421.

Another remarkable case of zooerasty is published by Howard (*Alienist and Neurologist,* 1896, vol. 17, no. 1). It refers to a young man of sixteen years of age who only found sexual gratification with pigs.

The rarity of cases of real zooerasty seems to be remarkable. This may be explained, however, by the ease with which they are kept secret.

The present state of our knowledge does not permit a final judgment as to whether zooerasty is an original anomaly or a perverse condition acquired through fetishistic influences.

Moll (*Libido sexualis,* p. 432) is inclined to believe that it is an arrest of undifferentiated sexuality coupled with hypersexuality directed to beasts (analogous to masturbatory impulses), and that this craving for sexual dealings with beasts is permanent and inhibits the development of libido toward the human female. Practically speaking, sexual feeling and psychic potency seem to be absent, as well as the power to differentiate between the male and female beast as an object for sexual accomplishment. Cf. Howard's case, in which only a certain species of animal was preferred.

The forensically important distinction between bestiality and zooerasty can never be difficult in actual cases.

One who seeks and finds sexual gratification exclusively with animals, when the opportunities for the normal act are at hand, must immediately be suspected of having a pathological condition of the sexual instinct. This is even more the circumstance here than for the sexually inverted person, because in sexual acts with animals the psychic infection is absent; i.e., the possibility of the perversion of one partner leading to the perversity of the other does not exist.

It may be assumed, however, that the number of cases of zooerasty is small compared to those of sexual inversion. This follows *a priori* from the character of both perversions. The zooerast, when compared with the sexual invert, is much farther removed from the normal object. This would qualify the perversion of the zooerast as a much graver condition – because it is more degenerative – than the perversion of the sexual invert.

[b] with persons of the same sex (pederasty; sodomy in its strict sense).

Although German law takes cognizance of unnatural sexual relations only between men, Austrian law makes illegal such relations between any persons of the same sex. Thus, unnatural relations between women are punishable.

Among the immoralities between men, pederasty (**insertion of the penis into the anus**) claims the principal interest. Indeed, the jurist thought only of this perversity of sexual activity; and, according to the opinions of distinguished interpreters of the law (Oppenhoff, *Stfgsb.*, Berlin, 1872, p. 324, and Rudolf and Stenglein, *D. Stfgsb. f. d. Deutsche Reich*, 1881, p. 423), **insertion of the penis into a living body** must take place to establish the criminal act covered by Paragraph 175.

According to this interpretation, legal punishment would not follow other improper acts between male persons, *so long as they were not complicated by offense to public decency, force, or undertaken with boys under the age of fourteen.* Recently this interpretation has again been abandoned, and the crime of unnatural abuse between men is assumed to have been committed whenever acts *similar to cohabitation* are performed.[40]

The study of antipathic sexual instinct has placed male love for males, particularly pederasty, in a very different light from the one in which it was seen at the time the statutes were framed. The fact that there is no doubt about the pathological basis of many cases of inverted sexual instinct shows that pederasty may also be the act of an irresponsible person. This makes it necessary to examine not only the deed but also the mental condition of the perpetrator in court.

The principles laid down previously must also be adhered to here. Only an anthropological and clinical judgment of the perpetrator can permit a decision as to whether we are faced with a perversity deserving punishment or an abnormal perversion of the mental and sexual life. Such a perversion, under certain circumstances, excludes punishment.

The next legal question to settle is whether the antipathic sexual feeling is congenital or acquired; and, if acquired, whether it is a pathological perversion or a moral perversity.

Congenital sexual inversion occurs only in predisposed (tainted) individuals as a partial manifestation of a defect evidenced by anatomical or functional abnormalities, or by both. The case becomes clearer and the diagnosis more certain [1] if the individual, in character and disposition, seems to correspond entirely with his sexual peculiarity; [2] if the inclination toward persons of the opposite sex is entirely absent, or horror of sexual intercourse with them is felt; and [3] if the individual, in the impulse to satisfy the antipathic sexual instinct, shows other anomalies of the sexual sphere, such as more pronounced degeneration in the form of periodicity of the impulse and impulsive conduct, and is a neuropathic and psychopathic person.

Another question concerns the mental condition of the homosexual. If this condition removes the possibility of moral responsibility, then the pederast is not a criminal, but is instead an irresponsible, insane person.

In congenital homosexuals this condition appears to be less frequent. These cases usually present elementary psychic disturbances that do not remove responsibility.

This does not settle, however, the question of responsibility in the homosexual. The sexual instinct is one of the most powerful organic needs. There is no law that looks upon its satisfaction outside of marriage as punishable in itself. If the homosexual feels perversely, it is not his fault; instead, it is the fault of an abnormal condition that is natural to him. Although his sexual instinct may be aesthetically repugnant, it is natural from his morbid standpoint. Again, in the majority of these unfortunates the perverse sexual instinct is abnormally intense, and their consciousness recognizes it as nothing unnatural. Thus, moral and aesthetic ideas fail to assist them in resisting the instinct.

Although innumerable normally constituted men are in a position to renounce the gratification of their libido without suffering from diminished health, many neuropathic individuals – and homosexuals are almost always neuropathic – become nervously ill when they do not satisfy sexual desire, either as Nature prompts or in a way that is to them perverse.

The majority of homosexuals are in a painful situation. On the one hand, there is an impulse toward persons of their own sex that is abnormally intense, the gratification of which has a good effect and is natural to them; on the other hand, there is public sentiment, which stigmatizes their acts, and the law, which threatens them with disgraceful punishment. Before them lies mental disrepair – even insanity and suicide – and, at the very least, nervous disease; behind them, shame, loss of position, etc. Under these circumstances, conditions of stress and compulsion are undoubtedly created by an unfortunate natural disposition and constitution. Society and the law should understand and appreciate these facts. Society should pity, not despise, these unfortunates, and the law must cease to punish them – at least while they remain within the limits set for the activity of their sexual instinct.

As a confirmation of the opinions and demands concerning these stepchildren of Nature, it would be appropriate to reproduce here the entreaty of a homosexual to the author. The writer of the following lines is a man of high position in London:

"You have no idea what a constant struggle we all must endure – particularly those of us who have the best minds and finest feelings – and how we suffer under the prevailing false ideas about us and our so-called 'immorality.'

"Your opinion that the phenomenon under consideration is primarily due to a congenital 'pathological' disposition will, perhaps, make it possible to overcome existing prejudices and awaken pity for poor, 'abnormal' men, instead of the present repugnance and contempt.

"Much as I believe that the opinion expressed by you is exceedingly *beneficial* to us, I am still compelled, in the interest of science, to repudiate the word 'pathological.' Permit me, if you will, to express a few thoughts with respect to this.

"Under all circumstances the phenomenon is anomalous; but the word 'pathological' conveys another meaning, which I do not think suits this phenomenon; at least as I have had occasion to observe it in very many cases. I will allow that, *a priori*, a far higher proportion of cases of insanity, nervous exhaustion, etc., may be observed among homosexuals than among other normal men. Does this increased nervousness necessarily depend upon the character of homosexuality, or is it not, in the majority of cases, to be ascribed to the effect of the laws and the prejudices of society, which prohibits the indulgence of their sexual desires due to a congenital peculiarity, while others are not thus restrained?

"The youthful homosexual, when he feels the first sexual promptings and naïvely expresses them to his comrades, soon finds that he is not understood; he shrinks into himself. If he tells his parents or teacher what moves him – that which is as natural to him as swimming is to a fish is described as wrong and sinful – then he is told it must be fought and overcome at any price. Then an inner conflict begins, a powerful repression of sexual inclinations; and the more the natural satisfaction of desire is repressed, the more lively the fantasy becomes, painting the very pictures one wishes to banish. The more energetic the character that carries on this inner conflict, the more the whole nervous system must suffer. Although such a powerful repression of so deeply implanted an instinct cultivates, in my opinion, the abnormal symptoms that are observed in many homosexuals, this does not necessarily follow from the homosexual's disposition.

"Some continue the conflict for a longer or shorter time, and thus injure themselves; others come at last to the knowledge that the powerful instinct born in them cannot possibly be sinful, and, therefore, they cease to try to do the impossible – to repress the instinct. Then, however, the constant suffering and excitement begins. When a normal man seeks satisfaction of his sexual inclination, he knows how to find it easily; it is not so with the homosexual. He sees men that attract him, but he dares not say – nay, not even betray by a look – what his feelings are. He thinks that he alone in all the world has such abnormal feelings. Naturally he seeks the society of young men; but he does not venture to confide in them. Thus he comes to provide himself with a satisfaction that he cannot otherwise obtain. Masturbation is practiced inordinately, and is followed by all the evil results of that vice. When, after a time, the nervous system has been injured, the abnormality is again not the result of homosexuality, but is produced by the masturbation to which the homosexual resorts as a result of the public sentiment that denies him opportunity to satisfy the sexual instinct that is natural to him.

"Or let us suppose that the homosexual has had the rare fortune to soon find a person like himself; or that he has been introduced by an experienced friend to the events of the world of homosexuals. Then, although he is spared much of his inner conflict, fearful cares and anxieties follow his footsteps. Then he knows that he is not the only one in the world who has such abnormal feelings; he opens his eyes and in wonderment meets so many of his kind in all social circles and in all callings; he also learns that in the world of homosexuals, as in the other, there is prostitution, and that men as well as women can be bought. Thus there is no longer any lack of opportunity for sexual satisfaction. But what a difference there is between the way experience is gained here and how it is obtained in the normal manner of sexual indulgence!

"Let us consider the happiest case. After longing all one's life, a friend of similar feeling is found. But he cannot be approached openly, as a lover approaches the girl he loves. In constant fear, both must conceal their relations; nay, even intimacy that might easily excite suspicion must be kept from the world, especially if they are of different ages or belong to different classes. Thus, even within this intimate relation, a chain of anxiety and fear is forged that the secret will be betrayed or discovered, which leaves them no joy in their indulgence. The slightest thing, an event that would not affect others, makes them tremble with fear that suspicion might be aroused and the secret discovered, destroying social position and business. Could this constant anxiety and care be endured without leaving a trace, without exerting an influence on the entire nervous system?

"Another less fortunate man does not find a friend of similar feeling, but falls into the hands of a handsome man, who toys with him until his secret is discovered. Then the most refined blackmail is extorted. The unfortunate, persecuted man, brought to the alternative of paying, or losing his social position and bringing disgrace on himself and his family, pays; and the more he gives, the more voracious the vampire becomes; until at last there remains nothing but absolute financial ruin or dishonor. Who can wonder that nerves are not equal to such a terrible struggle!

"They give way; insanity ensues, and the miserable man at last finds the rest that he could not find in the world in an asylum. Another, in the same situation, driven to despair, finds relief in suicide. One can only guess how many of the suicides of young men can be attributed to this combination of circumstances.

"I do not think that I am in error when I declare that at least one half of the suicides of young men are due to such conditions. Even in those cases where homosexuals are not persecuted by a heartless villain, but where a happy relation between two men exists, discovery, or even the fear of it, very often leads to suicide. How many officers, how many soldiers, who have such relations with their subordinates or companions, have sought, at the moment when they have believed themselves discovered, to escape the threatened disgrace by means of a bullet! And it is the same in all callings.

"Therefore, if it has to be admitted that more mental abnormalities and more cases of insanity are actually observed among homosexuals than among other men, this nevertheless does not prove that the mental disturbance is a *necessary* accompaniment of the homosexual's condition, and that the latter induces the former.

"According to my firm beliefs, the greater number of cases, *by far,* of mental disturbance or abnormal disposition observed in homosexuals are not to be attributed to the sexual anomaly; instead, they are caused by the existing notions about homosexuals, the resulting laws, and the dominant public sentiment concerning the anomaly. Anyone with an adequate idea of the mental and moral suffering, the anxiety and care that the homosexual must endure; the constant hypocrisy and secrecy he must practice in order to conceal his inner instinct; the difficulties that meet him in satisfying his natural desire – can only be surprised that more insanity and nervous disturbance does not occur in homosexuals. The greater part of these abnormal states would not be developed if the homosexual could find a simple and easy way, like any other man, in which to satisfy his sexual desire; if he were not forever troubled by these anxieties!"

With regard to established law, as far as the homosexual is concerned, the paragraph with reference to pederasty should not be applied *without the proof of actual pederasty;* and psychic and somatic abnormalities should be examined by experts with respect to an estimation of the individual on the question of guilt.

With regard to proposed law, the homosexuals wish a repeal of the paragraph. If the jurist remembers that pederasty is much more frequently a disgusting vice than the result of a physical and mental infirmity, he would not consent to this. Furthermore, many homosexuals, though driven to sexual acts with their own sex, are nevertheless not compelled to indulge in pederasty – a sexual act that must stand as a cynical, disgusting and, when passive, a decidedly injurious one, under all circumstances. *Whether it would not be opportune for reasons of expediency* (difficulty of fixing the guilt, encouragement of blackmail, etc.) *to strike the legal punishment of the male-loving man from the statutes is a question for the jurists of the future.*[41]

My reasons for abolishing the laws referred to above are as follows:

[1] The offenses referred to in these laws generally spring from an abnormal psychic condition.

[2] Only a most careful medical examination can distinguish cases of sheer perversity from those of pathological perversion. As soon as the individual is charged with the offense, he is socially ruined.

[3] The majority of homosexuals are the victims of a perverse instinct of abnormal quality. They are irresistibly forced by the physical compulsion that characterizes their sexual instinct.

[4] Many homosexuals are incapable of considering their sexual instinct as unnatural; on the contrary, their own instinct seems the natural way, while the one permitted by law seems against nature. Thus, the moral means of correction that might otherwise prevent the sexual transgression are absent.

[5] The definition of what constitutes an immoral offense is defective and allows the judge too much latitude. In Germany, for instance, the interpretation of Paragraph 175 grows more subtle and ingenious every day, directly proving the uncertainty of its proper legal understanding.

The deed in itself ought to be decisive, and the verdict should be in accordance with it. (As a rule, the motive is scarcely ever scrutinized.) But how is this to be established when the deed is usually committed in secret and in the absence of witnesses?

[6] Theoretical criminal reasons for the retention of the paragraph are never advanced. It does not deter from crime and has no corrective influence, inasmuch as pathological manifestations are not removed by penal remedies. It is definitely not an atonement for a criminal act, which can only be considered criminal under certain and mostly false presumptions, and thus it may lead to acts of gross injustice. It must be remembered that in many civilized countries this paragraph is no longer in vogue. In Germany it only exists as a concession to a public morality that is based on false principles and frequently confuses perversion with perversity.

[7] In my opinion, public morality and youth are sufficiently protected in Germany by other paragraphs of the statutes, and I am inclined to believe that Paragraph 175 does more harm than good, insofar as it favors and abets blackmail – one of the basest and vilest vices.

Although, of course, the blackmailer may be punished, he always has chance in his favor; his victim will never resort to the extreme measure of appealing to the law. At worst, the blackmailing scoundrel, without having risked losing the honor he never possessed, is briefly confined to prison, while his victim has lost all – i.e., his good name and the respect of others – and thus is brought to ruin and often self-destruction.

[8] If the German lawmaker should deem public morality endangered by the abrogation of Paragraph 175, then surely the extension of Paragraph 176.1 to include *male* persons should be sufficient (at present this paragraph only deals with immoral acts committed on females either with force or under threats). The French penal code has such a paragraph. The age of fourteen years mentioned in paragraph 176.3 – after which immoral actions committed on still youthful persons go unpunished – might eventually be raised to a more mature age. This would also benefit the female portion of society, who scarcely possess, at the age of fifteen, sufficient maturity of mind and judgment to protect themselves against evil. This would further insure more efficient protection of young people in general (say up to the end of the sixteenth year) than is now granted by Paragraph 175, which, after all, is only directed against pederasty (and, according to more recent interpretation, against other acts of a coitus-like nature) while regarding masturbation and other immoral acts with impunity. Although perverse people seldom use pederasty to endanger the morality of the young, they commit other acts of immorality much more frequently. Beyond a certain age, say eighteen, when a sufficient degree of moral and intellectual ripeness has been attained, the law has neither the right nor the duty to impugn immoral acts that are committed between husband and wife, behind closed doors, and with mutual consent. The individual himself is responsible for such acts, inasmuch as they do not violate either public or private interests.

What has been said about congenital sexual inversion and its relation to the law is also applicable to the *acquired* abnormality. The accompanying neurosis or psychosis should have much diagnostic and forensic weight when applied to the question of guilt.

It is of great interest psychopathologically and, under certain circumstances, criminally, that individuals of antipathic sexuality (when unfortunate in their love affairs, or when meeting with deception on the part of the beloved) are subject to all the same psychic reactions (in the form of jealousy and vindictiveness) that occur in the love affairs between man and woman. Such reactions frequently lead to acts of violence, in order to revenge the affront or punish the robber of happiness.

Nothing else could prove more clearly the constitutionality of these inverted sexual feelings; their dominating power over sense, thought and aspiration, and their complete substitution for normal heterosexual feeling and development. The following is such a case of unrequited and betrayed love, taken from recent American criminal acts, the report of which was sent to me by Dr. Boeck of Troppau.

Case 236.

A sexually inverted girl kills the girl she loves because she was rejected.

In January 1892, Alice M., a young girl from one of the best families of Memphis, Tennessee, USA, killed her girlfriend, Freda W., also of the best society, on a public street of that town. She made several deep gashes with a razor in the neck of the girl.

The trial elicited the following facts:

Alice inherited taint from her mother. In addition, an uncle and several first cousins were insane. The mother was psychopathic, with puerperal dementia after each confinement. The worst attack followed the birth of the seventh child (Alice, the accused). Afterward, she declined mentally, suffering from persecutory dementia.

A brother of the accused suffered from mental derangement for some time after an alleged sunstroke.

Alice was nineteen years of age, of medium height, and not pretty. Her face was child-like, "almost too small for her size," and asymmetrical, with the right side more developed than the left. Her nose was "of striking irregularity," her eyes piercing. She was left-handed.

With the onset of puberty, severe and continued headaches were of frequent occurrence. Once a month she suffered from nosebleeds, and had frequent attacks of tremor, which still occur. During one of these attacks she lost consciousness.

Alice was a nervous, irritable child, with very slow physical development. She never enjoyed children's or girls' games. At four or five years old she took much pleasure from tormenting cats, suspending them by one leg.

She preferred her younger brother and his games to her sisters, and competed with him in spinning tops, playing baseball and football, shooting at targets, and playing silly pranks. She loved to climb trees and roofs, and was good at such things. Above all, she loved to amuse herself in the stable among the mules. When she was six or seven her father bought a horse, which she took great delight in feeding and tending. Like a boy, she would ride around the paddock astraddle its back, without using a saddle. She would also groom the horse and wash its hoofs. She would lead him along the street by the halter, gear him up in the buggy, and became quite an expert at harnessing him when required.

At school she was slow and faulty, incapable of continued occupation with the same subject, did not grasp things easily, and had no memory. She had not the slightest talent for music and drawing, and hated feminine occupations. She never cared for reading of any kind. She was stubborn, capricious, and considered abnormal by her teachers and friends.

As a child, she did not care for boys, and had no companions among them. As an adult, she never cared for men, and had no lovers. She was indifferent, even abrupt, toward young men, and they in turn looked upon her as being "cracked."

"As far as she can remember," however, she had an extraordinary love for Freda W., a girl of her own age who was the daughter of a friend of the family. Freda was tender and sweet, and although the love was mutual, it was more violent on Alice's part. From year to year it increased until it became a passion. A year before the catastrophe, Freda's family moved away to another town. Alice was steeped in sorrow, and a tender love correspondence began.

Alice went to visit Freda's family on two occasions, during which the two girls showed "disgusting tenderness" for each other. They were seen swinging together in a hammock by the hour, as well as hugging and kissing; "they hugged and kissed ad nauseam." Alice was ashamed of doing this in public, but Freda upbraided her for this.

When Freda paid a visit in return, Alice made an attempt at killing her by trying to pour laudanum down the sleeping girl's throat. This attempt failed because Freda woke up in time. Then, however, while Freda watched, Alice took the poison herself, and became violently ill. The attempted murder and suicide had been triggered by Freda's show of interest in two young men. Alice declared that she could not live without Freda's love and "wanted to kill herself in order to find release from her tortures and make Freda free." After this incident, they resumed their amorous correspondence with even more fervor than before.

Presently Alice proposed marriage to Freda. She sent her an engagement ring, and threatened death if Freda should prove disloyal. They were to assume a false name and escape to St. Louis. Alice planned to wear men's clothes and earn a living for both. In addition, if Freda were to insist upon it, she would grow a mustache, which she felt sure she could do by shaving frequently.

Just before the attempted elopement the plot was discovered and prevented; the "engagement ring" was returned to Alice's mother along with other love tokens, and all interaction between the two girls was stopped.

Alice was completely broken up. She was unable to sleep, refused food, and became listless and confused (at shops she purchased goods under the name of her beloved). She concealed the ring and other love tokens (among them a thimble of Freda's filled with the latter's blood) in a corner of the kitchen, where she spent hours contemplating them, alternately bursting into peals of laughter and floods of tears.

She became emaciated, her face assumed an anxious expression, and her eyes showed "a peculiar strange luster." When she learned of an intended visit by Freda to Memphis, she firmly resolved to kill her *if she could not possess* her. She stole a razor from her father and carefully concealed it.

In the meantime she started a correspondence with Freda's admirer in which she simulated friendship with him in order to find out about his relations with Freda. She then kept herself informed about these relations.

All attempts made by Alice to see or hear from Freda during the girl's sojourn in Memphis failed. She waylaid Freda in the street, and one time almost succeeded in carrying out her purpose, but was prevented by an accident. On the very day, however, that Freda was on her way to the steamboat to leave town, Alice overtook her.

She felt mortally hurt because Freda, though she walked beside the buggy in which Alice was riding, never spoke a word to her, giving her instead only an occasional glance. Alice then jumped from the vehicle and cut Freda with the razor. When Freda's sister tried to beat her off, she became frantic and blindly cut deep gashes into the poor girl's neck, one of which extended almost from ear to ear. While everyone attended to Freda, she drove off furiously through the streets. Upon reaching home, Alice immediately told her mother what had happened. She could not comprehend the awfulness of the deed, and was cold and unmoved at the consequences pointed out to her. When she heard of the death and the funeral of her beloved Freda, however, thus realizing her loss, she burst into tears and passionate wailings, kissed the picture of the dead girl, and spoke as if she were still alive.

During the trial her callous behavior struck everyone. The deep sorrow of her own people did not affect her in the least, and she showed absolute indifference to the ethical points of her deed.

At times, however, her passionate love for Freda and her jealousy awoke, and she yielded to boundless grief and emotion. *"Freda has broken her faith!"* "I have killed her because I loved her so!" The experts in this case found her mental development to be equal to that of a girl of thirteen to fourteen years. Although she comprehended that no children could have sprung from her "union" with Freda, she would not admit that a "marriage" between them would have been an absurdity. She absolutely denied that sexual intercourse between the two (even mutual masturbation) had ever taken place; nothing definite, however, about this point or about her previous sexual life could be learned. No gynecological examination was performed.

The verdict was insanity (*Memphis Medical Monthly,* 1892).

cultivated pederasty. [42]

This is one of the saddest pages in the history of human delinquencies.

There are various motives that bring pederasty to a man who was originally sexually normal and of sound mind. It is used as a temporary means of sexual satisfaction in the absence of something better (as in infrequent cases of bestiality) where abstinence from normal sexual indulgence is enforced.[43] Thus, it occurs on board ships during long voyages, in prisons, in spas, etc. Among men subjected to such conditions, it is highly probable that individuals of low morals and great sensuality, or actual homosexuals, seduce the others. Lust, imitation and desire further their purpose.

The strength of the sexual instinct is most markedly shown by the fact that such circumstances are sufficient to overcome repugnance for the unnatural act.

Another category of pederasts is made up of old *roués* who have become super-satiated in normal sexual indulgence, and who find in pederasty a means whereby sensual pleasure can be excited, because the act provides a new method of stimulation. Thus, the power that has been psychically and physically reduced to so low a state is temporarily renewed. The new sexual situation makes them relatively potent, so to speak, and makes pleasure that is no longer found in normal intercourse with women possible again. Power to indulge in pederasty also eventually flickers out. Thus, the individual may finally be reduced to passive pederasty as a stimulus to make temporary active pederasty possible, just as flagellation or looking on at obscene acts (Maschka's case of mutilation of animals) is used as a stimulus.

The termination of sexual activity expresses itself in all kinds of abuse of children – cunnilingus, fellatio, and other enormities.

This is the most dangerous kind of pederast, because he *deals mostly with boys* and ruins them in body and soul.

The experiences of Tarnowsky (op. cit., p. 53ff.) gathered from St. Petersburg society are terrible with reference to this. Pederasty is cultivated in institutes. Old *roués* and homosexuals play the role of seducers. Although at first it is difficult to carry out the disgusting act, fantasy assists by calling up the image of a woman. With practice, the unnatural act gradually becomes easy, until at last the individual (like one *debased* by masturbation), while relatively impotent for women, becomes lustful enough to find pleasure in the perverse act. In some circumstances, such individuals give themselves for money.

As Tardieu, Hofmann, Limon and Taylor show, often such fiends are found in large cities. Numerous statements made to me by homosexuals demonstrate that actual prostitution and houses of prostitution for male-loving men exist in large cities. The arts of coquetry that are used by these male prostitutes to attract pederasts and homosexuals are noteworthy – ornament, perfumes, feminine styles of dress, etc. Such imitation of feminine peculiarities is spontaneous and unconscious in congenital as well as in (some) acquired cases of (abnormal) antipathic sexual instinct.

The following, of interest to the psychologist, may also give the officers of the law important clues concerning the social life and practice of pederasts:

Coffignon, *La corruption à Paris,* p. 327, divides active pederasts into *amateurs, entreteneurs* and *souteneurs.*

The *amateurs* (*"rivettes"*) are debauched persons, frequently of congenital sexual inversion, who have position and fortune, and who are therefore forced to guard against detection in the gratification of their homosexual desires. For this reason they visit brothels, lodging houses, or the private houses of female prostitutes, who are usually on good terms with male prostitutes. In this way they escape blackmail.

Some of these *amateurs* are bold enough to indulge their vile desires in public places. Although they thus run the risk of arrest, in a large city there is little risk of blackmail. Danger is said to add to their secret pleasure.

The *entreteneurs* are old sinners who cannot deny themselves the pleasure of keeping a (male) "mistress," even though there is the danger that they will fall into the hands of blackmailers.

The *souteneurs* are pederasts who have been punished. They keep *"jesus,"* whom they send out to entice customers (*"faire chanter les rivettes"*), and then appear, at the right moment if possible, to pluck the victim for themselves.

They often live together in bands, and the members, in accordance with individual desire, live together as husbands and wives. In such bands there are formal marriages, betrothals, and banquets, as well as introductions of brides and grooms into their apartments.

The *souteneurs* train the *"jesus."*

The *passive* pederasts are *"petits jesus," "jesus,"* or "aunts."

The *petits jesus* are lost, depraved children who are placed by accident into the hands of active pederasts. The active pederasts seduce them and reveal to them the horrible means of earning a livelihood, either as *entretenues* or as male street-walkers, with or without *souteneurs*.

The slyest and choicest *petits jesus* are those trained by persons who instruct these children in the art of female dress and manner.

In order to become *femmes entretenues,* the *petits jesus* gradually emancipate themselves from the teacher and master, often by anonymously denunciating their *souteneurs* to the police.

It is the object of the *souteneur* and the *petit jesus* to make the latter, through all the arts of the *toilette,* appear young for as long as possible.

The age limit of the *petits jesus* is about twenty-five years, after which they become *jesus* and *femmes entretenues* and are often sustained by several *souteneurs*. The *jesus* fall into three categories: *"filles galantes"* (those who have fallen again into the hands of a *souteneur*); *"pierreuses"* (ordinary streetwalkers, like their female colleagues); and *"domestiques."*

The *domestiques* hire themselves out to active pederasts, either to gratify the pederasts' desires or to obtain *petits jesus* for them.

A subgroup of the *domestiques* is formed by those who entered the service of *petits jesus* as *femmes de chambre*. Their principal object is to use the position to obtain compromising knowledge with which they later practice blackmail. In this way they assure themselves ease in old age.

The most horrible class of active pederasts is made up of the "aunts," who are the *souteneurs* of (male) prostitutes. Although sexually normal, they are morally depraved, and practice (passive) pederasty only for gain or the purpose of blackmail.

The wealthy *amateurs* have reunions and other such gatherings at which the passive ones appear in female attire and where horrible orgies take place. At these events, all of the waiters, musicians, etc. are pederasts. Although the *filles galantes* do not venture (except during the carnival) to show themselves in the female attire on the street, they know how to lend to their appearance (through style of dress, etc.) something indicative of their calling. They use gesture, peculiar movements of their hands, etc., to entice their victims, after which they lead them to hotels, baths, or brothels.

What the author says of blackmail is generally known. There are cases where pederasts have allowed their entire fortune to be wrung from them.

The research of Laurent (*Les bisexués,* Paris, 1894) demonstrates that these urban monstrosities, in the shape of *"petits jesus,"* are not only the product of professional training, but are also the result of a degenerated mental condition. On page 172 of his book, under the heading of *"hermaphroditisme artificiel,"* he describes manifestations of effemination and *"infantilisme."* Such manifestations refer to boys who, with incipient puberty, show no further development of the frame and the genital organs, have no growth of hair around the face or pubes, do not experience a change in the voice, and are retrograde in their mental faculties. It often happens in such cases that secondary physical and psychic characteristics of female sexuality are developed. Postmortem examinations of such *"petits garroches"* (Brouardel) have revealed a small bladder, mere rudiments of the prostate, an absence of the ischio and bulbo cavernosi muscles, an infantile penis, and a very narrow pelvis.

Without a doubt these are heavily tainted individuals who experienced a sort of rudimentary sexual change at the time of puberty.

Laurent (p. 181) makes the interesting remark *that the professional passive pederasts* ("petits jesus") *are recruited from the ranks of these* infantiles *and* effeminates.

It is therefore evident that, by virtue of degenerative and anthropological factors, these human monstrosities are predestined and prepared for this abominable career.

The following notice from a Berlin newspaper (February 1884), which fell into my hands by accident, shows something of the life and customs of pederasts and homosexuals:

"*The Woman-haters' Ball.* – Almost every social element of Berlin has its reunions – the fat, the baldheaded, the bachelors, the widowers – so why not the woman-haters? This species of men, so interesting psychologically and none too edifying, had a great ball a few days ago. The notice ran: 'Grand Vienna Fancy Dress Ball.' The sale of tickets was rigorous; they wished to be very exclusive. The rendezvous was a well-known dance hall. We enter the hall about midnight. The merry dancing is to the strains of a fine orchestra. Thick tobacco smoke, veiling the gaslights, does not allow the details of the moving mass to become obvious; only during the pause between the dances are we able to obtain a closer view. Masks are by far in the majority; black dress coats and ball gowns are only seen now and then.

"But what is that? The lady in rose-tarlatan who just now passed us has a lighted cigar in the corner of her mouth and puffs like a trooper; she also wears a small blonde beard, lightly painted out. And yet she is talking with a very *décolleté* 'angel' in tricot who stands, with bare arms folded behind, likewise smoking. The two voices are masculine, and so is the conversation; it is about the 'd—— tobacco smoke that permits no air.' Two men in female attire! A conventional clown stands, against a pillar, in soft conversation with a ballet dancer, his arm around her faultless waist. She has a blonde 'Titus-head,' a sharp-cut profile, and a seemingly voluptuous form. The brilliant earrings, the necklace with a medallion, and the full, round shoulders and arms do not raise a doubt about her 'genuineness' until, with a sudden movement, she disengages herself from the embracing arm and, yawning, moves away, saying in a deep bass, 'Emile, you are too tiresome today!' The ballet dancer is also a male!

"Suspicious now, we look about further. We almost suspect that here the world is topsy-turvy; for there goes, or rather trips, a man – no, not a man at all, even though he wears a carefully trained mustache. The well-curled hair; the powdered and painted face with the blackened eyebrows; the golden earrings; the bouquet of flowers that reach from the left shoulder to the breast to ornament the elegant black gown; the golden bracelets on the wrists; the elegant fan in the white-gloved hand – all these things are anything but masculine. And how he toys with the fan!

How he dances and turns and trips and lisps! And yet kindly Nature made this doll a man. He is a salesman in a large sweet shop, and the ballet dancer is his 'colleague.'

"At a little corner table there seems to be a great social circle. Several elderly gentlemen press around a group of *décolleté* ladies who are sitting over a glass of wine and – in the spirit of fun – making jokes that are none too delicate. Who are these three ladies? 'Ladies!' laughs my knowing friend. 'Well, the one on the right, with the brown hair and the short, fancy dress, is called "Butterrieke." He is a hairdresser. The second one – the blonde in the singer's costume, with the necklace of pearls – is known here by the name of "Miss Ella of the tightrope," and he is a ladies' tailor. The third – that is the widely celebrated "Lotte".'

"But that person cannot possibly be a man! That waist, that bust, those classic arms, the whole air and person are markedly feminine!

"I am told that 'Lotte' was once a bookkeeper. Today she, or rather he, is exclusively 'Lotte,' and takes pleasure in deceiving men about his sex for as long as possible. 'Lotte' is singing a song (that would hardly do for a drawing room) in a high voice acquired by years of practice that many a soprano might envy. 'Lotte' has also 'worked' as a female comedian. Now the former bookkeeper has become so involved in his female role that he appears on the street almost exclusively in female attire and, according to the people with whom he lodges, sleeps in an embroidered nightdress.

"On closer examination of the assembly I discover, to my astonishment, acquaintances on all sides. My shoemaker, whom I would have taken for anything but a woman-hater, is a 'troubadour' with sword and plume; and his 'Leonore,' in the costume of a bride, routinely places my favorite brand of cigars before me in a certain cigar store. When 'Leonore,' during an intermission, removes her gloves, I recognize with certainty her large, blue hands. Right! And there is my haberdasher, who moves about in a questionable costume as Bacchus and is the swain of a repugnantly bedecked Diana, who works as a waiter in a beer restaurant. The real 'ladies' of the ball cannot be described here. They associate only with one another and avoid the woman-hating men, who are exclusive, amuse themselves, and absolutely ignore the charms of the women."

These facts deserve the careful attention of the police, who should be placed in the position *of coping with male prostitution in the same way that female prostitution is currently handled.*

Male prostitution is certainly much more dangerous to society than is the prostitution of females; it is the darkest stain on the history of humanity.

From the statements of a high police official of Berlin I learned that the police are conversant with the male *demimonde* of the German capital and do all they can to suppress blackmail among pederasts – a practice that often does not stop short of murder.

On the other hand, the hope that *the lawmaker of the future will abandon the prosecution of pederasty, at least for reasons of utility,* is justified by the foregoing facts.

It is worth noting with reference to this point that the French code does not punish pederasty, so long as it does not become an offense to public decency. Probably for political and legal reasons, the new Italian penal code passes over the crime of unnatural abuse in silence, as do the statutes of Holland and, as far as I know, Belgium and Spain.

To what extent such cultivated pederasts are to be regarded as mentally and morally sound may remain an open question. The majority of them suffer from genital neuroses. *In these cases, at least, there are stages of transition that lead to acquired pathological antipathic sexual instinct* (see p. 240). Generally speaking, the responsibility of these individuals, who are certainly much lower than the women who prostitute themselves, cannot be questioned.

With respect to the manner of sexual indulgence, the various categories of male-loving men may thus be generally characterized as follows:

The *congenital* homosexual becomes a *pederast only exceptionally,* and then eventually resorts to it after having practiced and exhausted all other possible immoral acts with males.

For him, passive pederasty is the ideally and practically adequate form of the sexual act. He practices active pederasty only to please another. The most important point here is the congenital and unchangeable perversion of the sexual instinct.

It is otherwise with the *cultivated pederast*. Having once acted normally sexually, or at least having had normal inclinations, he occasionally has intercourse with the opposite sex. His sexual perversity is neither congenital nor unchangeable. He begins with pederasty and ends in other perverse sexual acts, induced by weakness of the centers for erection and ejaculation. At the height of his power his sexual desire is for active rather than passive pederasty. He yields to passive pederasty only to please another; for money, in the role of a male prostitute; or as a means to make active pederasty still occasionally possible when virility is declining.

In conclusion, a horrible act that must be alluded to is the act of pederasty with a woman[44] and even with a wife. Sensual individuals sometimes do this with hardened prostitutes, or even with their wives. Tardieu gives examples in which men who usually practiced coitus sometimes indulged in pederasty with their wives. Fear of a repetition of pregnancy may occasionally induce the man to perform and the woman to tolerate the act.

Case 237.

Imputation of pederasty that was not proved. Résumé from the legal proceedings:

On May 30, 1888, S., chemist, of H., was accused by his stepfather in an unsigned letter of having immoral relations with G., aged nineteen, the son of a butcher. S. received the letter and, astounded by its contents, hastened to his employer, who promised to proceed discreetly in the matter, and to ascertain from the authorities what was being said about it by the public.

The next morning G., who lived in the house of S., was arrested. He was suffering at the time from gonorrhea and orchitis. S., advising caution, tried to induce the authorities to release G., but was refused. In his statement to the judge, S. said that three years previously he had become acquainted with G. on the street, and then saw no more of him until the fall of 1887, when he met him in his father's shop. After November, G. supplied S.'s kitchen with meat; coming in the evening to get the order, and delivering the meat the next morning. Thus, over time, S. became well-acquainted with G. and developed a friendly feeling for him. When S. fell ill and was mostly confined to his bed until the middle of May 1888, G. gave him so much attention that S. and his wife were much attracted to him because of his harmless, childlike and happy disposition. S. showed and explained to him his collection of curiosities, and they spent pleasant evenings together, usually in the presence of S.'s wife. In addition, S. and G. experimented in making sausages, jelly, etc. In February 1888, G. fell ill with gonorrhea. S., as his friend, having studied medicine for several terms, took care of G. and procured medicine for him, etc. In May, because G. was still ill and was inclined, for a number of reasons, to leave home, S. and his wife took him into their own home to care for him. S. denied the truth of all suspicions raised by this circumstance, and defended himself by pointing to his life of previous respectability and his education, as well as to the fact that G. had been suffering at the time from a disgusting, contagious disease, and that he himself had a painful affliction (nephritic calculus, with occasional attacks of colic).

It must be mentioned that S.'s statement was contradicted by facts that led to a conviction in the first trial.

Because of its obviousness, the relation of S. to G. had given cause for remark by many of the townspeople. G. spent almost all of his evenings with S.'s family and came to be quite at home there. They took walks together. Once, while out on such a walk, S. said to G. that he was a pretty fellow, and that he (S.) was very fond of him. There was talk at this time of sexual matters and also of pederasty. S. said that the only reason he touched on these subjects was to warn G. Regarding the interaction at home, it was proved that occasionally S., while sitting on a sofa, embraced G. and kissed him. This happened in the presence of the wife as well as in front of the servant girls. When G. was ill with gonorrhea, S. instructed him in the method of using a syringe, and at that time took G.'s penis in his hand. G. testified that when he asked S. why he was so fond of him, S. answered, "I don't know myself." One day, when G. did not come home as expected, S., with tears in his eyes, complained of it to him when he returned. S. also told him that his marriage was unhappy; he tearfully begged G. not to leave him and said that he must take the place of his wife.

From all this resulted the just accusation that the relation between the two men had a sexual direction. According to the complaint, the fact that all was open and known to everybody spoke more for the intensity of the passion of S. than for the harmlessness of the relation. The spotless life of the accused was considered, as well as his honesty and gentleness. The probability of S.'s unhappy marriage was raised, and his highly sensual nature was demonstrated.

During the course of the trial, G. was repeatedly examined by the medical experts. He was scarcely of medium size, of powerful frame, pale; his penis and testicles were large and perfectly developed.

In consonance with the accusation, it was found that the anus was pathologically changed, inasmuch as there were no wrinkles in the skin that surrounded it. In addition, the sphincter was relaxed. It was presumed that these changes pointed to the probability of passive pederasty.

The conviction was based on the above facts. The judgment recognized that the relationship between the culprits did not by itself necessarily point to unnatural abuses, any more than did the physical conditions found on G.'s body.

The combination of the two facts, however, convinced the court of the guilt of both culprits, and held it proved: "That the abnormal condition of G.'s anus had been caused by the frequently repeated introduction of the penis of S., and that G. had voluntarily permitted the performance of this immoral act on himself."

Thus the conditions of Paragraph 175 seemed to be covered. In passing sentence, S.'s education, which made him appear to be G.'s seducer, was considered; in G.'s case, this fact and his youth were given weight; and the previous respectability of both was held in view. Thus S. was sentenced to imprisonment for eight months, and G. for four months.

They appealed to the Supreme Court at Leipzig and, in the meantime, prepared themselves to collect sufficient evidence to call for a new trial should the appeal be denied.

They subjected themselves to examination and observation by distinguished experts, all of whom declared that G.'s anus presented no signs of indulgence in passive pederasty.

Because it seemed important to those interested that the psychological aspect of the case, which had not been touched on at the trial, be made clear, the author was entrusted with the examination and observation of S. and G.

Results of the Personal Examination, from December 11 to 13, 1888, in Graz: S., aged thirty-seven; two years married, without children. Ex-director of the City Laboratory of H. He came from a father, said to have been nervous due to great activity, who had an apoplectic attack at age fifty-seven, and died at age sixty-seven from another attack of apoplexy. His mother was living and was described as a strong person who had been nervous for years. Her mother, who lived to a relatively old age, was said to have died from a cerebral tumor. A brother of the mother's father was said to have been a drinker. The paternal grandfather died early from softening of the brain.

S. had two brothers who were in perfect health.

He reported having a nervous temperament and a strong constitution. After articular rheumatism in his fourteenth year, he suffered for several months from great nervousness. He often suffered thereafter from rheumatic pains, palpitation, and shortness of breath. With sea bathing, these symptoms gradually disappeared. Seven years ago he had gonorrhea. This disease became chronic and for a long time caused bladder difficulty.

In 1887 he had his first attack of renal colic and had such attacks repeatedly during the winter of 1887 and 1888, until May 16, 1888, when quite a large renal calculus was passed. Afterward, his condition had been quite satisfactory. During the time he suffered from stones, he had felt severe pain in the urethra at the moment of ejaculation (during coitus) and when urinating.

With reference to his life, S. reported that although he attended the *Gymnasium* until he was fourteen, he studied privately thereafter due to the results of his illness. He then spent four years in a chemist's shop, and studied medicine for six semesters at the university, serving as a voluntary hospital assistant in the war of 1870. Because he had no certificate of graduation from the *Gymnasium,* he gave up the study of medicine, and obtained instead the degree of doctor of philosophy. He then worked for the Museum of Minerals in K., and was later an assistant at the Mineralogical Institute of H. Thereafter he made special studies in the chemistry of foodstuffs and became director, five years ago, of the City Laboratory.

He made all these statements in a prompt, precise manner and did not think long about his answers, so that one was led more and more to think that he was a man who loved and spoke the truth. His consistent statements on the following day further supported this conclusion. With reference to his sex life, S. stated in a modest, delicate, and open way that in his eleventh year he began to have a knowledge of the difference between the sexes, and was given to masturbation until his fourteenth year. He first had coitus at eighteen and indulged moderately thereafter. Although his sensual desire had never been great, until lately the sexual act had been normal in every way, accompanied by gratifying pleasurable feeling and full virility. Since his marriage two years ago, he had cohabited with his wife exclusively. He had married his wife out of love, still loved her, and had coitus with her several times a week. His wife confirmed these statements.

Exhaustive cross-questioning of S. regarding a perverse sexual feeling toward men was answered repeatedly in the negative, without contradiction or any thought about the answers. He stuck to his statements even when he was told, in an effort to trap him, that proof of a perverse sexual instinct would help him in the trial. Thus, one gained the important impression that S. did not have the slightest knowledge about the facts of male love. It was learned that his lascivious dreams had never been about men; that he was interested only in female nudity; that he liked to dance with ladies, etc. No traces of any kind of sexual inclination for his own sex could be discovered. With reference to his relations with G., S. expressed himself exactly as he had in his examination before the court. In explanation of his partiality for G., he could only say that he was nervous, a man of feeling and great sensibility, and very sensitive to friendliness. He had felt very lonesome and depressed during his illness; his wife had frequently been with her parents; and thus it had transpired that he had become friendly with G., who was so gentle and kind. He still had a weakness for him and felt remarkably quiet and content when in his company.

He had previously had two such close friendships; one, when he was still a student, with a corps brother, a Dr. A., whom he also embraced and kissed; the other with a Baron M. When it turned out that he could not see him for a few days, he became depressed and even cried.

He also had a similar feeling and attachment for animals. Thus he had mourned, as if it had been a member of the family, the loss of a poodle that died a short time ago; he had often kissed the animal. (On relating this, tears came to his eyes.) His brother confirmed the statements regarding his brother's remarkable friendship for A. and M. with the remark that, in these instances, there had not been the slightest suspicion of sexual coloring or relation. The most careful and detailed examination of S. did not reveal the slightest reason for such a presumption.

He stated that he never had the slightest sexual feeling for G., to say nothing of erection or sexual desire. He explained his partiality for G., which bordered on jealousy, as merely due to his sentimental temperament and his inordinate friendship. G. remained as dear to him as a son.

It is worth noting that, according to S., when G. told him about his love adventures with girls, it had only hurt him because G. was in danger of injuring himself and ruining his health by dissipation. He had never felt personally hurt by this. He would be glad, if he knew of a good girl for G., to rejoice with him and do all he could to promote their marriage.

S. stated that it was during the course of his legal examination that he began to see how he had been careless in his intercourse with G., thereby causing gossip. He explained his openness as due to the innocence of their friendship.

It is worth mentioning that S.'s wife never noticed anything suspicious about the intercourse between her husband and G., even though the most simple wife would have instinctively noticed anything of such a nature. In addition, Mrs. S. had not opposed receiving G. into the house. On this point she remarked that the spare room in which G. lay ill was on the second floor, whereas the living quarters were on the fourth floor. She further declared that S. had never been alone with G. the entire time he was in the house. She was convinced of her husband's innocence and loved him as before.

S. freely stated that he had often kissed G. and talked with him about sexual matters. G. was very attracted to women and, in friendship, S. had often warned him about sexual dissipation, particularly when G., as it often happened, did not look well. Although he had once said that G. was a handsome fellow, it was in a perfectly harmless manner.

The kissing of G. had been due to inordinate friendship, or when G. had shown him some particular attention, or when he had pleased him especially. In this he had never had any sexual feeling. He had now and then dreamed of G., but in a perfectly harmless way.

It was of great importance to the author to form an opinion of G.'s personality as well. On December 12 the desired opportunity was given, and G. was carefully examined.

G. was a young man, aged twenty, of delicate build, whose development corresponded with his years. He appeared to be neuropathic and sensual. His genitals were normal and well-developed. The author thought he might be permitted to pass over the condition of the anus, as he did not feel called upon to pass judgment about it. Prolonged association with G. gave one the impression that he was a harmless, kind and artless man. Although he seemed light-minded, he did not appear to be morally depraved. Nothing in his dress or manner indicated perverse sexual feeling. One would never suspect him of being a male courtesan.

G. stated that when he was questioned as the case was proceeding, he had described the situation as it actually was, inasmuch as he and S. felt they were innocent. It was on this account that the whole trial had been based.

At first, S.'s friendship, and especially the kissing, had seemed remarkable, even to him. He later convinced himself that it was merely friendship and thought no more about it.

Because S. was so unselfish and loved him so, G. viewed S. as a father-like friend.

The expression "handsome fellow" was made when a love affair of G.'s prompted S. to express his fears about a happy future for G. At that time S. comforted him, saying that G.'s appearance was pleasing, and that he would make an eligible match.

Once S. complained to G. that his wife was inclined to drink, after which S. burst into tears. G. was touched by his friend's unhappiness. On this occasion S. had kissed him, begged for his friendship, and asked that G. visit him frequently.

S. had never spontaneously directed the conversation to sexual matters. G. once asked what pederasty was, about which, while in England, he had heard a great deal; and S. had explained it to him.

G. acknowledged that he was sensual. At the age of twelve he had become acquainted with sexual matters through his schoolmates. He had never masturbated. He first had coitus at the age of eighteen and had since visited brothels frequently. He had never felt any inclination for his own sex, and had not experienced any sexual excitement when S. kissed him. He had always enjoyed coitus performed normally. His lascivious dreams had always been of women. With indignation, and pointing to his descent from a healthy and respectable family, he repelled the insinuation that he had enjoyed passive pederasty. Until he heard the gossip about them, he had been innocent and devoid of suspicion. He tried to explain his anal anomalies as he had at the trial.

It should be noted that Mr. J. S. maintained that he was no less astonished by the charge of male love against his brother than were those more closely associated with S. Nevertheless, he could not understand what attracted his brother to G. All the explanations that S. made to him concerning his relation to G. were in vain.

The author took the trouble to observe S. and G. in a natural way while they were dining in the company of S.'s brother and Mrs. S. in Graz. This observation did not reveal the slightest sign of improper friendship.

Although the general impression that S. made on me was of a nervous, sanguine, and somewhat overstrained individual, he was, at the same time, kind, open-hearted, and very emotional.

S. was physically strong, somewhat corpulent, and had a symmetrical, brachycephalic cranium. The genitals were well-developed; the penis somewhat bellied; the prepuce slightly hypertrophied.

Opinion. Although, unfortunately, pederasty is not infrequent among mankind today and still occurs among the peoples of Europe, it is nonetheless an unusual, perverse, and even monstrous method of sexual gratification. It presumes a congenital or acquired perversion of the sexual instinct, as well as a defect of the moral sense that is either original or is acquired as a result of pathological influences.

Medico-legal science is thoroughly conversant with the physical and psychic conditions from which this aberration of the sexual instinct arises. Thus, for both the concrete and the doubtful case it would seem imperative to ascertain whether the empirical, subjective conditions necessary for pederasty are present. It is essential to distinguish between active and passive pederasty.

Active pederasty occurs:

[I] As a *non-pathological* phenomenon:

[1] As a means of gratifying great sexual desire when there is enforced abstinence from natural sexual intercourse.

[2] In old debauchees who, having become satiated with normal sexual intercourse, are not only more or less impotent, but also morally depraved. They resort to pederasty in order to excite their lust with a new stimulus, as well as to aid a virility that has sunk so low psychically and physically.

[3] Traditionally, among certain barbarous races that are devoid of morality.

[II] As a *pathological* phenomenon:

[1] Upon the basis of congenital sexual inversion, with a repugnance for sexual intercourse with women or even an absolute incapability of it. According to Casper, however, even under these conditions pederasty is very infrequent. The so-called homosexual satisfies himself with a man through either passive or mutual masturbation or coitus-like acts (e.g., coitus between the thighs), only rarely resorting to pederasty as a result of intense sexual desire, because of a low or lowered moral sense, or from a desire to please another.

[2] On the basis of acquired pathological sexual inversion:

[a] As a result of masturbation which, having been practiced over the course of many years, finally causes impotence toward women with a continuation of intense sexual desire.

[b] As a result of severe mental disease (senile dementia, brain-softening in the insane, etc.) in which, experience dictates, an inversion of the sexual instinct may take place.

Passive pederasty occurs:

[I] As a *non-pathological* phenomenon:

[1] In individuals of the lowest class who, having had the misfortune to be seduced in boyhood by debauchees, endured pain and disgust for the sake of money. They thus became morally depraved to the extent that, even when they are more mature, they take pleasure in being male prostitutes.

[2] As a remuneration to an individual who has allowed active pederasty (under the circumstances of [I], [1]).

[II] As a *pathological* phenomenon:

[1] In individuals affected with sexual inversion who endure the act, with pain and disgust, in order to reciprocate for the bestowal of sexual favors.

[2] In homosexuals who feel like women in relation to men, out of desire and lust. For these female-men there is not only *horror feminae,* but also absolute incapability in sexual intercourse with women. The character and inclinations are feminine.

All of the empirical facts gathered by legal medicine and psychiatry are included in this classification. It would be necessary to prove that a man belonged to one of the above categories to convince the court of medical science that he was a pederast.

One searched in vain for signs in the life and character of S. that would place him in one of the categories of active pederasts established by science. He was neither forced into sexual abstinence nor made impotent toward women by debauchery. He was not congenitally male-loving. He had not become alienated from women through masturbation and thus attracted to men through a continuation of sexual desire. Finally, he was not sexually perverse as a result of severe mental disease.

Furthermore, the general conditions necessary for the occurrence of pederasty – moral imbecility or depravity on the one hand and inordinate sexual desire on the other – were lacking in him.

It was likewise impossible to classify G. in any of the empirical categories of passive pederasty, inasmuch as he possessed neither the peculiarities of the male prostitute nor the clinical marks of effemination. Further, he lacked the anthropological as well as clinical stigmata of the female-man. He was, in fact, the very opposite of all this.

For a pederastic relation between these two men to be plausible from a medico-scientific perspective, it would have been necessary for S. to present the antecedents and marks of the active pederasts of [I], [2], and for G. to present those of the passive pederasts of [II], [1] or [2].

Thus, from a psychological standpoint, the assumption on which the verdict was based is legally untenable.

By the same prerogative, every man might be considered a pederast. What is left to consider is whether the explanations of S. and G. regarding their remarkable friendship are psychologically valid.

That so sentimental and eccentric a man as S. could entertain a transcendental friendship without any sexual excitement whatsoever is not without psychological parallel. When one considers the friendship of schoolgirls, the self-sacrificing friendship of sentimental young persons in general, or even this sensitive man's partiality for domestic animals, one does not then think of sodomy. For a man of S.'s mental character, his extraordinary friendship with the youth G. can be easily comprehended. The openness of the friendship permitted a conclusion that it was an innocent one, and not one that depended upon sensual passion.

The defendants succeeded in obtaining a new trial. The new trial took place on March 7, 1890. There was much evidence presented in favor of the accused.

The previous moral life of S. was generally acknowledged. The Sister of Charity who cared for G. in S.'s house never noticed anything suspicious about the interaction between S. and G. Friends of S. testified to his morality, his deep friendship, and his habit of kissing them upon meeting or leaving them. The anal abnormalities that had been found on G. were no longer present. Experts called by the court allowed for the possibility that they had been simply due to digital manipulations; at any rate, their diagnostic value was contested by the experts who were called for the defense.

The court recognized that the imputed crime had not been proved and exonerated the defendants.

l e s b i a n   l o v e. [45]

Sexual intercourse between adult women is of minimal legal importance. It could come into consideration only in Austria. In connection with homosexuality, this phenomenon is of anthropological and clinical value. The relation is the same, *mutatis mutandis*, as between men. Lesbian love does not seem to approach the frequency of male homosexuality. The majority of female homosexuals do not act in obedience to an innate impulse; instead they develop under conditions analogous to those that produce the homosexual by cultivation.

These "forbidden friendships" especially flourish in penal institutions for females.

Krausold (op. cit.) reports: "The female prisoners often have friendships that extend to mutual masturbation, when possible.

"But temporary mutual gratification is not the only purpose of such friendships. They are entered into systematically, so to speak, and are made to be enduring. Intense jealousy and passion are developed to an extent that could scarcely be surpassed between persons of opposite sex. The most violent scenes of jealousy, even beatings, are often the result of the friend of one prisoner merely being smiled at by another.

"When, in accordance with the prison regulations, the violent prisoner has been put in irons, she says 'she has had a child by her friend.' "

I am indebted to Parent-Duchalelet (*De la prostitution*, 1857, vol. 1, p. 159) for interesting communications concerning lesbian love.

According to this experienced author, it is often a repugnance for the most disgusting and perverse acts that men perform on prostitutes (**coitus in the armpit, in the mouth, between the breasts,** etc.) that is responsible for driving these unfortunate creatures to lesbian love. His statements indicate that it is essentially highly sensual prostitutes who come to indulge in the practice because they are unsatisfied by intercourse with impotent or perverse men and repelled by their disgusting habits.

In addition to this, there are prostitutes who want to be known as preferring tribadism, as well as women who, in prison for years, acquire the vice in these hotbeds of lesbian love due to abstinence.

It is interesting to note that although prostitutes hate those who practice tribadism (just as men abhor pederasts), female prisoners do not regard the vice as indecent.

Parent mentions the case of a prostitute who tried, while intoxicated, to force another into lesbian love. The latter became so enraged that she denounced the indecent woman to police. Taxil (op. cit., pp. 166, 170) reports similar instances.

Mantegazza (*Antropologisch-kulturhistorische Studien*, p. 97) also finds that sexual intercourse between women has the especial significance of a vice that arises from unsatisfied sexual hyperesthesia.

With the exception of congenital sexual inversion, however, one gains the impression that in many cases of this kind the cultivated vice gradually leads to acquired antipathic sexual instinct, with repugnance for sexual intercourse with the opposite sex, just as it is in men.

At least Parent's cases were probably of this nature. The correspondence with the lover was as sentimental and exaggerated in tone as between lovers of the opposite sex; unfaithfulness and separation broke the heart of the one abandoned; jealousy was unbridled and led to bloody revenge. The following cases of lesbian love from Mantegazza are certainly pathological and may possibly be examples of congenital antipathic sexual instinct:

[1] On July 5, 1777, a woman was brought before a court in London. She had been married to three different women while posing as a man. She was recognized to be a woman and sentenced to imprisonment for six months.

[2] In 1773, another woman dressed as a man courted a girl and asked for her hand; the trick, however, did not succeed.

[3] Two women lived together as man and wife for thirty years. On her deathbed the "husband" confessed her secret to those around her.

Coffignon (op. cit., p. 301) reports that lately this vice is quite the fashion, partly because of novels on the subject, and partly because of excessive work on sewing machines, female servants having to sleep in the same bed, seduction by depraved pupils in schools, or seduction of daughters by perverse servants.

The author declares that this vice ("sapphism") is more frequently seen among ladies of the aristocracy and prostitutes.

He does not differentiate physiological from pathological cases and, among the pathological cases, he does not make a distinction between the acquired and congenital cases. The details of a few cases, which are certainly pathological, correspond exactly with what is known about men of inverted sexuality.

The sapphists have their places of meeting and recognize each other by peculiar glances, carriage, etc. The members of a sapphistic pair like to dress and ornament themselves alike, and are thus called *"petites soeurs"* ("little sisters").

Moraglia makes a strong distinction between *cunnilingus* and *tribadism.*

He generally finds cunnilingus in women with normal sexual instinct but hypersexual feelings (e.g., in girls who have no opportunity for or are afraid of coitus, pregnancy), or in married women whose sexual desires remain unsatisfied as a consequence of the husband's impotence or because of the absence of sexual desire due to masturbation. Thus, there is no question here of love or intense jealousy, unless the individuals have an *acquired* antipathic sexual instinct; it is merely an ephemeral union for the purpose of mutually satisfying libido coupled with all sorts of other acts to obtain the desired goal.

Tribadism (**mutual contact and rubbing of the genitals**) is only practiced by women of antipathic sexual instinct who are in a permanent bond of love as a means of sexual satisfaction in which the active individual always assumes the male role in relation to the female consort. These women are much more subtle and persevering in their campaigns of conquest and coquetry with heterosexual women than man could ever be under similar (reversed) circumstances.

If this assumption is true, the method of sexual intercourse would establish at once an easy means of distinguishing perversity from perversion. The individuals referred to by the author were, without exception, either viragoes or gynandromorphs.

Chevalier very drastically characterizes the perversity and distinguishes it from the perversion in the following words (cf. *L'inversion sexuelle,* p. 268, Paris, 1895):

". . . whether one is a pederast or a lesbian due to overstimulation of exhausted senses, mercantile debasement, the need to 'stave off hunger,' feeble-mindedness or dilettantism, the result of this analysis is that the aberration does not originate with the individual at birth, does not appear during childhood, seldom exhibits itself all at once, but exhibits itself little by little, gradually, at a certain age, after normal sexual experiences; is neither permanent nor absolute, can exist with the full knowledge and integrity of the person's intelligence, can possibly improve and disappear, is not originally accompanied by any outstanding physical or psychic defect, has no other objective criterion other than itself, is neither fatal nor irresistible in its urges, and ultimately constitutes a particular state of being more social than individual.

"Lack of instinctiveness, spontaneity, incoercibility and immutability; absence of or belated organic and correlative mental defects; delayed and artificial acquisition, premeditation of acts and conscience; genesis of a semi-logical order, necessity of a previous initiation, and especially no trace of heredity – these are most certainly the characteristics of pure passion and unadulterated vice. To sum up, there is nothing pathological; the liability should therefore be prevented, or at least repressed."

[8] necrophilia. [46]

[Austrian statutes, Paragraph 306.]

This horrible kind of sexual indulgence is so monstrous that the presumption of a psychopathic state is, under all circumstances, justified; and Maschka's recommendation that the mental condition of the perpetrator should always be investigated is well-founded. In any case, an abnormal and decidedly perverse sensuality is required to overcome the natural repugnance that man otherwise has for a corpse, and which thus permits a feeling of pleasure to be experienced in sexual congress with a cadaver.

Unfortunately, however, in the majority of the cases reported, the mental condition was not examined; therefore, whether necrophilia is compatible with mental soundness must remain an open question. In the absence of further consideration, however, anyone who has knowledge of the horrible aberrations of the sexual instinct would not venture to answer the question in the negative.

[9] incest.

[Austrian statutes, Paragraph 132; Austrian abridgment, Paragraph 189;
German statutes, Paragraph 174.]

The preservation of the moral purity of family life is a product of civilization; and feelings of intense displeasure arise in an ethically intact man at the thought of lustful feeling toward a member of the same family. Only great sensuality and defective ideas of laws and morals can lead to incest.

Both conditions may, in tainted families, be operative. Drinking and a state of intoxication in men; weak-mindedness that prevents the feeling of shame and that is sometimes associated with eroticism in women – these facilitate the occurrence of incestuous acts. External conditions that facilitate their occurrence are due to defective separation of the sexes among the lower classes.

As a decidedly pathological phenomenon, the author has found incest in states of congenital and acquired mental weakness and infrequently in cases of epilepsy[47] and paranoia.

It is not possible, however, to find in most of these cases a pathological basis for the act that so deeply wounds not only the tie of blood, but also the feeling of a civilized people. In many of the cases reported in literature, however, to the honor of humanity, the presumption of a psychopathic basis is possible.

Case 238.

Z., aged fifty-one, superintendent; enamored with his own daughter since her puberty. She had to leave home and reside with relatives abroad. He was a peculiar, nervous man, somewhat given to drink, without manifest taint. Although he denied being in love with his daughter, he acknowledged behaving like a lover toward her. He was very jealous of every man who ever approached her. He threatened to commit suicide if she ever married, and once proposed that they should die together. He knew how to arrange things so that he could always be alone with her and overwhelmed her with presents and caresses. No signs of hypersexuality. Did not keep a mistress and was looked upon as a very decent man.

In the Feldtmann case (Marc and Ideler, op. cit., vol. 1, p. 18), where a father constantly made immoral attacks on his adult daughter and finally killed her, the unnatural father was weak-minded and probably subject to periodic mental disease as well. In another case of incest between father and daughter (loc. cit., p. 247), the daughter, at least, was weak-minded. Lombroso (*Archiv. di Psichiatria,* vol. 8, p. 519) reports the case of a peasant, aged forty-two, who practiced incest with his daughters, aged twenty-two, nineteen, and eleven. He even forced the youngest to prostitute herself and then visited her in a brothel. The medico-legal examination showed predisposition, intellectual and moral imbecility, and alcoholism.

There was no mental examination in the case reported by Schürmeyer (*Deutsche Zeitschr. für Staatsarzneikunde,* vol. 22, no. 1), in which a mother had her five-and-a-half-year-old son lay on top of her, after which she practiced abuse on him; nor in that reported by Lafarque (*Journ. méd. de Bordeaux,* 1874), where a girl, aged seventeen, had her brother, aged thirteen, lay on top of her, at which time she brought about **contact of the genitals** and performed masturbation on him.

The following cases involve tainted individuals:

Legrand (*Ann. méd.-psych.,* May 1876) mentions a girl who at fifteen seduced her brother into all types of sexual excesses upon her person. When her brother died after two years of this incestuous practice, she attempted to murder a relative. The same article relates the case of a married woman, aged thirty-six, who hung her exposed breasts out of a window, and indulged in abuse with her brother, aged eighteen; and also the case of a mother, aged thirty-nine, who practiced incest with her son, with whom she was madly in love. She then became pregnant by him and induced abortion.

A case that was published by Kölle and taken from a criminal psychiatric opinion of the psychiatric clinic of Zurich refers to incest committed by a father on his imbecile adult daughter. This man suffered from chronic alcoholism.

Thoinot (op. cit.) reports a case of a nymphomaniac, aged forty-four, who attempted suicide because of unrequited love of her own son, aged twenty-three. She pestered him with kisses and caresses and tried one night to force him to engage in coitus, which he refused. Other similar attempts followed, accompanied by periodic spells of sanity. When all her efforts had failed, she made an attempt on her own life.

An even more horrible case is reported by Tardieu. A chronic nymphomaniac mother, apparently homosexual, often masturbated her little daughter, aged twelve, **in the vagina and anus** for hours in the middle of the night. During this time she was highly excited.

Through Casper we know that depraved mothers in large cities sometimes treat their little daughters in a most horrible fashion in order to prepare them for the sexual use of debauchees. This crime belongs elsewhere.

[10] immoral acts with persons in the care of others at wards; seduction (austrian).

[Austrian statutes, Paragraph 131; Austrian abridgment, Paragraph 188; German statutes, Paragraph 173.]

Allied to incest, though less repugnant to moral sensibility, are cases in which persons seduce those who are entrusted to them for care or education, and who are more or less dependent upon those who commit or tolerate vicious practices. Only rarely do such acts, which are especially deserving of legal punishment, seem to have psychopathic significance.

seven

appendix

[1] case histories from the seventh edition of "psychopathia sexualis"

(*Case histories and text from the seventh edition of* Psychopathia Sexualis [*originally published in 1892 by Ferdinand Enke, Stuttgart, Germany; English edition translated by Charles Gilbert Chaddock, M.D., and published in 1893 by The F. A. Davis Co., Philadelphia, Pennyslvania] that were eliminated by Krafft-Ebing in subsequent editions. Note: case history numbers are specific to the seventh edition only.*)

general pathology.

Case 3.

D., aged thirty-three, had a mother who suffered from persecutorial insanity. The mother's father also suffered from persecutorial insanity, and committed suicide. Her mother was also insane, and this woman's mother became insane during childbirth. Three of her mother's children died at a very young age, and those that lived longer had an abnormal character. As early as his thirteenth year, D. was troubled by the thought that he would become insane. At fourteen he attempted suicide. Later, vagabondage, and, as a soldier, repeated insubordination and crazy pranks. His intelligence was very limited; no sign of degeneration, genitals normal. At seventeen or eighteen he had emissions of semen, had never masturbated or had sexual feeling, and had never sought intercourse with women.

Case 30.

(Communicated by Dr. A. Moll, Berlin.) L. T., aged twenty-one; merchant in a Rhenish city. He was from a family in which several members were nervous and psychopathic. A sister suffered from hysteria and melancholia.

The patient was always timid and had a quiet disposition. At school he often stayed away from other pupils, particularly when they talked about girls. In the presence of ladies he thought that every expression he uttered was an offense against decency. Thus, for example, he thought it was very improper, in the presence of ladies, whether they were married or unmarried, to speak of going to bed, rising, etc. In the elementary classes the patient learned well. Later he became more indolent and did not make good progress.

On August 17, 1890, the patient visited Dr. Moll because of abnormal symptoms of a sexual nature. He did this on the advice of a physician, X., a relative in whom he had previously confided. From Dr. Moll's report: "The patient conveyed the impression of being extremely apprehensive and shy, and in answer to questions stated that he was extremely timorous to the point that, particularly in the presence of others, he lost all his self-confidence and assurance. Dr. X. confirmed this statement.

"The patient was able to pinpoint his seventh year as the beginning of his sexual life. At that age he frequently played with his genitals, and was often punished for it. As a part of this masturbation, during which he said he had erection, he constantly thought of whipping a woman with a rod on the naked buttocks until welts were raised on her skin. 'It delighted me,' said the patient, 'to imagine that she was a *proud,* beautiful lady, and that I performed the act in the presence of others, especially women, particularly with the idea *that she might feel the power I had over her.* For this reason, early on, I read about punishment; e.g., about the abuse of Roman slaves. I only had erections, however, when the conceived abuse consisted of blows delivered on the back or buttocks. At first I thought this kind of excitement would eventually disappear, and so I said nothing about it to anyone.'

"The patient continued to practice masturbation, and always with the same thought. After his thirteenth or fourteenth year he had ejaculation with the act. **When he was seventeen he first approached a woman for sex, but he could not carry out intercourse** since passion and erection were lacking. Soon, however, he again tried to have sex with another woman, with no success. Then he forcibly whipped the woman. So greatly was he aroused that he did not stop whipping the woman, although she was screaming and groaning in pain. He never thought of any legal punishment for his acts, and, in fact, escaped it. During this procedure erection, orgasm, and ejaculation occurred. The patient took the woman between his knees so that his penis was in contact with her body, but without his penis in her vagina, which seemed entirely superfluous to him.

"Afterward, however, the patient experienced such a feeling of shame about the beating, and was overcome with such great depression, that he often contemplated suicide. Although he still visited women occasionally, in the following three years he never again asked a woman to allow him to beat her. He sought to obtain erection by thinking of the beating; but this was without result, and masturbation by the woman did not induce erection. After an unsuccessful attempt of this kind, the patient was finally determined to confide in a physician.

"The patient made several other statements concerning his sex life. His abnormal sexual desire had troubled him with its intensity. He went to sleep with sexual thoughts. They troubled him through the night and were still with him when he awoke. He was never safe for any length of time from the impulsion of the abnormal ideas that excited him. Indeed, he gave himself up to them willingly, and was only able to free himself, for a short time, through masturbation.

"In response to my question, the patient stated that no other means of punishment of women, aside from beating the back and buttocks, had any charm for him. Neither binding them, walking on them, nor striking them, gave him much pleasure. This should be emphasized, inasmuch as a whipping given to a woman afforded him sexual pleasure because of its "humiliating, mortifying" effect on her, and because of his belief that she "felt herself to be completely in his power." It also gave the patient no pleasure to beat a woman on any other part of her body than those mentioned, or to cause her pain in any other way than by blows. It brought him much less pleasure to be whipped on the buttocks by a woman; this act often brought about an ejaculation of semen, although he thought this happened without an erection. When he inserted his penis into the vagina between the whippings, he ejaculated semen as soon as his penis made contact; he thought, however, that he experienced no pleasure from any part of the woman's body. Just as in beating the woman his pleasure was in humiliating her, so (with the relations *reversed) was he sexually excited by the fact that the beating humiliated him and that he felt himself to be completely in the woman's power.* No other personal humiliation, aside from a beating on his buttocks, excited him. Allowing himself to be bound or walked on by a woman was repugnant to him.

"The patient's erotic dreams were similar to his sexual inclinations while awake; in them, actual ejaculation often took place. Whether the perverse sexual thoughts first occurred in dreams or while awake, the patient was not able to state, due to the fact that his memory only went back to his seventh year. He believed, however, that these thoughts first occurred to him while awake. In his dreams it had frequently seemed to him that he was striking a man, which also caused ejaculation. While awake it *barely* excited him to think of striking a man. The nude form of a man had *no attraction whatsoever* for him, while the nude form of a woman had a decided charm, though his libido found its real satisfaction only when the acts previously described took place. He reported that he felt no desire for vaginal coitus.

"The treatment of the patient was directed to attaining normal coitus with normal desire, where possible. It was assumed that, with success in making his sexual life normal, the patient's shyness and apprehensiveness, which had caused him great annoyance, could be removed much more easily. The treatment followed by me, during three and a half months, was as follows:

"[1] The patient, who had a great desire to be cured, was strictly forbidden to indulge in perverse thoughts. Of course, I did not give him the foolish advice to not think of blows at all. The patient could not follow such advice, because the thoughts would come to him unbidden, even when he would accidentally read the word "blow." I only forbade him from indulging voluntarily in such thoughts. I specifically advised him to do everything he could to turn his ideas in another direction.

"[2] I allowed him, even commanded him, to think of nude women, because many nude females interested him, even though he thought they did not excite him sexually.

"[3] I used hypnosis, which was hard to induce, and suggestion to fortify the patient in this as far as possible. All attempts at coitus were forbidden in order to save the patient from a discouraging result.

"Within two and a half months, the patient reported that the perverse ideas occurred much less frequently and were constantly retreating to the background. Indeed, according to the patient's statement, erections occurred with thoughts of nude women, became more frequent, and often induced him to masturbate while thinking of coitus and without any idea of blows. Erotic dreams occurred but infrequently. Some included normal coitus, others included blows.

"After two and a half months of treatment I advised the patient to attempt coitus. Four such attempts were made. I advised him to always choose a woman who pleased him, and I attempted to increase his sexual excitement before coitus with a tincture of cantharides. The four attempts, the last of which took place on November 29, 1890, resulted as follows: In the first attempt, prolonged manipulation of the penis by the woman was necessary in order to induce erection. Insertion into the vagina and ejaculation with orgasm then took place. During the whole act no thought of beating the woman or being beaten occurred; instead, the woman herself excited him sufficiently for the performance of coitus. In the second attempt, the result was better and more quickly attained; manipulation of his genitals by the woman was not required for long. In the third attempt, coitus was attained only after the patient had thought of beating for a long time, thus inducing erection; no beating occurred. In the fourth attempt, coitus was attained without any thought of beating and without any manipulation of his genitals.

"Of course, the patient still could not in any way be regarded as cured. Although he was able to perform coitus in a normal or nearly normal way, this does not mean that he will always be able to do so in the future. Furthermore, the thought of beating still affords him great pleasure, even though it occurs much less frequently than before. Yet there is a possibility that the abnormal desire, having been weakened, will remain so in the future, and perhaps disappear."

†

Case 36.

A man always announced his intended visits to a public prostitute. She had to stand at the window, awaiting him with her face done up in a cloth bandage, and, upon his entrance into the room, complain of a severe toothache. He would be sorry for her, ask particularly about the pain, and take the cloth off and put it back on again. He never had coitus, however, and found his satisfaction exclusively in this act.

general pathology – masochism.

The following detailed autobiography of a masochist gives an exhaustive description of a typical case of this remarkable perversion:

Case 44.

"I come from a neuropathic family where, in addition to all kinds of peculiarities of character and manner of life, there are several abnormalities of a sexual nature. My imagination has always been very lively, and was directed very early to sexual matters. As far as I can remember, I enjoyed masturbation long before puberty. Even at that time my thoughts were directed, for hours at a time, to intercourse with females. My relations with the opposite sex, however, were entirely peculiar. I fantasized that I was a prisoner and absolutely in a woman's power, and that this woman used her power to hurt and abuse me in every possible way. Whipping and blows played an important part in my fantasy, as did many other acts and situations, all of which expressed the condition of bondage and subjection. I saw myself constantly kneeling before my ideal, trod upon, loaded with chains, and imprisoned. Severe punishments of all kinds were inflicted on me, to test my obedience and to please my mistress. The more severely I was humiliated and abused, the more I indulged in these thoughts. (At the same time I developed a great preference for velvet and fur, which I liked to touch and smooth, and which likewise excited me sexually.)

"I remember well that as a child I received many actual whippings at the hands of females. Because they never caused me any feeling other than pain and shame, I have never thought to connect such realities with my fantasies. A threat to severely punish and correct me agitated me painfully, but in my fantasy I assumed that my 'mistress' wanted to enjoy my suffering and humiliation, which entranced me. I have also never used as a part of my fantasies the acts and orders of the females who have taken care of me. I discovered early the truth about the relation of the sexes, but this knowledge made no impression on me. The idea of sensual pleasure remained connected with my first fantasies. I also had the desire to touch females, to embrace and kiss them, but I looked for the greatest delight only in their maltreatment, and in situations where they would make me feel their power. I soon came to realize that I differed from other men, and preferred to be alone and absorbed in my dreams. In my boyhood, real girls and women held little interest for me because I saw no possibility of having them act in the way I desired. On lonely paths in the forest I whipped myself with fallen branches, and allowed my imagination to play in the habitual way. I reveled in the sight of pictures of command-ing women, particularly if, like queens, they wore furs. I read everything related to my cherished ideas. Rousseau's *Confessions,* which then fell into my hands, was a great discovery. I found a condition described that essentially resembled mine. I was still more astonished at the similarity of my ideas to those I read about in the writings of Sacher-Masoch. I devoured them all with avidity, though the bloodcurdling scenes often far outdid my imagination, and then excited my aversion. Later, in order to supply new food for my fantasy, I began to write descriptions of erotic scenes to my taste, and to make drawings of situations that until then I had only painted in my imagination. In this, reality was an entirely indifferent matter to me. In the presence of a woman I was devoid of every sensual feeling; at most, the sight of a feminine foot would bring a fleeting wish to be trod upon by it.

"This indifference, however, was only in relation to pure sensuality. In late boyhood and early youth I was subject to an enthusiastic partiality for young girls of my acquaintance, with all the extravagances common to this youthful fervor. But it never occurred to me to connect the world of my sensual thoughts with these pure ideas. I never had to overcome such a thought; one never came to me. This is all the more remarkable, because although my lustful fantasies seemed very strange and unattainable in reality, they were in no way vile or obnoxious. This, too, was a kind of poetry to me; but it was divided into two worlds – in one was my heart, or, rather, my aesthetically excited fantasy; in the other, my sensually inflamed imagination. While my 'elevated' feeling always had a certain young girl for its object, at other times I saw myself at the feet of a mature woman who treated me as previously described. I never placed any lady of my acquain-tance in this role. Although in dreams the two spheres of my erotic ideas alternated, they never combined. Only the images of the sensual sphere induced pollutions.

"In my nineteenth year I allowed myself, with outward reluctance, but with inward desire, to be taken by friends to visit prostitutes. While there, however, I experienced nothing but repugnance and aversion, and left as soon as possible, without having felt the faintest trace of sensual excitement. Later, on my own initiative, I repeated the attempt, in order to determine for myself whether or not I was impotent, because I was much troubled by my first unexpected failure. The result was always the same – I felt no excitement at all, and did not have the slightest erection. In the first place, it was not possible for me to regard a real woman as an object of sensual gratification; furthermore, I could not renounce the conditions and situations that were sexually the principal things for me, and about which nothing could induce me to speak a word. Insertion of the penis – the act that was to be undertaken by me – seemed to me absolutely senseless and unclean. In the second place, there was my repugnance for common women, as well as my fear of infection.

"Meanwhile, in secret, my sexual life went on in the old fashion. Whenever my old fantasies came to mind, violent erection occurred, and I had ejaculations almost daily. I began to suffer from all kinds of nervous troubles, and then regarded myself as impotent, in spite of powerful erections and intense desire when I was alone. Nevertheless, from time to time I continued my experiments with prostitutes. Although in time I overcame my timidity and some of my aversion of contact with common women, I remained absolutely cold.

"After I had, with advancing years, overcome to some extent my shyness and my inclination to indulge in dreams, my sexual thoughts reflected an approach to the normal when I began to direct my interest to real persons. I was even successful in directing sensual thoughts toward women of my acquaintance, without carrying over any of my peculiar ideas from the other sphere. Thus I had some affairs with respectable girls. Embracing and kissing occurred, desire was excited, but not the power; it was, at least, too weak to allow me to think that under normal circumstances I could be virile. Of course, the attention I gave to the excitation of my sexual power was not calculated to favor this. Thus, always greatly ashamed, I would break off relations.

"With this, my old habit continued. I was still a great masturbator, although with lessened power. My fantasy, however, no longer entirely satisfied me. I began to follow both respectable women and others on the street; in the winter, I particularly followed women wearing velvet and furs. I often followed prostitutes to their homes and had them masturbate me. I always thought I could find more real pleasure in that than in my fantasies, but I always found less. When the woman took off her garments, my interest followed the garments. Although clothing by itself has never attracted me very strongly, it attracts me more than the nude female. The real object of my interest is the attired woman. In this, velvet and furs play the most important part, but all other articles of attire attract me also, particularly the form that is brought out by lacing and padding. I scarcely had any interest in the nude female form other than an aesthetic one. I have always had a very great interest in the shoes of women, particularly slippers with high heels, which are always connected with the thought of being trod upon, or with submissively kissing the foot.

"I finally overcame the last vestige of my shyness, and one day, to realize my dreams, had myself whipped, trod upon, etc., by a prostitute. The result was a *great disappointment*. What was done to me I felt to be rough, repugnant and silly. The blows caused me nothing but pain; the situation, repugnance and shame. Nevertheless, I induced an ejaculation mechanically, and, with the help of my imagination, I transformed the real situation into the one for which I longed. This desired situation differed from the actual essentially in that I created in my imagination a woman who abused me with the same pleasure as I experienced in her maltreatment of me.

"All my sexual fantasies were built on the expectation of a woman with a tyrannical, cruel disposition, to whom I wished to be subject. The act used to express the relation was a secondary matter to me. After the first attempt at an impossible realization, it was perfectly clear to me where my longing was directed. In my lustful dreams, of course, I had often passed beyond all ideas of abuse to conceive of a commanding woman with an imperious mien, a word of command, a kiss on the foot, etc.; now, however, I fully realized what it was that attracted me: flagellation was only the strongest means of expressing the principle, and by itself of secondary importance.

"In spite of this disappointment, I did not after the first step abandon my efforts to realize my erotic ideas. I was confident that, once accustomed to the new reality, my fantasy would find food for more intense activity. I sought the most suitable women for my purpose, and instructed them carefully in a complicated comedy. Occasionally I found that the way had been prepared for me by predecessors of similar disposition. The value of these comedies for the effect of my fantasy upon my sensuality remained problematic. By intensifying the subsidiary circumstances of the desired situation, these acts and scenes caused an unfortunate diminution in the intensity of the principal element, which my unaided fantasy, without the consciousness of planned, coarse deception, could more easily summon. My physical sensations, under the various punishments, were changeable. The more perfect the self-deception, the more perfectly the pain was felt as pleasure.

"In other words, the punishment was then conceived as a symbolic act. From this arose the illusion of the desired situation, accompanied by an intense psychic feeling of pleasure. The lustful feeling then spread over my whole body in lustful physical sensations, thus overcoming the perception of the painful quality of the punishment. The process of the moral punishments – the humiliations to which I subjected myself – was similar, but simpler, because it was confined to the mental sphere. These punishments were also attended by pleasurable feelings when the self-deception succeeded. It seldom succeeded well, however, and never perfectly; there always remained a disturbing element in my consciousness. Therefore, in the intervals I returned to solitary masturbation. Also, when punishment was used, the conclusion of the act was usually ejaculation provoked by masturbation, often without the aid of mechanical means.

"Thus I went on for many years, with diminishing power but only slightly diminished desire, and with the strength of my peculiar sexual idea unchanged. Today the condition of my sex life is the same. Coitus, which I have never performed, still seems to me a strange and unclean act. I learned about it from descriptions of sexual dissipation. My own sexual ideas seem natural, and do not in the least offend my sensitive taste. Their realization, as previously mentioned, leaves me unsatisfied for various reasons. I am pleased with pretty girls and women of respectability, but for a long time I have ceased to approach them. I have never attained, not even partially, a direct, actual realization of my sexual fantasy. As often as I have come into close relation with females, I have felt the woman's will to be beneath mine, never the reverse. I have never met a woman who manifested a desire for mastery in sexual things. Women who wish to rule in the household and exercise petticoat sovereignty are entirely different from my erotic ideals.

"My whole personality presents many abnormalities in addition to the perversion of my sex life; my neuropathic condition is expressed in many mental and physical symptoms. Besides, I think I recognize in myself an original abnormality of character in the nature of a resemblance to the feminine type; at least, I interpret as such my great weakness of will, and my great lack of courage in the presence of men and animals, which is in contrast with my coolness in the face of peril. My external appearance is entirely masculine."

The author of this autobiography also sent me the following communication:

"I always sought to find out whether the peculiar ideas that ruled me sexually were entertained by other men. Since the first stories about it accidentally came to my ears, I have sought everywhere to learn about it. Because it is a process of inner consciousness, it is not easy to identify, and cannot always be done with certainty; but I assume the existence of masochism where I find perverse sexual acts that cannot be explained except by this dominating idea. I look upon this anomaly as widespread.

"I have heard numerous stories about it from prostitutes here in Berlin, as well as in Vienna; and I have learned in this way how numerous are my fellow sufferers. I am always careful not to describe my own experiences, or ask whether they know of such; instead I allow these persons to relate their experiences just as they will.

"Simple flagellation is so common that almost every prostitute is familiar with it, but cases of real masochism are also frequent. The men subject to this perversion submit themselves to the most refined cruelties. The same farce is always played out with the instructed prostitutes – humiliating subjection of the man; treading upon him; commands, threats, and scoldings that have been committed to memory; flagellation; blows on various portions of the body; punishment of all kinds; pricking with needles; etc. The scenes often end with coitus, but they more frequently end with ejaculation without coitus. Twice prostitutes have shown me heavy iron chains with handcuffs that their patrons wanted to have put on them; the dried peas, on which they kneeled; the seat set with needles, on which they were commanded to sit; and many other such things. Often the perverted man wishes the woman to tie his penis tightly enough to cause pain; to prick it with needles, make cuts into it with a knife, or beat it with a stick. Even the act of hanging is employed, and cut short at just the right moment. Others have themselves scratched with a knife or dagger, but during the act the woman must also threaten them with death. In all these things the symbolism of subjection is the most important factor. The woman is usually called 'mistress'; the man, 'slave.'

"A man of high social standing, dressed as a servant, sat on the box of a carriage and drove his mistress around. Here there may have been a conscious imitation of *Venus im Pelz*. It seems to me that the writings of Sacher-Masoch have done much to develop this perversion in those who are predisposed. It is peculiar that the inexplicable enthusiasm for furs is so frequently combined with this perversion. A passion for furs and velvet has been peculiar to me from my earliest youth.

"For masochists, all these comedies with prostitutes are only troublesome substitutes. Whether there is such a thing as a realization of masochistic dreams in love relations or not, I do not know. If it occurs, it is certainly infrequent; for this taste in women (sadism in women, as described by Sacher-Masoch) is very difficult to find. In addition, the expression of sexual abnormalities finds greater obstacles in such things as women's modesty. I myself have never noticed the slightest indication of anything of this kind, and I have never been able to attempt an actual realization of my fantasies. Once a man told me confidingly of his masochistic perversion, and said he had found his ideal."

†

Case 49.

Autobiography. In January 1891 I received the following letter from a gentleman in Hungary:

"In depression and despair over a life that shuts me out from all that makes human happiness, I come to you with the last gleam of hope of rescue from a condition that can only end tragically if it continues.

"I am thirty years old, and come from a mother who suffered from periodic insanity. As early as my fourteenth year, abnormal sexual tendencies were noticeable in me. It always gave me a certain lustful pleasure to be whipped by boys of my own age, particularly when I was taken over the knee and spanked. It particularly delighted me when this was done by handsome young persons or boys with well-formed legs and closely fitting trousers. By means of such ideas I also came to masturbate. I practiced masturbation quite frequently – almost daily, and, in fact, in absolute ignorance of the terrible results of the vice. Thus it continued until my eighteenth year, at which time I was made aware of the vicious results of this practice.

"From this time began the terrible struggle with the desire to give it up, abandoned only too often. The fantasies did not leave me; I longed to be whipped by handsome young persons aged from twenty to twenty-two years, wearing tight trousers. My fantasy was filled especially with young soldiers and hussars. Although at times I was able to repress my imagination and avoid masturbation, I then had pollutions with dreams of the same nature.

"After my twentieth year, to my astonishment, the sexual inclination toward women that I had noticed in comrades of my own age and expected in myself did not appear. I was cold toward women, and embarrassed in their presence. At the same time, feminine nudity was not unpleasant; on the contrary, there was something attractive about it, but my sensuality was not excited.

"I twice attempted coitus; I was not troubled about being in bed with the girl; instead, I kissed and embraced her with pleasure, and even had traces of erection, but that was all. Since then I have had no hope, and have occasionally returned to masturbation, which I had previously avoided for some months. Nevertheless, I cultivated social intercourse with ladies, particularly young girls; I was esteemed in society, and liked for my graceful dancing. I was always hoping that in this way my unhappy tendency would be successfully overcome, but in vain; instead, it grew constantly stronger. Thus I have lived hours of wretchedness, and the ghost of suicide has passed before me. Although I once confided in a physician in Pest, he had only the usual remedies for persons suffering from sexual weakness – cold baths, quieting medicines, intercourse with women, etc.

"I tried everything in vain, until by accident a book on contrary sexual instinct fell into my hands, and gave me the last ray of hope. I have a respected position as a merchant, and appreciate thoroughly the joys of family life; I have an opportunity to marry, under the most favorable circumstances, a young girl whom I love, and who loves me. But I feel the cruel impossibility of this step. I suffer terribly when thinking about these repulsive abnormalities. My only hope lies in a cure by means of hypnosis. May it not be in vain!"

Pity and a scientific interest induced me to invite the writer of the preceding lines to come to see me. Early in February Mr. D. came. He was distinguished, pleasing, and masculine in appearance. Examination of the case showed it to be one of masochism. He distinctly remembered once seeing fellow pupils whipped by a teacher, and he remembered that it gave him a feeling of lustful pleasure. He could not remember if he was ever whipped by a teacher. His masochism had been an *absolutely primary manifestation,* and incomprehensible to him. Only gradually, and for lack of anything better, had he come to practice masturbation, during which ideas of being flagellated filled his mind. He had never had a desire to be whipped by the teacher; he always wished to be flogged by fellow pupils and well-developed young persons. Since reaching maturity he had never been able to induce himself to satisfy his masochistic inclinations.

In intercourse with prostitutes he had repeatedly had the thought of having himself whipped by them; because, however, this was not accompanied by sensual feeling, it was not carried out. The patient declared that his inclination toward persons of his own sex was purely masochistic. In other respects he found nothing interesting in men. Until his eighteenth year the patient also had sadistic tendencies. He was enthusiastic about the position of the pedagogue and wanted to be a teacher in order to be able to flog boys. *This ideal sadism later disappeared entirely.* The patient complained of feeling alone in the world, like a pariah, and of being different from other men. His libido toward women had greatly diminished, possibly as a result of his masturbation. Although he had no erection at the sight of feminine charms, the sight of a riding whip or a cane powerfully excited him sexually. When he attempted coitus, no masochistic ideas occurred. Such ideas arose, however, whenever he saw attractive young men. He believed that if he were freed from his ideas of flagellation he could be helped, for then his sensuality would direct itself in a normal path.

The patient had neuropathic eyes, but was free from all degenerative signs. Regarding hereditary taint, it was noteworthy that his maternal grandfather was peculiar, and shot himself while in a psychopathic condition. The patient felt well, except for slight neurasthenic troubles. Patellar reflex increased. His genitals were perfectly normal. His dreams with pollutions were exclusively about being flagellated by young persons, particularly soldiers with tight trousers.

The following principles of treatment were imposed: [1] Removal of the symptoms of neurasthenia. [2] Suggestive treatment to achieve [a] avoidance of masturbation; [b] indifference toward his own sex and absence of thoughts of flagellation when awake and when asleep; [c] libido exclusively toward persons of the opposite sex, occurrence of erections at the sight of beautiful women, complete power with women, and dreams of women exclusively. At the first sitting, Bernheim's method caused the patient to pass quickly into a state of deep lethargy. At the second sitting (February 5), a cataleptic condition of the muscles was induced. Sittings occurred almost daily. It was seen that stroking the brow induced deeper hypnosis, with catalepsy, that did not, however, go beyond deep lethargy. Suggestion was begun in the third sitting.

February 10. The patient said that he no longer had any interest in men, but had a growing interest in women. He began to dream of women.

February 13. He felt himself free from masochism during the day, and canes and whipping no longer interested him. Although at night he still had "weak" dreams of flagellation concerning men, they were without lustful feeling or pollution. A short time ago he had a dream, unusual in all respects, with no erotic coloring, in which he whipped himself.

February 19. The patient attempted coitus with a prostitute pleasing to him. Erection was incomplete, and ejaculation did not occur, so he gave up the attempt. The patient's libido toward women was still weak. He was not discouraged by his failure, however, and expected ultimate success, for he felt free from his abnormal tendencies and like a different man. On February 20, unfortunately, the patient had to discontinue treatment because he was called home by duties there.

The fact that traces of sadism were simultaneously present here lends certainty to the diagnosis of masochism in this rudimentary case. The purely psychic character of masochism is unquestionable. At the same time, the case is combined with incompletely developed contrary sexual instinct, a frequent association in masochists and sadists.

†

Case 52.

A man found satisfaction in the following manner: Occasionally he visited a public prostitute and had a porcelain ring, similar to those used in hanging curtains, placed on his penis. Two cords were attached to the ring, drawn backward between his legs, and attached to the bedstead. He then told the woman to beat him mercilessly with a whip, cry "whoa" to him constantly, and treat and abuse him as if he were an unruly horse. The more the woman, with shouts and blows, spurred him on to pull, the greater his sexual excitement became. Erection occurred (probably mechanically favored by compression of the dorsal vein of the penis that was closed by the pressure of the hard ring when the cords were strained). With increasing erection, the whole member was compressed by the ring, after which ejaculation, with lustful feeling, occurred.

†

Of the numerous established cases of shoe fetishism, the following one, reported by Dr. A. Moll of Berlin, (corresponding in many respects with Hammond's case, but described in more detail and observed more carefully here), seems especially suited to show the connection between masochism and shoe fetishism:

Case 60.

"O. L., aged thirty-one, bookkeeper in Wurtemburg; from a tainted family.

"The patient was a large, powerful man, of ruddy appearance. Although in general he had a quiet temperament, he would, on occasion, become violent; he said himself that he was quarrelsome and inclined to assert himself. L. was kind and generous, and would weep easily. At school he passed classes as a talented pupil, with good powers of comprehension. Although the patient had occasional congestion of the head, he was otherwise healthy, except that he was very depressed and melancholic as a result of his sexual perversion, described below.

"Few details could be learned about the nature of any hereditary taint.

"The following facts concerning the development of his sexual life were gathered from the patient's own statements:

"In early youth (eight or nine years old), L. had the desire to lick his teacher's boots like a dog. Although L. thought it was possible that this idea was excited by his once having seen a dog actually do this, he was unable to state this with certainty. The patient seemed much more definite that the first ideas of this kind came when he was in a waking state, not in dreams.

"From his tenth to his fourteenth year he constantly sought to touch the shoes of his fellow pupils, as well as those of little girls; he always chose, however, boys who had wealthy and prominent parents. One of these, the son of a rich landed proprietor, had riding boots; in the boy's absence, L. took these in his hands, struck himself with them, and pressed them against his face. L. did the same thing with the elegant boots of an officer of the dragoons.

"After the onset of puberty, the desire was transferred exclusively to the boots of females. Thus, while skating, the patient's attention was entirely occupied with putting on and taking off the skates of the ladies there. He always chose, however, only such women who were rich and prominent socially, and who wore elegant boots. On the street and everywhere else, L. constantly looked for elegant boots. His love for them went so far that he often put the sand and mud that bore their imprints in his purse, and even in his mouth. As a boy of fourteen, L. visited brothels, and he often visited a café singer with the sole purpose of exciting himself with the sight of her elegant boots (low shoes were less attractive). In his schoolbooks and on the walls of closets, L. drew boots. In the theatre he saw nothing but the shoes of the ladies. On the street and aboard steamboats, for hours at a time, L. would run after ladies who wore elegant boots; he thought with delight of how he might get a chance to touch the boots. This peculiar love for boots remained unchanged. *The thought of having himself trod upon by ladies in their boots, or of kissing the boots, would give L. the most intense sensual delight.* In front of shoe stores he would stand and stand, merely to look at the boots. He was particularly excited by their elegance.

"Although the patient preferred high-buttoned or laced boots with high heels, less elegant boots, even with low heels, also excited him if their wearer was a wealthy, distinguished and proud lady.

"At the age of twenty L. attempted coitus, but was not successful 'in spite of the greatest efforts,' according to him. During the attempt the patient had no thought of shoes; on the contrary, he had first tried to excite himself sexually with shoes, and blamed too much excitement for his lack of success in coitus. Up to his present age of thirty-one, he had attempted coitus only four or five times, and always in vain.

"On one occasion the patient, already much to be pitied because of his disease, had the misfortune of contracting syphilis. When asked what he regarded as the most lustful act, the patient said: '*It is my greatest delight to lie naked on the floor and have myself trod upon by girls wearing elegant boots;* this, of course, is only possible in brothels.' Furthermore, according to the patient's statements, such sexual perversions of men were well-known in many houses of prostitution – proof that they were not so infrequent. The prostitutes called these men 'boot lovers.' The patient had only rarely had the lustful act actually performed, however, notwithstanding the fact that it was a most beautiful and pleasant thing for him. The patient had no thoughts that impelled him toward intercourse; at least, not in the sense of inserting his penis into the vagina – an act that afforded him no pleasure whatsoever. Indeed, he gradually developed a fear of coitus, which could be sufficiently explained by his numerous unsuccessful attempts, for the patient himself said that his inability to complete coitus embarrassed him exceedingly. The patient had never practiced real masturbation. With the exception of a few occasions where the patient satisfied his sexual desire by masturbation with boots or in a similar way, he was innocent of such satisfaction because in his enjoyment of boots there was scarcely ever anything more than erection. At most, only a slight discharge of fluid would slowly take place, which the patient took to be semen.

"The sight of a shoe alone excited him, but not nearly as intensely as when it was worn by a woman. New shoes that had not been worn excited him much less than those that had been used; but used shoes had to be free from wear and look as new as possible. Shoes of this kind excited him the most. As has been said, ladies' boots alone excited him. Under such circumstances, in fantasy, L. created a lady for them; he would press them against his lips and penis. He said he would 'die with delight' if a proud, respectable lady were to tread upon him with her shoes.

"Aside from the previously mentioned characteristics of the women (pride, wealth, social prominence) that constituted an especial stimulus in connection with the elegance of the boots, the patient was by no means indifferent to the physical charms of the female sex. Although he was enthusiastic about beautiful women without thinking of boots, this love was not directed toward sexual satisfaction. The bodily charms played a part, however, in connection with the boots; a homely old woman wearing the most elegant boots could not affect the patient. The rest of the attire and other circumstances also played an essential role, shown by the fact that elegant boots worn by proud, distinguished women especially excited the patient. A common servant girl in her working dress wearing the most elegant shoes would not excite him. Men's shoes and boots no longer affected the patient, and he never felt attracted at all to men sexually.

"Yet the patient had erections very easily. When he would take a child in his lap, when he would pat a dog or horse for some time, when he would travel on the streetcars, or when he would ride – erections would occur. In the latter case he thought it was due to the shaking. He had erections every morning; and he could quickly induce erection by thinking of the acts with boots that were so pleasing to him. Previously, nighttime pollutions had frequently occurred – about every three or four weeks; now they were less frequent, and occurred about once every three months.

"In his erotic dreams the patient was almost always sexually excited by the same thoughts that excited him in the waking state. He thought that for some time he had felt ejaculation during erection; he drew this conclusion, however, only because he felt a little moisture at the end of his penis. Books that touched the sphere of the patient's sexual ideas especially excited him. Thus, when reading *Venus im Pelz*[1] by Sacher-Masoch, he was so excited "that the semen just *ran* away from him." Moreover, for L., the kind of ejaculation he had while reading decidedly satisfied his sexual desire. When he was asked if blows received from a woman's hand would also excite him, the patient thought he had to answer in the affirmative. Although the patient had never attempted such, playful taps had always been very pleasing to him.

"It would give the patient a particularly intense pleasure if he were to be kicked by a woman, even one with bare feet. He did not think that the blows, as such, would cause the excitement, but rather the thought of being maltreated by a woman; and that the excitement would follow scolding as well as actual blows. In addition, blows and cross words had an exciting effect only when they came from a proud and distinguished lady. In general it is the *feeling of humiliation and slavish subjection* that gave the patient lustful pleasure. 'Were a lady,' the patient told me, 'to command me, even with distant coldness, to wait on her, I would nonetheless feel sensual pleasure.'

"When he was asked whether the feeling of humiliation came over him with boots, the patient answered: 'I think that this general passion for self-humiliation has been concentrated especially on ladies' boots; for it is symbolic of one's being "unworthy to loosen the latchet of another's shoe"; and, besides, a subject kneels.'

"Women's stockings also had an exciting effect on the patient, but only to a slight extent, and perhaps only through awakening an idea of boots. Although in the past the patient's passion for ladies' boots had constantly increased, in recent years he thought he had noticed a decrease. For example, he seldom visited public prostitutes, and he was also more capable of self-restraint. Yet this passion still ruled him absolutely, and every other pleasure was spoiled by it. A pretty female boot would attract his glance away from the most beautiful landscape. He often went about at night, in the corridors of hotels,[2] seeking elegant ladies' shoes. He would kiss the shoes and press them mostly against his penis, but would also press them against his face and neck.

"The patient, who was very well-to-do, voluntarily went to Italy a short time ago, with the sole thought of becoming the servant of a rich and distinguished lady unacquainted with him; the plan, however, failed. The patient, who came for consultation only, had not yet been treated medically.

"The foregoing history includes events almost up to the present time, and the patient has communicated with me by letter concerning his condition in the intervening period. It does not require an extensive commentary. It seems to me to be one of the best cases that illustrates the relationship between shoe fetishism and masochism as set forth by

Krafft-Ebing. Without being asked leading questions, the patient always emphasized that the principal charm for him was his subjection to a woman, who had to be as far above him in pride and position as possible."

†

In the following case, communicated by a professional friend, the masochistic significance of a disgusting act is clear:

Case 69.

H. v. G., landed proprietor; major; died in his sixtieth year; came from a family in which irresponsibility, tendency to run in debt, and defect of morals were hereditary. He was given to reckless dissipation in his youth (he was known as the leader of "naked balls"). Although he always had a cynical and brutal nature, he was punctilious and exact in his military service, which he had to leave because of a disreputable affair that was not made public. He then lived in private life for seventeen years. Not needing to earn his living, he led the life of a man-of-the-town everywhere, and was widely avoided because of his lascivious nature. Ostracized by the best society – which, in spite of his independence, he noticed – he preferred instead the ordinary society of fakirs, artisans, and loafers. It could not be ascertained whether he had sexual intercourse with men, but it was certain that in his later years he arranged symposiums with mixed company and was known as a *roué*. In the last few years of his life he would hang around new buildings in the evening, and, of the women working there, he would ask the dirtiest to accompany him. He would have the woman undress, and he would then suck her toes. His libido was excited and satisfied by the act.

†

The following case was reported to me by a physician:

Case 72.

A notary, known from his youth as peculiar and misanthropic. During his school days he enjoyed masturbation. According to his own story, he excited his sexual desire by spreading pieces of toilet paper that he had used on the cover of his bed. He then induced erection by regarding and smelling them, and finally masturbated. After his death, a large basket of such papers, with dates marked on them, were found by the side of his bed. There were probably fantasies here in the realm of acts previously described in cases of masochistic coprolagnia.

general pathology – antipathic sexuality.

Case 96.

X., aged nineteen; mother nervous; two sisters of mother's father insane. Patient of nervous temperament; well-endowed mentally; well-developed; normally formed. When he was twelve years old, an elder brother seduced him into mutual masturbation.

After this, the patient continued the vice alone. In the last three years, during the act of masturbation, he had had peculiar fantasies in the domain of "contrary sexual instinct."

In these fantasies, he imagined himself as a female. He would, for example, imagine himself as a ballet dancer engaging in the act of coitus with an officer or a circus rider. These perverse fantasies had accompanied the act of masturbation since the patient became neurasthenic. He understood the harm of masturbation, fought desperately against it, but always surrendered to the impulse.

If he was able to withstand the impulse for a few days, a normal desire for sexual intercourse with females was awakened; but a certain fear of infection always checked these desires, and drove him again to masturbation.

Remarkably, this unfortunate's lascivious dreams only concerned females.

Over the course of the last few months, the patient had become very neurasthenic and hypochondriacal. He feared tabes.

I advised treatment of the neurasthenia, suppression of masturbation, and marital cohabitation, if possible, after improvement of the neurasthenia.

†

Case 103.

A middle-aged woman in the asylum at Greifswald thought she was a man, and acted out her belief. She cut her hair short, and parted it on one side in the military fashion. A sharply cut profile, a somewhat large nose, and a certain heaviness of all the facial features combined with the short hair combed smoothly over her ears to give the whole head a decidedly masculine appearance. She was tall and lean; her voice low and rough; the larynx angularly prominent; her attitude erect; her gait, like all her movements, heavy without being awkward. She looked like a man in female dress. Asked how she had come to think she was a man, she would almost always cry excitedly: "Just look at me! Don't I look like a man? I feel like a man, too. I have always felt so, but only gradually have I come to understand it clearly. The man who should be my husband is not a real man. I raised my children myself. I always felt somewhat like this, but I came to understand it later. Have I not always worked like a man? The man who passed for my husband only helped. He did what I planned. From my youth I have been more masculine than feminine. I have always had more of a liking for the garden and farm than for work in the house and kitchen. But I never understood the reason. Now I know I am a man, and I shall bear myself like one. It is a shame to always make me wear women's clothes."

C a s e   1 0 4 .

X., aged twenty-six, tall, and of handsome appearance. From his earliest youth he loved to wear female attire. As he grew up, when he was a participant in theatricals, he always managed it so that he had a female part. After an attack of mental excitement, he imagined that he was actually a woman, and tried to convince others of it.

He liked to undress himself, put on female clothing, and dress his hair. In this state he had a desire to go out on the street. In other respects he was perfectly reasonable. After costuming himself in a nightgown to appear as much like a woman as possible, he would spend the whole day arranging his hair and looking at himself in the mirror. He imitated the walk of women. One day, when Esquirol acted as if he were about to lift up his dress, X. flew into a rage and upbraided him for a lack of modesty (Esquirol).

C a s e   1 0 5 .

Mrs. X., widow. Because of the death of her husband and the loss of her fortune, her mind had been greatly troubled. She became mentally disturbed and, after attempting suicide, was admitted to the Salpêtrière.

Lean, thin, and constantly maniacal, Mrs. X. believed she was a man, and became angry if she was addressed as "madam." Once, when male clothing was placed at her disposal, she was beside herself with joy. She died in 1802 of a consumptive malady. She had expressed her delusion of being a man until shortly before her death (Esquirol).

†

I am indebted to a physician, aged thirty, for the following autobiography, which is noteworthy in another respect:

Case 108.
Mental hermaphroditism; abortive contrary sexual instinct.

"In my ancestry I am somewhat predisposed hereditarily. My grandfather on my father's side was a speculator and lived the high life. My father was a man of character, but for more than thirty years he suffered from recurrent dementia. He was not, however, much hindered by it in business. My mother suffers from cardiac attacks, as did her father. My mother's father and brother are said to have been sexually hyperesthetic. My only sister, about nine years older than myself, was twice subject to attacks of eclampsia, was religiously exalted during puberty, and was probably also sexually hyperesthetic. She suffered for many years from a severe hysterical neurosis, but is now completely well.

"As an only son, and born late, I was the apple of my mother's eye. I have her indefatigable care to thank for my surviving childhood, after having passed through all the childhood diseases (hydrocephalus, measles, croup, smallpox, and, at thirteen, chronic intestinal catarrh that lasted a year). My very religious mother raised me, without spoiling me, in a religious way, and implanted as my guiding moral principle an unyielding devotion to duty. This was further carried to an extreme for me by a teacher whom I still call a friend. Due to my delicate health, the greater part of my childhood was spent in bed; thus I indulged in quiet occupations, especially reading. As a boy I thus came to be – if not blasé – at least precocious. As early as eight or nine the parts of books that excited me most were those describing injuries or operations that had to be endured by beautiful girls or ladies. Thus I was thrown into great excitement by a story's illustration that showed a maiden who had run a thorn into her foot and a boy removing it. Indeed, every time I looked upon this picture, which was in no way lascivious, I had an erection. Whenever possible, I went to see chickens killed; if I had missed that, I looked at the spots of blood and, with pleasurable shudders, stroked the warm bodies of the birds. I would emphasize the fact that I have always been a great lover of animals, and that I have felt disgust and pity while killing larger animals, as well as during vivisections of dogs.

"The killing of chickens is still a great sexual stimulus for me. I am especially excited by holding them, during which I suffer from palpitations of the heart and precordial oppression. It is worth noting that my father had a passion for binding together the hands of girls and young women.

"I think that another of my sexual abnormalities can be attributed to this strain of cruelty. As I shall clearly describe, one of my favorite games was that of an improvised doll theatre, where I prescribed the parts of my companions. The story almost always involved a young girl who, at the command of her papa (played by me), had to have a painful operation done on her foot. The more the girl cried, the more satisfaction I had. I came to hit upon the foot as the constant object of operation in the following way. As a very young boy, I happened to see my eldest sister change her stockings. When she hastily hid her feet, my attention was attracted, and the sight of her bare feet immediately became the ideal of my longing. Naturally, this made my sister very careful; there was thus occasioned a constant quarrel that I provoked with all the wiles of cunning and flattery, and even explosions of anger, until my seventeenth year. In other respects I was indifferent to my sister. Indeed, her kiss was repugnant to me. For lack of anything better, I made use of the feet of servants; masculine feet had no effect on me. My greatest desire would have been to cut the nails or (pardon the expression) the corns, from the beautiful foot of a woman. My lustful dreams were concerned with these things. Indeed, I applied myself to the study of medicine with a real expectation of gaining an opportunity to satisfy or cure my desires. I cured them, thank God. After undertaking my first dissection of the lower extremity of a female, this unfortunate desire was removed from me. I was unhappy because I was always deeply ashamed of this impulse. I think I can safely refrain from giving further details about it, because this peculiar enthusiasm, which even inspired me to write verses, has been sufficiently described by others.

"Concerning the last phase of my sexual errors: I was about thirteen, and had just begun to mature, when a schoolmate who happened to be our guest one night teased me by kicking me under the covers with his bare feet. I seized his foot, immediately became greatly excited, and afterward had a pollution – my first. The boy was peculiarly girlish in form, as well as mentally effeminate. In addition, another comrade with very small, delicate hands and feet, whom I once saw in a bath, caused unusual excitement in me. I thought it would be a great piece of good fortune to be in bed with either of these men, although nothing closer to sexual intercourse than embracing them ever came into my mind. Moreover, I always thrust such thoughts aside with aversion. Some years later, at about sixteen or eighteen, I made the acquaintance of two other boys who awakened my sexual feeling. When I played with either of these boys, I immediately had an erection. Both were energetic and lively, but delicately formed and childlike. With puberty I lost interest in both of them, though a warm friendship was preserved. I could have never allowed myself to indulge in vicious practices with them.

"After I went to the university I completely forgot these errors of my sexual desire, and abstained on principle from sexual intercourse until I was twenty-four, in spite of the contempt of my companions. When pollutions became too frequent, I feared cerebral neurasthenia due to abstinence, and subsequently surrendered to normal sexual indulgence. Although somewhat mechanical, it was, of course, very beneficial to me.

"I blame the special field of work to which I have devoted myself for the fact that I am almost impotent with street prostitutes, and also for the fact that the naked form of a woman disgusts rather than excites me. The act of coitus always satisfies me the most if, during it, I can maintain a view of the woman's face. Because, however, I find unbearable the idea that the girl near me has been enjoyed by another, for years my mental comfort has depended upon my keeping a (virgin) mistress, in spite of the financial sacrifice involved. Otherwise the most terrible jealousy would leave me absolutely incapable of work. I must also mention that, at thirteen, I fell platonically in love for the first time; and since then I have often languished in chaste love. What distinguishes my case from all others is the fact that I have never masturbated in my life. Some weeks ago, while asleep, I was frightened by a dream of a naked boy, from which I awoke with an erection.

"In conclusion, I shall undertake the difficult task of describing my present condition: Medium height, gracefully formed. Skull dolichocephalic, with prominence in the occipital region; circumference, fifty-nine centimeters; frontal prominence marked; glance somewhat neuropathic; pupils medium; teeth very defective; musculature strong and tense; abundant hair, blonde. Varicocele on the left side of the scrotum; frenulum too short, hindering me in coitus. I severed it myself three years ago. Since then ejaculation is retarded, and pleasurable feeling much diminished. Temperament choleric. Quick at comprehension; good at drawing conclusions; energetic; very persevering for one hereditarily predisposed. I learn languages easily, and have a good ear for music, but otherwise I have no talent for the arts. I am always ambitious to do my duty, but I am constantly troubled with *taedium vitae,* and only kept from attempts at suicide by my religion and the thought of my mother. Otherwise I am a typical candidate for suicide. I am ambitious, jealous, have a fear of paralysis; left-handed. I am filled with socialistic ideas. I like adventures, and I am courageous. I have decided to never marry."

Case 109.

Psychic hermaphroditism. Autobiography. "I was born in 1868. The families of both my parents are healthy; at any rate, mental disease has never occurred in them. My father, who was a merchant, is now sixty-five years old; for years he has been nervous and especially inclined to be melancholic. It is said that my father lived fast before his marriage. My mother is healthy, though not very strong. There are two other healthy children.

"Sexually I developed early, and in my fourteenth year was so much troubled by pollutions that I was frightened. I am no longer able to state under what circumstances these pollutions occurred, or the particular nature of the dreams that were connected with them. The fact is, for years I have felt myself drawn sexually only toward men; and, with every effort and terrible struggle, I am still unable to overcome this unnatural impulse that is so repugnant to me. It is said that I had many severe illnesses in my childhood, and that I often came near death. This is probably why I was spoiled and very delicate. I was always in the house, preferred to play with dolls rather than with soldiers, and liked playing quietly in the house better than playing noisily in the streets. I entered the *Gymnasium* at the age of ten. Though I was lazy, I was among the best scholars because I learned very easily and was the favorite of my teacher. From my earliest childhood (seventh year), I took pleasure in little girls. As late as my thirteenth year, I remember that I had formal love affairs with them and was jealous of those who associated with them; that I took pleasure in looking under the petticoats of my sister's friends and the servants; and that I had erections when touching the bodies of my female playmates. I recall with certainty that boys attracted and excited me sexually just as early and just as powerfully. I always took great delight from reading and from the theatre. I had a doll theatre, and playing with it was a preferred activity. I knew whole pieces by heart, copied the actors I saw, took the female parts especially, and was delighted to put on female attire.

"As my sexual life became more pronounced, my inclination for boys won the upper hand. I fell completely in love with my companions, and had lustful feelings if a companion who pleased me touched my body. I became very shy, and refused to take gymnastic and swimming lessons. I thought I was different from my comrades, and did not like to undress in front of them. I liked to look at the penises of my companions, and had erections easily. I have masturbated only once, in my youth. It occurred after a friend told me that one could have pleasure without women; I tried it, but found no pleasure in it. Also, at that time a book that warned against the effects of masturbation fell into my hands. After that one time, I never did it again. In my fourteenth or fifteenth year I made the acquaintance of two younger boys who excited me sexually to the highest degree. I was especially in love with one of them. In his presence I became sexually excited, and was restless when I did not have him near me. I was jealous of those who associated with him and embarrassed in his presence. He had no suspicion of my condition. I felt very unhappy, and was often glad to weep, after which I felt relieved. I could not understand this feeling, however, and always felt its irregularity. I was also especially unhappy because all at once my ability to work disappeared. Where before I had learned with ease, suddenly I had difficulty; my thoughts were never on the subject. Only by straining every nerve could I get anything through my head. I had to study aloud in order to keep my attention on the matter at hand. My previously excellent memory often left me in the lurch. Nevertheless, I continued to be a good scholar, and I still pass for a talented man; but I have terrible difficulty in learning anything. I exerted all my energy to free myself from this sad condition. I went swimming daily, practiced turning, often rode, practiced fencing, and in all of these activities I enjoyed myself very much. I still like to be on a horse's back, though I know nothing about horses, and have no particular talent for physical exercises. I was never absent from a drinking party, and I smoked. I was much liked. In cafés I associated a great deal with waitresses, and liked to amuse myself with them. I was not, however, sexually excited by them. Among my friends and teachers I passed as a man who was experienced with women, as well as spoiled by them. Unfortunately, this was not true.

"At the age of nineteen I went to the university. My first semester was spent at the University of B., and it is still terrible to recall it. My sexual appetite powerfully excited me, and I ran about at night, for hours at a time, looking for men, especially when I was intoxicated. The next morning I would be crazy because of it. Fortunately, I found no one. In the second semester, I went to M. This was my happiest time. I had pleasant friends and, to my surprise, took pleasure in women, about which I was very happy. I had a love affair with a young girl of spoiled character, with whom I spent wild nights. I was extraordinarily virile. I had formerly been chaste, but now I associated with women as never before. I felt fresh and well after coitus. I was not charmed so much by the female figure, which was never beautiful to me, as by – I know not what. That is, I knew women whose touch immediately induced erection. This joy and state of delight did not last long. I was foolish enough to take rooms with a friend. We had one bedroom. My friend was very talented and amiable, and a favorite with women; these were the characteristics that at first so strongly attracted me. In fact, I love only highly educated men; uneducated, powerful persons are only momentarily able to excite me, but they cannot retain my affections. I soon fell in love with my friend. Then came the terrible time that destroyed my health. Because I slept in the same room with my friend and had to see him undress every day, it required all my strength to keep from betraying myself. I became nervous, cried easily, and was jealous of those who associated with him. Although I still associated with women, it was only with difficulty that I could perform coitus, which, like woman, was repugnant to me. The same women who had excited me intensely no longer had any effect on me. I followed my friend to W., where he met another friend he had known before me. I became jealous and sick with love and longing. At the same time, I associated again with women, but indulged in coitus seldom, and only with difficulty. I became terribly depressed and almost insane. Work was out of the question. I led a foolish, wild life, and spent a great amount of money, almost throwing it away. After six weeks of this, I broke down and had to visit a water-cure, where I spent many months. There I came to myself again. Because I can be very gay, and take great pleasure in the society of educated ladies, I soon became much liked. In conversation I prefer married women over younger girls. I am also very gay in the society of gentlemen at the beer table and in the bowling alley.

"At the sanitarium I met a man of twenty-nine who was apparently constituted like myself. The fellow forced himself upon me, and wanted to embrace and kiss me. Although he excited me, his touch causing erection and even ejaculation, I found him repugnant. One evening he got me to perform mutual masturbation. Afterward I spent a frightful, sleepless night; I was terribly disgusted with the whole affair, and thought I would never do such a thing with a man again. All day long I could get no rest. It was terrible to me that, in spite of this, and against my will, this man so excited me sexually. On the other hand, it gave me satisfaction that he was in love with me, and that he was apparently having to go through struggles similar to my earlier ones. From that time I was successful in keeping him away from me.

"I went again to various universities, as well as many water-cures, with temporary, but never permanent, benefit. I fell in love, too, with many friends, but never so deeply as with the friend from M. I no longer had sexual intercourse with women – I was incapable of it – or with men: I had no opportunity for it with men, because I forced myself to avoid it. I still often meet my friend from M.; we are the same good friends as ever, and, much to my delight, he no longer excites me. This is usually what happens; when I have not seen a person who excites me for a long time, the sexual influence disappears.

"I passed my examinations with distinction. A year before they took place, when I was twenty-three, I began to practice masturbation, because I could find no other way of gratifying my burdensome sexual appetite. Still, I did it infrequently, for I was always disgusted afterward, and then would spend a sleepless night. When I have had too much to drink, however, I lose all strength; I run about for hours seeking men, and finally surrender to masturbation. The next morning I awake with a dull head and a horror of myself, and go about all day in a melancholy state. As long as I have control of myself, I use all my strength to combat my nature. It is terrible when one cannot enjoy the simple pleasure of associating with friends, and when every erect soldier or butcher boy makes one tremble and throb. It is frightening when night comes, to watch at the window for someone to urinate against a wall across the way so that I may have an opportunity to see his genitals. In addition to those terrible thoughts, there is the consciousness of the immorality and criminality of my state of mind and my longing. I have a repugnance for myself that I cannot describe. I consider my condition abnormal; I cannot think that it is congenital, but believe that the impulse was bred in me by faulty education. My suffering makes me reckless and egotistical; it takes away all kindness of disposition, and makes me careless about my family. I am moody, and frequently almost insane; I am often so depressed that I do not know what to do, and am then easily moved to tears. And yet I have a horror of sexual intercourse with men. One evening after a drinking party, drunk and excited and in a half-conscious state, I was wandering around full of desire when I met a young man who got me to perform mutual masturbation. Although he excited me, after the act I was beside myself. When I go by the place now, I am overcome with horror: when I rode by it recently, I fell from my gentle horse, whom I know so well, because I was so overcome by the memory of my unworthy deed.

"I love family life, children, and social intercourse; and, with my position in society, I am suited to have a family. I must, however, give all that up; and yet I cannot abandon hope of a cure. And so I vacillate between hopeful gaiety and frightened hopelessness, neglecting business and family. Indeed, I do not wish to marry and have a family; I only wish to overcome my terrible inclination for the male sex, associate quietly with my friends, and learn to respect myself again.

"No one has any suspicion of my condition; rather, I pass as a great *roué* – a reputation I try to maintain. I try to have relations with girls, for which I have ample opportunity. Although I have known many who have loved me and would have sacrificed their honor for me, I have no love to offer them and nothing sexual to give. I can, however, love a man. I am only excited by young men between the ages of seventeen and twenty-five, preferably clean-shaven, or at least without full beards. I can only love those who are educated, respectable and amiable. I am, in short, proud, quick, enthusiastic, and easily led by persons who please me. I try to imitate these persons, but I am very sensitive with them and easily hurt. I put a great deal of value on appearances, love beautiful furniture and dress, assume a distinguished manner, and keep an elegant address. I am unhappy because my neurasthenic condition keeps me from doing and learning what I would like."

Last fall I made the patient's acquaintance. He had no degenerative signs, and presented a perfectly masculine appearance, even though he was delicately formed and slender. Genitals were perfectly normal. Appearance distinguished, with nothing striking. He was very troubled about his sexual perversion, and wanted to be freed from it at any price. In spite of the greatest efforts of both physician and patient, only a slight degree of hypnosis, insufficient for suggestive treatment, could be induced.

Case 110.

Psychic hermaphroditism – mouth fetishism. "I am thirty-one years old, and an official in a factory. My parents are healthy and have nothing abnormal about them. My paternal grandfather is said to have had brain disease; my maternal grandmother died melancholic; a cousin of my mother was given to drink; and several other blood relations are mentally abnormal.

"My sexual appetite was awakened when I was four years old. A man between twenty and thirty years old, who played with us children, took us in his arms, exciting in me the desire to embrace and kiss him passionately. The desire for sensual kissing on the mouth is characteristic of me, and still forms the chief charm of my sexual gratification.

"At about nine I experienced a similar desire for a man who was ugly, dirty, and who a red beard. A characteristic peculiar to me was manifested here for the first time, and is still present – i.e., how odd the stimulus of coarseness – the filthiness of a person in dress and conduct – is to my senses at times.

"From my eleventh to my fifteenth year, while in the *Gymnasium,* I was affected with a passion for a comrade. It was my greatest pleasure to embrace him and kiss him on the mouth. I was often seized with a desire for him as intense as what I now feel for persons I love. During these years, as I have said, I only had the desire to embrace and kiss; **the desire to see or touch the genitals of others, however, was plainly lacking.** I was a perfectly innocent, naïve boy, and, until my fifteenth year, did not know the meaning of an erection; I now think, however, that I had my first erections in my thirteenth year. I never once ventured to kiss the beloved person, for I felt that it would be doing something strange. I felt no desire to masturbate, and also had the good fortune not to be seduced into it by older comrades. I have never masturbated; I feel a certain repugnance for it.

"In my fourteenth and fifteenth years I was seized with a passion for several young persons, some of whom still attract me. Thus I was very much in love with a boy to whom I had never spoken. It was even a delight to meet him on the street.

"That my passions were of a sensual nature is shown by the fact that I had powerful erections when I pressed and caressed the hands of those I loved. But it had always been my greatest pleasure **to embrace and kiss the mouth;** I desired nothing else.

"At the time I did not know that what I experienced was sexual love; I merely said to myself that it was impossible that only I felt such stimuli.

"Until my fifteenth year, a woman had never excited me. One evening, however, when I was alone in a room with our servant girl, I experienced the same desire that I had for many boys. At first I played with her; and, when I found that she liked to be kissed, I covered her with kisses. I felt an intensity of sensual pleasure that I seldom experience now. Mouth to mouth, we kissed each other, and after about ten minutes ejaculation occurred. Thus I gratified myself two or three times a week. I soon began a similar relation with our cook, as well as with other servant girls. Ejaculation always took place after kissing for about ten minutes.

"In the meantime, I had taken dancing lessons, where I was first charmed by a nice girl; this love, however, soon disappeared. I fell in love with another girl with whom I never became acquainted, but at the sight of her I felt an attraction that was the same as what I felt for boys, and unlike the purely brutal passion I felt for other girls. At this time my impulse for girls was at its acme; I was pleased by about an equal number of girls and boys. As mentioned above, I gratified my sensuality by kissing the servant girl and inducing ejaculation. This is how I spent my time from my sixteenth to my eighteenth year. The departure of the servant deprived me of opportunity.

"Then came two or three years during which I had to give up sexual pleasure. In general, girls pleased me less; also, now that I had grown older, I was ashamed to surrender myself to the servant girls.

"It was not possible for me to obtain a mistress. In spite of my age, I was carefully watched by my parents, rarely associated with young men, and thus had little independence. With lessening desire for women, the attractiveness of youths increased.

"From my sixteenth year I had experienced frequent pollutions at night with dreams that involved both women and men. Because I was extremely weakened and depressed by these pollutions, I desired to end them by means of normal coitus. Scruples and the belief that prostitutes would have no effect on me, however, kept me from the brothel until my twenty-first year. For two or three years I went through a daily struggle, although if there had been male houses of prostitution, no scruples would have hindered me. Finally I visited a brothel. I could not even induce erection, partly because the girl, though she was unusually fresh and pretty for a prostitute, did not affect me, but primarily because she would not kiss me on the mouth. I was very much depressed, and thought I was impotent. Three weeks afterward I visited another prostitute, whose kiss immediately induced erection. She stood erect, had thick lips, and was much more sensual than the first one. After only three minutes of simple kissing, mouth to mouth, ejaculation was induced – before the act, of course. Thus it was only after I had visited prostitutes about seven times that I was successful in coitus.

"Sometimes I would have no erection at all, because the girl made no impression on me; at other times I would ejaculate prematurely. The first few times I was reluctant **to insert my penis;** and, even after I was successful in normal coitus, I found no pleasure in it. For me, sensual satisfaction comes from kissing on the mouth; this is the principal thing, and coitus is only secondary to embracing. No matter how much the woman might charm me, coitus would be an indifferent matter without kissing. Indeed, erection disappears, or does not occur at all, when the woman will not kiss on the mouth. I cannot kiss every woman, however; I can only kiss those who have faces that please me. A prostitute whose appearance I find repugnant cannot excite me with any amount of kissing; she can only disgust me.

"Thus, during the last four years, I have visited brothels about every ten days or two weeks. I have learned my peculiarities, and in the choice of a prostitute I know immediately whether she will excite me or have no effect. Thus, coitus rarely fails. It has again happened recently that when I thought the woman would stimulate me, no erection occurred. This happened whenever I had to forcibly repress my desire for men on the previous day.

"When I first went to brothels, the sensual pleasure was slight; I had true lustful feeling only a few times (with kissing). Now, however, for the most part I experience sensual pleasure. The lower houses have a particular charm for me; lately I have found the coarseness of the women, the dark entrance, the yellow light of the lamps, and all the surroundings to be strangely enchanting. This is probably because my sensuality is unconsciously excited by meeting the soldiers who frequent such places, and who at the same time lend a certain charm to the women. If I then find a woman whose face attracts me, I can have intense lustful pleasure. In addition to prostitutes, my desires can be excited by peasant girls, servant girls, working women, and girls of the lower classes – in general, by those in common dress. Red cheeks, thick lips, and erect forms particularly please me. I am absolutely indifferent to respectable women and young ladies.

"My pollutions now are usually without lustful pleasure, and often occur with dreams of men, but seldom – almost never – with dreams of women. Thus, in spite of regular coitus, my desire is still for young men. Indeed, I can say that it has only increased, and very markedly. Although immediately after coitus girls have no charm for me, the kiss of a pleasing woman can nevertheless immediately induce erection again. For the first few days after coitus, young men seem the most attractive to me.

"Sexual congress with women does not satisfy all my sensual desires. I have days when I have frequent erections with an intense desire for young men; then come quieter days, with moments of complete indifference for women and latent desire for men. On the other hand, too much sensual rest makes me melancholy; that is, when such rest follows moments of repressed excitement. I then only feel lighthearted when the thought of beloved youths again causes erection. My serenity changes to intense nervousness; I feel depressed, and sometimes have a headache (after repressed erection). This nervousness often increases to ungovernable restlessness, which I seek to overcome with coitus.

"Last year an essential change took place in my sexual life when I dared to enjoy male love for the first time. In spite of pleasurable coitus with women (more correctly, pleasurable kissing with resultant ejaculation), my desire for young men gave me no peace. I was determined to go to a brothel often frequented by soldiers and, driven to extremes, buy a soldier for myself. I was fortunate to immediately meet one like myself, who, notwithstanding his much lower station, was not unworthy of me in character and behavior. What I experienced (and still experience) with this young man is something different from what I feel with women. The sensual pleasure is not greater than with prostitutes, whose kisses and embraces excite me extraordinarily; but I am able, at any time, to experience lustful pleasure with him, and I have a feeling for him that is lacking for women. Unfortunately, I have been able to embrace and kiss him only about eight times.

"Although we have been separated many months because he was sent to a garrison in Hungary, we have not forgotten each other, and keep up a regular correspondence. In order to possess him, I risked exposure by daring to embrace him in a brothel.

"Early in our acquaintance there was a time when I did not hear from him because he thought he could not trust me. During these weeks I endured a level of pain, depression, and anxious restlessness that I had never before experienced. To have scarcely found a lover and then to lose him seemed to me to be the greatest misfortune. When, thanks to my efforts, we met again, my joy was unbounded; indeed, I was so excited that, in his embrace again for the first time, I could not induce ejaculation in spite of my sensual lust.

"**Sexual activity only consisted of kisses and embraces; he was also allowed to play with my penis** (while the touch of a woman's hand on it is unendurable to me, and I never allow it). It should also be noted that in the company of my lover I immediately have an erection; the pressure of his hand, or even his look, is sufficient. I have gone about with him in the evenings, for hours at a time, and never tired of his society for a moment, despite his inferior station. With him I feel happy, and the sexual satisfaction is merely the crowning of our love. Although I had so long sought and finally found a man like myself, and could enjoy male love at last, I have not become insensitive to women; I still visit brothels when I am too sorely troubled by desire. I had hoped to be able to spend this winter in the city where my lover is; unfortunately, this is impossible, and I am now forced to be separated from him for an indefinite period. Nevertheless, we shall try to see each other once or twice a year, if only for a short time, and I hope that in the future we may be together again for a longer time. This winter, then, I am compelled to be without a friend like myself. Indeed, because of the danger of discovery, I had resolved to never try finding another homosexual; but this is impossible. Sexual intercourse with women does not satisfy me, and my desire for young men constantly increases. I am often afraid of myself; afraid of discovery from asking all prostitutes, as I do, whether they know others like me. Yet I cannot keep from seeking a youth like myself, and I know that if it becomes necessary I shall buy a soldier, although I know perfectly well the penalty meted out to one caught in such circumstances.

"I can no longer do without male love; without it I would always be out of harmony with myself. Although my ideal is to be associated with a number of men who are like me, I would be satisfied if I could have unrestrained intercourse with one lover. If I had regular male satisfaction, I could easily dispense with women; but I think that occasionally I would like to embrace a woman for the sake of variety, as my nature is absolutely hermaphroditic in a psychosexual sense (where I can only sensually desire women, I can sensually desire, as well as love, young men). If there were marriage between men, I think I would not avoid a lifelong union; while marriage with a woman seems to me to be something impossible. In the first place, even if the woman charmed me, the charm would soon be lost in regular intercourse, and then all sexual indulgence, if not impossible, would certainly be devoid of pleasure for me. In the second place, true love for the wife would be absent; that is, it would lack the attraction that I feel toward young men I love, which makes the intercourse that is not simply sensual seem desirable to me. A constant association with a youth who is physically pleasing and in mental harmony with me, who could understand all my feelings and share my intellectual opinions and desires, would, it seems to me, be the greatest happiness.

"The young men who please me must be between eighteen and twenty-eight; although as I have grown older, the age limit of such men has also increased. Aside from this, I am pleased with a wide variety of types. The face plays the most important part. Blondes excite me more than dark persons. They must have no beard, and if they have a mustache, it must be small and not too thick. Certain kinds of faces please me. Faces with large, straight noses are excluded, as are those with pale cheeks (although there are exceptions). I regard soldiers with favor, and many who do not affect me when in civil dress please me when in uniform. Just as, with women, certain ordinary articles of dress (like light-colored jackets) please me, so, with men, does the military costume attract me. Visits to dance halls (usually beer halls) where there are many soldiers; mixing with the crowd of soldiers and boys who please me; trying to get a kiss and an embrace, would, of course, excite my sensuality; intellectually and socially, however, everything common in speech and conduct is repugnant to me.

"With young men of higher position, my sensual desire is less prominent.

"What I have said about the attractiveness of certain kinds of dress is not meant in the sense that the clothes attract me in themselves. Instead, I mean that the dress may help to enhance the attraction exerted by the face, when, perhaps, the same face, by itself, would not attract me to the same extent. I may say the same thing, though with a different meaning, about the odor of lighted cigars. In persons to whom I am indifferent, the odor of cigars is repugnant rather than pleasing to me, while it is exciting in those sexually attractive. The kiss of a prostitute smelling of cigar smoke gives me great pleasure because I am reminded (unconsciously) of the kiss of a man. I took pleasure in kissing my lover just after he had smoked. (I myself have never smoked a cigar or cigarette, and have never even tried to smoke.) I am tall and thin; my face is masculine; my eyes are restless; and in the way I carry myself I am aware there is often something girlish. My health leaves much to be desired, as it is influenced a great deal by my sexual anomaly. I am very nervous, as previously mentioned, and I often have paroxysms of onomatomania. I also suffer from terrible depression and melancholia when I see the difficulty of gratifying my male-loving nature, and also when I have overcome great sexual desire because of the impossibility of male gratification. At other times, my depression is associated with an absolute lack of sexual desire. In work I am industrious, though often too quick, because I am inclined to work too rapidly and violently. I have a lively interest in art and literature. Among poets and writers of fiction, I typically prefer those who describe refined feelings, peculiar passions, and farfetched impressions; an artificial or hyperartificial style pleases me. Likewise, in music, it is the nervous, exciting music of a Chopin, a Schumann, a Schubert, or a Wagner, etc., that is in most perfect harmony with me. Everything in art that is not only original, but *bizarre,* attracts me.

"I do not like physical exercise, and do not practice it.

"In character I am kind and compassionate; and, although with my anomaly I suffer greatly, I am not unhappy because I love young men, but because the satisfaction of such love is considered improper, and therefore I cannot gratify it without restraint. I cannot regard male love as a vice, though I can well understand why it is considered vicious. Because this love is regarded as criminal, although I am in harmony with myself in gratifying it, I am not in harmony with the times. Therefore, I must necessarily be somewhat depressed; all the more because I have a frank character that hates a lie. The pain of always having to hide it within me has induced me to confess my anomaly to a few friends, whose silence and appreciation I trust. Nevertheless, my situation often seems sad. Because of the difficulty of gratification and the general abhorrence of male love, I often feel a trace of pride that I have such anomalous feelings. Of course, I shall never marry. This is not a misfortune, even though I love family life, and have thus far lived only with my parents. I live in the hope that some day I shall have a lover; I must have one; without one, the future seems dark and barren, and all the ambitions usually cherished – honor, position, etc. – seem empty and unattractive. If I should not have this hope fulfilled, I know I shall be unable to devote myself for long to my business with pleasure, and I shall soon be in a state of wanting to sacrifice everything to obtain male love. I no longer have any moral scruples because of my anomalous inclination; in fact, I have never been troubled because I felt attracted to boys. I am much more inclined to judge morality and immorality in accordance with my feelings than in accordance with fixed principles, for I have always been prone to skepticism, and still have not studied out a fixed belief for myself. Thus far, only what injures others seems to me to be evil and immoral, as well as that which I would not have inflicted on myself. Accordingly, I try to infringe on the rights of others as little as possible, and find that I am capable of great indignation at injustice inflicted on another. Why love of men should be something immoral, however, I cannot understand; purposeless activity of the sexual instinct (if the immoral is to be seen in all that is useless and unnatural) is also found in intercourse with prostitutes, and even in marriage when means to prevent conception are used. Thus, it seems to me that the sexual interaction of men must be placed on the same level with all sexual congress that does not have procreation as an end. It seems questionable to me that only sexual gratification having this purpose is moral. Certainly, sexual satisfaction not directed to procreation is not contrary to nature; it is possible it may have other purposes; and, even if it were purposeless, it would not necessarily be despicable (it is not certain that the measure of a moral act is its usefulness).

"I am certain that present prejudice will one day disappear, and that when such individuals experience male love, the right of unrestricted love will be acknowledged. For the possibility of such recognition one need only recall the Greeks and their friendships, which were nothing but sexual love. Further, one has only to think that, despite such unnatural vice practiced by their greatest men, the Greeks are still regarded as an unattainable example in intellectual and aesthetic matters, and are held up for imitation.

"I have already thought of having my anomaly cured by hypnotism. If it were to be of any use, which I doubt, I would still want assurance that I could have a lasting love for women. For even though I cannot satisfy myself with men, I still prefer to feel the capability of inordinate lust and love, even if ungratified, to being absolutely without feeling. Thus I maintain the hope that I shall find opportunity to satisfy the love I desire, the love that would make me happy; and I would not prefer the suggestive removal of homosexual feelings (without the simultaneous substitution of a heterosexual equivalent) to my present condition. Finally, I should like to add that I, at least (in contrast to the statements of homosexuals in published biographies), find it very difficult to recognize those like myself. Although I have described my sexual anomaly somewhat in detail, I think that the following notes are important for a better understanding of my condition:

"Recently I have given up **inserting my penis,** and have confined myself to **coitus between a girl's thighs.** Ejaculation occurs earlier than **contact between the genitals,** and I experience a certain lustful feeling in my penis itself. If this manner of sexual intercourse is quite pleasant to me, it is, perhaps, partly because the gender is not important in this kind of sexual indulgence, and I am unconsciously reminded of masculine embrace. This memory is absolutely unconscious, however, and only obscurely felt. This is because I am not indebted to my imagination for my pleasure; instead, pleasure immediately comes from kissing the woman's mouth. I feel that the charm exercised by the brothel and prostitutes is also beginning to fade; but I am convinced that certain women will always be able to excite me with their kisses. Still, no woman is, or ever will be, attractive enough to induce me to overcome obstacles and win her, while even the danger of discovery and disgrace can barely keep me from seeking a man's embraces.

"Thus I recently allowed myself to be induced to buy a soldier at a prostitute's house. Although the lustful pleasure was strong, the subsequent feeling of satisfaction was especially exhilarating. The next day I felt similarly strengthened (capable of erection at any moment); and though I have not yet been able to meet the soldier again, the thought that I shall venture to purchase another gives me peace. I could be perfectly satisfied, however, simply to find one who feels like myself, and who is of my own position and education.

"I have not yet mentioned that I am not attracted to the female form (with the exception of the face) and genitals (to touch the latter with my hand would be disgusting to me); but **I have always wanted to touch a penis while my mouth kisses another man's mouth;** indeed, to kiss the mouth of a very pleasing man would not be disgusting to me. Masturbation, as I said before, would be quite impossible for me."

Case 112.

The following is an extract from a circumstantial autobiography, put at my disposal by a physician affected with contrary sexual instinct:

"I am now forty years old, from a healthy family.[3] I have always been healthy and a model of physical as well as mental strength and energy. I have a powerful build, but only a moderate beard, and, with the exception of hair in my armpits and on my mons pubis, my body is hairless. My penis, unusually large even soon after birth, measures twenty-four centimeters long by eleven centimeters in circumference when erect. I am a skillful rider, athlete, and swimmer, and have gone through two great campaigns as a military surgeon. I have never experienced any taste for female attire and vocation. Up to the time of puberty I was shy toward the female sex, and I am still shy with new acquaintances.

"I have always had a distaste for dancing. In my eighth year an inclination for my own sex made its appearance. I next experienced pleasure in regarding my brother's genitals. I induced my brother to indulge with me in mutual fondling of the genitals, as a result of which I had an erection. Later, in bathing with the schoolchildren, the boys excited a lively interest in me; the girls did not. I had so little interest in them that, as late as my fifteenth year, I believed that they also had a penises. In company with boys like myself, I took pleasure in mutual masturbation. At eleven and a half years I was given a strict tutor, and thereafter could only rarely steal away to my friends. I learned very easily, but could not get along with my teacher. When, one day, he made it too hard for me, I became furious, struck at him with a knife, and would have gladly stabbed him if he had not fallen into my arms. In my thirteenth year, for a similar reason, I escaped from the teacher, and wandered about in the neighboring country for six weeks.

"I then entered the *Gymnasium.* By that time I was already sexually developed, and while bathing with my comrades I amused myself in the way mentioned above, and later with imitation coitus between the thighs. I was then thirteen years old. I felt absolutely no pleasure with girls. Violent erections caused me to play with my genitals, and I would put my penis in my mouth, which I succeeded in doing by bending over. This induced ejaculation. I thus learned masturbation. I was extremely frightened, looked upon myself as a criminal, and confessed to a companion of sixteen. He encouraged and quieted me, and entered into a love bond with me. We were happy, and satisfied ourselves with mutual masturbation. At the same time, I masturbated. After two years the bond was broken; but to this day, when we occasionally meet (my friend is a high official), the old fire lights up anew.

"That time with my friend H. was a happy one, and I would gladly pay for its return with my heart's blood. Life then was a pleasure, learning was mere play, and I had a feeling for everything beautiful.

"During this time a physician, a friend of my father's, seduced me on the occasion of a visit by caressing me and practicing masturbation on me, and by explaining the sexual act. He advised me to never practice masturbation, because it was injurious to health. He then practiced mutual masturbation with me, explaining that this was the only method by which he could perform the sexual function. He had a horror of women, and had lived unhappily with his deceased wife. He gave me a pressing invitation to visit him as often as possible. The physician was a pompous man, and the father of two sons aged fourteen and fifteen respectively, with whom in the following year I entered into love relations similar to those I had with my friend H.

"Although I was ashamed of my unfaithfulness to him, I nevertheless continued my relations with the physician. He practiced mutual masturbation with me, and showed me our spermatozoa under the microscope. He also showed me pornographic works and pictures, which, however, did not please me, because I only had interest for male forms. On the occasion of later visits, he asked me to do him a favor that he had never yet enjoyed, but which he very much desired. Because I loved him, I acquiesced in everything. He dilated my anus with instruments, and practiced pederasty on me; at the same time he masturbated me, so that I experienced pleasure and pain at once. After this discovery I immediately went to my friend H. with the idea that this beloved man would be able to give me still greater pleasure. We practiced pederasty on each other, but were both deceived and did not repeat it; for passively I had only pain, and actively no pleasure, while mutual masturbation gave us both the greatest enjoyment. Thereafter, out of gratitude, I was often still exclusively at the disposal of the physician. Up to my fifteenth year I practiced passive or mutual masturbation with my friend. Now I was quite grown, and although I was given all kinds of signals from women and girls, I fled from them as Joseph did from Potiphar's wife. At fifteen I came to the capital, but I had only rare opportunities for the satisfaction of my sexual inclination. I reveled in the sight of pictures and statues of male forms, and could not keep from kissing the beloved statues. The fig leaves on the genitals were my principal annoyance.

"At seventeen I went to the university. There, again, I lived for two years with my friend H.

"In my eighteenth year, while in a state of mild intoxication, I was determined to have coitus with a woman. I forced myself to do it, but immediately afterward I fled the house overcome with disgust. Just as after the first active masturbation, I had a feeling as if I had committed a crime. On the occasion of another attempt, while in a sober condition, I could not get an erection in spite of the efforts of a beautiful naked girl; the mere sight of a boy or the touch of a man's hand on my thigh, however, would always throw my penis into violent erection. A short time before, my friend H. had had a similar experience. We racked our brains in vain to discover the reason for it. Thereafter I left women alone, and found enjoyment in passive and mutual masturbation with friends, as well as other behavior with both of the sons of the physician, who had used his sons for pederasty after my departure.

"At the age of nineteen I made the acquaintance of two genuine homosexuals:

"A., aged fifty-six, of effeminate appearance, beardless, of small mental endowment, possessed a powerful sexual desire that had materialized abnormally early (he had indulged in homosexual love since his sixth year). Once a month he visited the capital. I had to sleep with him. He was insatiable in mutual masturbation, and made me take part in active and passive pederasty. The passive pederasty was an unpleasant part of the bargain for me.

"B., a merchant, aged thirty-six, of masculine appearance, was as passionate as I was. He knew how to make his manipulations on me such a stimulus that I had to serve him passively in pederasty. He was the only one with whom I ever had any pleasure in passive pederasty. He confessed to me that just knowing I was near gave him the most painful erections; and that when I could not serve him, he was compelled to satisfy himself with masturbation.

"While pursuing these love affairs, I was clinical assistant at the hospital, and was considered ambitious and skillful in my work. I naturally searched throughout literature for an explanation of my sexual peculiarity. I found it generally regarded as a crime deserving punishment, while I could only recognize in it the natural satisfaction of my sexual desire. I had an awareness that this was congenital with me. Feeling myself in opposition to the whole world, however, and often near insanity and suicide, I again sought to satisfy, with women, my powerful sexual desire. The result was always the same – either lack of sufficient erection, or, when it became possible to force myself into the act, disgust and horror at its repetition. As a military surgeon, I suffered terribly from the sight and touch of thousands of naked male forms. Fortunately, I formed a love bond with a lieutenant similarly affected, and again passed a time of happiness. Out of love for him I consented to pederasty, for which he longed. We loved each other until, at Sedan, he discovered he no longer loved me. From that time I never gave myself to active or passive pederasty, although I had many love affairs, and was a person who was much sought.

"At twenty-three I went to the country as a physician, and was sought and esteemed. I satisfied myself with boys over fourteen. I interested myself in political affairs, made an enemy of the clergyman, and, betrayed by one of my lovers, was denounced and compelled to flee. The legal investigation, fortunately, did me no harm. I was able to return, but I was greatly shaken. I went to war (1870) as a soldier with the hope of meeting my death. I returned, however, with many distinctions, much matured, and I found even more pleasure than I had before in the earnest work of my profession. I hoped that the extinction of my excessive sexual desire was near at hand, exhausted by the great hardships of the campaign.

"I had scarcely recovered when the old unbounded desire again appeared, and led to a new unbridled satisfaction. Although, of course, it was often on my mind, the inclination that was so revolting to the world did not seem that way to me.

"By means of the greatest exercise of my will, I abstained for a year. I then went to the capital to force myself to cohabit with a woman. I, who at the sight of the dirtiest (male) ragamuffin would have painful erections, could scarcely induce one with the most beautiful woman. Overcome, I returned home and obtained a young manservant for my personal service and satisfaction.

"The solitude of life as a country physician and the longing for children drove me to marriage; besides, I wished to make an end to gossip, and I hoped to finally triumph over my fatal desire.

"I knew a young girl, and was convinced of her respect and love for me. Through my esteem and honor for my wife, I was enabled to perform the conjugal duties, and begot four boys. The boyish appearance of my wife was of effectual assistance. I called her my 'Raphael.' I forced into my mind images of boys in order to induce erection. If my fantasy ceased for a moment, the erection failed. I was unable to sleep with my wife. Within the last few years, coitus has become increasingly more difficult to attain, and for two years we have given up all attempts. My wife knows of my mental condition, and her esteem and love for me may become estranged.

"My sexual inclination for my own sex is unchanged; unfortunately, it too often forces me to become untrue to my wife. To this day, the sight of a youth of sixteen throws me into a state of violent sexual excitement with painful erections, so that occasionally I am compelled to help myself by masturbating him and myself.

"The sufferings I endure are indescribable. For lack of something better, I have my wife practice masturbation on me; but what my wife's hand accomplishes with great effort in half an hour is produced by the hand of a boy in a few seconds. Thus I live, miserable, a slave of the law and the duty to my wife! I have never had pleasure in active or passive pederasty. I only practiced or suffered it from gratitude or a desire to please."

The physician to whom I owe the preceding autobiography assured me that up to the present time he had enjoyed sexual intercourse with at least six hundred homosexuals. Indeed, among them were many who today occupy high and respected positions. Only about ten percent of them later came to love women. Although another portion did not avoid women, they were more inclined to their own sex. The remainder were exclusively and lastingly homosexuals.

This physician asserted that among the six hundred, he never found abnormal formation of the genitals; there were, however, many approaching the female form, as well as states of incomplete growth of hair, delicate complexion, and higher voice. Development of the breasts was not infrequent. He asserted that from his thirteenth to his fifteenth year he had milk in his breasts, which his friend H. sucked out. Only about ten percent of this number showed any inclination for female occupations, etc. All his acquaintances were affected with a sexual desire that was abnormally powerful and made its appearance abnormally early. The vast majority saw themselves as the man in their relations with the other, and satisfied themselves by mutual masturbation, or by masturbation on the person of the lover, or by masturbation at his hands. Although the majority were inclined to active pederasty, frequently the law and aesthetic feeling were reasons for the nonperformance of the act. Those who saw themselves as women in relation to others were few, and the inclination to passive pederasty was rare.

In the beginning of 1887 this physician was arrested for having committed acts of indecency on the persons of two boys under fourteen years of age. The crime consisted in his having first rubbed **his member between the thighs of a man** until he **ejaculated,** as well as **rubbing his member between the thighs of a boy.** Although at the examination it was recognized that an abnormal instinct was in play, it was also shown that the culprit was not mentally unsound, and was not deprived of free will; at least, he had not acted in obedience to an uncontrollable impulse. Therefore, he was sentenced to prison for one year, the mildest possible punishment.

Case 113.

Mr. X., Hungarian, merchant, consulted with me because of neurasthenia and sleeplessness, which had existed for years. The investigation of the cause of his trouble led the patient to confess that he had an abnormal sexual instinct for his own gender, that he was very passionate, and that his nervous trouble might have resulted from this. The following, taken from the history of this intelligent patient, possesses scientific interest:

"My abnormal sexual instinct goes back to my childhood. At the age of three, I got ahold of a journal of fashions. I kissed the beautiful pictures of the men until the paper was torn to tatters, but paid no attention to the female figures. I did not like to play with boys. I preferred to play with girls, because they always had dolls. I especially liked to cut out dolls' clothes; and today, in spite of my thirty-three years, dolls still possess an interest for me. As a boy I would lurk for hours around places where I would be likely to get a glimpse of male genitals. When I succeeded, a strange, dizzy feeling came over me. Weak, unattractive men or boys made no impression on me. At thirteen I began to masturbate. From my thirteenth until my fifteenth year, I slept with a handsome young man. That was happiness. At night, for hours at a time, I would wait, with erections, for his return. In bed I was delighted if he happened to touch my genitals. At fourteen I had a schoolmate whose instincts were like my own. During school hours, for hours at a time, we would hold each other's genitals. Ah, those were happy hours! I lingered in bathhouses as often as I could. That was always a feast for me. The sight of male genitals induced violent erections. At sixteen I came to the metropolis. It charmed me to see so many handsome men. In my eighteenth year I attempted coitus with a prostitute, but disgust and fear made it impossible. Other attempts were failures until my nineteenth year, when I tried again with success. The act afforded me no pleasure, however; instead, it induced a feeling of disgust. I conquered myself, and was proud of my success at being a man, which I had gradually begun to doubt.

"Subsequent attempts were not successful. The disgust was too great. When the woman was undressing, it was necessary to put out the light because of my feeling of repugnance. I now considered myself impotent, and because I still did not know what to think of it, I consulted physicians, and visited baths and sanitariums to cure it. I took pleasure in the society of ladies, perhaps out of conceit, for I impressed most ladies as being sympathetic and amiable; but I valued in them nothing more than mental and aesthetic qualities. Although I liked to dance with them, if, while dancing, one pressed against me, I experienced a feeling of repugnance, and even disgust, and felt like striking her. If, in jest, I happened to dance with a gentleman, I always took the part of the lady. I would press and rub against him, and take a perfect delight in it. When I was eighteen, a gentleman who came into the office said, 'That is a fine youth; in the East he would bring a pound sterling every time!' I was puzzled by this remark. Another gentleman liked to joke with me, and steal kisses from me as he was going away; kisses that I would only too gladly have given him. He later became my lover. These circumstances excited my attention, and I waited for an opportunity.

"When I was twenty-five years old, it happened that a man who had previously been a Capuchin monk became attracted to me. For me he was like a Mephistopheles. Finally he spoke to me. To this day I can still almost feel the beating of my heart and the light-headed feeling that he caused in me. He arranged a rendezvous for that evening at a public house. I went, but at the threshold I turned back, afraid. On the next evening we met. He overcame my scruples, and took me to his room. I was scarcely able to walk due to my excitement. My seducer made me sit on his sofa, and, smiling at me, he fixed his wonderful black eyes on me, at which time I lost consciousness. The delight; the ideal, divine sense of pleasure that filled my whole being – I could never write enough about it. Only an innocent youth, head over heels in love, who has his love's longing fulfilled for the first time, could be as happy as I was that night. As a joke, my seducer demanded my life; at first, however, I thought he was in earnest. I begged him to let me be happy for a time, and then, united with him, I would end my life. It would have been entirely in accordance with the high-flown ideas I entertained at that time. For five years after that, I kept up a relation with the man, who is still very dear to me. Oh, how happy, and yet, often, how unhappy I was during those years! If I merely saw him speak to a handsome young man, I became wildly jealous.

"At twenty-seven I became engaged to a young lady. Her mind and aesthetic feeling (as well as financial considerations), induced me to think of marriage. I am also very fond of children, and, whenever I meet even the commonest day laborer who is accompanied by his wife and a pretty child, I envy the man his good fortune. Thus I made a fool of myself. I managed to get through the time of courtship; when kissing my bride I felt more anxiety and fear than pleasure. On one or two occasions, however, after luxurious dinners, I had erections while kissing her passionately. How happy I was at that! I already saw myself as a father. Twice I came near breaking off the engagement. On my wedding day, when all the guests had assembled, I locked myself in a room, cried like a child, and felt that I could not proceed with the ceremony. Persuaded by all the relatives, to whom I made the best excuses that occurred to me, I allowed myself to be taken, in ordinary street clothes, to the altar.

"As great good fortune would have it, at the time of the marriage, my wife was menstruating. Oh, how thankful I was for this excuse! I am now convinced that this circumstance is all that made later cohabitation possible. How it later became possible for me to cohabit with my wife, and have a lovely boy, I do not know. He is the comfort of my ruined life. I can only thank God for the happiness of having a child. I was a cheat, so to speak, in the marriage bed. Although my wife, whom I respect for her high qualities of character, has no suspicion of my condition, she often complains of my coldness. Aided by her goodness of heart and simplicity, it was possible for me to make her think that the conjugal duty should only be performed once a month. Because she is in no way sensual, and my nervous condition provides me with excuses, I am successful in keeping up the swindle. Cohabitation is the greatest sacrifice for me. By taking considerable wine, and by making use of the erections that occur in the morning as the result of an overfilled bladder, it is possible for me to perform coitus once a month; but if affords me no pleasurable feeling. Afterward I am worried, and for the rest of the day I experience an increase of my nervous difficulties. The consciousness of having fulfilled my duty toward my wife, whom I love in all other respects, affords me moral consolation and satisfaction. With a man, it is different. With him I am able to perform the act several times in a night, always taking the sexual role of a man. In this, I experience the greatest pleasure, the purest happiness. I feel myself refreshed and invigorated. Lately, my desire for men has somewhat decreased; in fact, at this moment, I would have the courage to avoid even a handsome young man who approached me. Will it last? I fear not. I am absolutely unable to exist without male love; if I am compelled to forgo it, I become depressed, weary and miserable, and have pain and pressure in my head. I have always regarded my pitiable peculiarity as something congenital, and I would feel happy if only I had not married. I pity my good wife. Often the fear seizes me that I can no longer endure life with her; then thoughts about divorce, suicide, and flight to America come to me."

No one who saw this patient would suspect his condition. His outward appearance was, in all respects, masculine; he had a well-developed, full beard; strong and deep voice; normal genitals. Cranium normally formed; signs of degeneration absolutely lacking; only exquisitely nervous eyes made one suspect a neuropathic condition. The vegetative organs performed their functions normally. The patient presented the usual symptoms of neurasthenia, which may essentially be ascribed to sexual excesses with persons of his own sex in a man abnormally passionate, as well as to the injurious influences of forced, though infrequent, coitus with the wife when *horror feminae* existed.

The patient declared that he came from healthy parents, and that he had no knowledge of neuroses or mental disease in his ancestry. His elder brother was married three years. Because the husband never had sexual intercourse with his wife, there was a separation. He married a second time. Although the second wife also complained of neglect on the part of the husband, she had four children whose legitimacy was never doubted. A sister was hysteropathic.

The patient said that he suffered as a young man from momentary attacks of dizziness, during which it seemed to him as if he were about to die. He said that he had always been very excitable and emotional, and was an enthusiast for the arts, especially poetry and music. He described his own character as enigmatic, abnormal, nervous, restless, extravagant, and undecided. He was often exalted without any real reason, after which he was again depressed, even with thoughts of suicide. He could pass through quick and sudden changes – "religious and frivolous, optimistic and cynical, cowardly and brave, credulous, amiable, and suspicious; inclined to do others harm, and sorrowful to the point of tears over the misfortunes of others; generous to excess, and then miserly *à la Harpagon.*" The patient was certainly a tainted individual. He was seemingly very well-endowed intellectually, which confirmed his statement that, at school, he had learned easily, and had been among the first in his class.

The marriage of this man was not happy. Notwithstanding the fact that only rarely had he performed the inadequate and injurious sexual act with his wife, and that he sought and found a substitute in male lovers, he remained neurasthenic. His disease, at times, presented marked exacerbations, which even manifested itself into a state of despairing depression about his matrimonial, sexual and mental condition, to the point of violent *taedium vitae.*

His wife became hysteropathic and anemic, and the patient attributed this to sexual abstinence. In spite of efforts to force himself, in recent years he was not able to perform coitus, with erection failing completely. At the same time, in intercourse with male lovers, he was very potent.

The son of these unfortunate parents, now over nine years old, was developing well. The patient added that when he engaged in coitus with his wife, he was potent only when he thought of a beloved man (from the author's *Lehrb. der Psychiatrie*).

Case 114.

Autobiography. "The writer of this is a congenital homosexual. Even though I have not consorted with other homosexuals, I am, nevertheless, fully informed about my condition, for it has been my lot to see almost all the literature on the subject. Your work, *Psychopathia Sexualis,* was sent to me a short time ago. I saw in the book that you were working and studying without prejudice in the interest of science and humanity.

"If I cannot tell you much that is new, I will still speak of a few things that I trust you will receive as one more brick to be used in your work; in your hands, I am confident, this will aid in saving us.

"When you presume that there is often a hereditary tainted condition, perhaps you are right. My father was subject to spinal disease before my birth; later, he became mentally unsound, and took his own life.

"Another point, which I am inclined to doubt, is the one you have mentioned elsewhere; i.e., that masturbation practiced from youth may lead to perverse instinct.

"I (merchant, owner of a small business, unmarried) am in the beginning of my thirtieth year. I am apparently healthy, and show scarcely any deviation from the normal masculine type. My first sexual impulses were immediately and exclusively directed to the male sex, and I experienced them from my tenth year. I have masturbated since my twelfth year. Because coitus with women, in spite of all attempts, was always absolutely impossible for me; because I have never had a desire for women (on the contrary, I have had an aversion); and because my attempts have never resulted in the slightest erection, I have been compelled to satisfy myself with masturbation.

"If I am now to confess the manner of my sexual satisfaction, I will say that in my earlier years my fellow pupils and companions excited me sexually. My impulse now consists mostly of a desire for youths from fifteen to twenty years, but also for boys of about ten.

"For a long time, strong and healthy cadets of fine form have had a particular charm for me; and with their handsome uniforms and fine presence, they especially excite my desire. Although I have no opportunity to approach them, or even to enter into distant social intercourse with them, I am compelled to satisfy myself by following them in the streets and squares, or by sitting near them in restaurants, horsecars or railways, and, when under such circumstances it is possible to do so unnoticed, by practicing masturbation. My most ardent wish has often been to become the friend, servant, or slave of such a young man.

"I have never even dreamed of direct pederasty; my desire has always been bodily contact, embrace, masturbation of my genitals by my lover, and, on my part, a kiss on his genitals or behind.

"I often have the desire, however, to act the part of Sacher-Masoch in his *Venus im Pelz*. There a man makes himself the voluntary slave of a woman, and feels an intense thrill of lustful pleasure only if he is chastised and humiliated by her. I naturally feel, however, that under no circumstances could I become the slave of a woman. Instead, I could become the slave of a man; more correctly, of a young man; further, of a young man for whom I would have such an infinite love that I could completely surrender to his mercy or cruelty.

"The lustful images that float before my mind during masturbation are those of any young man I have just seen. As a sad and incomplete substitute for actual relations, I practice this masturbation constantly.

"I pass into a lustful dream in the following way (and I will reveal everything here, because I wish to write only the truth and the whole truth): I choose a young man whose form pleases me, and in my imagination I involuntarily submit to his domination. I imagine that he wishes to humiliate me, and that he commands me, for example, to kiss his feet, or compels me to smell his socks. For lack of the desired effect, I take my own socks, smell them, put them into my mouth, and rub them all over my genitals; then erection and ejaculation, with sensual pleasure, takes place.

"Yes, I am so dominated by this mental imagery that I imagine the young man to be my confessor, who, in order to humiliate me, commands me to eat his excrement. Here again, lacking actuality, I eat my own excrement, but only a small amount. Then, with an imperfect feeling of disgust and violent palpitation of the heart, erection and ejaculation take place.

"I only come to this vile, feverish imagery and the performance of these acts, however, when it has not been possible, for a long time, for me to satisfy myself with masturbation in the immediate vicinity of a young man, which I consider more natural. I have more pleasure because of it, and I experience a more perfect physical and mental benefit, given the circumstance that my ideal of actual and direct satisfaction from mutual understanding has never been bestowed upon me.

"I almost believe that the above-mentioned disgusting imagery is simply the evil result of a constant absence of normal satisfaction (i.e., my normal satisfaction as a homosexual); and that with regular satisfaction, body to body, the imagery that becomes almost insane would be less intense; at least it would certainly not progress to such extravagance. Or, the imagery is the ultimate result of an attempt at abstinence, inasmuch as these idiotic, sensual images only come after a long period of it.

"I sincerely believe that under different social conditions I would be capable of great and noble love and self-sacrifice. My thoughts are in no way exclusively carnal or diseased. How often, at the sight of a handsome young man, I am seized with a deep feeling of impatience, and I breathe at once the sweet words of Heine:

"'Thou are like any flower, so sweet, so beautiful, so pure,' etc.[4]

"And once, when I was compelled to part with a young man who had honored and valued me as his friend and protector (my love had remained unknown to him), those fine verses by Scheffel kept passing through my mind, especially the last – *mutatis mutandis:*

"'Lowering like the heavens, frowns the world on me,
Yet blest or cursed will be the fate I meet,
With trusting heart, dear friend, I think of thee!
God keep thee, dear! it would have been too sweet,
God keep thee, dear, such happiness was not to be!'[5]

"I have never independently revealed my love to a young man, and have never spoiled or injured one morally; but I have, now and then, made the way easy for many. Under such circumstances, nothing is too much trouble, and I obtain victims any way I can.

"When I have an opportunity to have such a beloved friend to educate, protect and help, if my recognized love should find a (natural, non-sexual) return, then all my disgusting mental imagery becomes less and less intense. My love then changes into something almost platonic and ennobled, sinking again into the mire, however, when this worthy satisfaction is removed.

"Without overestimating myself, I can say that I am not one of the worst of men. Mentally brighter than the average man, I take interest in all that moves humanity. I am amiable, easily moved to pity, and incapable of injuring an animal, much less a man; instead, I do good wherever I can.

"When I have nothing in my own conscience with which to reproach myself, and must, at the same time, set myself in opposition to the judgment of the world, I suffer very much. Indeed, I have done no one harm, and I consider my love, in its noblest activity, to be quite as holy as that of a normal man. With the unhappy lot that impatience and ignorance cast upon us, however, I suffer, even to the extent of *taedium vitae.*

"No pen, no tongue can describe all the misery, all the unhappy situations, the constant fear of having this peculiarity recognized, and of being cast from society. The thought that, with discovery, one's existence could be lost, that he could be cast away from all, is as terrible as any thought can be. Then all the good that one had ever done would be forgotten; then, in the pride of his great morality, every normal man would be moved to scorn, even though the object of such scorn had never been as frivolous with his love as the normal man.

"So what does our misery amount to? We may, cursing man, end our unhappy lives. Truly, I often long for the quiet of an asylum. Let my life end when it will, the sooner the better; I am ready.

"To refer to one more point: I also believe, like the others who have written to you, that our nervousness is first acquired as a result of our unhappy, unspeakably miserable lives among our fellow creatures.

"And still another: At the conclusion of your work, you write about the repeal of pertinent legal enactments. Indeed, humanity would not be destroyed if these were repealed. In Italy there are no such laws, as far as I know; and Italy is not a wilderness, but a culti-vated nation.

"As for myself, compelled though I am to undermine my life with masturbation, the law could not touch me; I have never sinned against a letter of it. At the same time, however, I suffer under the accursed scorn to which we are all subjected. How can the ideas of society be changed as long as there is a law that strengthens society in its immorality? Although, of course, the law must correspond with public opinion, it should not be in harmony with the erroneous opinion of ignorance. It should, instead, accord with the ideas of the best and most scientific thinkers, and not with the wish and prejudice of the vulgar. True thinking minds cannot much longer be satisfied with the old idea.

"Pardon me, Professor, if I close without a signature. Do not try to find me. I could tell you nothing more. I give you these lines in the interest of future sufferers. In the interest of science, truth, and justice, publish what seems to you to be necessary."

†

Case 119.

Autobiography. "[1] *Descent:* I am now in my twenty-third year. I have chosen as an occupation the study of the technical arts, and am completely satisfied with it. I only had the mild childhood diseases; the other children in my family, however, who are now healthy, had to pass through severe illnesses. My parents are both living, and my father is an advocate. He and my mother are, shall we say, nervously hypersensitive. In my father's family there were two other children, who died early.

"[2] *My person:* Physically I am of robust figure, without being especially handsome; eyes, gray; hair, blonde; my hair and beard correspond with my sex and years. My breasts and genitals are normally developed. My gait is firm and almost heavy; my bearing, careless. It is worth noting that the breadth of my pelvis is exactly equal to that of my shoulders.

"I am naturally well-endowed mentally. In one of my certificates my talents are, in fact, called 'excellent.' Without any particular desire to excel in them, I passed my examinations with distinction. I have an interest in everything that concerns the well-being of humanity, and in science, art, and industry. With my energy it is comparatively easy to postpone for a time the satisfaction of my desires, which will be described hereafter. Intentionally and consciously, I curse the morality of today, which forces those who are abnormal sexually to break laws that are voluntarily established, and regards the sexual congress of two persons of the same sex as a matter that results from the individual's choice, and a matter in which lawmakers have a right to interfere. From my studies I have found the most earnest incentives to construct, on the basis of the Darwinian theory, after Carneri's method, a system of morals, which, to be sure, does not harmonize with the prevailing system, but which seeks to elevate and improve mankind in accordance with natural law.

"I think that there are not many marks of hereditary taint in me. There is a certain hypersensitiveness. A very intense dream life is perhaps important. In general, it is occupied with indifferent matters, and never has so-called sensual images as a subject; at most it is concerned with female attire and putting it on, which for me is a lustful thought. Furthermore, until my sixteenth year, my dream life often developed to the extent of somnambulism, or, frequently (as is still often the case), to loud talking during sleep.

"[3] *My inclinations:* The above-mentioned abnormal proclivity is the fundamental factor in my sexual feeling. When I am dressed like a woman, I feel perfectly satisfied. A peculiar feeling of peace and comfort comes over me, which allows me to work mentally with greater ease. My libido for indulgence in sexual intercourse is extremely slight. I also have much love and taste for female handiwork. I learned, without assistance, to crochet

and embroider, and I like to do these things in secret. I also like other female employ-
ments, like sewing, etc. Thus, at home, where I keep my proclivity perfectly concealed,
and guard against indulging it by involuntary activity, I have often won the praise of
being as good as a servant girl. This did not make me ashamed, however; instead, it
filled me with secret pride. I get nothing out of dancing with women; I enjoyed dancing
only with my schoolmates, and was given the opportunity to do so through the manner of
our instruction in dancing. This gave me pleasure, however, only when I could dance as a
lady. A multitude of other desires and dreams, which seem to have something characteristic about them, I will omit, because they seem exactly similar to those described in
Psychopathia Sexualis. . . . In other respects my inclinations are not different from those
of my sex. I smoke and drink moderately, love delicacies, and take no pleasure from
physical exercises.

"[4] *Development:* After this brief description of my personality, I can now proceed to an
analysis of the developmental history of my abnormality. As soon as I had some ability to
think independently, and understood the difference between the sexes, it was my secret
and fixed desire to be a girl. In fact, I believed I was one. In the bath, however, when I
saw the same genitals on other boys, the impossibility of my idea became apparent. I
reduced my wish, and hoped to be at least a hermaphrodite. Notwithstanding my abundant opportunities to read writings on the subject, I was able to entertain this hope,
because I had a certain shyness about looking closely at pictures or descriptions of the
genitals. Later, my studies compelled me to become more closely acquainted with the
subject. During this time I read everything I could find about hermaphroditism, and
longed to be in the place of the female who, as the newspapers often reported, had been
raised as a male and restored to her sex by accident. The recognition of my masculinity
brought this dreaming to an end, and did not fill me with any special delight. I tried to
destroy my sexual glands by gradual pressure, but pain soon caused me to desist. My
longing is still for the external characteristics of the female sex – for a pretty coiffure, a
rounded breast, a slim waist.

"My first opportunity to put on female attire came at the age of twelve, and I soon came
to drape myself (by means of fashioning bedclothes, bed linen, etc.) with female petticoats. When I grew older, it was my greatest delight to secretly put on my sister's
dresses, even if it could only be for a few moments, and with constant danger of detection. Later, much to my delight, I had an opportunity to play a female role in a love
scene; and it is said that I was not at all bad in the part. When I began to lead an inde-

pendent life as a student, I immediately obtained female dresses and linen, which I cared for myself. At night, safe from discovery, when I can put on one article after another, from corset to apron and bracelet, I am perfectly satisfied, and devote myself to some quiet employment, inwardly happy and full of delight while doing it. As I am dressing, an erection usually occurs, but it is never followed by ejaculation, and soon disappears. I also try to approximate the female appearance externally, by arranging my hair appropriately and by removing the beard, which I would prefer to tear out.

"[5] *Sexual inclinations:* Before proceeding to the description of my sexual proclivities, I first wish to note that, in general, puberty occurred normally, judging from the occurrence of pollutions, the change of voice, etc. Pollutions still regularly occur, usually no more than once every three weeks. With them I never experience any lustful feeling. I have never practiced masturbation; until recently I knew nothing more of it than its name, and I had to seek direct information about it in order to understand it. Any touch on my erect penis is disturbing and painful to me, and without lustful feeling.

"Previously I behaved very shyly toward women. Now I am quiet, but associate with them as with my kind. Although sexual excitation by a woman has sometimes occurred, it seems to me when I try to analyze it that it was never her person that affected me; instead, it was her attire alone. I would fall in love with a woman's dress, and the thought of wearing one like it was heavenly. Thus sexual excitation never took place, not even in brothels that I was led to by friends, and in spite of the sight of the greatest voluptuousness and beauty. But friendly feelings for the female sex were in my heart. I imagined how, dressed as a woman and unrecognized, I could stay with them, associate with them, and take pleasure with them. I prefer the impression made on me by girls whose breasts have not yet fully developed, particularly those who wear their hair short; for such girls appear more like me. Once I was fortunate enough to find a girl who felt unhappy with her gender. We formed a firm bond of friendship, and often took delight in the idea of exchanging places. Perhaps it is not inappropriate or unimportant, for the purpose of characterization, to record the following: Some months ago, when the story was running through the newspapers of a Hungarian countess who, dressed as a man, had married, and felt like a man, I seriously thought of offering myself to her, in order to contract an inverted marriage – she as husband, I as wife. . . . I have never attempted coitus, and have never felt any desire for it. Because I foresaw that the erection necessary with a woman would be lacking, however, I thought of putting on some of her clothing; then, I think, the expected result would occur.

"As for my behavior toward male persons; first of all, I must emphasize that I had the warmest friendships during my school days. If I could do some small service for the object of my devotion, my heart was full of happiness. I really worshiped him passionately. I displayed terrible jealousy over the slightest incident, however; and while my anger lasted I felt as if I could neither live nor die. When reconciliation occurred, I was, for a short time, the happiest of creatures. I also tried to make friends with younger boys, whom I bribed with sweetmeats, and whom I would have gladly kissed. Though my love always remained platonic, it was still abnormal. An expression that I unconsciously made at that time about an elder friend, whom I worshiped, illustrates this. I said I loved him so much that I would have enjoyed marrying him. And even now, on the infrequent occasions when I indulge in intercourse, I am easily taken with a handsome man who has a fine beard and refined features. Yet I have never met a person who feels as I do, in whom I could confide, and with whom I could live as a female friend. I have never attempted to exercise my inclinations directly, and have never committed any foolish act of this kind. I finally ceased visiting museums where nude male figures were displayed, for the erections, which were sure to occur, were exceedingly annoying. I had often secretly wished to sleep with a man, and often found opportunity. I was asked by a rather unattractive elderly man to sleep with him. **When I laid down next to him, he touched my genitals;** and although this person was unattractive to me, I was filled with an intense feeling of lust. I felt as if I had completely surrendered to him; in a word, *I felt like a woman.*

"If I may be permitted to add a concluding word to what I have already said, I wish to expressly state that, though I am conscious of the abnormality of my inclinations, I have no desire to change them; instead, I long for a time when I can give free rein to my desires more easily and with less danger of discovery, and experience a delight that will harm no one."

Case 120.

Miss Z., aged thirty-one; came for consultation because of neurasthenic symptoms. She was remarkable for her coarse, masculine features: a deep voice, short hair, a masculine style of dress, masculine gait, and self-consciousness. In other respects she was feminine, with well-developed breasts and a female pelvis, and without any indication of a beard.

Examination with reference to contrary sexual instinct indicated a positive result:

The patient stated that even as a little girl she preferred to play with boys; particularly "soldier," "merchant," and "robber." Although she was wild and unrestrained in these games with boys, she never had any proclivity for dolls or female employment, about which she learned only the most ordinary things (knitting, sewing).

In school she made good progress, and was especially interested in mathematics and chemistry. She had a precocious desire for sculpture, and showed talent for it. Her greatest ambition was to become a real artist. In her dreams of the future, she never thought of marriage. Although she was interested as an artist in handsome men, she was otherwise attracted exclusively by female forms; she saw male forms only "in the distance." She could never endure "trumpery"; "manly dress" was all that pleased her. The ordinary society of girls was repugnant to her, because their talk of *toilette,* ornaments, and love affairs with men seemed stale and tiresome to her. On the other hand, since childhood she had had enthusiastic friendships with certain girls; at the age of ten she was in love with a girl companion, and wrote her name everywhere. Since then she had had numerous female friends with whom she indulged in passionate kissing. She pleased the girls, as a rule, because of her masculine bearing. She wrote poems to her female friends, and would have done anything out of love for them. It was remarkable to her that she was embarrassed before girls, especially when they were friends. She could not undress in front of them. The more she loved a friend, the more she was modest in front of her.

She had such a relation at the present time. She often kissed and embraced her Laura, walked by her window, and suffered pangs of jealousy, particularly when she saw her conversing with men. Her only wish was to always live with this female friend.

The patient stated, however, that twice in her life men had made an impression on her. She thought that if she had been pursued, there would have been a marriage, for she was very fond of family life and children. If a man wished to possess her, it would be necessary for him to win her; her preference was to win a female friend. She thought woman was more beautiful and ideal than man. In her infrequent erotic dreams, the subject had always been a female. She had never dreamt of men. At the present time, she did not think she could love a man; for men were false, and she herself was nervous and anemic.

Although she considered herself a woman in all respects, she regretted that she was not a man. Even at the age of four it had been her greatest pleasure to put on boys' clothes. She certainly had a masculine character, and had never wept. Her greatest passions were riding, gymnastics, fencing, and driving. She suffered a great deal because no one around her understood her. Conversation about feminine things seemed silly to her. Many of her acquaintances thought that she should have been a man.

The patient said that she was never sensual. In embracing female friends, she had often experienced a peculiar lustful feeling. Embracing and kissing had been her only manner of expressing her friendship.

The patient stated that she came from a nervous father and an insane mother who, as a young girl, had been passionately in love with her own brother, and had tried to induce him to flee with her to America. The patient's brother was an eccentric, peculiar man.

The patient presented no external degenerative signs; her head was regular. She said her menses began at fourteen, and that, although they were regular, they had always been painful.

Case 121.

"In order to immediately designate my unhappy diseased condition with its correct name, I will state at the beginning that it bears all the marks of what you have named *effemination* in your work, *Psychopathia Sexualis*.

"I am now thirty-eight years old, and, thanks to my abnormality, I look back on a life that has been so full of indescribable suffering that I am often astonished when I think of the extent of man's capacity for pain. Consciousness of the suffering I have endured has recently become the source of a kind of self-respect, which, in itself, makes my life bearable, to a degree.

"I shall nevertheless endeavor now to truthfully describe my condition. I am physically healthy, and, as far as I can remember, have never had any severe illness. I come from a healthy family. Each of my parents, however, has an excitable nature. My father has a so-called choleric temperament, and my mother has a sanguine temperament; with, however, a strong tendency to mild melancholia. Although she is a lively woman, loved for her good-heartedness and active benevolence, she is still extremely dependent and lacking in self-confidence. All these peculiarities were marked in her father. I mention this fact because I am told that I resemble them both, and I can acknowledge the resemblance myself as far as the last two peculiarities are concerned. When, by means of my inner strength and by thinking of my own power, I have made attempts to rend the bond that draws me to men with a magic force, there has always remained a residuum that I cannot eradicate. As far as I can remember, I have always had this elementary longing for a male lover. To be sure, its first expressions were of a coarse, sensual nature. When I was about ten years old, lying in bed in the daytime, I suddenly discovered how, by applying pressure on my genitals, I could induce a new and intoxicating feeling while fantasizing that a man of my acquaintance performed sensual manipulations on me. It was only many years afterward that I learned that this was masturbation. At first I was so frightened and so depressed by the inexplicability of my longing, that I then made my first attempt at suicide. If I only had put it into execution! For since then there has been such an incessantly violent agitation of mind and body that my heart has felt as if it is bound with a chain and been made cold. Up to the present time, masturbation has not loosened me from its clutches; it has overcome all attempts and efforts to escape, and my desire to resist it is almost destroyed. On three or four occasions I have given it up for a month at a time, usually under the influence of mental excitement.

"When I was about thirteen, I had my first love. Today it seems as if my greatest wish then was to kiss my schoolmate's fresh, rosy lips. It was a passion full of romantic dreams. At the age of fifteen or sixteen it became more violent, when I first experienced the insane pangs of a jealousy more terrible than the jealousy of natural love. This second period of my life lasted for years, though I spent only a few days with the object of my passion, after which we did not see each other for fifteen years. Gradually my feeling cooled, and I then fell passionately in love with a succession of other men, who, with the exception of one, were about my own age.

"My love – if you will kindly allow this expression for a feeling condemned by the majority of mankind – has never been returned; I have never had intercourse with a man that would not, in any way, bear the light of day; never has anyone shown even extraordinary interest in me, though one of my friends discovered my secret longing; and yet I have maintained a burning desire for masculine love. In this longing my feelings seem to me to be entirely those of a loving woman; and I notice, with horror, that my sensual ideas grow more and more like those of a woman. During the periods when I am free from any particular love, my longing degenerates so that I conjure up only coarse, sensual ideas in my masturbatory manipulations. But I am still finally able to overcome these. My efforts to repress the love, however, are absolutely in vain. At the present time I am again suffering from this kind of an exaggerated state of feeling. It has existed for months, and I have pondered so much over its peculiarities that I think I can describe my feelings truthfully. This is how I came to make the peculiar observation that I have never loved a bearded man. Although it might easily be presumed from this that I am given to so-called boy-love, that is not the case. For, with closer association, a mental interest is added to the sensual charm. With this begins the mental pain. I am seized with such a passionate longing that I am willing, in a way, to sacrifice myself. I excite confidence in myself, and from the mutual feeling that results, a heartfelt friendship might be engendered, were it not for the demon sleeping deep down in my soul who impels me toward the closest of relationships, allowed only between human beings of opposite sex. My whole being, every fiber of my body, longs for it, and I am consumed by a hot, glowing passion. I wonder about my ability to here again describe, with unfeeling words, the feelings that coursed through my whole being. Of course, I have been forced by the struggle of years to learn to conceal my inclination, and to smile when torn by pain. For, in never having my love returned, I have learned to know all the sufferings of love. Jealousy – insane, blinding jealousy – of each and every person who casts even a friendly glance at the object of my secret love!

"I have emphasized the mental element, in order to show how deeply rooted my abnormal impulse is. I have never felt the slightest touch of sensual love for the opposite sex. The idea of being forced to associate sensually with women is repugnant to me. At times I have suffered from merely being assured of the love of young girls. Like every young man, I have had abundant opportunity to enjoy the modern social pleasures, dancing among them. I like to dance; but I would be really happy if I were able to dance with men as a girl.

"I wish to remark once more that my love is entirely sensual. How else could I explain the fact that the pressure of my lover's hand, and often merely his glance, causes palpitation and erection! I have done everything to eradicate this love from my – let us say 'heart.' I have tried to still it by means of masturbation, thus dragging it in the mire in order to raise myself above it. (About ten years ago, during such a time of love, I avoided masturbation, and felt that my feeling of love elevated me.) I still entertain the delusion that if the object of my love were to tell me he loved me – that he loved me, and only me – I would willingly give up sensual gratification to repose in faithful arms. But this is certainly a self-deception.

"Honored sir, I have a responsible occupation, and I think I can give the assurance that my abnormal inclination has never, even by a hair's breadth, caused me to deviate from the duty imposed on me. Aside from this abnormality, I am not insane, and I might ulti-mately become contented; but I have, particularly in recent years, suffered too much not to look on the future with painful feeling. For the future will certainly not bring a fulfill-ment of the desire that constantly glows under the ashes – the desire to possess a lover who understands and returns my love. Such a relation would make me truly happy. I have thought a great deal about the origin of my abnormality, particularly because I think I am forced to assume that it was not inherited. I believe that masturbation has changed my inborn feeling into a burning passion. I might have long ago put an end to my misery, because I have no fear of death, and because in religion – which, strange to say, has not departed from my impure heart – I find no warning against suicide. The consciousness that I am not alone responsible, however, and that a worm has nipped my whole life in the bud (a certain comfort that has recently sprung up out of indescribable suffering), leads me to see whether comparative happiness in life cannot be obtained on an entirely new basis: something which fills the whole heart. I think I could be happy under the influence of a quiet family life. But I dare not conceal from you the fact that the thought of married life with a wife is terrible to me, and that I make the attempt at a change of life with a bleeding heart; for, in doing it, I absolutely abandon the hope that is now always awake; namely, the delusion that fate may yet bring me desired happiness.

"This delusion is so deeply rooted in me that I think nothing but hypnotic suggestion could help me. If you could advise me, you would make me unspeakably happy. Of course, your strictest injunction would be to abandon masturbation. How gladly I would follow it! But were I not to have some direct physical or mechanical means at hand to help me, I should certainly be unable to free myself from this vice; all the more so because I fear that by long years of habit, my nature has become accustomed to it. Of course, I have not escaped the effects of it, even though they are not as terrible as they are often described. I suffer from mild nervousness; I am, indeed, weakened, and have periodic disturbance of digestion; but I can still endure hard work, and take a certain pleasure in it when it is not too great. I am depressed, but I can also be happy. Fortunately, I take pleasure in my calling, and am interested in various things, particu-larly music, art, and *belles lettres.* I have never indulged in female pursuits.

"As may be seen from the foregoing, although I like to associate with men, especially with those who are handsome, I have never had intimate relations with them. A wide gulf separates me from them!

"*Postscript:* I feared that in the foregoing I had not described my sexual life with sufficient exactness. Although it consists only of masturbation, with it I abandon myself to almost every imaginable repugnant act, such as **coitus between the thighs, ejaculation into the mouth,** etc.

"My role is passive. When I am seized by a passion, the ideas change and become a desire to be impregnated. The struggle against such a passion is so terrible because my mind is also implicated. I long for the closest, most complete union that can be conceived of between two men – always together, common interests, unlimited confidence, sexual union. I think that natural love is different from this only in its degree of warmth; i.e., it does not reach the boiling point of our passion. Just now I am fighting the battle again; I forcefully stifle the insane passion that has enthralled me for so long. All night long I walk around, followed by the image of the man I love; for whose love I would give up all I possess. How sad it is that the noblest feeling given to man – friendship – is sullied by common sensual feeling!

"I wish to state once more that I cannot come to the determination to transform my sexual life by means of sexual intercourse with the opposite sex. The thought of such intercourse fills me with repugnance and disgust."

Case 122.

"I will write, as well as I can, the history of my suffering. I am driven only by the desire to clear up, to some extent, with this autobiography, the misunderstanding and errors concerning 'contrary sexual instinct' that are still so widely prevalent.

"I am thirty-seven years old, and come from healthy parents, both of whom were very nervous. I only mention this because I have often had the thought that my contrary sexual instinct came through inheritance. This, however, is nothing more than a vague notion. About my grandparents, whom I did not know, the only remarkable thing I can mention is that my maternal grandfather was known as a great Don Juan.

"I was a rather weak child, and during my first two years I suffered severely from fits, as a result of which my understanding and memory may have been damaged; for I learn but slowly things that do not particularly interest me, and forget them easily. I should also mention that during the time before I was born, my mother was subject to violent mental excitement, and was often frightened. From my third year I have been perfectly well, and have escaped severe illness. As a boy, from the age of twelve to sixteen only, I had peculiar, indescribable nervous sensations, which made themselves felt in my head and fingertips, and in which it seemed to me as if my whole being were about to end. For many years, however, these attacks have ceased to occur. I am a rather powerful man, with abundant growth of hair, and masculine in all respects.

"Even as a boy of six years, I independently learned to masturbate, and practiced the vice quite persistently until my nineteenth year. Even now, for lack of something better, I frequently resort to it, notwithstanding the fact that I understand the vileness of the passion, and always feel somewhat weakened after it. But sexual intercourse with a man does not affect me in the least; on the contrary, it gives me a feeling of strength. I began school at the age of seven, and although I soon experienced an intense feeling of sympathy for my companions, I had no impression beyond that. In the *Gymnasium,* at the age of fourteen, my companions explained to me the sexual life of man, which, up to that time, was absolutely unknown to me; but I was not much interested in the matter. At this time I also practiced mutual masturbation with two or three friends who had seduced me into it, and it had an extraordinary charm for me. I was still perfectly unconscious of the perversity of my sexual instinct, and considered my vices as sins of youth, like those committed by all boys of the same age. I thought an interest in the female sex would come in time. Thus I became nineteen years old. During the following years I fell insanely in love three times — first with a very handsome actor, then with a bank employee, and then with one of my friends. The last two were men who were nothing less than beautiful, and were chosen because they excited my sensual feeling. This love was merely platonic, however, and occasionally found expression in glowing poetry. It was, perhaps, the most perfect period of my life, for I regarded everything with pure, innocent eyes. In my twenty-first year I gradually began to notice that I was not exactly constituted like my comrades, for I found no pleasure in masculine pursuits. I cared little for smoking, drinking, and card playing, and I was frightened to death by a brothel. I still have never been in one; I have always been able to avoid going on some pretext or other. But I began, then, to think about myself; I often felt terribly lonesome, miserable, and unhappy, and longed for a friend constituted like myself, without, however, ever thinking that there could be other men like me. At twenty-two I made the acquaintance of a young man who finally explained to me contrary sexual instinct and the individuals affected with it. He was also a homosexual, and was in love with me. It was as if scales had fallen from my eyes, and I bless the day this explanation came to me. From that time I saw the world with different eyes; I saw that many others were given the same fate; and I began to learn, as well as I could, to content myself with my lot. Unfortunately, I did not succeed very well, and I am still often seized with bitterness and a deep hatred for the modern ideas that treat us poor homosexuals with such terrible harshness. For what is our fate? In most cases we are not understood, and are derided and despised. Even when all goes well, and we are understood, we are still pitied like invalids or the insane — and pity has always been sickening to me. Thus I began to play a role in order to deceive my fellow men about my state of mind. It always gave me great satisfaction to succeed in this. I made the acquaintance of several men like myself, with whom I established relations. These relations never lasted long, however, for while I was fearful and cautious, I was also very particular and wearied easily.

"I have always absolutely despised pederasty as something unworthy of a man, and I only wish that all those like me would do the same; unfortunately, however, for many this is not the case. If everyone like me were to think as I do, then the contempt and scoffing of men who feel differently would be an even greater injustice to us than it is now.

"My feelings toward the men I love are completely like those of a woman, and, therefore, in the sexual act I am quite passive. In general, my whole sensibility and feelings are feminine. I am vain, coquettish, fond of ornament, and like to please others. I love to dress myself beautifully, and, in cases where I wish to please, I even make use of the arts of the *toilette*, in which I am quite skilled.

"While I have only a slight interest in politics, I am passionately fond of music and an inspired follower of Richard Wagner. I have noticed this preference in the majority of us; I find that this music is perfectly in accord with our nature.

"I play the violin quite well; I like reading, and read a great deal, but I have little interest in anything else. Because of the deep resignation that more and more takes possession of me, I am quite indifferent to everything else in life.

"Even though I should have reason to be satisfied with my fate, in that I have an assured position in technical employment in a large city of Germany, I still take no pleasure in my calling. It would suit me best if, independent and free, I could travel about with a handsome lover, living for music, literature, and particularly the theatre, which seems to me to be one of the greatest pleasures. I think a connection with a court theatre would be very acceptable.

"The only position or calling that seems really desirable to me is that of a great artist – singer, actor, painter, or sculptor; and it seems to me that it would be even finer to be born to the throne of a king – a wish that is in harmony with my pronounced desire for power. (If there is really such a thing as transmigration of souls, a subject I have studied extensively, and which seems to me to clear up a great deal; I must have lived at one time as an emperor or ruler of some kind.) A man must be born to all this, however; and since I was not, I am without ambition for so-called social honors and distinctions.

"I must mention a painful oddity regarding my tastes. Handsome, intellectual young men of at least twenty years, who must be of my own social station, seem to me to be more correctly suited for platonic love; and with them I satisfy myself completely with a straightforward, though ideal, friendship, which seldom goes beyond a few kisses. But I can be sensually excited only by coarse, powerful men who are at least of my own age, and who are mentally and socially beneath me. The reason for this strange phenomenon may be that my pronounced feeling of shame and innate apprehensiveness, when combined with my cautious disposition, produce an inhibitory effect with men of my own social position, so that with them I can only rarely and with difficulty induce sexual excitement in myself. This diversity is painful to me because I am always afraid to reveal myself to these simple men, below me in station, who may often be bought with money. I cannot imagine anything worse than a scandal, which would drive me at once to suicide. For I can think of nothing more terrible than to suddenly be branded before the world, and be powerless to avert it, because of some slight act of carelessness or a particular man's enmity. What is it that we do that is so different from what normally constituted men are free to do without embarrassment or shame? That we do not feel as the crowd feels is not our fault, but a cruel trick of nature.

"Innumerable times I have racked my brains to figure out whether science, or any of her free and unprejudiced devotees, could somehow give us stepchildren of nature a more endurable position before the law and mankind. But I have always reached the same sad conclusion: when one enters the lists on behalf of anything, he must first thoroughly know and be able to explain that for which he contends. And who is able today to perfectly explain and define contrary sexual instinct? Yet there must be some correct explanation of it; there must be some way in which the mass of mankind can be brought to a milder and more reasonable judgment of it; and, most important, there must be some way to show that contrary sexual instinct should not be regarded as meaning the same as pederasty, which is how the majority of men – I could even say all men – regard it. With such an act, a man could erect an immortal monument in his own honor, which would be justified by the gratitude of thousands of men of present and future generations; for there have always been homosexuals and there will always be homosexuals, perhaps in a greater number than has been suspected.

"In Wilbrand's work, *Fridolin's heimliche Ehe,* a very plausible theory is given in explanation of this matter; for I myself have repeatedly had the opportunity to observe that all homosexuals do not love men with the same intensity. Instead, there are innumerable sub-varieties – from the most feminine man to the man who is equally sensitive to female charms. This may also account for the so-called difference between congenital and acquired contrary sexual instinct, which, in my inadequate opinion, does not exist. Nevertheless, the fifty-five individuals with whom I have become acquainted in the three years since I came to understand this matter have all shared the same peculiarities of temperament, disposition, and character. Almost all of them are more or less idealists: they smoke minimally or not at all; they are bigoted, vain, desirous of admiration, and superstitious; and, unfortunately, I must confess that they embody more of the defects and reverse sides of both sexes than the good qualities. I experience a feeling of true horror for a woman in a sexual role, which I could never overcome, even with the help of my extremely lively imagination. I have never attempted it, because I am thoroughly convinced of the fruitlessness of such an attempt, which seems to me unnatural and sinful.

"In purely social and friendly relations, I like to associate with ladies and girls, and I am gladly welcomed in ladies' society, for I am much interested in ladies' fashions, and know how to talk of such things with great skill. Although I can be very gay and amiable when I wish to be, my faculty for conversation is only assumed for the most part, and always tires me. I have always had an interest in and have shown great skill for female work. As a child, and up to my thirteenth year, I was passionately fond of playing with dolls, whose clothes I made myself; and it still affords me much pleasure to work at beautiful embroidery, which, unfortunately, I can only do in secret. I have the same preference for knickknacks, photographs, flowers, sweetmeats, toilet articles, and other such feminine things; and my room, which I arranged and decorated myself, is like the overcrowded boudoir of a lady.

"I wish to mention as particularly remarkable that I have never suffered from pollutions. I dream abundantly and intensely almost every night. Although I occasionally have lascivious dreams, with men as the only subjects, I always wake out of them before it comes to ejaculation. In reality I am not very passionate sexually, and have periods that last from four to six weeks in which I have almost no sexual desire. Unfortunately, however, these periods are infrequent, and are usually followed by a violent awakening of my already strong sexual desire, which, when unsatisfied, causes intense physical and mental suffering. I then become moody, depressed, sensitive, irritable, and retiring. These peculiarities, however, again disappear with the first opportunity I have for sexual gratification. I must also mention that often the slightest incident can cause my mood (like April weather) to change several times during the day.

"I dance well, and love to dance; but only because of its rhythmical movement, and because of my partiality for music.

"In conclusion, I wish to speak of something that always arouses repugnance in me. We are usually considered diseased, and this view is absolutely incorrect. In every disease there is a means of cure or amelioration; but no power in the world can take from a homosexual his perverse natural constitution. Even suggestion, which has been used with so much apparent success, cannot induce any enduring change in the mental life of a homosexual. In us, effect is mistaken for cause. We are considered diseased because eventually the majority of us actually become ill. I am almost convinced that two-thirds of us in later life (if we live so long) have a mental defect of one kind or another; and this is only too easily explained. Consider what strength of will and nerves is required for one to constantly dissimulate, lie, and play the hypocrite all of his life! How often in the society of normal men, when the conversation turns to contrary sexual instinct, must one agree with the words of abuse and contempt, while every one of them wounds the heart. In addition to this, there are always the tiresome and indecent jokes and talk about women that are so popular today in so-called 'good society' – and one must show interest and give attention to them! To daily and hourly see so many handsome men and not be able to reveal oneself; to be compelled to go without a friend, an intercourse we desire so much; to say nothing of the constant and fearful anxiety of betraying oneself before the eyes of the world, only to then stand covered with ignominy and shame! It is really no wonder that the majority of us are incapable of real work, inasmuch as we need all our strength of will and all our power of endurance for the struggle with our own fate. How injurious it is to our nerves to constantly be compelled to shut up all such thoughts and feelings in our hearts; where, feeding on it all, our lively fantasy plays all the more intensely, so that as we go about, a fire burns within us that only too often threatens to consume us! Happy are those of us who are never denied the strength to lead such a life; but happy, too, are those who have passed beyond it."

Case 123.

Autobiography. "In what follows, you will find a description of the character, the mental tendency, as well as the sexual disposition of a homosexual – an individual who, in spite of his masculine form, feels as a woman does, whose senses are not excited by women, and whose sexual desires are constantly directed toward men.

"Convinced that the enigma of our existence can be solved (or, at least, illuminated) only by the unprejudiced thought of scientific men, my only aim in describing my life is to perhaps clear up this cruel error of nature, and to possibly do a kindness to people like me in generations to come; for as long as men are born, there will be homosexuals. It is a fact that they have existed in every age. With the progress of science in our age, men will see me and those like me as objects of pity, not as objects of hatred, who deserve the compassion rather than the odium of their more fortunate brothers. I shall be as brief and objective as possible in my communication; and, above all, with reference to my caustic, often cynical, style, I shall be honest. Thus, I will not avoid strong expressions; for they are most happily suited to the subject at hand.

"I am in my thirty-fifth year; a merchant, with a fair income. I am somewhat above average height, slim, weak-muscled, with a full beard, a quite ordinary face, and, at first sight, no different from ordinary men. On the other hand, my gait is feminine, and particularly mincing in fast walking; the movements are awkward, displeasing, and indicative of an absence of manly feeling. My voice is neither feminine nor shrill, but rather a baritone.

"This is my external appearance.

"I do not smoke or drink, and can neither whistle, ride, do gymnastic feats, fence, nor shoot. I have absolutely no interest in horses or dogs, and have never had a gun or sword in my hand. My inner feeling and sexual desire is completely that of a woman. Without a thorough education – I passed only a few classes in the *Gymnasium* – I am still intelligent, like to read well-written, improving books, and have good judgment. I nevertheless allow myself to be carried away by the feelings of the moment, and I am easily influenced by anyone who knows my weakness and knows how to make use of it. Although constantly making resolves, I never have the energy to carry them out; like a woman, I am moody and nervous, often irritated without reason, and sometimes mean. I am arrogant, unjust, and often shamefully insulting toward persons who do not please me.

"In all my conduct I am superficial, often frivolous, and have no deep moral feeling. I have little consideration for parents, brothers and sisters. I am not egotistical, but can be self-sacrificing on occasion. Although I cannot withstand tears, I can (like a woman) be won by amiability and entreaty.

"In my earliest years I avoided playing soldier, gymnastics, or the rough games of my manly comrades, and ran around instead with little girls, with whom I was much more in sympathy than boys. I was retiring, bashful, and blushed frequently. When I was no more than twelve or thirteen years old, the close-fitting uniform of a handsome soldier gave me the most peculiar feeling. During the next few years, while my comrades were always talking about girls, and even engaged in love affairs, I would run after a well-built man with well-rounded hips for hours at a time, and feast my eyes on the sight.

"Without thinking much of these impressions, which were so different from the feelings of my comrades, I began to masturbate, during which I always thought of a heroic, handsome form. This continued until my seventeenth year, when I learned from a companion (who was constituted like myself) the true explanation of my condition. Although since that time I have been with girls eight or ten times, it was always necessary, in order to have an erection, to think of a handsome man of my acquaintance. And I am thoroughly convinced that today, even with the help of my imagination, I would be unable to have intercourse with a girl.

"Shortly after my discovery, I preferred to associate with mature, powerful homosexuals, for at that time I had neither the mind nor the opportunity to associate with real men. Since then my taste has changed entirely; and men, real men, of twenty-five or thirty-five years, with supple, powerful forms, are the only ones who ravish my senses, and charm me as if I were a woman. Circumstances have allowed me, during these years, to make about a dozen male acquaintances who, for a gulden or two per visit, serve my purpose. If I am alone in a room with a handsome youth, my greatest pleasure is **to take in my hands his member, especially if it is big and fat, and to grasp and press it, and to touch his swelling buttocks and thighs and cover his entire body – moving into his buttocks – with burning kisses. If his member is big and clean, however, and its master is pleasing** to me, I can suck his penis, taken into my mouth, with burning passion for several hours. I am not pleased, however, if semen is ejaculated into my mouth, although a very great number of those who are called 'homosexuals' are not only pleased with this, but sometimes even swallow the semen.

"The most intense delight, however, is experienced when I find a real man **who takes my member in his mouth and yields his mouth to my erection.**

"Improbable as it sounds, I have not yet been able to find some coarse fellows who will allow themselves to be used for this purpose. They learn these sexual acts while in military service, because there homosexuals know that other men can be made to do the most for money. Once the fellows are trained, however, in spite of their passion for the opposite sex, circumstances often compel them to continue the practice.

"With certain exceptions, homosexuals make no impression on me, because everything feminine is repugnant to me. At the same time, there are some who know how to give me the most intense pleasure, just as a real man can; and I prefer to consort with them, for the reason that they sometimes return my passionate caresses. When in a *tête-à-tête* with such a person, my excited senses cause me to lose complete control and give my animal passions free rein: **I kiss, I press, I embrace him. I insert my tongue into his mouth, a mouth trembling with desire, and suck his upper lip. I place my face in his buttocks and, with a voluptuous odor emanating from his buttocks, I become senseless with pleasure.** Real men, in close-fitting uniforms, make the deepest impression on me. If I have an opportunity to embrace and kiss such a ravishing fellow, ejaculation immediately takes place – a weakness that I attribute to my frequent masturbation. In my earlier years I practiced it frequently, almost every time I saw a man pleasing to me, and during the act I kept his image before my eyes. With this my taste is by no means difficult to please – I compare it to what a servant girl might have in finding her ideal in a dragoon guard. Although a handsome face is a pleasant supplement, and inflames my sensual desire, it is in way essential. The requisite remains: **a man with a robust and very beautiful lower half of his body, with swollen thighs and hard buttocks,** while the upper portion of the body can be slim. Corpulence disgusts me. A sensual mouth with pretty teeth affects me more intensely; and if the person also has a **big, beautiful and equally well-shaped member,** all my demands – the most far-reaching included – are fulfilled.

"When I was younger, ejaculation took place from five to eight times a night with men who pleased me and excited my passions intensely, and now it occurs from four to six times. I am unusually strong sensually, and even the clinking of a hussar's sword, for example, can excite me. At the same time, I have a very lively fantasy where, using force, **a man endowed with a big penis has coitus with a girl in my presence; he has been persuaded by me that my senses would be vehemently and passionately affected by this sight. While he had coitus with the girl, I would touch the body of the beautiful youth and, if it were allowed, I would climb on top of him while he lay with the girl and do the same with him by inserting my member into his anus.** The accomplishment of these cynical ideas – with which my mind is often filled – is hindered only by my limited means; otherwise, I would have enjoyed the reality long ago.

"Although soldiers have the greatest charm for me, I also have a weakness for butchers, fakirs, drivers, circus riders, and boat captains; all must be supple and powerfully built. I hate homosexuals in intimate relations, and for the majority of them I have an inexplicable and unjust aversion. I have never had even one homosexual as an intimate friend. On the other hand, I have the most affectionate and enduring ties with men of my own age, in whose company I delight, but with whom I have no sexual relations, and who have no idea of my condition.

"I hate conversation about politics, economics, and every other earnest subject, though I gossip with considerable sense and peculiar pleasure about the theatre. At operas I see myself on the stage, feel myself applauded by the public, and would prefer to sing as either a passive heroine or in the dramatic role of a woman.

"For me, and for those who are like me, however, the most interesting subject of conversation is always men; for us the topic is inexhaustible. Their secret charms are described in the most minute details, and **their penises are appraised – how big they are in size and fatness. We confer about their shape and rigidity, and we learn from one another who ejaculates quicker and who ejaculates slower.** I might add that, of my four brothers, one gave himself to the service of homosexuals, without being one himself. All four are ladies' men, and indulge in sexual excesses. Without exception, the genitals of the men of our family are unusually developed.

"In conclusion, I repeat the words with which I began these lines. I could not choose my expressions, because my object here has been to furnish material for the study of the homosexual's existence, and therefore absolute truth was essential. I beg the numerous cynics to keep this circumstance in mind."

In October 1890 the writer of the foregoing lines presented himself to me. In all essentials his appearance corresponded with his description. Genitals large, with abundant growth of hair. His parents had been psychically well. One brother had shot himself because of nervous trouble; three others were intensely nervous. The patient came to me in a state of despair. He could not endure such a life any longer, for he had been admonished about engaging in intercourse with men who could be bought; with his extreme sensual nature, he was unable to abstain. He could also not understand how he could be made to love women, and to enjoy the nobler joys of life. He had enjoyed love for men since his thirteenth year.

He felt like a woman in all respects, and longed to be won by men who were not homosexuals. When he was with a homosexual, it was just as if two girls were together. He preferred being sexless to living longer the way he was. Would castration not help him?

An attempt at hypnosis with the highly excited patient induced only a slight degree of lethargy.

†

Case 125.

On May 1, 1880, G., Ph.D., writer, was brought by the public authorities to the clinic for mental diseases at Graz. On his return from Italy, G. found a soldier in Graz who sold his services, but ultimately denounced G. to the police because G. had openly confessed his love for men. The authorities considered his mental condition doubtful, and sent him to alienists for examination. G. told the physicians, with cynical openness, that he had had such an affair with the police years before, in M., and was in prison fourteen days. He stated that there was no danger from such people in the south; only in Germany and Austria was it regarded as evil.

G. was fifty years old, tall and powerful. He had a humorous expression and a cynical, coquettish manner; his eyes had a neuropathic, swimming expression; his teeth of the lower jaw sat further back from those of the upper jaw. His cranium was normal, his voice masculine, and his beard abundant. His genitals were well-formed, though his testicles were somewhat small. With the exception of slight emphysema of his lungs and external fistula in his anus, there were no remarkable anomalies of his vegetative organs. G.'s father was subject to periodic insanity. His mother was a high-strung person, and she had an insane sister. Four of the children died in childhood.

With the exception of scrofula, G. asserted that he was healthy. He obtained the degree of doctor of philosophy; afterward, at twenty-five, he had hemoptysis, and went to Italy, where he has since lived, with slight interruption, by writing and giving private lessons. G. said that he often had congestions, as well as some spinal irritation – i.e., pain in his back – but he otherwise had a genial disposition. He was not much of a financier, however; at the same time, like all old prostitutes, he had a very good appetite. He further stated, with great satisfaction and remarkable cynicism, that he had congenital contrary sexual instinct. At only five years old, his greatest pleasure was to observe penises, and he hung around appropriate places in order to enjoy that pleasure. Even before puberty he practiced masturbation. At the time of puberty he noticed an inward feeling toward his friends. An obscure impulse pointed out to him the course his love would take. He was impelled to kiss young men, and to now and then caress their genitals. At twenty-six years old, he first began to have sexual intercourse with men, toward whom he felt like a woman. Even as a child, it was his greatest delight to put on female attire. He was often chastised by his father because, in an effort to satisfy this impulse, he put on his sister's clothing. If he happened to see a ballet, only the male dancers interested him. For as long as he could remember, he had had a *horror feminae.* If he happened to visit a brothel, it was only to see young men. He was, indeed, a rival of prostitutes. If he saw a young man, he first looked at his eyes, to see if they pleased him; then he looked at the mouth, to see if it was well-formed for kissing; then he would look at the genitals, to see if they were well-developed. G. pointed, with a great feeling of self-satisfaction, to his poetic works, and tried to make it appear that persons with attributes like his were poetically endowed. He gave as examples Voltaire, Frederick the Great, Eugene of Savoy, and Plato, as well as numerous distinguished men of the present, who, according to his opinion, were homosexuals. His greatest pleasure was to have a sympathetic young man read his verses to him. During the last summer he had had such a lover. When he had to part with him he was quite undone, and did not eat or sleep until, gradually, he recovered his former condition. He said that the love of homosexuals was a passionate, inner fire. He pointed out that the *effeminelli* in Naples shared living quarters, just as in Paris the *grisettes* lived with their lovers. They sacrificed themselves for their lovers, and cared for the household, just as the *grisettes* did. On the other hand, a homosexual repelled a homosexual, "just as one prostitute does another — that is the curse."

G.'s need for intercourse with males occurred about once a week. He was happy in his peculiar sexuality, which he certainly considered peculiar, but which he did not regard as abnormal or wrong. He thought that nothing remained for him and those who were like him, except to raise what was unnatural in themselves to the supernatural. He looked upon the love of homosexuals as the higher, the ideal; as godlike; an abstract love. When shown that such a love was far from the purpose of nature and the preservation of the race, he expressed the pessimistic thought that "the world should die out, and that the earth should turn round on its axis without men, who were on earth only to cause trouble." As reason and explanation for his unnatural sexual feeling, G. referred to Plato, "who certainly was no beast." Plato expressed allegorically the idea that men were originally balls. The gods had divided each of these balls into two hemispheres. For the most part, man was suited to woman, but sometimes man was suited to man. In the latter case, the impulse to union was just as powerful as in the former, and the parts of the union strengthened each other in the same way. G. further related that his erotic dreams never had women, but only men, as their subjects. Male love was the only kind that could satisfy him. He considered it disgusting for one human being to be prodding about with his penis in the abdomen of another, since he had heard that it was in this disgusting fashion that coitus was usually carried out. He had never had the curiosity to inform himself concerning the female genitals; the subject was disgusting to him. He did not consider the indulgence of his sexual appetite a vice, but the result of a natural impulse that compelled him. It was conducive to self-preservation. Masturbation was a poor substitute, and, moreover, injurious, while homosexual love was morally elevating and conducive to physical well-being.

With a moral indignation that appeared ridiculous in contrast with his cynicism in other directions, he protested the classification of homosexuals with those who indulged in pederasty. He looked on the behind with disgust, because it was a secreting organ. The intercourse of homosexuals always took place in front, in the form of combined masturbation.

This was the extent of G.'s disclosures, whose mental condition was certainly congenitally abnormal. As proof of this, his cynicism can be cited; his incredible frivolity in applying his vices to religion, in which direction we could not follow him without overstepping the bounds set by scientific inquiry; his perverse philosophical ideas with reference to his sexual perversion; his perverse manner of looking at the world; his ethical defect in all directions; his vagabondage; and his perverse mind and exterior. G. made the impression of an original paranoiac (personal case, *Zeitschrift für Psychiatrie*).

†

Case 132.

Count Z., aged fifty-one, from a psychopathic mother, was sent, when young, to a military school, and was taught masturbation there. Although he developed well and had normal sexual feelings, he became somewhat neurasthenic in his seventeenth year as a result of masturbation. He enjoyed intercourse with women, was married at twenty-five, but became neurasthenic after a year, and absolutely lost his inclination for women. In its place came contrary sexual instinct. Involved in an accusation of high treason, he was sent to prison for two years, and then to Siberia for five years. During these seven years, under the influence of continued masturbation, neurasthenia and contrary sexual instinct constantly increased. At the age of thirty-five, with his freedom restored, the patient began to visit all kinds of health resorts because of his great neurasthenia; afterward, this was his sole occupation. In all those years his abnormal sexual feeling had not changed in any way. For the most part, he had lived away from his wife. Although he esteemed her for her mental qualities, he had avoided her, as he had every other woman. His contrary sexual feeling was purely platonic. "Friendship," sweet embraces, and kisses had sufficed him. His occasional pollutions were induced by lascivious dreams that involved persons of his own sex. Also, during the day, the most beautiful woman had no charm for him, while the mere sight of handsome men induced erection and ejaculation. Only athletes and male dancers in the circus and ballet interested him. At times of greater excitability, even masculine statues gave him erections. He had occasionally resumed his old vice of masturbation. This man of aesthetic culture had a horror of pederasty.

Although he had always felt that his perverse sexual feeling was something abnormal, with his apparently much weakened libido and virility, he had not been unhappy.

The examination gave the usual findings of neurasthenia. Development, manner, and attire presented nothing remarkable. Electrical massage was unusually successful. After a few sittings the patient was mentally and physically much better. After twenty sittings his libido was again awakened; not in the same way, but normally, as the patient had felt until his twenty-fifth year. Lascivious dreams were thereafter only concerned with women, and one day the patient joyfully gave the information that he had engaged in coitus, during which he had the same natural feeling of twenty-six years before. He then began to live with his wife again, and hoped that he was lastingly freed from neurasthenia and contrary sexual instinct. His hope was fulfilled for the six years during which I was able to keep the patient under observation.

Physical treatment, although morally reinforced by good advice with reference to the avoidance of masturbation, the repression of homosexual feelings and impulses, and the encouragement of heterosexual desires, will typically not prove sufficient, even in cases of acquired contrary sexual instinct.

In such a circumstance, a method of mental treatment – hypnotic suggestion – is all that can bring benefit.

The following case is interesting; and it is an example of successful autosuggestion that gives encouragement for the milder forms of the anomaly:

Case 133.

Autobiography of a psychic hermaphrodite. Successful struggle against homosexual inclinations made by the patient himself.

"My father once had a stroke, but has recovered except for paralysis of the face. My mother was very anemic and melancholic. Both suffered severely from hemorrhoids, and my father ascribed this trouble to the lumbar pain with which he suffered from time to time after his marriage.

"I am, if I may say so myself, a passive character. As a child, I indulged in all kinds of fantasies, religious as well as others. I suffered from incontinence of urine, and it is said that while asleep I handled my genitals, so my father fastened my hands to the bed! (I was then a mere child, and had not masturbated.) I was always very shy and embarrassed in social intercourse. At about fourteen or fifteen years old, I was seduced into masturbation. The impulse and desire for women that occurred in connection with awakening sexual feeling were actually only of a platonic nature; I was also without the society of ladies. At about eighteen, I attempted to satisfy my sexual desire in the natural way, more in obedience to a feeling of curiosity than from inner longing. Since that time, without having experienced any real inclination for women, I have satisfied my desire as often as possible by means of sexual intercourse.

"Soon after puberty I became very anemic, and appeared much older than I really was. Then came melancholic and peculiar ideas. It was a delight for me to fantasize about being humiliated in the extreme. It may be of interest to add that I was troubled with religious doubts at the time, and only later found the courage to rise above religion. I fell in love with young men. At first I opposed these ideas; later they became so powerful that I became a genuine homosexual. Women seemed to me to be human beings of the second class. I was in a state of despair. My sickened soul was filled with *taedium vitae* and thoughts inimical to humanity. One day I read: 'What will it come to?' And before I knew it, I was a socialist; but an ideal one. Life had value for me again, for I had an ideal – the joyous struggle for the social elevation of the proletariat. This caused a powerful revolution in me. As I had in my best years (from the age of sixteen to seventeen), I again pursued an interest in art, particularly in dramatic art. I am, at the present time, writing a play and a story, and I am occupied with the grandest thoughts. I read a remark of Schlegel's concerning Sophocles, who was indebted to his physical exercise for his energy and creative power, and to music for his artistic proportions. In another place I read: 'The dramatist must, above all things, be mentally intact.' This depressed me; for my contrary sexual feelings could not arise from a perfectly normal mind.

"I thought of having myself treated hypnotically; but shame held me back. Then I said to myself that I was a weakling, indeed, to have so little confidence in myself, and began in earnest to combat my abnormal desires. At the same time, I struggled against my nervousness by leading the proper kind of life. I rowed, fenced, and was often in the open air. I was delighted when I awoke at last and seemed to be an entirely different man. When I thought of the time from my twentieth to my twenty-sixth year, it seemed to me that a strange and depressed being had been dwelling within me during those years.

"I was astonished that the handsomest rider or the trimmest waiter excited almost no interest in me; even the muscular masons had no effect on me. I was disgusted when I thought that, at one time, such men had seemed handsome to me. My self-respect has increased; I am good-natured, and my character is entirely active. Since my twentieth year my appearance has steadily improved. My appearance now corresponds perfectly with my years. Although there have been recurrences of my abnormal inclinations, to be sure, I have struggled against them energetically. I satisfy my libido only by means of natural intercourse, and I hope that, by continuing to lead a proper life, my pleasure in natural coitus will increase."

†

Case 135.

Acquired contrary sexual instinct. Marked improvement under hypnotic treatment. Mr. P., born in 1863, official in a manufactory. He came from a highly respected patrician family of Middle Germany, in which nervousness and insanity have frequently occurred.

His great-grandfather on his father's side and his sister died insane; his grandmother died of apoplexy; his father's brother died insane, and a daughter of the latter died of cerebral tuberculosis. His maternal grandmother was melancholic for years; his maternal grandfather was insane. A maternal uncle took his own life in an attack of insanity. The patient's father was very nervous. An elder brother was very neurasthenic, and had anomalies in his sex life; another was the subject of case 155 [case 180 of twelfth edition, p. 394]; a third was eccentric in conduct, and was said to be subject to fixed ideas. A sister suffered from convulsions, and another died from convulsions as a small child.

The patient was constitutionally predisposed, for at an early age he had been peculiar, irritable, irascible, and had impressed those around him as being abnormal.

His sex life appeared very early and with great intensity, and, without any seductions, was satisfied by masturbation. From his sixteenth year the prematurely developed boy visited brothels in the capital, using his permissions to go out on Sundays and holidays for that purpose. Although he took pleasure in coitus, during the week he satisfied himself with masturbation. After his twentieth year, when he became independent, the patient excessively indulged in prostitutes. As a result, he fell ill with sexual neurasthenia, becoming relatively impotent and unsatisfied in coitus, due to weakness of erection and premature ejaculation. His sexual libido then became more powerful than ever, and was satisfied by masturbation. Early in 1888 the patient made the acquaintance of a young man. "With his pleasing face, attractive manner, and beautiful form, he conquered me entirely. I wished to speak to him, and was happy just to see him. I was completely in love with him. With this, my love for women was extinguished. A man could excite me to such an extent that, for some moments, I would stammer and feel my memory fail.

"Soon after this I made the acquaintance of another very attractive gentleman, who had a decided influence on my future life. He was male-loving. I confessed to him that I no longer felt anything but aversion for the female sex, and that I was attracted to men.

"Once, when I asked my companion how he caused soldiers to surrender themselves to him, he answered that the principal thing was skill; almost any of them could be brought to it. Late in 1888, thinking of these words, I was attracted by an officer's servant, and although I was intensely excited by him, ejaculation never occurred. Because I saw that the soldier would surrender himself without trouble, I approached him. **Once I asked another soldier, who I had enticed into my bedroom, to strip off his clothes and sleep with me in bed. He did what I wanted when I asked, and we rubbed each others' penis.**

"Though I misused many persons after this success, I was never really in love, so to speak, with any of them except one. He was a very handsome young fellow of seventeen. I found his voice so attractive, and his manner so delicately proper, that I cannot forget him. In my dreams I thought only of handsome young men, and often I could not sleep at night because of sensual feeling."

Early in 1889 the patient's conduct awakened a suspicion of male love. A threatening communication frightened him, and plunged him into deep depression, so that he contemplated suicide. At the advice of the family physician, he came to the capital. Because the patient was unable to overcome his habitual desires by his own will, hypnotic treatment was undertaken. It induced only mild lethargy, and, in opposition to the seduction of former lovers, it had but little effect.

At that time the patient was lacking in earnest desire. In the face of the disgrace with relatives and the prospect of a legal examination that was actually threatening, however, matters improved somewhat. The patient was determined to attempt a cure with the author.

I found him to be a delicate, pale, very neurasthenic man, much depressed, and despairing about the future. He was without degenerative signs. He realized his perverted situation, and seemed to be willing to do anything in order to again become a decent, moral man.

He exceedingly regretted his sexual perversion, which he regarded as abnormal, but also as having been acquired. He made no attempt to conceal the fact that he could not control himself with young men, and likewise would not say that he could abstain from masturbation, to which he was driven for lack of anything better. Only a powerful, imperious will could keep him from it.

Thus far, his male love had consisted exclusively of mutual masturbation. Erections occurred only when he touched men he loved. Although ejaculation resulted early, simple embrace was not sufficient. He had never felt himself in any particular sexual role in relation to a man. Genitals and vegetative organs normal.

On April 8, 1890, in addition to treatment directed toward his neurasthenia, hypnotic suggestion was begun. Hypnosis was easily induced by simply looking at him, with verbal suggestion. After thirty seconds the patient passed into deep lethargy, with a cataleptic state of the muscles. The awakening was brought about by suggesting it at the count of three. Post-hypnotic suggestions were always successful. The intra-hypnotic suggestions were:

[1] The interdiction of masturbation.

[2] The command that male love should be regarded as disgraceful and despicable, and that it should be impossible.

[3] The command to regard only women as beautiful; to approach them, to dream of them, and to have libido and erection at the sight of them.

The sittings occurred daily. On April 14 the patient announced, with thankfulness and a kind of moral satisfaction, that he had had pleasure in coitus, and had ejaculated tardily. On April 16 he felt free of any inclination to masturbate, was attracted to women, and perfectly indifferent to men. He dreamed of female charms and coitus with women. By May 1 the patient seemed and felt himself to be sexually normal. He had become a different man mentally, full of courage and self-confidence. He had coitus with complete satisfaction, and thought that he was insured against relapse.

In a later letter Mr. P. wrote: "As was only to be expected, I find myself lastingly freed from my errors. All that remains to remind me of my unhappy time are my dreams, which, though infrequent, come from my past, and I have no power to banish them.

Indeed, they sometimes pleasantly occupy my thoughts. I still hope, however, to soon succeed in freeing myself from them absolutely, with my own will. Should I ever become weak again, the ideas you have impressed on me would, I am sure, make an energetic resistance, and I would not succumb."

On October 20, 1890, P. wrote me: "I am completely cured of masturbation, and I have no pleasure in male love. Yet complete virility does not seem to have been reestablished, notwithstanding the fact that I lead a virtuous life. Nevertheless, I feel satisfied."

✝

Case 137.

"I was born out of wedlock in 1858. I was only recently able to trace my obscure origin, and obtain knowledge of my parents; unfortunately, this knowledge is very obscure and imperfect. My father and mother were cousins. He later married and, as far as I know, had several healthy children. He died three years ago.

"I do not think that my father had contrary sexual feelings. Without knowing that he was my father, I often saw him when I was a child. He was a powerful, masculine man. It is said that he was sexually ill at the time of my birth, or before.

"Although I often saw my mother on the street, I did not know then that she was my mother. At the time of my birth she may have been about twenty-four years old. She was tall, physically quick and energetic, and had a decisive character. At the time of my birth, she was reported to have often gone about in male attire, worn short hair, smoked a long pipe, and in general to have been remarkable for her eccentric character. She was exceedingly well-educated, and is said to have been beautiful in her youth. Although she left a fortune – a considerable one, even when measured by our present ideas – she died unmarried.

"In any case, all this would point to homosexual inclinations or, at least, to abnormalities. In addition, several years before my birth, my mother took care of a little girl. This stepsister, whom I never knew, married young, but poisoned herself early in her married life for reasons unknown to me.

"I am 1.7 meters tall, measure 92 centimeters around the waist, and 102 centimeters around the hips, and I therefore think my pelvis is somewhat overdeveloped. Subcutaneous fat has always been abundant. Skeletal form is strong. Although my muscular system is well-formed, it is not well-developed, either from lack of exercise, or perhaps because of the influence of early, long-continued, and frequent indulgence in masturbation. Thus I appear stronger than I really am. Hair of head and face is normal; genital hair, somewhat thin. The upper portion of my body is nearly without hair. In all other ways my appearance is fully masculine. My gait, attitude, and voice are those of a fully developed man, and other homosexuals have often told me that they never would have suspected my passion. I served in the army, and always found pleasure in all knightly exercises – riding, fencing, swimming, etc.

"My early training was under a priest. I had few real playmates. The family life of my foster parents was faultless. In October 1861 I entered the institute. Here I indulged in my first perverse acts, which I shall describe more fully when I come to the development of my sexual life.

"I finished the *Gymnasium,* served my voluntary years in the army, studied forestry, and I am now a director of estates. During my early years my mental development was very slow. Because I did not learn to speak until my third year, the supposition that I had hydrocephalus was strengthened. From the time I began school, my mental development was abnormal. Although I learned easily, I have never been able to concentrate my activity on any particular subject. I have a great interest in art and aesthetics, but almost none in music. In my early years my character was the worst possible. Without being able to give any reason for it, there has been a complete transformation during the last twelve years. Today there is nothing I hate more than a lie, and I never speak untruth even in jest. Without being avaricious, I have become an economical manager in financial matters.

"It is enough that I look back on my past with a deep feeling of shame; and, if I could be freed from my unhappy sexual perversion, or perversity, I would justly regard myself as a true gentleman. I am kind, and always ready to be charitable to the extent of my means; I am gay-spirited, and socially regarded with favor. I have no trace of the nervous irritability that is so often noticeable in others who are like me. I am also not lacking in personal courage. There is nothing in the early period of my development that points to abnormality. To be sure, I liked to lie in bed on my abdomen as a child, and often took delight in rolling about on my abdomen in the morning, much to the amusement of my foster parents; but I cannot recall that I ever had sensual feeling at such times. I never tried often to play with girls, and I never played with dolls. Although I early heard talk about sexual matters, I never thought anything about it. In my dreams of that time there was nothing sexual, nor was there anything of that kind in my associations with boys of my own age. I think that my sex life was really first awakened after I had been seduced into mutual masturbation, in my thirteenth year, by a roommate at the institute. Although at that time ejaculation did not take place, it did, for the first time, about a year later. Nevertheless, I passionately gave myself up to the vice of masturbation. At this time the first signs of homosexual inclination were manifested. Youthful, powerful men, market-helpers, workmen and soldiers took hold in my dreams, and played an important role in my fantasies when I masturbated. I was also first shown, then, the tendency to pederasty, especially passive. Up to my fourteenth year I made frequent attempts at mutual pederasty with my seducer, but neither of us were successful in bringing about insertion. There was also, at the same time, a weak inclination for the female sex. On one occasion (about a year after my first indulgence in masturbation), I was with a prostitute, but I had neither ejaculation nor any special feeling of sensual pleasure. Thereafter, and up to my nineteenth year, I performed coitus in public houses about six times. Erection and ejaculation occurred promptly, but without marked sensual pleasure. I liked masturbation, particularly mutual masturbation, quite as much. I have never had any love for athletes. About ten years ago, while at H. (a spa), I thought I was in love with a beautiful lady of a highly respectable family; I was happy in her presence, and thought myself happy in finding my love returned. For a time this affair kept me from masturbating; I was afraid, however, that weakened by years of masturbation, I would be incapable of performing my marital duty. When we became widely separated, my feeling quickly cooled. I found that I had deceived myself; and, after about two years, I was able to hear, without jealousy, that the lady had married. My inclination for women – if I have actually ever had any – grew colder and colder. Two and a half years ago, when visiting a public house with very virile friends, I was the last to perform coitus. There was erection, but no ejaculation. Women have become a matter of indifference to me. A prostitute who acts coarsely excites my repugnance. Although I like to converse with intellectual women, particularly when they are elderly, I am often unskillful, awkward, and devoid of tact in their society. I have never been able to find any charm in woman's physical form.

"To return, however, to my perverse inclinations. When I went to H. at the age of four-teen, I lost sight of my lover and seducer. He was some years older than I, and an official. He was traveling in this capacity when I, at nineteen, met him once again on the railway. We immediately cut the journey short, and lodged together, attempting mutual pederasty. Because of pain, however, insertion was not successful. We amused ourselves in mutual masturbation. In H. I had sexual intercourse with two fellow students, but this intercourse was confined to frequent mutual masturbation because neither was inclined to pederasty. During the last year of my stay (when I was nineteen), although I had intercourse with another person, which likewise consisted of masturbation, our intercourse was more intimate. We always retired and practiced mutual masturbation in bed. I had no lover from Easter 1869 until July 1870. I practiced masturbation alone. When the war broke out, I offered myself as a volunteer, but was not accepted. At the same time a former schoolmate offered himself. He had developed into a remarkably handsome man. I had to spend one night with him in an overcrowded hotel. Though as students we had never associated sexually, he was not averse to my desire, and attempted pederasty. Although in this instance pain prevented success, **ejaculation in front of my anus** occurred in the attempt. Even now I can recall the pleasurable feeling I had from it – a feeling I had not previously known. After the war I frequently met this friend, though our intercourse was then limited to masturbation. During the following eighteen years I had only two opportunities for homosexual intercourse. The first was in the winter of 1879, when I met a handsome hussar in a railway carriage. I induced him to sleep with me at a hotel. He later confessed to me that he had previously practiced mutual masturbation with the son of a landed proprietor of his town. I could not bring him to engage in pederasty. I induced ejaculation in him, however, by **putting his penis into my mouth.** This caused me disgust rather than satisfaction. I have never tried it since; nor have I ever allowed **my penis to be inserted into another's mouth.** In 1887, again on the railway, I made the acquaintance of a sailor, and induced him to stay with me at a hotel. He said that although he had never practiced pederasty, he was ready for it. He was apparently sensually excited, inasmuch as he had an erection immediately, and performed the act with evident passion. It was the first time I had successfully performed pederasty. Although I had terrible pain, I also had indescribable pleasure.

"Because of my sojourn here, my sex life has undergone a complete change. I have learned how easy it is to find persons who, partly for money and partly from desire, yield to our inclinations. I have not been spared, however, annoying experiences with cheats. Until the end of the last year, I enjoyed male love to the full extent, particularly in passive pederasty. Since then, I have not gone beyond mutual masturbation because of a fear of venereal infection. Because I have found no one able to endure the pain, I have never practiced active pederasty.

"Generally, I seek my lovers among cavalrymen and sailors, and, eventually, among workmen, especially butchers and smiths. Robust forms, with healthy facial complexions, attract me especially. Leathern riding trousers have a particular charm for me. I have no partiality for kissing and the like. I also love large, hard, calloused hands.

"I also wish to mention that I have great control of myself under certain circumstances.

"As the director of an estate, I lived in a large house. My personal servant was a very handsome young man who had served in the hussars. I once spoke in general terms with him on the subject, and found that he could not be approached. Then, although for years I lived in close intimacy with him, and enjoyed his beauty, I never touched him. To this day, I think he knows nothing of my passion. Likewise, two and a half years ago, in C., I made the acquaintance of a sailor, who is still regarded by me and my acquaintances as one of the handsomest men we know. He had been absent for more than two years when I invited him to visit me a few weeks ago. I knew how to arrange matters so that we slept in the same room, and I burned with desire to be nearer to him. First, however, I sounded him out in confidential talk; and, when I found that he despised everything connected with male love, I did not have the heart to approach him more closely. For weeks we slept in the same room, and I took constant delight in his divine form (I was, in fact, sexually excited at first). Although I even bathed with him, in the Roman manner, in order to see his beautiful form naked, he never learned anything of my passion. I still have an ideal, platonic relation with this young man who, for one of his position, has an unusual education and a fine talent for poetry.

"Until my thirty-eighth year I did not have a clear understanding of my condition. I always thought that I had become averse to women because of early and frequent masturbation, and I always hoped that, when the right woman came along, I would find pleasure in her and thus be able to abandon masturbation. It was after making the acquaintance of others suffering and feeling like myself, however, that I first came to fully understand my condition. Although at first I was frightened, I later came to look upon my fate as something independent of myself. I also made no further effort to resist temptation.

"Two or three weeks ago *Psychopathia Sexualis* fell into my hands. The work has made an unexpectedly deep impression on me. At first I read the work with an interest that was undoubtedly lascivious. I was uncommonly excited by, for example, the description of the cultivation of *mujerados.* The thought of a young, powerful man being emasculated in this manner so that later he could be used for pederasty by a whole tribe of wild, powerful, and sensual Indians, excited me to the point that I masturbated five times during the next two days, fantasizing myself as a presumptive *mujerado*. The farther I read in the book, however, the more I saw its moral earnestness, the more I felt disgust with my condition, and the more I saw that I must do everything possible to bring about a change in my condition. When I had finished the book, I was determined to seek assistance from its author.

"The reading of this work has had an undeniable effect. Since then I have masturbated only twice, and have practiced masturbation with cavalrymen only twice. In each instance I have had less real pleasure and satisfaction than before, and have always had the feeling: 'Ah, if only I could be free from it!' Nevertheless, even now I confess that I immediately have erections in the society of handsome soldiers.

"In conclusion, I should add that in spite of masturbation, or, perhaps, because of it, I have never had pollutions. The ejaculation of semen, which has usually only consisted of a few drops, only takes place after prolonged friction. Ejaculation takes place quickly, and is more abundant if I have not masturbated for a long time. About twelve years ago Hansen tried in vain to hypnotize me."

In the spring of 1891 the writer of the foregoing autobiography visited me, declaring that he could live no longer in his condition; he looked to hypnotic treatment as the only hope of salvation, inasmuch as he lacked the strength to resist his impulse to masturbation and satisfaction with persons of his own sex. He felt like a pariah; like an unnatural man; like one outside the laws of nature and society, and in danger of criminal prosecution. Although he felt moral repugnance when performing the act with a man, the sight of a handsome soldier electrified him. For years he had not had the slightest physical (or mental) sympathy with women.

The patient exactly resembled, both physically and mentally, the person described in his autobiography. His head was exquisitely hydrocephalic, as well as plagiocephalic. Attempts at hypnosis met with difficulties at first. Only by Braid's method, with the help of a little chloroform, was deep lethargy attained at the third sitting. From that time, simply looking at a shining object was sufficient. Hypnotic suggestions were given to the patient to achieve: [1] the avoidance of masturbation; [2] the removal of homosexual feelings; and [3] the inclination for women only, with subsequent virility and pleasure from such heterosexual intercourse. Masturbation was indulged in only once; after the eighth sitting the patient dreamed of a woman.

Although, after the fourteenth sitting, the patient had to return to his home because of pressing business, he declared that he was quite free from any inclination to masturbate or indulge in male love. He also stated, however, that he was by no means absolutely free from his partiality for men. He felt a returning interest in the female sex, and ultimately hoped to be freed from his unhappy condition by continuance of the treatment.

Case 138.

Psychic hermaphroditism. Mr. von P., aged twenty-five, single; came from a neuropathic family. As a child he had convulsions. He recovered, but remained weak, emotional, and irritable. No severe illnesses. Sexuality was manifested before his tenth year. His earliest memory concerning it was of having had lascivious feelings in the company of the servants of the house. When he was older, he had sensual dreams involving intercourse with men. In circuses, only the male performers interested him.

Youthful, powerful men were most enticing to him. He often could scarcely resist the longing to fall on their necks and kiss them. Recently, simply the touching of such persons had become sufficient to give him pleasure and induce ejaculation. Fortunately, he had thus far resisted the impulse to engage in "affairs" with men. The patient was a psychic hermaphrodite, insofar as he was not insensitive to the charms of women, and found men more pleasing than women. In fact, however, feminine nudity had never pleased him, and he could remember only dreaming once of coitus with a woman.

Because of his great sexual desire, and because he was ashamed to give himself up to men, he began to have sexual intercourse with women after his twentieth year. Afterward, although he had rarely indulged in manual masturbation, he had often indulged in mental masturbation, during which the forms of handsome men floated through his fantasies.

He had coitus with success, but without pleasure or sensual feeling. Circumstances forced him to abstain from his twenty-second until his twenty-fourth year. This abstinence was painful, and occasionally he relieved himself by mental masturbation.

When he again had an opportunity to engage in coitus a year ago, he noticed a failure of libido for women, imperfect erection, and premature ejaculation. Finally he gave up coitus, at which time libido for men was manifested.

Irritable weakness of the ejaculatory center caused a circumstance in which the mere touch of a sympathetic man was sufficient to induce ejaculation.

The patient was an only child. The circumstances of his family demanded that he marry. He justly hesitated, thought he was mentally impotent, and asked for advice and help.

He pointed out that, to help him, his feeling for men had to be eradicated.

The patient's appearance was, in all respects, masculine. His head was slightly hydro-cephalic and rhombic. Abundant growth of beard. Genitals normal; cremasteric reflex could not be excited. No manifestations of neurasthenia. Neuropathic eyes. Pollutions infrequent. Erections occurred only as a result of contact with men.

On July 16, 1889, hypnotic suggestion, after Bernheim's method, began. Deep lethargy was induced at the beginning of the third sitting.

Suggestions: "You no longer have any desire for men. Only woman is beautiful and desir-able. You will love a woman, marry, be happy, and make her happy. You are fully potent; you feel that already."

In daily hypnosis, which never went beyond lethargy, the patient accepted the sugges-tions. On July 24 he announced that he had had pleasure in coitus, and that male servants no longer interested him. At the same time, he still found men more beautiful than women. On August 1, 1889, it was necessary to discontinue treatment. Result: Completely potent; complete indifference for men, but also for women.

The same treatment met with decided success in a case of psychosexual hermaph-roditism, reported by me in volume 1 of the *Internat. Zentralblatt für die Physiol. u. Path. der Harn- und Sexualorgane.*

†

Case 140.

Psychic hermaphroditism; improvement with hypnotic treatment. Mr. von K., aged twenty-three; from a distinguished family; mentally well-endowed; scrofulous as a child. His father was said to have been dissipated. His father's brother was said to have been subject to contrary sexuality.

The patient stated that he had a peculiar inclination for male persons when he was only seven years old, particularly for coachmen and servants who had mustaches. He experienced a peculiar delightful sensation when he pressed himself against such persons.

The patient entered the cadet corps early, where he was seduced into mutual masturbation. He also learned **imitation coitus between a man's thighs.** At the age of seventeen he had coitus with a prostitute for the first time. Although he performed the act perfectly, he did not enjoy it in the slightest. He learned that this kind of gratification either amounted to nothing, or that he had to be different from other young men.

Nevertheless, he had coitus often, and subsequently contracted gonorrhea. After this he experienced an increasing aversion for the female sex, and indulged in coitus less and less frequently. It only occurred, in fact, when he was burdened with intense libido and lacked the opportunity to engage in intercourse with men. His inclination for men predominated more and more, and he was attracted exclusively by those who were handsomely formed, and who had as little beard as possible. He descended to the most revolting practices – fellatio, active and passive pederasty.

The patient was deeply ashamed of such depravity, and constantly endeavored to improve his situation by means of coitus with women. He came to the despairing conclusion, however, that his moral strength was insufficient, he was indifferent about intercourse with women (or it was repugnant to him), and he was created for sexual intercourse with persons of his own sex only. In fact, he had always dreamed of men, and never of women. Furthermore, he had done this at a time when he had no suspicion of the difference between the sexes.

The patient came for consultation because he saw that he was jeopardizing the happiness of his whole life, and recognized the unnaturalness and immorality of his sexual life. He did not regard his condition as hopeless, for he had no horror of women, and three weeks previously he had successful coitus with one, although it was devoid of pleasure and mental satisfaction. He was certain that he was really created to love men; but, due to acquired neurasthenia, he no longer experienced the pleasure he had once enjoyed in the sexual act with a man. He had given up his position as an officer, because the soldiers excited him sexually to the point that he feared he would perhaps compromise himself.

The patient was devoid of degenerative signs. His appearance was perfectly masculine, and his genitals were normal. Examination of his semen revealed an abundance of spermatozoa. His penis was large and well-developed, with abundant growth of hair on his genitals, as well as on the rest of his body. Although the patient had masculine tastes, he had never been partial to drinking and smoking. A neuropathic gaze was all that pointed to a nervous condition.

He stated that in his sexual acts with men he had typically felt as a man would feel, and had only occasionally felt as a woman would feel.

An attempt at hypnosis led to lethargy with a cataleptic condition of the muscles, and the opportunity was used to impart suitable suggestions.

After the fourth sitting he expressed satisfaction, and was astonished that men no longer made an impression on him. He wanted to try his fortune with women, but was afraid that he was impotent.

After the sixth sitting, without advice, he attempted coitus with a woman. Although his libido was very great, he lost it, with his erection, during the act.

After the ninth sitting the patient was forced to discontinue treatment because of business that called him home. He was satisfied, inasmuch as he felt indifferent and capable of resisting men. He felt sure that he would not relapse into his former vices. At the same time, however, he had not the slightest interest in the female sex.

Case 141.

Mr. X., aged thirty-one, chemist; came from a neuropathic family. Since childhood he had been nervous, emotional, apprehensive, and afflicted with migraines. He remembered distinctly that, as a very small boy, he experienced a lustful feeling at the sight of half-naked men in the workshop at his father's house, and felt drawn to them. When he began school, he felt the same way toward his companions. At the age of eleven, without instruction, he began to masturbate, during which he thought of his comrades. Later there were enthusiastic friendships. His sex life gained the upper hand. As he grew up, women also interested him; his chief interest, however, was for men in the higher circles of society. He felt that this inclination was abnormal, and sought the acquaintance of prostitutes. He often had coitus, but never with any real pleasure. Thus he became more and more inclined to contrary sexuality, practicing mutual masturbation and **coitus between a man's thighs.** He occasionally gave himself up to passive pederasty, which he soon abandoned because of the pain it caused him.

He asserted that he felt perfectly masculine, and had never had female inclinations. Skeleton and attitude perfectly masculine; strabismus; abundant beard; genitals entirely normal. No aversion to the female sex. Occasional coitus with prostitutes, but without satisfaction. The patient felt exceedingly unhappy, and clearly recognized his abnormal position. He wished to be freed from his homosexual inclination at any price, and become suitable for marriage. "It is terrible to have to constantly act a farce." At the first attempt at hypnosis, after Bernheim's method, the patient passed into a state of deep lethargy. He proved to be very susceptible to suggestion, and suitable suggestions were imparted. After the fourth sitting, he stated, with gratitude, that he had become indifferent to men, and that he was beginning to have pleasure in coitus. Because he was limited to prostitutes, however, he did not feel mentally satisfied. After the fourteenth sitting, he declared that he required no more treatment. He was in love with a young lady, and wanted to marry. He asked for her hand, and was refused. Soon after, while he was on a journey in Italy, men interested him again. He had a relapse, and asked for further treatment. A few sittings reestablished the previous status quo.

Case 142.

Psychic hermaphroditism; successful treatment by hypnotic suggestion. Mr. von Z., aged twenty-nine. He asserted that he came from healthy grandparents, a healthy father, but a nervous mother. An only child, he was petted by his mother. At the age of eight he was powerfully excited sexually by a male servant, who showed him pornographic pictures as well as his penis.

At twelve years old, Z. fell in love with his tutor. The imagined naked form of this man appeared before him as he was going to sleep at night. He thought of himself in a female role in relation to him, and imagined how he would marry him some day.

At the age of thirteen, at a private ball, his fancy was excited by a young governess. At fifteen, he fell in love with a young lady. Although he remained very excitable sexually, it was, thereafter, exclusively in regard to men pleasing to him. Masturbation was not practiced.

At the age of twenty the patient became neurasthenic (due to abstinence?). He then attempted coitus, but was not successful. On the other hand, he experienced intense desire on the occasion of seeing a naked man in a steambath. The man noticed his excitement, approached him, and performed masturbation on him, giving the patient intense pleasure. He felt powerfully attracted to this man, and subsequently allowed him to repeat the act. There were, in the meantime, attempts at coitus with females, which always ended in a fiasco. The patient was much troubled by this and consulted physicians, who explained his impotence as due to nervousness that would soon pass.

Until his twenty-fifth year his sexual indulgence consisted of masturbation by the beloved man about once a month. He then, at last, felt attracted to a woman, a young peasant girl. She would not accede to his wishes. Because his lover was also unattainable, the patient began to masturbate alone. With this, his neurasthenia increased. For this reason he was unable to finish his studies; he became shy, dysthymic, abulic, and vainly tried cures at various hydropathic establishments. Because of continued severe (cerebro-spinal) neurasthenia, the patient came to me for advice in the latter part of February 1890.

He was a tall, slim man, of aristocratic and decidedly masculine manners. Neuropathic appearance; large ears, the lobes of which ran into and lost themselves in the skin of the cheeks. Genitals perfectly normal. The usual picture of cerebro-spinal neurasthenia of moderate degree. Great depression; complaint of being dissatisfied with life, even to *taedium vitae*; he was pained by his sexual anomaly, especially because he was urged by his family to marry.

He was interested in women only mentally, not physically. Sexually, his only interest was in men of distinction. His dreams had never been about persons of the opposite sex, but only about those of his own sex. In these lascivious dreams he had always seen himself in the role of a woman.

The most refined woman had never been able to induce erection or even libido in him.

His sexual intercourse with men had consisted of passive or mutual masturbation. He had practiced solitary masturbation only infrequently and for lack of anything better. During the last five months he had abstained, and had not engaged in male intercourse since August 1889.

An attempt at hypnosis, after Bernheim's method, failed; prolonged stroking of the brow induced deep lethargy, with catalepsy.

This method was used in order to carry out suggestive treatment of this patient, who was so worthy of compassion. The hypnotic state was always the same; he could not be brought into a state of somnambulism.

At the third sitting the patient was given these suggestions: forever despise masturbation and male love; find women beautiful, and dream of them.

After the sixth sitting (March 10) a moral transformation took place in his mind. The patient became quieter, felt more free, occasionally dreamt of women exclusively, finding that he had become indifferent to men. He gratefully stated that he had no more inclination to engage in masturbation. Although he approached women, he noticed that he did not have the least attraction to them.

On March 19, business called the patient home; treatment had to be discontinued.

On May 17, 1890, the patient returned for treatment. He asserted that he had not masturbated in the interval, and that he had resisted his inclination toward men. He had also not dreamed of men, and had twice dreamed of women, though only platonically. His cerebral asthenia (due to abstinence?) had increased. He apparently now suffered from the absence of mental and sensual satisfaction of his sex life, inasmuch as homosexual love and masturbation had become impossible for him, and intercourse with women was denied him. The patient was thus painfully depressed, to the extent of *taedium vitae.*

He was then subjected to anti-neurasthenic treatment (hydrotherapeutic and electro-therapeutic), and the treatment by hypnosis was resumed. Only after ten weeks of painstaking treatment did the neurasthenic symptoms disappear. Parallel to this, there was a progressive change in his mental personality.

The patient was gratified to note that he grew stronger, and that his sexual life no longer played a dominating part. Although he felt more drawn toward men than women, he easily resisted homosexual desires. His boudoir became a workroom; instead of adornment and frivolous reading, he entertained himself with walks in the mountains and forests. Because of the danger of a fiasco, initiative in heterosexual attempts was left to the patient.

It was not until the fourteenth week of treatment that the patient made an attempt. It was perfectly successful. The patient became happy, sound in body and mind, expressed the best hope for his future, and even had thoughts of marriage.

He experienced increasing pleasure in normal sexual intercourse; occasionally he had lascivious dreams of women, and he no longer dreamed of men.

The patient stopped treatment at the end of September. He felt perfectly normal in heterosexual intercourse, was devoid of neurasthenia, and had thoughts of marriage. Yet he freely confessed that he still always had erections at the sight of a naked, handsome man, although he could easily resist the desires that arose, and in dreams had *"relations avec la femme"* exclusively.

I saw the patient again in April 1891, and he was in the best of health. He regarded his sex life as perfectly normal, for he regularly had coitus with pleasure and full virility, dreamed only of women, and had no inclination to masturbate. Nevertheless, he made the interesting confession that frequently, after sex, he still had a temporary *"gout pour l'homme"* ("taste for men"), which he could easily control. He thought he was lastingly cured, and was occupied with thoughts of marriage.

Case 143.

Congenital contrary sexual feeling. Successful removal of homosexual feelings by suggestion. L., doctor of philosophy, aged thirty-four, German; consulted with me in the spring of 1888 because of perversion of his sex life, and asked if he could be freed from it by means of hypnotic treatment.

Patient came from a healthy mother, in whose family, for generations, there had been neither insanity nor nervous disease. He closely resembled his father mentally, as did his only brother. His brother was very sensual, psychically abnormal, and given to overindulgence in drink.

His father was a neuropathic, eccentric man. Although nothing was known of any abnormal sexual manifestations in him, he had a tendency to overindulge in alcohol, as did all his brothers.

This vice seemed to have been inherited from his mother (the grandmother of the patient), who was a notorious drinker. The father of this woman (the great-grandfather of the patient) was also a great drinker. No other ancestral history was obtainable.

Patient stated that from childhood he was nervous and easily excited. He learned very easily, and had a talent for languages. He was always interested in art, particularly in music and poetry. His education was excellent, and given at home. When he was thirteen, his father told him that he should never touch his genitals, for it was wrong to do so, and might bring unhappiness.

Occasionally his father showed him pictures of syphilitic diseased conditions, etc., in an anatomical museum, and the patient was disgusted and frightened. He believed that his later fear of sexual intercourse with women was partly nourished by this early erroneous teaching.

The patient, however, thought that the principal cause of his sexual perversion was to be found in a defect of organization. As a small boy, he had a silly enthusiasm for companions. He also remembered that he had a desire only for girlish games at that time, and preferred the society of girls. As a boy, he had a passion for crocheting and embroidering. At fourteen he was still without any sexual knowledge, and fell into the hands of a pederast. He ran away, frightened, when he learned what was going to be done with him. At fifteen, a sympathetic companion would lay his head in the patient's lap. This gave the patient a peculiar pleasurable feeling, but he did not know why. At sixteen he had his first erections – at the sight of men.

At twenty he first learned that his sexual condition was perverse, and recognized the fact that what he had taken for friendship was love. He was much frightened and pained by the discovery. His sympathies were directed toward young men of the upper class who were handsomely formed and of pleasing appearance.

The society of ladies had no effect on him. He was never attracted by the charms of the opposite sex. In his fifteenth year, however, he had a sensual dream, in which he imagined a girl with an elegant figure sat opposite him on a sofa.

In the theatre, although he admired the art of the actresses, it was the actors who excited his real interest.

Drinking and smoking had always been repugnant to him. He had no interest for hunting, gymnastics, and other masculine occupations. He did not enter the army, because his general physical weakness precluded it.

The patient had little sexual desire. He had never had any impulse to satisfy himself with persons of his own sex. Some years ago, when he first tried to embrace a man lovingly, he had a powerful erection and became greatly excited. He was able, however, to control himself and repel his lover. He thereafter always avoided such attempts. He only seldom became powerfully excited sexually, and even then was not driven to satisfy himself. He was never given to masturbation. During the establishment of puberty, the patient had frequent dreams with pollutions, but these were not induced by erotic fantasies of any kind.

Although for a lengthy period, some years ago, the embrace of a sympathetic man always induced ejaculation, this condition of irritable weakness disappeared. The patient had always had a desire for marriage and a family. As the years passed, however, he became anxious because of his conviction that the anticipated inclination toward females would never come. As it then became more and more clear to him that he was abnormal, he began to have fears about his virility and his future happiness in life.

In order to test the matter, he sought a brothel. He found a prostitute of beautiful form. He attempted to find out if he was virile; the woman did all she could, but it was in vain. There was no erection and, ashamed, he withdrew. New attempts, under the most favorable circumstances, were likewise failures, though the patient brought his imagination to his aid, and pictured himself embracing a man instead of a woman.

He then realized that his ideal of consummating marriage was impossible. He saw himself as unfortunate, and was dissatisfied with life. He was also forced to see himself as morally low, inasmuch as he could not overcome his inclination for his own sex, and because the friendship he felt toward the respectable men of his circle was degraded by sexual feelings. In his consultation with me, the patient was unending in describing his painful situation. His ideal was marriage. He longed for it for purely ethical reasons. He thought of it as something holy. The begetting of children, however, the sexual act, was extremely repugnant to him. At the same time, he saw that he could not really marry without being potent. Would not hypnotic suggestion exercise a favorable influence on his sexual life? He did not have the energy of a man with a normal sexual condition. He seemed to himself to be all wrong. He would endure all – even poverty and misery – in exchange for a normal sexual inclination.

When the patient was gently told of the deep congenital and constitutional significance of his sexual anomaly, and shown that the creation of a normal sexual condition was therefore doubtful, he thought that he would be satisfied remaining in his condition. He wished to know, however, whether it would be possible to eradicate his inclination for men without attempting to create an equivalent for women; and if, in hypnosis, it could be suggested to him that, in the future, men be a matter of indifference to him, and that he no longer be excited sexually in intercourse with his friends. Such a result would significantly elevate his moral feeling, and make him satisfied and unembarrassed in social relations with his friends.

Although the possibility of such suggestive removal of feelings by hypnosis could not be denied, he doubted that he could be hypnotized, because the hypnoscope had previously had no effect upon him.

Out of pity and scientific interest, I decided to make an immediate attempt at hypnosis, after Bernheim's method.

The patient easily passed into a state of deep lethargy and, in a drawling voice, repeated the following suggestion: "I feel that, from this time, I am sexually indifferent to men, and that I am as sexually indifferent to a man as I am to a woman."

At the previously suggested count of three, the patient came to himself, as if out of a deep sleep, and immediately performed the post-hypnotic suggestion to open the door of the stove. He said that although he had not lost consciousness entirely, he had felt paralyzed and without will, with a peculiar creeping sensation in all his limbs.

After five days the patient came again. His manner had changed, and he joyfully said that he felt like a different man. His energy and willpower – the loss of which he had felt so keenly – had returned. He now felt entirely unembarrassed toward men, and had a new joy in living.

He was then hypnotized on each of the following seven days. Although the hypnosis was no longer as deep as at first, the suggestion was always accepted and repeated. He was quite profoundly influenced, however, for when the suggestion was given, he slept on, in a state of lethargy, for ten minutes, and had to be awakened by suggestion. This always occurred as if from a deep sleep – slowly, and through a stage of somnolence.

After the eighth sitting, the patient found himself well and happy, and in possession of full self-confidence. He had the feeling and the evidence that men had no influence on him.

He then thought he could dispense with hypnotic treatment and, gratefully taking his leave, he promised that he would come again should the influence of the suggestion fade. I have since then heard nothing more of this interesting patient, and have reason to hope that he remains improved.

The patient was, in all respects, of masculine appearance; beard abundant. Physically he presented nothing remarkable, with the exception of slight neurasthenic symptoms. Genitals normal (personal case, *Internat. Zentralblatt,* etc., vol. 1, no. 1).

Case 144.

X., aged thirty-three; single; tall. Of small endowment mentally; from a tainted family. His paternal grandfather died at thirty-four from a mental disease that was said to have developed as a result of masturbation and spermatorrhea. His father and brother suffered from disturbances of the sexual functions. There was insanity in the mother's family; other branches of the family were noted for their irritable and eccentric character.

The patient had too small a head, a retreating brow, abnormal ears, sparse growth of hair, and a hernia that was probably congenital. Genitals large and normally developed.

Great impressionability; neuropathic constitution; occasional *taedium vitae.* For several years he had peculiar, imperative ideas: that he was a locomotive; a horse; a velocipede;

and had to act accordingly. Congenital contrary sexual feeling from his earliest youth. *Horror feminae;* sexual inclination toward boys; satisfaction by sensual contact and, for lack of anything better, masturbation. One day he had an affair with a boy dressed in gray, which made a deep impression on him. Afterward, while masturbating, the image of the boy had entered his mind, and he could not see gray clothes without having powerful erections. Although on the advice of physicians he attempted coitus with women, he was cold and impotent, notwithstanding the assistance of memory-pictures of the boy dressed in gray. He finally gave up his efforts.

March 27, first hypnotic sitting. Small result. He resisted, and said his fantasy kept him from going to sleep.

In a further series of sittings in which he declared that he experienced unfavorable effects, he was more excited, and was troubled by imperative ideas and the desire to masturbate. He made fun of the physician and hypnotism, and offered much resistance, inasmuch as he expressed that hypnotism was good for nothing and only made people crazy.

Gradually, however, it became possible to induce somnambulism. After twenty-five sittings the patient confessed that he was better, and that he was less troubled with imperative ideas and masturbation. The sittings were repeated every week or two. At the end of the treatment, though the patient felt mentally and morally well, and had ceased to masturbate, he was indifferent toward the opposite sex (Dr. Ladame, *Revue de l'hypnotisme,* September 1, 1889).

In the two foregoing cases there was successful suggestive removal of homosexual feelings. This result means a great improvement for such unfortunate individuals, as case 143 shows, in that it protects them from shame and the law. An entirely different and phenomenal result is presented by the following case, reported by Dr. Schrenk-Notzing in the *Wiener internat. klin. Rundschau,* October 6, 1889, no. 40, which is a case of effemination. Although it discloses a new method of treating homosexuals, it is necessary to guard against illusions. Only when hypnosis can be deepened to somnambulism are decided and lasting results to be expected:

Case 145.

Congenital contrary sexual instinct improved by hypnotic suggestion. R., official, aged twenty-eight. On January 20, 1888, he sought medical advice. He was the brother of the patient who is the subject of case 135, and as such, came from a badly tainted family (see above, p. 596). He confessed toward the end of treatment that he was the author of the autobiography published as case 83 in the fifth edition of this work, which is reproduced here:

"In brief, my abnormality consists of this; in sexual relations I feel myself to be completely feminine. In sexual acts and fantasies from my earliest youth, I have always had before my eyes only images of masculine beings and masculine genitals.

"I found nothing peculiar in this until I went to the university (I had never spoken with others about my fantasies while at the *Gymnasium;* instead, I lived a silent and retired life).

"It struck me while at the university that female persons did not make the slightest impression upon me. I have since then attempted coitus in houses of prostitution, etc.; I have also attempted to merely obtain an erection with women; always, however, in vain.

"As soon as I was alone in a room with a woman, erection ceased immediately. Although at first I considered it impotence, I was, at the same time, so sexually excited that I had to masturbate several times during the day in order to sleep.

"The development of my feelings toward the masculine sex, however, has been quite different, and has grown stronger every year. These feelings first expressed themselves in extraordinary, enthusiastic friendship for certain persons; under whose windows I would wait at night for hours; whom in all possible ways I would try to meet on the streets; and with whom I sought to come in contact. I wrote such persons the most passionate letters; I was shy, however, about expressing my feelings too plainly. Later, after my twentieth year, I came to understand the essential nature of my inclinations; particularly from the sensual pleasure I experienced as soon as I came in direct contact with any of these friends. These persons were all finely built men, with dark hair and eyes. I have never had my feelings excited by boys. Real pederasty is absolutely incomprehensible to me. About this time (twenty-second to twenty-third year) the circle of my beloved friends grew more and more extensive. I can now scarcely see a handsome man on the street without the wish to possess him becoming excited in me. I especially love persons of the lower classes, whose powerful forms attract me – soldiers, policemen, car drivers, etc. –

i.e., all those who wear uniforms. If one of these men returns my look, I feel a kind of thrill go through my whole body. I am especially excitable in the evening, when the heavy tread of a soldier is enough to induce the most powerful erections. I take a peculiar pleasure in following such persons and looking at them. As soon as I learn that they are married, or that they consort with girls, my excitement frequently ceases.

"A few months ago I was able to control my inclinations so that they were not directly noticeable. About this time I followed and spoke to a soldier who seemed likely to acquiesce to my desire. For money he was ready for anything. I was filled at once with a most violent longing to embrace and kiss him, and the danger of being noticed did not deter me from doing so. He had scarcely grasped my genitals when ejaculation followed. I had finally attained, with this meeting, the long-desired goal of my life. From this time, knowing that my whole nature would find its happiness and satisfaction, I gave myself entirely to the effort of finding a person whom I could love, and from whom I would never part. I do not experience the slightest twinge of conscience because of my actions.

"In quiet moments, of course, I very well appreciate the difference between my way of thinking and the way of the world. Also, as a lawyer, I naturally recognize the dangers of a relation of the kind I desire. As long as my entire nature does not change, however, I shall not be able to give up the opportunities offered me. Nevertheless, I would be willing to undergo any cure to be freed from my abnormal condition.

"I recognize my feminine feeling in the fact that any sensual idea in connection with a woman must be forced and seems unnatural to me, among other things. I am also sure that my respect for a woman (I move a great deal in the society of ladies, and enjoy it) would immediately change to repugnance if I were to notice in her any sensual inclination toward me. In my dreams and sensual fantasies of men, their faces are always toward mine. Mustaches, abundance of hair, and even dirt, seem to be especially enticing. My greatest delight would be to have a powerful man, undressed, take me in his arms with a force I could not resist. I always think of myself in a passive role in such situations, and have to force my feelings in order to think of myself in any other position. In this way I am truly feminine. As great as my desire may be to approach certain persons, my struggle to hide it is just as great. It is hardly necessary to say that I view my condition with reference to society as absolutely desperate, and life would scarcely be endurable if I did not have the hope of finding a being who could understand me. I feel that sexual commerce with a man is the only means of successfully combating my impulse to masturbate. Though this has a very bad effect on me, I cannot constantly keep myself from it, because I will then be even more weakened by pollutions at night and persistent erections during the day, as I have often discovered.

"Up to this time I have only truly loved two men. Both were officers, remarkably endowed mentally, handsomely and gracefully formed, with dark skin and eyes. I became acquainted with the first at the university. I was madly in love with him, and suffered unspeakably because of his indifference. I spent nights under his window, simply to be near him. I was in despair when he was officially transferred.

"I became acquainted soon afterward with an officer who resembled him, and who likewise enchained me at first sight. I sought every opportunity to meet him, spending the day in the streets and in places where I hoped to catch a glimpse of him. I was aware of how the blood came into my face when, unsuspected, I saw him. When I watched him be friendly with others, I could scarcely contain my jealousy. When I sat near him, I was impelled to touch him. I could barely conceal my excitement when I touched his knee or thigh. I never ventured, however, to express my feelings to him, because I was convinced from his conduct that he would not understand or share them.

"I am twenty-seven years old, of medium height, well-developed, and would be considered handsome. My chest is somewhat narrow, my hands and feet are small, and my voice is weak. I think I am well-endowed mentally, inasmuch as I passed the state examination with distinction, speak several languages, and am a good painter.

"In my calling I am considered industrious and conscientious. My acquaintances think me cold and peculiar. I do not smoke, do not play games, and cannot sing or whistle. My gait, like my voice, is somewhat affected. I have a taste for elegance, jewelry, sweetmeats and perfumes, and I prefer the society of ladies."

From Dr. Schrenk-Notzing's notes of the case, it was further learned that social and criminal deterrents on the one hand, and uncontrollable desire for his own sex on the other, caused violent mental struggles, making life unendurable. For this reason the patient confided in the physician. On January 22, 1889, hypnotic treatment with suggestion, after the method of Nancy, was begun. It gradually became possible to induce somnambulism.

Suggestions were made that urged an indifference to men, an ability to resist them, and an increase of interest in women. Masturbation was thus forbidden, and women substituted for men in lascivious dreams. After a few sittings, pleasure at the sight of women was induced. At the seventh sitting, successful coitus was suggested; this was subsequently fulfilled.

During the next three months, under the influence of occasional hypnotic suggestions, the patient remained in the full possession of normal sexual functions. On April 22, 1889, a relapse was induced by a companion. At the next sitting, he had remorse and shame that was then expiated by coitus with a woman in the presence of his seducer.

The patient complained that coitus with women who were below him in class did not satisfy his aesthetic feelings. He hoped to find satisfaction in a happy marriage. After forty-five sittings the patient considered himself cured (May 2, 1889). Treatment ceased. Some weeks later he became engaged to a young lady, and after six months he presented himself again as a happy bridegroom. In his happiness with his wife, he thought he had a sure preventive against relapse.

The author emphasized that the hypnotic treatment had had no injurious collateral effect, and left undecided the question of the cure's permanence, given R.'s bad heredity. He expressed the conviction, however, that in the case of relapse, renewed hypnotic treatment would not be contraindicated.

Because the incredible result of this case, as well as its further course, interested me exceedingly, I wrote to the author and requested information concerning his patient.

Dr. Schrenk-Notzing very kindly placed at my disposal the following letter, received from the patient in January 1890:

"By means of suggestive treatment given me by Baron Schrenk-Notzing, I became possessed for the first time of a psychic condition that permitted me to have intercourse with a woman. Up to that time, in spite of repeated efforts, I had been unable to do this successfully.

"Because my aesthetic needs were unsatisfied by intercourse with prostitutes, I thought to find my real salvation in matrimony. A previous friendly inclination toward a lady I knew in my youth offered me the opportunity, all the more because I believed that she alone would be in a position to awaken feelings for the opposite sex that had been absolutely foreign to me. Her character – i.e., our harmony – is in such accord with my inclinations that I am fully convinced I shall also find complete psychic satisfaction. This conviction has not changed during the eight months of our engagement.

"I intend to be married in about four weeks.

"As far as my position toward my own sex is concerned, my power of resistance – and this is the lasting positive result of this treatment – is absolutely changed in degree. While it had previously been impossible for me to overcome an intense sexual excitation upon seeing a finely formed streetcar driver, I am now without sexual excitement when in the company of my former lovers. I must add, however, that now, as before, I find in their society a certain attraction, though it does not compare with my earlier passion.

"In addition, I have refused repeated persuasions to indulge in sexual intercourse with men without expending much force in resistance – persuasions that I would have previously been unable to resist. Indeed, it is a feeling of compassion for my former lovers – lovers who have proven their passionate devotion to me – that keeps me from directly repulsing them. My action seems to be due to a feeling of duty rather than one of inner need.

"I have not consorted with prostitutes since the conclusion of treatment. This circumstance, as well as the numerous letters and persuasions from my former lover, may well be the reason why I have allowed him to persuade me to have sexual intercourse on three or four occasions in the eight months that have elapsed. At these times I have always been conscious of being a complete master of myself, as compared with my earlier passionate condition in similar situations, as the violent reproaches of my friend have convinced me. *I always feel a certain unconquerable repugnance, which cannot be based on moral grounds, but which, I believe, must be attributed to the treatment.* I no longer feel a love for him as I did before. Besides, since the treatment, I have sought no opportunities for sexual intercourse with men, and I feel no need for it. Previously, however, not a day passed in which I did not feel impelled to engage in homosexual intercourse, to the point that at times I was unable to think of anything else. Awake or dreaming, ideas of sexual content are now very infrequent.

"I believe that my marriage (which will take place in a few weeks), as well as the much-desired change of place bound to it, will entirely remove the residuum of my earlier condition. I conclude these lines with the honest assurance that I am, subjectively, another man, and that this change has restored the mental equilibrium that was previously absent."

The foregoing words (which Dr. Schrenk-Notzing completed with the patient's verbal statement that he had not since practiced masturbation) are brilliant proof of the lasting effect of post-hypnotic suggestion. I consider the heterosexual instinct of the patient to be the artificial creation of his excellent physician. The patient himself seemed to recognize this, inasmuch as he spoke of a repugnance that "cannot be based on moral grounds, but must be attributed to the treatment."

The further fate of this interesting patient can be learned from the following letter, kindly submitted by Dr. Schrenk-Notzing:

"Honored Sir: Having been home for a few days after my wedding journey, I wish to send you a short report of my present condition. During the week before my wedding I was greatly excited, because I feared that I would be unable to perform certain duties. The impelling thoughts of my friend, who at any price wished for another meeting with me, had no effect. We had not seen each other since I last heard from you. I had been much troubled, however, by the thought that my marriage was doomed to be unhappy. I now have no anxiety. Success was difficult on the first night, of course, because it was difficult to induce sexual excitation in myself. On the following night and since, however, the influences needed for a normal man, I believe, would have been sufficient for me. I am also convinced that the harmony between us, which, of course, is mentally of long standing, will become more and more complete. A relapse to the former condition seems impossible. Significant, perhaps, in regard to my present condition is that although I dreamed one night of my former lover, the dream was not sensual, and did not excite me sensually.

"I am satisfied with my present circumstances. I am, of course, well aware that my present inclinations are far from being equal to what they formerly were. I believe, however, that they will grow stronger daily. Already my former life is incomprehensible, and I cannot understand why I did not think earlier of overcoming my abnormal sexual instinct by normal sexual indulgence. A relapse would only now be possible with an entire change of my mental life. In a word, it seems impossible.

"Your obedient servant, ———d."

From a December 7 letter of Dr. Schrenk-Notzing's I extract the following:

"In this case the cure seems to be of a longer duration than I expected, for, on speaking with the patient some months ago, he said that he was perfectly happy in marriage, and, I hear, he soon expects the happiness of being a father."

Dr. Schrenk-Notzing has reported in the *Wiener internationalem klinischen Rundschau*, 1891, no. 26, further facts of interest concerning his patient, which are therapeutically complete.

special pathology.

The imagination of debauchees when actively or passively picturing immoral acts is exceedingly lively. It is doubtful whether the following enumeration of the kind of sexual acts that are known to law exhausts all the possibilities. Most frequently the abuse consists of sexual handling (under some circumstances, flagellation),[6] active masturbation, seducing children by inducing them to perform masturbation, or lustful handling of the seducer. Less frequent acts are cunnilingus, fellatio of boys or girls, female pederasty, coitus between the thighs, and exhibitionism.

In a case reported by Maschka (*Handb.*, vol. 3, p. 174), a young man had naked girls, from eight to twelve years old, dance around in his room and urinate before him until he ejaculated. Boys are abused by sensual women who try to achieve contact with the boys' genitals and, by means of friction or masturbation, satisfy themselves.[7]

Tardieu saw one of the most disgusting examples. A servant, in the company of her lover, masturbated children entrusted to them; performed cunnilingus on a girl of seven, as well as putting parsnips and potatoes into her vagina; and introduced similar things into the rectum of a baby of two years!

Case 185.

Z., aged sixty-two; deeply tainted, masturbator. He stated he had never had coitus, but had frequently practiced fellatio. He was in an asylum because of paranoia. It had been his greatest pleasure to entice girls, aged from ten to fourteen years, and practice cunnilingus and other vile acts on them. During these acts he had orgasm and ejaculation. Masturbation did not give him the same satisfaction, and induced ejaculation only with difficulty. For lack of anything better, he also practiced fellatio with men, and was occasionally an exhibitionist. Phimosis; asymmetrical cranium (Pelanda, *Arch. di Psichiatria,* vol. 10, fasc. 3, 4).

Case 186.

X., priest, aged forty. He was accused of enticing girls, aged from ten to thirteen, undressing and lustfully fondling them, and finally masturbating. He was tainted, and had been a masturbator from childhood; he was morally an imbecile; had always been very excitable sexually. Head somewhat small. Penis unusually large; indications of hypospadias (Pelanda, loc. cit.).

Case 187.

K., aged twenty-three; laborer. He was accused and convicted of repeatedly enticing boys, and occasionally girls, to an out-of-the-way place where he then practiced abuses with them (mutual masturbation, **performing fellatio on the boys,** fondling of the genitals of the girls).

K. was an imbecile, and physically deformed, being scarcely 1.5 meters tall; cranium rachitic and hydrocephalic; teeth bad – furrowed, defective, and irregular. Large lips, idiotic expression, stuttering speech, and an awkward attitude completed the picture of psycho-physical degeneration. K. behaved like a child discovered in some mischievous act. Scarcely any growth of beard. Genitals normal and well-developed. Although he had a superficial consciousness of having done something improper, he was unconscious of the moral, social and legal significance of his crimes.

K. came from a drunken father, and from a mother who became insane from the abuse of her husband and died in an asylum. As a baby he was almost blinded by corneal ulcers. After his sixth year, he grew up with an almoner, and later with difficulty earned his living as an organ grinder. His brother was good for nothing, and the culprit himself was considered a surly, quarrelsome, evil, moody, and irritable man. The opinion emphasized the intellectual, moral, and physical defect of the culprit.

Unfortunately it must be admitted that the most revolting of these crimes are done by sane individuals who, by reason of satiety in normal sexual indulgence, lasciviousness, brutality, and often intoxication, forget that they are human beings.

A great number of these cases, however, certainly depend upon pathological states. This is particularly true when old men become the seducers of children.[8]

I agree with Kirn, who believes a mental examination is necessary under all circumstances in cases of this kind, inasmuch as a reawakened, perverse, abnormally intense and uncontrollable sexual desire is frequently enough shown to be one of the manifestations of senile dementia.

[2] the significance of menstruation in the manifestation of psychopathic states
by richard von krafft-ebing, m.d.

THE SIMULTANEOUS occurrence of a criminal act and the onset of menstruation has not found sufficient mention in the literature of this field. Nevertheless, it is a well-known fact for any experienced physician that menstruation has a powerful effect on the psyche of countless women, and in many cases can result in acute psychopathic states.

It is therefore a duty and a necessity to not only determine whether a connection exists between a criminal act and the onset of menstruation, but also to arrive at a theory concerning what might have been the nature of an individual psychological reaction in general as well as in a particular set of circumstances.

The following case studies justify the author's proposal outlined in his work *Kriminalpsychologie,* second edition, p. 41; namely, when a woman of legal age has been committed to an institution, the date of her last menstrual cycle should be determined.

The majority of women manifest a heightened nervous and emotional excitability before, during and after menstruation. In any case, it can be stated that their central nervous system, as well as their vasomotoric nervous system and their emotional well-being, are enormously taxed. Stimuli, which can otherwise lead to no response, provoke strong reactions; latent neuroses such as hysteria and epilepsy reappear. An abnormal irritability of the emotions (which can reach unmanageable and even pathological states), anxiety attacks, neurotic fixations and obsessions, psychological dysesthesia and anesthesia with impulses leading to hostile reactions to the outside world, are regular occurrences.

Normally occurring symptoms in the cases of countless female individuals include an inability to get along with husbands and servants, mistreatment of the other-wise beloved children and the environment in general, explosions of rage, insult-ing behavior and disturbance of domestic peace, insubordination against superiors and official persons, scenes of jealousy directed against the husband, and cravings for alcoholic drinks due to acute neurasthenic conditions, as well as anxiety attacks and states of intoxication. These individuals can intermediately be perceived as well-behaved wives and mothers, and in general can be pleasant elements of society, whereas they are true furies and Xanthippes when in their "state," and are avoided and feared.

In its fluid transitions we can discern cases in these daily and pathological reac-tions – that nevertheless demand the application of mercy at the hands of a judge – in which states of complete (transitory) mental dysfunction are reached, whereby the subjects thus afflicted cannot be held legally responsible for their actions.

One may be dealing with a free-floating form of acute mental disease, which may be, depending on circumstances, recurrent with each menstruation. In some cases it may be highly variable (periodic menstrual insanity); or there may be an acute increase of a mild chronic and preexisting mental dysfunction.

Both of the cases here present the danger of misdiagnosis of a state that may be of a very short duration (sometimes lasting only hours or days), and thus may be unjustly categorized.

The intensity of the psychological reaction to menstruation is mainly based on the degree to which a frequently hereditary condition strains the central nervous system. Further etiologically significant indications are impairments of the ovaries, chronic metritis, flexions, versions, as well as many other related neuroses (neurasthenia, hysteria).

Menstrual insanity can appear in various forms[9] – mostly mania, especially *mania furiosa,* and more rarely acute melancholia, accompanied by more or less pronounced states of anxiety (*raptus melancholicus*), acute hallucinatory insanity, stupor, epileptic hysteria, epileptic delirium, pathological states, etc.

In cases of menstrual insanity, the frequency with which fixations and impulsive motivation lead to criminal acts can be explained on the basis of a degenerative condition of the central nervous system. This also results, with each recurring menstruation, in a great danger to society at the hands of such individuals.

The diseased impulses manifest themselves mostly through acts of arson, murder or suicide.

The following theses can be postulated as some of the main arguments:

[1] The mental integrity of the menstruating woman is forensically questionable.

[2] In the case of female prisoners, a determination whether the incriminating act was committed during menstruation is suggested. The time of menstruation is not limited to the days of actual blood flow, but also includes the days before and after menstruation.

[3] A mental evaluation is suggested if the criminal act and the time of menstruation coincide; such an evaluation is essential if there are other clues that suggest previous psychopathic incidents during previous periods of menstruation, or if other unusual facts are to be observed.

[4] Due to the powerful influence of menstruation on the mental state, the defendant should be granted judicial leniency, even in cases when no acute menstrual insanity can be proven.

[5] In cases of crimes committed by the mentally insane that coincide with the time of menstruation, the defendants are not to be held accountable, especially when such crimes are committed in the heat of the moment.

[6] Individuals who, because of menstrual insanity, are not criminally charged, must be considered a threat to society and carefully supervised during the time of

menstruation. It is highly recommended that they be committed to an asylum; due to the care and treatment provided there, recovery is usually achieved.

The following case studies may provide a welcome illustration of the forensic reality of menstrual insanity. Included is a case that was evaluated by the medical faculty in Vienna, as well as some other remarkable cases taken from existing literature.

[1] murder of the husband during menstruation. questionable menstrual insanity in the physically and mentally insufficiently developed female perpetrator.

On June 27, 1888, the coroner of Banjaluka reported to the local court that he had detected a strangulation mark on the neck of Malje C., who was reported to have died a sudden and unexpected death; he therefore concluded that the victim could not have died of natural causes.

The local constable, J., reported that on the morning of June 27 he had arrived at the house of the deceased in order to fulfill his duties, and had encountered there the wife and mother-in-law of the deceased, who had shown no sign of mourning. He subsequently determined that the deceased had strangulation marks. When he declared that he did not believe in a natural death in this case, the widow C. began to sob and finally blurted out the words, "I don't know, he had a sudden fever and then he died."

J. had the corpse transported to the hospital and arrested the widow. On their way to prison, she confessed to him that she had strangled her husband, and that a certain St., who was employed at the time by Hadschi M., had helped her by holding the hands of the sleeping person while she was strangling him. This St. had promised to marry her after the deed had been accomplished. Her actions were said to have been motivated by the fact that her husband had had a fight with her the night before and had hit her twice with his hand.

She had been angry with her husband, but had not known what she was doing when she had committed the murder. She later stated that she had strangled the man before dawn with a candy cane ribbon. The evening before, her mother's brother, Ivo M., had been visiting. She had told him she was thinking about strangling her husband because he was abusing her and she couldn't live with him any longer. Ivo had assisted her without protest by holding the man's hands. After the deed Ivo had left; he went to her mother and told her everything, whereupon the mother became angry.

Mara C. later denied that St. had been her accomplice. She said it was true that St. had visited her on November 21, and he had asked her whether she would marry him if he helped her strangle her husband.

In the hearing of June 27, Mara C. stated that she had been forced by her mother to marry this man, but that she had to leave their shared apartment a month later because the landlord's wife had accused her of having an affair with another man. She had started to work, but returned to her husband on June 20 because of sore feet and an inability to continue working. She had then peacefully coexisted with him until the evening of June 26, when he had struck her twice on the shoulders with his hand because she had refused to light a fire. After that, the husband had fallen asleep. She went out of the house and into the garden in order to have dinner.

"That's when Uncle Ivo came and asked me if I wanted to strangle my husband. I thought it was a good idea, even though I wasn't angry with my husband, and I went into the room with Ivo, put a rope around my husband's throat, and strangled him like that for a quarter of an hour while Ivo held his hands. My husband, God rest his soul, could only cry 'O joj,' whereupon his eyes came out of their sockets. When we saw that he was dead, we stopped. Ivo ran home and I went to bed, fell asleep at once and slept until sunrise. In the morning I went to my mother's house. She scolded me for what had happened and abused me. I strangled him because he hit me and because I had been wrong about marrying him. I have never had an affair and have never had sexual intercourse with anyone except my husband.

"Last night St. came into the garden, spoke to me of immoral things, and asked if I wanted to be his wife. When I told him he mustn't have anything to do with me, he left.

"My Uncle Ivo never asked me anything like that and I never had an affair with him."

On July 3, Mara C. declared that she became angry with her husband as a result of his abuse of her, decided to kill him, and set out to accomplish the deed after he had fallen asleep. He did not regain consciousness and did not resist. After the deed she had lain down next to the corpse; she could not sleep and was crying, however, because she was sorry about what she had done.

She stated that although she had unjustly accused Ivo and St., she had committed the murder by herself. She had only accused the two because she had been upset and quite beside herself. She had never considered killing her husband before the night of June 26.

The forensic examination determined that death had occurred as a result of suffo- cation due to strangulation. Because there were no other exterior marks of violence on the body, the assumption that strangulation had occurred while the victim was sleeping and unconscious seemed to be justified.

Witness (female) K. confirmed that Mara C. had returned to her husband on June 20 of her own free will.

Her mother, Josipovic, stated that her daughter had never been able to learn even the simplest of household tasks and that she, the mother, had always been required to help her out wherever she was employed so she wouldn't be chased away. Her daughter was not particularly bright. When the victim proposed, her daughter did not like him initially because he was much older, but later agreed to the marriage. Her son-in-law had never complained about the fact that his wife refused to sleep with him. The mother stated that she noticed bloodstains on her daughter's under- wear eight days before the murder. On the morning after the deed the daughter had told her very nicely and quietly how her husband had died the night before.

She said that two years earlier her daughter had stolen from her.

As long as her daughter had been unmarried she had menstruated very regularly, without any unusual occurrences.

The prison warden has since stated that there were no unusual occurrences at the time of Mara C.'s menstruation. Her cellmates stated that Mara C. sometimes said immoral things and behaved immorally, doing such things as exposing her private parts.

Observation Journal: Mara C., twenty-two years old, is the child of a sickly yet mentally stable father and a healthy mother.

She was sickly as a child, but did not suffer from epilepsy. She was put in charge of herding the cattle at age twelve, and later helped with household chores. She had always been industrious, willing and obedient.

Later she entered into the service of Muratbeg K., and served there until she was twenty-one. She menstruated for the first time when she was eighteen or nineteen years old.

In the middle of April 1888, Mara entered into the service of Dr. Hadj in Banjaluka, where she stayed for just one month.

While serving there she became acquainted with Malje K. Mara remained indifferent to her suitor's efforts. Her employer had no knowledge that she had been coerced into marriage by her mother. Marriage resulted on July 20, 1888. Mara followed her husband to live in the mill he was leasing and fled to her mother's house after fifteen days, telling her a story about having been chased away by the female owner of the mill. The husband confirmed that there had been differences between the owner and Mara, and asked the mother to keep her daughter until he had time to find another mill to lease. Since the mother had no means to provide for her daughter, Mara went into service after three weeks, returned to her mother during Christmas 1888, stayed with her until March 1889, and then was employed by Hadj and stayed there until June 1889. On June 20 she returned to her husband.

The mother stated that Mara began to menstruate at the age of eighteen or nineteen, that she menstruated every four weeks for three or four days, and that she experienced no pain during that time.

In general her daughter was feeble-minded and could not learn to perform simple chores such as mending, sewing, and other household tasks. She never attended school.

Mara herself stated that she suffered from headaches for two or three days before menstruation, experienced occasional vomiting, and in general was excitable and moody. She did not want to get married, and was talked into marrying Malje, whom she did not care for, by her mother.

According to the official records of October 8, 1889, Mara is small (1.33 meters), strong and well-nourished. She stated that she had never been sick as a child (except for the chicken pox), that she had always slept well and generally felt fine, and that there were no disturbances in her vegetative organs.

The mucous membranes at the opening of her vagina, inside the vagina itself and at the portio vaginalis, were reddened and covered with a creamy greenish secretion. In the vicinity of the pubic area there was a painful erythema. Her uterus was unusually small, with a slight deviation to the left.

Mara told her cellmates that her mother had been after her quite a bit with regard to the marriage and had told her: "If you don't marry Malje, you are not my daughter." This threat made her marry Malje, even though he was three times her age.

She told her mother she would marry him with the remark: "If I should live unhappily with him, my misfortune will be on your conscience."

Her mother had made her promise to the priest that she would marry Malje of her own free will, and that is how they were married.

She said that she had fled to her mother's house because the couple lived in want and because she could not love her husband.

During the first night, Mara said, Malje wanted to force her to engage in coitus, even though she was menstruating. He had later complained about her reluctance to her mother. Mara made excuses, saying that she had been menstruating, that she did not love her husband, and that she did not really like to sleep with him. During the following thirteen nights, Malje attempted to force her into cohabitation; he succeeded only once. Because of the unbearable situation, Mara fled to her mother's house on the fifteenth day after her marriage. When, at the insistence of Mara P. and her mother, she returned to her husband on June 26, 1889, Malje again wanted to force her to cohabit. She felt that she resented him even more than she had right after her marriage. She found herself in a very difficult situation, because she realized that she could not continue to live like this. Also, Mara P. and the mother had threatened her, and said that they would bring her back to him by force if she chose to leave her husband.

"While struggling with all these thoughts, I fell asleep on June 26 in the afternoon and dreamt that I had strangled Malje, and then I was happy. When I awoke later that evening, all I could think about was how to make this dream real; I found a cord and put it underneath my husband's pillow before he went to sleep. Again, that night, Malje tried to force me into coitus; I refused him and finally went to sleep. In the middle of the night I awoke because I was thirsty. I saw my husband sleeping; I twined the cord around his neck and pulled on the ends. Malje awoke with a sigh and stretched his limbs. I pulled a second time while straddling his chest. In the end, when Malje showed no more sign of life, I twisted the cord twice around his neck and pulled at it very hard."

Mara stated that she started her period on June 26 and finished menstruation at the time of the murder. She had suffered from a severe headache.

It was determined in jail (from June 27 to June 29) that she still had an expulsion of blood from her genitals.

During the night of October 21 her cellmates were disturbed by a fearful nightmare of Mara's, from which she could only be awakened after a quarter of an hour. She could not be shaken out of it completely, and even in her half-sleep was tearing her hair out with her right hand while holding on to her hay mattress with her left. She was laughing, pushing back her cellmates, and repeatedly shouting: "Malje, what do you want!" She stared blindly into the space before her and did not respond to any questions. After a few minutes she came to and recounted that she had been dreaming that Malje had wanted to force her into coitus. She prayed and sighed, then complained about a backache and remained sleepless for the rest of the night. During the doctor's visit in the morning it was determined that she was menstruating. Mara was quiet and seemed to be very sad; her complexion was pale. She remembered her dream, but did not recall having struggled with her cellmates.

The cellmates stated that every night Mara was afraid to go to bed. When asked about this, Mara stated she was afraid because she always had a vision of her husband. He came to her each night, right after she lay down; he came through the window and lay down beside her. He said nothing and then suddenly disappeared.

On October 25 Mara was still very pale and depressed. She complained about sleeplessness because her husband kept appearing to her. She had no appetite, complained about pain in the pit of her stomach and in her forehead; she had no fever. On the last night of menstruation she fell asleep at eight o'clock, then became stiff in all her limbs and, completely chilled, could only be fully awakened after repeated attempts had been made to shake her out of sleep. After this she was not really herself and, when repeatedly addressed, only reacted after about half an hour. She complained about pains throughout her body and remained (how long?) without sleep.

Beginning October 26 (termination of menstruation), these symptoms subsided, although she still had the frightening dreams in which her husband wanted to force her into coitus. She still saw him, his whole body naked and black, while she was half-awake.

When she did not have her period, she slept quietly and generally felt good; her behavior was friendly and she diligently completed her days' work. Only occasionally was she sad not to be with her siblings and enraged at her mother, who had forced her to return to her husband.

Beginning November 10 she menstruated, with the previous burning sensations during urination and dysmenorrheic complaints, which were identified by the physicians as originating from the left side of her uterus. She was pale, sometimes sleepless, and depressed.

On November 15 her menstruation stopped and all physical complaints ceased; her sleep was undisturbed and her good mood had returned. There were no frightful dreams or cramps of any kind.

She never exhibited remorse for her deed or showed any sign of affection for her husband. She avoided conversations of an erotic nature.

Her previous employer described Mara as moral and obedient, but feeble-minded inasmuch as she either quickly forgot the orders given to her or failed to execute them.

The medical testimony stressed her very small size, her noticeably small and misaligned uterus, her late sexual development, her feeble-mindedness (naïveté, lack of willpower, childish demeanor, weak memory, lack of repentance concerning her deed, moodiness), as well as the symptoms during her menstruation of October 22 and November 13, 1889, that led to the conclusion of menstrual insanity.

She was forced into marriage and intimidated by threats, which made a deep impression on her because of her gullibility. She was made to return to her husband, felt herself to be in a desperate situation and, moreover, was menstruating on the day of her crime. The hatred she felt toward her husband was tremendously aggravated by the fact that he had forced her to cohabit. She had physically struggled with the fifty-year-old man until he fell asleep, exhausted. Mara fell asleep as well, awoke during the night thirsty and suffering from a headache, and then proceeded to commit the crime.

It is likely that the occurrence of the crime coincided with an episode of menstrual insanity.

The symptoms of headaches and thirstiness on the night of June 26 presage the symptoms of October 22. Because there were no witnesses to the crime, however, it is not clear whether other symptoms of menstrual psychosis were present during that particular time.

It is noteworthy that on January 25, 1890, a female cellmate reported that she had frequently seen Mara standing on her head, laughing, or jumping around. When Mara was asked about this, she was reported to have said: "What am I supposed to do?"

This particular cellmate considered Mara a normal, healthy woman, whose health was not altered by menstruation.

The same impression was gained by her other cellmates.

On August 5, 1890, Mara was sentenced to death. At the instigation of her defense lawyer, the above evaluation was provided. Because this evaluation was not deemed sufficient, the medical faculty was called in for an evaluation.

e v a l u a t i o n .

Concerning the evaluation of the physical-mental personality of Mara C., it is necessary to include two separate argumentative strains in the assessment (as documented in the files). They are:

[1] The individual's general mental and physical state;
[2] The individual's state at the time of the criminal act.

a r t i c l e   [1]

Even though the material documented in the files was incomplete and a personal exploration of the accused was not possible, one cannot help but gain from the material at hand the definite impression that this individual was not normally developed in terms of her mental state; she was, in fact, intellectually deficient and a feeble-minded person. In this respect her mother's testimony – that her daughter was not able to learn simple household chores, and that the mother had to assist her so she would not be chased away from her place of work – was significant. Important, also, was the deposition of her employer, according to which Mara was feeble-minded, forgot the orders given to her, or was not able to complete them to his satisfaction. All this speaks in favor of this assumption.

Further indications are that she was gullible, dependent on others and easily intimidated by threats, and that she was forced to enter into a marriage in spite of her strong resistance.

Other incidents that occurred in prison, such as her exposing her private parts, standing on her head, and imbecilic jumping about cannot be interpreted other than as manifestations of a mentally immature and weak personality.

In addition to these manifestations of intellectual defectiveness, there were other symptoms that indicated moral atrophy.

It is worth noting that, during her imprisonment, Mara never showed signs of real, deep remorse concerning the severe crime she had committed.

Even her ludicrous attempt to blame others for the origination of the idea of the murder, and to generally cast suspicion on others, speaks in favor of the assumption that her personality was intellectually and ethically deficient.

In addition to the psychological anomalies and character defects, there were other indications; Mara was of very small stature, and – even considering her heritage and that she did not have a fully developed uterus (which, in addition, was dislocated) – started menstruating at an abnormally late age.

In relation to the mass and configuration of her skull, we are unfortunately lacking sufficient information, but one can conclude that Mara was not only mentally but also physically retarded as a person; these indications of deficiency can be easily combined to conclude that they are an expression of a mental as well as a physical state of degeneration.

The official records of her sexual life contained only limited notes; we can deduce from these, however, that Mara never wanted to engage in sexual intercourse, which in itself indicates a significant deviation, considering her age (twenty-two years old), and may very well point to a diseased tendency in her sexual development.

This mentally weak, physically defective, and possibly sexually abnormal predisposed person was entrusted to a man because of her feeble-mindedness. With the aid of certain threats, she subsequently defected, after which she was reattached to this man as a result of renewed threats. She then found herself unable to fulfill her marital obligations. Desperate, she was then incapable of withdrawing from her relationship with this man (in spite of her predicament, which was based on these very conditions).

A woman in full command of her powers would not have been intimidated by such threats, would have attempted to flee again, eventually would have made things impossible through domestic war, and, in general, would have known to fight for her liberation in a legally accepted manner; the intellectually and morally deficient Mara, however, saw murder as her only means of extracting herself from a situation that seemed unbearable to her, and therefore treacherously and clumsily killed her hated husband, thus liberating herself.

Even if premeditation cannot be discounted, it must be admitted that a powerful affect was at work during the time of the crime, and that the criminal motivation was powered by a strong sexual impulse. Her reduced intelligence and insufficient development of the moral sense could not really stand in the way of its execution.

The present case offers many analogies that have been reported in Hitzig's *Annalen der Strafrechtspflege* (September 1847), one of which is the following:

"Anatrine, sixteen years old, hardly developed, scarcely educated, of a gentle but introverted character disposition, was forced into marriage with a stable hand. The marriage turned out to be unhappy, and three months later the wife inflicted a four inch cut on her husband's throat, intending to kill him while he was asleep. Even before her marriage, Anatrine had been afraid of coitus as a painful and possibly deathly occurrence. Her husband deflowered her anyway. She hated him for this and wanted to kill herself because she was not able to fend him off. She decided, however, to kill her husband instead, in case he attempted to force coitus again.

"The evaluation did not conclude mental disease; it did, however, determine that her body had not arrived at its full sexual maturity.

"Anatrine was sentenced to six weeks in prison.

"The judges assumed that Anatrine had acted out of desperation and at the height of her impulses; they also assumed that because of her immature age, her non-acquaintance with her marital duties, and the childish idea that coitus could in fact lead to her death, she had acted out of a state that bordered on self-defense."

article [2]

The forensic judges cast their vote, stating that Mara had most likely committed her crime in a state of menstrual insanity. This assumption cannot be dismissed, but at the same time it cannot be completely proven.

In favor of such a judgment one can recount the following: the fact that she was menstruating at the time of the crime; the frequency and degree to which a mentally and physically predisposed individual such as Mara was incapacitated at the time of menstruation; the fact that during menstruation, which lasted from October 21 to October 25, and then again from November 10 to November 15, disturbances of the central nervous system and related disturbances of the mental functions were observed.

The facts observed impel one to take the utmost care as to whether menstrual occurrences, which were undoubtedly present in Mara at the time of the crime, played a significant role in her mental state during the occurrence of the crime.

Every experienced physician knows that the psychic state of a menstruating woman is different than any other time outside the term of menstruation, and that abnormal moods and a greater excitability and inclination to certain affects are normal under these circumstances. If the person is abnormally predisposed, such states can expand, little by little, into conditions of extraordinary mental confusion and even complete mental paralysis. This condition may only last for a few hours, and its manifestation may be so insignificant as to be almost overlooked.

A case reported in Hitzig's *Zeitschrift für Kriminalrechtspflege* (July and August 1827) is significant in this respect. A mother killed her child by throwing the infant into the water. Nobody even surmised insanity at the time of the crime. The unfortunate mother confessed and was sentenced to death. Shortly before the execution, she told her fellow inmates that she had been ashamed to tell the judge that she had been having her period; this was a time for her when she was routinely plagued by an inner fear and restlessness and was tired of life in general. The execution of the sentence was suspended and the woman was kept under medical supervision during various menstruation cycles, from which it was concluded that she suffered, when menstruating, from sleeplessness, headaches, anxiety, suicidal thoughts, an increased pulse rate of up to one hundred and thirty beats a minute, and other symptoms of deep melancholia. The unfortunate creature was thereupon released.

Returning to our defendant (Mara C.), we can assume that her statements concerning her symptoms before the beginning of her period (headaches, vomiting, excitability, moodiness) are significant, inasmuch as they correspond to general experience.

It can also be concluded that on June 26 the nervous system of the menstruating Mara was in a state of great excitability. She had a dream in the afternoon that predisposed her to commit the murder; she also suffered from headaches and woke up thirsty. There is not sufficient material available about her emotional state during the night of June 26 to evaluate it with complete certainty. It is noteworthy, however, that the usually timid and dependent Mara acted cruelly and energetically; she also stated that she lay down next to the corpse after the murder and spent the rest of the night in this position; these are circumstances that can be interpreted in terms of a temporarily diseased emotional state (psychic anesthesia). Her indifference and calmness during the morning hours of June 27 also speak for this interpretation.

We can therefore conclude this evaluation by stating that Mara C. is, intellectually and morally, incompletely developed, and that she is a feeble-minded and physically degenerative person who was not conscious of the significance of her crime.

The crime must be seen in relation to the abnormal nature of her sexual life and her developmental difficulties, as well as to the pathological abnormalities of her sexual organs; it was committed in the heat of the moment during which her poor intellectual and moral powers could not provide sufficient counterbalance. Furthermore, the possibility exists that we are dealing with a menstrual melancholic depression that exerted significant influence.

[2] simulation of insanity on the part of a mentally diseased female charged with attempted murder. menstrual insanity.

On January 10, 1877, Frau P. seemingly set out for work, accompanied by her four-year-old son. On the way she bought him some bread, after which she led him to the water and pushed him in. The child was saved. During the first hearing on January 11, she declared that the child had been a burden to her, that she was living within very limited means, and that she had wanted to kill the child and then herself. The thought had come to her that very morning. She could see that she deserved severe punishment.

On January 17 she acknowledged that she had not been in an emergency situation on January 10, and she stated that she frequently suffered from headaches, especially on January 9 when she had started her period. The night before January 10 had been good. The unfortunate idea had been formed the next morning. She did not recall the details of her crime and could not explain her motive. She said she loved her child very much.

Not much is known about P.'s history. It was said that as a young girl she loved men and liquor. Ten years ago she seemed to have undergone a brief period of insanity and was not considered normal. A remark to that effect was also made in an otherwise good work reference. Her marriage was tense, the financial situation unfavorable. Frau P. did love her child very much, and nobody thought she would be capable of such an action. Her husband had noticed a character change in her for about a year before the incident; she complained about headaches and was neglecting her household. She seemed to him and others to be mentally abnormal. She often spoke in a confused manner. On January 9 and 10, P. seemed to her employer to be acting very strangely. She did not manage to do any work. On January 10 she had to go home at two o'clock in the afternoon because of severe headaches.

The reports of eyewitnesses of the crime correspond with P.'s statements. While trying to drown the child she was heard to say, "I am crazy." When the child was sinking she said, "The poor creature, it has to die," and was seen pushing him under the water. When the child was rescued she said, "Leave it alone, it is better off if it dies."

From February 21 to April 17, P. was under observation in the mental institution. During the first two days she did not seem to know her environment or her past. On February 23 she tore up some work and started to sigh and walk around like any other patient. During the doctor's visit, she acted imbecilic, as she had during her first days at the institution; she mistook one of the doctors for her husband, and cried about the fact that her three children had been taken away to the mountains. In the evening she did not remember any of this. Up to March 1 she acted anxious in the presence of the doctors; during morning visits she acted dumb, and during evening visits she acted pleasant. She worked well, her bodily functions were normal, but she slept only every other night. It was assumed that she simulated sleep, and she was reprimanded. She then became organized and slept regularly until March 6. She then escaped. She was brought back that day in the same state as she had been in the beginning. She spoke of her situation to the personnel, however, and expressed fear of being sent back to prison. She was like this until March 22. She then became excited, incoherent, spoke about angels, and shouted: "Man, let's drink!"

When faced with the doctors, her agitation doubled. She became exhausted after a very short time, was then calm for a few hours, and grew agitated again in the evening when a particular remark pertaining to her was made. She then remained calm until April 7. She was allowed to see her child. She embraced him but did not really recognize him. When the child claimed that Frau P. was not his mother, she lost her composure and embraced and kissed him tenderly. When it was pointed out to her that her behavior was contradictory, she again pretended not to know him.

When the child was led away, there was a stormy scene in which she admitted to her crime. On April 11 she again attempted to stand out by talking nonsense. On April 17 she was brought back to prison. Frau P. did not have her period while in the institution. Her ears are noticeably deformed, her skull is asymmetrical, and her forehead is low.

The evaluation of the accused shows evidence of simulation and, at the same time, mental imbalance (melancholy) during the time of the crime. Although on January 11 she was still sick, on January 17 she started to lie and simulate.

She was not convicted and was recommitted to the mental institution. Nothing further of significance occurred until May 23, at which time she started to complain again about headaches, did not work or eat, and could not sleep. During the day of May 24 she was sad, anxious and melancholic, and remained so until after her period stopped. One month later this menstrual melancholic state was repeated.

One day the public prosecutor happened to visit the institution. She became terribly frightened and could not be calmed down. On the following day she began to simulate as she had before and continued her behavior until she thought that no one was watching her.

(Marandon de Montyel, *Journal l'Encéphale.*)

[3] repeated arson committed by a seventeen-year-old girl during menstruation. later full-blown melancholy with suicidal tendencies.

Adele K., eighteen years old, had a father who was addicted to brandy. Her mother suffered from headaches and sleeplessness. Her grandfather was epileptic and mentally disturbed.

K. started menstruation when she was fourteen years old. Since then she was menstrually psychologically disturbed. On June 11, June 27, and October 31, while employed, she committed arson four times. She admitted to her crimes; she offered negligence as an excuse and declared that she experienced an irresistible pleasure in fire and bright red objects during the time of her period. She satisfied this lust by playing with matches. She said she had a feeling, while menstruating, of needing to see fire or blood.

These assertions were verified. The incidents of arson corresponded to her menstrual episodes. When K. appeared before the investigating judge on November 1, she seemed to him to be mentally disturbed. From March 12 until October 29 she was committed to the mental institution for observation and treatment. She seemed physically well-developed and showed no signs of degeneration; she was very quiet, seemed depressed, and was constantly driven to attempts to take her own life. During menstruation her psychological symptoms worsened; she became anxious and agitated, as well as suicidal. Other symptoms: irregular blood circulation, dizziness, sleeplessness.

Menstrual insanity led to the crisis at the time of the incidents of arson.

(Pelman, *Vierteljahrschrift f. gerichtl. u. öffentl. Medizin,* 1887.)

[4] premenstrual psychopathic states during puberty. two incidents of arson.

The sixteen-year-old Pl., without a negative family history, mentally and physically well-developed, committed arson on two occasions: on February 7, 1877, in the house of her employer, and on March 24, 1878, in the house of her parents. Although she initially denied the act, she later admitted it. No motive could be found. She became moody while in prison, stayed in the corners of rooms, rocked back and forth in her chair, and complained about boredom and earaches.

Her crime seemed inexplicable. It was determined that the dates of the arson coincided with the first and second occurrences of her menstruation. Previous to her first menstruation she experienced three days of moodiness, boredom, strong fear and a general feeling of sickness, as well as strong aches in her head and body. At night she heard a voice commanding her to start a fire. She fought this command for twenty-four hours and finally succumbed. Then her period started and all her ailments disappeared. The second menstruation was not accompanied by such ailments. Previous to her third period she experienced the same ailments, with the exception that her fear continued throughout the entire duration of her period. When examined by a physician, it was found that her skin and mucous membranes were generally without feeling (numb), and that her reflexes had disappeared. She was under medical observation in the mental institution from June 1878 until May 1879. She repeatedly experienced premenstrual anxiety, accompanied by destructive acts, until the end of 1878. She never had a more destructive desire, however, than the one to commit arson. Her general numbness continued. With the beginning of her period on March 12, 1879, her numbness suddenly disappeared. Her subsequent periods went by without any disruption. Her genitalia did not show any abnormalities.

(Dr. Rousseau, *Annales médico-psychol.,* November 1881.)

[5] premenstrual psychopathic states during puberty. three incidents of arson.

From May 13 to June 3, 1877, there were three incidents of barns burning in the village. Anonymous letters, which a servant girl had found in front of a house, led to the suspicion that a certain M., and then a certain G., were the writers of these letters. G. admitted that she had committed these arsons because she had been upset about having been reprimanded. The defense argued that she could not be held accountable for her actions. G. was examined by a forensic physician.

Seventeen years of age, she had menstruated since she was sixteen, had come from a healthy family, and was physically well-developed. Her period had always been accompanied by pains, hot flashes in her head, and frequent nosebleeds. G. was feeble-minded, but her moral sense was well-developed. She regretted her actions, denied revenge as a motive, and stated that she was confused in her head when the incidents occurred.

She was menstruating on May 13 and June 5, 1877, set fire to the barns on May 13 and June 3, and wrote the letters of denunciation on June 5.

During the night of May 12, she awoke from a terrifying dream. Shaking, she left her bed, experienced severe headaches, saw flames, was aware of a boiling sensation in her ears, and heard voices threatening her with death. She did not sleep for the rest of the night. In the morning she could not get up because she felt severe chest pains. On the morning of May 13 she started her period, at which time the severity of her ailments increased, and she experienced strong anxiety. A woman (her employer) reprimanded her that same day. In the evening she discovered the story of an incident of arson on a shred of newspaper. She was immediately haunted by the idea of setting a fire. She fought this obsession, but eventually succumbed. Only some hours after the arson did her nervous state dissipate, but she then became plagued by her conscience. Until June 3 nothing significant occurred; she only suffered from a slight headache.

On June 3 she worked hard at the stove. As a result, the blood pressure in her head increased, and the state of May 12 and 13 recurred. When she worked in the barn that evening by the light of a lamp, she again thought of setting a fire. She followed this inclination. During the night she experienced remorse and anxiety, but did not hear voices. On June 5, with the beginning of menstruation, she relapsed. She saw M. pass by and wrote a letter in which she denounced her as the arsonist. On June 6, as her psychopathic state continued, she again denounced her by letter. She was delirious, and convinced that she was injured. A nosebleed ended the entire diseased state on June 7. In prison she did not manifest any psychopathic symptoms, with the exception of two transitory outbreaks of anger. She had her periods regularly and without complications. Although from October 1878 until February 1879 her periods occurred irregularly, she then experienced hallucinatory, delirious anxiety attacks. On February 27, 1879, return of her period. In its wake, great pains and mutism. Subsequent attacks became increasingly rare. Patient was released as healthy in June 1879.

(Dr. Rousseau, Annales médico-psychol., November 1881.)

[6] giraud, "annales médico-psychologiques," september 1889.

Girl, twenty years of age, predisposed, imbecilic; menstrual obsession with suicide and arson. Repeated arson during menstrual insanity.

[7] combes, "annales médico-psychologiques," march 1880.

Girl with moral and intellectual stuntedness. Menstrual psychological excitability, during which impulsive and unconscious acts were committed (such as insults, theft, disruption of domestic peace).

[8] philoindicus, "journal of mental science," january 1882.

Predisposition, hysteria, extraordinary menstrual excitability and sexual arousal. Impulses to murder and suicide. Due to a state of menstrual excitement, attempted murder of a girlfriend, who rejected the advances of the (probably) homosexually inclined patient.

[9] mabille, "archives de neurologie," january 1889.

Heavy genetic predisposition, hystero-neurasthenia; thefts motivated by menstrual impulsiveness; amnesia for these incidents.

[10] krafft-ebing, "friedrich's blätter," vol. 40, no. 5.

Feeble-mindedness. Persecutorial paranoia. Periodic menstrual insanity. Murder at the time of menstruation.

[11] giraud, "annales médico-psychologiques," may 1887.

Predisposition. In 1879, adolescent mania. Since 1882, incidents of menstrual hallucinatory-delirious insanity.

Since 1884, obsession to kill her children, aggravated by menstruation.

In 1885, murder of the children during menstruation (severing of head, three children dead, one saved) and suicide attempt with atropine. Lengthy period of choleric melancholy without delirium already present before the crime.

[12] tuke, "journal of mental science."

Predisposition. Melancholy without delirium for months after the death of two children; inclination to alcoholism. During menstruation and after, an excessive consumption of alcohol, anger at the six-year-old daughter; murder of the daughter due to a pathological affect, which was aggravated by intoxication.

notes

preface to the first german edition (1886).

[1] "Einstweilen bis den Bau der Welt
Philosophie zusammenhält,
Erhält sie das Getriebe
Durch Hunger und durch Liebe."

[2] Hartmann's philosophical view of love, in *Philosophie des Unbewussten*, p. 583, Berlin, 1869, is the following: "Love causes more pain than pleasure. Pleasure is illusory. Reason would cause love to be avoided were it not for the fatal sexual instinct; therefore, it would be best for a man to have himself castrated." The same opinion, minus the consequence, is also expressed by Schopenhauer (*Die Welt als Wille und Vorstellung,* 3d ed., vol. 2, p. 586ff.).

[3] "Aucune misère physique ou morale, aucune plaie, quelque corrompue qu'elle soit ne doit effrayer celui qui s'est voué à la science de l'homme et le ministère sacré du médecin, en l'obligeant á tout voir, lui permet aussi de tout dire."

one. fragments of a system of psychology of sexual life.

[1] Cf. Lombroso, *Der Verbrecher,* German translation by Fränkel, p. 38ff.; Westermarck, *Geschichte der menschlichen Ehe,* 1893; Ploss, *Das Weib in der Natur- und Völkerkunde,* 3d ed., vol. 2, pp. 413-90, 1891, Leipzig; Josef Müller, *Das sexuelle Leben der Naturvölkur,* 2d ed., 1902; idem, *Das sexuelle Leben der alten Kulturvölker,* 2d ed., 1902 (Leipzig, Grieben).

[2] According to Westermarck, *Geschichte der menschlichen Ehe,* it was "not the feeling of shame that suggested the garment, but the garment that engendered shame. The desire to make themselves more attractive originated the habit among men and women to cover their nakedness."

[3] This assertion may be modified insofar as that the symbolical and sacramental character of matrimony was clearly defined only by the Council of Trent, although the spirit of Christianity always tended to raise woman from the inferior position that she occupied in previous centuries and in the Old Testament.

The tradition that woman was created from the rib of the sleeping man (see Genesis) is one of the causes of delay in this direction, for after the fall she is told "thy will shall be subject to man." According to the Old Testament, woman is responsible for the fall of man, and this became the cornerstone of Christian teaching. Thus the social position of woman had to be neglected, as it were, until the spirit of Christianity had conquered tradition and scholastic tenets.

It is a remarkable fact that the Gospels (barring divorce, Matt. 19:9) contain not a word in favor of woman. The clemency shown toward the adulteress and the penitent Magdalen do not affect the position of woman in general. The epistles of St. Paul definitely insist that no change can be permitted in the position of woman (2 Cor. 11:3-12; Eph. 5:22, "woman shall be subject to man," and 5:23, "woman shall fear man").

How much the fathers of the Church are prejudiced against woman because of Eve's part in the temptation may be easily learned from Tertullian: "Woman, thou shouldst ever go in mourning and sackcloth, thy eyes filled with tears. Thou has brought about the ruin of mankind." St. Jerome has everything but good to say about woman: "Woman is the gate of the devil, the road of evil, the sting of the scorpion." (*De Cultu Feminarum*, vol. 1, no. 1.)

Canon law declares: "Man only is created in the image of God, not woman; therefore woman shall serve him and be his handmaid."

The Provincial Council of Macon (sixth century) seriously discussed the question whether woman had a soul at all.

These opinions of the Church had a sympathetic influence upon the peoples who embraced Christianity. Among the converted Germanic races the *dower value* of woman fell considerably (J. Falke, *Die ritterliche Gesellschaft*, Berlin, 1862, p. 49. Regarding the valuation of the two sexes among the Jews, cf. 3 Moses, 27:3-4).

Even polygamy, which is distinctly recognized in the Old Testament (Deut. 21:15), is not definitely prohibited anywhere in the New Testament. In fact, many Christian princes (e.g., the Merovingian kings: Chlotar I, Charibert I, Pippin I and other Frankish nobles) indulged in polygamy without a protest being raised by the Church at the time (Weinhold, *Die deutschen Frauen im Mittelalter*, vol. 2, p. 15; cf. Unger, *Die Ehe*, etc., and Louis Bridel, *La femme et le droit*, Paris, 1884).

[4] Cf. Friedländer, *Sittengeschichte Roms;* Wiedemeister, *Der Cäsarenwahnsinn;* Suetonius; Moreau, *Des aberrations du sens génésique.*

[5] Friedreich (*Hdb. der gerichtsärztl. Praxis,* 1843, vol. 1, p. 271) is of a different opinion, for according to him the Red Indians of America are addicted to the practice of pederasty. Cf. also Lombroso, op. cit., p. 42, and Bloch, *Beiträge zur Aetiologie der Psychopathia sexualis,* pt. 2, 1903.

[6] Cf. Friedreich (*Gericht. Psychologie,* p. 389) who quotes numerous examples. For instance, Blanbekin, the nun, was constantly tormented by the thought of what could have become of the part of Christ that had been removed in circumcision.

Veronica Juliani, beatified by Pope Pius II, in memory of the divine lamb, took a real lamb to bed with her, kissed it and suckled it on her breasts.

St. Catharina of Genoa often burned with such intense inward fire that in order to cool herself she would throw herself upon the ground crying, "Love, love, I can endure it no longer." At the same time she felt a peculiar inclination toward her confessor. One day, when lifting his hand to her nose, she noticed a peculiar odor that penetrated her heart with "a heavenly perfume that could awaken the dead."

St. Armelle and St. Elisabeth were troubled with a similar longing for the Infant Jesus. The temptations of St. Anthony, of Padua, are known to the world. Of significance is an old Protestant prayer: "Oh! that I had found thee, bless'd Emmanuel; that thou wert with me in my bed, to bring delight to body and soul. Come and be mine. My heart shall be thy resting place."

[7] Cf. Friedreich, *Diagnostik der psych. Krankheiten,* p. 247ff.; Neumann, *Lehrb. d. Psychiatrie,* p. 80.

[8] This may be observed in the actual life as well as in the fiction and the plastic arts of degenerate eras. For instance, Bernini's carving representing St. Theresa "sinking in a hysterical faint upon a marble cloud, while an amorous angel plunges the arrow (of divine love) into her heart." – Lübke.

[9] Cf. Max Müller, who derives the word *fetish* etymologically from *factitius;* i.e., artificial, insignificant.

[10] *Deutsches Montagsblatt,* Berlin, August 20, 1888.

[11] Magnan's *"spinal cérébral postérieur,"* who finds gratification with any sort of woman, is only animated by lust. Meretricious love that is purchased cannot be geniune (Mantegazza). Whoever coined the adage *"Sublata lucerna nullum discrimen inter feminas"* ("When the lamp is removed, there is no difference between women") was a cynic, indeed. The power to perform love's act is by no means a guarantee of the noblest enjoyment of love.

There are homosexuals who are potent with women, as well as men who do not love their wives, but are nevertheless able to perform the marital "duty." In the majority of these cases even lustful pleasure is absent, for it is simply a masturbatory act rendered possible by the aid of imagination substituting another beloved being. Although this deception may, indeed, superinduce sexual pleasure, as a rudimentary gratification it can only arise from a psychic trick, just as in solitary masturbation voluptuous satisfaction is obtained chiefly with the assistance of fantasy. As a matter of fact, the degree of orgasm that completes the lustful act is entirely dependent upon the intervention of fantasy.

Where psychic impediments exist (such as indifference, disgust, aversion, fear of contagion or impregnation, etc.) the feeling of sexual gratification seems to be absent altogether.

[12] "Madame, vos beaux yeux me font mourir d'amour."

[13] "De gustibus non ext disputandum."

two. physiological facts.

[1] The olfactory center is presumed by Ferrier (*Funktionen des Gehirns*) to be in the region of the gyrus uncinatus. Zuckerkandl (*Ueber das Riechzentrum,* 1887), from researches in comparative anatomy, concludes that the olfactory center has its seat in the hippocampus major.

[2] Later researches by Müller ("Klin. u. experim. Studien, etc.," *Deutsche Zeitschr. f. N. heilkde.,* vol. 21) seem to render it more probable that the center of erection does not lie in the conus medullaris of the spinal cord, but rather in the sacral ganglia; thus constituting a sympathetic reflex.

[3] Cf. Albert Hagen, *Die sexuelle Osphresiologie,* Charlottenburg, 1901 (Verlag H. Basdorf), a most interesting monograph on the relations between the olfactory senses and odors and the sexual acts in man. Albert Moll, *Untersuchungen über Libido sexualis,* p. 377. (Literature and studies on the olfactory sense as a stimulating cause of the sexual instinct.)

[4] See also further interesting observations on the aphrodisiac effects of sweat on both sexes. Féré, *L'instinct sexuel,* p. 127 (Paris, 1899).

[5] Cf. Laycock (*Nervous Diseases of Women,* 1840), who found that in women the love for musk and similar perfumes was related to sexual excitement.

[6] The following case, reported by Binet, seems to be in opposition to this idea. Unfortunately nothing is said concerning the mental characteristics of the person. In any event, it is certainly confirmatory of a connection between the olfactory and sexual senses:

D., a medical student, was seated on a bench in a public park, reading a book (on pathology). Suddenly a violent erection disturbed him. He looked up and noticed that a lady, redolent with perfume, had taken a seat on the other end of the bench. D. could not attribute the erection to anything except the unconscious olfactory impression made upon him.

[7] Meibomius, *De flagiorum usu in re medica*, London, 1765; Boileau, *The History of the Flagellants*, London, 1783; Doppet, *Aphrodisiaque externe*, Paris, 1788; Cooper, *Der Flagellantismus u. d. Flagellanten;* Hansen, *Stock und Peitsche in XIX. Jahrhundert* (Dohrn, Dresden), 2 vols.

[8] Corvin, *Hist. Denkmale des christlichen Fanatismus*, vol. 2, Leipzig, 1847; Förstemann, *Die christlichen Geisslergesellschaften*, Halle, 1828.

[9] Cf. Roubaud, *Traitè de l'impuissance et de la stérilité*, Paris, 1878.

three. anthropological facts.

[1] Bardach, *Die Physiologie als Erfahrungswissenschaft*, 1826-40; Ploss, *Das Weib*, 1891, 3d ed.; Havelock Ellis, *Man and Woman*, 1894; A. Moll, *Die konträre Sexualempfindung*, 3d ed., p. 3; idem, *Untersuchungen über die Libido sexualis*, 1897-98.

[2] Laurent, *Les bisexués*, Paris, 1894; idem, "De l'hérédité des gynécom.," *Annales d'hygiène*, 1890.

[3] Cf. Moll, *Libido sexualis*, pp. 335-350, where he gives a large number of cases of perverted sexual characteristics of a physical as well as a psychic nature, and even of sexual inversion.

four. general pathology.

[1] Literature: Parent-Duchatelet, *Prostitution dans la ville de Paris*, 1837; Rosenbaum, *Entstehung der Syphilis*, Halle, 1839; idem, *Die Lustseuche im Altertum*, Halle, 1839; Descuret, *La médécine des Passions*, Paris, 1860; Caspar, *Klin. Novellen*, 1860; Bastian, *Der Mensch in der Geschichte;* Friedländer, *Sittengeschichte Roms.;* Wiedemeister, *Cäsarenwahnsinn;* Scherr, *Deutsche Kultur- und Sittengeschichte*, vol. 1, chap. 9; Jeannel, *Die Prostitution*, German translation by Müller, Erlangen, 1869; Krafft-Ebing, *Neue Forschungen auf dem Gebiete der Psychopathia sexualis*, 2d ed., Stuttgart, 1891; Taxil, *La Prostitution contemporaine*, Paris, 1884; Frank Lydston, *Philadelphia Med. and Surg. Reports*, 1889; Urquhardt, *Journal of Mental Science*, January 1891; Antonini, *Archiv. di Psichiatria*, vol. 12, nos. 1 and 2; Cantarano, *Zeitschr. "La Psichiatria,"* vol. 5, nos. 2 and 3; Krauss, *Psychologie des Verbrechens*, 1884; Kiernan, *Medic. Standard*, November 1889; Delcourt, *Le vice à Paris*, 1889; Lombroso, *L'uomo delinquente*, 2d ed., 1878; Toulmouche, *Annal. d'hygiène*, 1868; Giraldès and Horteloup, ibid., 1876, p. 419; Eulenburg, *Klin. Handb. d. Harn- und Sexualorgane*, 1894, 4th ed., p. 36; Moll, *Untersuchungen über die Libido sexualis*, 1897; idem, *Archivio delle psicopatie sessuali*, Naples, 1896, vol. 1; Tardieu, *Des attentats aux moeurs*, 7th ed.,

1878; Emminghaus, *Psychopathol.*, pp. 98, 225, 230, 232; Schüle, *Handb. der Geisteskrankheiten*, p. 114; Marc, *Die Geisteskrankheiten*, German translation by Ideler, vol. 2, p. 128; Krafft-Ebing, *Lehrb. d. Psychiatrie*, 6th ed., vol. 1, p. 77; idem, *Lehrb. d. ger. Psychopathol.*, 3d ed., p. 279, *Archiv f. Psychiatrie*, vol. 7, no. 2; Moreau, *Des aberrations du sens génésique*, Paris, 1880; Kirn, *Allg. Zeitschr. f. Psychiatrie*, vol. 39, nos. 2 and 3; Lombroso, *Geschlechtstrieb und Verbrechen in ihren gegenseitigen Beziehungen*, (Goltdammer's *Archiv*, vol. 30); Tarnowsky, *Die krankhaften Erscheinungen des Geschlechtssinnes*, Berlin, 1886; Ball, *La folie érotique*, Paris, 1888; Sérieux, *Recherches cliniques sur les anomalies de l'instinct sexuel*, Paris, 1888; Hammond, *Sexuelle Impotenz*, German translation by Sallinger, 1889; Krafft-Ebing, *Über sexuale Perversionen*, Leyden's *Deutsche Klinik*, 1901, vol. 6; Schrenk-Notzing, *Die Suggestionstherapie*, 1892; idem, *Zeitsch. f. Hypnotismus*, vol. 7, nos. 1 and 2, vol. 8, no. 1; Moll, *Die konträre Sexualempfindung*, 3d ed., 1889; idem, *Untersuchungen über die Libido sexualis*, 1897-98; Hirschfeld, *Jahrb. f. sexuelle Zwischenstufen*, vols. 1-4; Bloch, *Beiträge z. Aetiologie der Psychopathia sexualis*, pt. 2, 1903.

Among modern novelists who deal with the subject of sexual perversion the French are most preeminent, namely: Catulle Mendès, Péladan, Lemonnier, Dubut de la Forest (*L'homme de joie*), Huysmans (*Là-bas*), Zola.

[2] An interesting instance of how an imperative conception of non-sexual content can exert an influence is related by Magnan (*Ann. méd. psych.*, 1885): Student, aged twenty-one, strongly predisposed hereditarily, previously a masturbator, constantly struggled with the number thirteen as an imperative conception. As soon as he would attempt coitus, the imperative idea would inhibit erection and render the act impossible.

[3] Louyer-Villermay speaks of masturbation in a girl of three or four years, and Moreau (*Aberrations du sens génésique*, 2d ed., p. 209) discusses masturbation in a girl of two years. See further Maudsley, *Physiologie und Pathologie der Seele*, German translation by Böhm; Hirschsprung (Copenhagen), *Berlin. klin. Wochenschr.*, 1886, no. 38; Lombroso, *Der Verbrecher*, German translation by Fränkel, p. 119ff., cases 10, 19, and 21.

[4] Cf. Kirn, *Zeitschr. f. Psych.*, vol. 39; Legrand du Saulle, *Annal. d'hyg.*, October 1868.

[5] Cases, see Lasègue; "Les exhibitionistes," *Union médicale*, May 1, 1871.

[6] Legrand du Saule, *La folie devant les tribunaux*, p. 530.

[7] Kirn, Maschka's *Handb. d. ger. Med.*, pp. 373, 374; idem, *Allg. Zeitschrift f. Psychiatrie*, vol. 39, p. 220.

[8] *Die Welt als Wille und Vorstellung*, 1859, vol. 2, p. 461ff.

[9] No doubt Swift, the great satirist, was a case of sexual anesthesia. Adolf Stern says in his

biography of Swift (*Aus dem 18. Jahrhundert; biographische Bilder und Skizzen,* Leipzig, 1874): "It seems that he was totally devoid of the sensual elements of love; his candid cynicism, found in many of his letters, is almost definite proof of this. Whoever properly grasps certain passages in *Gulliver's Travels,* and especially the account which Swift gives of the marriage and progeny of the Houyhnhorses, the noble steeds of the last chapters, can scarcely doubt that this great satirist abhorred marriage, and never felt the impulse which draws the sexes together." Practically speaking, the enigmatic side of Swift's character, and several of his works, namely, *Diary to Stella* and *Gulliver's Travels,* can only be understood if Swift is considered sexually anesthetic.

[10] "Ueber männliche Sterilität," *Wiener med. Presse,* 1878, Nr. 1. "Ueber potentia generandi et coeundi," *Wiener Klinik,* 1885, no. 1, p. 5.

[11] For individuals in whom intense sexual hyperesthesia is associated with acquired irritable weakness of the sexual apparatus, it happens that simply the sight of a pleasing female figure, without peripheral irritation of the genitals, may cause the psychosexual center to excite into action not only the mechanism of the erection, but also that of ejaculation. For such individuals, all that is necessary to induce orgasm or even ejaculation is to imagine themselves in a sexual situation with a female who sits opposite them in a railway carriage or a drawing room. Hammond (op. cit., p. 40) describes several cases of this kind who came to him for treatment of subsequent impotence, and he mentions that these individuals used the term "ideal coitus" for the act. Dr. Moll of Berlin told me of a similar case, and in this instance the same designation was chosen for the act.

[12] So named from the notorious Marquis de Sade, whose obscene novels treat of lust and cruelty. In French literature the expression "sadism" has been applied to this perversion. Eulenberg (*Klin. Handb. der Harn- und Sexualorgane*) uses the term "active algolagnia" in connection with these phenomena.

[13] Moll, *Kontr. Sexualempfindung,* 3d ed., p. 160; Krafft-Ebing, *Arbeiten,* vol. 4, p. 106; idem, Leyden's *Deutsche Klinik,* vol. 6, sec. 2, p. 137; Eulenberg, *Grenzfragen des Nerven und Seelenlebens,* vol. 21, p. 1.

[14] Cf. also Alfred de Musset's famous verses to the Andalusian girl: "How proud she is in her disorder – when she falls, her breasts naked – How one sees her, gaping, twisting – passionately raging and biting – Howling unknown words!"

[15] During the excitement of battle the idea of lust forces its way into consciousness. Cf. the soldier's description of a battle, by Grillparzer:

"And as the signal rang out, the armies met, breast to breast – lust of the gods – here, there, the murderous steel slays enemy, friend. Given and taken – death and life – with wavering change – wildly raging in frenzy." (*Traum ein Leben,* act 1.)

[16] Schulz (*Wiener med. Wochenschrift,* no. 49, 1869) reports a remarkable case of a man, aged twenty-eight, who could perform coitus with his wife only after working himself into an artificial fit of anger.

[17] Concerning analogous acts in rutting animals, see Lombroso, *Der Verbrecher,* German translation by Fränkel, p. 18.

[18] Among animals it is always the male who pursues the female with proffers of love. Playful or actual flight of the female is not infrequently observed; and then the relation is similar to the one between the beast of prey and its victim.

[19] The conquest of woman takes place today in the social form of courting, in seduction and deception, etc. From the history of civilization and anthropology we know that there have been times (as there are savages today that practice it) where brutal force, robbery, or even blows rendering a woman powerless were used to obtain love's desire. It is possible that tendencies toward such outbreaks of sadism are atavistic.

In the *Jahrbücher für Psychologie,* vol. 2, p. 128, Schäfer (Jena) refers to the reports of two cases by A. Payer. In the first case, states of great sexual excitement were induced by the sight of battles or paintings of them; in the second, by cruel torturing of small animals. In addition: "The pleasure of battle and murder is so predominantly an attribute of the male sex throughout the animal kingdom that there can be no question about the close relation existing between this side of the masculine character and male sexuality. I also believe it can be shown, by unprejudiced observation, that for men who are mentally and physically absolutely normal, the first indefinite and incomprehensible precursors of sexual excitement may be induced by the reading of exciting scenes of the chase and war – i.e., such scenes give rise to unconscious longings for a kind of satisfaction in warlike games (wrestling), in which the fundamental sexual impulse to the most perfect and intense contact with a companion is expressed, with the secondary thought of conquest more or less clearly defined."

[20] It sometimes happens that an accidental sight of blood, etc., puts into motion the preformed psychic mechanism of the sadistic individual and awakens the instinct.

[21] Cf. Metzger's *Ger. Arzneiw.,* edited by Remer, p. 539; Klein's *Annalen,* vol. 10, p. 176, vol. 18, p. 311; Heinroth, *System der psych. ger. med.,* p. 270; *Neuer Pitaval,* 1855, pt. 23 ("Fall Blaize Ferrage").

[22] Michéa, *Union méd.,* 1849; Brierre, *Gaz. méd.,* July 21, 1849; Moreau, *Aberrations du sens génésique,* p. 250; Epaulard, *Vampyrisme* (*nécrophilie, nécrosadisme, nécrophagie*), Lyon, 1901.

[23] A similar case is related by Neri (*Archivio delle psicopatie sessuali,* 1896, p. 109). A man, fifty years of age, used in a brothel only girls who, clad in white, lay motionless feigning death. He violated the body of his own sister **by putting his penis into the corpse's mouth until ejaculation was attained!** This monster also had fits of fetishism for **the pubic hairs of girls,** and for the trimmings of their fingernails; eating them caused strong sexual emotions.

[24] Simon (*Crimes et délits,* p. 209) mentions an experience of Lacassagne's, to whom a respectable man said that he was never intensely excited sexually except when he was a spectator at a funeral.

[25] Taxil (op. cit.) gives more detailed accounts of this sexual monster, which must have been a case of habitual satyriasis accompanied by perverse sexual instinct. Sade was so cynical that he actually sought to idealize his cruel lasciviousness and be the apostle of a theory upon which it was based. He became so bad (among other things, he made an invited company of ladies and gentlemen erotic by serving them chocolate bonbons containing cantharides) that he was committed to the insane asylum at Charenton. During the revolution of 1790 he escaped. He then wrote obscene novels filled with lust, cruelty and the most lascivious scenes. When Bonaparte became Consul, Sade made him a present of his novels, magnificently bound. The Consul had the works destroyed and the author committed to Charenton again, where he died at the age of sixty-four. Sade was inexhaustible in his lascivious publications, which were markedly intended for advertisement. Fortunately it is difficult today to obtain copies. Extant are: *Histoire de Justine,* 4 vols.; *Histoire de Juliette,* 6 vols.; *Philosophie dans le boudoir,* London, 1805. Interesting is Sade's biography by J. Janin, 1835.

A scientific and very thorough study of sadism has recently been made by Dr. Marciat, *Bibliothèque de criminologie,* vol. 19, 1899 (Paris, Masson). It gives an analysis and table of contents of Sade's writings. Cf. also Dühren, *Der "Marquis de Sade",* 1900.

[26] Cf. Krauss, *Psychologie des Verbrechens,* 1884, p. 188; Dr. Hofer, *Annalen der Staatsarzneikunde,* vol. 6, no. 2; Schmidt's *Jahrbücher,* vol. 59, p. 94.

[27] According to newspaper reports, in December 1890 several similar attacks were made in Mainz. A young fellow between fourteen and sixteen years of age pressed against women and girls and stabbed them in the legs with a sharp-pointed instrument. He was arrested, and seemed to be insane. Further details of the case are not known.

[28] Leo Taxil (*La Corruption,* Paris, Noiret, p. 223) makes the same statements. There are also men who demand **insertion of a prostitute's tongue into the anus.**

[29] Leo Taxil (op. cit., p. 224) relates that in Parisian brothels instruments are kept ready that look like leather whips, but that are merely tubes filled with air, such as clowns use in circuses. Sadistic men use them to create the illusion for themselves that they are whipping women.

[30] Dimitri, the son of Ivan the Cruel, derived unspeakable pleasure from witnessing the death struggles of sheep, chickens and geese (*Bibliothèque de criminologie,* vol. 19, p. 278).

[31] The legend is especially spread throughout the Balkan peninsula. Among the modern Greeks it has its origin in the myth of the *lamiae* and *marmolykes* – bloodsucking women. Goethe made use of this in his "Braut von Korinth." The verses referring to vampirism, e.g. "suck thy heart's blood," etc., can only be thoroughly understood when they are compared with their ancient sources.

[32] Another case of female sadism is given by Moll, third edition of *Die Kontr. Sexualempfindung,* p. 507, case 29. It is the exact counterpart of masochism in man and represents the ideal desire of the masochist.

[33] The gifted Heinrich von Kleist, who was beyond a doubt mentally abnormal, gives a masterly portrayal of complete feminine sadism in his *Penthesilea.* In scene 22, Kleist describes his heroine pursuing Achilles in the fire of love, and when he is betrayed into her hands, she tears him into pieces with lustful, murderous fury, and sets her dogs on him: "Tearing the armor from his body, she strikes her teeth into his white breast – she and her dogs, the rivals, Oxus and Sphynx – they on the right side, she on the left; and as I approached, blood dripped from her hands and mouth." And later, when Penthesilea becomes satiated: "Did I kiss him to death? No. Did I not kiss him? Torn in pieces? Then it was a mistake; kissing rhymes with biting [in German, *Kuß, Biß*], and one who loves with the whole heart might easily mistake the one for the other." In recent literature we find the matter frequently treated; particularly in Sacher-Masoch's novels, of which mention is made later on, and in Ernest von Wildenbruch's *Brunhilde,* Rachilde's *La Marquise de Sade,* etc.

[34] Literature: Krafft-Ebing, *Neue Forschungen auf d. Gebiet d. Psychopathia sexualis,* 2d ed.; idem, *Arbeiten aus d. Gesamtgebiet d. Psychiatrie u. Neuropath.,* vol. 4, pp. 127-160; Moll, *Die Kontr. Sexualempfindung,* 3d ed., p. 276; Eulenburg, *Grenzfragen des Nerven- u. Seelenlebens,* vol. 19, "Sadismus u. Masochismus," 1902; Fuchs, *Therapie der anomalen vita sexualis* (Stuttgart, Enke), cases 5 and 6; Schrenk-Notzing, *Die Suggestionstherapie,* 1892; Seydel, *Vierteljahrsschr. f. gerichtl. Med.,* 1893, vol. 4, no. 2 (interesting letter by a masochist); Bloch, *Beiträge z. Aetiol. d. Psychopath. sexualis,* pt. 2, Dresden, 1903.

[35] Cf. for corroboration the Sacher-Masoch biography by Eulenburg, *Grenzfragen des Nerven- und Seelenlebens,* 1902, vol. 29, pp. 46-51.

[36] Cf. above, "Physiological Facts," p. 35.

[37] This difference of courage in the face of events in nature, on the one hand, and in the face of conflict with willpower, on the other, is certainly remarkable, even though it is the only indication of effeminacy that is apparent in this case.

[38] "Transactions of the Colorado State Medical Society," quoted in the *Alienist and Neurologist*, April 1883, p. 345.

[39] Instructive instances are given by Seydel, *Vierteljahrsschr. f. ger. Med.*, 1893, no. 2, pp. 275-276.

[40] Léo Taxil (op. cit., p. 228) describes masochistic scenes in Parisian brothels. The man affected with this perversion is also called "slave."

Coffignon (*La corruption à Paris*) has a chapter in his book entitled "Les Passionels," which contains contributions on this subject.

The strongest proof of the frequency of masochism lies in the fact that it openly appears in newspaper advertisements. For instance, the following advertisement appeared in the *Hannoversches' Tageblatt*, December 4, 1895:

"*Sacher-Masoch.* 109 404. Ladies interested in the works, and who embody the female characters, of this author are requested to send their address, under no. R. 537, to the offices of this paper. Strictest discretion." Another similar advertisement appeared in the same issue.

[41] The domain of masochism, however, must be sharply differentiated from the principal subject of that work, namely, that love contains an element of suffering. Unrequited love has always been described as "sweet, but sorrowful," and poets speak of "blissful pain" or "painful bliss." This must not be confounded, as Z. does, with the manifestations of masochism, any more than an unyielding lover should be characterized as "cruel." It is remarkable, however, that Hamerling (*Amor und Psyche,* canto 4) uses perfect masochistic pictures, flagellation, etc., to express this feeling.

[42] Cf. his recent paper on "Passivisimus" in the *Archives d'Anthropologie criminelle,* 1892, vol. 7, p. 294.

[43] Moll, *Untersuchungen über Libido sexualis,* vol. 1, pt. 2, case 36, p. 320. Against the theory, however, that foot and shoe fetishism is a manifestation of (latent) masochism, Dr. Moll (op. cit., p. 136) raises the objection that it is still unexplained why the fetishist so often prefers boots with high heels to boots and shoes of a particular kind – buttoned or laced. To this objection it can be remarked in the first place that the high heels characterize the shoes as feminine, and, in the second place, that in spite of the sexual character of his inclination, the fetishist demands all kinds of aesthetic qualities in his fetish; also the interesting theories advanced by Restiv de la Bretonne (himself a foot fetishist), and quoted in Moll's work, op. cit., pp. 498 and 499, footnote.

[44] Compare the instructive case of Moll, *Libido sexualis,* p. 320.

[45] There is apparently a connection between foot fetishism and the fact that certain persons of this kind, whom coitus does not satisfy, or who are unable to perform it, find a substitute for it in **rubbing the penis between a woman's feet.**

[46] This disgusting impulse is also referred to in case 68 of the eighth edition of this work. It seems to occur especially with coprolagnists and fetishists.

[47] The laws of the early Middle Ages gave the husband the right to kill his wife; those of the later Middle Ages, the right to beat her. The latter right was used freely, even by those of high standing (cf. Schultze, *Das höfische Leben zur Zeit des Minnesangs*, vol. 1, p. 163 and the following page). At the same time, however, the paradoxical chivalry of the Middle Ages remains unexplained (see below, p. 172).

[48] Cf. Lady Milford's words in Schiller's *Kabale und Liebe*: "We women can only choose between ruling and serving; but the highest pleasure power affords is but a miserable substitute, if the greater joy of being the slaves of a man we love is denied us!" (act 2, scene 1).

[49] Seydel, *Vierteljahresschr. f. ger. Med.*, 1883, vol. 2, quotes as an instance of masochism the patient of Dieffenbach, who repeatedly and purposely dislocated her arm in order to experience lustful sensations when it was being set (anesthetics not being known then).

[50] Analogous facts are found in the animal kingdom. *Pulmonata Cuv.*, for instance, possess a small calcareous staff that lies hidden in a special pouch of the body. At the time of mating, however, it is projected and used as a means of sexual excitement, unquestionably producing pain.

[51] Cf. the author's article, "Über geschlechtliche Hörigkeit und Masochismus," in the *Psychiatrische Jahrbücher*, vol. 10, p. 169 and the following page, where this subject is treated in detail, and particularly from the forensic standpoint.

[52] The expressions "slave" and "slavery," though often used metaphorically under such circumstances, are avoided here because they are the favorite expressions of masochism, from which "bondage" must be strictly differentiated.

The expression "bondage" is not to be construed to mean J. S. Mill's "bondage of woman." What Mill designates with this expression are laws and customs, social and historical facts. Here, however, we always speak of facts that have peculiar individual motives that often conflict with prevalent customs and laws. In addition, this type of "bondage" can refer to either sex.

[53] Perhaps the most important element is that by the habit of submission a kind of mechanical obedience (without consciousness of its motives, and which operates with auto-

matic certainty) can be established. This obedience has no opposing motives to contend with, because it lies beyond the threshold of consciousness; and it may be used by the dominant individual like an inanimate instrument.

[54] Sexual bondage, of course, plays a role in all literature. Indeed, for the poet, the extraordinary manifestations of the sexual life that are not perverse form a rich and open field. The most celebrated description of masculine "bondage" is that by Abbé Prévost, *Manon Lescault.* An excellent description of feminine "bondage" is in *Leone Leoni* by George Sand. But first of all comes Kleist's *Das Käthchen von Heilbronn,* who called it the counterpart of (sadistic) *Penthesilea.* Halm's *Griseldis* and many other similar dramas also belong here.

[55] Cases can occur in which the sexual bondage is expressed in the same acts that are common in masochism. When rough men beat their wives, and the wives suffer for love (without, however, having a desire for blows), we have a pseudo form of bondage that may simulate masochism.

[56] It is highly interesting, and dependent upon the nature of bondage and masochism – which essentially correspond in external effects – that to illustrate bondage, certain playful, metaphorical expressions are in general use; such as "slavery," "to bear chains," "bound," "to hold the whip over," "to harness to the triumphal car," "to lie at the feet," "henpecked," etc. – all things which, when literally carried out, form the objects of the masochist's desire. Such metaphors are frequently used in daily life and have become trite. They are derived from the language of poetry. Poetry has always recognized, within the general idea of the passion of love, the element of dependence in the lover, who practices self-sacrifice spontaneously or from necessity. The facts of "bondage" have also always presented themselves to the poetical imagination. When the poet chooses such expressions as those mentioned, to depict the dependence of the lover in striking metaphors, *he proceeds exactly along the same lines as does the masochist;* that is, in order to intensify the idea of his dependence (his ultimate aim), he creates such situations in reality. In ancient poetry, the expression *"domina"* is used to signify the loved one, with a preference for the metaphor of "casting in chains" (e.g., Horace, ode 4, 11). From antiquity through all the centuries to our own times (cf. Grillparzer, *Ottokar,* act 4: "To rule is sweet, almost as sweet as to obey"), the poetry of love is filled with similar phrases and metaphors. The history of the word "mistress" is also interesting. But poetry reacts to life. It is probable that the courtly chivalry of the Middle Ages arose in this way: in its reverence for women as "mistresses" in society and in individual love relations; its transference of the relation between feudalism and vassalage to the relation between the knight and his lady; its submission to all feminine whims; its love tests and vows; its duty of obedience to every command of the lady – in all this, chivalry appears as a systematic, poetical development of the "bondage" of love. Certain extreme manifestations, like the deeds and sufferings of Ulrich von Lichtenstein and Pierre Vidal in the service of their ladies; or the practice of the fraternity of the "Galois" in France, whose members sought martyrdom in love and subjected themselves to all kinds of suffering – these clearly have a

masochistic character, and demonstrate the natural transformation of one phenomenon into the other.

[57] If it may be considered that, as shown above, the phenomenon of "sexual bondage" is observed much more frequently and in a more pronounced degree in the female sex than in the male, the thought arises that masochism (if not always, at least as a rule) is an inheritance of the "bondage" of feminine ancestry. Thus it comes into a relation – though distant – with antipathic sexual instinct, as a transference to the male of a perversion really belonging to the female.

It must, however, be emphasized that "bondage" also plays no unimportant role in the masculine sex life, and that masochism in man may also be explained without any such transference of feminine elements. It must also be remembered here that masochism, as well as its counterpart, sadism, occurs in irregular combination with antipathic sexual instinct.

[58] Cf. cases 57 and 58.

[59] Cf. case 70 in Schrenck-Notzing; case 20 in Féré, *L'instinct sexuel,* p. 262.

[60] Cf. case 67 in Schrenck-Notzing; Moll, *Kontr. Sexualempfindung,* 3d ed., p. 265 (gentleman who pestered an officer with letters in which he begged to be allowed to clean the officer's boots); ibid., p. 281 (gentleman who was agitated by two wishes, namely: [1] to be a woman so that he might have coitus with the man he loved, and [2] to be maltreated by the man he loved); ibid., case 17; ditto, p. 283 (man who finds satisfaction in the act with another man only when the latter rubs his back with a hard brush until the blood flows); p. 284 (coprolagnia); p. 317; Krafft-Ebing, *Psychopathia Sexualis,* 6th ed., case 43; 8th ed., cases 46, 114, 115; idem, *Jahrb. f. Psychiatrie,* vol. 12, pp. 339 and 351; idem, *Arbeiten,* vol. 4, p. 134.

[61] Of course, both have to contend with opposing ethical and aesthetic motives in their own minds. After these have been overcome, active sadism immediately comes in conflict with the law. This is not the case with masochism, which accounts for the greater frequency of masochistic acts. The instinct of self-preservation and fear of pain, however, prevent the realization of the latter. The practical significance of masochism lies only in its relation to psychic impotence, while that of sadism lies beyond this, and is principally forensic.

[62] Schrenck-Notzing, who in his explanation of all perversions lays particular stress upon the "occasional momentum," gives preference to the theory of acquired perversions over the congenital, and allows the manifestations of sadism and masochism only a subordinate position. Although he admits that many cases can only be explained on the assumption of congenital predisposition, he nevertheless contends that circumstances or a timely coincidence control their acquirement (op. cit., p. 170).

His arguments are based upon observations. Quoting two cases of *psychopathia sexualis* (29 and 37 of the seventh edition), he contends that the accidental sight of a girl bleeding or a boy being whipped that coincides with a strong sexual emotion can be sufficient cause for continued pathological associations.

Against this it may, however, be decisively held that in every hyperesthetic individual, early and strong sexual emotions have often coincided with numerous heterogeneous things, while *pathological associations are always coupled with only a few definite* (sadistic and masochistic) *things*. Numerous pupils indulge in sexual emotions or gratifications during lessons in grammar and mathematics in the classroom (as well as elsewhere) without thereby contracting perverse associations.

From this it clearly follows that although the sight of a whipping or similar scenes may provoke pathological associations already present but latent, it cannot produce them. Moreover, the aroused sexual instinct is not associated with the numerous *indifferent* things that are always present, but only with such things that normally excite disgust.

The same argument refers to the opinion of Binet, who also seeks to explain these manifestations by accidental associations.

[63] Every attempt to explain the facts of either sadism or masochism as being due to the close connection of the two phenomena demonstrated here must also be suited to explain the other perversion. An attempt to offer an explanation of sadism, by the American J. G. Kiernan (see "Psychological Aspects of the Sexual Appetite," *Alienist and Neurologist,* St. Louis, April 1891) meets this requirement, and for this reason may be briefly mentioned here. Kiernan, who cites several authorities in Anglo-American literature for his theory, starts from the assumption of several naturalists (Dallinger, Drysdale, Rolph, Cienskowsky) that conceives the so-called conjugation, a sexual act in certain low forms of animal life, to be cannibalism, a devouring of the partner in the act. He brings into immediate connection with this the well-known facts that at the time of sexual union crabs tear limbs from their bodies and spiders bite off the heads of the males, as well as other sadistic acts performed by rutting animals with their consorts. From this he passes to lust murder and other lustful acts of cruelty in man, and assumes that hunger and the sexual appetite are, in their origin, identical; that the sexual cannibalism found in lower forms of animal life has an influence on higher forms and on man, and that sadism is an atavistic rebound.

This explanation of sadism would, of course, also explain masochism; for if the origin of sexual intercourse is to be sought in a cannibalistic process, then both the survival of one sex and the destruction of the other would fulfill the purpose of nature, and thus the instinctive desire to be the victim would be explained. It must be stated in objection, however, that the basis of this reasoning is insufficient. The extremely complicated process of conjugation in lower organisms, into which science has delved only during the last few years, is by no means to be regarded as simply a devouring of one individual by another (cf. Weismann, *Die Bedeutung der sexuellen Fortpflanzung für die Selektionstheorie*, p. 51, Jena, 1886).

[64] In Zola's *Thérèse Raquin*, where the lover repeatedly kisses his mistress's boot, the case is quite different from that of shoe and boot fetishists, who, at the sight of every boot worn by a lady, or even alone, are thrown into sexual excitement, even to the extent of ejaculation.

[65] Cf. *Arbeiten*, vol. 4, p. 172, case of ring fetishism; p. 174, mourning crepe fetishism in homosexual persons.

[66] Though Binet (op. cit.) declares that every sexual perversion, without exception, depends upon such an "accident acting on a predisposed subject" (where, under predisposition, only hyperesthesia is generally understood), such an assumption for perversions other than fetishism is neither necessary nor satisfactory. For example, it is not clear how the sight of another's chastisement could sexually excite even a very excitable individual, if the physiological relationship of lust and cruelty had not been developed into *original* sadism in an abnormally excitable individual. Just as sadistic and masochistic associations are performed in the mind of the subject from homogeneous elements in adjacent spheres, so is the possibility of fetishistic associations prepared by the idiosyncrasies of the object and thus easier understood. In nearly every instance it is impressions of parts of the female form (including garments) that are in question. Fetishistic association originating by mere accident can only be traced in a few special cases.

[67] When young husbands who have associated often with prostitutes feel impotent in the face of the chastity of their young wives – a thing of frequent occurrence – the condition may be regarded as a kind of (psychic) fetishism in a wider sense. One of my patients was never potent with his beautiful and chaste young wife, because he was accustomed to the lascivious methods of prostitutes. When he now and then attempted coitus with girls he was perfectly potent. Hammond (op. cit., pp. 48, 49) reports a similar interesting case. Of course a bad conscience and hypochondriacal fear of impotence play an important part in such cases.

[68] Great sexual hyperesthesia.

[69] This is also sexual hyperesthesia. Any intense excitement affects the sexual sphere (Binet's *"dynamogénie générale"*). Concerning this, Dr. Moll provides the following case: "A similar thing is described by Mr. E., aged twenty-seven; merchant. While at school, and afterward, he often had ejaculation with pleasurable feeling when he was seized with a spell of intense anxiety. In addition, almost every other physical or mental pain exerted a similar influence. E. reported that although he had a normal sexual instinct, he suffered from nervous impotence."

[70] Exceptions are the cases of latent masochism in the form of coprolagnia, in which case

the fetishistic stimulus is not to be found in the clean naked foot but in its opposite; cf. case 80.

[71] Garnier ("Sadifetishism," *Annal. d'hyg.*) knew a degenerate whose fetish was the hair of the mons pubis. His greatest delight was to tear it out with his teeth. He collected specimens and used them for renewed sexual gratification by biting and chewing them. He bribed housemaids of hotels to let him search the beds in which ladies had slept for such hairs. While searching for them he became erotically excited and trembled with happiness upon making a successful find.

[72] Moll (op. cit., p. 131) reports: "A man, X., becomes intensely excited sexually whenever he sees a woman with her hair in a braid; loose hair, no matter how beautiful, cannot produce this effect."

Of course, it is not justifiable to consider all hair despoilers fetishists, for in a few cases such acts are done for the purpose of gain – i.e., stolen hair is not a fetish.

[73] Cf. Goethe's remarks about his adventure in Geneva ("Briefe aus der Schweiz," sec. 1, conclusion).

[74] The fact that the partly veiled form is often more charming than when it is perfectly nude, is the same literally, but quite different psychically. This depends upon the effect of contrast and expectation, which are common phenomena, and in no sense pathological.

[75] On page 262 (op. cit.) Dr. Moll writes concerning this impulse in heterosexual individuals: "The passion for handkerchiefs may go so far that the man is entirely under its control. A woman tells me: 'I know a certain gentleman, and when I see him at a distance I only need to draw out my handkerchief so that it peeps out of my pocket, and I am certain that he will follow me as a dog follows its master. Go where I please, this gentleman will follow me. He may be riding in a carriage or engaged in important business, and yet, when he sees my handkerchief he drops everything in order to follow me – i.e., my handkerchief.'"

[76] Another case of temporary, i.e., periodic handkerchief fetishism accompanied by anxiety and severe sweating, is related by Dr. Moll in the *Zentralbl. f. d. Krankheiten der Harn- und Sexualorgane,* vol. 5, no. 8. This might be a case of latent epilepsy. (Head injury at the age of ten, imbecility, repeated fainting fits, later on partial amnesia for fetishistic conditions, accompanied by anxiety and sweating, etc.) In these attacks of morbid impulse to steal ladies' handkerchiefs, which set in after an attack of typhus at the age of thirty, the patient would wipe his face with the stolen article, producing erection as well as occasional ejaculation. A physician whom he consulted had given him the advice never to wear linen shirts again, inasmuch as his peculiar impulse was caused by them.

[77] Other cases of shoe fetishism without distant relations to masochism are given by

Alzheimer, *Archiv f. Psychiatrie u. Nerven Krankheiten,* vol. 28, p. 350. This same case was declared by Kurella, "Fetischismus oder Simulation," ibid., vol. 28, p. 964, to be simulation, but the reasons given are trivial and easily refuted. See also Moll, *Untersuchungen über Libido sexualis,* case 32.

[78] In the novels of Sacher-Masoch, fur plays an important role; in fact, it serves as a title in some of them. The explanation given is that fur (ermine) is the symbol of sovereignty, and therefore the fetish of the men described in these novels seems unsatisfactory and far-fetched.

[79] Garnier (*Anomalis Sexuelles,* Paris, pp. 508, 509) reports two cases (cases 222 and 223) that are apparently opposed to this assumption; particularly the first, in which despair about the unfaithfulness of a lover led the individual to submit to the seductions of men. The case itself clearly shows, however, that this individual *never found pleasure in homosexual acts.* In case 223, the individual was effeminate from birth, or was at least a psychic hermaphrodite.

Those who hold to the opinion that the origin of homosexual feelings and instinct is exclusively to be found in defective education and other psychological influences are entirely in error.

Although an *untainted* male may be raised as a female, and a female as a male, they will not become homosexual. *The natural disposition is the determining condition; not education and other accidental circumstances, like seduction.* There can be no thought of antipathic sexual instinct, except when the person of the same sex exerts a psychosexual influence over the individual, and thus brings about libido and orgasm – i.e., has a psychic attraction. Quite different are cases in which, lacking anything better, and with great sensuality and a defective aesthetic sense, the body of a person of the same sex is used for a mastubatory act (not for coitus in a psychic sense).

In his excellent monograph, Moll shows very clearly and convincingly the importance of original predisposition in contrast with exciting causes (cf. op. cit., pp. 212-231). He knows "many cases where early sexual intercourse with men was not capable of inducing perversion." Moll further says, significantly: "I know of such an epidemic (of mutual masturbation) in a Berlin school, where a person, who is now an actor, shamelessly introduced mutual masturbation. Though I now know the names of many homosexuals in Berlin, I nevertheless could not ascertain, with anything even approaching probability, who among all the pupils of that school at that time had become homosexual. On the other hand, however, I have quite certain knowledge that many of those pupils are now sexually normal, in feeling as well as in intercourse.

[80] Cf. author's *Experimentelle Studie auf dem Gebiet des Hypnotismus,* 3d ed., 1893.

[81] Cf. Sprengel, *Apologie des Hippokrates,* Leipzig, 1792, p. 611; Friedreich, *Literärgeschichte der psych. Krankheiten,* 1830, p. 31; Lallemand, *Des pertes séminales,* Paris, 1836, vol. 1, p. 581;

Nysten, *Dictionn. de médecine,* 11th ed., Paris, 1858, art. "Éviration et Maladie des Scythes"; Marandon, "De la maladie des Scythes," *Annal. médico-psychol.,* March 1877, p. 161; Hammond, *American Journal of Neurology and Psychiatry,* August 1882.

[82] An abstract of this can be found in case 103 of the ninth edition of this book.

[83] Cf ibid., cases 104 and 105.

[84] Literature (besides works mentioned hereafter): Tardieu, *Des attentats aux moeurs,* 7th ed., 1878, p. 210; Hofmann, *Lehrb. d. ger. Med.,* 6th ed., pp. 170, 887; Gley, *Revue philosophique,* 1884, no. 1; Magnan, *Annal. méd-psychol.,* 1885, p. 458; Shaw and Ferris, *Journal of Nervous and Mental Diseases,* April 1883, no. 2; Bernhardi, *Der Uranismus,* Berlin (Volksbuchhandlung), 1882; Chevalier, *De l'inversion de l'instinct sexuel,* Paris, 1885; Ritti, *Gaz. hebdom. de médecine et de chirurg.,* January 4, 1878; Tamassia, *Rivista sperim.,* 1878, pp. 97-117; Lombroso, *Archiv. di Psichiatr.,* 1881; Charcot and Magnan, *Archiv. de neurologie,* 1882, nos. 7 and 12; Moll, *Die Konträre Sexualempfindung,* Berlin, 3d ed., 1899 (numerous bibliographic references); Chevalier, *Arch. de l'anthropologie criminelle,* vol. 5, no. 27, and vol. 6, no. 31; Reuss, "Aberrations du sens génésique, *Annales d'hygiène publique,* 1886; Saury, *Etude clinique sur la folie héréditaire,* 1886; Brouardel, *Gaz. des hôpitaux,* 1886 and 1887; Tilier, *L'instinct sexuel chez l'homme et chez les animaux,* 1889; Carlier, *Les deux prostitutions,* 1887; Lacassagne, art. "Pédérastie," in the *Dict. encyclopédique;* Vibert, art. "Pédérastie," in the *Dict. de médec. et de chirurgie;* Coutagne, *Lyon mèdical,* 1880, nos. 35 and 36; Blumer, *Americ. Journ. of Insanity,* July 1882; Krafft-Ebing, *Zeitschr. f. Psychiatrie,* no. 38; Blumenstock, art. "Konträre Sexualempfindung," *Realenzyklop. d. ges. Heilkunde,* 2d ed., vol. 6; Brouardel, *Gaz. des hôpiteaux,* 1887; Kriese, inaugural dissert., Würzburg, 1888; Hofmann, art. "Päderastie," *Realenzyklop. d. ges. Heilkunde,* 2d ed., vol. 15; Tarnowsky, *Die krankhaften Ercheinungen des Geschlechtsinnes,* Berlin, 1886; Magnan, "Séance de l'académie de médecine du 13 Janvier, 1884"; idem, *Annales médico-psychol.,* 1886 ("Anomalies du sens génital"; "Discussion sur la folie héréditaire"); Sérieux, *Recherches cliniques sur les anomalies de l'instinct sexuel,* Paris, 1886; Chevalier, *L'inversion sexuelle,* Lyon and Paris, 1893; Ladame, *Revue de l'hypnotisme,* September 1889; Peyer, *Münch. med. Wochenschr.,* 1890, no. 23; Lewin, *Neurol. Zentralbl.,* 1891, no. 18; Schrenck-Notzing, *Die Suggestionstherapie,* etc., Stuttgart; Eulenburg, op. cit., p. 66, "Homosexuelle Parerosie"; Raffalovich, *Die Entwicklung der Homosexualität,* Berlin, 1895; idem, *Uranisme et Unisexualité,* Paris, 1896; Schrenck-Notzing, *Klin. Zeit- und Streitfragen,* vol. 9, no. 1 (Vienna, 1895); Laupts, *Perversion et perversité sexuelles,* Paris, 1896; Ellis, *Das konträre Geschlechtsgefühl,* Leipzig, 1896; Legrain, *Des anomalies de l'instinct sexuel,* etc., Paris, 1896.

[85] Dr. Moll of Berlin called my attention to the fact that in Mortiz's *Magazin für Erfahrungsseelenkunde,* vol. 8, Berlin, 1791, references are made to antipathic sexual instinct in man. Two biographies of men are reported who manifested an enthusiastic love for persons of their own sex. In the second case, which is particularly noteworthy, the patient explains his aberration by the fact that as a child he was caressed only by grown persons, and as a boy of

ten or twelve years only by his schoolmates. "This, as well as the lack of association with persons of the opposite sex, caused my natural inclination toward the female sex to be entirely diverted to the male sex. I am still quite indifferent to women."

It cannot be determined whether such a case is one of congenital (psychosexual hermaproditism?) or acquired antipathic sexual instinct.

[86] *Vindex, Inclusa, Vindicta, Formatrix, Ara spei, Gladius furens* (Leipzig, H. Matthes, 1864 and 1865); Ulrichs, *Kritische Pfeile*, 1879, commissioned by H. Crönlein, Stuttgart, Augustenstrasse 5.

[87] Tarnowsky (op. cit., p. 34) records a case demonstrating that antipathic sexual feeling, as a concomitant manifestation with neurotic degeneration, may also affect the descendants of parents having no neurotic taint. Syphilis of the parents played a part in this instance, as well as in a similar case of Scholz (*Vierteljahrsschr. f. ger. Med.*), in which the perversion of the sexual desires stood in causal relation to an arrest of psychic development that had been caused by trauma.

[88] Klaus' research in zoology (*Zoologie*, 1891, p. 490) shows that not only does hermaphroditism exist in the lower grades of the animal world, sexual exchange (physiological?) within one individual may also occur. Klaus states that the *cymothoideae* (classified under Crustacea) perform the functions of the male during the first part of their life, and then – with many, even secondary, changes in the sexual character – perform the functions of the female during the second part of their life.

[89] A monosexual psychic apparatus of regeneration in a monosexual body belonging to the opposite sex does not, of course, mean a "feminine soul in a masculine brain," or vice versa – this would simply contradict all monistic and scientific thought. Likewise, a feminine brain in a masculine body contradicts every anatomical fact. Instead, such a circumstance is merely a feminine psychosexual center in a masculine brain, and vice versa.

[90] Josef Müller, in a clever brochure (*Ueber Gamophagie*, Stuttgart, 1892), offers an inducement for further research in this direction. He advances the opinion that a union of the organs and their qualities occurs because of a certain law that is established by necessity, and that progresses in a normal fashion. This union would explain how, in the struggle of the development of mono- and bisexuality, those organs and their qualities – which belong together as a whole with regard to their functional capacity – suffer the common fate of conquest or defeat. In persons subject to organic taint, the defect of the elements connecting the organs during the struggle for superiority could only be explained as a negative result of this hypothetical law.

[91] That inversion of the sexual instinct is not uncommon is proved by its frequent use as a subject of novels, among other things. The neuropathic foundation of this sexual perversion

does not escape the writers. This theme is treated in German literature in *Fridolin's heimliche Ehe*, by Wilbrand; in *Brick-a-Brack oder Licht im Schatten*, by Emerich Graf Stadion; and also in *Prinz Klotz*, by Balduin Groller. The oldest homosexual romance is probably the one published by Petronius in Rome, under the Empire, under the title *Satyricon*.

[92] Cf. author's work, "Ueber psychosexuales Zwittertum," in the *Internationalen Zentralblatt für die Physiologie und Pathologie der Harn- und Sexualorgane*, vol. 1, no. 2.

[93] This idea is supported by the statements of an unmarried homosexual kindly communicated to me by Dr. Moll of Berlin. He could report a number of cases of his acquaintance in which married men also had "relations" with men.

[94] Literature: Havelock Ellis, *Alienist and Neurologist*, April 1895; idem, "Das konträre Geschlechtsgefühl," *Bibliothek für Sozialwissenschaft*, German translation by Kurella, vol. 7, 1896, p. 184; Moll, *Konträre Sexualempfindung*, 3d ed., p. 504; Moraglia, *Neue Forschungen auf d. Gebiet der weibl. Kriminalität*, Berlin (Skopnik), 1897; Krafft-Ebing, *Jahrb f. sexuelle Zwischenstufen*, vol. 3, p. 20.

[95] Observations: [1] Westphal, *Arch. f. Psych.*, vol. 2, p. 73; [2] Gock, op. cit., no. 1; [3] Wise, *The Alienist and Neurologist*, January 1883; [4] Cantarano, *Zeitschr. La Psichiatria*, 1883, p. 201; [5] Sérieux, op. cit., observ. 14; [6] Kiernan, op. cit.; [7] Müller, Friedreich's *Blätter f. ger. Med.*, 1891, no. 4; [8-19] Moll, *Konträre Sexualempfindung*, 2d ed., cases 18-23; [20] Meyhöfer, *Zeitschr. f. Medizinalbeamte*, vol. 5, no. 16; [21-22] Zuccarelli, *Inversione congenita in due donne*, Napoli, 1888; [23-33] Moll, *Untersuchungen über Libido sexualis*, cases 10-12, 40-44, 47, 56, 57; [34-36] Havelock Ellis, *Alienist and Neurologist*, April 1895; [37] Penta and Urso, *Archiv. delle psichopatie sexuali*, p. 33; [38] Penta, ibid., p. 94; [39-40] Féré, *L'instinct sexuelle*, observ. 15, p. 242, observ. 22, p. 291; [41] the Urban case of the 18th century, reported by Moll, *Konträre Sexualempfindung*, 3d ed., p. 533; [42-43] Krafft-Ebing, *Jahrb. f. sexuelle Zwischenstufen*, vol. 3, pp. 27 and 29.

[96] Paul, Epist. and Rom.

[97] Ploss, op. cit.

[98] It is a remarkable fact that lesbian love is frequently used in fiction as the leading theme, namely: Diderot, *La Religieuse;* Balzac, *La fille aux yeux d'or;* Th. Gautier, *Mademoiselle de Maupin;* Feydeau, *La Comtesse de Chalis;* Flaubert, *Salammbô;* Belot, *Mademoiselle Giraud, ma femme;* Rachilde, *Monsieur Venus.*

The heroines of these (lesbian) novels appear to the beloved persons of the same sex in the character and the role of a *man;* their love is most intense.

The oldest case of sexual inversion recorded thus far in Germany is one of viraginity that dates as far back as the beginning of the eighteenth century. It is that of a woman who was married to another woman, and who cohabited with her consort by means of a leather priapus. See Dr. Müller in Friedrich's *Blätter f. ger. Med.*, 1891, no. 4.

[99] Cf. the expert medical opinion of this case, by Dr. Birnbacher, in Friedreich's *Blätter f. ger. Med.*, 1891, no. 1.

five. special pathology.

[1] For numerous cases, see Henke's *Zeitschr.*, vol. 23, supplement, p. 147; Combes, *Annal. méd psychol.*, 1866; Liman, *Zweifelh. Geisteszustände*, p. 389; Casper and Liman, *Lehrb.*, 7th ed., case 295; Bartels, Friedrich's *Blätter f. gerichtl. Med.*, 1890, no. 1.

[2] Other cases of pederasty, see Casper, *Klinische Novellen*, case 7; Combes, *Annal. méd psychol.*, July 1866.

[3] Sander, *Vierteljahrsschr. f. ger. Med.*, vol. 18, p. 31; Casper, *Klin. Novellen*, case 27.

[4] Arndt (*Lehrb. der Psych.*, p. 410) especially emphasizes the passionate element in epileptics: "I have known epileptics who behaved in a most sensual way toward their mothers, and others who were suspected by their fathers of having sexual intercourse with their mothers." When Arndt declares, however, that the thought of an epileptic element should come into consideration whenever there is a peculiarity of the sexual life, he is in error.

[5] Cf. also Liman, *Zweifelhafte Geisteszustände*, case 6; Lasègue, "Exhibitionists," *Union méd.*, 1877; Ball and Chambard, art. "Somnambulisme," *Dict. des scienc. méd.*, 1881.

[6] Literature: Bienville, *Traité de la nymph.*, Amsterdam, 1771; Louyer-Villermay, art. "Nymphomanie," *Dict. des sciences med.*, volume 30, p. 563; Magnet, *Dict. en 60 vol.* (vol. 36, p. 580); Meyer Alexis, *Des rapports conjugaux*, Paris, 1882, 7th ed.; Guibout, *Traité clinique des malad. des femmes*, Paris, 1886; Icard, *La femme pendant la période menstruelle*, 1890; Marc, *Die Geisteskrankheiten*, German translation by Ideler, vol. 2, p. 138; Ideler, *Grundriss der Seelenheilkunde*, vol. 2, p. 488; Foville, *Dict. de méd. et de chirurg. pratique;* Legrand du Saulle, *La folie devant les tribun.*, 1864; Ball, *La folie érotique*, 1888; Moreau, *Aberrations du sens génésique*, 1884; Thoinot, *Attentats aux moeurs*, p. 487; Legrand du Saulle, *Les hystériques*, 1883.

[7] Thoinot, *Attentats aux moeurs*, p. 498.

[8] See case of Merlac, in the author's *Lehrb. d. ger. Psychopathol.*, 3d ed., p. 322; Morel, *Traité des malad. mentales*, p. 687; Legrand, *La folie*, p. 337; "Process la roncière," *Annal. d'hyg.*, ser. 1, vol. 4; ser. 3, vol. 22.

[9] The incubus in the witch trials of the Middle Ages depended on them.

six. pathological sexuality in its legal aspects.

[1] S. Weisbrod, *Die Sittlichkeitsverbrechen vor dem Gesetz*, Berlin, 1891; Dr. Pasquale Penta, *I pervertimenti sessuali nell' uomo*, Napoli, 1893; Seydel, "Die Beurtheilung der perversen Sexualvergehen in foro," *Vierteljahrsschr. f. ger. Med.*, 1893, no. 2; Viazzi, "Dui reati sessuali," *Biblioteca antropologica giuridica;* idem, "Strafgesetzbücher und Unzuchtsdelikte," *Archivio di Psichiatra*, vol. 19, fasc. 1.; Schrenk-Notzing, *Archiv f. Kriminalanthropol.*, vol. 1, no. 1.

[2] Cf. Casper, *Klin. Novellen;* Lombroso, Goltdammer's *Archiv*, vol. 30; Oettingen, *Moralstatistik*, p. 494.

[3] Boisser and Lachaux, "Perversions sexuelles á forme obsédante," *Archives de neurologie*, October 1893; Schäfer, *Vierteljahrsschr. f. gerichtl. Med.*, issue 3, vol. 10, no. 1; Thoinot, *Attentats aux moeurs*, 1898, p. 366-398; Seiffer, *Arch. f. Psych.*, vol. 31, nos. 1 and 2.; Cramer, "Die Beziehungen des Exhib. zum § 51. des deutsch. Stfgab.," *Zeitschr. f. Psych.*, vol. 54, p. 481; Bassenge, "Der Exhibitionismus," Inaug. Dissert., Berlin, 1896; Hoche, *Neurolog. Zentralbl.*, vol. 2, 1896.

[4] Laségue, *Union médicale*, May 1877; Laugier, *Annal. d'hygiéne*, 1878, no. 106; Pelanda, "Ueber Pornopathiker," *Arch. die Psichiatr.*, vol. 8; Schuchardt, *Zeitschr. f. Medizinalbeamte*, 1890, no. 6; Duchateau, *Bulletin de la société de médecine de Gand*, February-March 1897; Garnier, *Annal. médico-psychol.*, January-February 1894; Vigouroux, ibid.; Hoppe, *Vierteljahrsschr. f. gerichtl. Med.*, issue 3, vol. 20, no. 2; Leppmann, *Die Sachverständigentätigkeit*, p. 101; Rayneau, *Annal. médico-psychol.*, May-June 1895; Schrenck-Notzing, *Arch. f. Kriminalanthropol.*, vol. 1, nos. 2 and 3, cases 4 and 5; Strassmann, *Vierteljahrs. f. geriehtl. Med.*, issue 3, vol. 10.

[5] Instructive case reported by Morselli, *Bolletino della R. Accademia medica di Genova*, vol. 9 (1894), fasc. 1; Moeli, *Über irre Verbrecher*, p. 22, 1888; Garnier, *Annal. médico-psychol.*, vol. 19, p. 97, 1894; Molet, *Annal. d'hyg.*, p. 202, 1866; Pribet, *De l'exhibit. chez les épilep.*, Paris, 1894.

[6] Cf. Krafft-Ebing, "Ueber transitorisches Irresein bei Neurasthenischen," *Zeitschr. "Irrenfreund,"* no. 8, 1883, and "Arbeiten," *Wiener Klin. Wochenschrift*, vol. 1, no. 50, p. 21, 1891.

[7] *Recherches sur les centres Nerveux*, ser. 2, Paris, 1893.

[8] Analogous case: Boissier and Lachaux, *Archives de Neurologie*, October 1893.

[9] Dr. Moll calls this perversion (?) *mixoscopia* (from μιξις, *cohabitation;* and σκεπτειν, *to look*). Merzejewsky, in his *Gynécologie médicolégale*, relates the case of an old castellan who, in order to excite himself, made his servants violate women and girls in his presence (Ivankow, *Archiv. d'Anthropol. criminelle*, vol. 13, p. 697).

[10] *Annal. médico-psychol.*, 1849, p. 515; 1863, p. 57; 1864, p. 215; 1866, p. 253.

[11] Cf. the cases of Tardieu, *Attentats,* pp. 182-92.

[12] Cf. Holtzendorff, *Psychologie des Mords.*

[13] Tardieu, *Attentats,* case 51, p. 188.

[14] Cf. the complete medico-legal opinion on this case reported in Friedreich's *Blätter,* no. 6, 1891.

[15] Schweizer, *Archiv f. Tierheilkunde,* no. 1, 1889.

[16] As Herbst (*Handb. d. österr. Strafrechts,* Vienna, 1878, p. 72) remarks, there are, nevertheless, crimes conditioned by the absence of assent on the part of the injured individual, which cease to be such as soon as the injured individual has given consent – e.g., theft, rape.

Herbst also enumerates here, however, the limitation of personal freedom (?).

Recently a decided change of views on this point has taken place. The German criminal law regards the consent of a man to his own death to be of such importance that a very different and much milder punishment is inflicted when such circumstances occur (Paragraph 216); and it is the same in Austrian law (Austrian abridgment, Paragraph 222). The so-called double suicide of lovers was the act considered. In cases of bodily injury and deprivation of freedom, the consent of the victim must also receive consideration at the hands of the judge. Certainly knowledge of masochism is of importance in making a judgment about the probability of asserted consent.

[17] According to Austrian law, this crime should fall under Paragraph 411, as *slight* bodily injury; according to the German criminal law, it is bodily injury (cf. Liszt, *Lehrb.,* p. 325).

[18] Abstracts from a paper read before the International Congress at Paris.

[19] Cf. cases 211, 212, 213, 214, 221, 225, 226, 228. (Cases by Marc, Ideler, Friedreich, Giraud.)

[20] Cf. cases 10, 23.

[21] Cf. cases 12, 172, 174, 175, 176; Chevalier, *L'inversion sexuelle,* p. 362; Fére, *Les epileptique,* p. 81.

[22] Cf. cases 196-200.

[23] Tardieu, *Attentats aux mouers;* Casper, *Klin. Novellen,* case 1; Maschka, *Handbuch,* vol. 3, p. 175; Casper, *Vierteljahrsschr.,* 1852, vol. 1.

[24] Lop, *Archives d'antropol. crimin.,* vol. 10, p. 55; idem, *Annales d'hygiéne,* vol. 35, p. 462; Bernard, "Attentats à la pudeur sur des petites filles," Thèse de Lyon, 1886; *New York Med. Journ.,* December 13, 1893.

[25] Albert, Friedreich's *Blätter f. ger. Med.,* 1859, p. 17.

[26] Cases 163-165 quoted in this book.

[27] Leppmann, *Die Sachverständigentätigkeit,* p. 96; Lombroso, *Archivio di psichiatria,* vol. 8, p. 519.

[28] Cf. above, page 390, and my *Arbeiten,* no. 4, p. 96 ("Incest," immorality with children).

[29] Cases 182, 183, above; Liman, *Zweifelhafte Geisteszustände,* case 6.

[30] Cases 174, 175.

[31] Case 176.

[32] Casper's *Klin. Novellen,* p. 161, 193, 272; Leppmann, op. cit., p. 115; Henke's *Zeitschr.,* vol. 23, "Ergänzungsh.," p. 147; cf. above, pp. 367, etc.; 420, etc.

[33] See above, cases 193 and 194, 10th ed., and case 209 above, *Vierteljahrsschr. f. ger. Med.,* vol. 49, no. 2.

[34] See above, cases 178, 179, 184, 185. Also, Krafft-Ebing, *Arbeiten,* vol. 4, p. 97 ("Schändung von Kindern im epil. Dämmerzustand des Täters").

[35] Cf. author's original article in Friedreich's *Blätter f. ger. Med.,* 1896, and *Arbeiten,* no. 4, p. 105.

[36] Fuchs, *Therapie der anomalen Vita sexualis,* p. 11.

[37] Cf. *Zeitschrift f. Psychiatrie,* vol. 58, no. 4.

[38] I follow the usual terminology in describing bestiality and pederasty under the general term of sodomy. In Genesis (chapter 19), whence this word comes, it exclusively signifies the vice of pederasty. Later, sodomy was often used synonymously with bestiality. The moral theologians, like St. Alphonsus of Ligouri, Gury, and others, have always distinguished correctly, i.e.,

in the sense of Genesis, between sodomy, i.e., **sexual intercourse with a person of the same sex,** and bestiality, i.e., **sexual intercourse with an animal** (cf. Oelfers, *Pastoralmedizin,* p. 78).

The jurists brought confusion into the terminology by establishing "sodomy according to sex" and "sodomy according to genus." Science, however, should assert itself here as a slave of theology, and return to the correct usage of words.

[39] For interesting histories, see Krauss, *Psychol. des Verbrechens,* p. 180; Maschka, *Handb.,* vol. 3, p. 188; Hofmann, *Lehrb. d. ger. Med.,* p. 180; Rosenbaum, *Die Lustseuche,* 5th ed., 1892.

[40] How difficult, unpleasant, and dangerous it can be for the judge to form a proper judgment of these "coitus-like" acts for the establishment of the objective fact of the crime is clearly shown by an article on the punishability of male intercourse in the *Zeitschr. f. d. gesamte Strafrechtswissenschaft.,* vol. 7, no. 1, as well as by a similar article in Friedreich's *Blätter f. ger. Medizin,* 1891, no. 6. Further, see Moll, *Konträre Sexualempfindung,* p. 223ff.; Bernhardi, *Der Uranismus,* Berlin, 1895; Van Erkelens, *Strafgesetz u. widernatürl. Unzucht,* Berlin, 1895; Schäfer, *Vierteljahrsschr. f. gerichtl. Med.,* issue 3, vol. 17, no. 2.

[41] Cf. the author's pamphlet, *Der Konträrsexuale vor dem Strafrichter,* Leipzig and Vienna (Deutike), 2d ed., 1895.

[42] For interesting histories and notes: Krauss, *Psych. des Verbrechens,* p. 174; Tardieu, *Attentats;* Maschka, *Handb.,* vol. 3, p. 174. This vice seems to have come through Crete from Asia to Greece and was widespread in the time of classic Hellas. Thence it spread to Rome, where it flourished luxuriantly. In Persia and China (where it is actually tolerated) it is widespread, as it also is in Europe (cf. Tardieu, Tarnowsky et al.).

[43] Lombroso (*Der Verbrecher,* German translation by Fränkel, p. 20ff.) shows that, in the case of animals, intercourse with the same sex also occurs when normal indulgence is impossible.

[44] Cf. Tardieu, *Attentats,* p. 198; Martineau, *Deutsche Med. Zeitung.,* 1882, p. 9; Virchow's *Jahrb.,* vol. 1, 1881, p. 533; Coutagne, *Lyon mèdical,* nos. 35, 36. Eulenburg in Zülzer's *Klin. Handbuch d. Harn- u. Sexualorgane,* sec. 4, p. 35, relates cases of his own experience, in which women brought actions for divorce on the grounds that the husband, in order to avoid offspring, practiced pederasty only.

[45] Cf. Mayer, Friedreich's *Blätter,* 1875, p. 41; Krausold, *Melancholie und Schuld,* 1884, p. 20; Andronico, *Archiv. di psich. scienze penali et anthropol. crim.,* vol. 3, p. 145; Chevalier, *L'inversion sexuelle,* Paris, 1893, p. 217 (searching description of "sapphic love" in modern Paris); Moraglia, op. cit., p. 24.

[46] Cf. Maschka, *Handb.,* vol. 3, p. 191 (good historical notes); Legrand, *La folie,* p. 521.

[47] Vallon, *Annal. méd. Psych.*, 1894, p. 116. (Immoral assault by a father on his own little daughter.)

seven. appendix.

[1] In this story the writer describes a man whose greatest pleasure lies in being treated as a slave by a beautiful woman whom he loves. Besides numerous scenes in which the man is whipped by the woman, there are others in which he is trod upon by her. It is this act that forms the principal means of excitement in the case described above.

[2] In continental hotels the guests customarily put their shoes in the corridors at night to be cleaned.

[3] Later it became known that a near relative died insane, and, further, that eight of his parent's children had died of acute or chronic hydrocephalus at ages ranging from one to fifteen.

[4] "Du bist wie eine Blume, so hold, so schön, so rein," etc.

[5] "Grau wie der Himmel, steht vor mir die Welt,
Doch wend' es sich zum Guten oder Bösen,
Du, lieber Freund, in Treuen denk' ich Dein!
Behüt Dich Gott!, es wär' zu schön gewesen,
Behüt Dich Gott, es hat nicht sollen sein!"

[6] Cases, see Friedreich's *Blätter f. ger. Anthropologie,* vol. 3, p. 77.

[7] Cases, Maschka, *Handb.,* vol. 3, p. 175; Casper, *Vierteljahrsschr.,* 1852, vol. 1; Tardieu, *Attentats.*

[8] Cf. Kirn, *Allg. Zeitschr. f. Psych.,* vol. 39, p. 217.

[9] Cf. Krafft-Ebing, *Archiv für Psychiatrie,* vol. 8, no. 1.

defemination 248

defilement of women 104

development, psychic impediments of 385

diagnosis 365

effemination 315

ejaculation, center of 55

   affections of 55

epilepsy 391

erection 30

erection center, affections of 54

erogenous zones 38

eviration 248

exhibitionists 423

   acquired, mental debility of 424

   hereditary degenerates 431

   neurasthenics 428

fanaticism, religious 10

fellatio 422

fetish 18

   animals 235

   apron 214

   dress 209

   eye 191

   foot 21, 196

   fur 230

   hair 203

     despoilers 205

   hand 21, 192

   handkerchiefs 215

   in woman 23

   kid gloves 232

   material 225

   nose 192

   odor 22

   petticoat 215

   physical defects 199

   relations to other sexual perversions 192

   shoe and foot fetishism as latent

     masochism 151

   shoes 219

   silk 230

   skin 202

   soul 21

   velvet 229

   voice 22

fetishism 18, 187

   as an acquired perversion 189

   erotic 18

   essence of 189

   explanation of 187

   of beasts 235

   of parts of the body 191

   of the hair 207

   of things and clothes 209

   physiological 18

   religious 18

   robbery, theft 455

   violation of the body 455

flagellants 35

flagellation as excitant 34

   caused by masochism 127

     sadism 98

fondness of dress 17

friendship 14

frottage, explanation of 437

frotteurs 437

girl-stabbing 100

gynandry 329

gynecomastia 46

RICHARD VON KRAFFT-EBING was born on August 14, 1840 in Mannheim, Germany. After receiving a doctorate in medicine and neurology, he began his career as a professor of psychiatry in Strasbourg in 1872. A year later he was appointed the director of the Feldhof Asylum near Graz, Austria, and from 1892 until shortly before his death on December 2, 1902, he was the head of the psychiatry department at the University of Vienna. A pioneer in the study of syphilis, hypnosis, epilepsy and criminal psychopathology, Krafft-Ebing popularized, with the publication of *Psychopathia Sexualis,* the terms *masochism, sadism,* and *fetishism.* His other books include *Lehrbuch der Psychiatrie auf klinischer Grundlage für practische Ärzte und Studirende* (3 vols., 1879-80), and *Arbeiten aus dem Gesammtgebiet der Psychiatrie und Neuropathologie* (4 vols., 1897-99).

BRIAN KING was born in 1962 and was educated at the California Institute of the Arts. He is the author of *Lustmord: The Writings and Artifacts of Murderers* (1996).